DIVORCING THE DICTATOR

DIVORCING THE DICTATOR

AMERICA'S BUNGLED AFFAIR WITH NORIEGA

FREDERICK KEMPE

G. P. PUTNAM'S SONS

New York

For my mother and father

G. P. Putnam's Sons
Publishers Since 1838
200 Madison Avenue
New York, NY 10016

Library of Congress Cataloging-in-Publication Data

Kempe, Frederick.
Divorcing the dictator / Frederick Kempe.
p.   cm.
Includes index.
1. Noriega, Manuel Antonio, 1934– .   2. United States—Politics and
government—1977– .   3. Panama—Politics and government—1946– .   4. United
States—Relations—Panama.   5. Panama—Relations—United States.   6. Political
ethics—United States.   7. Political ethics—Panama.   I. Title.
ISBN 0-399-13517-0
F1567.N67K46   1990   89-77131 CIP
327.7307287'09'048—dc20

Printed in the United States of America
1 2 3 4 5 6 7 8 9 10

This book has been printed on acid-free paper.

∞

CONTENTS

Foreword: BLOOD UNDER THE PILLOW   1

1. LAST RESORT   8
2. BUSH'S RECURRING NIGHTMARE   27
3. THE ABANDONED CHILD   35
4. A SPY IS BORN   47
5. THE NOT-SO-LOYAL SERVANT   55
6. THE NORIEGA UNDERWORLD   73
7. THE CARTER COVER-UP   90
8. THE ARROGANCE OF POWER   113
9. THE SPADAFORA KILLING   126
10. THE BARLETTA OUSTER   143
11. NORIEGA AND THE CONTRAS   157
12. THE FIFTH HORSEMAN   183
13. PLAYING THE U.S. CARD   207
14. FOREIGN POLICY BY INDICTMENT   236
15. THE WRONG HERO   258
16. THE KEYSTONE COUP   273
17. U.S. POLICY FOLLIES   289
18. THE MISSED OPPORTUNITY   309
19. BUSH'S TAR BABY   332
20. PSYCHOLOGICAL WARFARE   350

21. UNFINISHED BUSINESS   369
22. NORIEGA AND THE NUNCIO   398

Epilogue: OUR OWN WORST ENEMY   418
Notes   425
Index   457

NOTE TO READERS

This is a reporter's book. Although I urge the reader to investigate the notes in the back, this book's heart is original reporting from more than three hundred interviews with sources ranging from the papal nuncio to drug dealers, from Noriega's oldest friends to political prisoners who have been tortured by his thugs. When other sources aren't cited in the notes, interviews conducted for this book are almost invariably the source.

None of the dialogue or description has been invented. When any doubt remained about quotes, the quotation marks have been left off. The rule has been to check quotes either with the source, two witnesses to the meeting or exchange, or with notes or documents recording the exchange. Other valuable sources of information were the transcripts from congressional hearings, particularly those convened by Senator John Kerry's drug subcommittee.

Many sources who provided information in this book are anonymous, both due to the sensitive nature of the information and to the fact that General Noriega still ruled when most of the manuscript was completed. To preserve the independence of the project, no one involved in the story was given the right to review the manuscript before publication. Certain sections were provided to key sources during an extensive fact-checking exercise.

ACKNOWLEDGMENTS

This book never would have happened without the patience and support of Norman Pearlstine, the managing editor of *The Wall Street Journal.* I am deeply grateful for his willingness to humor my curious passion for Panama, to provide a leave of absence to produce the book, and then to enthusiastically support articles written from the isthmus.

The discerning reader will recognize shades of *The Wall Street Journal* style throughout the manuscript. And indeed, the book was an outgrowth out of work and thinking done for the paper during my time as diplomatic correspondent. The Panama story intrigued me as a fascinating case study of American foreign policy failure and the tale of one of our more unsavory allies, General Noriega. No newspaper is better suited for such a story. *The Wall Street Journal,* at its best, is a newspaper that fosters in-depth reporting, rich detail, good writing, meaningful analysis, and unconventional insights.

In that vein, thanks also to Karen House, Albert Hunt, and Lee Lescaze, my *WSJ* bosses and friends who sacrificed their own daily demands to free me for this project. Hunt was particularly generous in offering use of office resources and space whenever it was needed. I owe special thanks to Tom Petzinger, one of the best editors I know, whose touch can be seen in my Panama articles and in some of this book.

My attorney/agent, Robert Barnett, believed in this project from the beginning and taught me the trade. Neil Nyren was a masterful editor and a talented psychiatrist for an insecure author.

Good friends are few. Those who can edit proficiently are far fewer. Muchas gracias to David Ignatius's deft touch and instincts which helped shape the theme and writing. The reader should be glad Alan Murray's sharp eye spotted the mistakes and possibilities I would have missed. Peter Chase, my friend and brother, was at hand with his manuscript-saving red pen as each new page rolled off the printer. Thanks above all to Kyle Gibson, who endured the project happily and supportively, spending long nights with bleary eyes and editing pencil in hand.

Two reporters provided invaluable assistance—James Dorsey and M. Scott Malone. Dorsey's friendship and help on the ground was irreplaceable. Malone provided information that made several chapters far richer. I learned from both.

In Panama, Queenie Altamirano took me on voyages that placed her in more danger than she wanted. A big hug. Thanks also to courageous Louis Martinz (may he never sit in jail again) and Sarah Simpson (and her caterers) for their friendship and help. Thanks also to Panama expert Eva Loser who saved me from embarrassment.

A project of this size demands plenty of research. Carolyn Rhodes devoted endless hours when it counted. Thanks also to Mary Motta, Bellinda Vallarino, Steve Stine, and Kathleen Wills. David Dolinger and William Hoover gave me the computer know-how. (How did Dostoyevsky do it without a hard drive?)

For their special interest in the project, "cheers" to Gil Pimentel, Judd Rose, Forest Sawyer, and Scott Willis of ABC. Thanks also to Richard Smith, Maynard Parker, and David Alpern of *Newsweek* for well-edited and well-chosen excerpts. Thanks also to Kenneth Adelman and Robert Hawkins for the friendship and Institute for Contemporary Studies office.

Stewart Powell emptied computer and memory banks to help, and Linda Creighton provided, as always, the right light.

Most of all, to Jeanie, Patty, and Teresa, who always believed.

A number of sources in Panama and in Washington, who know who they are, can't be mentioned here. Forget macaroni and cheese. Forget roast beef sandwiches. I'll cater for you anytime.

You provide the drinks.

And God bless the nuncio.

BLOOD UNDER THE PILLOW

*I will only tell you honestly that the higher cosmic con-
sciousness which is God is with me. I have prayed every
day since my mother taught me. It is my moral principle.*
—MANUEL ANTONIO NORIEGA, MAY 26, 1989

I found Ivan Trilha down the dingy hallway from the pet toucans munch-
ing on papaya, across the room from the fake Salvador Dali originals and
underneath a life-sized poster of General Manuel Antonio Noriega, who
was pictured in a uniform so white that the doves appeared gray as they
fluttered beside it.

The inscription on the poster, in the General's unmistakably bold but
childlike handwriting, read, "To my brother, compadre, guide, and light,
Ivan Trilha, 1984." Trilha smiled as he ran his finger lovingly over the
lettering, as if to draw energy from it. Under the brim of the white,
high-peaked, military cap, Noriega's dark snake's eyes seemed to dart
around the room.

Trilha was a Brazilian sorcerer whose gold-plated business card read,
"The World's Premier Mentalist, Astrologer, and Tarot Card Reader."
According to Noriega's fellow officers, he was also the cosmic force who
provided the General a magic weapon against American and domestic
enemies. Trilha wasn't shy about taking credit.

"All the sorcerers of the world were after Noriega and me," he said, "and we were able to win. I have helped him with my spiritual support. He and I communicate mentally. He has a very high capacity for clairvoyancy."

The Brazilian psychic threw back wild shocks of shoulder-length black hair, stringy with sweat from having just performed an operation without anesthesia. He had cut out a tumor with sewing scissors, using only the energy of his hands to numb the surrounding area. He then showed a video taken from a previous operation to prove this unusual skill, explaining that the subject's cries were cosmic screams of joy and not an indication of pain.

Noting that his listener had some doubts and wanted additional proof of his prowess, Trilha showed a letter of thanks from the United Nations Recreation Council for speaking to its parapsychology club. He also walked me to his wall, where he showed off two phony diplomas manufactured at the Mendez Print Shop in New York.

Having thus established his credentials, he turned to his favorite subject: Manuel Antonio Noriega Moreno. Noriega, he said, was one of the four strongest men in universal politics, along with Gorbachev, Castro, and Qaddafi. "Noriega is a Christian, a Rosicrucian, a Freemason, a Buddhist, a Taoist, a man protected by God and the Son of God." Noriega hedged his bets, pursuing all spiritual and superstitious paths, so as not to be caught having forgotten the one that might bring him salvation. Trilha called him a "synchrotist": he has put all faiths together, thus believing in everything and nothing.

"There is something I want you to write," said Trilha, staring down at my notebook. "If Noriega were to choose any single religion, I don't have any doubt he would be a Latin-American Christ. He has been persecuted so much that the demon has become an angel. It has been a modern-day crucifixion. He even speaks in parables, like Christ."

It was in the mid-1970s, when Noriega was head of Panamanian intelligence, that Noriega first met Trilha. The Brazilian mentalist had healed Noriega's adoptive mother of debilitating arthritis, and she'd suggested that her surprisingly successful son go to this phenomenon to cure his migraines. "People think because he wears sunglasses all the time he is a drug addict," said Trilha. "That isn't true. It is because of his headaches."

After putting spells on his demon headaches, Trilha then told Noriega something he wanted to hear. He said the introverted and homely spy chief would become more famous internationally than Panama's popular and handsome dictator Omar Torrijos. At the time, Torrijos was making quite a name for himself by negotiating the new Panama Canal Treaties. Noriega privately thought Torrijos a windbag and a drunkard. To hear a psychic voice his most secret desires was the omen Noriega had waited for, and he immediately adopted Trilha as his brother and spiritualist.

Trilha abruptly stopped talking. He was having a premonition, a vision. He saw something out in that cosmic beyond, and it seemed to make him happy. His clammy hands touched the arm of his visitor. The room was too hot, as steamy as the streets outside, covered with the muggy blanket of Panama's rainy season. Trilha was sweating through his sheer white shirt and pants, and the water dripped off the black beads hanging around his neck. While everyone in the world was predicting that Noriega would soon fall, Trilha was tuned to a different channel.

"At age twelve, I predicted the death of Kennedy with absolute precision," says Trilha. "In 1971, I predicted the date of the fall and death of Allende, and last year I predicted the fall of Stroessner. I now predict that Noriega will stay."

Trilha jumped from his seat and paced the room. He looked at the ceiling. He was having another vision. This time it was about my book—this book. "I am having a vision. I see the book cover. The title of the book will be 'The Big Truth about Noriega and Panama.' You could sell a million copies of the book. I have very good contacts with editors all over the world. I have written three books, and more than thirty-five million have been sold."

Trilha offered to provide photographs of Noriega as a child. Of Noriega at the Peruvian military academy. Of Noriega as the strongman behind Omar Torrijos. Trilha would arrange the publisher and the advance: twenty thousand dollars, he said. But that would be just the beginning. "All that is required is that the truth come out impartially."

It wasn't much of a bribe, considering his dictatorial friend's vast financial means; but rather than negotiate, I protested that I already had a publisher and an advance. Trilha said he could offer Spanish rights. I told him those had been sold as well. Then Trilha offered to put me up at Panama's lush Contadora Island to write the book. He would provide lodging and food, and would send regular shipments of goat's milk.

When that, too, was rejected, Trilha lost interest in the interview and, frowning, told me he was going to give me the same sort of massage that so relaxes Noriega. Over my protestations, he lowered me to the floor, onto a matting of damp towels, and began a massage so violent that I almost passed out. A merciful patient stopped him just before the world went dark for me.

I beat a hasty retreat.

That afternoon, I continued my research with a lawyer who represented drug figures from Cali, Colombia. He, too, knew Noriega well, and was frustrated by the problems his clients were having with the General. Noriega favored the Medellín cartel, and he used his position to promote its members in their competition with Cali bosses. Noriega would feed American drug enforcement agents information on Cali figures to set them up, he complained. This pleased his drug partners and U.S. authorities. Noriega had even shut down a Panamanian bank for money laundering in 1985, the first time such a thing had been done in Panama. One of the bank's owners had been a Cali kingpin—his competition.

The lawyer told of one client who hadn't cooperated with Noriega. The client had been visited at midnight in his plush seaside condominium by Lieutenant Colonel Nivaldo Madriñan, the vicious head of Panama's FBI who would be charged with murder after Noriega was ousted. The lawyer alleged that Madriñan proceeded to take several million dollars in $100 bills that were stacked in the client's closet and had been brought to Panama for laundering—and then vanished back into the night. Part of the capital flight from Panama hadn't anything to do with the troubled banking system or American sanctions against Noriega, the lawyer said. Rather, many launderers feared Noriega's men would rip off the money before they could get it into banks.

"Who was my client going to call for help, the police?" laughed the lawyer. "The police are Panama's thieves."

At the end of the interview, the lawyer became alarmed when told this information would be used in a book. He had provided names and dates. I assured the lawyer his identity would be camouflaged, but it didn't calm him. "I don't think you understand the dangers in what you are doing," he said. "This could be very dangerous for me—and for you. You Americans are all too naive to understand Noriega's capabilities."

I returned to my apartment hotel, watched David Letterman joke lamely about Dan Quayle on American armed forces television, and then, exhausted, shut off the light. But as I put my left hand under the pillow, I felt something cool and wet. I turned on the light to discover that my hand was covered with blood. There was a small puddle of it under the pillow.

Someone was sending me a message.

Had Ivan Trilha decided his effort to influence the book required less subtlety? Was it the drug lawyer? It even may have been the apartment hotel's receptionist, whom I had vilified a day earlier for withholding messages to me from Noriega's opponents (while keeping them on a neat list in his drawer). One of his colleagues had said he was from military intelligence.

I had been told Noriega believed in Santeria, a Cuban black-magic religion that involved animal sacrifice, so I wrapped up the pillowcase in the bed pad, which was also damp, and hid both inside a tennis bag in the closet, planning to have the blood tested for its origin upon returning home.

Using an armchair to block the entry door, I switched Letterman back on and moved to the adjacent twin bed for a fitful night's sleep.

After a short breakfast the next morning, I returned to the room to find everything as I had left it. It was still only 8 A.M., and the maid hadn't come yet. But the pillowcase and the bed pad were gone.

It was the perfect caper: I had been intimidated but hadn't any idea who had done the intimidating, or for what reason. Nor was there any proof. If I had told Panamanian friends, they would have shied away from me. If I had told the American embassy, and American diplomats had protested, my ready access to government officials would have been cut off. I did tell others, and they told me to leave Panama.

But by Panamanian standards, the message seemed almost too playful for much concern. Around the same time I was discovering the blood, Noriega's men had dumped the decapitated body of a Panamanian on the front driveway of a Panamanian-American lawyer who had accused the military of Panama Canal Treaty violations. The black head stood on its neck next to the torso, neatly wrapped in plastic.

Somehow, though, the blood under the pillow seemed a fitting metaphor for Noriega's Panama. Until the December 1989 invasion, the General controlled the country indirectly through intimidation, yet most often the repression was carefully hidden from view by his style of ruling from the shadows. When Noriega's most outspoken political opponent, Hugo Spadafora, was beheaded in 1985, the General, in the shadows, permitted the decapitated corpse to be found in an American mailbag just across the border in Costa Rica. The killing was never investigated. When vice presidential candidate Billy Ford was beaten with a pipe and his bodyguard was shot dead in an apparent assassination attempt in 1989, the perpetrators were plain-clothed "Dignity Battalions." Again, no one was arrested, but no one could prove the orders from offstage. Noriega left no fingerprints.

Noriega's life's goal has been to remain an enigma, a sphinxlike mystery man. Like a stealthy spouse, he has vowed devotion to the U.S. while promiscuously courting other mates: the Cubans, the Nicaraguans, and Libyan and Israeli intelligence agencies, to list a few. While helping the Americans fight the drug trade, he was only turning in his competition, as he skimmed off the profits from a multibillion-dollar industry. Yet all his partners in the end would discover that this laconic military man was loyal only to himself, not to any country or ideology.

He created himself, a combination of Frankenstein, Richard III, and the Wizard of Oz.

As Frankenstein, Noriega was a monster the United States helped build.

Communist-fearing Americans funded and trained an influential military—which most Panamanians never wanted—and then turned the other way as it seized power, stole elections, and repressed democracy. It was the United States military that gave Noriega much of the training he needed to rise through the ranks and then control his country. It was from the Americans that he first learned about intelligence, counterintelligence, and psychological warfare.

As Richard III, Noriega was a man misshapen by nature and society. His appearance and character were already scarred in childhood, the one by acne, the other by poverty, his father's abandonment, and the premature death of his mother. Like Richard III, Noriega sought vengeance against society and his ridiculers by becoming a virtuoso in evil who dazzled through the sheer audacity and enormity of his competency in crime. Noriega, like Richard III, pursued corruption with such a whole-souled quality that it achieved an almost inverted moral significance. He worked hard at being a perfect villain, a deceiver of all sides, and an intimidator of friends and enemies alike.

As the Wizard of Oz, Noriega built a facade that made him seem larger than life. He sat behind it, manipulating all the levers of power and fury, hoping his true, vulnerable, and troubled self wouldn't be discovered. He seemed to wilt out of uniform, and he was far shorter when not wearing one of his high-peaked hats. He supported the facade by cleverly spreading the riches of a spoils system and expertly conducting psychological warfare. The voice from behind the screen claimed to be the symbol of Panamanian nationality itself, the modern-day Simón Bolívar; but behind it sat a man with a migraine headache in his private world of insecurities. Yet to leave his chair, to dismantle the front, would certainly mean disgrace. More to the point, to surrender the facade would likely mean death for the wizard at the hands of the drug traffickers and intelligence services he had so long manipulated and too often deceived. In the end, the wizard opted for the safety of a Miami jail.

From unruly cadet in Peru, to shadowy double agent leeching off the CIA and Fidel Castro, to drug trafficker and corrupt dictator, Noriega had been a thorn in the side of every American administration since Eisenhower.

For the United States, it was a sordid marriage of convenience from the beginning. Neither partner ever felt great affection for the other, but each had its own reasons for maintaining the tie. For the U.S., the partnership with Noriega was first maintained because of fears of communism; then was protected by the Ford and Carter administrations so as not to undermine the Panama Canal Treaties talks; and finally was promoted because of the Reagan administration's greater concern with the Nicaraguan Contras than with Panamanian democracy.

Even after the 1988 drug indictments and increasing evidence of other crimes made the relationship untenable, many in the administration balked. The Drug Enforcement Administration said he was still cooperating with them; the Pentagon feared that taking on Noriega could ruin base agreements all over the world; and the CIA privately worried about the intelligence cooperation they'd lose and the threat that Noriega might reveal much of what he knew: he had many of the administration's secrets.

The American war on Noriega hence took on an intimacy and a seaminess that made it seem more of a bedroom fight than a foreign policy struggle. Many Washington individuals and agencies who profited from a relationship with Noriega quietly resisted the idea of ending it, or at least didn't want to end it in a way that humiliated a longtime friend. And Noriega, feeling like the wronged lover, opted to fight back. Even if it meant breaking all the furniture and destroying the house, Noriega refused to budge. America's effort to unseat Noriega had more the feel of divorce court than diplomacy.

No one understood this seaminess better than Joel McCleary, a former Carter White House aide who provided Noriega paid political advice in 1985 and 1986 to help democratize Panama before helping the General's opponents plot their ill-fated strategy to destroy Noriega in 1987.

"Everyone was sleeping with Noriega," says McCleary now. "Noriega was a lovely hooker. But then he grew old and got a wrinkled ass. He grew more corrupt; he started selling drugs. He wasn't fun to take to parties anymore. So you had to get rid of him."

CHAPTER
ONE

LAST RESORT

Enough is enough.

—President George Bush,
December 17, 1989

The war began at a makeshift roadblock in Panama City's slums. The battlefield was Avenida A, a narrow artery through a shantytown of rotting wood, peeling paint, and decaying corrugated tin roofing. It was growing dark, and the poor *pueblo,* as was their custom, had evacuated their steamy homes for the cooler doorsteps and rickety balconies of the Chorrillos barrio.

Yet an unfamiliar tension filled the air. Noriega's troops were jumpy, checking cars and patrolling the streets. Just a day earlier, the General had declared himself "maximum leader" of Panama, removing the last vestiges of constitutional rule, and had asserted that a "state of war" existed with the United States, thus feeding the siege mentality of his men. Noriega had received intelligence that a coup was being planned against him for this day, December 16, 1989.

Fearing the worst, Noriega had surrounded his headquarters with men from the Machos del Monte—the macho men of the mountains. They had been trained for jungle combat by the Cubans, but Noriega had brought many of them into the city after a rebel officer, Major Moisés Giroldi, almost unseated him in a coup attempt two months earlier. The Machos were the only troops that had remained entirely loyal to him. At the roadblocks around his cement headquarters complex, they stood with AK-47 semiautomatic machine guns like Latin Rambos, many of them wearing crisscrossing bandoliers, tanktop T-shirts and wild, black beards. Many had been drinking in celebration of December 16, which Noriega had made a national holiday, "Loyalty Day," when he'd taken power in 1983.

Just after 9 P.M., four American Marines took a wrong turn and unwittingly found themselves at the Machos' roadblock. Only two hours from their military curfew, they had raced across town from Fort Clayton for a quick drink at the Marriott Hotel before turning in. Marine Captain Richard Haddad was behind the wheel of a car that had gringo written all over it: a cream-colored, beat-up Chevrolet Impala with Michigan license plates—and a large blue decal in the windshield identifying him as a U.S. military officer. Captain Haddad was a gung-ho Marine out of central casting. He lifted weights, collected pistols, and bragged to superiors that he would never stop for a Panamanian roadblock; the Panama Canal Treaties didn't require it, and he wasn't about to let the Panamanian wimps get their grimy hands on him. But now, in the mean, mazelike streets of the Panamanian barrios, he found himself third in line at a roadblock on a street too narrow to allow a U-turn.

Captain Haddad's foot rested uneasily on the gas. One of his companions—First Lieutenant Robert Paz, the twenty-four-year-old son of Colombian missionaries—fidgeted as a group of Panamanians surrounded the car, shouting curses and threats. "We stopped the car, and one guy immediately locked and loaded," Haddad, a twenty-six-year-old Marine assigned to Southern Command intelligence, later told a superior officer. When the two cars in front drove off, Haddad gunned the gas, running the roadblock. "I put the pedal to the metal to get the hell out of there."

The Machos fired at the rear of the car as it barreled down Avenida A toward Noriega's nearby headquarters, where the General was celebrating his holiday. Panamanian history would change forever because of one of the wildly fired bullets which penetrated the trunk, the back seat, and then Lieutenant Paz's back.

As the car raced past the Comandancia itself, where Noriega was present with other officers, more soldiers joined in the shooting. One bullet grazed Captain Haddad's ankle. The Impala squealed around the corner toward Southern Command Gorgas Army Hospital, on a hill just a couple of miles away. But the car took yet another wrong turn, this time on July 4 Avenue, the dividing line between Panama's barrios and the rich homes of the old Canal Zone. Paz was bleeding badly in the back seat. A few minutes after they arrived at Gorgaz, Lieutenant Paz became the first American soldier to be killed by one of General Noriega's troops in a two-and-one-half-year war of nerves between the dictator and Washington. The tripwire had set in motion preparations for the biggest American military operation since the Vietnam War. It would be the largest U.S. invasion ever to be targeted so exclusively at one man.

* * *

This wasn't an isolated act that American officials felt they could afford to ignore. For in addition to killing Lieutenant Paz, Noriega's troops subjected an American couple who had witnessed the incident to some trauma of their own.

They were a navy lieutenant and his wife, who had just finished a dinner at a restaurant called La Cascada, a tacky gringo hangout with phony waterfalls, papier-maché animals, a sixteen-page menu (in English and Spanish) and $2 piña coladas. The lieutenant's wife, a graduate student in Latin studies, had arrived only that day for the Christmas holidays. The lieutenant had also taken a wrong turn, ending up behind the roadblock, where they witnessed the confrontation.

The Machos seized them, wrapped masking tape around their mouths, and bundled them off to the military intelligence headquarters around the corner. Your wife has nice tits, said one of the interrogators. Too bad that you won't enjoy them for a while.

"They kicked me in the groin fifteen or twenty times. They hit me in the stomach and they beat my feet and head with a hammer and did the same number on my ears," he said later. "They threatened to kill me and asked if I wanted to die. They had me blindfolded, so you really didn't know where the next blow would come from."

The Panamanian soldiers also threatened to sexually abuse the lieutenant's wife, but her only injury was a gash to the head when they pushed her against a cement wall. "They didn't really get too bad," said the lieutenant. "But they would insinuate they were going to touch her in other places and they rubbed up against her and things like that." She passed out after being made to stand against a wall with her hands over her head.

On Sunday morning, December 17, President Bush read intelligence reports about the incidents of the night before. If outraged, he didn't show it to his family, friends, and a multitude of their children, whom he'd invited to a Christmas brunch. The president sang carols with them, and he took groups of children on a guided tour that left out only the presidential bedroom.

It wasn't until midafternoon, when all his guests had departed, that the president retreated with his closest advisers to his private study in the White House living quarters, a cozy office where he spent most of his evenings catching up and writing notes to friends on his electric typewriter. The last, straggling guest to leave the White House spotted some familiar faces heading to the elevator for the meeting: Joint Chiefs of Staff Chairman Colin Powell, Secretary of Defense Dick Cheney, National Security Adviser Brent Scowcroft, and White House spokesman Marlin Fitzwater.

Secretary of State James Baker and Vice President Dan Quayle, who had
attended the brunch, joined them upstairs.

"Business as usual," the woman remarked.

Hardly.

President Bush was about to take the biggest risk of his political career.
The president had grown convinced that Noriega was a problem that
would only grow worse with time—an obvious lesson since his time as CIA
director in 1976, when he had paid Noriega as an "asset." Already, he had
taken some steps toward a solution. Following the failed coup attempt
three months earlier, when he had balked at helping the rebel officers at
the most critical moments, Bush had been creating a military alternative.

Senior officials had rewritten agreements with congressional intelligence
committees to give the White House greater freedom of action in Panama—including loosening the restrictions on assassinations. But more
importantly, General Maxwell R. Thurman had been brought out of retirement to replace General Frederick Woerner, a self-styled officer-diplomat
who, as head of the Southern Command, had opposed military action
against Noriega. Thurman was a fifty-eight-year-old bachelor known to
some of his men as "Mad Max" for his crazed devotion to military discipline. Thurman reviewed the contingency plans that Woerner had drawn
up—and ditched them. He thought they brought troops too slowly to
Panama to be practical. And after the Paz killing, Colin Powell, the chairman of the Joints Chiefs of Staff, abruptly reversed his reluctance to use
military force against Noriega.

Now Bush had everything in place. It was only a question of what would
provoke him. And the events surrounding the Paz killing were sufficient.

"Enough is enough," Bush told his assembled aides.

Three military alternatives were available to Bush, and contingency plans
were available for each. The most limited action envisioned the capture of
Noriega in a surprise commando-type raid by special operations forces,
supported only by conventional troops already in Panama. Its advantage
was limited casualties and the greater likelihood of maintaining secrecy,
but Bush couldn't be given any assurance that the troops would be able to
find Noriega, whom he was told was "moving around like a Mexican
jumping bean" to prevent just such an attack on him. The middle course
foresaw using only the 12,000 troops already stationed in Panama. They
could surely decapitate the defense forces and capture Noriega's cronies.
Casualties would be low and secrecy protected. The danger was that such
a limited force might not prevent prolonged fighting outside of Panama
City nor prevent threats to the Panama Canal.

In the end, President Bush joined Powell in preferring the sledgehammer approach: massive force. There was, to be sure, less chance of secrecy, but greater assurance of finishing off Noriega and his allies for good, whether or not he was seized at the moment of invasion. Powell agreed this was the only way to "guarantee success rapidly"—which an impatient American public would demand. The only problem: this option posed the greatest risk of military and civilian casualties. But while the danger of deaths increased, the danger of failure disappeared altogether.

Bush quizzed Powell methodically throughout the thirty-minute meeting. What kind of equipment? Could it be brought in without tipping off Noriega? What kind of troops? Could Noriega be captured just as the invasion began? Bush wanted Powell to assure him there'd be no repeat of the failure at Desert One, the disastrous mission launched by Jimmy Carter to rescue the hostages in Iran. He also talked about the tragic errors in invading Grenada and how they had to be avoided in Panama.

In the end, however, Bush made the decision alone, without awaiting a consensus among his advisers. "Let's do it," he said. The original name of the operation was "Blue Spoon." But that wouldn't do for the history books. A more fitting title was chosen: "Operation Just Cause."

At 2 P.M. Tuesday, Bush called a meeting that was tellingly described as a session to discuss "the use of the military in the war on drugs." By that time most of the details were in place, and the key troops had all been put on alert and separated from any phones. The circle of senior officials who knew about the invasion plan was cautiously expanded, but Bush would still keep his secret from Congress until 10 P.M. that night. National Security Adviser Brent Scowcroft gave each of the advisers a document identifying the tasks to be conducted from 6 P.M. to 1 A.M., when the invasion would be launched—H-Hour. Once again, to the outside world, George Bush acted naturally. That evening, just a few hours before a massive attack involving more than 20,000 troops, he spent two hours greeting 300 guests at one of many White House Christmas receptions. Wearing a bright red and green tie, he joined the guests in the East Room to hear the Army Chorus sing Christmas carols. The last guest in the line, *New York Times* reporter Maureen Dowd, whispered to a friend that she wanted to ask the president something about Panama. But she thought better of it at the festive affair.

The question could wait.

Meanwhile, the best-kept secret in Washington was rapidly becoming common knowledge inside Noriega's circle.

General Noriega's first hint of danger came from Nicaragua's intelligence chief, Ricardo Wheelock, who arrived Sunday evening on one of his increasingly frequent visits. "We believe Wheelock warned Noriega that he was going too far," said one Southern Command officer. He said that the Soviets had grown convinced from spotting increased activity at American military bases that the U.S. would act soon, "But we don't believe Wheelock's report was definitive." Spotted by a reporter at Panama's airport en route to Managua on December 19, the day before the invasion, Wheelock pointed to his duty-free bag and explained he had come to Panama only for shopping.

Further advance warning came more than twenty-four hours before the attack, at 10 P.M. on Monday, December 18, from Vice Minister of Health Orlando Allen. Allen, a close ally of Noriega's, had graduated from medical school in Moscow and was known to have close links to Soviets who were believed to be KGB agents. Allen's warning was phoned into the Comandancia hotline. Separately, a report was registered from retired Sergeant Israel Gonzalez, who "overheard two Hispanic U.S. soldiers talking about H-hour and called it into the Comandancia." H-hour, Noriega was told, would be 2 A.M. Tuesday, barely an hour later than it would actually begin. But still, "Noriega basically did not believe the U.S. would attack Panama and discounted the warning," according to a U.S. intelligence report. The U.S. had cried "wolf" so often in threatening Noriega that he never believed Bush would risk U.S. lives over him.

But the warnings grew more explicit on the eve of the invasion. Noriega was in the city of Colón, where his intelligence chief, Rafito Cedeño, briefed him on information obtained from the Cubans. The data was indisputable, he said. At that moment C-130 transport planes were flying to Panama with men and equipment—ten minutes apart through air space well within Cuba's intelligence-gathering reach. The Cubans were logging each craft, and estimating the tonnage. This was either a very costly bluff or the beginning of the end. By 5 P.M. on December 19, General Noriega grew convinced an attack was imminent. A later report on a debriefing of one of Noriega's strategists said: "Source said Noriega was worried about being captured by the Delta Force, fearing a surgical operation. Noriega's greatest fear was the drug charge, and he felt he would not get a fair trial if taken to the U.S." He doubted Cedeño's estimate of the invasion's probable size. But he knew he would be the first target.

So Noriega went on the lam. He slipped out of a friend's home in Colón and drove overland in a white van. The driver would occasionally steer off the main road, just to check if he were being observed. Back in Panama City, he borrowed a Hyundai and drove toward the airport like a moth to the flame; American paratroopers were well on their way. It was the perfect getaway vehicle: Noriega was known for always driving BMWs or four-wheel-drive vehicles with darkly tinted windows. The gringos weren't looking for a South Korean subcompact car.

A team from the crack Delta Force of the 82nd Airborne, which had flown secretly to Panama several days earlier, worked with the world's most sophisticated electronic eavesdropping equipment and satellite surveillance in a vain attempt to locate their quarry. At times he used a double, who was spotted through the tinted glass of a four-wheel-drive jeep just like that belonging to the General. "As unlikely as it sounds, there's another guy who looks as ugly as Noriega," said one military officer, "and we think he's been used as a decoy." He sent helicopters, often empty, flying from his places of refuge, sending American forces on wild-goose chases. He changed his clothing several times daily to throw off his spotters. To confuse gringo eavesdroppers, he had recorded his voice and had it played over office phones he hadn't used for weeks.

Ultimately, by Tuesday night, he wound up at a sleazy military recreation center called La Siesta, near Tocumen airport, where the Rangers and the 82nd Airborne would drop down in less than four hours. But the U.S. Special Forces had failed to pick up Noriega's trail. The invasion would go ahead, but hitting the target would have to wait.

Thus, as H-hour approached, the emphasis on nabbing Noriega shifted to destroying the General's military infrastructure so that even his escape couldn't endanger the operation. To achieve this, nothing was more important in the first minutes of battle than destroying his headquarters, and, with it, command and control.

At 7 P.M. Monday evening, barely six hours to H-hour, Lieutenant Doug Rubin of Virginia Beach briefed the two dozen–odd men in his platoon for what he foresaw as a bloody and perhaps fatal engagement. He posed them in front of their APCs and took snapshots with his Pentax. He told them to write letters home and leave them behind on their sleeping bags or bunks—where they would be easily discovered, just in case. Then Rubin—twenty-six years old and mature beyond his years—prayed with his men. Rubin saw this war as a classic conflict of good and evil, like the ones he'd read about in the Old Testament. He viewed his armored personnel carrier as God's modern weaponry against Satan's new envoy. Rubin's men had never faced fire before, and he wanted to convince them that God was in their camp. "I don't know how some of you feel about God taking sides in combat," he prayed. "But God has always wanted evil eradicated from the world." And Noriega was evil.

At 12:30 P.M. he pulled his M-113 armored personnel carrier up to the "LD"—the line of demarcation. The first vehicle rolling into battle is always the most likely to be wiped out, so only four men manned this M-113, while at least eight occupied each of the vehicles behind it. The LD, appropriately enough, was Fourth of July Avenue, the road between the Panamanian ghetto and the rich homes of the former canal zone, which Panamanians had renamed Avenue of the Martyrs, for students killed in clashes with the Americans in 1964. Lieutenant Rubin searched the heavens for assistance. There they were, right on cue: two AC-130 Spectre gunships. The lumbering, stubby, propeller-driven planes carried weaponry made pinpoint precise with star-wars guidance systems—"surgical firepower" that would wipe out Noriega's headquarters in the ten minutes it would take for Rubin and company to reach the target from July 4 Avenue. The soldiers had an affectionate nickname for the planes: "Puff the Magic Dragon."

Finally, at 12:45 P.M., the order came: *Roll.*

Rubin watched the Spectre gunships, from the 1st Special Operations Wing from the Florida panhandle, perform. Six targets were hit immediately. However, the forewarning had allowed most of the men and officers to vacate Noriega's headquarters. Rubin's APCs rolled over blockades of cars that Noriega's soldiers had put up that evening, while gunfire, mortar, and grenades rained down from the slum houses that surrounded the Comandancia. Tracer bullets whizzed back and forth, the Americans' red streak of light crisscrossing the Panamanians' green.

Either from the tracer bullets or Molotov cocktails, the shantytown was quickly alight. The conflagration could be seen from luxury high-rises miles away.

Rubin commanded his platoon to the back of the headquarters, where his job was to blow up the wall and secure that side. But all three of his vehicles were soon disabled, and Rubin was taking refuge under one of them, radioing for help as grenades exploded all around. Twenty-one of his twenty-four men were injured, fifteen of them sent home for treatment. Yet no one was killed—an outcome Rubin considered miraculous.

The attack on the Comandancia was perhaps the most brutal in an invasion that had remarkably few slipups, considering its size and its nighttime launch. In a series of simultaneous attacks that included two widely separated parachute assaults, the overnight invasion not only captured Noriega's headquarters in downtown Panama City but blocked reinforcements from outside, crippling the Panamanian Defense Forces and the paramilitary "Dignity Battalions." The Panamanian Defense Forces counted some 15,000 personnel, but only 3,300 were capable of combat, and only a few hundred actually resisted the invading American forces. Most either gave up or fled when the skies over Panama filled with the roar of assault helicopters, Air Force fighters, and transport planes that swooped low, dropping heavily armed paratroopers. Sometimes it almost seemed too easy, more like a military exercise than a war. Some whole companies were found missing from their headquarters. And the U.S. was able to try out some of its highest-technology equipment, such as the top-secret Stealth F-117 fighters that surgically attacked the perimeter of RioHató Air Base, stunning the Panamanians into submission with two-thousand-pound charges.

Noriega was being entertained by a prostitute at La Siesta when he heard the first explosions at just before 12:45 A.M., one of his companions would later tell American investigators. "He pulled up his pants, jumped in his Hyundai, and fled," said one U.S. military man who traced the General's steps later. "He basically drove around in circles all night." Noriega remained just ahead of troops as they rolled into town. "The escaping Hyundai was fired on by tracers at one point and had to turn off its headlights to escape," the report says, not indicating whether those firing knew Noriega was inside.

Noriega kept moving. The report says he stopped at Los Andes #2, on the road from the airport into town, where a local politician, Lucho Gómez, helped hide him; at the home of the San Miguelito mayor, Balbina Periñan, who was known for her brutal rule on behalf of Noriega; and at the home of his lawyer, Ramón "Tinto" Arosemena; and at the plush and sprawling house of arms dealer Jorge Krupnick, who was already on the U.S. wanted list for alleged narcotics and drug connections.

Two hours after the attack, at either the first or second home, Noriega phoned a clandestine radio station and issued a blustery statement that he would fight "to the end." But despite the bravado of the declaration, he was flat on his belly when he called his allies to arms—the hideout was a small house without curtains. "Noriega had to low-crawl across the room to get to the phone during the day," said a U.S. intelligence report. Noriega also phoned the Cuban ambassador from his hideaway. "Noriega really wanted to get to the Cuban residence or Cuban embassy, according to source," the document read.

Another call from the cold marble floor of the safe house went to mistress Vicky Amado, who had become more his wife. The Amados, in fact, had become his adopted family. Her mother, Norma Amado, was attending to his business, his appointments, and even his cooking—so that he could avoid poisoning. He tried to call his most beloved daughter,

Sandra, but without luck. "He did not call his wife, according to source," the cable said dryly.

When the dust had settled on the morning of December 20, one big blemish remained visible to the world: Noriega was still at large. So the Bush administration posted a reward—one million dollars for information leading to the seizure of the fugitive dictator. Since most of Noriega's friends had been in it for the money, it seemed the perfect solution. Indeed, his friends vanished with his power. Noriega didn't contact fellow officers to issue orders, not knowing if they could be trusted.

On Wednesday, at Noriega's hideout, the General suspected the U.S. was onto him when the phone went dead. Once again he got into his Hyundai, and he continued to drive, fearing every face was that of an enemy. "He was highly agitated and actually avoided contact with several PDF officers his group bumped into, out of paranoia," the intelligence report said, quoting a source captured later, who was with Noriega at the time.

The source told U.S. intelligence agents that Noriega was particularly concerned that he didn't have any of his religious totems with him that he believed could ward off evil. He had forgotten them at a home where he had changed clothes, and he didn't dare turn back. All he had were the protective black beads around his neck that he gave to his allies as gifts. "Source related that Noriega regularly wears red underwear to ward off the 'evil eye,' " the report said.

Later on Wednesday Noriega moved into the locker room of the health club at Jorge Krupnick's luxurious home on Avenida 3L Sur, in one of the city's richest neighborhoods. While Noriega was in lavish but exhausted isolation, the contingency plan he had worked on for many weeks was put into play, but only partially due to the rash of surrenders and defections in the first hours of combat. Some units took to the hills for potential guerrilla war, aware that tons of weapons had been pre-positioned around the country. And within Panama City, Noriega's plan to destroy the business and middle class, and then to rule with his own followers and the poor of Panama, was being executed. Members of the Dignity Battalions would break into stores, remove the money from registers, and pile the most valuable goods into trucks. They would then stand guard as looters picked clean what remained on the shelves. The most glaring oversight of the U.S. invasion was the failure to deploy Military Police with tear gas against looters. The mistake was a costly one: more than a half billion dollars in damage that the United States would later have to help repair.

Yet the second part of this plan—guerrilla warfare—wasn't to be. The deputy chief of Noriega's security, Capt. Ivan Castillo, sitting near the pool at Krupnick's home, asked the General whether they shouldn't take to the jungles or mountains to mount a guerrilla war. "Noriega's reaction to this idea was tentatively favorable," said an intelligence report on this exchange. "But he stated that they (Castillo and Noriega) would probably both get heart attacks if they tried it."

Noriega was once a star pupil at the U.S. army jungle training center at Fort Gulick in Panama. Just before the invasion, Noriega was seen wearing a camouflage jacket bearing the distinctive patch from his 1967 jungle training class there. Yet since his training heydays, he had put on weight and developed a strong taste for the good life and his favorite brand of whiskey, Old Parr.

"Noriega realized the jig was up," according to the U.S. intelligence report, when he learned terribly disturbing news listening to a small radio: Lieutenant Colonel Luis del Cid was surrendering in Military Zone Five.

Del Cid, a handsome if corpulent officer with a regal nose and penetrating eyes, was the only officer besides Noriega to have been indicted on drug charges in the United States. He knew he would be enemy #2 for the drug-fighting gringos. On the night after the invasion, del Cid was growing alarmed that he hadn't heard a word from his Comandante, who seemed more interested in saving his own skin than fighting for his dignity. Del Cid had to make some quick decisions.

After the initial attack, Colonel del Cid followed the contingency plan that had been established months before for such an invasion. His troops laid mines at the local airport to prevent American planes from landing, and he retreated with loyal officers to the mountains outside David City, the capital of Chiriquí province, where a young major named Tony Noriega had once fought opposition guerrillas. It was the natural place for Noriega to retreat to lead his own resistance movement. But del Cid and his officer corps decided within twenty-four hours that Mr. Noriega was no latter-day Che Guevara.

"The whole infrastructure of our forces was destroyed in the first hour," said Major Ivan Gaytan, who at age thirty-seven was one of Noriega's smartest and fastest-rising officers, and who was del Cid's right-hand man. "The only thing we could do is react to existing plans. Nothing more."

Major Gaytan had spent 1985 through 1987 teaching psychological operations and other courses to Salvadoran officers at Fort Benning, Georgia. He had also taken management courses at Emory University in Atlanta. But it didn't take a graduate course for him to understand that lengthy guerrilla warfare wasn't in the cards. Major Gaytan decided with the other officers that the U.S. wasn't about to engage itself in a bloody ground-war against guerrilla forces.

"I personally know the Americans quite well," Major Gaytan told the others. "They aren't going to put troops up against our guerrillas because they wouldn't put soldiers in another Vietnam. They will simply bomb the hell out of our area."

Something else dawned on him: Although they had plenty of weapons and men, they lacked the high-tech shoulder-held missiles needed to hold off the 82nd Airborne Division. At one point he turned to his fellow officers and said, "It would be impossible to confront the U.S. invasion with these fossils of weapons." Just as meaningfully, the troops lacked the popular backing essential to sustain a guerrilla war.

So del Cid and the others decided to end the war in Chiriquí. Ivan Gaytan turned to his family for help. From his mountain hiding place, he phoned his thirty-year-old brother, Moisés, a Catholic priest. He told Moisés that the officers had decided to work out a deal with the gringos, but that they wanted the Church's assistance. Ivan then reached a second brother, Eliecer, who was head of Noriega's special forces and personal security. No officer was more loyal to Noriega. Ivan told Eliecer that del Cid was quitting, and a day later Eliecer himself sought refuge at the Vatican's embassy in Panama City, removing yet another of Noriega's critical allies from the field.

The colonel's surrender wasn't the usual act of self-humiliation. In a series of telephone linkups to the U.S. military in Panama City, del Cid pursued a novel form of plea bargaining. What he had to offer, in brief, was peace in Panama's most important and treacherous outlying province. Thus he could hand over Noriega's last best hope of holding out militarily against the U.S. In exchange, Lieutenant Colonel del Cid would later say, he won a U.S. promise not to dispatch troops against him—and a pledge, as he put it, to "respect my rank." He also received assurances that his cooperation could help reduce drug charges against him in Miami.

Then Major General Marc Cisneros of U.S. Southern Command went to work.

Cisneros, a Mexican-American born in Texas, was impressing State Department officials with his diplomatic skills. He worked the telephone around the country, convincing local commanders to surrender rather than engage in a war with the Americans that they could only lose. He promised them dignity and the possibility of their troops joining the new security forces, all the while making it clear that the alternative was an American shellacking.

Before taking del Cid's bait, Cisneros wanted proof of the Noriega loyalist's goodwill. Cisneros wanted a white flag flying over his headquarters. He wanted del Cid to give interviews to Western reporters about his surrender. And he wanted del Cid to collect weapons from the Dignity Battalions of his province, over whom he ruled.

Late on Thursday December 21, not quite two days after the invasion, Cisneros dispatched planes to conduct a flyby over the concrete command post, located in the city of David. U.S. military men learned to their relief that they weren't likely to face a long guerrilla struggle in the Panamanian countryside. The white flag was fluttering in the warm tropical breeze. Reporters were allowed in the following day, and del Cid began to collect the weaponry. By the time of his first press conference, del Cid still hadn't had time to remove a poem that he had inscribed "with love and respect" for the General. Entitled "If I Call Myself Your Friend," it read in part:

> *When shadows are running over your soul,*
> *And you think everything is lost*
> *I want you to know that if you call me*
> *Your friend, I'll be there.*

But Noriega's friend was gone.

Early on Sunday, December 24, del Cid was flown to Panama City on a military aircraft. His phone calls had led him to believe he would be greeted warmly and be offered soft treatment. Instead, DEA agents frisked him, took him inside a military transport plane, and made him strip. While he was handcuffed to the ceiling, doctors unceremoniously checked out his health and then cleared him for flight as a captured fugitive to the United States. If it came to a trial, he would be a state's witness against Noriega. Del Cid cried.

Yet that didn't lessen the U.S. victory in Chiriquí province. Ironically, it had been gained through just the sort of bargaining with an indicted drug trafficker that for months Washington had refused to engage in with Noriega. The biggest American triumph since the first day of the fighting was won without firing a shot. Noriega was left without a place of retreat or resistance.

The State Department's Michael Kozak, who had overseen Panama policy since the end of the Reagan administration, saw Cisneros repeat his telephone warfare with different commanders around the country. "The 82nd Airborne conquered Panama City and Río Ható—and Marc Cisneros conquered the rest of Panama on the telephone," he laughed.

And, with each defection, the heat grew on Noriega, who was increasingly confused by the suddenness of his demise. He had not only lost command of a country, he had lost command of himself. His two bodyguards took over his fate, telling him when he had to move and when to lay low.

During the last two days of his four-day flight, the fallen dictator was moving primarily between Krupnick's lavish home and another comfortable chateau a few miles away, near the popular Panama City horse track. The home was owned by the sister of the singer Ulysses Tason, but intelligence sources believed the real hostess to be Noriega's plump and likable secretary, Marcela Tason, who was Ulysses' wife. Marcela, a photography enthusiast, had become a millionaire through dictation, shorthand, and a loyal friendship that made her one of the few people to have access to Noriega's files. Noriega was a generous and jealous boss. At first he had opposed her marriage to the singer, who had spent two decades carousing and singing in New York City bars. Ulysses Rodriguez also seemed to be a gold digger, and he happily accepted his wife's last name of Tason as his own. The secretary's influence was far greater than his own in a country where all assumed her demands were those of the General.

Another one of Noriega's companions during his four days in hiding was Ivan Castillo, one of the General's bodyguards, whom Noriega's allies had grown to suspect in recent weeks. Castillo was growing nervous, fearing an attack on Noriega would take his life as well. Noriega was so frightened of capture on the night of December 23 that he contemplated suicide. At 6:30 A.M. on Christmas Castillo talked Noriega into letting him go to get help and "come back in an hour." He never returned.

"Although ostensibly loyal to Noriega," said an intelligence report on Castillo's actions, "in the end he walked away out of self-interest. But if he had clearly understood that a one-million-dollar bounty was being offered for Noriega, he would have turned himself in." For Noriega's friends, loyalty always had a price tag.

The one-million-dollar offer had brought a rash of crackpot reports to the Special Forces' contingents searching for the General. The hundreds of calls were mostly fanciful. Panamanians reported Noriega dressed as a woman in the mountains of Chiriquí province, as a patient hiding in the back of an ambulance, and in whorehouses with ladies of the night. They were sure he was in Cuba, Nicaragua, and the Dominican Republic. One had seen his dead body—he'd supposedly committed suicide. But by midmorning of Christmas eve, Lieutenant Colonel Harry B. Axson, the forty-four-year-old commander of an 82nd Airborne battalion, had a lead worth taking seriously.

An informant had come in with details so precise on Noriega's location that Axson, a six-foot-six-inch, 225-pound officer, put his men into motion. The informant said Noriega was at Jorge Krupnick's house, and he drew a blueprint of the home so detailed that he must have spent many hours there with Krupnick. The man was a worker—not one of Noriega's cronies—and the million dollars seemed to be his lure. He said Noriega's mistress, Vicky Amado, was traveling with him—as was her teenage daughter. Axson threw a bag over the informant's head, a camouflage cloth with two holes cut in it, and they hopped into an all-terrain vehicle to approach the home. He prepared two four-man teams to storm the front and back, and the rest of his platoon of thirty men would surround and isolate the Spanish-style estate, not far from the shore of the Pacific and a two-minute drive from the Marriott, where the debriefing of the informant had taken place.

When the troops went in, at about noon, they stormed a home that looked more like a resort: there was a rock steam bath, a huge wine cellar, a weight-lifting room, a swimming pool, a large billiards table, five Mercedes-Benzes, a candy-red Porsche, and the largest satellite dish Axson had ever seen. They even found Noriega's hideaway, a comfortable retreat in the "locker room" for the pool area. He had a quadraphonic sound system, two televisions, and a comfortable bed. The entire pool area was still decorated for the wedding of Krupnick's daughter a week earlier—lots of bows all around and decorative Spanish moss in the pool. Axson thought it looked like a scene from *Miami Vice*. The pool area was inhabited by toucans on the banisters and a couple of monkeys swinging in the palms.

But there was no Noriega.

Axson's troops had missed him by less than half an hour. Neighbors and Mrs. Krupnick would later say he had taken off from Krupnick's spacious backyard in a tiny tuna-hunting helicopter, a white-and-blue craft of the sort that fly low over the ocean to spot schools of fish. The bodyguards drove off separately in a green Mitsubishi. Axson believed Vicky Amado escaped in the craft with Noriega—airborne getaway for a broken Bonnie and Clyde.

Axson doubted this story at first, but neighbors and the observation tower that the 82nd Airborne had posted atop the nearby Marriott had spotted the helicopter and reported its short flight hugging Panama City's shoreline. "I'm positive that's the way he got out," said Axson. The chopper flew up the coast from Panama City, setting down no more than six miles away.

But although Axson missed Noriega, he found a collection of hangers-on. At first, Mrs. Krupnick protested that Noriega had never been there. She said she needed to return to her turkey, which was in the oven. "While you're cooking that turkey, I'm chasing this turkey," Axson laughed.

A teenage girl finally spilled the beans. Sarita Sossa, the daughter of Vicky Amado, pleaded with the soldiers not to do anything to her mother. Just two months earlier, Noriega had deported a nun who had failed the teenage girl in a course at her parochial school, raising a local controversy. But now the young girl, spoiled by the riches that Noriega had showered on her family, was turning on the General, providing the details of his departure. "All my mother wants is peace," she said.

Axson then questioned a young boy playing a computer game. Did he know General Noriega? "Yes, he's my godfather," the boy said. Quite a family, Axson thought.

Finally, Mrs. Krupnick started talking, making clear that Noriega was a guest no one wanted. He had only twenty families to whom he could turn in a country of two million people. He was traveling primarily among five of them. "He will always be my friend—he has been good to us," she said. "You people have to understand. I would help any human being. And he is a human being. When will you give up?"

"We won't, ma'am," said the lanky lieutenant colonel. He warned Mrs. Krupnick that if Noriega were at her home again, troops probably wouldn't be able to hear cries of surrender as they stormed in. He said they would fire so many shots that the roof would fall in. He wanted to dissuade the woman from providing safe harbor in the future.

She seemed more interested in the house than Noriega. "But I have worked so hard for so many years on this home," she protested, bringing Axson a piece of holiday fruitcake that she had baked for the General. Axson thought the fruitcake was good, and remarked that it was too bad the former dictator wasn't there to enjoy it.

Mrs. Krupnick said the General wasn't a danger to anyone anymore. "He has no will of his own," she said. "His bodyguards control his movements and tell him when and where to go."

About then the phone rang. Vicky Amado wanted to speak to her daughter. Two special agents picked up two other phones to listen in. Amado said that Noriega was exhausted. "He's tired," she said. "He's giving himself up."

At about 1:30 P.M., a friend of Noriega, Mario Rognoni, phoned the papal nuncio, José Sebastián Laboa, on his private line. With the Cuban and Nicaraguan embassies and residences surrounded by troops, Monsignor Laboa was his last hope of gaining asylum in a third country. And Noriega knew Laboa well, a man who had always kept his door open to the errant General. He knew Laboa wasn't on his side, but he knew the papal nuncio had been critical of the United States' manner of handling the General.

Noriega, a man of many superstitions and beliefs, still returned to Catholicism in the end. A giant painting of St. George, his patron saint, hung at one of his offices, and he would take off his black Santeria beads and don a crucifix whenever he visited Laboa.

At sixty-seven, Laboa didn't seem to the layman to be the archbishop that he was. He was an elfish monsignor, a Spanish Basque with a taste for good food and laughter. He had come to Panama in February 1983, just seven months before Noriega had come to power, and he was the dean of the diplomatic corps and by far its best-informed ambassador. He also had a way of cutting through the finery of diplomatic life to the truth. His last job at the Vatican had been running a tribunal that investigated reports of miracles in the process of canonizing new saints. Laboa was the *Abogado del Diablo*—the "Devil's Advocate." He was the priest who cut to shreds imposters and their fake miracles.

Noriega dragged the nuncio into his drama at about 2 P.M. on Christmas Eve, when he called from a pay phone at a gas station. He said that he would send one of his bodyguards in ten minutes to the Vatican residence. Noriega wanted the nuncio to come pick him up and grant him refuge. The bodyguard would drive the nuncio to Noriega in the Vatican's own light-blue 1983 Toyota Crown, with its fluttering white-and-yellow papal flag. U.S. soldiers would be unlikely to stop the diplomatically protected car. Noriega wouldn't disclose his location to the nuncio for fear he would be turned in.

"You are out of your mind," said the nuncio. "I can't do that."

Noriega spoke quickly. You have ten minutes to decide, he said. If you don't come, I will go into the jungles. There will be a bloodbath in Panama. A massacre.

The nuncio briefly tried to call General Cisneros, but he had been unable to reach him at the numbers he had for more than a day. He decided to send his car to Noriega, but it was too risky for the nuncio himself to go with the bodyguard. So Father Javier Villanueva, the most outspoken anti-Noriega priest in Panama, was disguised in the vestments of the nuncio. He was a Spanish Basque, like Monsignor Laboa, and he was about the nuncio's height and age. He sat in the nuncio's spot in the rear right seat of the car. Father Joseph Spiteri, the nuncio's personal secretary, hopped onto the front seat beside the bodyguard. The bodyguard assumed the nuncio was his passenger.

After driving just a few blocks, Father Spiteri noticed the car was almost out of gas, and all filling stations were closed because of the war. The priests finally flagged down the car of a fellow cleric, and they siphoned off enough gasoline to get them to their meeting place: a Dairy Queen in a working-class suburb of Panama City, just eight miles from the Nunciatura. The gas problem had delayed the priests, and they saw no Noriega. Fearing he had left, they asked to use a phone at the Dairy Queen. But no phone was available.

When they returned to the car, beside the brightly colored plastic slides of the children's playground, a dark Mitsubishi Montero arrived with windows so darkly tinted that the priests couldn't recognize the driver. The passenger, who climbed out quickly, was familiar to them even in his disguise: a gray T-shirt, blue-and-white Bermuda shorts, and a large white baseball cap pulled down to his eyes. He had an Uzi submachine gun and a grenade hidden under a blanket. A backup weapon, a tiny lady's pistol, was tucked into his belt, under his shirt against the small of his back.

As was prearranged, Noriega's bodyguard jumped into the Montero, and Father Joseph took over the wheel of the Toyota. Noriega climbed quickly into the back seat, so as not to be seen, and he turned toward the man who should have been the nuncio.

"Do you know me?" asked Father Javier Villanueva.

"*Lamentable, sí,*" said Noriega. Unfortunately, he did. The nuncio had tricked him.

While riding in the back seat of the nuncio's Toyota with Noriega, Father Joseph inspected the fallen dictator's face in an effort to read his thoughts. He thought about the irony of history, of how the Catholic Church was now protecting this sinner's life. Having lost all friends and hope, the prodigiously prodigal son was seeking shelter from the Church. Father Joseph searched the face for signs of tension, for any warning that Noriega might react violently or take him or Father Javier hostage. Instead, said Father Joseph, "I saw a scared little face under a baseball cap."

They drove in silence to the Vatican embassy, where the nuncio was nervously waiting. The Noriega chase was over. The General had eluded the gringos. But, fittingly enough, the anti-Christ had surrendered to an archbishop.

The American invasion of Panama was more successful than any of its planners could have hoped. Noriega's military had been destroyed, most of his cronies were captured or on the run, and the General himself was off the streets, perhaps never to be free again.

But at such a cost. Twenty-five Americans lay dead. Perhaps as many as 1,000 Panamanians were killed. Some $1.5 billion in property had been destroyed.

For all its apparent success, this war, like most, was more the result of failed policy than brilliant strategy. It came only after the Reagan and Bush administrations bungled several opportunities to remove General Noriega at far less cost. And for more than a quarter of a century before that, American officials had done much to create Noriega: they recruited him as a young spy in 1960, they helped him form a small, provincial intelligence operation in 1967, they provided him all the training an aspiring intelligence chief and Comandante could want. Then they put him on the payroll, paying his intelligence service up to $200,000 a year by 1985— equal to the American president's salary.

With the December 1989 invasion, the United States had brought down Noriega, but it had also destroyed a little of itself.

CHAPTER
TWO

BUSH'S RECURRING NIGHTMARE

I've got Bush by the balls.
> —MANUEL ANTONIO NORIEGA,
> AUGUST 12, 1988

For George Bush, pushing the Noriega problem under the carpet had become a habit, dating back to his days as director of the Central Intelligence Agency under President Gerald Ford.

The last thing that Bush wanted to hear then was that a two-bit intelligence chief from a banana-and-banking republic was buying intelligence from his CIA agents, but that's exactly what the resourceful Noriega was doing. Even worse, Noriega was doing it at the same time that he was on Bush's CIA payroll.

President Gerald Ford had hired Bush in January 1976 with a simple mandate: damage control. The CIA was reeling from the shocks of Watergate and the Church committee hearings, which had left the agency scattered and demoralized, with too much bad press about corruption, assassination plots, and illegal clandestine activities against domestic enemies. Bush also had an unspoken partisan role: as the former Republican National Committee chairman, he would avoid any more scandals that might prevent a Republican victory in the 1976 presidential elections.

Idaho Senator Frank Church, the Democratic head of the senate Intelligence Committee, fumed at the Bush appointment. "How peculiar it is," said Church, "that we are being asked to confirm as CIA director an individual whose past record of political activism and partisan ties to the president contradict the very purpose of political impartiality and objectivity for which the agency was created." President Ford appeased angry senators somewhat by promising he would not consider Bush as his running mate, but that didn't reduce the Republican loyalist's political role.

Then just three months after Bush took office, he learned that the army had launched an inquiry into Noriega's misadventures, details of which might embarrass the Ford administration and cause the Republicans long term political damage. Code-named "Canton Song," the investigation revealed that Lieutenant Colonel Manuel Antonio Noriega, Panama's chief of intelligence, had been buying reel-to-reel audio tapes from members of the army's 470th Military Intelligence Brigade, which conducted high-tech eavesdropping throughout the region on behalf of the Defense Intelligence Agency. The 470th was specifically tasked to tape Panamanian officials involved in Canal treaty negotiations. At the time, former California governor Ronald Reagan was already winning points in presidential primaries by denouncing Ford for aiming to give away "our Panama Canal." If "Canton Song" were to hit the newspapers, Ford's campaign would suffer a severe blow.

The details were relatively simple: Noriega, who at the time was being paid by both the CIA and the Defense Intelligence Agency, had discovered the U.S. wiretap operation. Instead of blowing the whistle, Noriega had had a better idea. He allowed the Americans to continue recording, and he purchased copies of some of the tapes on behalf of his boss, Panamanian dictator Omar Torrijos. Buying American agents in Panama had never been much of a problem. Many were Puerto Rican–born and had no loyalty to their largely WASP superiors. Noriega remembered them and their children at Christmas with small gifts, and he phoned on their birthdays—more attention than gringo officers ever paid them.

Lew Allen, Jr., then the head of the National Security Agency, was in charge of international electronic surveillance when the case, which would soon be known as the "Singing Sergeants" affair, came to light. To send a message to other would-be traitors, Allen wanted to prosecute harshly and publicly. In a memo, Allen urged Bush to back his plan. But the CIA director balked. He said he lacked authority. This was an army matter, he said, and the embarrassed army had opted to keep the lid on. At the time, however, the CIA feared that Noriega had sold the sensitive intelligence— which may have included wiretaps on Cuban and other leaders in the region—to Fidel Castro's intelligence service, which also had Noriega on its payroll.

Bush not only let the officers and Noriega go unpunished, he also opted to continue paying Noriega some $110,000 annually for his liaison relationship with the CIA.

"Noriega must have appeared to Bush as a bad guy from the very beginning," says Stansfield Turner now, the retired admiral who took over the CIA from Bush in 1977. "We had caught him red-handed with his fingers on our cookie jar. While establishing a close relationship with us, he was willing to cheat on us."

Turner said that this and other suspicions about Noriega's misadventures had prompted him to cut contractual payments to Panama's intelligence service. It was part of President Carter's general housecleaning at the CIA that demoralized many agents but, Turner thought, made the United States less blackmailable. Turner would recall this with some ire some eleven years later when Bush, running for president, suggested that the last seven American administrations had paid Noriega. "Bush is in the government during the Ford administration, and Noriega is on the payroll," Turner says. "Bush is out of the government during the Carter years, and Noriega is off the payroll. Bush comes back, and so does Noriega. Those are the facts, and you have to figure out for yourself what they mean."

Even back in 1976, Bush realized that paying Noriega didn't mean buying him. "Canton Song" wasn't even the worst of it. New intelligence in the fall linked Noriega to a chain of three bombings aimed at American property and civilians. He'd been ordered to stir up things by Torrijos, who was angry over the foundering talks on the Panama Canal Treaties. With elections coming, the Ford administration had decided to step back from the widely unpopular treaty negotiations. As a result, Panamanian dictator Torrijos had come under domestic pressure on his political left to get tough with Washington. Torrijos was also enraged by a comment by candidate Carter, who had said in a debate with Ford that he would "never" give up "practical" control of the Zone. Just prior to the bombings, one of Torrijos's chief negotiators, Rómulo Escobar Bethancourt, went to poolside at Contadora Island to warn his U.S. interlocutor, Michael Kozak. "I would advise you to get out of this," he said. "I think there is no good left in this for reasonable people." He said Panama would be turning to "direct action"—a term that had already become terrorists' shorthand—to make its feelings known.

As was his habit, Torrijos assigned Noriega his dirty work. The targets would be in the American-controlled Panama Canal Zone, a red-neck preserve of baseball fields, country-and-western bars, and Southern Baptist churches, where racism had a good name and political lobbying against the treaties was most reactionary. The "Zonians," a unique race of people who had settled in the American zone in the early 1900s, had always been a thorn in nationalist Panamanians' sides. The Zonians realized that Panama's independence had come in 1903 only because Teddy Roosevelt had sent warships to dissuade the Colombians from interceding. And without American engineering, the Panamanians wouldn't ever have had a canal. They considered the waterway American property in perpetuity. They stole it fair and square, they liked to laugh to each other. Zonians' salaries were higher, few spoke Spanish, and they swaggered through Panama with the arrogant air of colonial masters when they weren't in their spacious homes attending to well-groomed lawns. The most outspoken proponent of these views was William Drummond, a Canal Zone policeman whose lobbying in Washington and speeches in Panama increasingly angered Torrijos.

Noriega's G-2 planted three bombs in forty-eight hours. The first destroyed the car of Drummond, who had just filed a civil suit demanding a halt to treaty negotiations that named President Ford and Secretary of State Henry Kissinger as codefendants. The second exploded in the parking lot of an American hospital near the Atlantic coast at Coco Solo. One of Noriega's men threw the third from a car near an American housing area on the Monday evening before the Carter-Ford elections.

A few days after the bombings, American intelligence agents handed Washington's ambassador to Panama, William J. Jorden, proof positive of the Noriega connection. It was the first known government-sponsored terrorism against the U.S. ever in Panama, and Noriega had indirectly executed the violence. But as so often in matters regarding Noriega, the U.S. looked the other way.

In his final month as CIA director, George Bush had to confront Noriega on the troublesome issues of the bombings and "Canton Song." Although Bush had prevented any new CIA scandals from emerging, Ford had lost to Jimmy Carter in November anyway. However, neither Ford nor Carter wanted trouble during the transition. So, even though Noriega flew to Washington fearful of a tough rebuke from the CIA chief, their meeting was instead surprisingly cordial.

The two met for a private lunch in December 1976 at the elegant stone residence of the Panamanian ambassador in Washington. Years later, in 1988, after Noriega was indicted on drug charges in Florida, Bush would at first deny having ever met Noriega. He thereafter recalled the meeting, but none of its details. His three lunch guests have better memories, and one of them insisted this was the third meeting between the two men.

The session, requested by Noriega, was arranged by Panama's ambassador to the United Nations, Aquilino Boyd. The host was Ambassador Nicholás Gonzalez Revilla, Torrijos's thirty-two-year-old envoy to Washington. Boyd acted as interpreter for the two spy chiefs, both of whom he knew well. As Panamanian foreign minister in 1957, he had given Noriega his first big break by writing the letter of recommendation that had gained him entrance to the Peruvian Military Academy. His relationship to Bush was more recent. Boyd and Bush had served together as their countries' ambassadors to the United Nations in 1971.

The two intelligence chiefs contrasted in style and substance. Bush was lanky and refined, raised by a Brahmin New England family. He towered over the five-foot-five-inch Noriega. Noriega was mean-streets mestizo, the bastard son of his father's domestic. Noriega offered his usual damp, limp handshake to Bush's firm grip. They were clearly uncomfortable with each other.

Their missions were disparate as well. Bush wanted to convince Noriega and Torrijos they would have to change their provocative ways. Noriega's mission was to protest that he and Torrijos were innocent of all charges, and to pass on a letter for president-elect Carter, promising warm relations in the future.

Noriega opened almost plaintively, assuring Bush that Torrijos and he weren't communists. "What interest would we have in causing the animosity of such a large and dangerous neighbor?" he said. He then made a technological argument against his own complicity: American explosives and techniques had been used that the Panamanians hadn't mastered. But Bush knew Noriega had studied "special demolitions" at the Americans' Fort Gulick in Panama, and he had used American explosives and procedures he had learned there to mask the G-2's involvement. Then Noriega, using a technique he had learned during psychological warfare training at Fort Bragg in 1967, planted rumors that Drummond had bombed his own car. Bush knew from his own briefings that Noriega was lying, but he didn't challenge him. His instructions were to be firm, but cooperative. Bush listened courteously, and never said what he really thought.

"I take your explanation in good spirit," Bush said. "Our only interest is that these things don't happen again."

As for "Canton Song," Noriega turned the tables on U.S. complaints that he had been spying on Washington. After all, he suggested, the U.S. had spied on him first. "Aquilino," he said to Boyd, "ask your friend who were the ones who made these denunciations about these terrorist acts?" Noriega correctly suspected he'd been fingered by a U.S. agent operating within his own G-2. He smiled across the table at Bush, who smiled back sheepishly. It was spy versus spy.

But Noriega had also committed a comic slipup: Noriega was asking how Washington knew about an operation he was denying existed. Boyd now remembers Bush replying that he had received the information on the bombings "from his man in the field." Bush's thinly veiled message to Noriega was that the CIA had infiltrated Panamanian intelligence.

The meeting ended with the two sides even more suspicious of one another. Boyd was shocked to hear the American so openly concede that he had agents inside the G-2. After Bush left, Boyd turned to Noriega and remarked, "We must tell Torrijos that the U.S. has eyes and ears everywhere in Panama." Noriega was surprised at Boyd's naiveté; how could he have thought otherwise? After all, Noriega also had his agents inside American intelligence.

The last problem CIA director George Bush had with Noriega was what to do with a golden medallion the Panamanians had given him at the end of the luncheon—a memento to a fellow spy chief who was leaving office. To make the gift more palatable, Noriega had told Bush it was from Torrijos's puppet president, Demetrio Lakas—a man known to have long-standing links with American intelligence. Bush returned the medallion to his friend Boyd with an explanation: "I wish I could keep it and proudly display it," Bush wrote, but he said U.S. rules required him to turn such gifts over to the General Services Administration. He wrote that the medallion would only "gather dust on some shelf" there. He was sending it to Boyd to give back to Lakas. "Gosh, Aquilino, I hope you understand," Bush wrote.

Only in the twisted mind of Manuel Antonio Noriega could that 1976 luncheon with George Bush be construed as the beginning of a beautiful friendship. A decade later, Noriega would recall their meeting as proof that he and Bush could get along, that they could avoid crises together, and that Bush valued him.

For Bush, however, Noriega was a recurring nightmare. The Panamanian continued to haunt Bush in all his incarnations. For Bush the intelligence chief, Noriega was a troublesome "asset" who was easier to ignore than rebuke. For Vice President Bush, Noriega was the intelligence chief-turned-dictator whose connections to drug trafficking, election fraud, and murder had made him a growing embarrassment. For presidential candidate Bush, Noriega was a campaign threat. And for President Bush, Noriega was a reminder of American impotence and already a danger to his run at a second term at a time when fighting drugs had become a national passion.

On the fifth anniversary of Noriega's rule, August 12, 1988, Noriega threw a party for himself at the Atlantic-Pacific Convention Center, known better as Atlapa. About 2,000 of his best friends were there. He had the goods on George Bush, Noriega told a small circle that hovered around him. If Bush were elected president, all of his problems would be over. He said Carlos Duque, his business partner, had contributed large amounts of money to the Bush campaign through a third party. Noriega could embarrass Bush with this information whenever he wanted.

Well oiled by his trademark Old Parr whiskey (the more expensive, fifteen-year-old version in the bell-shaped bottle), Noriega was at his sadistic best. He had stared down a superpower, and his nemeses—Assistant Secretary of State Elliott Abrams and President Ronald Reagan—were on their way out. He told friends visiting from abroad for the event that he had won against American sanctions and threats because he still had friends in Washington who prevented the administration from turning completely against him. Since many of them owed him debts as well, they had no reason to doubt Noriega.

Now, said the General, he wanted George Bush to be elected over Michael Dukakis. He said Dukakis had sent an emissary to gather dirt on the vice president. Noriega had refused. Bush would have to be more conciliatory. "I've got Bush by the balls," he said. Noriega's Strategic Military Council, the CEM—a body he had created to support his own military rule—even debated whether to begin a campaign against Bush that would tie the campaign in knots. Even if Noriega didn't have the goods on the vice president, as he said, misinformation could have put Bush on the defensive. But Noriega held back, expecting better times ahead if Bush was elected. Noriega relished his potential position in the middle of the American election campaign, and he expected Bush to reward him for remaining on the sidelines.

What Noriega failed to understand was that Bush's pragmatism, which made him a reluctant ally in the 1970s and the early years of the Reagan administration, now would make him an enemy. With drug indictments against Noriega in Florida, Bush hadn't any option but to pursue Noriega's ouster, and he in the end pressured Noriega far more effectively and consistently than Ronald Reagan ever had, with sustained psychological operations against him, military pressure, and a more successful effort to rally more Latin American leaders to join in sending anti-Noriega messages to Panama.

Interviewer David Frost questioned President Bush on his apparent change of heart toward Noriega. "You've met him a couple of times," said Frost. "Would you call General Noriega one of the few people you'd call an evil man?"

"I would now," said Bush, adding bashfully. "I hadn't always had him characterized as this. But when he got immersed into the international drug business, I would have to say that, yeah."

By late 1989, Bush knew Noriega had become his biggest foreign policy embarrassment and a remaining political land mine. Noriega stuck in Bush's craw, and the president expressed frustration time and again at his inability to budge him. Noriega's continued survival blemished Bush's anti-drug efforts and underlined the increased American impotence in the region—an impotence emphasized even more by the abortive October coup, when Bush reacted slowly and ineffectively. Finally, President Bush had to launch an invasion to destroy a man he had unwittingly protected more than a decade earlier.

But then Noriega had always been a problem—even as a young man.

CHAPTER
THREE

THE ABANDONED CHILD

Tony was born the 11th of February in this dear city of Panama.

His ambition: to be a psychiatrist and President of the Republic.

Interests: the skirts and eating in the Casa China [a restaurant].

Favorite musical piece: "Torna Sorrento[sic]."

Representative to the First Extraordinary Congress of Students.

. . . He is a labor leader in embryo.

— NORIEGA'S HIGH SCHOOL YEARBOOK, 1953

Felicidad Sieiro de Noriega wept so uncontrollably that she could scarcely tell her story. The bulge in her stomach, from seven months pregnancy, heaved with each successive shriek of anger and revulsion. Rodrigo Miranda Morales, the Sieiro family lawyer, regarded Felicidad nervously. He feared she might deliver the child right there, the way she was shaking. He tried to calm her. "What's the matter, *Muñeca,*" he said, using her nickname, which meant "little doll." Miranda frowned. "Nothing could be that bad."

"I want a divorce," she sobbed. "He has been very cruel to me."

"He" was Captain Manuel Antonio Noriega, the young chief of the police transit department in David, the capital of Chiriquí province.

Tears running down her pale face, Noriega's fragile wife was adamant as she threw the long, dark strands of her hair from her face. She had come home early from a shopping trip, having forgotten her money. She'd walked in on her husband while he was having his way with a part-time Indian house girl on their nuptial bed. The location bothered her as much as the act itself. "Can you imagine, on our own bed," she cried. "On our own bed!"

Miranda wanted to help. He'd first met Tony Noriega after hiring him as an expert witness for a criminal defense. He paid Noriega up to $50 per court appearance—the equivalent of a week's salary for a poor police captain. And Noriega was worth it. Unlike the largely illiterate crowd that populated the National Guard, Noriega was smart, serious, technically minded, believable, and obsessed with the sort of detail that wins over juries. This was a cop who was going places, Miranda thought.

Miranda's relation with the Sieiro family went back even further. The Sieiros were a proud, middle-class clan of Basque extraction. They ran a local grocery and liquor store where the service was always friendly and the prices fair. The family wasn't happy that their daughter, a local grade-school teacher of pure Basque breeding, had married this homely police-man of dark and cratered skin and uncertain parentage. He never talked about his father or mother, and they guessed he didn't even know who they were—not an unusual thing for Panamanians of his class.

Yet what drew their daughter to Noriega was a shared introversion. They had met at a dance for local schoolteachers, which National Guard members always attended in their sharply ironed uniforms. The young couple hadn't danced, however. Instead, they'd talked for hours in the corner. It was an unusual couple for Chiriquí province, two overly serious young people who discussed books and ideas. Throughout his life, Noriega was rarely attracted to the mindless beauties that appealed to fellow offi-cers.

Now as Felicidad sobbed and heaved, Miranda figured that his friend, young Tony, had just grown a little restless after two years of marriage. Felicidad had given birth to a daughter in that time, and Tony was only doing what comes naturally to Latin men. Miranda left the woman in his office with a box of tissues and phoned Noriega from his receiving room.

If Noriega was upset about Miranda's call, he didn't show it. He apolo-gized for the trouble. He had made a mistake, and he would make it up to Felicidad. He instructed Miranda to prepare the divorce papers, but only as a way to console Felicidad: he shouldn't file them. The police captain said he needed a little time to patch things up.

So Miranda interviewed Felicidad and dutifully wrote down her an-swers, all the time knowing that he would abide by Captain Noriega's wishes. It paid to stay on the right side of the transit department.

Noriega's scheme hit a glitch, however, when he ran across Felicidad's angry brother at Club David, a local watering hole. Ramón Sieiro, drunk and angry, accused Noriega of soiling his family's good name. Ramón had a degree in agricultural engineering, and he considered himself superior to Noriega in breeding and education. One witness remembers Ramón raging that he would kill Noriega for so besmirching his sister. Noriega then pulled a pistol on his brother-in-law. Before he could pull the trigger, Noriega's friends intervened. A near murder was averted.

About a month later, Felicidad phoned Miranda from the hospital. She had given birth to a baby girl, whom they had named Sandra. She asked Miranda if he could stop the divorce procedure. Tony had gone down on his knees at her bedside to beg forgiveness on the morning after Sandra's birth. How could she refuse? She pledged Miranda to secrecy.

For General Noriega, the story was an early example of his patience and cunning sense of timing. He controlled the situation from the beginning, always holding more information than the other participants in the drama. And he waited for the right moment to make amends. This was no ordinary cop. This was a master tactician.

Felicidad still winked at Miranda for years thereafter, thinking they had shared a dirty little secret that she had once tried to divorce the man who ultimately made her and her family rich and influential beyond their wildest expectations. "You are my secret weapon," she laughed. "I will call you when he mistreats me." Miranda laughed too, aware that Noriega had been in on the secret all along.

From his earliest days, Noriega showed a penchant for manipulation and clandestine relationships that would later become the hallmarks of his personal life and his political career. Too shy to take on the world directly, he cleverly used intelligence to outmaneuver friends and foes during his determined rise to power. Too ugly to charm, he still philandered and wooed, sometimes scoring through guile and other times through simple intimidation.

Noriega came by all these traits honestly, however. He was the misshapen product of a country whose history was one of conspirators and pirates from the days when Columbus first landed in Panama in search of gold and a passage to the Orient in the early sixteenth century. Noriega was born on February 11, 1934, the son of a philandering and alcoholic father, into a poor and disenfranchised piece of Panama that few foreigners ever saw, near the city's century-old market.

The one-room apartment where Noriega was raised was just around the corner from an ugly, narrow alley where the smell of urine stung the air, a passageway so unappealing that it was called Sal Si Puedes—translated, "Get out if you can." Noriega was of mestizo blood, a mixed breed of Indian, black, and Spanish. The mestizo stock grew out of the workers brought in from neighboring countries in order to build the railway, the Canal, and the roads that had made foreigners and better-born Panamanians rich.

Embarrassed by his humble roots, Noriega had classified stories of his youth as top secret. Most of his childhood acquaintances would speak only anonymously before his ouster in December, 1989. Noriega's resentment about his childhood years had colored his whole character, leaving him distrustful of the oligarchs who historically controlled the country, resentful of a world that allowed him to be born ugly and underprivileged, and determined above all to achieve control over his life and that of others— control that he so lacked during childhood. He had achieved money and power, but they were only the offshoots of his search for control.

When Tony Noriega was born, there wasn't any reason to believe this child would rise any further than his father, who had abandoned him. Ricaurte Tomás Noriega had been a lower middle-class civil servant who worked as a government accountant. He was an alcoholic whose hunger for women matched his thirst for booze. He frequently stayed home from his government job to satisfy one yearning or the other. Ricaurte had lost his first wife to pneumonia; he had married her when she was just fifteen, and she had borne him several children. At least two had died in infancy. Three boys survived: Julio, Tomás and Rubén. The wife's death had isolated the father, however, and after a string of affairs, mostly casual, he married a jealous and bitter woman. She worked at a nearby office to help keep the family fed, so a domestic from the small town of Yaviza, Darién province, whose name was Moreno, delivered and prepared meals for the elder Noriega, who by this time was surviving on disability payments.

After Moreno had worked in the home for about a year, she quit to deliver a child. The Noriegas didn't think much about her departure. She wasn't married, but around the Central Market illegitimate children were more the rule than exception. What Ricaurte's family didn't know was that he had sired the child. He promised Moreno occasional money for support, and she left.

Noriega's father wouldn't recognize the child as his own, and his mother died—apparently of tuberculosis—when he was either four or five. After she contracted the disease, she asked a local schoolteacher—who was Tony's godmother and was from Moreno's hometown in Darién province—if she would take the five-year-old boy. Noriega's natural mother returned to Yaviza, where she died. Noriega's friends consider it significant that he never visited his mother's grave until he was an officer. He clearly felt little warmth toward her. However, he grew to revere his adoptive mother, Luisa Sanchez, and she showered him with love and attention.

They lived in a single room in an old wooden building that dated back to the French canal period. The house today is marked 3-36 12th Street. The one-room apartment on the second floor remains, tucked around the corner from a rickety wooden staircase. The room measures no more than twenty feet in length and fifteen in width. A dingy hallway leading to it is painted white and turquoise. Barroom sounds rise from a cantina downstairs called Chucu-Chucu, and the smells of the sea mix with those of the nearby market as they waft up to the always-open doorway.

The room where Noriega was raised has no commemorative plaque. The building's residents know nothing of their historic predecessor. Yet Noriega's friends remember playing with him there.

Legend persists in Panama that Tony was cruelly treated by his mother and homosexually raped by one of his brothers, but the truth about Noriega's childhood isn't as rich or dark as the rumor. Luisa Sanchez adopted Tony Noriega and coddled him, and turned him out for school more clean and neat than almost any of his friends. "He was almost always well washed and groomed, and he was well liked by other parents for being so well behaved," said Hector Manfredo, his closest childhood friend in the early 1940s. At age seven, both attended the Escuela República de Méjico, a converted convent where Manfredo's father was principal, and he remembered that he and Tony were above-average students, "but not brilliant."

The two friends were attracted to each other by a shared bashfulness. "We immediately liked each other," said Manfredo. "We were both of humble origins—my family also lived over a cantina. Tony was introverted, and I was introverted. We liked being with each other because we didn't need to talk too much."

Tony Noriega was, in fact, an oddly serious child. Sometimes Hector and Tony would spend the whole day together without doing or saying much of anything. Hector doesn't remember any games that were played. "It was a relationship mostly of talking and just being with each other. He wasn't athletic by any means—and neither was I."

Tony Noriega's marks were good enough to land him a place at the Instituto Nacional in 1947, a Panamanian high school that throughout its history had been a hothouse for political activism and the breeding ground for nationalist politicians. However, the most important event of Tony Noriega's first year there was intimately personal: he met a brother he never knew he had.

Luis Carlos Noriega, five years Tony's senior, was one of the best-known students at the Instituto Nacional. He was in his final year of studies, and was known by all the students as the leader of political demonstrations and the most gregarious of socialist activists.

Luis Carlos was taller, heavier, darker, and more extroverted than his brother. Luis Carlos also was better off economically, although the son of a lower middle-class family. Their common father had met Tony only a year earlier, and although he acknowledged paternity, he had kept it a secret from his other sons and his jealous wife. Even though the two brothers now attended the same school, it wasn't likely they would have discovered the truth on their own. Luis Carlos Noriega Hurtado and Manuel Antonio Noriega Moreno didn't look, act, or behave like brothers. Their shared family name was just common enough to be considered coincidental. It took one of Tony's more gregarious friends, Pedro Brín Martínez, to bring them together.

Pedro Brín had joined Luis Carlos's socialist student organization, and Luis Carlos, singling him out as a promising leader, invited Brín to lunch at his home. Brín did a double-take, however, when he saw Luis Carlos's father, who looked like an older and fatter version of his friend Tony Noriega. The old man was about the same height as Tony and even had a similarly scarred complexion. Brín didn't have a doubt that they were father and son.

Proud of this discovery, Brín excitedly arranged for Luis Carlos to meet his brother Tony at a cantina near the Instituto Nacional called El Atlas. Brín remembers buying each of them a beer, "at ten cents a glass."

"This is your brother," he said to Tony. "Get to know him." From that moment on, Luis Carlos played a critical role in Tony's life. If Tony Noriega had never met his brother, he might never have been introduced to student politics, or have received a scholarship to the Peruvian military academy. Americans likely would never have heard of him. Luis Carlos was Tony Noriega's political instructor and trusted confidant as he rose in power and influence. Their meeting was Tony Noriega's first break in a previously unexciting life.

Luis Carlos was also openly homosexual, a quickly recognizable trait in macho Latin society. Both he and his bastard brother were ostracized by the Noriega family, Luis Carlos for his sexual proclivities and Tony for his parentage. The three eldest Noriega sons, born of a different mother, had never been close to Luis Carlos. When he grew up to be homosexual, they shunned him even more. They ignored Manuel Antonio altogether, once they'd learned of him. The three boys were bitter enough about their alcoholic father and unaccepting stepmother, and they had no interest in widening the family circle. One brother, Tomás, would provide Manuel Antonio some belated help later on, and the forgiving General Noriega rewarded him by sending his son to Hong Kong as Panama's consul general. But the other two lived to regret their unkindness to the country's future dictator.

Luis Carlos and Tony formed a bond of trust, and many think Tony Noriega's problems only careened out of control when Luis Carlos died in 1984. "Luis Carlos was the guy who shaped Manuel Antonio," recalled Hector Manfredo. "Tony looked up to him. Meeting those people [the socialist youth] made him change his views about life. He became very interested in the students' movement. There would be no General Noriega without Luis Carlos." It was rumored in the school that Luis Carlos and two of his cohorts—Jorge Illueca and Rómulo Escobar Bethancourt, both of whom would serve General Noriega later as political leaders—even stole an election for young Tony. It was probably a rigged vote that put him in the National Congress of Students in the 1949–50 school year: many more popular students lost. Noriega launched his political career by fraud, and so it would continue.

From 1948–49, Luis Carlos was the president of the National Students' Congress. At the time Tony met him, he was leading a movement against a secret agreement Panama was preparing to sign with Washington. It would give the American military continued control over most of the bases it had established in Panama during World War II.

The Instituto Nacional students viewed the World War II base agreement as the oligarchy's pact with the American devil, selling out sovereignty for greenbacks just as they had when they allowed the Americans not only to build the Canal in 1913 but also to exercise sovereignty over the land around it. The students got word of a treaty, concluded secretly in 1947, that allowed the U.S. to keep its military bases and facilities, and student and teacher groups mobilized a nationalist coalition against the agreement. Luis Carlos planned a march on the National Assembly and, in his first political demonstration, his newly-found brother Tony tagged along. The Panamanian cavalry was called out, and it killed four or five students.

Then the National Assembly backed down and refused to ratify the treaty. Luis Carlos was a hero, and his little brother was in awe. "Noriega had just discovered his brother, and his brother was doing great things," says Pedro Brín. "It seemed the natural thing for all of us to do: fighting for liberty and against imperialism."

At that time, the University of Panama had just opened as a night school, and it shared classrooms on a split shift with Instituto Nacional students. The socialist and communist leaders of the university roamed the hallways each day looking for recruits: police were much less likely to beat those with younger faces. Noriega was always first in line, hoping to emulate his brother.

Tony left behind his childhood friend, Hector Manfredo, and their silent alliance. He began giving speeches, organizing marches, and planning political campaigns. In his last year at the high school, Tony and his friend Pedro Brín started publishing a newspaper that they shipped back to Darién province. It was socialist in tone, and promoted land reform. "At the Instituto Nacional," remembers Hector Manfredo, "Noriega underwent a transformation. He wanted to be recognized. He became an extrovert."

Manuel Antonio Noriega looked almost handsome in his high school yearbook picture. An artist's airbrush has smoothed over his acne-scarred face, and a boyish smile is full of hope and innocence.

He was the only student who wrote an essay that was published in the book, extolling the virtues of peasantry and warning that agrarian discontent would fuel a revolution. "In Panama, the agrarian problem has become a great collective burden," he wrote. "The Panamanian plantation system stifles the population, paralyzes economic progress, and reflects itself in our backward, oligarchical, and invidious politics."

The white shirts and thin black ties that were the school uniform made the students in the yearbook all appear much the same. They included Boris Martínez, the future military leader who masterminded the 1968 coup that paved Noriega's way to power; César Rodriguez Maylin, a man who would be chief of aeronautics under Noriega and his ambassador to Bogotá (a position in which he allegedly dealt in drugs and arms smuggling with Noriega); Carlos Bolívar Pedreschi, then a young fellow socialist and high school graduation speaker who forty years later would be one of Noriega's most outspoken opponents; and Carlos Duque, who would be his business partner and a presidential candidate in 1989.

Boris Martínez was everything Noriega was not in high school—macho, handsome, happy-go-lucky, and comparatively brilliant. Noriega was softer, almost effeminate, and more average. Their yearbook entries betray grand ambitions. Martínez's entry says he wanted to be the first Panamanian to win a Nobel Prize for medicine; however, in the same entry, his expressed predilection for crime and horror stories suggests his military future. Noriega wanted to be a psychiatrist and president, but he is also described as having a weakness for "the skirts." Martínez was a conservative student, while Noriega moved leftward.

Predictably, after graduation in 1952 Martínez rose to prominence faster than Noriega. After attending military school in Mexico, he became Noriega's commanding officer in Chiriquí province before leading the 1968 coup with Omar Torrijos. Martínez saw leadership capabilities in the quiet Noriega, even in high school. He didn't know Noriega would use these capabilities years later to help form a coup against him.

"Noriega had a good mind and the desire to lead people," he said. "You don't need much more."

Even in a school where none of the students were well-off, Noriega was known to be particularly disadvantaged. "We knew for sure he was poor," said Martínez. "His clothes never fit him properly. They always looked like hand-me-downs. But he was also very popular. His problem with acne didn't seem to faze him. He flirted with girls, and he had girlfriends. He didn't pay any attention to the problem with his face."

He would come back for more no matter how often girls rebuffed him; and even then he had a taste for social climbing. He ignored girls of his mestizo coloring and gravitated toward blonde Panamanians. "He always preferred milk to coffee," said one friend from that period.

Boris Martínez said that although Noriega was noticeably poorer than other students, there was nothing unusual about his anti–U.S. views. "The school had no upper classes," he said, "so we had no way to be sympathetic to the gringos. Many of us had unemployed fathers, or came from single-parent households. Many came to school hungry because they had no breakfast. It affects the way you think about government. Instituto Nacional students tended to be more nationalist than others. We knew who the enemy was: it was those who had the money and those who had the Canal. It was the oligarchy and the Americans. If the Soviets had the Canal, they would have been the enemy."

Noriega quietly rose in his brother's footsteps to become the leader of the socialist youth movement. He was elected twice to the National Students' Congress. In his speeches, he would often quote Ralph Waldo Emerson's words engraved in Spanish on the large bronze plaque outside the school, beside the two sphinxes that guard the gates. "Only those who build upon ideas build for eternity."

He repeated that slogan to friends throughout his career. In his high school years, Noriega would write with fervor—in his yearbook and elsewhere—about "the weapon of theory, of precepts."

Friends remember him as a young man who would read books and write poetry when other students were wasting time or playing games. He was always serious, not given to much laughter. His writings and poetry were sappy and emotional.

One poem, unearthed from his high school years, reveals his odd intellect. It is a love poem to a bullet.

THE BULLET WITH A SOUL

The bullet that will wound me
will be a bullet with a soul

And the soul of that bullet
will be like a rose,
if flowers could sing
Or like topaz
if stones had a smell

If I am shot in the brain,
then it will say to me
that it wanted to explore my thoughts

And if it sears my breast,
then tenderly, it will say to me
that it looked to know
the beatings of my heart

The bullet that wounds me
will be your love

At the Instituto Nacional, Noriega also discovered the father figure he never had: the founder of Panama's small Socialist party, Demetrio Porras. To many leftists in Panama, Porras had disgraced himself by accepting the government's offer to serve as ambassador to London. He had returned with British Labour Party philosophies, which he then tried to pass on to Instituto Nacional students, who tended to be much further to the left. Porras saw promise in young Tony when Luis Carlos first brought him to the Socialist office.

Hector Manfredo remembers a class where students were reading Rousseau's *The Social Contract.* Noriega was one of the few students who understood it, and he offered to bring Porras to class to explain the book. Students, looking for help to pass exams, thought this was a fine idea; but they were disappointed when Porras spoke only of socialism and not at all about the book. He talked about the profound coincidences between capitalism and communism and why both should be rejected. He talked of agrarian reform. "After that, I saw Noriega with Porras all the time," says Manfredo. "People even said that he was Demetrio Porras's son."

Ironically, as a student Noriega campaigned energetically against the

man who would consolidate military control of the country and be the
father of the National Guard that would later be Noriega's path to power.
When populist Arnulfo Arias was ousted in 1951, after two years of rule,
by Colonel Remón—again with Washington's blessing—Noriega went to
the streets to throw rocks. When Remón ran for president in 1952, Noriega
helped campaign against him and for the Socialists' favored candidate,
Remón's cousin Adolfo Chiari. Chiari lost, however, and the country had
its first military leader. Remón transformed the police into a National
Guard to take advantage of new U.S. legislation that provided aide to
Latin-American militaries—legislation aimed at thwarting communism.

"Noriega was the most anti-military person I had ever met in my life,"
laughed Pedro Brín years later. "He was the anti-military prototype."

During the campaign, he also came into his first political money. The
Chiaris had given $2,000 to $3,000 to the students for their campaign.
Students from that period remember that Noriega and Pedro Brín threw
the best parties, and everyone would come.

Although Noriega's graduation photograph is in the 1952 Instituto Nacional yearbook, he actually didn't finish school until 1953, after he and
a number of other students failed mathematics. "We both were bad at
math," said Brín. "They wouldn't give us our diplomas unless we took an
additional year of mathematics. It wasn't because we didn't study, although we weren't brilliant students. I think it was more because we were
poor. We were unable to buy the textbooks."

Numbers weren't what interested the poetic young Noriega. What
friends remember most about young Tony Noriega was his voracious
reading appetite. Hector Manfredo had a photographic memory but little
desire to read the assigned books. Noriega was one of the few students who
loved to read; so Manfredo would ask Noriega to give him a summary of
a book before taking a test about it. "He had a fantastic ability to summa-
rize novels," remembers Manfredo. "He read everything and could give
from his head a complete summary of what he had read. Yet I got the
better grades on my written compositions, just from hearing his summary,"
laughs Manfredo now. "He got so angry."

Noriega often would give books to his friend Pedro Brín Martínez, who
would later be a Noriega-backed legislator from Darién province. Brín
remembers that Noriega's favorite book was Machiavelli's *The Prince*.
Noriega thought the book applied to Panama, so he badgered Brín until
he read it, so he could have someone to discuss it with him. Noriega wrote
a long paper about *The Prince*. He wrote about how Machiavelli had
become obsessed by the need for Florence to build a strong militia of its

own instead of relying on mercenary troops and outside allies. Panama should do the same, and not rely on the United States, he wrote. He wrote about *realpolitik,* not of ideals or beliefs, but of how principalities are actually best conquered and ruled.

Although Noriega's paper is disjointed, it provides glimpses into the young student's thinking. Foreshadowing his rise in the shadow of dictator Omar Torrijos (or perhaps referring to his relationship to his brother), he quotes Machiavelli that "a prudent man must always follow in the footsteps of great men and imitate those who have been outstanding. If his own prowess fails to compare with theirs, at least it has an air of greatness about it. He must behave like those archers who, if they are skillful, when the target seems too distant, know the capabilities of their bow and aim a good deal higher than their objective, not in order to shoot so high, but so that by aiming high they can reach the target."

Noriega was most taken by Machiavelli's story of Agathocles, the Sicilian, who rose from the lowest classes through the ranks of the militia and to power. He quotes Machiavelli: "Agathocles, the Sicilian, not only from the status of a private citizen but from the lowest, most abject condition of life, rose to become king of Syracuse. At every stage of his career this man, the son of a potter, behaved like a criminal; nonetheless he accompanied his crimes with so much audacity and physical courage that when he joined the militia, he rose through the ranks to become praetor of Syracuse."

Noriega, however, doesn't quote the portion of *The Prince* that would apply most to his later career: "One might well wonder how it was that Agathocles, and others like him, after countless treacheries and cruelties, could live securely in his own country and hold foreign enemies at bay, with never a conspiracy against him by his countrymen, inasmuch as many others, because of their cruel behavior, have not been able to maintain their rule even in peaceful times, let alone in the uncertain times of war. I believe that here it is a question of cruelty used well or badly."

Years later, Brín said he doubted Noriega still read Machiavelli. "I continue to read *The Prince,* " says Noriega's friend. "But he wrote his own version. He surpassed Machiavelli."

CHAPTER FOUR

A SPY IS BORN

He had an elegant uniform with gold buttons in a country where there was a cult of militarism, where officers were the elite, with special privileges.

—DARIÉN AYALA, NORIEGA'S FRIEND IN PERU

During the summer of 1960, an American military intelligence agent, serving under diplomatic cover at the U.S. embassy in Lima, Peru, wired home a secret cable with some disturbing news.

One of his more promising recent recruits, a young Panamanian cadet at the Chorrillos Military Academy, had been arrested for beating and raping a prostitute. She had nearly died.

The recruit: Manuel Antonio Noriega.

Although the cable didn't go into much detail, two of Noriega's friends from Peru and one former American intelligence agent recreate the story:

That summer, Noriega and two friends had sought some relief from the rigors of their military training in the local bars. Noriega had spent most of his weekend allowance on Peruvian beer and couldn't meet the escalating price of a whore who had already serviced his two friends, so she rejected the young cadet, not expecting any danger from this short, skinny Panamanian whose face was so pockmarked that his friends privately called him "Cara de Piña," or "Pineapple Face." His unusually tiny, oval skull appeared so small for his body that fellow cadets also heckled him as "Cabecita," or "Little Head."

However, in his peaked military cap and neatly pressed, French-made academy uniform, Noriega felt more handsome and powerful than ever before in his underprivileged life. He considered himself intellectually superior to most other cadets at the academy, and he was older, having subtracted four years from his own birthdate to gain entrance into the academy. He knew it would be a humiliation to return to the barracks without having had sex with the woman. So he beat the prostitute until she submitted.

Years later, he would tell a U.S. intelligence agent exactly how it all happened, acting out how he threw his fist directly into the middle of the prostitute's face. "But I was very straight after that," he immediately explained. "I knew they were watching me."

It was a rare breach of discipline for the elite academy, which had been founded in the early 1900s by the French military mission in Peru and still held to tenets of European military order. The mostly Peruvian cadets, many of whom came from well-off families, called the poorer and more playful Panamanian students "tropicals."

If concerned by the event, however, Noriega's case officer also knew him to be a good catch. He was smarter than other cadets, so his reports were better. He resented his richer fellow cadets and the harsh officers, so he had both the motivation to provide intelligence and the need for the American agents' modest payments.

Noriega's first U.S. intelligence payment came in either 1958 or 1959 through his brother, Luis Carlos, who was already being paid by U.S. intelligence agents for other services. "The man who found Noriega should either be shot or decorated," laughs one intelligence agent who inherited the Noriega account at one point during the 1970s. "He was the perfect find: smart, devious, amoral, resourceful, and reliable." He was a bright young officer who might be able to serve the U.S. in the future. A little whore-beating in Peru was hardly something to worry about.

What preceded this historic point for Noriega, his first service for American intelligence, had been five of the worst years of his life, between his high school graduation at age nineteen in 1953 and his entry into the Peruvian military academy. They had turned an optimistic, ambitious student with grand political dreams into a resentful, depressed laboratory technician at Santo Tomás Hospital with little hope of advancement. He had been a young man determined to accomplish great things in life, but he had found the barriers to his class overwhelming. His friends remember him caught in a downward spiral of circumstance: female rejection, job disappointment, drinking binges, and occasional barroom fights, most of which he lost to larger opponents. Noriega earned his first police record after one such brawl, a record which he later expurgated. The psychological scars of his childhood began to resurface in a new meanness and cruelty his friends hadn't seen before.

Noriega had told friends that he wanted to be like Arnulfo Arias, the nationalist Panamanian leader who had studied medicine in the United

States before turning to politics. Noriega had gone to the streets to throw stones at the military when Arnulfo Arias had been ousted in 1951 by Colonel Remón. Ironically, nearly two decades later, Arias would be elected again, and overthrown again. Among those joining that coup: Tony Noriega.

But in those days, just after high school, while Noriega still revered Arias, he quickly realized that he lacked Arnulfo Arias's advantages: money and family connections. Medical studies in Panama in the 1950s were a family affair, and new students either came from the right families or were sponsored by them. Noriega lacked the money for medical school, and he didn't have the connections or the grades for a scholarship.

Noriega turned to his half-brothers for economic help, but they failed him, adding to his resentment. The two older brothers, who were both engineers, could have funded young Tony, but they never felt any kinship toward him and turned him away. Half-brother number three, Julio, had just married and was starting a family; he didn't have the money to help. And Noriega's favorite brother, the fellow family outcast Luis Carlos, was just finishing his university studies.

Noriega took occasional night courses from the university's science faculty, hoping that if he did well he could turn to medical studies, but his below-average marks and poverty prompted him to drop out. Through a politician for whom he'd once campaigned, Noriega landed a job as a laboratory assistant in Santo Tomás Hospital's pharmacy in Panama City. But again, he found himself excluded by the closed community that ran the pharmacy. Many of its employees were linked by either family or contacts to pharmaceutical suppliers, and they would push specific products, mark up the prices to the hospital for extra profit, and even sell some of the most sought-after drugs outside the hospital for personal gain.

One former employee remembered that Noriega was once accused of stealing drugs, although his superiors never proved the charge. "The point wasn't that he had committed a crime," said the former employee. "He simply wasn't part of the inner circle." Noriega saw that those who got ahead were part of a health services mafia in Panama, and young men of his underclass couldn't sign on.

Yet despite these disappointments, doctors at the hospital remember Noriega as one of the brightest and hardest-working of the assistants. His ambition and drive persisted. He told friends that he had tried to join a training program to become a pharmacist, but been rejected. He'd applied to begin training as a male nurse, but been turned down there as well. And all the time he continued to write friends and family for help. Now he was embittered. He hated the oligarchy for not giving him the chance for a medical career; he hated the U.S. for giving only the sons and daughters of the oligarchy scholarships; and he resented his half-brothers for treating him as a second-class relative. A class hatred began that would shape his actions for years to come, a hatred that friends say they never noticed until his time at the hospital.

Then one day his high school friend Boris Martínez came in for medical tests, dressed in a sharply creased cadet's uniform from the Mexican military academy. Noriega riddled him with questions. He envied Martínez's success, and Martínez expressed surprise that Noriega hadn't done more with his life. It was then that Noriega began pressing his brother Luis Carlos—who had recently become a diplomat in Peru—to find him a military scholarship.

Luis Carlos finally wrote to his brother that there was one chance: the Chorrillos Military Academy was offering two scholarships to Panamanians. Manuel Antonio was already too old to be accepted, and it appeared that the two successful candidates had already been chosen. However, when Manuel Antonio begged him to, Luis Carlos consented to falsify his brother's birth date and to find a sponsor important enough to edge out one of the already-chosen candidates. Everything in Panama depended on connections, and Luis Carlos found one of the most important sponsors available: Aquilino Boyd, a man whose letter would assure the appointment. In 1956, the thirty-five-year-old Boyd had been appointed foreign minister. He was Luis Carlos's boss, but also a close friend of Luis Carlos from his rabble-rousing days as head of the university's student association.

Boyd had graduated from Holy Cross College in New Orleans, and had studied law at the University of Havana before Castro took power. He had already worked at the embassy in Washington and had won election to Panama's National Assembly four successive times. He viewed himself as a future president, and he bestowed favors on those who could help him later—in this case both Luis Carlos and Tony Noriega. Boyd wrote Noriega a letter of recommendation, figuring it wouldn't hurt to have a young officer as a friend to an aspiring politician. He never guessed how profitable that note would be in the years ahead.

The most popular theory in Panamanian salons is that Noriega's first service to the CIA was spying on fellow high school students at the Instituto Nacional. But a former U.S. intelligence agent, who for years was the liaison to Noriega, calls those reports "utter rubbish and fabrication." Noriega's first service came at the Peruvian Military Academy, and he emerged as a volunteer.

It is unusual for U.S. intelligence agents to recruit cadets. They consider their time far better spent on young officers, who can offer a far more certain return on initial investment of time and payments. But Luis Carlos Noriega, anxious to promote his brother, offered him up to the local station chief and military attaché.

It was a time when events in the West Indies had refocused American concerns on the area.

From his mountain bases, Fidel Castro had led a guerrilla movement that on January 1, 1959, after a decade of setbacks, had finally overthrown Cuban dictator Fulgencio Batista. America's worst Cold War fears were becoming reality. Communism had a base only ninety miles from Florida; and even worse, Castro almost immediately announced a policy of exporting revolution. Fear of Castro came to dominate Latin American affairs late in Eisenhower's term and throughout the Kennedy administration. These were the years that Noriega spent in Peru. CIA stations throughout the region were ordered to keep close watch on revolutionary seedbeds. None were more important than military academies, where Latin America's future coup-makers were being trained.

And few were as important as those in Peru. The local station chief was extraordinarily pleased to have eyes and ears inside the Peruvian military academy, which was already thought to be infiltrated by leftist instructors. Noriega would provide regular reports on their pro-Fidel teachings, offering names of officers who several years later would be involved in the 1968 coup that would bring Juan Velasco Alvarado to power, who would nationalize American-owned companies, expropriate landed estates, and open diplomatic relations with nations of the communist bloc. Noriega's information didn't help stop any of this, but it did feed the giant maw in Langley that couldn't get enough data on Latin communists.

Manuel Antonia Noriega was the perfect informant—and not just because he was smarter than his fellow cadets, many of whom had been sent there by their rich families as if it was a sort of reform school. (It was joked that every important Peruvian family would have one son who became an officer and one a priest.) Noriega's shy personality was fittingly unobtrusive. He had an archival memory and a brother who could act as the perfect intermediary for intelligence reports and payments. Intelligence sources say Noriega never even met with his American minders. Luis Carlos gathered the information from his brother and passed it on, sometimes merely in casual conversation.

And Tony Noriega was a cheap buy. He joked to a friend at the Peruvian military academy that he would buy all the beer one weekend with his "North American rewards."

Laughed Noriega's friend, "We were very disappointed that the beer ran out so quickly and we said that he should seek a raise." Noriega's reports on the leftist leanings of instructors and students were good enough to keep the small payments coming. Besides, buying into a future Panamanian officer was almost as important as the information he provided.

Noriega viewed his Peruvian years as some of the best in his life. His uniform made him feel more manly than ever before. His brother's position gained him invitations to diplomatic parties, and his scholarship lightened his financial burden. He was also happy to capitalize on Peruvian women's mistaken notion that he was rich. "The girls knew the military academy students had money, and they figured the foreigners must have more money than anyone else," laughs Darién Ayala, Noriega's close friend who was studying agriculture engineering in Peru at the time. "He had an elegant uniform with gold buttons in a country where there was a cult of militarism—where officers were the elite, with special privileges."

Yet Noriega's eyes were also opened to a world of riches and repression that he hadn't known in Panama. The social strata were far more extreme. Peruvian cadets invited him to visit their families on farms that even had their own cemeteries and jails; while the Indians lived in straw houses and their children went without shoes.

Noriega had trouble adjusting to the Peruvian school, however. It was far more European in discipline and academic demands than anything he had experienced before. It was at the school that he saw brutality used as a means of control for the first time. Instructors and officers would punish cadets severely for the most minor infractions. Those who were caught cheating on tests might only be forced to perform a couple of hundred pushups, but some were also beaten if their discipline slipped too far.

The young Panamanian cadets also saw a repression of civilians that far exceeded anything they had known before. Troops fired live ammunition on demonstrations, and they enforced curfews with brutal force that shocked the more placid Panamanians. "We saw very strong repression for the first time," says Ayala. "We understood for the first time what curfew was."

But the bruises and humiliation dealt him by Peruvian officers were softened by his gentle brother, who played mother hen to all the Panamanian students in Lima. For the first time in his life, Noriega had the security of an older brother—a father figure—who took him under his wing, protecting him from punishment and inviting him, in his ill-fitting suit, to diplomatic parties where he got his first taste of high society.

Noriega also met friends he would trust and promote for years to come. He brought his friend Darién Ayala into government as vice agricultural minister. Ayala would later become head of the politically critical community development program, and a minister of state. Another friend from the Peruvian period, Elías Castillo, would become commander of his ground forces. Even his future enemy and chief of staff, Colonel Roberto Díaz Herrera, was in Lima, although at the less-respected police academy.

Noriega was closest, however, to Francisco Rodriguez, a top student at the agricultural university with Ayala. Rodriguez didn't feel he really knew Noriega, although he had been chosen as his mentor and tutor during the year. Noriega, a born intelligence agent, would sit quietly in the corner, studying and listening to others without joining in conversations or expressing opinions.

"I always wondered what really motivated him," says Rodriguez. "He never told me. He was thoughtful and analytical, but he was also very introverted. He has always been an enigma, even then. We were the ones who did the talking and told the jokes. He spoke only when it was necessary. He wasn't an extrovert whom you could understand and penetrate."

Instead, Noriega sat quietly and read biographies of great military men, such as José de San Martín, a South American revolutionary leader of the early nineteenth century, and Simón Bolívar, the Venezuelan hero in the South American movement for independence from Spain.

Yet at the time, Rodriguez tried to convince Noriega to leave the military academy and pursue a civilian career. Once, after they had gotten drunk on pisco sours, Rodriguez told Noriega only delinquents and criminals joined the military. "You have excellent intelligence," he remembers telling Noriega. "Those who study the military don't have any future in our country. Only those of high social class become senior officers. Those of lower classes become cops. When I come back to Panama, I will be driving a Cadillac, and I will pass you on the street corner blowing your whistle."

More than twenty years later, in 1983, Rodriguez was invited to celebrate the naming of Noriega as the commander in chief of the National Guard. Rodriguez, by then elevated to be Panama's comptroller, congratulated his old friend. Noriega was full of himself, strutting and smiling proudly as he received congratulations in an almost regal manner.

"Do you remember what you told me in Peru about blowing whistles?" Noriega asked.

Rodriguez didn't remember, so Noriega reminded him, having stored every word in the computerlike archive of his memory. "Who is driving Cadillacs now?" he laughed.

Rodriguez was surprised and a little embarrassed. "What happens, Tony, is that when we get drunk we speak a lot of foolishness," he replied.

"Noriega keeps everything inside of him forever," said Rodriguez. "He knows those who have been his friends and those who are disloyal. In ten years, twenty years, he will always remember everything."

Rodriguez stayed on Noriega's good side throughout the years, by loyally serving him in government jobs that included overseeing the country's finances and making sure the General got his share. After weeks of not speaking to each other, Noriega would call and ask plaintively, "Why don't you call me more often? Why don't you ask me for more favors?" In a world where he had grown to distrust everyone, Rodriguez and other friends from Peru became the few people he felt he could depend upon.

On September 1, 1989, Noriega repaid Rodriguez's loyalty by naming him as his fifth president in only six years as Comandante. His erstwhile tutor had become his loyal puppet. Noriega considered civilians with more political reputation than Rodriguez's to be either disloyal or a threat. Rodriguez, whom he had known for almost three decades, wasn't likely to join any coups or plots against him. Yet it was clear to all that Noriega was still driving the Cadillac. He removed Rodriguez when his puppet National Assembly named him "maximum leader" in December 1989, just a few days before the U.S. invasion.

Noriega's five years in Peru, which ended in 1962, were his life's turning point. The degree, the knowledge, and the contacts he acquired—most importantly his new relationship with the Americans and friends like Rodriguez—would provide the first paving stones for his path to power. He had suited America's narrow needs by gathering intelligence—of dubious value and at small prices—regarding Latin American leftists. More importantly, Washington fulfilled his need for an early sponsor and an enthusiastic promoter in the years to come. Full of new hopes and ambitions, he returned to Panama to pursue a career that he now hoped would make him commander of the armed forces.

Noriega's next big break in trying to reach that goal would come seven years later, when he and his brother would again join forces to save a dictatorship and assure Noriega's place in Panama's history.

CHAPTER FIVE

THE NOT-SO-LOYAL SERVANT

The best preparation to be a man of authority is to have been an obedient man, to bow to duty. Those who have never learned to command their own selves will never be able to command others.

—FROM NORIEGA'S PAMPHLET
*THE PHILOSOPHY OF THE
TALENT TO BE IN COMMAND*

It was 2 A.M. on the morning of December 15, 1969, when Major Manuel Antonio Noriega, the commander of the Chiriquí province garrison, got the call. On the phone was Major Alejandro Araúz, Panama's military intelligence chief and a man known to have been recruited, trained, and well paid by the CIA. Araúz said dictator Omar Torrijos wasn't coming back from his "vacation" in Mexico, where he had flown to enjoy the Caribbean Classic horseraces. Torrijos was out—overthrown.

Was Noriega with the coup makers? asked Araúz.

Noriega was silent. If he sided with the rebel colonels and they failed, he would be imprisoned and executed for treason. Yet if Noriega opposed a successful coup, his promising career and grand ambitions would be dashed. The rebels would be watching him carefully. Torrijos had been like a father to Noriega, nurturing and promoting his career as his commanding officer for most of his years in the National Guard. Because of that, Noriega's chances of promotion were dismal under this new leadership.

Noriega, trying to buy time, told Araúz that he needed a chance to consult his troops. "It should be their decision," he said. What he really needed was a chance to plot his own strategy. Should he side with officers he didn't like and their gringo allies, or should he cast his lot with a father figure who might never return to Panama?

For the previous seven years, Noriega had loyally served both Torrijos and the Americans in Colón and then Chiriquí province. Both relationships had served him well. Now it seemed he had to choose between them. The thirty-five-year-old major faced the most important decision of his life. A misstep could leave him in exile, in prison, or dead.

Legend has it that Noriega first met Omar Torrijos in February 1962 at the Atlantic port city of Colón, Panama's second largest city, where Torrijos was commanding officer of the National Guard garrison. Noriega had a particularly attractive girlfriend in tow to celebrate Carnival in her hometown. He was flush with money for the first time in his life: the Americans, perhaps in gratitude for his good work in Peru, had helped him land a well-paying road-surveying job in the American-controlled Canal Zone. American salaries were the best in Panama, and a junior officer's billet hadn't been available anyway when Noriega returned from Peru.

At a particular lively Carnival party in the free-wheeling Caribbean city, Torrijos immediately set his eyes on Noriega's beautiful date. A notorious womanizer, he flirted extravagantly with her, figuring the skinny, short, and ugly Noriega was more likely to be her brother than her boyfriend. But when she left the table, Noriega started to talk. The local commander, already well-known in Colón, was impressed with Noriega's intelligence and credentials. Torrijos spoke eloquently about his plans to transform the National Guard into a socially progressive force, and said he needed men of Noriega's caliber to help him.

Noriega was taken with this handsome, charismatic major, and agreed to quit his better-paying American job. Torrijos hadn't the budget to hire a new man, so he would pay Noriega from petty cash. Noriega flew to Colón in September 1962.

However, Noriega's new career ended almost as quickly as it began. One of his first assignments was to monitor the Caribbean port city's bountiful population of prostitutes. The profitable prostitution business was run by the National Guard, and Torrijos was the local equivalent of a madame. Noriega considered access to the whores a perquisite of the office; and after a few months, he ran into trouble for raping and beating a prostitute—the same problem he had had in Peru. The story leaked out in a local newspaper that was campaigning against Torrijos at the time.

"That was something kind of ugly for us, but not terrible," says Boris Martínez, who read of the incident in Noriega's files when he became his commander in Chiriquí province. Martínez says the most troublesome aspect of the rape was that Noriega had done it in a police car and the prostitute had taken its license number. There had also been witnesses.

General Bolívar Vallarino ordered Torrijos to remove Noriega from the National Guard. Torrijos's wife, Raquel, had taken to young Noriega, however, and she felt sorry for him. She told her husband that Tony needed another chance. How could he expect him not to have some complexes, what with his sad upbringing and his homeliness?

So Torrijos saved him. His style of leadership wasn't that of a military disciplinarian anyway. Noriega, his most efficient and clever young officer, now would be even more loyal. A few months later, Torrijos was promoted to take over the Chiriquí province garrison in David city. On February 1, 1963, Noriega joined him, and soon thereafter became chief of the transit police department.

Chiriquí was the most important National Guard garrison in the Panamanian countryside. The province was the country's most important livestock and agricultural producer. Its porous frontier with Costa Rica attracted trade—legal and illegal—and Chiriquí province was also a stronghold of support for the "Arnulfistas," the backers of former President Arnulfo Arias, who had been ousted after he had tried to dismantle the country's military. General Vallarino wanted Torrijos to keep watch on Arnulfo's supporters, as did key businessmen in the region who didn't want their sweetheart deals with the military disrupted.

The CIA wanted Torrijos, who was on their payroll, to monitor something else: communist influence among banana growers in Puerto Armuelles and Bocas del Toro. The plantations were owned by the United Fruit Company, a powerful American company that still had the power to make or break political leaders in Panama.

In 1964 and 1965, officers from the 470th Military Intelligence Brigade helped Torrijos establish an intelligence capability. One or two American agents were permanently stationed in his headquarters. Torrijos picked Noriega, his transit police chief, to oversee the modest intelligence-gathering operation. The Americans were pleased with the choice as well: their files showed he was an inactive former asset who had served American intelligence well in the past.

In his position as transit police chief, Noriega had already begun collecting the files that were the first raw material upon which he would build his career. For instance, he knew which prominent citizens had been arrested for drunk driving, and which of them had been caught in the company of mistresses. He also controlled the licenses of cab drivers, bus

drivers, and chauffeurs. Not only would they be among his early informants, but in the 1964 elections, Noriega used them to make it more
difficult for voters from known opposition strongholds to get to polling
stations.

The 470th MI's liaison to Torrijos was a Puerto Rican–born American
named Efrain Angueira, who paid the Chiriquí commander $250 a month
for his services. Angueira would provide occasional bonuses of appliances,
food, or alcohol from American PXs and commissaries, for jobs well done.
The amount doesn't seem much, but Torrijos's salary at the time was only
about $500 monthly. Noriega's starting salary was $50 to $100 a month.

Now that Noriega was working with American intelligence people
again, they put him through a series of American finishing schools. But as
with so many other Latin American military officers, the American training was more successful in teaching him the technical skills of how to
control the Panamanian population than in transmitting democratic ideas
or procedures. Noriega's curriculum vitae, which was printed in 1983 but
which he later classified as secret, shows that he studied intelligence and
counterintelligence under American officers at Fort Gulick in Panama in
July 1967 and psychological operations at Fort Bragg in September 1967;
and then returned to the School of the Americas in Panama, where he took
a two-month course in "military intelligence for officers."

Noriega took every course available in order to broaden his knowledge
and give himself an edge over other young Panamanian officers. His CV
also shows courses in administration of documents and archives, basic and
advanced cartography, military engineering, jungle warfare and counterinsurgency battle, and American special forces and parachute training. He
also took military, special intelligence, and police investigative courses
elsewhere—primarily in Israel and Taiwan.

Noriega's instructors at the time, however, remember that it was psychological warfare that interested him most. The high school student who
dreamed of being a psychiatrist decided this was the form of warfare most
befitting modern times. At Fort Bragg, he spent seven weeks learning the
art of media manipulation to conquer adversaries and control people. In
their course catalogue, his instructors called this "purposeful communication." The emphasis was on disarming internal enemies, who in 1967 the
Americans considered to be communists. Noriega studied alongside Persian officers who feared the Soviets and Kurds, with Taiwanese who worried about the mainland Chinese, and with Latin American officers busy
fighting off Cuban infiltration.

Noriega learned about gray communications—the art of spreading news
and rumors for which the source is fuzzy—and "black" communications,

in which the information is made to sound as if it is coming from some other source entirely. Later, in 1975, Noriega would write Panama's first manual for psychological operations.

Noriega also developed police skills of his own. Torrijos's orders before the 1964 elections were for Noriega to intimidate Arnulfista leaders, so after the bombing of a local electrical station, Noriega arrested a small number of them and charged them with the crime.

Two eyewitnesses report seeing criminals in the jail using Coke bottles to rape the Arnulfistas from behind. One also used a splintered stick. Noriega supervised, watching silently as the prisoners screamed. Sometimes, he would wear a bag over his head, so that his distinctive face wouldn't be easily recognized afterward.

The 1964 sexual torture triggered such animosity that local women organized a downtown march. Panama was still under civilian rule and a local prosecutor began an investigation, causing Torrijos to ship Noriega off to Bocas del Toro for six weeks—from March 11 to April 26—to allow matters to cool down before the May elections.

Major Boris Martínez inherited the eager Noriega and his fledgling intelligence operation when he took over the Chiriquí garrison from Torrijos in 1966. Martínez was surprised to read of Noriega's misadventures, in his file, but he was impressed with the long list of services Noriega had performed for Torrijos. Martínez's only complaint was that Torrijos hadn't used this talented intelligence agent enough against local communists and the Arnulfistas.

Torrijos had been too soft, he thought, and the times called for a steady hand. Torrijos was an unusual military man, who seemed to Martínez something of a cross between Humphrey Bogart and W. C. Fields. Martínez viewed himself as more of a Latin George Patton, who frowned upon Torrijos's philandering and drinking.

One of Martínez' first meetings with Noriega let the new Chiriquí commander in on the young officer's belief in witchcraft. He was told he could find Torrijos and Noriega together at the home of a woman named Billings, who ran the local lottery together with the military. He found the two men sitting in a tub in the backyard, leaves, berries, and herbs floating beside them, while Billings said incantations. "He said it was important to go to those people for advice and for intelligence on others who visit them," remembers Martínez. "Noriega was well connected with such people."

Martínez remembers disciplining Noriega only once. The young first lieutenant, naked and in a drunken rage, had chased his wife, Felicidad, around the neighborhood, shouting sexual epithets while swinging a belt at her. A neighbor had complained. The incident was only the latest one of many in a common theme: Noriega's Dr. Jekyll would become Mr. Hyde under the influence of alcohol. Just a few months earlier, Noriega had stopped by the roadside of a farm and, while drunk, shot a couple of cows and a horse. On several occasions, Noriega would come to the prison cells intoxicated, and order prisoners to take off their clothes and run around the courtyard naked. He didn't do anything to them most of the time—no sexual torture or even violence. It was just good-natured humiliation. "People started wondering if something was wrong with him," said a local lawyer who had at first befriended the young first lieutenant.

Major Martínez ordered Noriega to cut down on his drinking immediately or be fired. Noriega obeyed, and he never had another discipline problem under Martínez. No former superior of Noriega's remembers his not fulfilling an order, no matter how difficult or dangerous the assignment. "Noriega was the most reliable and loyal servant I ever had," Martínez says of the Chiriquí days.

"If he has a boss, he pleases the boss," said Martínez. "If the boss wants coffee, he brings it. If the boss wants efficiency, he provides it. If he wants brutality, Noriega is brutal. I don't like people who kiss my foot, but I do like an officer who delivers. I gave Noriega many assignments. I don't know how he completed them all, but he did. Whenever I wanted to be informed of any movement in Chiriquí province, he kept me informed."

Martínez expanded Noriega's already ambitious mandate and provided him with more resources. His assignment: to infiltrate the banana workers' unions and keep their communist members under surveillance.

In the weeks that followed, Noriega organized a network of informants in every town and village, all eager to fight communism. Noriega gave the villagers simple instructions. When union organizers came through, informants were instructed to write down the time of the visit and the license number of the jeep. They were not to question the visitors personally, but only to listen to the villagers' gossip about the meetings later. His new recruits sent information to central headquarters every week.

"It was an interesting job, and Noriega was very good at it," said Martínez.

Noriega's intelligence allowed Martínez to avoid problems. On one occasion, Martínez told Noriega that he had heard that a union leader would be leading a march of 25,000 farmers on Labor Day. They were planning to carry machetes and farm tools, and Martínez feared they would provoke a riot. Noriega was told to investigate, and he returned three days later with a complete report. Noriega feared trouble as well.

"What do you suggest we do?" Martínez asked.

Noriega pulled out a file. He claimed that the union boss was having an affair with his deputy's wife. The two men had fought privately over the affair, but their feud hadn't come into the open. Maybe we can use this to demoralize them, Noriega suggested.

First Noriega studied the workers' vernacular and collected previous handbills they had printed; then he launched a smear campaign against the union leader, using the appropriate workers' slang and even their paper. His people posted the handbills where the men were accustomed to looking for messages from their union leaders, and before long, all the banana workers knew of the sexual struggle between their leaders, with each leader blaming the other for starting it. In one act, Noriega had divided the entire union.

"The most important thing was that the slander was real," says Martínez now. "Noriega knew this made it more effective."

When the banana-union boss arrived in David a week or two later to pick up his permit for a demonstration, Martínez demanded that the workers leave all their tools at home. The union leader agreed, but he demanded that his own workers—wearing armbands—provide security. Martínez refused.

"If I see anything like that," he said. "I'll arrest you first." The union boss was weakened, and he no longer had the full backing of his people. The usually combative labor leader looked tired and demoralized. Noriega had softened him up.

"It was like a play on Broadway," laughs Martínez. "Noriega managed the whole thing. He was superb. Noriega was an expert at bribing and blackmailing people. And he knew when valuable information should not be used and just held."

A case in point: the CIA would tip off Noriega whenever any Panamanian returned from a Soviet school or suspicious training program. In 1967, the CIA informed Noriega of a schoolteacher returning to Chiriquí province who had studied in Moscow at Patrice Lumumba University. She was taking a job in a banana growers' area, where her assignment would be to mobilize teachers and workers. Noriega put her under surveillance in a rundown hotel room, and he collected recordings of some energetic love-making and political planning with a male visitor. The visitor was Moisés Torrijos, the older brother of Noriega's former commander and Panama's future dictator. Noriega was so proud of this find that he brought along Boris Martínez to listen in. When the two conspirators left the room, Noriega and Martínez entered and found an explicit love letter to Moisés, who had also spent considerable time in Moscow. Martínez said he didn't want the letter in his office files, so Noriega took it home. Martínez thinks it was the beginning of a thick private file that Noriega kept on Torrijos, that would later make it impossible for the dictator to rein him in.

"Over the years, Torrijos never showed as much loyalty to anyone in the military as he did to Noriega," said Martínez. "He would often change people's jobs or reduce their power, but Noriega always remained and gained in influence. Torrijos often made clear to his friends that he didn't trust Noriega, but yet he was also always Torrijos's darling. The explanation can only be intelligence—he must have had something on him."

In 1968, nothing was more important to General Vallarino, the last member of the country's oligarchy to rule the armed forces, than preventing the election of Arnulfo Arias. Vallarino sent orders to Major Martínez to coordinate election fraud with some local businessmen. But the business community hated Martínez, who had as viciously rooted out their sweetheart deals with the National Guard as he had repressed the Arnulfistas. Martínez turned the job over to Noriega. Noriega set up an operation to intimidate Arnulfista leaders through random arrests and threats: he used his power over the transit department to scare taxi and bus drivers from transporting opposition voters from rural communities to polling places; and, in places where Arias was the clear loser, he helped prepare fake ballot books.

Yet this time, all the tricks of the military and its partners in the Chiriquí business community couldn't shift the landslide. Arias won, with 175,000 votes to 134,000 for the government candidate, David Samudio. Even General Vallarino was forced to endorse the results. The National Guard was concerned, knowing that Arnulfo previously wanted to dismantle the military and create a secret police loyal only to him.

Plotting against Arias began immediately in the National Guard, by a group known as "the Combo." Major Martínez was its most powerful and strident member, a popular commander who had won the loyalty of troops, not only in Chiriquí province but in other garrisons where he had served. His top co-conspirator was Torrijos, who was senior in rank but who lacked command over troops. Noriega was among the junior officers who joined the Combo.

However, General Vallarino argued for caution and convinced the younger officers that Arias might not decimate their ranks. Consequently, they set aside their plotting for a while and, at age sixty-seven, Arias was inaugurated as president for the third time, on October 1, 1968. He served only eleven days.

Shortly after taking office, Arias made clear he would indeed purge the

National Guard, ordering Torrijos with his family to El Salvador and having Martínez transferred to Chitré province, a far less important posting.

A frightened Torrijos visited Martínez, with his friend Demetrio Lakas and businessman Juan David Morgan. Torrijos pleaded with Martínez to take action—before it was too late—to stop Arias from destroying the National Guard.

"But your rank is higher than mine," said Martínez.

"But you have the troops," said Torrijos. As the secretary to Vallarino, he hadn't commanded soldiers for two years. Martínez was also a logistical magician, while Torrijos's skills were more political. Before long, thirty officers had joined the plotting with Martínez and Torrijos.

That same week, after the inauguration, the U.S. ambassador to Panama, Charles Adair, sent reassuring cables home to Washington saying that the National Guard wouldn't rebel. These messages were based on faulty intelligence, planted by the Combo through American friends such as Efrain Angueira of the 470th Military Intelligence Brigade, who gathered most of his intelligence over cocktails with Torrijos and Rory Gonzalez at the U.S. Officers Club. He had sponsored their memberships there. Gonzalez and Torrijos found the Americans hopelessly easy to manipulate. American intelligence officers would take and relay whatever information they provided.

Torrijos even took Angueira to the airline office, where he bought tickets for himself and his family to Mexico. Martínez had shipped his goods ahead to Chitré as well, another move intended to mislead the Americans and Arias into thinking that everything was under control.

Ironically, the strategy Martínez used to seize the country was patterned on a plan the Americans had helped him put together in order to prepare for communist invasion. He had been running counterinsurgency maneuvers for two years, and the morale of his troops was high. "We were prepared for taking over the country," said Martínez. "The plan was to prepare for communists, but we used it on Arnulfo." First Lieutenant Noriega was responsible for intelligence and for seizing communication facilities.

Fearing that Torrijos was backing down, Martínez began the anti-Arias plot at 8 P.M., an hour before the scheduled starting time. Arias was at the Iris movie theater with a young mistress, but once he discovered what had happened, he fled to the American Canal Zone and caught a military flight to Miami. It seemed a strange irony that this politician, who had campaigned against the U.S. for so long and who had twice been ousted in U.S.–endorsed coups, was now turning to Washington for safety.

The coup had been easier than expected. Martínez was particularly pleased with Noriega's work. Noriega had seized Arias's radio station, helped arrest tens of Arias's backers, sent a group of his men to burn down the Arias farm, and rounded up many of Arias's crop workers.

One of the first politicians Noriega arrested after the 1968 coup was Rodrigo Miranda, the local lawyer who had saved Noriega's marriage several years earlier. After leaving Miranda in jail for three days, Noriega called him to his office as the first of about a hundred captives to be interrogated. The prisoners watched fearfully as Miranda walked by; they knew Noriega's reputation for brutality. The door slammed behind the popular lawyer, sending an echo through the cement prison building. Noriega smiled at Miranda, pulled out his gun, and aimed it at his head. He then raised the barrel and fired a shot straight at the ceiling. The noise reverberated through each of the cells, sending waves of fear through the other prisoners. Noriega laughed maniacally. "It was typical Noriega," says Miranda, who was released unharmed the next day.

The 1968 coup also saved Noriega from facing more rape charges, this time before the Progreso village community court. Juan B. Ibarra, the Third Circuit Court magistrate, had already prepared the case, in which documents alleged Noriega had come to the village for the rice harvest party that year, where he was appointed to crown the queen, and late in the evening, Noriega had taken the queen to a nearby field and raped her. The villagers had denounced him and pretrial proceedings had begun, but when Arias was overthrown the case was dropped. From 1968 on, the Chiriquí courts rarely prosecuted crimes committed by National Guard members.

After the October 1968 coup, Torrijos and Martínez put Noriega atop the list of those to be rewarded. The two promoted him to major for his role in supporting their overthrow of President Arnulfo Arias, even though Noriega had been a lieutenant for only three years. On January 3, 1969, they named Noriega commander of the First Company of Engineers and deputy to the National Guard's general staff. A month later, Noriega also had command over the Second Infantry Company.

Noriega accepted command with relish. His first assignment was to help Martínez round up a new band of ragtag guerrillas fighting on behalf of Arnulfo Arias. They were led by two foreigners, Uruguayan guerrilla leader Walter Sardinia and Costa Rican Adolfo Aguilar, but their ranks were made up of no more than a few dozen local farmers and their sons. Yet Martínez, with Noriega's eager help, pursued them like dangerous invaders. Those that fell into Noriega's hands suffered the cruelest fates. Noriega had several of them tied down naked, on their backs, in a sunbaked courtyard of the Chiriquí province prison until their skin began to bubble.

Noriega also used psychological warfare, spreading word that he had ordered his troops to bring back the ears of any guerrillas they caught, preferably cutting the ears off before killing the insurgents. "He planted the stories," said Martínez. "He realized the value of this terrorism of information." Noriega also kept quiet certain stories that he and his commander knew would have terrorized his own troops: the guerrillas had captured two of his men, cut off their testicles, put them in their mouths, and then hung them upside down from trees.

Noriega also worked more closely with the Americans than ever before during this time. Without a helicopter force of its own, the National Guard turned to the Americans for help in hunting down the guerrillas in the backwoods with night vision devices.

It was still Martínez who was running the anti-guerrilla war, but his loyal servant Noriega fulfilled all his commands better than any sub-officer he'd ever had.

Yet Noriega would soon have to choose between Torrijos and Martínez, a team predestined to divorce.

Martínez embodied the highly organized military man, who was often brutal but honest to the point of naiveté. He couldn't countenance weakness or disloyalty. His ideology was discipline.

Torrijos, the disorganized, heavy-drinking womanizer, led his troops by his charisma. He liked people in his company with enough weaknesses to make them interesting. He was a romantic, who wanted power without pain. His ideology was vaguely socialist.

Martínez openly worried about Torrijos's drinking and his ability to lead the country, and suggested to military allies that Torrijos might be unfit for office. That was bad enough for Torrijos, but Martínez shocked him most when he went alone before a national television audience to announce a new economic program that included land reform to benefit Panama's peasant farmers and a more comprehensive health care program. Torrijos resented not being included in the announcement of this popular plan. Torrijos decided to act, and his American intelligence friend, Efrain Angueira, helped him prepare the ground for Martínez's ouster.

On February 24, 1969, Martínez walked into a trap set in Torrijos's office. One colonel stuck a Thompson submachine gun in Martínez's gut; another officer hit him over the head. They wrapped thick military green tape around his mouth and put him, along with three other officers, on a plane to Miami. Four other officers were exiled to Spain. Noriega, once Martínez's loyal servant, had been part of the scheme: he even personally had set up one of Martínez's allies for the sting in Panama City so that he himself could become commander of the Chiriquí garrison.

When Martínez arrived in Miami, it was clear the U.S. was in on his ouster as well. All the immigration papers had been prepared, and Martínez was quickly cleared through Customs. Torrijos sent an emissary to meet Martínez in Miami and offer him a cushy job at the Inter-American Defense Board in Washington.

Martínez turned him down, still hoping to fight his way back to power. But he told the emissary that he worried about the well-being of Noriega. "I am very sad," Martínez said, "because I am sure they have killed Tony Noriega." But Noriega had gauged the situation properly, and had carefully measured the strength of each of his former commanders before casting his lot with Torrijos.

"It was a surprise to me about Noriega," sighs Martínez now, sipping an Amstel Light at Terminal B of the Miami International Airport. His chest still juts and his shoulders are square, but now he wears the uniform of El Salvador's Taca Airlines, where he is in the freight department. "I was very naive. Torrijos was a politician in uniform. I was just a soldier. But I always thought Noriega and I were on the same line of thinking. His talent was in gaining my trust. One of the things Noriega didn't have is loyalty. Not to anyone or anything."

Now, less than ten months after Martínez's ouster, Noriega had to choose right again. This time the situation was far less clear and his decision was much more critical. This time, the coup makers were against Torrijos, apparently backed by some influential Americans, and they were phoning to ask for his assistance. As so often in his life, he turned to his brother Luis Carlos for advice.

Luis Carlos, then a well-connected foreign ministry official in Panama City, was close to the usurpers. The rebels didn't have much backing among other officers or troops, the two brothers agreed. Luis Carlos concluded the coup would fail unless Washington was fully behind it. But that was a real possibility. The Nixon administration feared Torrijos was moving Panama too far left.

Furthermore, Araúz was more American than Panamanian. He golfed almost daily with American officers at their Fort Amador Country Club, a lush course fittingly named after Panama's first president, whom Theodore Roosevelt had helped into power. During the bloody 1964 anti-American riots, Araúz had taken his own troops to the American embassy to protect diplomats from violent students and had been close to the Americans ever since. Some of the other officers involved—Ramiro Silvera, Amado Sanjur, and Luis Nentzen Franco—had often been seen using the "red phone" that connected Panama's military with the U.S. Southern Command.

In Panama City, coup leader Amado Sanjur had called the cabinet members to the presidential palace at 1:30 A.M. The rebels listed three reasons for removing Torrijos. They feared Torrijos's support of compulsory unionism, and charged Torrijos was creating a Perón-like populist system in Panama with himself as the head of the "shirtless ones"; they were angry that Torrijos had named known communists to cabinet positions; and finally, they accused Torrijos of concentrating too much power in his own hands. They promised to move quickly toward democracy.

The coup makers gave the cabinet members a choice of quitting or joining their junta. Two cabinet members at the time, Fernando Manfredo and Nicholás Ardito Barletta, would recall later that they joined ranks with new leadership because they felt the country could fall apart if they resigned. They had no faith in the new regime.

One of the rebel colonels, José María Pinilla, phoned Torrijos at 4:30 A.M. to inform the dictator that he was out of a job. Standing near Pinilla, Fernando Manfredo picked up another phone to listen in. Pinilla told Torrijos his wife was safe, his mortgage would be paid, and he should stay abroad. "I can't leave this poor country in your hands," Torrijos replied. "I'm coming back." Pinilla lied to the civilian leaders waiting in the next room that Torrijos had accepted their seizure of power. Manfredo whispered to the others what he had heard.

True to tradition, Americans tinkered. At one point, Araúz took a call from American military intelligence agent Efrain Angueira. He reported to his fellow conspirators that Angueira was prepared to offer support if it was needed. This was powerful information, although evidence never surfaced that the Nixon administration itself was behind the coup. Angueira was the American closest to Torrijos. They were drinking buddies, and their wives were best friends.

"We have the gringos on our side," Araúz said.

The key for the Noriega brothers was how far American commitment went. Would the gringos support the coup makers with arms? Neither of them knew, although they doubted Panama was important enough to Nixon—whose focus was on China and the Soviet Union—to merit such attention. They also didn't know Torrijos's plan, and their efforts to reach him in Mexico had failed. They devised a strategy that would serve them no matter who triumphed.

Noriega phoned back Araúz less than an hour after the first call. He would cooperate if his brother Luis Carlos was named as a minister of government, he said. That move would provide him a protector in the new regime, if it lasted, and it would also give him a spy in the coup. The coup makers, who liked Luis Carlos and needed Manuel Antonio, agreed to the deal.

Nevertheless, Major Noriega privately rooted for his mentor, General Torrijos, under whom he stood far better chances of advancement. Torrijos had rewarded Noriega's role in the Martínez ouster on October 22, 1969, by naming him commander of the 5th Military Zone, with its headquarters in David, the capital of Chiriquí province. Few Panamanian officers had ever risen so quickly in such a short time. But Noriega couldn't even get a phone call out to Torrijos. The rebels had cut foreign lines. So he waited, nervously, for his brother's first reports.

In Mexico City, Torrijos paced his hotel room furiously. The rebels had reached him first through Panama's ambassador to Mexico, who had awakened him with the bad news. Ever since, he had been in a rage. Former foreign minister Fernando Eleta, a horse-racing fanatic also in Mexico at the time, found Torrijos in his hotel room, angrily throwing furniture, vases, paintings—anything not nailed down. "It's impossible for Silvera and Sanjur to do this to me," he shouted so loud at the predawn hour that others in the hotel were coming to their doors. Nothing was open yet in Mexico City; Torrijos couldn't get a phone call through to Panama; and the dictator was destroying everything in sight.

Eleta sifted his way through the havoc to the phone and dialed the INTERCOMSA (International Communications Satellite) central exchange. He was an INTERCOMSA board member. He asked the operator to connect him to Chiriquí province and Major Manuel Antonio Noriega. Torrijos knew Noriega, his most loyal junior officer, was his best hope for a return to Panama. While the two men plotted Torrijos's counter-coup, Eleta found an air charter company in the Yellow Pages. Noriega would provide the landing field, and now Eleta had to find a plane. A night watchman answered the phone and gave Eleta the name of a pilot. "General Torrijos's mother is dying in Panama," Eleta said. "He needs to get back right away." The drowsy pilot said he would help, but he would have to stop in El Salvador to refuel. A young embassy employee, Emilia Arosemena, provided the check to pay for the plane, which would later bounce. No matter. She was later promoted to ambassador for her service, a position she served in for more than a decade.

In Chiriquí province, Noriega already knew that money in Panama was always the first step to gaining or preserving power. Noriega knew Torrijos would have to feed troops and perhaps operate for some time in Chiriquí province, and the new leaders had frozen National Guard accounts, so Noriega phoned Torrijos's long-time friend and personal doctor Jorge

Abadía Arias to raise funds. Torrijos had lots of rich friends in Chiriquí province: as garrison commander, he had protected their contraband schemes, ignored questionable businesses, and helped them steal local elections. Dr. Abadía quickly raised $1 million, the Abadía family providing most of the money, but four or five others gave $150,000 each, as well.

Abadía called on his brother, Aristides, who owned the American Motors Corporation franchise for Panama. Noriega wanted Aristides to provide a fleet of jeeps, and he needed AMC dealerships throughout the country to provide him intelligence through their independent network of CB radios. Soon, the dealers began reporting to Noriega on troop movements and on support for the coup in their cities. Noriega also dispatched several jeeps along the road to Panama City to scout the potential route of Torrijos's return.

The intelligence was favorable: eighteen hours after the coup, the rebels still hadn't put any troops on the streets. They clearly didn't think Torrijos would come back. Or perhaps they weren't yet ready to test their hold on the National Guard by issuing orders to seize vital roadways.

At Torrijos's request, Noriega sent a pilot to meet the dictator in San Salvador for the final leg of his trip home. Torrijos wanted a pilot he trusted, an American crop-duster named Red Gray who had been a wing commander with the British Royal Air Force during World War II. Gray knew Panama's landscape without maps and could find Chiriquí province at night. His Spanish nickname, in honor of his fire-red hair, was "Gallo Chiricano"—the Chiriquí rooster.

Torrijos and Red Gray took off for Chiriquí after dark. Noriega was so nervous that he phoned Lakas, who had stayed behind in El Salvador, every half-hour. "Noriega was afraid the plane wouldn't get there on time," says Lakas. "He kept saying, 'It's getting late. Where's Omar? It's time. He should be here.' "

Finally, as Noriega watched the dark sky from the control building beside Chiriquí's dirt landing strip, he heard a crackle, and then a familiar American voice identifying the plane. But he didn't want to take any chances.

"How do they call you?" Noriega said to the copilot.

"I'm El Gallo Chiricano," he said.

Torrijos was back.

Noriega fired a pistol in the air. The shot in the dark was the signal for the drivers of the AMC jeeps and other cars lined up along the runway to turn on their headlights. It was early morning on December 16, 1969. Torrijos remarked to Red Gray that the landing strip looked like two long strings of Christmas lights. Torrijos still wasn't sure he wouldn't be killed when he stepped onto the tarmac, however; and Noriega, equally nervous, had ordered his soldiers to point their guns at the plane. But when it was Torrijos who climbed out, Noriega embraced him. "Now you are in Panama," he said. "Now we can take over this place."

The next day, in Jorge Abadía's personal Wagoneer, Torrijos started the drive to Panama City. Word spread through Panama of his return. Much of the country arrayed itself behind him as he drove up the highway. Television crews had come along to record Torrijos's comeback. Noriega stayed in David, watching television. If Torrijos made it back, he was a hero. If he didn't, he hoped his brother could save him.

After Noriega took military command on August 12, 1983, he would make December 16 a national holiday—"Loyalty Day"—and he would install a plaque beside the landing strip where Torrijos had triumphantly returned. It reads: "16 December 1969. General Torrijos came back to the country, reconquering the political and military power of the nation in twenty-four hours, an odyssey never exceeded by any other Caudillo of America. It was thanks to the decision and the courage of the 5th Military Zone, at that time under the command of Major Manuel Antonio Noriega, today General of the Panamanian Defense Forces. He wrote the most glorious page of the institution in high civic and patriotic spirit, loyalty without price or doubt. On 16 December 1969, Torrijosism was born."

But what few Panamanians knew was that even on this most important of days to General Manuel Antonio Noriega, he was hedging his bets and playing both sides.

Noriega's role in foiling the failed coup was just the break the ambitious major needed.

Several weeks earlier, Noriega had complained to a cabinet minister that he wanted Torrijos to promote him. Noriega was tired of the backwoods, he said, and he didn't understand why Torrijos didn't bring him to Panama City.

The cabinet minister had asked Torrijos why he kept Noriega in Chiriquí province, and Torrijos had replied that Noriega had too much ambition and too little principle for high office. But December 16 had left Torrijos with a heavy debt to repay and new confidence in Noriega's loyalty. Torrijos now owed his dictatorship to Noriega. Eight months later, in August 1970, Torrijos named Noriega head of the country's military intelligence, or G-2. Torrijos also promoted him to lieutenant colonel, only eighteen months after he had been named a major, and he made him a member of the general staff. The National Guard had never known such a meteoric rise.

December 16 also shaped Panama's political landscape. By triumphing over his rivals, Torrijos gained a new aura of leadership. He was stronger and more confident—and also more anti-American. Torrijos was convinced Washington had encouraged—if not helped to plan—the coup against him, and ordered Noriega to transform the country's military intelligence service into a sophisticated national spy service. He wanted Noriega slowly to improve strained relations with the CIA, but he also instructed him to diversify: Noriega should develop closer ties to the Israelis, the Cubans, and other intelligence services.

In the coming weeks, Noriega would see Torrijos play all sides with a deftness that he himself would later build upon. Despite Torrijos's certainty that the gringos wanted him out, he sent a message of reassurance to President Richard Nixon, saying one of his basic principles was "total repudiation of communism and all other extremist ideologies." He said the country's development programs would "identify completely with the philosophy of the Alliance for Progress" launched by President Kennedy.

At the same time, he told Noriega, "Panamanians should never be American servants again. You see to that." Torrijos bragged that his coup, and the defense of it, might be the first time in Panama that forces had come to power and thereafter successfully defended it despite American opposition.

Noriega participated in an investigation, led by Colonel Rodrigo Garcia, that proved U.S. involvement in the coup, particularly that of Torrijos's erstwhile friend Efrain Angueira. Torrijos had trusted Angueira so much that his wife, Raquel, had fled to Angeuira's home for safekeeping during the abortive coup. The U.S. withdrew Angueira from Panama in embarrassment.

"Relations were very poor," says Nicholás Gonzalez Revilla, who would later become Torrijos's ambassador in Washington. "There was no treaty, no ambassador; there was nothing. Torrijos thought he had U.S. support. When he found out he didn't, he started rethinking policies."

Torrijos wanted to start from scratch on new Panama Canal Treaties, despite talks which had made considerable progress in the late 1960s. He named prominent leftists to lead the negotiations: the University of Panama's rector Rómulo Escobar Bethancourt and Aristides Royo. Erasing forever the inequity of the 1903 Panama Canal Treaties would be at the center of his populist campaign, which included costly reforms in agriculture, social welfare, and education.

Noriega chose his first intelligence task for himself: he gathered the telegrams of congratulations that obsequious Panamanians had sent to the coup makers during their less than forty-eight hours in power. "Noriega kept all of them," says Aristides Abadía, the son of the AMC dealer who helped Torrijos regain power. "I saw them. A lot of people who said they were loyal to Torrijos weren't. Noriega knew who they were, and what they did."

The secret Noriega files, upon which he would build his rise to power, began to grow. The Noriega-Torrijos relationship, which would provide the setting for Noriega's accumulation of power and influence, was set in cement.

CHAPTER
SIX

THE NORIEGA UNDERWORLD

Well, do I look like a monster?
—NORIEGA TO *WASHINGTON POST* REPORTER
SALLY QUINN, MARCH 8, 1978

General Omar Torrijos ruled over Panama with a tropical laissez-faire. Hardly a military dictator, he was more a populist, happy-go-lucky lay-about who was determined to make history by creating a generous social welfare system and new Panama Canal Treaties. But his hands-off approach allowed corruption to spread within the ranks of his military and the nation like jungle fever. Noriega's intelligence service was the only full-time monitor.

From the beginning, Torrijos and Noriega were the Caribbean Odd Couple. Torrijos was a lazy, disorganized, but charismatic and handsome dictator. Noriega was the detail-oriented, workaholic confidence man. Torrijos sought the klieg lights; Noriega preferred the shadows. Torrijos mixed in crowds with populist comfort, trudging across streams with peasants and marching across the Libyan desert with nomads. Noriega shied away from human contact, and preferred quiet meetings in occluded places.

Everyone knew Torrijos and most loved him. Few knew Noriega, and those who did know him, feared him. Ironically, though, it would be Torrijos who created the system of corruption and broad military power that Noriega would later exploit to repress a nation. Even more troubling, Washington would discover the problem early but nevertheless encourage the development of a financial system and military that would misshape Panama.

Torrijos had seized political power from the country's traditional oligarchy, thus forcing them from political and military leadership for the first time in the country's history. They acquiesced, partly because he allowed them not only to maintain their economic strength but also to expand it. Torrijos backed new banking laws that ensured strict secrecy and anonymity and made Panama the Switzerland of Latin America. From only twelve banks before the 1968 coup, the number expanded to more than 100 by the mid-1970s. Illicit funds flowing to Panama grew commensurately, and dummy corporations multiplied like rabbits.

"Suddenly, banks were opening whose sole purpose was handling slightly or completely suspicious money," said Jack Blum, a congressional investigator for Senator John Kerry's narcotics subcommittee, who years later would piece together how Panama had evolved into a drug money laundering center. "Immediately, Panama became a place where corporations and individuals parked illegal money. Noriega might never have been any more than a somewhat sadistic and relatively small-time military strongman if it hadn't been for the Panamanian banking system."

The irony, Blum says, was that Washington encouraged and even assisted this means of development. Again, Washington's shortsighted policies were laying the groundwork for its future problems in Panama. For the clever criminal mind, Panama provided everything: anonymous shareholders, dollar accounts, and shell corporations.

The basic concept was that shady figures throughout the Hemisphere could move money to Panama from areas where regulatory controls were stricter. "That is the place where all good criminal planning begins," says Blum. "And Noriega came into this situation with one of the most remarkable criminal minds of our time."

At first, three sorts of money came to Panama. Latin money used Panama for flight capital from taxation and political unrest. Corporations would use Panama to mask their profits; for instance, Colombian coffee growers would sell at an enormous loss to Panamanian companies they had established; the loss went onto their books at home; and then the coffee would be resold in America at a large, untaxed profit. Third, companies in the Hemisphere would establish a bank in Panama which would lend them capital at extremely high interest rates. The interest would be a tax write-off at home for the company, and it would be a big profit for that company's bank in Panama. The only limit to the schemes in Panama was the executive's imagination.

Panama's geographical location, its fifty-one-mile-long canal from the Atlantic to the Pacific, and its Colón Free Trade Zone, where contraband of any nature and nationality could be easily traded, made it a good place for transactions of every sort. From the days of the Spanish Camino Real to the Americans' Panama Canal, the narrow isthmus had been a magnet to fortune seekers. Torrijos liked to tell Noriega that Panama was "like a thin-waisted woman—everyone wants to fuck her." Now, however, Panama was all Torrijos's to offer to those lusty foreigners.

After the Torrijos coup, Panama began replacing pre-Castro Cuba as a magnet for Mafia money laundering, drug racketeering, arms smuggling, and various other contraband operations, ranging from the repacking of embargoed Cuban shrimp under Panamanian coverings for the U.S. market to falsifying end-user certificates in order to pass American high technology to Castro. For some time during Prohibition, Cuba was fueled with millions of dollars from Mafia moonshiners, but the amount of money and business that would pass through Panama in the 1970s would dwarf that of pre-Castro Havana.

However, Torrijos never cared much for the money himself. On his travels, he would occasionally turn to his "bodyguard," a communist poet named José de Jesús Martínez, for a reading of their financial condition. Martínez, whose nickname was "Chuchu," would merely hold his thumb and forefinger as far apart as their stack of hundred dollar bills was high. When the gap shrank to an inch, Torrijos would order more money from the Treasury.

Noriega, however, would get full reports from his banker every month on his wife's credit card charges, and he'd receive computer printouts from the National Bank on whatever businessman or foreigner he wanted to bribe, blackmail, or co-opt. His G-2 meticulously gathered the data on the quickly expanding financial center. "Every one in Panama has something to hide," Noriega told his G-2 officers. "What I want to know, in every case, is what that something is."

Noriega's attraction to the world's seamier side got him into early trouble with the Americans, almost as soon as he took over Panamanian intelligence in August 1970. The Nixon administration was on the lookout for expanding communism and drug dealing throughout Latin America, and Panama seemed to fit both bills. The Bureau of Narcotics and Dangerous Drugs (BNDD), the forerunner to today's Drug Enforcement Administration, started to trail one of Noriega's G-2 informants and, apparently, an employee, and that trail led to the top of Panama's government.

The head of air traffic control at Panama's international airport, Joaquín Him Gonzalez, had two weaknesses: drug trafficking and softball. When American anti-drug agents discovered the first, they decided to lure him into an arrest by using the second.

By 1971, American agents had collected sufficient evidence to believe that Him Gonzalez oversaw a flow of heroin from Europe, the Far East, and South America through Panama and on to the United States. Him Gonzalez, whose nickname was "Chino," because of his oriental looks, was a wheeler-dealer whose partners were government officials. Agents suspected that his arrest would also provide more information on his boss, G-2 chief Manuel Antonio Noriega, whose connections to the drug world were raising alarm in Washington.

To protect against possible arrest, Him Gonzalez never flew to the United States—in fact, he rarely left Panama—so federal drug agents decided to draw him into the American-controlled Panama Canal Zone for a softball game between the Federal Aviation Administration and the Panama Civil Aviation Authority. The agents maneuvered so cleverly that Him Gonzalez even helped organize the game. But before the first pitch could even be thrown, he was arrested, handcuffed, and flown to the United States, where a sealed indictment awaited him in Texas. The Panamanians were livid. The game, not surprisingly, was called off.

Torrijos, steaming about this affront to his national sovereignty, publicly threatened military action against the Americans in the Panama Canal Zone and demanded the recall of 120 Peace Corps workers. He ordered the Bureau of Narcotics and Dangerous Drugs to close its office. The American ambassador to Panama, Robert Sayre, was also angry at this diplomatic embarrassment. He complained to the State Department that he hadn't been told in advance about this kidnapping plan, which had strained relations so much at a time when the Nixon administration was considering the reopening of Panama Canal Treaty negotiations.

However, it was the Nixon administration in its first term that was most worried about this new Torrijos-Noriega team.

Richard Nixon had entered office on an anti-crime platform in the 1968 elections. On June 17, 1971, he told Congress that the war on drugs was nothing less than "a national emergency," and his anti-drug enforcers considered Panama and Torrijos a clear threat: they said they had gathered information that Torrijos and his spy chief, Manuel Antonio Noriega, were facilitating the heroin trade through their embassies, consulates, airports, and customs offices in the Far East and the Américas. Even Torrijos's older brother, Moisés, was allegedly involved.

In addition, Torrijos posed Nixon a second, perhaps even more troubling, threat: the White House was wary of the spread of communism in Latin America. Torrijos had named known communists to his cabinet, had established a secret link to Fidel Castro's Cuba and, had in general—

despite the American Canal and bases—shifted leftward. Nicaraguan leader Anastasio Somoza warned his American friends that the Torrijos-Noriega duo would bring communism to Panama, and the added drug-dealing dimension only made matters worse.

Drugs might have been the legitimate excuse for the Nixon administration to target the Torrijos regime, but Panama's turn to the left provided additional motivation to enforce the law.

The air-traffic controller's arrest, among others, signaled that Washington knew what was happening in Panama and would try to stop it. Six months later, in New York, American agents arrested the son of a Panamanian diplomat, Rafael Richard Gonzalez, and they charged he had 154 pounds of heroin in his possession. Rafael Richard carried a diplomatic passport, personally signed by Foreign Minister Juan Antonio Tack, and he unsuccessfully tried to claim immunity. Investigators later would allege he had drug business connections with the Panamanian government and Moisés Torrijos, the dictator's brother. Richard was also allegedly connected to Noriega's G-2 intelligence service through his father.

In May 1971, the White House in a memo asked John Ingersoll, director of the BNDD, to draft a plan for "clandestine law enforcement" around the world. The minutes of the meeting left little doubt how far he should go. "This decisive action is our only hope for destroying or immobilizing the highest level of drug traffickers," it said.

In January 1972, Ingersoll asked his staff to draw up options for dealing with Torrijos and Noriega. Two agents, William Durkin and Phillip Smith, came up with five alternatives. A top secret, five-page report, buried beneath several layers of security at the Senate Select Committee on Intelligence, lists the options:

"Linking the official [Noriega] to a fictitious plot against General Torrijos; leaking information on drug trafficking to the press; linking his removal to Panama Canal negotiations; secretly encouraging powerful groups within Panama to raise the issue; and total and complete immobilization."

Anti-drug efforts at the time so exceeded acceptable bounds that several years later the Justice Department ordered an investigation into "allegations of fraud, irregularity, and misconduct in the Drug Enforcement Administration." The still secret document with the results of the probe is known as the "DeFeo Report," named for its author Michael DeFeo, a DEA investigator. It reveals embarrassing detail about drug enforcers, ties to Mafia figures and about CIA agents' infiltration of the DEA to pursue more political ends; and, in a separate section, many pages outline the involvement of Panamanian officials in drug trafficking. Most explosively, however, several memos regard the consideration of assassination and other measures to deal with Torrijos and Noriega.

The report includes a seven-page section called "Panama International Drug Traffic and Involvement of Panamanian Government Officials." It also includes a five-page section headed "Colonel Manuel Noriega concerning options w/respect to immobilization and/or neutralization of Noriega."

For instance, one DeFeo report memo reads:

"The Senate Permanent Subcommittee on Investigations inquired into reports that Phillip Smith and William Durkin participated in discussions within DEA regarding a proposal to assassinate the President of Panama, who was suspected of being involved in drug trafficking." The DeFeo report cites a Smith memorandum that denied any such plotting, but which claimed instead that he passed on to the CIA information he had received about a conspiracy to kill the Panamanian general.

"It was alleged that a discussion concerning assassination involved the possibility of killing Mr. Noryago [sic], the principal assistant to the President of Panama, and that Smith and William Durkin actually proposed that he be killed."

In the end, however, Ingersoll chose a far less controversial approach to Panama, one aimed at restoring his office in the country and improving relations with Torrijos. At the suggestion of Nixon's domestic counsel, John Ehrlichman, he flew to Panama in June 1972 to confront General Omar Torrijos. The diplomacy option had two goals: to stem drug trafficking and to repair relations, so that Panama would invite drug agents back to the country and begin to cooperate in international enforcement efforts.

The mood was tense at Torrijos's beach house, south of Panama City, as Ingersoll began his list of complaints. "There is a continuing problem concerning the abuse of diplomatic immunity," he said.

A secret memorandum of the meeting quoted Ingersoll as making some surprising allegations: "For example, BNDD received a report from Interpol indicating that on May 28, 1971, Armando Moreno Guillen, the Panamanian Ambassador to Egypt and India, entered Denmark with five suitcases. Four of the suitcases were seized containing 81 kilos of hashish. There is an outstanding warrant for his arrest in Denmark." Then Ingersoll turned to the problem of Torrijos's older brother.

The Americans knew that Omar Torrijos would be reluctant to rein in his brother unless he had all the facts. Moisés was nearly ten years older, and Omar had always respected him. Unlike Noriega's family, the Torrijos clan was close-knit, held together by parents who were schoolteachers. The Americans feared that if they secretly arrested Moisés, Torrijos might lash out at the Americans in the Canal Zone or the Canal itself. It was the beginning of a long cycle of excuses for not enforcing United States drug laws.

In fact, Ingersoll technically broke laws by briefing Torrijos on the details of an ongoing investigation. ". . . I am aware this will be a difficult thing for you to hear, and I am sorry that I have to be the one to tell you. I do it now because if it should become a matter of public record, I know how damaging this would be to you, your family and the GOP [government of Panama]."

He told Torrijos that his brother had been smuggling drugs since 1969, when he had been ambassador to Argentina. He said Moisés had become involved through a friend, Guillermo Gonzalez López, the ambassador to Taiwan, who had been arrested in the United States on drug charges in July 1971. Ingersoll said Moisés had been indicted by a New York City grand jury in a sealed indictment on May 16, 1972, for smuggling 155 pounds of heroin into the United States the previous year. Moisés would be arrested if he entered the U.S. "I am passing this to you in the hope you will investigate the matter further, recall your brother, and persuade him to remove himself from the illicit drug business." Ingersoll also sought permission for DEA agents to debrief Torrijos's brother.

Torrijos said that his brother was naive—an "intellectual idiot who does not understand the difficulties of life and how to survive." He rationalized that his brother had been duped by the unscrupulous Gonzalez, who was an enemy of Panama and allied with Cuban communists.

Ingersoll then raised the issue of Manuel Antonio Noriega. As he laid out how Noriega was facilitating the drug trade, Ingersoll noticed Torrijos's expression change to fear. "It was almost as if he were afraid to do anything about what I was telling him," Ingersoll recalled later. "Everybody was afraid of [Noriega]."

Moisés Torrijos remained at large. At one point, the State Department even forewarned Omar that anti-drug agents planned to arrest his brother while he was sailing through the Panama Canal on a boat. Panama's dictator was able to forewarn him. The indictment was quietly dropped by a New York district court in the late 1970s, during the Panama Canal Treaties negotiations, at the behest of senior Carter administration officials.

Thereafter, Torrijos, who never lacked a sense of humor, devilishly appointed his brother Moisés as his chief of Panama Canal Treaty information. He also kept him under diplomatic immunity as ambassador to Spain.

Any assassination plots considered for Torrijos and Noriega died their own quiet deaths as the Watergate scandal refocused the administration's energies from illegal activities to self-survival. After meeting Ingersoll, Torrijos did allow the DEA to reopen operations. But he reserved the right to name his own liaison to the DEA, who would keep him personally informed of anti-drug activities in Panama. He didn't want another embarrassment like the Him Gonzalez case.

As his liaison officer to the DEA, the mischievous Torrijos appointed Noriega, the man the Nixon administration had almost targeted for assassination. Within two years of his moving to Panama City, Noriega was Panama's liaison to the United States for all law enforcement and intelligence agencies, both military and civilian. Noriega was still far down on the pecking order of rank, but he was quickly becoming the second most powerful man in Panama.

Plots against Torrijos and other Panamanian leaders continued elsewhere in the Nixon administration for a little while, but they fizzled as Watergate took over national attention.

One of them, as happened so often in the Nixon White House when a secret operation was concerned, involved Gordon Liddy and E. Howard Hunt.

What is known is that Gordon Liddy's "Special Investigative Unit," which was so heavily implicated in the Watergate affair and its cover-up, was also tasked to fight a clandestine drug war. E. Howard Hunt, a retired CIA agent, went to work with Liddy as a private consultant, paid out of a secret $1.5 million White House Special Projects Fund.

To deal with Panama, Hunt reacquainted himself with Manuel Artime. The two had worked together in 1961 on the disastrous Bay of Pigs invasion, and Artime had also been implicated in later CIA plots to kill Castro and invade Cuba anew. In secret testimony before the Watergate grand jury in 1973, Artime said Hunt had asked him to help disrupt Panamanian drug trafficking, and had introduced Artime to "a friend of the White House" named Gordon Liddy. The mission to oust Torrijos was scheduled for after Nixon's reelection in 1972, which was when Watergate came along; and in any case, the White House group seemed to have only Torrijos in its sights—the anti-Noriega plot was apparently the work only of creative DEA agents.

In February 1977, when asked by a Boston television reporter about a Panamanian assassination plot, E. Howard Hunt made a surprising admission: "Panama was a drug trafficking area where drugs could move easily . . . with the blessing of the Panamanian government. There was a great deal of concern on the part of the drug officials and certainly on the

part of some of the Latin American drug informants. I think the feeling
was that if Torrijos didn't shape up and cooperate he was going to be
wasted. That never happened. I don't know any of the people asked to
participate other than the people in the Plumbers Unit. They had that as
part of their brief."

Torrijos and Noriega were the perfect match in this atmosphere of mutual
suspicion that would color U.S.–Panamanian relations during the 1970s.
Torrijos had grand ambitions of forging such impressive international ties
that Washington would be forced into more equitable Canal Treaties.
Noriega was his logistical master, and he happily created a worldwide
intelligence network and arranged security for Torrijos's endless overseas
missions.

Torrijos shied away from the nastier aspects of dictatorial rule, which
he delegated to Noriega. The best confirmed early incident was the murder
of Father Hector Gallegos in July 1971. The Colombian-born priest was
organizing a peasant cooperative at the time, and he ran afoul of a large
landowner who was a personal friend of Torrijos. Noriega is said to have
personally pushed Gallegos into the sea after the priest was shot by National Guard members—an event he proudly confirmed to friends. When
Roberto "Tito" Arias saw a photograph on Noriega's office wall that
showed him parachuting, he joked, "Was that jump before or after you
pushed Gallegos?" Noriega only smiled.

Even Torrijos's President Demetrio Basilio "Jimmy" Lakas knew that
Noriega's power was far greater than his own. When he'd walk up to
Torrijos and Noriega talking, they would turn silent, keeping him outside
their secret world. "I was just the president," frowned Lakas. "A puppet.
It's hard to say it, but I've got to be honest. Torrijos used me to reach out
to the Americans and the business community." Lakas chortled his bear's
laugh and continued in his Texas drawl. "Noriega knew everything Lakas
did, but Lakas knew nothing about Noriega's activities. After office hours,
it was the G-2 people who ran the country."

Noriega expanded his influence by tackling assignments that exceeded
his mandate, taking advantage of Torrijos's lack of interest in the day-to-
day control of the country and the general lassitude of the competing
officers. Within two years, he had transformed a purely military intelligence organization into an espionage network with tentacles throughout
the country and with contacts around the world. He created new G-2
departments for psychological warfare, civilian repression, and electronic
eavesdropping.

And he became the CIA's man in Panama, an alternative to the man considered a dangerous leftist by American intelligence, Omar Torrijos. The U.S. did much to finance the development of Panama's intelligence organization by providing both funds and free training for more than 350 Panamanian intelligence officers between 1973 and 1982 (Noriega thereafter leaned more on the Israelis) and for more than 80 men for special demolition teams. "Noriega told me that slots for training in the U.S. were more valuable to him than the money we could provide," said one U.S. intelligence agent who worked closely with him at the time.

He recalls one of his first meetings with Noriega at the Americans' Fort Gulick, when Noriega asked for books on how to create an intelligence service. He told the officer that he would be the president of Panama someday, so the Americans should help him.

Not more than two years thereafter, the intelligence agent ran into Noriega again—this time in a busy nightclub at about 2 A.M. Noriega was almost unrecognizable in a baseball cap and dark glasses, as he quietly observed a politician and his mistress. Within two years of starting his G-2, Noriega had infiltrated every faculty at the university, sometimes paying as much as $1,000 a month to his best informants. He had spies in all the important unions and organizations.

Noriega had a special obsession with the media, stemming from his conviction that communication in the modern age was the most powerful weapon. He monitored journalists for Torrijos and defined the art of character assassination through planted stories in government newspapers. "This is where his real power over society begins," said Mayín Correa, a journalist in exile who quit a government newspaper after Noriega ordered her to malign the reputation of a close friend of hers.

Noriega quietly placed allies in consulates around the world to expand intelligence and income; they provided passports to friendly espionage organizations. Panama's Vienna consulate, for example, became a factory of passports for Israeli agents working eastern Europe, and the Hong Kong and Singapore offices provided papers for Taiwanese hoping to infiltrate the People's Republic of China.

Noriega also had sufficient influence to gain important government positions for friends. For example, Torrijos named Noriega's brother Luis Carlos head of the Electoral Tribunal, a powerful position even when there wasn't much voting; the Tribunal issued identification cards. He placed Darién Ayala, his friend from his Peru days, as vice minister of agriculture and later as vice foreign minister—giving Noriega eyes and ears in important ministries. Ayala remembers when Noriega brought him from his lucrative job at a sugar plantation to Torrijos to be offered the job. You aren't going to say no to the old man, Noriega told Ayala.

Noriega cleverly jockeyed himself into a position that made him as indispensable to the Americans as he was to Torrijos. When Ambler Moss prepared to take over as U.S. ambassador to Panama in 1976, he found that Noriega was the liaison for the CIA, the FBI, Customs, and several military intelligence agencies. The Drug Enforcement Administration officials at the embassy told Moss to forget Torrijos. Noriega had the day-to-day power. "Torrijos was known as 'the lazy dictator,' " says Moss. "He kept control of certain things as his hobbies, but he really didn't run the country. This meant Noriega could run around and cultivate friendships and build up power."

But even while Noriega's power was growing, the bisexual side of his personality began to emerge more openly, still concealed by the macho image he was carefully cultivating. The macho officer, proficient in judo and parachuting, would perfume himself heavily on off-hours and wear yellow jump suits with yellow shoes, would travel the world with a pilot boyfriend, with whom he was widely rumored to be having a torrid affair, and would surround himself with openly gay ambassadors and personal advisers.

One friend of Noriega's says he liked homosexual advisers because they were easier to blackmail, but one of his gay advisers explains the attraction otherwise: "He is a spiritual and soft man and he likes to be around spiritual and soft people." Noriega would joke to this friend that the only Panamanians without balls were the heterosexual men; "the queers and the women are the only courageous ones," he would say.

Armchair psychiatrists credit Noriega's sexual confusion to his gay brother, Luis Carlos Noriega. Luis Carlos was the only person Noriega ever trusted completely, and Luis Carlos often interviewed close advisers before his brother did. Flamboyantly and unapologetically homosexual, Luis Carlos would often whisper to friends, with a twinkle in his eye, "I understand my brother Manuel Antonio is a bisexual." And he helped surround Noriega with a devoted cadre of gay consultants and ambassadors.

However, Luis Carlos was also a conduit for Noriega into the world of the political opposition; to well-off Panamanians around whom his younger brother felt uncomfortable. One was Louis Martinz, the son of one of Panama's most successful entrepreneurs, who had campaigned for years for Arnulfo Arias, the populist three-time president, whose popularity with Panamanians intrigued Noriega. On Luis Carlos's instructions, Martinz began by gossiping about his childhood encounter with Marilyn Monroe and his adult friendships with the Shah's former wife Soraya, about her beautiful green eyes and dazzling jewels; and Martinz spoke of European princes he knew. When Luis Carlos gave the signal, Martinz switched to the substance of the meeting—he wanted Noriega's help in starting a newspaper. Martinz would later be thrown in jail for long periods by Noriega's thugs, but at that time Martinz considered Noriega a notch above Torrijos intellectually.

Martinz never was part of Noriega's inner circle, but the two grew so friendly that Noriega later asked Martinz advice on improving his image, something that became the General's passion after he took power. "You frighten people, Manuel," said Martinz. "Yet you have such a beautiful smile. Why don't you smile more?" Martinz later blamed himself in part for Noriega's smile, which would be so often and inappropriately used in the years ahead.

Noriega's fondest, and most impossible, dream was for simple Panamanians to love him as they did Torrijos. Partly to achieve this, he invited *Washington Post* reporter Sally Quinn into his G-2 office, its decor a surrealistic homage to Fellini and Hugh Hefner.

Soft jazz and rock played from the state-of-the-art sound system. An ornate mirrored bar glittered against one wall as a centerpiece for an oddly decorated room. Oil paintings and photographs of suffering children cast a bleak pall on the setting—perhaps a throwback to Noriega's sad youth. Tables and bookshelves were littered with porcelain frogs, his *sapos,* Panamanian for informant.

For all his ability to recruit agents, Noriega lacked the ability to entice women—and that bothered him. A Guatemalan friend remembers inviting some prostitutes for an evening at a hotel in San José, Costa Rica, with Noriega and several others. The prostitute Noriega picked was the most beautiful, as usual; the other men weren't about to compete. But the woman looked at Noriega with disgust. Not knowing he was Panama's intelligence chief, she rejected him, despite his clear willingness and ability to pay.

I can't sleep with you, she said. You frighten me. You have the eyes of a killer. Noriega retreated to his room depressed, carrying a half-empty bottle of Old Parr whiskey. He watched television and drank while his friends frolicked in adjoining rooms.

By the time he met Sally Quinn in his office in 1978, he had already launched an effort to do something about his image. She noted his narrow eyes, high cheekbones, and wiry frame: "the swarthy, pockmarked complexion give him a rather Mongolian look," Quinn wrote.

Noriega said his job was to protect the people, so they could sleep at night and not be kidnapped by terrorists. He was almost flirtatious, sitting in tight-fitting slacks, his wavy hair slicked back in a shiny mound and reeking of perfume. He was also nervous, perspiring as he talked. He vainly lied about his age, telling Quinn that, at age thirty-eight, he was the youngest of Panama's seven colonels.

"I know," he said, almost with pleasure, "that I have an image problem. Mine is a position that doesn't attract sympathy. But somebody must do this job."

Noriega provided grist for every cocktail party. "The game was always to guess the next dictator, and always the worst possible scenario was Noriega coming to power," said General Frederick F. Woerner, the future head of the United States Southern Command in Panama, who in the 1970s traveled to Panama often from his posting in Washington. "The conventional wisdom at the time was that he would always elect to enjoy power from backstage without paying the price of being the number one man."

While Noriega schemed in the shadows, Torrijos basked in the limelight as he promoted new negotiations over the Panama Canal that aimed at closing American bases and transferring control of the Canal to Panama. On June 29, 1971, the United States and Panama had resumed the talks.

American negotiators saw Noriega rarely during the meetings, and when they did it usually meant trouble. Noriega was the ugly face of the revolution, carrying out the threats and missions Torrijos found distasteful. Nicholás Gonzalez Revilla, Panama's ambassador to Washington during much of the negotiations, remembers that Noriega would be brought in whenever matters seemed to be going badly, like an electric prod calculated to jolt Washington whenever it seemed to be losing interest.

One such instance came in March 1973 when Torrijos brought the United Nations Security Council to meet in Panama in his attempt to "internationalize" the Panama Canal problem. When the meeting produced a resolution that was patently unacceptable to the United States, American representative John Scali received instructions from Nixon's Deputy National Security Adviser Brent Scowcroft to cast an American veto. Scali, a veteran journalist from the Associated Press and ABC Television, reminded Scowcroft that the veto would only be the third by the United States in the U.N.'s history, and that it would anger the Panamanians and the Third World. But Scowcroft stood his ground.

As Scali was about to leave the U.S. embassy for the council chamber to cast his vote, he received a call from Lieutenant Colonel Noriega. If you are going to veto the resolution, you better do it at the airport, he said. Scali, reluctant to cast the veto before, became so angry that he was eager to act.

It was a little bit of psychological warfare that Noriega had cooked up with Torrijos, and it had gone off just as planned. Torrijos had decided that an angry U.S. veto was just the thing to dramatize Panama's plight on the world stage, and to that end, he had even scuttled a compromise resolution worked out with the Americans. Noriega himself concocted the provocation of Scali. Torrijos later apologized to Scali about the "misunderstanding," but Noriega had carried out his task perfectly.

A little later, in mid-August 1974, Torrijos grew angry again when he thought the U.S. was backing off agreements, known as the Kissinger-Tack Principles, that involved the Canal's independence. National Security Adviser Henry Kissinger had made substantial changes in the initial draft agreement that would ensure American military presence in perpetuity. "You are asking for the right to keep military troops in our country forever," complained Foreign Minister Juan Antonio Tack. The Panamanians also wanted international guarantees for the Canal's neutrality, but Washington wanted to avoid United Nations involvement.

"That was one of the worst moments ever in the negotiations," said then-Ambassador Gonzalez Revilla. "Kissinger screwed us. There was nothing we could even discuss. No one could believe it."

At the order of Torrijos, Panamanian negotiators abandoned the talks on Contadora Island to meet with the dictator in Panama City. Torrijos said that he had decided to send the United States a message by opening negotiations with Cuba. In so doing, he would defy the Organization of American States, which had cut ties with Castro. That would be the heavy cost of Washington's recalcitrance. The move would also burnish Torrijos's image as an independent leader who was reaching out to the nonaligned world.

In mid-August 1974, Torrijos's general staff, President Lakas, and other advisers almost unanimously opposed the move on anti-communist grounds. They also feared U.S. retribution. Noriega, however, remained silent, and privately told Torrijos later that he saw the wisdom in his action, that other military officers were hopelessly shortsighted. He was the only member of Torrijos's general staff who so clearly supported the dictator's move.

Tension surrounded the negotiators' return to Contadora Island. Ellsworth Bunker sat in the glass-enclosed front room of entrepreneur Gabriel Lewis's seaside home, waiting to hear Torrijos's response. "I was to reply with a position paper," said Gonzalez Revilla. "But instead I said, 'We are here to inform you that we are establishing full diplomatic relations with Cuba tomorrow.' Bunker almost jumped out of his goddamned seat."

Ambassador William J. Jorden found it impossible to dissuade Torrijos with arguments that the Organization of American States had cut off relations and that only a collective vote should resume them. Torrijos properly argued that Mexico had never severed relations, and that Argentina and Peru had already reestablished links. And that he was going to do it, whether the U.S. liked it or not.

A 100-person delegation of Panamanians set off on August 21, led by planning minister Nicholás Ardito Barletta, cleverly chosen by Torrijos to assuage the fears of the Panamanian business community. But ultimately more important to Panama's future was the man whom Torrijos had chosen to work on security and logistics: Noriega.

As detail man for the trip to Cuba, Noriega strengthened relationships that would grow even closer over time, as he worked out the visit and the opening of the embassies. It was in the summer of 1974 that Noriega established his first formal ties with Cuban intelligence.

Informal ties had already existed for a few years. Noriega had been one of Torrijos's two or three secret messengers to Castro since 1971, when he had first traveled to the country. Ironically, that first mission had come at the request of the U.S. The Cubans had seized two Panamanian-flagged vessels that the CIA had used in the region to gather intelligence, and Washington asked for Torrijos's help in getting the captains and the ships back. At first, Torrijos had sent the leftist rector of the University of Panama, Rómulo Escobar Bethancourt. Two years earlier, as Torrijos's first emissary to Castro, Escobar had successfully stopped Cuban support for anti-Torrijos guerrillas. But even he couldn't get Castro to give up the "fishing" boats.

So Torrijos decided to send Noriega to wheel and deal, and he got the boats and the captains back. With the blessing of Washington, he had established Panama's first intelligence contacts with Cuba. Without America's blessing, he was quietly expanding the relationship.

The Cuban message delivered, the negotiations with the U.S. got back on track, and Noriega's cameo appearances continued. When skeptical senators arrived to investigate treaty details, Torrijos would soften them up by talking about the evolution to democracy and cooperation with the United States. Noriega's job was as Torrijos's bad cop. At one point in 1977, he lectured Senator Howard Baker, and then pulled out a map and showed how holes could be punched in the dams and how easily the Canal could be mined. "Really, gentlemen," Noriega said, "you are very vulnerable."

In fact, it was no idle threat. Noriega had taken special demolition training from the Americans in the late 1960s, and he used that expertise and his military engineering knowhow to work out a plan for Torrijos to sabotage the Canal if the Americans didn't approve the treaty. He relished telling friends about the plan in intricate detail, expressing the ease with which shipping could be stopped for months.

Even after the April 1978 vote, Ambassador Ambler Moss asked Torrijos if he ever would have ordered Noriega to put into play his well-engineered sabotage plan. Surprisingly, Torrijos conceded that he would have, if only to recover some of his lost image. He said that while listening to the Senate hearings over the Voice of America, he had gone through two crates of Sony transistor radios. Every time a congressman said something against him, he'd throw the radio against the wall in anger and his aides would have to pull out another.

By the late 1970s, Noriega was still only a lieutenant colonel, maintained at that rank by a dictator who feared his knowledge and abilities as much as he needed them. However, with the blessing and assistance of the U.S., Torrijos was expanding the manpower and capabilities of his National Guard—and the changes placed even more power in the lap of Noriega.

In the first ten years of his rule to 1978, Torrijos expanded National Guard manpower threefold, from 5,000 to more than 15,000. The number of public servants grew from 50,000 to 150,000. The budget for the National Guard expanded from $10 million in 1968 to more than $100 million. Neither political parties nor the press could operate freely. Power intoxicates, and the military was getting drunk. In the 1960s, officers had been relatively poor and humble. By the late 1970s, even lower-level officers were driving expensive cars, keeping two or three mistresses, and finding that their sources of income were limited only by their postings and imaginations.

"This all permitted the comandante, whoever he was, to exercise irresistible pressure over civilian government to the point where he could determine its makeup," said Juan Materno Vasquez, a man who wrote Torrijos's first constitution, but then quit the regime when he saw that its early populist hopes were turning into just another form of Panama's historic corruption. "Latin American militaries can't benefit their countries. Civilians are educated to exercise liberal thought and flexibility and take academic professions. They have the capacity to survive in a marketplace of ideas and politics. Those who prosper are those with better ideas. Military officers are taught to fight wars and defeat enemies. They give orders and obey orders without any capacity to deliberate the future or compete in a marketplace of ideas."

American politicians unwittingly supported Panama's military dictatorship, because as necessary as it might have been politically to turn the Canal over someday to the Panamanians, the negotiations with Torrijos had the practical effect of legitimizing his reign. The talks allowed Torrijos to delay the domestic pressures on him to return to the barracks and democratize.

And the longer the military dictatorship remained, the more time Noriega had to build his own power base. Torrijos moved other officers from job to job, restricting their ability to challenge his influence. But Noriega had become his irreplaceable ally. Torrijos wouldn't trust anyone else in the intelligence job. So Noriega thrived quietly as Torrijos's shadow.

CHAPTER
SEVEN

THE CARTER COVER-UP

Noriega knows where we are, but we don't know where he is.

—OMAR TORRIJOS, 1975

From his first day on the job as President Carter's CIA director, Stansfield Turner had misgivings about some of his foreign allies. He thought good government money was being paid to some pretty questionable foreign espionage services for dubious gain. Iran's SAVAK caused him the most heartburn, with its torture and assassinations, but Noriega's G-2 wasn't too far behind.

Turner's briefing on Noriega's activities in Panama was enough to prompt him to sever contractual payments to Panama's G-2 intelligence service, a "liaison" relationship which was netting Noriega $110,000 annually by 1976. He heard reports about how Noriega had bought sensitive intelligence information from National Security Agency sources in Panama and how he had planted bombs in the Canal Zone. The explosions were engineered to protest Washington's recalcitrance over Panama Canal Treaty talks, but Noriega could have killed a number of Americans.

"In the world of intelligence, if you want to get information, you get it from seedy characters," he said. "The question is how much you get tied in with them, and whether they can extort you. It's a murky world. You almost don't turn down the devil. But you must ask yourself, what is the long-term cost to you of getting this information?"

Despite Turner's decision to cut off payments, Noriega thrived as never before under the Carter administration. Omar Torrijos grew to depend on him more than ever, and Washington chose to ignore mounting evidence that Noriega was involved in illegal arms dealings, relationships with drug traffickers, Cuban efforts to overcome the American economic and trade embargo, and a number of other threats to U.S. interests. Ending the contractual CIA relationship didn't mean going after Noriega's corrupt activities.

In the interest of ratifying the Panama Canal Treaties in 1978 and as a reward to Panama for taking the Shah off its hands in December 1979, Carter administration officials continued to play down and sometimes conceal Noriega's crimes. In addition, Noriega continued to provide data to American counterparts on Latin American militaries and growing guerrilla movements that they couldn't get anywhere else. Once the Sandinistas took over Nicaragua in 1979, he provided the most regular and reliable intelligence about them.

Noriega's buying off of American agents had begun under President Nixon, and was first discovered by George Bush, as President Ford's CIA director, but it was the Carter administration that had to wrestle publicly with the scandal the month after the president and Omar Torrijos had signed the Panama Canal Treaties on September 7, 1977.

Congressmen opposed to the Treaties learned that Torrijos's home and office had been bugged by U.S. agents in 1974, in an attempt to discover Torrijos's ties to communists and to see whether he could be trusted in negotiations. However, some of the tapes had been sold to Noriega by at least one, and probably three, U.S. sergeants. Panama was an important American listening post for the region, and treaty opponents figured that a great deal of valuable information could have been turned over to Noriega. Even more unnerving was the thought that Torrijos might have blackmailed American officials at critical points in the negotiations, by threatening to reveal his knowledge of the wiretaps if the Americans didn't offer concessions.

Senator James Allen of Alabama, recognized as one of the Senate's foremost political guerrillas, had described the Panama Canal Treaties as "shoving our flag into a broom closet" and "giving our vital canal to a banana republic." He decided to launch an investigation into the "Singing Sergeants" case. His platform was the Senate Judiciary Subcommittee on Separation of Powers, which he chaired.

The subcommittee issued subpoenas on September 26, 1977, a little more than two weeks after the treaties' signing. They included one of the suspect military intelligence agents, U.S. Army Sergeant Ilor Rodriguez Brustmayer of Brooklyn, New York, who had been honorably discharged from the military in August 1977 and was never charged with any misconduct.

Yet aside from demanding his presence at a hearing, the subpoena to him said, "You are further commanded to bring all books, documents, memoranda, notes, electronic recordings, or any other records in your possession of subject to your control pertaining to any contact you have had with the Government of Panama or any official thereof or pertaining to any matter regarding an alleged incident wherein the conversations of officials of the government of the Republic of Panama were made subject to clandestine interception by the government of the United States or by any agency thereof."

Others were also subpoenaed: CIA Director Stansfield Turner; FBI Director Clarence M. Kelley; Secretary of the Army Clifford I. Alexander; Lieutenant General Eugene Tighe, Jr., director of the Defense Intelligence Agency; Thomas M. Constant, secretary of the Panama Canal Company; Benjamin H. Civiletti, assistant attorney general in charge of the Justice Department's Criminal Division; and Brigadier General Robert S. Young, commanding general of the army's reserve component, personnel, and administration center. The subcommittee also hit the Intelligence Committee with subpoenas for witnesses and records pertaining to covert activities in Panama. Opponents of the Panama Treaties could hardly wait. Here it was: the proof that could so undermine the two countries' relations that the dreaded treaty would be killed once and for all.

But the inquiry fizzled. "Our jurisdiction is tenuous at best," said Allen, who was forced to cancel the subcommittee hearing in early October, 1977, when Attorney General Griffin Bell refused to turn over subpoenaed documents. Bell had leaned on the Judiciary Committee chairman, Democratic Senator James Eastland of Mississippi, to rein Allen in.

The Senate Intelligence Committee took on the complaints, but studied them in a more secret manner in closed sessions. Ambassador to Panama Ambler Moss and other treaty negotiators were forced to bring small mountains of transcripts of all the negotiating records to prove to committee members and staffers that there hadn't been any sudden shifts in position that could only be explained by blackmail. "They grilled us hard to pick any hole in the story," said Moss. Intelligence Committee chairman Daniel K. Inouye issued a statement afterward saying his committee had found no evidence the talks had been influenced by U.S. intelligence activities.

But the fight wasn't over. A year later, during congressional proceedings to ratify the treaties, conservative senators demanded a secret Senate session on Panama. Staff members were sent home and microphones turned off. The sanitized text of two days of sessions makes for lurid reading. The drug links of Torrijos's family, the secret Panamanian ties to Cuban leader

Fidel Castro, and a laundry list of other illegal Panamanian activities made clear that Panama under Torrijos was a haven for the Mafia, drug dealers, the Cubans, or anyone else engaging in shady activities.

"We are in the process of dealing with some of the most sensitive information, if not the most sensitive information, that has ever been made public to the U.S. Senate," warned the new Intelligence Committee Chairman Birch Bayh, an Indiana Democrat, whose report on Panama had been the focus of the session.

The senators again focused on Noriega's purchase of intelligence tapes and on its potential impact on negotiations.

"A U.S. military person stationed in the Canal Zone was found to be passing intelligence information to the Panamanians," said Bayh. "The investigation ultimately disclosed that, among other things, this person had passed to the Guardia Nacional information on U.S. intelligence operations including copies of sensitive intelligence from one of these operations."

Bayh reported that once Torrijos knew of the wiretaps, he decided to use them for his own purposes. His most dramatic use of American eavesdropping came in angry response to a newspaper's report that Ambassador Sol Linowitz had told reporters the treaties would defend America's right to defend the Canal unilaterally.

The enraged Torrijos had phoned his ambassador to Washington, Gabriel Lewis. Knowing his voice was being recorded by the Americans, Torrijos said that in response, he would reveal his knowledge of U.S. intelligence operations, and hold a press conference at which he would allege that high-level members of the legislative and executive branch had sought payoffs in return for arranging increases in the annual fees that would be paid Panama for use of the Canal. According to Bayh, the intelligence report was received by the White House and the State Department on the morning of July 16, 1977.

After seeing the report, senators on the Intelligence Committee demanded an investigation—but found no evidence of payoffs. Torrijos was merely unsettling negotiations. The senators also discovered no signs of sudden compromises at the negotiating table that could be attributed to blackmail. The only impact on foreign policy was that National Security Adviser Zbigniew Brzezinski, hoping to calm Torrijos, had issued a press statement that said newspaper reports quoting Linowitz were "incorrect in major details." Torrijos thereafter called off his press conference.

However, senators at the special session were as troubled by the American eavesdropping on a negotiating partner as they were by Noriega's infiltration of this effort.

"It is like if you are in a poker game and the other guy is looking at your hand," said Republican Senator Henry Bellmon in his Oklahoma drawl.

Responded Senator Bayh, "That is exactly what it is, and the one guy knows the other guy is looking at his hand in this particular instance."

The closed-door session also focused heavily on drugs. Senators heard about how Torrijos's family was heavily implicated, particularly his brother Moisés, who had been indicted but never extradited. In fact, shocked senators heard the tale of how the White House had tipped off Torrijos in 1973 that Customs agents were waiting to arrest his brother as he disembarked from a ship sailing into the American-controlled Cristobal port. But his brother had sent a helicopter to rescue him before the boat could dock.

As for Noriega, he was cited by one source as a man at the center of Panama's network a full decade before he would be indicted on drug charges in Florida. Noriega had been arresting many drug traffickers and extraditing some to the United States, but just as often he extorted traffickers before they could gain their release. One Colombian arrested in Panama had told the Colombian newspaper *El Tiempo* that he paid Noriega $235,000 for his freedom.

At the end of the session, Senator Jesse Helms—a conservative treaty opponent from North Carolina—was frustrated that too few of his brethren were moved enough by this catalogue of Panamanian corruption. He pleaded that passing the Panama Canal Treaties was just the beginning of America's problems with Panama. At the time, his warnings were ignored by most as the exaggerated claims of a far–right-winger who wanted to hang on to the Canal at all costs.

Ten years later, however, Helms's statements sound almost prophetic. "In this act, we become collaborationists with the crimes of the past. But we also become collaborators with Panama for the future. For the next twenty-two years, we become the close partners with a government that, on the grounds of past history, cannot be trusted. If, once the treaties are safely ratified, Panama once more becomes the center of crime for international trafficking, there will be nothing that we can do about it. Yet we will have joint administration of the Canal, joint defense of the Canal. We will find ourselves implicated in everything that Panama does. There will be no way that we can draw back without abandoning the Canal."

The treaty fight in Washington was one of the most emotional political battles ever on Capitol Hill, illustrating why Panama is as much a domestic as a foreign policy issue. Many pro-treaty senators lost reelection over the issue.

* * *

But the treaties survived, and so did Noriega. For the first time, however, the United States had debated the importance of Noriega's crimes, which were only beginning. After the treaties were ratified, the U.S. found new cause for concern: gunrunning. Noriega was believed to be assisting arms smuggling to the Nicaraguan guerrillas fighting to overthrow Anastasio Somoza. The U.S. would also have a new reason to protect Noriega: the Torrijos regime's willingness to take Iran's fallen Shah in exile.

In May 1979, Jerome Sanford, an assistant U.S. attorney in Florida, filed an indictment against five prominent Panamanians on gunrunning charges. The information for the indictment had been gathered by an undercover informant in a Miami gun shop, and the trail led clearly to the Panamanian government. Sanford was determined to prosecute this gunrunning case. The indictment named Noriega's close friend and business partner, Carlos Wittgreen, his wife's swarthy and corrupt first cousin. And the investigators were quickly closing in on Noriega himself. Sanford, in his thirties, was a Raymond Chandler–like character, a straight-shooting, public-minded attorney who belonged in a trench coat and a fedora. He was a trial lawyer, who loved the smell and the atmosphere of the courtroom.

Washington wasn't as eager as Sanford, however. A month after his indictment was delivered, in June 1979, U.S. military intelligence was again flirting with its longtime Latin American spy, whose information on the Cubans and the war in Nicaragua was growing more valuable each day. Noriega made plans to fly to Washington for a meeting with his counterpart in the Pentagon, Lieutenant General Eugene Tighe, Jr., director of the Defense Intelligence Agency. The visit wasn't unusual; the DIA often flew its better "assets" to the U.S. with their wives for schmoozing and shopping.

But Dade County and federal authorities, having caught wind that he would fly through Miami, started setting a trap aimed at arresting Noriega on the gunrunning charges as soon as he hit U.S. soil. It was a Friday in June, and Noriega's arrival was due the coming Monday. In only seventy-two hours, the agents would have Noriega behind bars.

Before that could happen, however, a State Department Panama desk officer intervened. After being routinely informed of the impending arrest by a Justice Department official, he called a friend at the Pentagon and briefed him on the danger to Noriega.

"That's terrible," said the Pentagon official, a veteran of many years of bureaucratic wars. He joked to the desk officer that there was an unwritten rule: crises only happen just before the weekend.

"Just thought you'd want to know," said the diplomat, deadpan. "But you never heard this from me." The phone clicked off.

The Pentagon official passed the problem upstairs. A senior officer in the DIA chief's front office thanked the Pentagon official and said he could forget about the problem.

The next word on the Noriega visit came Monday morning. A routine, unclassified message was cabled from the U.S. Army's military group commander in Panama. "Due to health reasons, Lieutenant Colonel Noriega has elected to postpone his visit to Washington."

The State Department's desk officer smiled at the message, knowing it had been his call that had done the trick. But the Pentagon official wondered even then if the Pentagon had done the right thing in forewarning Noriega.

"Now I really wonder," he said.

A former military intelligence agent showed documents that prove that American spies in Panama also knew exactly what Noriega was up to, but that the Carter administration didn't act on their reports, and Stansfield Turner's CIA sent messages that they should quit devoting so much time and energy to logging all the arms shipments to the Sandinistas that Torrijos and Noriega were facilitating. U.S. intelligence had detailed descriptions of equipment, the planes involved and their tail numbers, and the Panamanians who were working on arms deliveries to the Sandinistas, to ORPA guerrillas in Guatemala, and to communist FARC guerrillas in Colombia. One document shows a report of arms flown from Cuba to Río Ható field in Panama at Farallon, from which they were flown to Guanacate in Costa Rica, in the province of Liberia, where they were loaded for land delivery in Nicaragua.

The intelligence agent smiled at the amount of detail he was able to provide his superiors in Washington. "Guess how I knew," he said years later. "Noriega passed us all the information: pilots' names, Cuban companies involved, tail numbers, everything. He even provided some photographs." Noriega was playing all sides, but the prosecutors in Florida didn't know that.

The purchases they tracked, and tried to prosecute, began with orders from the Panamanian consul to Miami, Edgardo López, who was listed on G-2 computer printouts from the time as earning a $447 monthly salary from Colonel Noriega. López, who would become Noriega's military spokesman after he seized power, was also personally close to the G-2 chief.

A company owned by Carlos Wittgreen, Caza y Pesca—translated "Hunting and Fishing"—bought the weapons. It then flew them to Panama City on Air Panama—boxed, shipped, and passed through customs without a single check. Noriega was implicated by the statements of three defendants and by López, who wasn't indicted. One of the defendants, José Antonio Alvarez, told agents that he had been working for Noriega in the gun deals, and he provided copies of expense bills that were covered by the G-2. He said Noriega was a partner with Wittgreen in Caza y Pesca.

Before prosecutors could indict him, however, Noriega decided to go over the heads of U.S. attorneys to the secretary of state. He clearly thought he had done enough for the Americans to merit some protection, so Noriega quickly wrote a letter to Cyrus Vance, protesting the U.S. attorney's investigation, and saying that the consul had merely been buying the weapons for the use of his own Panamanian G-2. The then Deputy Secretary of State Warren Christopher wrote the response, admonishing Noriega that the proper way of purchasing weapons was by receiving an end-user certificate from the Munitions Control Office of the State Department.

"This showed the arrogance of Noriega," said Sanford years later. "A military man sends a letter to the Secretary of State of the United States, not through the foreign ministry, not through his superior Torrijos . . . but he, himself, doing that."

The case caused an immediate uproar, coming when Jimmy Carter was trying to push through the implementation provisions of the treaty. Again, Congressional hearings were called, this time on "Panama gunrunning," by the House Merchant Marine and Fisheries Subcommittee on the Panama Canal. The House committee was rich with treaty opponents who still hadn't given up their fight.

Its chairman was West Pointer John Murphy, an opponent who was even angrier now that he knew that the Panamanians were arming opponents of his fellow West Point graduate, Anastasio Somoza, with whom he had been close friends for years. However, the State Department denied to congressmen what the CIA knew to be true: Panamanians were smuggling guns and arming the Sandinistas.

Congressional hearings on the arms smuggling began on June 7, 1979, one month after Sanford's indictment. Meanwhile, the White House was pushing for implementation legislation hearings to be held on June 12— faster than House leaders had wanted.

Retired Lieutenant General Gordon Sumner, former chairman of the Inter-American Defense Board, testified that General Torrijos had surprisingly admitted his aid to the Sandinistas in a personal conversation, calling them "a bunch of good old boys," and told Sumner he would help other revolutionary movements as well. By that time, Torrijos had already put Noriega in charge of arms to be shipped to the Sandinistas from Cuba's Fidel Castro and Venezuela's Carlos Andrés Pérez.

"[Torrijos] stated that he would continue and increase this support," said General Sumner. "He said, you know there is a lot going on, socialism is the way of the future, and you people are behind the power curve on this." Torrijos also defended El Salvadoran insurgents and said he would "support and assist" them in trying to unseat the president at that time, Carlos Humberto Romero. Romero was ousted in a coup in 1979. "You know, my classmate, General Romero, wants to use tanks rather than talking," Sumner quoted Torrijos as saying. "I am going to do something about that situation, too."

Sumner was quite clear that, to a certain extent, he felt Torrijos was being manipulated by Lieutenant Colonel Noriega, who despite his introversion seemed to be the more revolutionary of the two. "I believed then, and do today, that [Torrijos] is under the influence of communists/Marxists within Panama and Cuba, particularly Colonel Noriega. . . . Noriega is not just an intelligence officer. He is the head of their intelligence, counterintelligence. He is like rolling the head of the FBI and the CIA all into one man."

But the then commander in chief of the U.S. Southern Command, Lieutenant General Dennis P. McAuliffe, and the Deputy Assistant Secretary of State for Inter-American Affairs, Brandon Grove, denied evidence of Panamanian government involvement in arms smuggling. "I don't have what I would consider conclusive evidence that these actions are other than the actions of individuals who are apparently trying to make money and capitalize on a situation," said General McAuliffe. "There is no evidence that the Panamanian government as such is behind this."

However, some in the administration knew the evidence against the Panamanian government was compelling. The Carter administration had in fact protested to Torrijos about the gunrunning at least a dozen times. General McAuliffe knew about these protests when he gave his congressional testimony and about extensive information concerning gunrunning to the Sandinistas. Now, however, Torrijos would always innocently deny any personal involvement and insist that no arms were crossing Panamanian territory. Ambassador Moss, who would make the demarches at the order of National Security Council staff member Robert Pastor, said that Torrijos "knew that we knew he was lying." But Torrijos would carry out the ruse so far that he once wrote down on a scrap of paper for Moss, "If anybody is caught running arms, I'll have him put into jail."

President Carter chose not to challenge Torrijos's lies publicly. The publicity would only hurt him and his controversial Panama Canal Treaties—not to mention Panama's protection of the Shah. Carter wanted Somoza out as well, although the administration preferred that the means be peaceful. "At the very least," said Moss, "we were in a public posture of not caring. No one was willing to save the day for Somoza."

* * *

Prosecutors in Miami didn't care about the politics; they only knew the law had been broken. But they had to restart their indictment efforts after another setback in October 1979. Their original indictment against Wittgreen, Noriega's friend, and the other four was dismissed on a technicality that hadn't anything to do with the merits of the case. It could be refiled using the same evidence, but that would take time. Yet now, along with reindicting Noriega's pal, Sanford intended to charge Noriega himself because of new evidence found by Customs agents that he was involved in the illegal purchase and smuggling of some $2 million in arms.

In January 1980, Sanford was summoned to a meeting with a man he was told was a Federal Bureau of Investigation agent. Washington had heard that Sanford was going to resubmit the case to another grand jury, but the FBI man's interests seemed more political than investigative. Panamanian dictator Torrijos, Sanford was told, had granted the Shah of Iran asylum in Panama as a favor to Washington. "We've got word from a prominent Cuban businessman here in Miami that the Shah of Iran is moving to Panama," said the FBI man. "Carlos Wittgreen, whom you have previously indicted and may indict again, has been named by General Torrijos to be the chief of security for the Shah when he comes to Panama. We kind of think it might be a bad idea if you indicted Wittgreen now."

Noriega thought he had pulled a master manipulative stroke to save his friend Wittgreen, although no one in Washington knew it at the time. It wasn't Wittgreen who would look after the Shah, but rather it was Noriega himself. Noriega had planted the misinformation to get Wittgreen off. How could the Americans prosecute someone whose job was to protect the Shah?

"Why can't I go ahead?" Sanford asked. "I don't care about Wittgreen: I want to indict Noriega, too."

The FBI man was alarmed. "Well, Jesus! How can you do that?"

Despite this discouragement, Sanford and other prosecutors pressed forward. By January, prosecutors had opened a second investigation that showed the Panamanians had bought some $10 million worth of weapons. It would have been enough to keep the Sandinista rebels going for months: 7,000 M-1 rifles, 3,000 M-16 rifles, jeep-mounted machine guns, and a million rounds of ammunition. During one meeting with a Panamanian officer that was monitored and recorded, the dealer told an informant, who was employed in the gun shop, that the Panamanian, "wished to purchase weapons . . . for General Omar Torrijos and Colonel Noriega, head of G-2, Panama's intelligence."

Agents planned to set up the Panamanian buyer for arrest on January 15, 1980. But again they feared a tip by Noriega's friends in the Carter administration warned the Panamanian off. The officer canceled his meeting to conclude the deal. He had been called back to Panama. Agents thought the officer had been tipped off by American officials. "It is the opinion of this investigator," said Donald Kimbler, of the Bureau of Alcohol, Tobacco and Firearms, "that the [Panamanian] was tipped off by someone unknown of the actual operation."

After prodding from Mr. Sanford, U.S. Attorney Jack Eskenazi sent to Washington a prosecution memo, which the Justice Department had requested on the case because of its political sensitivity. In an accompanying letter, he pleaded with officials to let the indictment proceed. "Unfortunately," Eskenazi wrote in a letter dated January 31, 1980, "those of us in law enforcement in Miami find ourselves frequently attempting to enforce the laws of the United States but simultaneously being caught between foreign policy considerations over which we have no control."

The prosecution memo made clear that Noriega was the conduit through which the arms were flowing to the Sandinistas from the Panamanian consulate in Miami. But after a long period without a response, Sanford asked what had happened. The Justice Department said it had lost the memo. So Sanford sent it again. "They were stalling," Sanford said.

After Sanford left his post in February, for unrelated reasons, another stall occurred. An even more aggressive assistant U.S. attorney, Wes Currier, took over the case. At age thirty-six, Currier was a former marine aviator whose powerful five-foot-nine-inch frame and closely cropped hair still made him appear more USMC than lawyer. Currier already suspected some political fiddling with the case, never having had to send a prosecution memo to Washington for such a case during more than a decade in the business. He was doubly suspicious when the prosecution memo was sent back in late spring with a request for more details.

"We felt we were just getting jerked around," he said. "The 'pros memo' was pretty comprehensive to begin with. This was a case worth prosecuting. The evidence was good."

But the politics, for the Carter administration, was bad.

The Carter administration never had to make the controversial decision to quash the indictment process. Instead, it continued to set up road blocks through the Justice Department until U.S. attorneys got the message. "The resistance gets too strong, and you have other fish to fry," said Currier years later.

Carl Perrian, then a staff member of the Merchant Marine and Fisheries Committee, said his panel's investigations at the time showed that the Justice Department blocked the indictment proceedings at the behest of the State Department. "We had no doubt it was all engineered by State," he said. "They came in and lied to us. And the worst was General McAuliffe." Perrian continued to push, but his boss John Murphy had been crippled politically by the Abscam scandal, an FBI bribery and corruption investigation.

In addition, the administration blocked the release of documents that might have conclusively proved a cover-up. "We cannot participate in any effort to damage our relations with a friendly government," the State Department said. "In this regard, certain information which may or may not be relevant to your inquiry must be classified for diplomatic or intelligence reasons."

Noriega was escaping his closest call yet with the United States, and he had every reason to believe that his service to the DIA and CIA were the critical factors. It would be a lesson he'd never forget, and he'd continue to buy protection for his crimes by serving his American intelligence counterparts.

Sanford later recalled one classified U.S. document that indicated that "Noriega was not overly concerned with the possible ramifications because of his association and contributions to the United States government." Frowned Sanford, "The implication was that Noriega, if he had to, would pull something out of the hat to stifle the investigation or indictment. I think if we had been allowed to go ahead then, we wouldn't have so many problems later," Sanford would say years later. "If he had been found guilty then, we could have nipped him in the bud."

Having saved Noriega from the Miami courtrooms, the Carter administration eagerly turned over Iran's wayfaring Shah to his safekeeping. Noriega loved logistical challenges, and none suited him better than the protection of the Shah during his 100-day stay in Panama from December 1979 to March 1980.

Torrijos wanted to make the Shah feel at home, so he appointed as his companion and bodyguard José de Jesús Martínez, known as Chuchu, who had spoken French fluently since his days studying mathematics at the Sorbonne. But there was also some devilish mischief in this choice. Martínez was a dedicated Marxist, who wanted to know what made a monarch tick. He was also a romantic poet, who was captivated by the story of this sad man, whom Omar Torrijos called a *chupón*—an orange with all the innards squeezed out.

Torrijos's choice of Noriega was a simpler matter. He wanted the Shah protected against the many dangers Khomeini's assassins posed, and Noriega was the best security man he had. Torrijos also might want to pull off some underworld deal regarding the Shah, and Noriega also had the corner on those contacts. Torrijos was a gambler, and the Shah was a valuable card that he might choose to play. American hostages being held in Iran—and the embarrassment of the Shah's stay in the United States— might stop his friend Jimmy Carter from being reelected. By taking the Shah, Torrijos was doing Carter a favor and also setting himself up for a little bit of international diplomacy.

The situation appealed to Torrijos's conspiratorial instincts and—after the signing of the Panama Canal Treaties—to his heightened sense of his own importance. He would mediate an international crisis, save American lives, and get his friend reelected. The world would love him for it.

Noriega's role was far simpler. Torrijos appointed him to keep the Shah alive, to monitor all his phone conversations, and to watch all comings and goings at his home on Contadora Island. Noriega appointed himself to help sell the Shah Panamanian real estate and, on at least one occasion, to organize the logistics for a midnight tryst with a tourist the Shah had met on a beach.

"Torrijos saw international stature in taking the Shah," says Robert Armao, the Iranian monarch's adviser and friend. "Noriega saw dollar signs." Armao, who was as determined to cut costs as Noriega was to increase them, clashed with the intelligence chief from the beginning. Armao was a cultured, eastern Republican—an insider in the Rockefeller clan—who never liked the idea of the Shah's coming to Panama. If incompetent Panamanian doctors didn't kill the Shah on the operating table, Armao feared Torrijos would ship the King of Kings to Khomeini.

Armao considered Noriega to be a low-class hoodlum, the kind of street tough not to be included in the company of Middle Eastern monarchs except under these, the worst of circumstances. Armao later remembered his first trip to Panama on December 13, 1979, to arrange for the Shah's stay. The party arrived from Lackland Air Force Base at Panama's Paitilla airfield on the Pacific Coast. "Noriega and his band of thugs were waiting at the airport," Armao said. "It was like out of a gangster movie. He pulled up in a six-passenger Mercury, a gun rack hooked over the front seat with an assortment of guns. He looked like an *Untouchables* series enforcer, except that Noriega was smiling like a hyena, and he was wearing a double-knit leisure suit."

Hamilton Jordan, whom Armao considered almost as crude and untrustworthy as Noriega, effusively greeted the intelligence chief with a Latin *abrazo,* and they all flew to Chiriquí province in Noriega's DC-9. Armao was repulsed by this good-ol'-boy Jordan and the Panamanian sleaze, the two of them downing their first Balboa beers for breakfast while G-2 men with machine guns stood outside Noriega's cinder-block office.

They in turn were disgusted with Armao, whom they considered an uptight pansy with no appreciation for the Panamanian good life. The Shah's chief bodyguard, Colonel Kiumars Jahanbini, was also uncomfortable with Noriega. Jahanbini had been trained in England at Sandhurst Military Academy and for fifteen years had served as an officer in the Imperial Guard. Jahanbini didn't look the part of bodyguard. He had glasses and a receding hairline. He didn't like the fact that Noriega did look the part of the corrupt Latin intelligence chief.

Noriega happily drove the American party through David, Chiriquí province, where he had served as garrison commander. "I was chief of the Red Devil division," he bragged, pointing to the red image painted on the headquarters' green wall. "At the crucial moment, I provided the crucial means to keep Torrijos in power." He then drove through well-off areas of the city, playfully offering Armao any house he wanted for the Shah. Noriega said often, "If you like this house, it's yours."

Ambassador Moss laughed about the situation afterward. "Noriega and I were in the real estate business. Our job was to sell a house to Jahanbini."

Armao refused time and again because of security concerns, shaking his head as Noriega boasted that he could protect the Shah anywhere in Panama. "He was Mr. Macho," says Armao. "He could protect the king anywhere. It might take two hundred men, but he would do it."

So Noriega—realizing he had a discerning customer—flew Armao and Jordan to Contadora Island. Armao was nervous about flying in the broken-down Electra plane which belonged to Torrijos, but Jordan warned him not to offend the Panamanians, so he reluctantly boarded what he viewed as the airborne Panamanian military equivalent of a love bus. He remembered that the tawdry furniture looked as if it had been bought at Ethan Allen—ten years earlier. The partition between the service area and passengers was ripped. Armao thought the stewardess looked like a prostitute, and then he decided that she was one, particularly after Torrijos's American friends jokingly called the plane the "Flying Whorehouse," because of both its appearance and its occasional carnal use by Panama's dictator and his intelligence chief.

Noriega next offered Armao the seaside home of Panama's former ambassador to Washington, Gabriel Lewis. After the uncomfortable officers' quarters at Lackland Air Base, Lewis's home would be heaven. The wide terrace overlooked the Pacific, over palms and hibiscus. It wasn't the palace, but it was the best the Shah would get in his fallen state. Armao accepted it in principle. Now U.S. officials wanted Torrijos to convince the Shah to come.

Armao remembers Torrijos as a sad character. As they arrived at one of his homes, he was bidding farewell to a woman who had probably been beautiful five years earlier. Torrijos absentmindedly handed her some bills from a roll of hundreds. He stood in white socks without shoes, and he wore wrinkled khaki pants. Torrijos, not trying to hide the transaction, finished paying her as they arrived.

Torrijos began chugging whiskey at 8 A.M., hoping to overcome the hangover from the night before. "His eyes seemed ready to pop out of his head," said Armao. "I could see he was nearly finished, and Noriega must have seen it as well." Yet Noriega stood quietly and obediently by Torrijos's side. He even lit Torrijos's cigar, wouldn't sit down until Torrijos did, and never spoke until the dictator was finished speaking. "I don't think Noriega liked being around Torrijos," remembered Armao. "He had to be totally subservient."

Torrijos handwrote a note inviting the Shah to Panama, a personal touch that so moved the Persian monarch that he willingly packed his bags for the move south.

For Noriega, the Shah's visit posed an unprecedented logistical challenge. He drew up plans, maps, and assignments with the vigor of a commanding officer planning the Normandy invasion. He built a shack on the water just off the shore of Contadora, in front of Lewis's house, for a PT boat, frogmen, and sonar devices that would stop any underwater intruders.

Whenever Noriega talks about writing a book on his unusual life, he always mentions that his relationship with the Shah will be a prominent chapter. "Oh, yes," he told one interviewer in 1989, "the first part of my book will be entitled, "I, Guardian of the Shah.""

Yet Noriega's protection of the Shah was less than impressive. "The frogmen looked like McHale's Navy," said Armao. "They were always sunning, drinking beer, and hanging their laundry"—directly in the Shah's line of sight to the sea.

Noriega also cleared a landing area for attack helicopters and installed anti-aircraft weapons at three points around the home. He stepped up security at airports and ports, closely monitoring passports from countries known to be enemies of the Shah. Noriega so strictly monitored tourists coming to Contadora Island that the local hotel manager complained that he lost $1 million in business in three months.

Lieutenant Colonel Noriega visited the Shah several times during the three months, but they never conversed much. Noriega preferred gathering his information on the Shah clandestinely. He was philosophically fascinated by this fallen dictator. In an interview for William Shawcross's book, *The Shah's Last Ride,* Noriega said, "I had the feeling that he was programmed to see himself as an extraterrestrial person, like the son of the Sun, not as a human being. A sort of divinity."

Noriega's friends say that seeing the Shah's desperation so close up had a profound effect on the young intelligence officer eight years later when he, too, would become a besieged dictator. Noriega saw then that there was little life after dictatorship. The message was continually reinforced thereafter as fallen rulers found sad exile, no matter how great their riches. Later that year, on September 17, Nicaragua's Anastasio Somoza Debayle would be blown to bits as he drove through Asunción, Paraguay, his home in exile. American intelligence agents say Noriega had been contacted by the Sandinistas to help with the assassination, but they insist that he didn't participate in the plot that resulted in Somoza's death.

Characteristically, Noriega was an entrepreneurial host for the Shah. He charged Armao $5,000 to $10,000 a month to rent two shanties in which Noriega's G-2 security men were housed. The Shah also picked up the cost of their meals at the nearby hotel, where the Shah's monthly costs were $21,000. The Shah even had to pay for the security system that was used not only to protect him but also to allow Torrijos to monitor his phone calls and conversations. The price tag: $68,000. A former accountant linked to the defense forces said Noriega also charged the military's account for these expenses and thus pocketed the money provided by the Shah. Colonel Díaz Herrera, who was chief of staff once Noriega rose to take over as Comandante in 1983, said Noriega pocketed $12 million that the Shah paid to be allowed to stay in Panama.

In a mobile van at the back of the house, Noriega installed a monitoring system. He tape-recorded reel-to-reel all the conversations in the house, an operation directed by his military ally Luis del Cid, who would later be indicted with him on drug charges.

The Shah complained that Noriega even forced him to pay $400 for this eavesdropping equipment. "Money pressures were anything but subtle. My staff complained about bills that seemed much too high. Friends of General Torrijos let me know that Contadora was for sale and had a $10 million price. We were shown property . . . at inflated prices."

Noriega arranged occasional trips for the Shah, from which his men tried to exclude Armao. On one such mission, the Shah was asked to give $35,000 to build a boys' school on a site he liked. The Shah told Jahanbini to give it to one of Noriega's cronies and not tell the tight-fisted Armao. When Armao discovered the Shah's largess, he leaked the information to a Panamanian newspaper to improve the Shah's image in Panama. Armao also thought the publicity would undermine what he suspected was

Noriega's true intention: to pocket the cash himself and never build the school.

Ambler Moss recalls how much Noriega and his G-2 men came to hate Armao. They complained that Armao wouldn't let them park their vehicles near the house, and that he would make obscene gestures at them. Finally they arrested Armao's aide, Mark Morse, and took him to Panama City. Ambassador Moss called Noriega to request his release.

"I just wanted to teach him a lesson," said Noriega. "He had been annoying my people. We were fed up. For you, I'll let him go. But he can't go back this morning. He'll have to spend the night in Panama City."

Noriega also did some pimping for the Shah. The Shah left the island one evening ostensibly to view real estate the next morning. Noriega's security people prevented Armao from tagging along, and they didn't say where they were taking the Shah. Armao was desperate about the disappearance. He feared the Shah was being packed into a crate for Teheran.

Under pressure from Armao, Ambler Moss frantically called all those closest to Noriega and Torrijos, and in desperation, finally called President Aristides Royo. Moss warned that the whistle was about to be blown in Washington on the Shah's disappearance.

Royo called back after a short time to reassure Moss. "Don't worry," he said. "The Shah's all right. Your Shah is perfectly happy and having a good time in the presidential suite in the Panama Hilton with a Canadian tourist he met on the beach."

Smiles Moss: "Noriega was the Shah's logistical expert for the rendezvous."

But Armao feared the Shah was unsafe in Panama. Torrijos was trying to save Carter by arranging the freeing of the hostages, and Torrijos had been told by Iranian intermediaries that locking up the Shah and charging him with a criminal offense might help. The Shah already disliked Torrijos, who had made no secret of his sexual desire for the empress through his oafish ogling and offers to visit her at any time—particularly when the Shah was incapacitated.

Torrijos had even ordered Noriega to make videotapes of the shapely empress waterskiing. The dictator kept the film in the bedroom at his home on Calle Cincuenta. Noriega also delivered all tapes of the empress's phone conversations to Torrijos. She talked all day on the phone to friends in Europe, the Middle East, and America—switching continents to suit the time of day. Torrijos saw her as a vulnerable, beautiful, and lonely woman. He was so obsessed with her that Shawcross reports that he asked to be brought her sheets after she left.

"We have a chance to get the hostages out," Torrijos told the Shah in

March. "But I may have to put you behind bars, take a few photographs, and say you are arrested."

Sighed the Shah to Armao, "When one is not well, such things are a strain."

"Your Majesty, over my dead body," Armao said. "I'm getting bad vibes." At that point, Armao decided that he needed to get the Shah out of Panama.

Armao also had to wrestle with a battle between Panamanian and foreign doctors over who would operate on the Shah's spleen and at what hospital. It involved one of the world's premier heart specialists, Dr. Michael DeBakey, and Panamanian specialists who resented being considered Third World butchers. DeBakey thought he was in charge of the surgery, but the Panamanians thought he had come as their consultant.

The Panamanians also didn't want the Shah treated at the American Gorgas Hospital, where they said they couldn't protect him. They considered the move an affront to their national pride. The Shah, however, feared private contacts between Panamanians and Iranians that had been aimed at gaining release of the hostages in exchange for Panama's readiness to hear Iranian extradition requests. At one point, Panama's president even announced that the Shah was under detention—a move engineered to please the Iranians, although the conditions of his stay in Contadora never changed.

Peace was finally made between doctors, and the Shah was admitted to Panama City's Paitilla Hospital under a false name: Manuel Antonio Noriega. But the Shah and his wife continued to worry that, for the right price, Panamanian doctors might sabotage an operation on the Shah. His non-Panamanian doctors delayed their operation, even though the cancer was worsening and the Shah's white blood count was down. They wanted to move him outside Panama, where the Shah faced fewer dangers of extradition and of murder on an operating table.

In his memoirs, the Shah was angry about his treatment. "I considered their attitude insane," he wrote. "My life was in jeopardy and I was not about to lose it to the personal insecurities of the Panamanians." He called the situation "a medical soap opera."

The decision was made to move the Shah. The Shah left Gabriel Lewis a handwritten note that Lewis still keeps framed in the living room, which overlooks the water and where the Shah would sit for hours staring at the sea. Jahanbini would sit in a chair slightly behind him, so that he wouldn't interrupt the view. "The Empress and I have difficulty to find the words to thank you and Mrs. Lewis for your unparalleled hospitality and graciousness and helpfulness. My regret is that I don't have a country where

I could invite you and your family to repay part of what you have done for us . . ."

Lewis never took a penny from the Shah during his stay. The Shah's entourage, however, didn't feel as kindly about Noriega, who had come to see them off at the airport at 2 P.M., Sunday, March 23, more than three months after the Shah had arrived. Noriega smiled absurdly at Armao as he wished him well. "I was ready to kill Noriega, but he hugged us all at the airport as we left," says Armao.

By the time the Shah left Panama, Torrijos was losing interest in power. He had achieved his Panama Canal Treaties, and had failed to help his friend Jimmy Carter with the Shah. What troubled him most, however, was that he was losing influence over the Sandinistas, who had seized power with his help but now were being controlled by the Cubans.

His worries began with intelligence reports relayed back to him by the head of a military assistance mission he had sent to Nicaragua, Colonel Rubén Paredes. Paredes had gone to Nicaragua with a team of fifteen officers, including Noriega, four helicopters, and a cargo transport aircraft to help the new Nicaraguan government. Paredes interpreted "help" as stopping Cuban-style communism and promoting Torrijos-brand populism. Torrijos had sent Kawasaki motorcycles and Peugeot cars for the police just so the Cubans couldn't argue that his support was a front for the Americans. Paredes was to organize a thirty-day training program for a new police force: Torrijos didn't see much need for Nicaragua to have a full-fledged military.

But Paredes soon reported back that he was little more than a tourist, watching the Cubans take over Nicaragua. He sent back intelligence on the surprising number of flights and advisers that arrived every day. Torrijos's worries mounted after the Spanish President Felipe Gonzalez flew to Panama from a stay in Nicaragua, to report much the same concern.

So Torrijos dispatched Paredes and Noriega to Cuba to question Castro. At first, Fidel Castro angrily denied the extent of Cuban involvement. When Paredes provided details, Castro lost control. "We have been involved in Nicaragua for twenty years," he told Paredes. "You can't take us out of there now. Who do you think you are?" Castro was angry. Torrijos had already begun to challenge his position as the hero to revolutionaries in the region. The Canal Treaties had made Torrijos popular enough to have meetings with leaders all over the world—even with the pope. Castro was still isolated and an outcast.

Castro broke up the meeting angrily. He was also determined to intimidate his visitors that night. His troops fired guns sporadically around the protocol house where they were staying at Los Colinos. In fear, Paredes turned the lights off and moved to a safer area of the home.

Throughout the visit, however, Noriega continued meeting happily with his Cuban counterparts in intelligence, Manuel Piñeiro Losada and José Abrantes. They would chat quietly and amicably in the corner of the conference room during hot discussions between their superiors.

Piñeiro visited Noriega privately on several occasions. They were close and intended to remain so, despite the current diplomatic war between their masters. By this time, Noriega had achieved the remarkable feat of convincing both the Cubans and the Americans that he was a more reliable and balanced friend than the romantic Torrijos, whom both Cuban and U.S. intelligence services viewed as disloyal. Castro saw Noriega as a valuable business partner, a man he could manipulate more easily, while Torrijos had become a political competitor.

Noriega's knowledge of the region was becoming legendary. In 1980 former Costa Rican president José "Pepe" Figueres paid a courtesy call on Fidel Castro. Figueres, the old man of Central American leftist politics, whose respect for Castro was great, praised the Cuban leader for being the best-informed man in the region. As Figueres absentmindedly picked at large lettuce leaves with his hands, he dropped one on his plate with surprise when Castro replied, "No, Noriega is the best-informed man. He knows everything the left and the right are doing."

In 1979 and 1980, Lieutenant Colonel Noriega's power increased as Torrijos retreated from the day-to-day running of the country. Torrijos would frown to friends that only Noriega knew everything about what was happening in Panama, and that he didn't even share the information with his boss. Torrijos, a man who didn't like to read, preferred that his briefings be given him on tapes. That way, he could turn them off when he got bored, and his advisers wouldn't ever know when he opted not to listen to their views altogether. When accused of keeping secrets from Torrijos, Noriega would reply that he couldn't make enough cassette tapes and Torrijos didn't have enough time to learn all that Noriega knew.

Torrijos was losing track of Noriega's many activities. The dictator knew less about what was happening in Panama than did Noriega. "The role of the chief of intelligence was for no one to see him, but that also gave Noriega a lot of power," said Juan Materno Vasquez, the lawyer who was Torrijos's first minister of justice. "Torrijos used to always tell me, 'Noriega knows where we are, but we don't know where he is.' "

Torrijos's worries about Noriega grew when a Panamanian government plane crashed in El Salvador loaded with weapons for FMLN guerrillas.

Torrijos wouldn't have had anything in particular against this mission, and in fact he backed the guerrillas' fight, but he had promised Carter that he would stop the deliveries for a time. He thought that Noriega had defied the agreement: this new embarrassment was a typical example of Noriega's private entrepreneurship. The guerrillas were flush with money from recent kidnappings, and they were turning it into weapons purchased through Noriega's cronies and then delivered by his pilots.

The pilots, Floyd Carlton Caceres and César Rodriguez Contreras, worked from the El Tamarindo airstrip on Costa Rica's Pacific Coast. Carlton flew a Piper Seneca and Rodriguez flew a Navajo Aerocommander. Noriega paid each pilot $35,000 per flight.

On this mission the guerrillas had come late to pick up the pilots from their hotel. They had already loaded the planes. Usually, the guerrillas would wait for the pilots to supervise the loading, but the guerrillas said they'd had problems with local police and needed to transfer the load from the trucks before they could pick up the Panamanians.

In addition to the AK-47 semiautomatic machine guns, ammunition, and other supplies for the FMLN, Rodriguez carried extra fuel so they could return the next day for Father's Day celebrations, a bit of luxury that cost them dearly. Overweight, Rodriguez's Aerocommando struggled to get off the ground and caught on electrical wires, breaking a hydraulic fuel line and disabling the brakes.

Rodriguez still flew the plane to El Salvador, and he landed, but without brakes, he rolled forward into a tree. The left side of the aircraft was crushed and Rodriguez broke both legs. Carlton dropped off his load of weapons, and then returned for his friend, assuming he was dead. Carlton pulled him out of the plane after breaking the cockpit windshield with his rifle butt, but he disregarded Noriega's explicit instructions that disabled planes with Panamanian markings be destroyed.

Two El Salvadoran air force helicopters hovered overhead, and the plane was still loaded with fuel and ammunition. Blowing it up could have killed them, so Carlton told the guerrillas to destroy the plane as soon as the pilots had taken off.

Carlton took Rodriguez to a hospital in Panama and called Noriega with the bad news. When Noriega asked if Carlton had destroyed the plane, Carlton lied that he had done so. Noriega called back a few minutes later, and he was furious. International news services were reporting that a Panamanian aircraft had been captured in El Salvador. "He was very, very angry," remembered Carlton. The plane's documents linked it to Noriega.

Rodriguez was moved to a military clinic to keep him away from the opposition press. Both men made statements only to the G-2 and the attorney general. The case was then dropped.

Torrijos thereafter assigned his head of political intelligence, José Blandón, to begin traveling with Noriega on all his foreign trips. His mistrust of Noriega grew each day. Blandón would give Torrijos a full report on cassette after each mission. Noriega was perfectly behaved, but he privately seethed at the humiliation of having this chaperone.

But Torrijos no longer had the energy to restrain Noriega. In early 1980, Torrijos sent a helicopter from Contadora Island to pick up his friend Rory Gonzalez for an urgent discussion.

I'm leaving the National Guard, he told him. I'm going to quit. I'm getting fed up with the military. It's too corrupt. It's out of control.

"But who will lead?" asked Gonzalez. "You can't quit."

They talked about alternatives. Díaz Herrera wasn't military enough and was always asking for more money. Paredes was too ambitious. Paredes at one point had tried to remove Noriega from office, and his sons had been set up in business in the Free Zone at ages eighteen and seventeen. Noriega was too sneaky.

Torrijos was particularly troubled by a letter from the Cuban ambassador, complaining about a $40,000 charge to be paid to Enrique Pretelt—Noriega's pilot—for helping to recover a Cuban Learjet that had been captured in Fort Lauderdale with Nicaraguan registration and a Cuban crew. The documents were falsified Panamanian ones.

Over the coming weeks, Torrijos told several friends about plans to retire the whole general staff. He said they had grown to love power too much over twelve years and that they would never let civilian leaders gain influence under the democratization plans he had promised in signing the Panama Canal Treaties.

"We are too accustomed to being dictators," Torrijos said.

Gonzalez, hoping to lighten the conversation, joked, "But what about the helicopter and the money? You'll have to rent planes like everyone else." He laughed and they sat down to figure out the budget an ex-dictator might need.

In June 1981, Omar Torrijos shared drinks with friends at Gabriel Lewis's house on Contadora Island. He was more depressed and disturbed than his friends had ever seen him, and his mood seemed to worsen with every day. A lawyer, Jaime Arias Calderón, asked him why he was taking so much time to democratize. "I first have to do something about the National Guard," he said. "I can't let those who are next in line take over the organization." At the time, Arias thought the statement was self-serving—an excuse to hang onto power.

Nicholás Ardito Barletta, Torrijos's long-time friend who was visiting from Washington, remembered the dictator toward the end as a man with a premonition that he would die soon. He hardly recognized Torrijos. He was drinking even more than usual, but he was also nicer to his wife; he had stopped fooling around. He had given a large piece of land to a close friend, and he had started serving drinks to his personal valet of many years.

Torrijos found the way out of his misery when his De Havilland Twin Otter plane crashed into the top of a mountain on the western part of the isthmus on July 31, 1981. Thirteen years of uninterrupted one-man rule came to an abrupt end.

Every Panamanian has a theory of how he was killed. The anti-Noriega crowd swears it was Manuel Antonio, who never properly performed his task of investigating the crash. Others say Castro killed a man who had grown bothersome. The leftists say it was the CIA (perhaps helping Noriega), and the rightists say it was the Nicaraguan leadership, avenging Torrijos's new support for Edén Pastora's anti-Sandinista plotting. Pastora had originally planned to be on the plane with Torrijos.

What is known is that American intelligence agents were pleased at his passing and hopeful that Noriega would rise to power. "I personally was glad he died," said one former intelligence agent, who operated closely with Noriega for more than a decade. "Torrijos was a pain in the ass. He once told me he didn't care a stitch for the U.S. except its women and money. Sure, Noriega worked for the Cubans, but we calculated he belonged twenty percent to them and eighty percent to us."

The most convincing case is that it was an accident: a crash into the top of a mountain on a stormy day with low visibility by a man who never took normal safety precautions. His usual pilot had flown home after his wife had given birth. And Torrijos would often force pilots to fly under the worst of conditions; they feared to refuse him and reveal themselves as lacking sufficient *machismo.*

The world may never know who, if anyone, killed Torrijos. However, what anyone can see is who profited most from his death: Manuel Antonio Noriega.

CHAPTER
EIGHT

THE ARROGANCE
OF POWER

Power in Panama is like a viper. You have to let go of it very cautiously . . . or it will bite you.
—GENERAL RUBÉN DARÍO PAREDES, 1989

Lieutenant Colonel Noriega seemed distracted and desperate at the Torrijos funeral. He sat on the edge of a church pew alone. His thumbs pressed and rubbed his temples. He didn't seem to know where to move, so he just held his place—almost catatonic. His confidence had crashed in the plane with Torrijos, and his usual introversion had become a full retreat into himself.

One friend said Noriega seemed a shadow which had lost its subject. Enrique Carreras, a Costa Rican politician who got no response when he put his hand on Noriega's shoulder, observed, "This is a man who usually records everything in a room, whose eyes dart from person to person. But now he wasn't noticing anything. He was very confused for several weeks."

Even in death, Torrijos was larger than life: the *macho caudillo,* master womanizer, signer of the Canal Treaties—hence the righter of wrongs dating back to 1903—and Panama's populist ruler for thirteen years. If he was corrupt, his corruption had a carefree timbre, and his rule had been more Mediterranean than dictatorial.

The question after his death wasn't who would be the next Torrijos, but rather who was the most "Torrijista." Who would be most loyal to Torrijos's traditions and make them live long past the dictator's death?

Noriega was a spy, more comfortable in the damp dark of the espionage underworld, yet now he was at the center of the speculation over who would win the post-Torrijos power struggle.

In terms of rank, Noriega was fourth in line, behind Colonel Florencio Flores, Colonel Rubén Darío Paredes, and Colonel Armando Contreras. The other competitor for power, Colonel Roberto Díaz Herrera, was one notch behind Noriega, but Díaz Herrera was the most political of the colonels, with close ties to leftist and union leaders, and he had the added advantage of being Torrijos's cousin.

In typical dictatorial fashion, Torrijos left no instructions for succession nor institutions that could facilitate change. Colonel Flores, Torrijos's chief of staff, took charge. While first in line, Flores did not pose a threat to the other colonels who had legitimate claims to the throne. Flores proved relatively weak: he led the National Guard—and hence Panama— for only the next eight months. He preferred baseball and basketball to politics, and his knowledge of American League batting averages exceeded his familiarity with Panamanian politics. He mixed most comfortably with lower-level officers and troops and avoided politicians and other senior officers, whom he correctly saw as circling sharks.

When his chief political adviser, José Blandón, suggested Flores promote himself to general to help consolidate his position, Flores balked. "Torrijos is Panama's only general, and no one else can fill that position," he said. "Out of respect for Torrijos, I cannot promote myself." Flores saw his role as keeping Torrijos's policies, people, and dreams in place.

Flores was right to distrust his senior officers. General Paredes whispered conspiratorially to other officers that the country needed a leader, not a museum keeper. Other officers, who all had to gain by Flores's removal, urged Paredes to act against him for the good of the country. "They saw Flores as a man who couldn't be a leader in the moment we were living," said Paredes later. "He wasn't giving solutions at the pace the country needed them." Paredes, then the chief of staff, also resented that Flores wasn't calling him for advice more often.

Paredes, handsome and intelligent, was far more articulate and political than Flores and had been Torrijos's agriculture minister during a revolutionary land reform. He was of mixed race and the middle class, and he felt more comfortable among the country's white civilian leaders than among fellow officers. Paredes was a horse breeder, which put him in higher-class circles, and he wanted legitimacy in their eyes by discarding his uniform and ruling as a civilian. Paredes wanted a transition to democracy, just as Torrijos had promised, but he wanted to be the president to bring it about. He saw the military as the only institution with the capability to rule Panama, and he viewed himself as the man who could smoothly transfer that power to the civilians as he took off his own uniform. But first he needed to become Comandante.

In conspiratorial Panama, however, all four colonels also suspected each other—so they worked out a three-page plan that would protect each of them. Paredes would be commander from 1981 to 1983, after which he would resign to run for president in the 1984 elections. Contreras would rule from 1985 to 1987, Noriega from 1987 to 1989 (when another presidential election would be held), and Díaz Herrera would take over in 1989. Noriega liked the agreement, because he would run the military through the country's first democratic elections since 1968, and he would resign in time to run for president in 1989, if that's what he wanted.

The agreement gave General Paredes certain backing to remove Flores in what was later called a "meeting room coup." Noriega encouraged Paredes, playing to his ego by repeatedly telling him he was the only man capable of running the military and the nation. Noriega utilized totally different approaches, pertinent specifically to the personality of each one of his rivals. Paredes's weaknesses were vanity and ambition.

On the morning of the planned coup, however, Noriega wasn't anywhere to be found. Díaz Herrera called Paredes at 4:30 A.M. to express his concern that Noriega might still side with Flores and undermine their plan. His fears grew at 6 A.M., when Noriega's Israeli-trained anti-terrorist forces, the UESAT, were scheduled to surround the Comandancia to prevent troops loyal to Flores from saving their commander. But Noriega and his forces were absent. The coup makers nervously waited for him, phoning his home and office without luck, and it wasn't until just before 7 A.M., when Noriega finally arrived looking patient and relaxed, that the action against Flores began.

Paredes now frowns about his action in 1981. "Flores was a good man, a good citizen, but he didn't have what it took to be a leader." Flores didn't argue at the meeting. He merely wished the officers luck, and asked them to "think of their country and not just themselves." Flores saw that individual ambitions were reversing Torrijos's goal of gradually transferring power to civilians, and he warned his senior officers against this.

"The UESAT surrounded only the lower part of the Comandancia," said Díaz Herrera. "I always thought that if Flores had won over us, the UESAT would have arrested us. Noriega was the only one of us who had left himself in a position to play either side."

The next step was to oust Torrijos's president, Aristides Royo. A year after Torrijos's death, Paredes informed him that he was through and would be sent to Spain as ambassador. He needed to put his own people in positions of power to prepare for his run at the presidency. Royo, planting his tongue firmly in cheek, explained that he was stepping down for health reasons. "I have a sore throat," he said at the time. "A general needs to do my talking for me." Paredes replaced him with Ricardo de la Espriella.

Paredes then unwittingly removed the next barrier to Noriega's rise, chief of staff Colonel Contreras. Using allegations that Contreras was weak and a homosexual, Paredes shipped him off to a foreign embassy. Noriega offered the means: Contreras could be retired after twenty-five years of service. Contreras offered no resistance; and Paredes was pleased at having Noriega as the head of the National Guard during his run for the presidency—a man he considered more loyal, efficient, and capable of mobilizing the National Guard to prepare the ground for 1984 elections.

"This is Paredes's doing," Noriega apologized to Contreras, playing all sides, as usual. "I'll make it up to you later."

Throughout his career, Noriega's strength had been patience and a knack for making superiors believe in his loyalty. Both gifts were useful in the two years following Torrijos's death, as one rival after another fell by the wayside. Noriega often lectured his more restless friends and allies that opportunities presented themselves to those willing to wait. Problems often disappear if left alone, he would say, or other events may alter the situation so much that the problems are no longer important. After Torrijos's death, Noriega knew that he was the most powerful officer in terms of knowledge and control of certain key commands and consulates. His ability to sell arms and his newly evolving ties to drug traffickers were increasing the size of his coffers and his ability to buy friends.

Officers and politicians alike feared Noriega, and he recognized the advantage of nurturing this image. At a critical meeting that Paredes called with his general staff and the country's leading businessmen, Noriega was the only one to arrive in uniform. He took a front row seat and he quietly but furiously scribbled notes of the proceedings. During three hours of talks, the businessmen nervously watched the intelligence agent record their every word. He ceremoniously handed the notes to an aide and asked him to type them up for General Paredes. But Noriega's performance had been all show: the aide had been taking the official notes, and Noriega's note pad was filled only with incoherent scribbles.

On August 12, 1983, Paredes stepped down from the National Guard. He planned to win the presidency with Noriega's help, then shift military and political power to civilian—i.e., his—control. He had already forced through constitutional reforms that increased democratic hopes in the country, and he assured American diplomats that only a strong man would be able to cut the military down to size and shift that power to the civilian sector.

What Paredes didn't realize was that Noriega already owned the military and wasn't about to hand it to a civilian—not even Paredes. He even inadvertently strengthened Noriega's hold by naming him General before he had even taken command, hence making him equal in rank. Other military officers also didn't like Paredes's plans to reduce military—and hence their own—power.

Paredes's worries regarding Noriega's loyalty began almost immediately, when he saw the celebration that Noriega threw for himself upon taking charge of the National Guard. Noriega turned Fort Amador and its American-built golf course into a stage for his "coronation," a festival of military parades, marching horsemen, beautiful women, and American generals. Military music from the opera *Aida* blared from loudspeakers as Noriega took to the microphone for his "inaugural" speech.

Noriega, smiling, raised a glass to his former boss, and offered Paredes a paratroopers' toast: *"Buen salto,* Rubén"—Good jump. Although the send-off seemed sincere at the time, it was soon Panama's favorite joke. Noriega, Panamanians said, had pushed Paredes from the plane without a parachute.

Within three weeks, Noriega finished off Paredes. He turned leftists against him by showing a letter sent by Castro, which said Cuba would sever diplomatic and economic relations if Paredes were elected. He turned Washington against him by insinuating that a former general could not usher in civilian, democratic rule.

Noriega's pincer attack worked. Ruling party leaders withdrew their support for Paredes's candidacy, seeing Paredes as a threat to their own power, as did many businessmen. Again, Noriega used others to do his dirty work. President Ricardo de la Espriella led the civilian fight against Paredes. Noriega encouraged de la Espriella's misguided belief that removing Paredes might allow him to run in the country's first presidential elections in sixteen years. Noriega also forced through cabinet changes that shifted support from Paredes. Díaz Herrera let Paredes know that the general staff no longer supported him but instead was behind Noriega. "We had to stop him before he took our power," said Díaz Herrera. "He was going to put us inside the barracks."

Noriega again remained in the background, pulling the strings of others. Paredes, like so many before and after him, had miscalculated Noriega. "I thought that I wouldn't be double-crossed because he couldn't find anyone else who could win," says Paredes now. "If they pulled the boards out from under me, they would be without a candidate.

"Power in Panama is like a viper," Paredes says. "You have to let go of it very cautiously. If you drop a viper in a careless way, she'll turn around and bite you. I made a great mistake by not fearing the viper." Without military support, Paredes's candidacy never had a chance.

Noriega thereafter neutralized Paredes through his sons, both of whom had been involved in drug trafficking with Noriega's business partner and friend César Rodriguez. One of Paredes's sons would later be assassinated with Rodriguez in Medellín in an attack the father blamed on Noriega, and another would be locked up when Paredes began speaking out against Noriega.

We can treat your son well, Noriega told him during the incarceration. But one thing you have to do is stick your tongue in your ass.

Two years after Torrijos's death, Noriega had outmaneuvered the three officers ahead of him in rank to rise to control of the National Guard. Many of Torrijos's allies were relieved at the time, knowing Noriega had been the underground protector of Torrijos and his service had advanced the dictator's causes.

But Noriega's rule in the months to come would be a far different one. Dictators, even the most corrupt, are normally motivated by a political ideology or plan. Nicaragua's Anastasio Somoza had been obsessed with fighting communism; Torrijos aimed to seize power from the oligarchy and to fight for the Canal. Noriega's only causes were money and power.

Noriega was exultant—the poor boy from the Panamanian barrios was military leader of Panama. But he was a Comandante who wasn't much attracted to politicians, economists, and legislators, with whom he was shy and withdrawn. Noriega was happiest with the conspirators, arms smugglers, drug dealers, prostitutes, and underworld figures who had served him well throughout the previous decade. At one of the celebrations of his rise to power, Enrique Carreras, the Costa Rican politician, Díaz Herrera, and Noriega—all drunk—talked about what era they most would have wanted to live in.

The Costa Rican said he would have preferred the heart of the Middle Ages, when no one knew what was going on within a hundred miles of his village. "That would have been a tremendous advantage in seeking a happy life," he said.

Díaz Herrera said he would have wanted to live during one of the Chinese dynasties, a time of real military discipline and new naval power. The rulers looked after their soldiers well.

Noriega, however, preferred America's Prohibition era in the Appalachian mountains. The families worked from dawn until dusk at their stills, but they banded together against the government, fooling the federal agents coming after them.

The hallmark of Noriega's leadership, revealed in the first three months of his rule, was a desire to control Panama's primary institutions and ministries as in a closely held corporation.

In an effort to be at the center of the web, Noriega simultaneously moved closer to the Cubans, the Sandinistas, the CIA, the Pentagon, and the Medellín cartel. Noriega wasn't double-dealing. He was quadruple- and quintuple-dealing. He had received payments from at least ten intelligence agencies in the world, say U.S. military intelligence sources, including Cuba, Nicaragua, Israel, Taiwan, France, England, and the United States. The Reagan administration put him back on the CIA payroll: he could be useful in helping to fight the Sandinistas.

Noriega immediately began converting the National Guard from a loosely run, corrupt organization into a closely held business. He renamed it the Panamanian Defense Forces at the suggestion of his business partner and adviser, Michael Harari, a former Israeli Mossad agent, who had regaled Noriega with tales about the Israeli Defense Forces. Noriega decorated Harari at a small luncheon for invited friends on the day he was named commander, and Harari provided Noriega plans for the PDF organization and his own personal security. Although Harari would later deny his importance to the General, Noriega's friends considered him central to Noricga's success.

Harari, a silver-haired man of military bearing, had been one of Noriega's most eager friends and useful supporters. He would become the adviser Noriega trusted most—aside from his own brother—now that he had to run the Panamanian military and, to a large extent, the country. Noriega also idolized the Israeli people and its military, and he wanted to copy the country's practices.

At first, Harari's posting to Latin America had been a political exile, after a covert mishap nearly ended his career. He had led an Israeli hit squad in Norway, whose aim had been to avenge the Black September murders of Israeli athletes at the 1972 Munich Olympics. But they had gunned down an innocent Moroccan waiter by mistake. Prime Minister Golda Meir, who was close to Harari, saved the Mossad man and made him Mexico City station chief. Harari grew close to Torrijos by mediating between him and his Jewish father-in-law, who had never approved of his daughter Raquel's marriage to a Panamanian dictator, by convincing Defense Minister Yitzhak Rabin to make a call on Torrijos's behalf. He served Israel by raising money and support—and by dealing arms—through well-heeled members of Panama's sizable Jewish community. He was so trusted by Torrijos that he attended a meeting in 1979 where Hamilton Jordan, an aide to President Carter, discussed Panama's plans to take the Shah of Iran in exile. Harari would be part of the assurance of the Shah's safety.

But Harari had grown far closer to his fellow intelligence expert Noriega than to Torrijos. He had provided Noriega with military equipment ranging from eavesdropping technology to lie detectors. In early 1984, shortly after the death of General Noriega's elder brother Luis Carlos, Noriega would call Harari his "mentor." Harari resigned officially from the Mossad in the late 1970s, but he stayed on in Panama City in an export-import business that served Noriega and the Israelis.

Harari's official business was importing Israeli-made solar heaters and farming equipment, primarily for three Israeli-managed farms in Panama growing strawberries and watermelons. He also had a company named Celidor—Celi for his daughter who had been in the Israeli army and Dor for his son the pilot. But intelligence sources say his real profits came from arms dealing in the region, often with the Mossad's Guatemalan station chief, Passat Ben Or. When Noriega wanted to send a message to a Panamanian civilian, and he didn't want the word to spread through his gossipy society, Harari delivered it. And Harari trained Noriega's bodyguards, who were armed with Uzis, the famed pistol version of the Israeli submachine gun. Noriega grew so close to Harari—and so respectful of Israel in general—that he sent his daughter to study Hebrew at the Israeli Albert Einstein School in Panama.

Noriega's first legislative act was to push through "Law 20," which ensured military control of ports, airports, immigration, and customs no matter who was elected in 1984 balloting. The law gave presidents the right to name their military commanders, but it didn't allow them to remove Noriega or any other incumbent Comandante. The law put the army, air force, navy, Canal defense force, police, traffic department, and even immigration officers permanently under Noriega's control. He increased the number of soldiers and military units, upgraded equipment and training for counter-terrorism and low-intensity warfare, and established more military installations, particularly in areas adjacent to the Canal. He also expanded training with American forces, and sent more officers to U.S. military finishing courses.

But at the same time, Noriega decided to play the Cuban and Sandinista cards more enthusiastically than had Torrijos, who was angered by Castro's heavy hand in Managua.

"Torrijos's own ego got in the way," said Ambler Moss, Washington's ambassador to Panama at the time of Torrijos's death. "Noriega didn't have the same hang-up. He's a person without any particular ideology. He didn't have Torrijos's messianic sense of destiny in the world. He is driven by simple principles: power and money."

This shift was apparent from the moment of Torrijos's death. Noriega invited Cuba's spy chief Manuel Piñeiro Losada, known as "Barba Roja" because of his red beard, to Panama for Torrijos's funeral. Next he yanked support away from Torrijos's favorite Nicaraguan, Edén Pastora Gómez, who had just begun moving to oppose the Sandinistas. Noriega was far closer to Tomás Borge, Nicaragua's interior minister and hence the overseer of its intelligence operations. One of his first acts after Torrijos's death would be to neutralize the Pastora threat to Borge.

On July 7, 1981, just before Torrijos's plane crash, Pastora and about a dozen men who had fought with him against Somoza had driven to Panama. Pastora told the Sandinista directorate that he was going off to join revolutionary guerrilla struggles in Guatemala or El Salvador. But instead he moved into the Panama City apartment of Hugo Spadafora, a fellow adventurer whose Panamanian brigade had fought alongside Pastora in Nicaragua. One of Torrijos's sons, Martín, had served in Spadafora's brigade at age fifteen. Torrijos, influenced by his son and Spadafora, had wanted to help Pastora regain influence in Nicaragua and perhaps even start combat against the Sandinistas.

Pastora believed the July 31 "accident" that killed Torrijos, his most important supporter, had been caused by the Sandinista directorate. Pastora had been scheduled to fly with Torrijos that day. After the crash, he and Spadafora fled to Torrijos's home at Farallon beach, near the Rio Ható base. Noriega phoned Pastora there to tell him that Venezuelan President Carlos Andrés Pérez was in town for the funeral and wanted to meet him in Panama City. He sent a plane to retrieve Pastora; Spadafora was left behind at Noriega's instruction.

When Pastora arrived at another Torrijos home near Panama's old golf club, he was shocked to find Noriega with Borge, not Andrés Pérez. Noriega had tricked Pastora into coming back to Panama City. Pastora tried to hide his concern by embracing Borge, his most dangerous enemy in Managua. Castro wanted Pastora to visit Havana, said Borge, and Noriega would provide the plane. In a single stroke, Noriega had shifted Torrijos's policy in Nicaragua to a stronger position of support for the Sandinistas—and the Cubans. "If I refused Castro's invitation, I would have been a dead duck," Pastora said later. "Yet I knew if I accepted, I would have trouble leaving Cuba again." After several weeks in Cuba, Torrijos's son Martín was able to get Pastora out to Caracas.

Noriega's assistance to the Sandinistas was a clear break with Pastora. "It was simple," said Ambassador Moss. "Borge had power and Pastora didn't. Affection didn't get in the way of Noriega."

Ideology was not the issue. Shortly thereafter, Noriega quietly supported Israeli efforts to help the anti-Sandinista Contras by providing landing strips and training areas. Within months of Torrijos's death, he was also enhancing his ties to—and income from—Colombian drug dealers, while simultaneously turning in more drug traffickers to the Drug Enforcement Administration. Noriega was pursuing a confusing array of links and allies whose only pattern was that they all increased Noriega's power, profits, and access to information.

The United States recognized Noriega's double-dealing early on, but it always believed his contention that Washington was getting the most out of his relationships. Washington's ambassador to Honduras, John Negroponte, knew Noriega was the conduit for messages from Fidel Castro to Honduran leaders. Noriega was as close to Leonides Torres Arias, the head of Honduran intelligence and a key facilitator of Contra aid, as he was to then Cuban Interior Minister José Abrantes, who led Castro's effort to undermine the Contras. "He has always played both sides," said Negroponte of Noriega.

After Noriega took over as commander on August 12, 1983, he quickly moved to prepare the government for May 1984 elections. To do so, he wanted more control over the cabinet and presidency. In early February 1984, on a flight between Chiriquí province and Panama City, Colonel Díaz Herrera told President de la Espriella that he would have to resign. He had stage-managed the flight so that the President's family was following in a separate helicopter. Díaz Herrera made clear that a quick decision to step down would be in President Ricardo de la Espriella's family interests. "Sometimes, threats finish a job more expeditiously than diplomacy," said Díaz Herrera later.

Yet in the same February, Noriega suffered a major personal setback, one whose implications only his inner circle fully understood. His brother, Luis Carlos, had felt a pain in his chest, so he started up his car and began driving to the hospital. He died of a heart attack en route. Noriega's adviser, father figure, and trusted friend was dead at age fifty-five, at a time when the newly risen General needed his help most. Michael Harari, perhaps the only other man who had Noriega's unalloyed trust, immediately flew in from Israel for the funeral, knowing there was a vacuum to fill. "Mike, I'm so glad you are here now," said Louis Martínz, a friend of Luis Carlos. "He's going to need you more than ever. Luis Carlos couldn't have picked a worse time to die."

* * *

Now more on his own, Noriega prepared for the country's first democratic elections in sixteen years, elections he didn't intend to lose. Noriega realized, however, that if he might have to steal the elections, he'd best pick a presidential candidate appealing to the Americans. Then they'd be less likely to turn on him over a few pilfered votes. In addition, he needed to pick someone close to Torrijos to win over his allies.

At first, Noriega turned to Fernando Manfredo, Torrijos's former commerce minister, who said he would run only if all parties were behind him. He wanted to run unopposed, not because he was against democracy, but because he figured that was the only way to have the strength to stand up to the military. Manfredo's request was unacceptable, so Noriega's ruling party picked World Bank Vice President Nicholás Ardito Barletta. Barletta also had old ties to Torrijos, having served as his planning minister. He was close to the Americans, with a Ph.D. in economics from the University of Chicago, where Secretary of State George Shultz had taught. And Noriega imagined that Barletta's ties to the international economic community might help Panama surmount its rising debt—the highest per capita sum in Latin America—and its limping economy.

Barletta wanted the job, but only if Noriega promised him the full support of the defense forces for civilian rule. Noriega did. Barletta then asked Noriega if he could try to form a coalition with the country's leading antimilitary candidate, Arnulfo Arias Madrid, running as vice president. After an hour-long meeting, Arias turned down the idea. After having been ousted three times following legitimate victories, Arias wanted to try again on his own. That left Barletta to run against Arias, arguably the most popular man in the country. Barletta nevertheless ran a good race and nearly won fairly, but the military didn't want to take any chances. Arias had tried to dismantle the National Guard before, and they were certain that he would do so again.

Noriega's chief of staff, Roberto Díaz Herrera, grew convinced that Barletta would lose by 11 P.M. on election night, and he put into action a plan to stop the counting and steal the election. "Barletta was more optimistic and he said he had won, but our data did not agree with his," said Díaz Herrera.

For Barletta, losing the election merely meant a return to his job at the World Bank or some other international financial position, but for Díaz Herrera and the military, winning was more critical. Díaz Herrera had already threatened members of one opposition party for not joining the government coalition, and he knew they would strip him of power and perhaps even arrest him if they won. "I was already exposed," said Díaz

Herrera. "I had to make Barletta win at any cost or risk. If Arnulfo had won, he would have sent me to hell."

Díaz Herrera feels Noriega might have been able to cut a deal with Arnulfo Arias, but he wouldn't have saved his chief of staff. "I knew that Noriega would never defend me," said Díaz Herrera. "He won't defend anyone when he is in danger." So although Noriega was blamed for stealing the 1984 elections, it was Díaz Herrera who did the dirty work.

However, Noriega sanctioned his paramilitary to fire upon opposition demonstrators who were converging on the legislative palace, where votes were being counted on the day after elections, leaving one demonstrator dead and forty injured. The military had slowed the count to a crawl, and the opposition suspected a fraud was being baked. By late evening, pro-Noriega gunmen, carrying pistols and shotguns, warned they would shoot at anyone who approached the counting board.

The president of the Electoral Tribunal, César Quintero, quit when he saw what was happening. "He was the only serious and respectable person in the group," said Díaz Herrera. "He was the only one we could not bribe."

Another, Supreme Court Judge Rolando Murgas, had been a law student of Quintero's at the University of Panama and was a reluctant vote fixer. Díaz Herrera alleged he personally gave Murgas $30,000 as a first payment to approve Barletta's victory. "He was a slippery fish that wanted to escape from my hands," said Díaz Herrera of Murgas. "He's quite a decent man, like me, or at least we try to be decent but things get in the way and we are not able." Díaz Herrera alleged the third, Yolanda Pulice de Rodriguez, was in the military's pocket and didn't need any convincing. She came up with the final winning margin for Barletta of 1,713 votes. "I can't remember why she picked that number," said Díaz Herrera. "I would have preferred a larger margin and a number that didn't end with thirteen. As you know, thirteen is a bad number." Díaz said many thousands of votes were altered in several provinces—San Blas, Veraguas, Coclé, Colón, and elsewhere.

Díaz Herrera said the military then had another problem: it feared Barletta's honesty might prompt him to turn down the presidency if he knew how many votes had been stolen. So Díaz Herrera kept him a safe distance from the operation, and to this day Barletta believes that he would have won even without the votes that the PDF stole for him, and he meticulously goes through computer printouts to prove his point, replaying videotapes of campaign rallies to demonstrate the massive crowds that came out to cheer him. "I think Barletta was deceived by the group that worked for him," said Díaz Herrera. "He really thought he had won and even brought with him files and documents that proved he had won the elections without much fraud. But we made him president. He should never have forgotten that."

U.S. intelligence agents on the ground didn't have any doubts who had won.

Reports filed back to Washington said that the Panamanian Defense Forces' own computers had given Arnulfo Arias a victory of more than 66,000 votes, a safe margin in such a small country. In fact, one State Department cable chronicling the fraud was in Secretary of State George Shultz's briefing book when he traveled to the inauguration several weeks later. The State Department decided to overlook this transgression, partly because Barletta was a former World Bank vice president with a Ph.D. from the University of Chicago, where Shultz had long been a professor. American officials also believed that Noriega would never let Arias take office, so a Barletta election was the best chance to help move the country toward democracy.

Noriega, however, could only conclude that he had looked after American interests well enough that Washington was also looking after him. But President Barletta would soon become a problem. Noriega and his officers felt they had created Barletta. And when they committed their most heinous crime, one of the most brutal killings in the country's history, they never expected their should-be puppet president would turn on them.

CHAPTER
NINE

THE SPADAFORA
KILLING

*—Major Luis Córdoba: "We have the rabid dog in our
hands."*
*—Noriega: "And what does one do with a dog that has
rabies?"*

—SEPTEMBER 13, 1985

Hugo Spadafora was the anti-Noriega.

Spadafora was charismatic and operatically handsome; Noriega was introverted and legendarily repulsive. Spadafora was optimistic and fun-loving—he knew no fear. Noriega's character was as scarred as his pock-marked face—paranoia and suspicion followed him like huge shadows.

Spadafora was a dashing physician-revolutionary. He'd received a medical degree from the University of Bologna, then traveled south to join guerrillas fighting for the independence of Guinea-Bissau. He'd written a book about his escapades, *Thoughts and Experiences of a Medical Guerrilla,* that had made him a national hero. Noriega had been refused entrance to medical school, and his only combat experience was the repression of three or four dozen halfhearted guerrillas in the late 1960s, an action that included torture so brutal that it has remained a state secret ever since.

Spadafora was Latin *macho* incarnate. He made women swoon and left men in awe. Noriega's handshake was limp and many of his movements effeminate. Even his parachuting, judo, and scuba diving seemed self-conscious, more contrived to enhance his image than to gladden an adventurous soul.

126

Spadafora and Noriega first met in 1975, at a Carnival celebration in Colón, the most Caribbean of Panamanian cities and a place where celebrations are free and easy. Noriega was the successful young intelligence chief and the senior officer at the event. He sent a message to Spadafora's table that he wanted to meet the famous guerrilla fighter, who had recently become vice minister of health.

Even loose Latin protocol required that Spadafora accept the invitation. But Spadafora was dancing with his wife and other attractive women, and didn't much like Noriega. He ignored the request. Those who knew Noriega best at the time said he acted like a rejected suitor. Friends thought Noriega's homosexual side was attracted to Spadafora's boyish exuberance and joie de vivre. Noriega sulked and left the party early.

Spadafora was everything Noriega wanted to be.

At age twenty-five, during Noriega's first year at the Peruvian military academy in the late 1950s, Spadafora had boarded a ship for Africa to join guerrilla forces fighting for independence in Portuguese Guinea. He had heard about the cause from some leftist Italian friends and wrote the Cuban and Soviet embassies in Egypt offering his assistance, but when they didn't respond he simply set off on his own.

"What made him most proud is he arrived before the Cubans," says Spadafora's half-brother Carmelo, an agricultural worker with a weather-beaten face, permanently callused hands, and a vise for a handshake. "The whole family lived vicariously from Hugo's adventures. We loved his craziness. We are a funny family. We all wanted to go with him."

Hugo returned to Panama in 1968 to fight against Torrijos's "revolution," which he considered merely a badly disguised military dictatorship. At first, he was imprisoned, but Torrijos eventually converted him with his seductive populism and made him a vice minister of health. Bored with bureaucracy and angry at government corruption in 1976, he recruited a band of Panamanian adventurers to fight alongside the Sandinistas in their struggle against Anastasio Somoza.

Spadafora's insurgents, whom he called the Victoriano Lorenzo Brigade, were fiercely independent and loyal above all to Nicaraguan resistance leader Edén Pastora Gómez known then as "Commander Zero." That was where he first crossed swords with Noriega. Torrijos had made Noriega his chief of operations for supporting the Sandinista resistance, and Noriega complained that Spadafora was operating outside his control.

"The Victoriano Lorenzo Brigade takes orders from no government, nor from any national or international organization except the Sandinista National Liberation Front, to which we are totally integrated and subordinated both politically and militarily," wrote Spadafora of his movement.

This curious brigade was to be motivated by ideas combining Panamanian nationalism, Marxism, and the teachings of Guinea-Bissau revolutionary leader Amilcar Cabral.

Spadafora then started gathering evidence against Noriega, who he believed was skimming profits from the sales of arms to the Sandinistas. After the 1979 overthrow of Somoza, Spadafora was convinced that Noriega and Costa Rican Public Security Minister Juan José "Johnny" Echeverría were making fat profits selling the surplus weapons left in stockpiles in Costa Rica. Spadafora resented this Panamanian officer, who had been in the struggle more for the money than for the cause, and now he saw the corruption turning worse. Noriega was using the pilots, landing fields, and arms suppliers established to help the Sandinistas in order to begin a far more lucrative arms and drug trafficking network.

Spadafora's rivalry with Noriega, and his outspoken charges against him, grew so troublesome that Torrijos brought the guerrilla fighter to his office for a meeting in January 1981.

José Blandón, the dictator's son Martín Torrijos, and Captain Felipe Camargo attended. Spadafora warned Torrijos that Noriega was involved in uncontrolled corruption and had even begun to plot against him. "Omar, you have to be very careful with Noriega," said Spadafora. "Noriega is controlling you. Noriega is involved with drugs. Noriega is trafficking in arms. Noriega is going to kill you."

Torrijos arranged another meeting with the same group, but expanded it to include Noriega, Rolando Armuelles Armudas, and Rodolfo Miguel Espinoza.

Spadafora accused Noriega of trafficking in arms and drugs. He said Noriega was investigating people's personal affairs to blackmail them. Noriega was shocked. No one had ever dared confront him so. Everyone knew Spadafora had driven the final nail either into Noriega's coffin or into his own. Noriega defended himself lamely, leading Torrijos to believe that perhaps his intelligence chief was out of control. Afterward, Torrijos met with Blandón, Armuelles, and Spadafora to hear more details.

Spadafora had declared war, and it escalated after Torrijos's death seven months later. Upon Torrijos's death, Noriega placed Spadafora and several others under house arrest at Torrijos's residence at Farallon. "His cruelty was especially directed against me," Spadafora told Radio Continente. "He kept us shut up for several days more, thus preventing my attending the funeral. This was clearly an attempt to terrorize me and let me feel his power."

Spadafora was the first person anywhere to accuse Noriega publicly of drug involvement, and he did it loudly and frequently. He was becoming

a threat to Noriega, the Medellín drug cartel, and—some say—even the
the CIA and its covert arming of the Contras, by speaking openly of
Noriega's help to the Israelis in the early years of the Contras' struggle.

Across Noriega's desk would come the following reports:

On December 21, 1981, Spadafora told the opposition newspaper *La
Prensa* that Noriega's G-2 was engaged in "arbitrary arrests, intimidation,
and the attempt to manipulate political groups and sectors." Never before
had the G-2 been so openly accused before Panamanian society.

On December 23, 1981, on Radio Continente, Spadafora made clear his
statements weren't a mistake. "I emphasize the problem of repression by
the National Guard's G-2 forces, headed by Colonel Noriega. . . . The
persecution carried out by Noriega against those who differ with him
personally has been aimed as often at members of the right wing as of the
left wing; no discrimination is practiced. From the time he first entered his
present position, Colonel Noriega has customarily abused his power."
Spadafora told the public that Noriega's second in command, Major Julian
Borbua Melo of the G-2, had relayed a message from his boss that to
meddle with him was to meddle with the National Guard. "I believe that
Noriega is doing great harm to the National Guard, looking for enemies
where none existed, as has occurred in numerous cases of which I am
aware."

Noriega answered by forcing newspaper editors to print articles ridicul-
ing Spadafora's role in Nicaragua's war and suggesting he was driven by
political ambitions.

Spadafora denounced Noriega's attempts at intimidation on January 18,
1982. He told Radio Continente that "on December 24, Noriega sent me
three 'Christmas presents.' The first was delivered through Major Julian
Melo, who called my friend Dr. Juliao and told him to inform me that I
have been 'tried and sentenced.' Later, Noriega himself told Dr. Juliao that
I should be careful. 'Hugo could die any day now, perhaps even by swal-
lowing a fishbone,' Noriega said. The third gift was sent to me through Mr.
Rodolfo Miguel Espinoza, who . . . left word with my brothers Winston
and Carmelo that they were looking for me that day in order to do me
harm.

"I'm tired of Lieutenant Colonel Noriega thinking he can play cat-and-
mouse with me," Spadafora said. "Because a mouse is one thing I've never
been nor ever will be. So I decided to let him know that I'm after him, too;
after him with the weapon of truth. And I paid a visit to his friend, Mr.
Carlos Duque, in order to tell him that what Noriega didn't know is that
I'm after him concerning drug trafficking, and that I'm already in possession of certain evidence—"

At that point, although just a little too late, Noriega cut off the radio station's electricity. It was the first time drug charges against Noriega had been carried over public airwaves.

Noriega tried to weaken Spadafora by co-opting his guerrilla brigade. In September 1982, he called together the ex-members of this brigade to gain political support for his struggle against presidential candidate Paredes. Some of them joined him. Noriega even offered Spadafora money to join.

But Spadafora resisted and kept talking, even after Noriega became commander. He told *La Prensa* in March 1984 that he considered Noriega "a pseudo-commander, who has arrived at the position and rank he now occupies through treason and opportunism, as the public is aware. . . . I, who have identified myself as a friend of the Guard for many years, feel it necessary to point out that it is truly shameful that today . . . the uniform of every single member of the National Guard is stained by the activities which Noriega has been carrying on for years now, activities such as drug trafficking, weapons contraband, and political manipulation."

Spadafora's words were thunderous in such a timid country. "It's time we shouted out loud that it is cause for national shame that an international trafficker is travelling around the world as our representative. . . . There are people who are well-informed on this situation in our country, but who do not dare speak out publicly. Nevertheless, I will say it for all to hear: Noriega is the main person responsible for the pressure, the intrigues, the deals, and the schemes—in a word, the corruption—which impedes democracy in this country." He then suggested that Noriega had participated in—or at the very least was happy about—Torrijos's death.

"Noriega was resentful of Torrijos at the time of Torrijos's death; he knew that he had lost Torrijos's confidence, and that he was going to be removed from the command of the G-2. These are facts which are well known within the National Guard."

After three months of fighting with guerrillas in Nicaragua, Spadafora returned to Panama to take on Noriega again. He told *La Prensa:* "I have joined with a group of citizens who are studying the possibility of formally accusing Manuel Antonio Noriega before the Tribunals of Justice, for abuse of power and full complicity in drug trafficking." He said it was clear Panamanian courts wouldn't condemn him, so the evidence they gathered would be put before "the supreme judge in our country: the people."

When asked why he would be so crazy to return to Panama at such risk, he replied: "The day I am not allowed to enter and freely move about my own country, I will enter Panama at the head of a battalion." He told Radio La Republica four days later, "The peace of our land is endangered because of the criminal and repressive politics carried out by Noriega and his groupies."

Spadafora had left Panama in voluntary exile in 1982, fearing Noriega and preferring to join Pastora's new struggle against the Sandinistas. After feuding with Pastora, he joined forces with Miskito Indian insurgents operating out of Costa Rica. But now Spadafora's focus was absolute, on Noriega.

Hugo Spadafora told his family that his struggle with Noriega was merely another form of the irregular combat that had become his trademark. On September 13, 1985, he left Costa Rica to launch his final offensive. He packed inside his canvas bag several copies of his 1980 book. He would hand them to admirers, and the books would immediately identify him and make it more difficult for enemies to kidnap him without being noticed.

He always regarded his murder as a possibility. He had befriended César Rodriguez, Noriega's business partner and drug pilot, who had been the source of much of his information on Noriega's underworld. Rodriguez had been murdered in Medellín, Colombia, just six months earlier. Spadafora believed Rodriguez's killing had been a setup, coordinated between drug world assassins and Noriega.

For many weeks, Hugo had been commuting from San José to his two fronts: helping the Miskito Indians fight the Sandinistas in Nicaragua and carrying on his personal offensive against Noriega in Panama. The usually optimistic Spadafora knew he might have already carried his fight too far with the General, but there was no turning back. Now he was coming to Panama for good—or at least until Noriega had been ousted. But his brother Carmelo heard something in his voice that had never been there before: fear.

I am scared, Melo, he said. The man wants to kill me.

On September 13, 1985, Hugo Spadafora did his yoga at the break of dawn, and then wrote a short entry in his vinyl-covered, book-sized diary. Fearing valuable notes might be stolen or that he might be arrested, he had sent copies of his diary to a friend, Joshua D'Baron, listing his meetings with DEA agents. He would travel to the border circuitously, using a light plane, minibus and taxi, then he would cross it on foot. He sent his wife by plane to Panama City.

But before he left, he phoned D'Baron, then a sergeant first class of the U.S. army, who had won the guerrilla fighter's allegiance through his uncanny knack of witchcraft. Sergeant D'Baron had grown close to Dr. Abdiel Juliao, Spadafora's closest friend, through their common belief in Santeria, a Cuban black magic religion with its roots in Africa. D'Baron was a Babalao, the highest rank of Santeria. "These Panamanian people are really into witchcraft," said D'Baron, who comes from a family of Santeria followers in the Dominican Republic. "They are really into it. And I was the best *brujo* [witch] in Panama."

D'Baron would play with seashells and look into a glass of water behind a candle to foretell the future and recall the past. When he met Spadafora in 1980, D'Baron didn't know who he was. "Tell your friend not to go to Guatemala," he said, "because he'll get killed." No one knew of Spadafora's secret plans to join Edén Pastora in Guatemala to open a new guerrilla front. "How did you know?" he asked, incredulously. He cancelled the trip, and started calling D'Baron "Candelo," in honor of the magic candle.

They grew close. Spadafora introduced D'Baron to his more famous friends, including the vice president of Guinea-Bissau. D'Baron opened up a nightclub in Panama with Spadafora that doubled as a source of funds for guerrilla activities for Edén Pastora's anti-Sandinista insurgents. D'Baron also provided Spadafora a monthly paycheck. In addition to the nightclub, the entrepreneurial American soldier said he indirectly owned three professional wrestling companies, each bringing him significant profits, some of which helped Spadafora.

Noriega ordered the nightclub shut down. The military withdrew D'Baron from Panama, questioning him on how much money he had sent to Pastora. He didn't know the amount, he said, but it was a lot.

After deft maneuvering, D'Baron was able to reenlist for Panama. He had contacts in the Pentagon who pulled strings, and he returned, ironically enough, as an official in the finance and accounting office. This time he stayed less than one month. On September 7, he phoned Hugo Spadafora, who said he was returning to Panama to reveal something important. Spadafora said he had talked to "the gringos" at the DEA and CIA, and to Felix Rodriguez, whom he called a CIA operative who had been visiting the Costa Rican embassy from Washington. Do you know this guy? he asked D'Baron, who said he didn't. Is he really a CIA agent?

The DEA hadn't offered Spadafora protection. The local agent later said that he found Spadafora's information fragmentary. Spadafora searched for more corroboration and detail. The DEA didn't offer him protection, and now he feared that his effort to provide the U.S. information had leaked to Noriega, who had close ties to the DEA in Panama.

He told D'Baron that he would bring a whole package of evidence to him in Panama, so he could hold a copy for safekeeping. If anything happened to Spadafora, D'Baron's job would be to take the papers to the press. D'Baron at first tried to dissuade him from the trip. Sitting with Spadafora in Costa Rica in 1983, D'Baron had filled a pumpkin with oil and then lighted it to Saint Norberto, patron of fighting and protection. He had told Spadafora then never to cross the border again because he would be killed. Spadafora's wife, Aris, remembers this advice. D'Baron didn't see any reason to reverse his original warning.

But now Spadafora was insistent, so D'Baron offered to meet Spadafora with his car at the border. "It's safer if I travel on a busy bus," Spadafora said. Spadafora had begun to have nightmares that Noriega would kill him. He carried a .38-caliber snub-nose on his leg, but he never thought it would do him much good. He dreamed that his killing would be unobtrusive, in an arranged automobile accident. He considered the bus a far more difficult target.

Hugo's half-brother Carmelo quit work early on the rice harvest at the border village of Progreso. He had always envied his brother's adventures, and privately wished he had fought as a guerrilla himself. Now the two brothers had arranged a rendezvous at the Restaurant y Café Los Mellos, an open-air cantina run by a family friend on the Panamanian–Costa Rican border.

Hugo had arrived early, however. He had forgotten that Costa Rica was one hour ahead of Panama, and was surprised to see how early it was when he looked at the clock on the wall, its black hands pointing straight up at noon over a Viceroy cigarette advertisement. His own watch showed 1 P.M. He didn't want to wait; Hugo considered the frontier area the most dangerous area of Panama, and he told the restaurant owner that he worried about his wife.

And Spadafora didn't think he needed his brother's protection. A week-long border festival had begun that day along the frontier town's streets, and it was Friday. Weekends weren't a time in Panama for evildoing, not even for Noriega's thugs.

The restaurant's owner, Ivan Garcia Gonzalez, walked with Hugo to the bus. Hugo gave him a copy of his memoirs. A family friend, Garcia Gonzalez didn't remind Spadafora that he'd given him two copies in the past. When Carmelo arrived two hours later, the owner, also known as El Guapo—"the handsome one"—told him the story. Carmelo shrugged, had a couple of drinks at the festival, and then headed back to Panama City. "I slept well," said Carmelo. "I didn't worry at all."

But there was no word from Hugo on Saturday. By 7 A.M. Sunday, Hugo's father was worried and wanted to take action. The elder Spandafora phoned his son.

"Melo, I think Hugo was taken in Costa Rica," the father said to the son.

"I'm sure that Hugo crossed the border," his son replied.

"Are you sure?"

"He's here in Panama. Yes. I'm sure."

"But he hasn't arrived. No one has seen him."

"They've killed Hugo then," said the son.

"Do you really believe that?"

"Yes."

"I want you to be absolutely sure. Go back to the border and talk to 'El Guapo.' Ask in more detail what happened. Find out more."

On Sunday, September 15, Rodrigo Miranda received a call from his friend in Panama City, lawyer Diogenes Arosemena. Arosemena wanted Miranda to prepare a writ of habeas corpus for the body of Hugo Spadafora, assuming, rightly, that Miranda was the only lawyer courageous enough—or crazy enough—to take on Noriega. Since Noriega had taken over, Miranda had started a rich collection of incidents documenting escalating human rights abuses.

Arosemena wanted Miranda to take depositions from those who had seen Hugo last: the restaurant owner, the bus drivers, the border guards. Carmelo and some friends would be Miranda's field investigators.

At 3 P.M., Monday, September 16, Miranda was ready to leave for his office when Carmelo, the mayor of the district of David, and two other Spadafora family friends arrived with the text of long interviews that established Hugo's entry into Panama. More troubling yet, Spadafora had clearly been trailed and detained by the PDF. Miranda prepared the copious notes in legal form to serve as proof of Spadafora's arbitrary arrest.

Just as he was about to finish the paper, Hugo's father called. Rodrigo could forget the writ of habeas corpus. Spadafora had been murdered.

Miranda recorded the call, as he did all his exchanges. "Rodrigo, don't continue working," said the father. "They just called me from Costa Rica. The body has been identified in a morgue in San José. And grab the window tightly because of what I have to say to you. You are the second person after me to know of this barbarity. Hugo was found dead in a ravine near the border with Panama and without a head, because his assassins decapitated him." The body had been stuffed in a U.S. mailbag. Even worse, the head was never found.

The Costa Rican coroner's autopsy was gruesome despite the dry anatomical language. Sharp objects had pierced the skin under Spadafora's fingernails, and then the nails were removed. His back was badly bruised. Two of his ribs were broken. His testicles were swollen. The groin muscles had been cut—"neat, symmetrical incisions"—skilled surgery to facilitate homosexual rape. The autopsy showed Spadafora's rectum badly deformed from forced entry—repeated and violent. Finally, a significant amount of blood was found in the stomach. The torturers had severed the head from the body while Hugo Spadafora was still alive; the dying body had swallowed the blood.

Had Spadafora's death been known earlier, fear would have silenced the witnesses, but the Spadaforas had notes from depositions done before the news came out, and names of other witnesses to contact. Noriega's thugs had been caught in their most infamous of crimes. Miranda phoned *La Prensa* columnist Guillermo Sánchez Borbón, and many of the details from his initial interviews appeared in the next day's newspaper. Noriega's people were shocked that Sánchez Borbón knew so much so quickly and concluded he had been fed by American agents.

A combination of fresh interviews and the reading of past depositions, hidden away by the Spadafora family and its lawyers, draws the following picture of Spadafora's last day:

—The restaurant owner, "El Guapo," told Carmelo that he had only one concern when Spadafora boarded the bus at David city. A notorious Panamanian Defense Forces officer, Francisco Eliecer Gonzalez, climbed in after him. Gonzalez's nickname was "Bruce Lee," given him more for his violent nature than for his martial arts prowess. Eliecer Gonzalez was a mixture of black and Indian, and his eyes were dark and angry. Spadafora didn't like entering the half-empty bus with him, so he walked across the street to a full bus ready to leave. So did "Bruce Lee." El Guapo took the license number, 4B-52. He knew the driver and his assistant.

—The bus passed two checkpoints, Jacu and Santa Marta: one was two miles south of the border and another seven miles further on. Officers routinely checked all identity cards, but they asked Spadafora to get off the bus at both checkpoints. Hugo had grown accustomed to this inconvenience. His name was on a list of those whom the guards at each post needed to report. Eliecer Gonzalez followed Spadafora off the bus and back onto it again at the first checkpoint. He didn't move from his seat the second time. The other passengers weren't bothered by the short delay. They knew that Hugo Spadafora was with them—the romantic guerrilla fighter. They all stared and some smiled and chatted with him amicably—or as amicably as one chatted in a bus without air conditioning in the midday heat. At the second checkpoint, a fellow guerrilla fighter from Nicaragua waved from a bus driving in the opposite direction. The many witnesses later made ludicrous the official claims that Spadafora hadn't ever entered Panama.

—Spadafora got off the bus in the main square of Concepción. The bus station, beside a cement building holding a dental clinic and shoe repair shop, was just a short walk down Avenida Centario from PDF headquarters. Hugo had a few more miles until his destination of David, but often changed buses if he suspected something was wrong. He apparently wanted to shake Eliecer Gonzalez before arriving at the headquarters of the Fifth Zone, which was commanded by Noriega's most vicious friend, Major Luis Córdoba.

Witnesses recounted the following scene:

Gonzalez got off, and insisted Spadafora come with him. Spadafora protested, and Gonzalez grabbed the handle of Spadafora's briefcase. Hugo then held up his identification to the bus so that all could see it. "I am Hugo Spadafora. I am Hugo Spadafora. This man of the Guardia is detaining me." He proudly walked ahead of Gonzalez toward the local headquarters, which was painted a dull white (it has since been repainted in camouflage colors). The bus driver's assistant chased after him. Hugo had forgotten to pay his fare. Hugo distractedly handed him a fistful of coins, well more than the $1.20 fare, and walked down Avenida Centario to the PDF station.

Carmelo wasn't surprised that his brother didn't fight detention. Hugo had been detained and released before, and must have thought they wouldn't dare harm him when so many had witnessed his arrest. And the beating didn't start then, not in Concepción. The headquarters there is closely surrounded by homes, and prisoners are rarely interrogated there.

Witnesses say the trip to his death came after dark, driving down the Interamerican Highway along a rural, asphalt road to San Martín. From San Martín, they took another rural road that runs parallel to the Interamerican Highway to Progreso. The first stop was the farm of Major Nivaldo Madriñan, the chief of police investigations, near San Martín. Madriñan was known by Panamanians as one of the two or three most brutal assistants of Noriega. He had flown to David after hearing Spadafora was detained. At least fourteen officers were involved in the interrogation and torture at one point or another. Most of them arrived at Madriñan's farm in three four-wheel-drive Toyota jeeps owned by the Agriculture Ministry. They began beating Spadafora at the farm, and then drove him to a nearby beach. Two lovers there, who had taken refuge behind a bush when they heard the cars, watched the homosexual raping of Spadafora. *La Prensa* printed names of other officers involved.

After he was already badly beaten and unconscious, Spadafora was thrown in the back of one of the cars and driven to a small village called Corozo. It's a lonely place. A vocational school had been built there several years earlier, but the school was never very successful. On a weekend, which is when Spadafora was taken there, the town was almost deserted. Witnesses saw only the body being dragged in: they couldn't tell whether it was alive or dead. But they did see the body still had its head. It was inside the school building that the head was severed.

When students came back to the school on Monday, they were surprised to find more PDF members in their small town than they had ever seen before—more than a dozen. A dog was digging furiously on the dirt patio outside one of the school buildings. One of the men, wearing a green uniform, walked up to the dog and shot it in front of the director of the school and the teachers.

The townspeople gossip that the dog was searching for Spadafora's head. More likely it smelled blood. Hugo's brother Carmelo blames *La Prensa* journalist Sanchez Borbón for the loss of the head. Villagers had told Carmelo and Miranda where it was, and Carmelo was gathering guns and men to retrieve it. Miranda mentioned the location to Sanchez Borbón, however, who wrote it into his reports.

On the morning the newspaper appeared, a tractor sent by the PDF turned over all the soil in the courtyard. The head was apparently removed or crushed. "Sanchez Borbón published the information without saying anything to us," says Carmelo, who visited the site too late with a group of armed men. "I think it was a big mistake. They erased whatever was there without a trace."

After the decapitation, the murderers dumped the torso in a ravine at Robalito, across the border in Costa Rica. It isn't much more than 1,000 meters from Corozo.

The killers washed themselves and their car at a cooperative farm called La Balsa. An eyewitness watched from afar, then came closer after the cars were gone and saw bloody footprints. He took photographs and showed them to Miranda.

Noriega's friends didn't understand. They knew Noriega, and this didn't seem like his work. Unlike many other dictators, Noriega hadn't sanctioned political killings as a weapon, and Panama's repression under him had been relatively mild and nonviolent. But Miranda knew Spadafora was a unique problem for Noriega—an enemy with too much knowledge and courage. Perhaps Noriega had even asked for his head. The reward was always great for satisfying Noriega. The act would also send a message to any others who might want to talk about their ties to Noriega's drug mafia.

"As a criminal lawyer, I have always tried to understand the criminal mind," said Miranda. "But this type of crime I haven't been able to understand. Why so much cruelty? The balls of Hugo were strangled; they cut the tendons of his thighs to make the rape easier. They hit him. They took his nails off. It's not the signature of Noriega, but that of Luis Córdoba, the Chiriquí garrison commander—a man of brutality. Córdoba was looking for a star."

The Spadafora family ran advertisements in local newspapers and on the radio asking for information, and the witnesses kept coming.

One sneaked into the back seat of Miranda's car and frightened him as he started to drive off. He had been one of the lovers on the beach who had witnessed the events.

Miranda charges $20 for an office visit for a new client, and one woman paid the fee before saying she had come to give information. In the middle of her deposition, she needed to take a break to vomit before she could go on.

Two mistresses of the killers met with Miranda clandestinely. One had confessed to her priest what she knew, and he had suggested that telling Miranda might be the right thing to do (he cautioned against going to the police).

The other mistress said she didn't know much about the Spadafora matter, but she gave information about another murder that her lover had carried out with fellow PDF officers a month earlier. "I suffer for that," she said. "I am a Catholic."

After *La Prensa* published the names of the bus driver and the assistant who had confirmed Spadafora's arrival in Panama and his arrest by "Bruce Lee," the PDF brought them in for interrogation. They were asked for the names of all those they knew who were in the bus. The bus drivers afterward denied Spadafora had boarded. After intercession by the Spadafora family, the union of bus drivers said it would defend the drivers. So they again told the truth: that Spadafora had gotten on. Noriega silenced the drivers again: they were moved to field-worker jobs, where the union couldn't protect them.

The PDF silenced the other witnesses. One woman on the bus thought she was too old to be bothered by the PDF. She was beheaded. A known alcoholic was charged with her killing and was put in jail, but the case was never tried.

After contacts from the PDF, other bus passengers and drivers lost their memories.

And the soldiers' alibi? Why, they were off target-shooting two miles outside Concepción at Bugavita. They were each other's witnesses. None of the townspeople heard shooting or saw the soldiers on the day of the killing.

"The proof existed, the eyewitnesses exist, all that didn't exist is the justice system that could get to the bottom of this," said Miranda. After

Noriega's ouster, Miranda hoped, he could reassemble the pieces of the case.

During the Noriega years, Miranda told all witnesses to remain silent— not even to talk to friends. Someday they may be able to testify, but to do so they must stay alive now.

But Miranda didn't follow his own advice. He told all.

At one point Córdoba called up Miranda. "Do you know who's speaking to you?" Córdoba said. "Your days are numbered."

Miranda responded, "You are a coward," and then hung up. He made a tape of the conversation, and he phoned Córdoba back to play it to him. Before Spadafora's death, Córdoba's men had destroyed Miranda's Toyota Cressida with an incendiary bomb. He ran outside to shoot at them. Then in October 1987, as Miranda collected more information for a human rights report, three men with machine guns fired indiscriminately through his stables. One of his horses died.

"It's like everything in life," he said. "There is a moment when you lose fear. My death would have been a very expensive political cost. I preferred to die resisting in front of people when they take me than to die like Hugo Spadafora."

Miranda viewed Spadafora as merely the climax in an escalation of repression. Human rights groups report that violations grew after Torrijos's death in 1981 and increased after Noriega took command in August 1983, but they began to multiply a year after that—when election fraud and problems with drug cartel leaders made the Noriega leadership more vulnerable. On May 17, 1984, shortly after the election, troops detained Edwin Eredia Amaya, thinking him a member of a guerrilla group that Hugo Spadafora was said to be organizing. His body was never found.

On May 20 and 25, unknown gunmen shot at the home of opposition legislator Bertilo Mejía, a Christian Democrat who had been elected by a large majority, and at opposition leader Edgar A. De Puy. Paramilitary soldiers also shot up the clinic of opposition dentist Luis B. de Arrco.

Two months later, armed gunmen shot dead Natividad Gonzalez. At a poker game with a local farmer, Major Córdoba was told that Gonzalez, a field-worker, had been an anti-regime guerrilla in 1969 and 1970. Someone knocked on the peasant's door that night and shot him through the chest with a high-powered rifle. The crime wasn't investigated.

In August 1984 the corpse of Diomedes Gonzalez was found at the side of the Volcan–Cerro Punto road with multiple wounds. He had also been an anti-military guerrilla. Again, the crime wasn't investigated.

In May 1985, incendiary bombs destroyed the Moisés Clinical Laboratory and the Chicas Boutique, two businesses associated with opposition movements. The owners of the laboratory were leaders of a new civic movement to stop Panama's moral decline.

In August 1985, opposition doctor Mauro Zuñiga, the national director of that same civic movement, Cocina, was arrested in a busy restaurant in Santiago de Veraguas. He was brought to Chiriquí by paramilitary troops along the well-traveled Interamerican Highway. He was tortured during the trip, and marked on the back with the initials: F-8. The initials would later recur on the beheaded torso of Spadafora. Zuñiga wasn't assassinated, but was instead thrown down at the entrance of the settlement of Remedios, where he was taken by passersby to a hospital in David. Intelligence sources later discovered that F-8 was a group of Noriega's most trustworthy men, a secret society bound by murder, torture, drugs, and illicit business connections.

The pain wasn't over for the Spadafora family. Two months after his son's death, Hugo's father took his campaign for justice to Chiriquí province. He was one of the few honest politicians in the country, a mayor and later governor in Chitré province. When a poverty-stricken friend asked him to reverse a traffic ticket, Carmelo Senior refused. He paid the ticket himself.

Hugo had been the heart and soul of his family, an Italian-Panamanian clan of two sisters and three brothers. "He's a little crazy, but that's okay," Carmelo, Senior, would tell his other children when talking about Hugo. Hugo's father wouldn't rest until the killers were punished.

Carmelo Senior was obsessed with finding Hugo's head. At first he refused to bury the body after the funeral at Don Bosco church until the head was found. His children would try to distract him with games of dominoes, but he would only pick up the pieces and mumble, "Where's the head, where's the head?" He would stop in the middle of a meal, and ask his son, Carmelo, Junior, "Where's the head?"

Despite a heart condition, he traveled around the country to rally support to bring the murderers to justice. President Eric Arturo Delvalle refused to help him; that made him work all the harder. His doctor told him to be careful, but his son's death made that impossible. Yet the fight was too much for his weak heart. Before he could speak to the crowd of 3,000 that had gathered at David city's cultural hall, he died in the arms of his son. Carmelo, Junior, considered his father's passing as much a murder as that of his brother.

"When burying him, I thought I wanted a vendetta," he said. "But now I just feel sick. To feel impotence is the worst thing in the world, and that is what I felt. I hope he is on Delvalle's conscience."

Noriega dissuaded friends of the family from helping. Few would hire Carmelo, Junior, and Noriega's people constantly monitored him. Restaurant owners were interrogated after they served him. Friends were told not to drive with him because he might have an accident. Hugo's brother Winston, a lawyer, had been the most active in fighting Noriega, but when friends offered him legal work in Panama, they found their cases took far longer to come to trial and often ended unsuccessfully. When Hugo's sister killed another driver in a car accident, the government-controlled newspaper played the story on the front page, calling her an "assassin" who was acting out her anger.

"The family was alone," Carmelo said. "Few of our friends could bear the PDF pressure."

Now Carmelo, Junior, is dying slowly of cancer.

Carmelo also wondered why Washington didn't help, although it seemed the U.S. knew what had happened. Two former intelligence officials who monitored Panama at that time have confirmed the existence of a tape monitoring a telephone conversation between Noriega in Paris and one of his officers in Panama on the evening of the killing. The call occurred at about midnight, Paris time.

Calls to Noriega were patched through satellite from Noriega's house in Panama City, so that those having his bedroom number could call him anywhere in the world. However, the use of the line, which was provided to Noriega by the Americans, also opened it up to interception.

A voice, which appeared to be that of Córdoba, said, "We have the rabid dog in our hands."

Noriega's voice is more distinguishable. "And what does one do with a dog that has rabies?"

The answer, obviously, is to exterminate it.

So why behead Spadafora?

Panamanians cite Noriega's belief in voodoo as one possibility. Among the lower classes that make up the bulk of the Panamanian Defense Force, superstitions run high. Some Panamanians speculate that Noriega believed a victim couldn't come back to haunt his killer if the head was severed from the body.

Noriega, a superstitious man, must wonder. For most Panamanians, the grisly death of Hugo Spadafora was Noriega's first fatal error en route to his own downfall. It was a subject he wouldn't discuss and his advisers wouldn't dare mention. But, once, when Noriega was drunk, he told a close friend that he sometimes saw Hugo's torso in his nightmares. It chased him down a nondescript street. No matter how quickly he ran, he couldn't escape. His legs grew heavy, and Hugo closed the gap. Noriega said he always awakened before being caught.

What can the dream signify? he asked the friend.

Noriega then changed the subject, not wanting to hear an answer.

CHAPTER
TEN

THE BARLETTA
OUSTER

*Listen to me. The day will come when you are sorry for
what you are doing. Remember my words.*

— PRESIDENT BARLETTA TO NORIEGA,
SEPTEMBER 27, 1985

A week after Hugo Spadafora's beheading, Manuel Antonio Noriega was
getting facial treatments in Geneva. Noriega had opted to sit out the
political storm in Europe, a characteristic response. The General calculated that not rushing back would prove his innocence and also put the
onus on his subordinates to solve the crisis.

In Switzerland, Noriega could also look after his twin passions: money
and dermatology. His chief financier worked out of Geneva, as did his
favorite skin doctor. His close aide and financial bookkeeper, Teresita
Chishan, had made the appointment. Noriega had tried every salve and
doctor possible in America and Europe to repair his pitted skin, convinced
that his appearance was the root of his political problems. Plastic surgeons
had said the problem was too extensive to be remedied by surgery. Miracle
salves from Switzerland seemed to help temporarily, but he needed to
return frequently for treatments.

Colonel Marco Justine gave Noriega regular reports on the Spadafora
situation—sometimes five times a day or more. On Saturday, September
21, he told Noriega that President Nicholás Ardito Barletta was planning
to appoint an independent commission to investigate the murder. Barletta
had long been friends with Spadafora's father. Justine told Noriega that
Barletta was frustrated he'd been unable to speak to Noriega. Barletta

insisted that they talk before he left on Monday for the United Nations General Assembly.

For Panamanians, Barletta was an unlikely president, and over his year of rule he had made enemies at an alarming pace through his stubbornness and honesty. His arrogance made him a hard man to advise on the byzantine needs of ruling Panama, requiring back-room dealing and corruption that baffled Barletta. He also expected Germanic traits of his Latin employees, who weren't accustomed to a hard-driving boss who wanted them to be at work early and to quit late. And many years in Washington at the World Bank had left him without the loyal political allies in Panama who might have protected him against the private intrigues of leftist politicians and military officers, with whom he hadn't shared the political wealth generously enough.

Barletta was a serious economist in a passionate country. Even his closest friends thought he would have been better off ruling Sweden than this Panamanian Phoenicia of wheeler-dealers, where mistrust and deception are the rules of play.

Noriega phoned this troublesome president from Geneva the day after Justine's warning. Noriega warned him not to allow the Spadafora case to be used as a political football. He spoke slowly, so Barletta wouldn't miss hearing. Remain close to the defense forces at this moment, he said. Don't play into the hands of the opposition.

Barletta asked Noriega to return to Panama. It wasn't good for both of them to be out of the country at this time of crisis, Barletta said. Noriega said he would return on Tuesday through New York, and that the two of them could discuss matters there before he returned to Panama.

Barletta then told him that he wanted to create a commission to investigate the Spadafora murder, and he waited to hear Noriega's response. Noriega didn't seem to oppose the idea, but merely listened, in silence, which Barletta saw as a green light to forge ahead—a costly miscalculation.

Consequently, on Monday, Barletta gave instructions to form an independent commission to investigate the Spadafora killing. He told subordinates, led by then vice president Eric Arturo Delvalle, to assemble its members. What Barletta didn't know was that Delvalle was already engaged in a conspiracy against him. The plotting had begun months earlier, after Barletta had found that he lacked the political backing—and, his enemies said, skill—to push through unpopular austerity measures needed to implement his economic reform package and gain International Monetary Fund support.

Yet when Barletta made a decision, he was maniacal about its implementation. He phoned his chief of staff, José Fierro, from an interim stop in Miami. "Has the commission been formed?" he asked.

Fierro protested that he had barely had time to return from the airport. "You have to hurry," said Barletta. "Move it."

Fierro, Barletta's closest confidant, thought Barletta wanted to use the controversy to recapture lost ground from the military. In April, he had been forced to give up several cabinet positions to Noriega in exchange for military and ruling-party support for his economic reform programs. PDF chief of staff Díaz Herrera considered Barletta's "compromise" a critical error that only a political amateur would have made: having supporters in powerful positions was far more critical than passing any transitory policy measure. "But we would have kicked him out then if he hadn't done it," laughs Díaz Herrera now.

When he arrived in New York, Barletta placed a call to a man regarded as the American official closest to Noriega in the U.S. government, Nestor Sanchez. Sanchez was the assistant secretary of defense for Latin America in the International Security Affairs Bureau of the Pentagon. Sanchez had also known Noriega as a Latin American expert at the CIA.

How are you getting along? asked Nestor.

Barletta said he was all right, but he needed some U.S. backing to keep the military in check. "You have to help me with these guys," he said.

Yes, we'll do it, Sanchez said, but he also insisted that Barletta himself had to make special efforts to get along with Noriega and his brass.

Barletta frowned at this less than wholehearted support. He was doubly nervous because an "F-8" had been painted in a rear window of the Panamanian government plane that had brought him to New York. It was the same F-8 that had been tattooed a month earlier on the shoulder of Dr. Mauro Zuñiga when he had been kidnapped and tortured after having started a civic action group against Noriega. The action against Zuñiga was on Barletta's birthday—a not so subtle message that Barletta should be tougher on political opposition. It was the same F-8 that had been found etched with a knife into Spadafora's headless torso. The repetition had raised worries among American human rights groups that some sort of death squad might be operating in Panama. Was Barletta the next target?

Noriega arrived in New York on Tuesday afternoon, September 24, and went to his usual suite at the Helmsley Palace hotel, a short walk from the United Nations. But meeting Barletta was the last thing on his mind. A CIA official had come to brief him. Noriega would later tell friends that it was Duane "Dewey" Clarridge, who had grown close to him as the chief of the Latin American directorate.

The agency was concerned by intelligence it had gathered in Panama that Colonel Díaz Herrera, Noriega's number two and a man Langley had pegged as a communist, was trying to turn the Spadafora killing into a military coup against Noriega. At the time CIA Director William Casey was in the middle of an operation with the NSC's Oliver North to sidestep congressional restrictions on arming and financing Nicaraguan Resistance fighters. Noriega had been helpful in allowing the use of airfields and in providing some funds, and he had recently agreed to train a small group of Nicaraguan Resistance officers who would serve on the Southern Front, Nicaragua's border with Costa Rica. Díaz Herrera was the enemy, and he had to be stopped.

Noriega's rivalry with Díaz Herrera had begun in Lima, Peru, in 1959, when Noriega had tried to steal Díaz Herrera's "Mrs. Robinson," an older woman who ironed for and fed the young cadet. Noriega had looked down on Díaz Herrera, who was at the police academy, a lesser school than his Chorrillos Military Academy. Díaz Herrera looked down on Noriega, a shy and homely cadet, whose brother at the embassy was homosexual.

From the beginning, their battle was more personal than political. Díaz Herrera was an inch shorter than Noriega, but his skin was lighter, his complexion smoother, and his language more flowing. Torrijos made his cousin Díaz Herrera a political officer, a front man presentable enough to deal with "popular movements"—leftist unions, student groups, and political factions. In contrast, Torrijos thought Noriega's introversion made him the perfect intelligence officer, who thrived in a world of dark deception. "I always thought he became an intelligence officer because he couldn't get information through normal conversations like other people," said Díaz Herrera years later.

Both men were obsessed with money and beautiful women, and they surrounded themselves with as much of both as possible. In the macho world of Latin American militaries, it was a measure of leadership capability. Díaz Herrera liked artists and dancers, and Noriega was jealous of his connections to both. Noriega took one well-known Panamanian ballet dancer to the side, after he had heard that Díaz Herrera was the Sugar Daddy sponsoring her career. "Find yourself another Godfather," Noriega said cryptically.

Noriega was particularly jealous of Díaz Herrera's relationship with a former Miss Panama, Gabriele DeLeuze, a strikingly beautiful woman with legs that seemed about as long as Díaz Herrera was tall. Noriega shipped her off to Panama's embassy in Paris to show Díaz Herrera who ruled the country—and its women. Díaz Herrera wondered why Noriega needed to do this: he was already having an affair with another Miss Panama. Why couldn't each have his own Miss Panama?

The Miss Panama affair reminded Díaz Herrera of an evening in Chiriquí province in late 1969. Díaz Herrera had come to a party with a woman more beautiful, blonde, and light-complected than Noriega's date. Noriega had been named commander of the province, and Díaz Herrera was on his turf. Noriega ignored his own date, and instead stared at Díaz Herrera's girlfriend until she grew uncomfortable and walked away. Within earshot of her, he asked Díaz Herrera, Do you mind if I take her.

"Yes, tonight I mind," said Díaz Herrera. "Later, I don't know."

Noriega was persistent, and a month later he began an affair with the woman.

"I sometimes think he doesn't have a real interest in sex or money, but he is just moved by power itself," Díaz Herrera would say years later. "I was never after his girls, but he always looked to mine. The problem is he never knew what he wanted from power. He had the economic power, status; he could have had the women he wanted—by conquering them or buying them. He shouldn't have had any complaints from life. But he was a man who was never pleased. I've rarely seen him relaxed. He was tense, even at parties."

The information the CIA provided Noriega on Díaz Herrera's plotting was fragmentary, but the General could at least be sure that Langley was firmly on his side. Much as Noriega hated him, Díaz Herrera's threatening presence as his number two was good insurance for American backing. As long as he remained, Washington was unlikely to turn on Noriega. After the meeting, Noriega asked his chief political advisers in Panama, José Blandón and Major Felipe Camargo, to fly to New York to brief him. He wanted to arrive in Panama fully prepared. They brought along Noriega's doctor, Carlos Garcia, and his barber, whose thankless task was to shave Noriega's uneven face.

Blandón walked into Noriega's usual suite at the Helmsley Palace at midday on September 25. Flower arrangements or fruit baskets sat on almost every table. Blandón knew they were either from Noriega's bankers, Luxembourg-based and Pakistani-owned Bank for Credit and Commerce International, who arranged all his travel and lodging in New York, or from Leona Helmsley herself (who had left a personal welcome note). Noriega was a good customer. An empty bottle of Dom Perignon champagne sat in a silver bucket on another table—leftovers from the previous evening's frolicking. Noriega emerged in a bathrobe, apparently having just awakened. He didn't seem in any hurry to return to Panama, and he told Blandón he planned to remain in New York a couple of days to attend to business.

Blandón's first question was predictable, but it still surprised Noriega. "Who killed Spadafora?" he asked.

I didn't kill him, insisted Noriega. It was Córdoba. He was trying to please me. Noriega didn't seem nervous. He simply stated fact. Blandón worried that Noriega didn't understand the political explosiveness of the killing.

Blandón summarized for Noriega the events since Spadafora's death: the opposition's propaganda efforts, the efforts to provide a false witness, Díaz Herrera's plotting, Barletta's move to create a commission, and the Spadafora family's outrage. "You have to return to Panama," he said. "The situation is more serious than you believe."

Noriega went into action. He told Blandón to hunt down the pilots and the chauffeur. They would fly home right away. But first Noriega would impress Blandón with his links to Langley. He said he would call his "friend Casey" to clear the plane for unhindered takeoff from La Guardia airport in New York. Noriega did call someone, but he spoke in Spanish. "We have a serious problem in Panama," he said. "We'll need some help at the airport."

Soon, Noriega, Blandón, and Camargo were sitting nervously in rush-hour traffic, in their stretch limousine. When they arrived at La Guardia their plane was bumped ahead of a long line on the runway, having been granted priority for takeoff, apparently after a call from the CIA's Langley headquarters.

En route to Panama, Blandón outlined how the Spadafora problem had gone from bad to worse. He recounted a meeting of Noriega's political intelligence group, led by Blandón, at which Major Nivaldo Madriñan reported that the CIA's Costa Rican station chief, Tomás Castillo, was providing someone who would prove Spadafora had never left Costa Rica. Madriñan's chief investigator, Domitillo Córdoba—no relation to Luis Córdoba—had left the meeting to pick him up.

The witness, a German-born electrician named Manfred Hoffman Wittenberg, had previously worked for the CIA in Costa Rica, but he had been a flop as an eyewitness. Domitillo Córdoba and Madriñan had questioned Hoffman before television cameras, and parts of the tape had been shown to a national audience. The result had been disastrous.

Díaz Herrera introduced him as a ". . . German citizen by birth but who carried a Panamanian identification card issued to foreigners, and who works in the area of Central America—Costa Rica, Honduras, and Panama." The electrician, who sometimes contradicted himself, said the El Salvadoran government had known about Spadafora's kidnapping and that leftist guerrillas from that country had been responsible for his killing in Costa Rica.

His tale was so unbelievable and disjointed that it only increased public suspicion of Noriega. El Salvadoran authorities denied any knowledge, and

Costa Rican investigators would state categorically that the murder had taken place in Panama. Hoffman was flown out of the country the next day, and the chief eyewitness for the government case never reappeared—increasing an almost universal conviction that Noriega was behind the killing.

"The guy in Costa Rica is a son of a bitch," said Blandón. "He was supposed to send someone serious. This problem will remain in the minds of people unless we make drastic changes."

In methodical fashion, Blandón listed Noriega's alternatives:

—He could prosecute and punish Spadafora's killers.

—He could allow Barletta to go ahead with his commission.

—Or—the alternative Blandón was pushing —Noriega could oust Barletta and replace him with Delvalle. Blandón had never liked Barletta and had actively conspired against him for several months. He considered Barletta incompetent and too tied to the economic reform ideas of the IMF and the World Bank, which the Panamanian left rejected. Barletta thought Blandón had turned against him because he had removed him from his lucrative and politically powerful job as head of the country's power company. Blandón, ambitious for power, was working with Díaz Herrera and Delvalle to provoke Barletta's downfall.

Blandón told Noriega that Barletta was finished as president, no matter what he did regarding Spadafora. "With Barletta, you will only have more chaos," he said. "He is a man without political skill." On the other hand, Blandón warned Noriega that if he ousted Barletta, he would have to retreat politically and allow Delvalle to strengthen civilian leadership. Noriega nodded. He would take Blandón's advice.

When Noriega landed at 2 A.M. on September 26, the stage had been set by Díaz Herrera, Blandón, and others. Key politicians and officers were called to a meeting at the National Assembly building, and Barletta's removal was presented as a fait accompli.

But Barletta assumed Panama's political struggle was now between Díaz Herrera and Noriega, and in this fight he was on Noriega's side. Barletta thought he had cleverly solved his conflict with Noriega at a meeting on September 3 where he had allowed the General to pick his favorite option for economic policy—ending months of debate over the matter and allowing Barletta to outmaneuver Díaz Herrera. What Barletta had overlooked again was that Panama's politics were highly personalized and conspiratorial. Policy is secondary to power. Economic policy was the last of the military's concerns. Preserving the PDF's unity and his own power was Noriega's primary worry. Civilian politicians were expendable; the military's unity was foremost.

Barletta's suspicions about the military rivalry were correct, but Díaz Herrera's coup efforts had already failed. Noriega's chief of staff had furtively sought support from several officers, each of whom said he'd go along if Díaz Herrera could co-opt certain key colonels who controlled troops, but Noriega's hold on the brass was firmer than Díaz Herrera had thought. He hadn't realized how far the spoils system of Noriega, Inc., had reached. Plentiful illicit funds had bought allegiance through the defense forces. Díaz Herrera said that the most senior officers received monthly cash bonuses—in brown envelopes, distributed by the PDF treasurer—that exceeded $20,000. Those closest to Noriega's businesses earned even more. Díaz Herrera had a silvery tongue, but Noriega had a Midas touch.

Díaz Herrera found that Noriega also had the gringos.

After Díaz Herrera had successfully moved some loyal troops to Panama City streets, a worried American general had phoned him. What are you up to? asked General John Galvin, the head of the United States Southern Command in Panama. What's going on there? Díaz Herrera, a nervous man anyway, worried that the Americans were onto him. He had to cover his tracks quickly and save his job, and he saw Barletta's ouster as the only way to deflect attention from himself and underline his loyalty to Noriega.

So Díaz Herrera began to set a trap for Barletta. He phoned his foreign minister, Jorge Abadía, who had been a Noriega ally since they had helped bring Torrijos back to power in December 1969. At Díaz Herrera's order, Abadía dutifully told Barletta that he should go back to Panama as soon as possible. But Barletta still balked. He had too many important meetings.

At his reception that night, Barletta learned that Hurricane Gloria could close New York airports all weekend and again tried in vain to reach Vice President Delvalle. Esquivel and Fierro both advised him to return home. So Barletta ordered his plane to be prepared for takeoff that night. He wanted to beat Hurricane Gloria, not realizing that a far more perilous political storm awaited him in Panama City.

Barletta phoned Noriega, but Colonel Justine said he was sleeping—jet-lagged from his trip. Justine said he was pleased Barletta was returning. We want to talk to you about "some things" privately, he said.

When former Ambassador Gabriel Lewis heard Barletta was flying home, he phoned from a booth on Madison Avenue. His friends in the military left no question in his mind that Noriega was setting the president up. Stay here, Lewis pleaded, figuring Barletta would have a better chance to hang onto his position after lobbying in Washington. Ever stubborn, Barletta refused. Heeding his aides' advice, he was obsessed with beating Hurricane Gloria to the airport, but he wondered throughout his flight home if he had made the wrong decision.

When Barletta arrived at Panama City's international airport just past dawn on September 27, he was worried that Delvalle hadn't come to greet him. More ominous yet was Díaz Herrera's phone call at the airport.

"We need to see you right away," he said. "Come to the Comandancia."

Barletta turned stone silent. Díaz Herrera knew he had been too pushy. "Nicky, don't worry," he said. "There's no problem. Everything is normal." But Barletta was now alerted to the danger.

The military could come to his office if they wanted to see him, Barletta thought angrily, but Foreign Minister Abadía came by Barletta's home, where the president was changing and showering, and urged Barletta to go to the Comandancia.

"They are suspicious enough about you," Abadía said. "If you go to see them at the Comandancia, it could help ease frictions." Noriega's spy in the cabinet was doing his dirty work, but Barletta didn't know the extent of Abadía's business and personal ties to the military. He took Abadía's advice, but said he first wanted to talk to Noriega. He feared Noriega might have been imprisoned by Díaz Herrera.

However, Noriega sounded cheerful when Barletta phoned him at 9 A.M. and apologized for not having contacted his president in New York.

I wanted to call you, said Noriega. But you were so busy with your meetings, and I thought I should hurry back here. So what's happened to you? We were expecting you to drop by.

Abadía then personally drove Barletta to Noriega's trap. After having flown all night, Barletta walked into the General's office at about 9 A.M.; he was Noriega's prisoner for the next fourteen hours.

Noriega's office was Barletta's spacious cell. The General had taken Torrijos's more modest quarters and then knocked down the walls of the two adjoining rooms to create a regal hall, carpeted in plush, tacky red and decorated with memorabilia from all over the world: a golden Buddha, a brass menorah from Israel, and Chinese vases. He also had his collection of porcelain frogs, the *sapos*. Photo books sat on a large coffee table, and pictures of Noriega with various world leaders and military commanders hung on the walls.

The office, as usual, was cold. Noriega always kept the air conditioner on its chilliest setting, explaining to guests that the low temperature kept him sharp. He wore a military jacket, but Barletta had only a thin shirt, in which he shivered.

Díaz Herrera and Colonel Marco Justine sat nearby, as Noriega broke the news to his president. A seditious movement had begun in Panama that Barletta had assisted, said Noriega. He said everyone in the room had concluded that Barletta should resign. "We are your friends, Mr. President," he said respectfully. "You can have anything you want from us. If you want to be ambassador, you can be ambassador."

Barletta answered simply. "Why should I go? I don't see any reason."

"We have to take care of this problem," said Noriega. "We can't do it with you."

Barletta replied. "If you tell me exactly what's going on, we could work together and get rid of it. It can only get worse without me."

Noriega didn't want Barletta to know what was going on, yet Panama's president was determined to resist the ouster effort and to buy time. Perhaps Washington would intervene if it knew democracy was in danger in Panama. Washington was his last hope, and he had to get word out so that the Reagan administration could act.

Barletta turned cold and silent. Noriega's soft sell was converted into Colonel Díaz Herrera's heavy pressure. Barletta's removal was a convenience for Noriega, but it was a matter of survival for his chief of staff.

"You have been a traitor to us," said Díaz Herrera. "Sedition is a national security problem. At times of national security difficulties, we have to defend the integrity of the defense forces. That integrity can't be maintained with you as president." Díaz Herrera said Barletta's treason was in trying to create a commission to investigate the Spadafora crime, a commission whose aim was to implicate Noriega and the defense forces. Díaz Herrera charged that Barletta was stacking the commission with "enemies of the defense forces."

"They are friendly to my government," Barletta said. He said only independent-minded commission members would ensure the commission's public credibility. "If you don't support this position, everyone in Panama is going to think you killed Spadafora," said Barletta.

"We, the general staff, and all the majors have come to the very delicate decision, that we support unanimously, that you have to go because you have been a traitor," Díaz Herrera repeated. "For the sake of saving the unity of the defense forces and the country, you must go. You choose how you want to do it, but it is an inflexible decision. You can resign or you can be removed by the National Assembly."

Barletta asked to call his secretary, seeing his situation might be irretrievable. He whispered to her that she should remove all his private papers from his office. She said Elliott Abrams had called. The conservative assistant secretary of state for Latin American affairs had taken his job only in July, and Barletta didn't know him well. Yet this was his chance. He took down the number and dialed it immediately, before Noriega could intervene.

"How are you?" asked Abrams, having received reports that Barletta had been called to the Comandancia and that Noriega was demanding his resignation because of the controversy regarding the Spadafora commission. Abrams wanted to buck up Barletta.

"How are you?" repeated Abrams with more urgency.

Barletta answered that the situation was difficult, but that he was all right.

"Hang on, hang tough," said Abrams. "Do not resign. We are supporting you."

Barletta's spirits were raised.

"That's exactly what I am doing," he said. "Now you get busy and do something about it, because I'm staying put." Barletta was more confident help might be on the way. But after he got off the phone, he feared he hadn't said enough. Was the message to Abrams sufficiently clear? Did he know that Barletta was being held hostage? He feared his circumspection had botched a key opportunity.

And he was right. "What we got out of it was no request for action at all on our part," said Abrams later. Yet a more explicit request might not have done him any good. Abrams, just six weeks in office, wasn't yet the forceful campaigner who would make so many enemies later. And most U.S. officials believed Barletta was in office only because Noriega put him there through a fraudulent election and that he hadn't been an effective politician thereafter. "There was nothing in it for the United States to move," Abrams said.

Díaz Herrera called in more firepower at 3 P.M., a group of prominent parliamentarians from the ruling Democratic Revolutionary Party, better known as the PRD. Most of them preferred Delvalle, having watched Barletta bungle the intricate politics of Panama as he tried to gain support for tax increases and an austerity program.

Barletta looked into their frightened eyes. Finally, Jerry Wilson, a friend of Barletta in the parliament, said what they were all thinking. "If you don't do this, we are all going to have to go," he said. The PRD, which had been losing faith in Barletta, had decided it was better to lose its troublesome president than to lose all power to the military. Barletta saw even his friends weren't ready to defend him.

"What excuse will you give for my resignation?" asked Barletta. "That there is a disagreement over the Spadafora commission?"

Rigoberto Paredes, the cruelest and most opportunist of those in the room, dismissed Barletta. "You honestly believe in the measures of IMF and the World Bank. And we disagree with that. That's what we will tell the outside world."

Díaz Herrera laughed malignantly as the parliamentarians trooped out of the room. "I told you the PRD is ours," he told Barletta. "Nobody else's."

Barletta, still waiting for Washington's charging white horses, stalled by asking to meet with Noriega's general staff. He also held out hope that the right appeal to Noriega's senior officers might still save him. They arrived an hour later.

"I have been called a traitor and asked to resign," he said. "I am not a traitor, and there is no reason for me to resign. Whatever problems we have, need to be solved together. My departure can only make matters worse."

He talked emotionally about the Torrijos period, how the father of their movement had entrusted him with economic planning. He spoke of December 16, 1969, when coup makers had taken leftist politician Rómulo Escobar Bethancourt into custody. He had looked out for Escobar at the time, he said, pointing to the politician who sat with him and the general staff. Escobar nodded assent.

But Díaz Herrera interrupted with another tirade. Even this artful persuasion was too late. The general staff left, and it was clear the die had been cast. Díaz Herrera gave Barletta the paper on which he was ordered to write his letter of resignation.

Noriega came in at 7 P.M., after a long absence, while Barletta continued to delay. Noriega answered a phone call from across the room, but he spoke loud enough for Barletta to hear clearly. "No, Nestor, yes, Nestor. It's all going to be constitutional, Nestor. Don't worry."

It was as if the conversation had been staged for Barletta. Nestor Sanchez, a senior Pentagon official, was carrying a message from the administration. Sanchez, chosen for the job because he knew Noriega well, later said he found the message urging constitutional measures was too soft, but his instructions—and message—had come from Elliott Abrams.

Abrams denies Sanchez's assertion. He said that Sanchez, who was a CIA official in Central America for more than three decades, would consistently resist putting pressure on Noriega in the months to come, to the point that the State Department stopped trusting him as the messenger to Noriega. "No single person in the course of 1985 and 1986 more strongly argued the view that State Department opposition to Noriega was hopelessly quixotic," said Abrams.

Whoever gave the orders, Sanchez's message helped seal Barletta's fate. "We would consider it very bad if you were to break the constitution," Sanchez said at the time. Noriega interpreted the call as giving him a free hand to remove Barletta, as long as he followed the constitution and replaced him with vice president Delvalle, a Jewish Panamanian who had many friends among pro-Israel lobbyist groups and senators on Capitol Hill. Delvalle would allow Noriega to cover his U.S. flank.

The call demoralized Barletta. Without realizing it, the U.S. was a silent
partner in the negotiations in Noriega's office, and it had just cast its lot.
But Barletta opted to use his own constitutional trick in his letter. Instead
of resigning, he would "separate" himself from office, which a president
is allowed to do for ninety days. Even if ousted, Barletta hoped this
maneuver might buy him time to make a comeback.

He finished writing at 8 P.M., pleased with having discovered this loophole, and Díaz Herrera offered him his first food in twelve hours. The wary
president refused the fish soup, however, unless he could see it spooned
from a communal pot. He was afraid of being poisoned. So he ate in the
mess hall with other officers.

When his letter was brought back, Barletta edited it and sent it back for
retyping—only to buy more time. At 9 P.M., Díaz Herrera allowed Barletta
to call his wife. She said government-owned TV 2 had announced his
resignation. Barletta was livid. He hadn't yet resigned, and he wanted to
announce the move himself, so that the subtlety of his "separation" language wouldn't be missed. Noriega had double-crossed him. He told his
wife to alert the press that he hadn't stepped down, and he refused to sign
the letter that he had written.

Barletta angrily rose from his chair and tried to leave Noriega's office
and return to the Presidential Palace. Díaz Herrera forcefully held him
back. Barletta could not leave unless he signed the letter, the colonel said.
Díaz Herrera also demanded that Barletta remove from the letter that the
PDF was responsible for his "separation." Barletta refused.

At 11 P.M., Colonel Díaz Herrera showed his trump card. "If you love
your family dearly, you'd better think twice about your decision not to
sign," he said. "Our decision is firm." Díaz Herrera stormed out of the
room and slammed the door behind him.

Rómulo Escobar walked in a few minutes later to underline the threat
in a softer tone. "These guys will do anything," he said. "Once they've
made a decision, there's nothing you can do about it."

Demoralized, weary and worried about his family, Barletta signed his
"separation" from office.

"Listen to me," he told Noriega. "The day will come when you are sorry
for what you are doing. Remember my words."

Barletta saw one last chance. He would go on television and say he had
been pressured to step down, but then explain that the "separation" wasn't
permanent. Barletta issued orders to the secretary who handled his TV
appearances. Noriega controlled the channels, however, and he wouldn't
allow a live message, so Barletta made a tape of his announcement with
cabinet members at 4 A.M. The "separation" nicety was lost. The official

U.S. embassy transcript even translated the Spanish word for separation as "resignation." Barletta was frustrated—and finished.

To avoid any misunderstanding, embassy officials, at that time, used the translation given them by the PDF. "The U.S. embassy translation was a political decision, not a translation mistake," Barletta said later. "My future wasn't a legal matter, it was a political matter."

After having his movements restricted for several weeks, Barletta flew to New York two months later to make a last stab at turning events around. Under his "separation," he thought he had ninety days to make a comeback. However, advisers to Barletta in Washington told him the Reagan administration's fixation on Nicaragua was total, and his own fate was final. Shultz might have come to his inauguration despite ample evidence of election fraud, but Shultz wasn't willing to fight now for "Nicky," as he called this former University of Chicago student. "We all basically thought he had compromised himself by resigning and by having taken the job in the first place," said Abrams later.

Barletta's ouster had spurred an interagency review of Panamanian policy, but the administration opted to put the problem on the shelf: Washington had to sacrifice democracy in Panama for the sake of the Contras. The administration would swallow the Barletta ouster, and Washington would instead press Noriega for free elections in 1989.

Assistant Secretary of State Elliott Abrams argued against the suggestion of Washington's ambassador to Panama, Everett Ellis Briggs, that the administration continue to recognize Barletta as the legitimate president. Briggs's proposal was essentially to do then what President Reagan would do more than two years later—to reject the military's removal of a sitting president and continue to recognize his regime as legitimate. But he was overruled by the Contra-mad Reagan administration.

What Barletta didn't know, even as president, was that Noriega had been quietly providing the CIA enough help in its Nicaraguan war to ensure his protection by some of Washington's most influential power brokers. He had convinced William Casey at the CIA and Oliver North in the White House that he could be an invaluable ally in their covert programs even if he did always promise more than he delivered. The intelligence community felt that the loss of a president, who had been elected through fraudulent means anyway, was far less dangerous to them than a Díaz Herrera dictatorship—which might have undermined their private Contra war.

They considered the Barletta ouster unfortunate, but perhaps the best possible outcome under the circumstances.

CHAPTER
ELEVEN

NORIEGA AND THE CONTRAS

Relations between Panama and the United States must be maintained because we are partners in a mission. . . . We are in a period which requires maturity and an official seriousness in this regard.

—GENERAL NORIEGA, OCTOBER 2, 1986

On the sunbaked morning of March 6, 1985, a series of explosions rocked Managua with such force that many residents feared an earthquake like the one that had flattened their city more than a dozen years earlier.

Many took refuge under tables. Others ran into the streets, so that their homes wouldn't collapse on top of them. A whole hillside was engulfed in flames. Soldiers ran wildly down the street from the area of the blast, while huge blocks of concrete fell around them.

The explosion ripped through Managua's military headquarters complex, which housed barracks, officers' quarters, and the munitions dump, where the blast had occurred. Miraculously, no one died, but that wasn't the aim anyway. The goal of the operation, which had originated in Oliver North's National Security Council office, was to show that the Contras could strike anywhere in the country at will. And it was precisely to avoid that impression that Nicaraguan investigators declared the explosion "accidental" after a superficial, week-long investigation.

As it happens, the Contras probably didn't have the capability to conduct regular urban raids on military targets inside Managua. In fact, only one foreign intelligence agency inside Nicaragua had the know-how, the means, and motivation. It belonged to Panama's Manuel Antonio Noriega.

In an effort to curry favor with Washington, the Panamanian General had helped carry out the sabotage in a scheme devised by British mercenary David Walker and North. Although Noriega hadn't masterminded the operation, he had proved indispensable to it; the United States, Walker, and the Contras lacked Noriega's ability to infiltrate Nicaragua. Noriega's network in Managua not only provided intelligence to map out the operation, but demolition experts to set and trigger the explosive devices.

By helping the March 1985 attack in Managua, Noriega was playing a game that had become familiar to him: he was offering American intelligence a minimum of help and extracting from it maximum protection. The environment at the time was perfect for breathing new life into a U.S.–Noriega marriage of convenience.

Noriega knew Washington's help had never been more vital to protect him while his domestic political fortunes declined and his role in the drug trade—and his problems with it—increased. And Oliver North and his allies, facing a congressional ban on military aid to the Contras, were desperate to find allies to prevent the Contras' defeat.

The Reagan administration hence trod a well-worn path; it overlooked mounting evidence of Noriega's crimes because he served narrow, immediate interests. The Reagan administration's covert operators were running full speed ahead with their Contra blinders on. Yet Noriega, whom the State Department officials had taken to calling "rent-a-colonel," continued to feed the appetite of Nicaraguan and Cuban intelligence services at the same time his men were helping to blow up the Sandinista arsenal. Noriega was characteristically playing all sides. The game was getting riskier as the stakes grew higher, but like a gambler who was too far in the hole to quit, Noriega couldn't stop rolling the dice now.

Oliver North knew Noriega was "double-dipping" and distrusted the General's assurances that the Americans always came first, but he hadn't anyone else to turn to in Nicaragua. Noriega had the only friendly and relatively reliable intelligence service in Managua, North told colleagues. Noriega regularly promised more assistance to the Contras than he delivered, but he also delivered more than others in the region. And North was taking help where he could get it—the Israelis, the Saudis, the Sultan of Brunei—so why not Noriega? This was a war—on communism and the Congress—and Noriega was an ally.

Noriega's covert partner for the March 1985 attack was David Walker, a veteran of British military special operations, who organized the assault. Walker, a former commander of the 22nd Special Air Services regiment, better known as the SAS, had served in Northern Ireland and South America before leaving the service in 1974 as a major. To all appearances, he had retreated to a quiet life as a Conservative party official in the Surrey town of Esher.

Unbeknownst to his neighbors, however, Walker had begun running his own sort of special operations, often with the blessing, if not the explicit instructions, of Her Majesty's government.

Walker's first job after retirement was with Control Risks, one of a new breed of powerful security companies that focused on kidnap negotiations. Control Risks' officials had spent much time in Panama, negotiating the resolution of kidnapping cases in which Noriega took some interest. Noriega would often act as broker between guerrilla groups in the region and families and governments of those they had kidnapped. Even when Noriega wasn't involved, Panama was often the stage for talks or for the payment of ransoms.

Even while at Control Risks, however, Walker was always more interested in its subsidiary, which he managed: the Kensington-based KMS, Ltd., "Keeny-Meeny Services." (The title comes from a Swahili word, roughly meaning "snake in the grass.") The company sold paramilitary skills to governments. In 1977, Walker bought the company and struck out on his own, taking on former SAS colleagues as his troops. The demand for his services, which included providing Saudi sheikhs with bodyguards and counterinsurgency troops with military training, made him rich.

His new occupation gave him reason to renew links to the United States that he had made years earlier. The British army had paid for Walker to study engineering at Cambridge, where he began a friendship with John Lehman, an American from a powerful Republican family, that had lasted twenty years. They had remained close as they'd both gained rank and influence. In 1981 President Reagan picked Lehman to run the navy and while in that position, Lehman brought Walker and North together.

In December 1984, North started to plan operations with Walker while sailing on a boat from the navy yard in Washington. They hit it off on the Potomac while sharing heady ideas about covert operations. North wrote a memo to National Security Adviser Robert C. McFarlane: "This weekend, at the request of Secretary John Lehman, I met with David Walker, a former British SAS officer. Walker suggested that he would be interested in establishing an arrangement with the FDN [the Contras] for certain special operations." North said he needed help to knock out new Russian attack helicopters that could devastate the Contras; Walker suggested a sabotage mission inside Nicaragua. Among other services he provided the Contras over a two-year period, Walker helped North organize an air attack on airports and a residential area of Nicaragua's capital. North told congressmen that the attacks were cleared by President Reagan's National Security Adviser, Vice Admiral John Poindexter. The *London Daily News* said KMS, Ltd. provided fifty military veterans to train and assist the Contras. In bold headlines, it called Walker "Britain's Colonel North."

Walker's ties to North first emerged in documents given the Iran-Contra committee in 1987. In answer to a question by Democratic Representative Thomas Foley of Washington, North reluctantly conceded the link to Walker. "David Walker was involved in support of the Nicaraguan resistance with international operations in Nicaragua and elsewhere," he said, "in an effort to improve the perception that the Nicaraguan resistance could operate anywhere that it so desired."

During the hearings, North only hinted at Walker's links with Noriega. When asked by House Intelligence Committee chairman Louis Stokes whether Walker was involved in the March 6 operation, North replied simply, "It is my understanding that Mr. Walker provided two technicians involved in that. We understand that those two technicians were Panamanians." North didn't mention it was Noriega who had provided Walker with the technicians and other logistical assistance. North said Walker—and hence also Noriega—had been paid by the Nicaraguan resistance out of funds the U.S. provided.

A narrowly circulated forty-two-page document known as a "stipulation," which summarized evidence from government documents for North's criminal trial, shed more light on Noriega's role in the 1985 sabotage. One excerpt also revealed an alarming Noriega offer to murder Nicaraguan leaders on Washington's behalf. Noriega was charting a new course: the tougher his political situation became in Panama, the more he would offer in helping the Contras, until even Oliver North had to refuse.

"In late August 1986, North reported to Admiral Poindexter that a representative of Panamanian leader Manuel Noriega had asked North to meet with him. Noriega's representative proposed that, in exchange for a promise from the USG [U.S. government] to help clean up Noriega's image and a commitment to lift the USG ban on military sales to the Panamanian Defense Forces, Noriega would assassinate the Sandinista leadership for the U.S. government.

"North had told Noriega's representative that U.S. law forbade such actions," the stipulation continues. "The representative responded that Noriega had numerous assets in place in Nicaragua and could accomplish many essential things, *just as Noriega had helped the USG the previous year in blowing up a Sandinista arsenal.*" [Italics added]

Noriega had become intimately involved in North's Contra network and had become privy to details of America's secret war whose revelation would be embarrassing. For instance, the unnamed "representative" mentioned in the North stipulation was Roberto Cordovez, a former Canal Zone policeman who carried out many of Noriega's most sensitive assignments. He was a chubby, brown-haired secretive man who spoke English with a pronounced American accent and drove a black Mercedes with tinted windows. Cordovez had grown close to Noriega through his wife's best friend Vicky Amado, who by this time had become Noriega's full-time mistress—a woman he clearly favored over his wife. And Cordovez's contacts with North were also intimate, arranged by Francis G. Gomez, a former State Department and United States Information Service employee whose public relations firm, International Business Communications, was secretly employed by North to raise funds and spread propaganda for the Contras. Gomez was careful not to be paid directly by Noriega or North for his Panama work. Cordovez's company, Impulso Turistico y Financiero, paid IBC $35,000 a month for a time, and Gomez cooperated by hiring Vicky's mother, Norma Amado, to assist in his work in Panama.

Elsewhere in the stipulation, the government shed more light on the Walker-Noriega-North connection. "North advised Admiral Poindexter that the British persons who had run the operation against the arsenal had used a Panamanian civilian ordnance expert. North noted that Noriega had the capabilities that he had proffered, and that the cost of any operation could be borne by Project Democracy." "Project Democracy" was a fund-raising effort for the Contras established after Congress had banned military aid to the Resistance.

So how did the Reagan administration reach this compromising situation, in which Panama's dictator would profit and help maintain his nondemocratic rule through Oliver North's "Project Democracy"? A reconstruction shows Noriega began helping the Reagan administration with its Contra war against the Sandinistas early in the 1980s by allowing the Israelis to use Panama as a conduit for funds and weapons, and his Israeli adviser Michael Harari played a key role. Noriega's role was small, but he increased it after becoming Comandante in August 1983. It grew more intensive in 1984 and 1985 when Noriega grew more desperate for friends. It was a time of desperation, both for Noriega and his American allies.

The story of the Noriega-North relationship—and the history of Panama's halfhearted support for the Contras—is a sad lesson in how easily a small-time dictator can gain leverage over the United States through participating in a covert operation whose revelation could embarrass an American president.

The Reagan administration's first step was putting Noriega back on the payroll in 1981, at an annual rate of $185,000, thus restoring a relationship that had been shaken during the Carter administration. CIA Director William Casey invited Noriega to his house for dinner on at least two occasions, and his chief for Latin American operations, Duane R. "Dewey" Clarridge, entertained him during his long evenings in Panama.

Casey had appointed Clarridge as his Latin American division chief, and it was Clarridge—with the advice of former CIA official Nestor Sanchez—who rebuilt the contractual relationship with Noriega that Stansfield Turner had torn down. Clarridge would arrive in the region, using the alias "Dewey Maroni," bearing cigars and cognac. Noriega, who appreciated the good life himself, enjoyed his company. From the beginning, Clarridge was Casey's man, and he had readier access to Casey than any other division chief. He regularly and extensively briefed Casey on Noriega's contributions and misadventures. It was clear that Casey and Clarridge were on Noriega's side, and they were pleased when the longtime intelligence asset became commander of the Panamanian Defense Forces in August 1983.

"Noriega traveled to Washington frequently after 1982 or 1983," said José Blandón, Noriega's adviser at the time. "Every time there were significant problems, Noriega traveled alone, and at his meetings with Casey, he was alone." Blandón said Noriega was also close to Clarridge and Joe Fernandez, the Costa Rican CIA station chief who used the alias Tomás Castillo, who also would be implicated in the Iran-Contra scandal.

Noriega, the new Comandante, made clear he was willing to be more cooperative than his predecessors. He was also feeling more heat for Panama's role in laundering money for international drug traffickers, and he interpreted a George Bush visit in December 1983 as an appeal for more help for the Contras. Although Bush's conversation was almost entirely with Noriega's puppet President Ricardo de la Espriella, Noriega quietly recorded that the two major themes were Bush's worry about the Nicaraguan threat and his Panama-specific concern about money laundering. In Noriega's mind, he thought Bush was saying that if Panama helped the Contras it could defuse criticism about money laundering. He passed this interpretation to a trusted adviser.

Coincidentally, perhaps, in December 1983 the Israelis allegedly started using a CIA front company in Panama to start funneling support to the Contras. That company was IFMA Management Company, which had originally been created in 1969 in Panama as a conduit for CIA "black" funds.

Noriega's importance to Casey and Clarridge increased even more after word leaked about the CIA's controversial mining of Nicaraguan harbors in January 1984. When senators discovered what they considered an act of war, even pro-Contra Republicans turned on the administration. Casey's former defenders now joined Democrats in condemning the mining, and on April 26, 1984, Casey formally apologized before a secret session of the Senate.

The Democrats had finally succeeded in halting the funding for the Contras after the money ran out in June, and in October Congress passed a tougher version of a measure known as the Boland amendment, which had first been approved in 1982. The new amendment banned the CIA or "any other agency or entity involved in intelligence activities" from spending money to support the Contras. "There are no exceptions to the prohibition," said its sponsor, Representative Edward P. Boland of Massachusetts.

William Casey and Oliver North found a loophole, however, and Noriega was to be part of their circumvention. They decided the White House wasn't covered by the Boland amendment, and North frantically led a search for funds, weapons, and assistance for the Contras. North would create a secret account in Geneva's Crédit Suisse for a company innocuously called Lake Resources. The man who established the account, Richard V. Secord, was a veteran of covert operations dating back to Vietnam's secret air war. Secord would call this new Contra aid business "The Enterprise." North, a man who knew the turn of phrase that could capture conservative dollars, gave his operation a different name: Project Democracy.

Secord already knew Panama's value for covert operations. In 1986, a Panamanian corporation linked to Project Democracy, Energy Resources International, would purchase 158 tons of assault rifles and ammunition for the Contras, and they were shipped on a boat purchased by another Panamanian company, Dolmy Business, Inc., owned by his partner Albert Hakim.

Noriega provided early help to the Reagan administration through the Israelis, who were training and arming the Nicaraguan resistance even before the Reagan administration had turned its full energy to the battle. According to a senior Panamanian official and to José Blandón, Noriega's political adviser at the time, Michael Harari, made contacts through CIA Latin American directorate chief Dewey Clarridge and President Bush's National Security Adviser Donald Gregg to establish a network of airfields and support for the Contras. Gregg denies all involvement or that he ever met Harari.

Blandón said Noriega, through Harari, offered landing rights at three different airstrips in Panama: in Chiriquí province, in Veraguas province, and at Paitilla airport in Panama City. The early arms came from the Soviet bloc and were brought to the region through Israeli connections.

A senator's mission to Panama in January 1983 served to confirm Noriega's early role in helping the Contras. Patrick Leahy, a Vermont Democrat then on the Senate Intelligence Committee, visited Panama as part of a regional trip dedicated to reviewing U.S. intelligence activities related to Nicaragua. The fact that he stopped in Panama at all raised eyebrows, since the country's role in the war wasn't publicly known at that time. It was a rumored super-secret Contra training center that had drawn Leahy to Panama.

When Leahy told the CIA's Panama station chief that he wanted a briefing on the Nicaraguan program in Panama, the agency's man said that Clarridge—who he said had left Panama a day earlier—had instructed him not to answer such queries. Leahy protested to Washington and said he wouldn't leave Panama until he had some answers. Clarridge finally appeared at 6 A.M., knocking on Leahy's hotel door. It appeared he hadn't left the country after all.

Clarridge said Noriega was going to allow the CIA to set up a Contra training facility in Panama, but it needed to be kept secret. Noriega, who was allowing the training only somewhat reluctantly, would use any leak as an excuse to shut down the program. (Although Noriega didn't say so, a news leak could also harm his close ties with Nicaraguan and Cuban intelligence services.) Panama might seem an odd place to train Contras, but Clarridge explained that this was to prepare insurgents to hit the Sandinistas from the south in Costa Rica.

Clarridge told Leahy more about Noriega. He said Noriega had long been a CIA provider and facilitator, but Noriega played both sides and also had cozy relations with the Cubans. The U.S. gained intelligence through these ties, but who knew what the Cubans got? Leahy came away from the trip surprised that even Panama was part of an anti-Sandinista network that Casey was putting together at significant cost and trouble. His trip throughout the region convinced him that "the Nicaragua program was growing beyond that which the committee had initially understood to be its parameters."

As the congressional ban neared, Casey clearly had his eye on Noriega as an alternative source for assistance and funding for the Contras. In a memo from Casey to McFarlane headed "Supplemental Assistance to Nicaragua Program" and dated March 27, 1984, the CIA director wrote that the first alternative was the Israelis, who could provide ordnance captured from the

Palestine Liberation Organization. "The second alternative we are exploring is the procurement of assistance from Panama," he said. Casey said that Noriega had "indicated that he may be able to make some equipment and training available to the Contras through the Hondurans."

Casey's desire for Noriega's help was so great—and his relationship with Noriega had grown so close—that he made an unusual trip to Panama with North from July 31 to August 2 to drum up backing for the Contras, according to previous information from a discovery document prepared by the CIA for the Oliver North trial. It would be the first in a series of meetings with Noriega, all of which revolved around North's desire for Panamanian help and Noriega's effort to gain politically and economically through his cooperation.

Documents released for the North trial show Noriega responded to American requests in midsummer 1985 by offering financial support for the Contras, apparently as a result of the Casey mission, at about the same time. Noriega was facing his political opposition's wrath following fraudulent May 1984 elections, and he had barely concluded Castro-mediated negotiations with the Medellín cartel to avoid a potential crisis with Colombian drug dealers. The story of joint desperation was nearing a crescendo.

The North trial stipulation revealed Noriega's dramatic cooperation dryly: "A Southern Front Resistance leader had received $100,000 from Panamanian Defense Forces Chief Noriega in July 1984 and $20,000 from a European official [probably Margaret Thatcher], who had previously given $40,000." Then Vice President George Bush was among those who received copies of documents that showed Noriega's financial assistance for the Contras.

After the Boland amendment cut off military aid to the Contras in 1984, Noriega's lawyer and business representative in Geneva, Juan Bautista Castillero, helped set up Udall Research Company, one of the ten dummy corporations formed by "The Enterprise" to support the Contras. It was formed to develop an airfield in northern Costa Rica for arming the Contras. Castillero, like Noriega, played all sides. He allegedly had set up companies for many Cuban officials and for Noriega. A handful of other Panamanian corporations was also created to assist Project Democracy.

In mid-January, 1985, Lieutenant Colonel North flew to Central America—and Panama—again, this time with National Security Adviser Robert McFarlane, "to discuss with his counterparts in those countries their continued willingness to support the resistance." Others on the mission were Vice Admiral Arthur Moreau and General Paul Gorman, the commander in chief of the United States Southern Command in Panama.

The trip was triggered by the Honduran government's threat to cease backing the Contras unless "it received a signal of U.S. government support." The meetings included a session with Noriega, during which the General expressed his willingness to continue supporting the Contras. The sabotage mission inside Nicaragua was carried out two months later, but it's unclear whether it was discussed at this meeting.

But North wanted more, and Noriega complied. By the summer of 1985, North was confident enough in Noriega's goodwill that he turned to him for help in training potential Contra platoon leaders for the Southern Front. In June 1985, Oliver North contacted Noriega again through political consultant Frank Gomez, who called the General's ally Roberto Cordovez.

North and Noriega met at Balboa Harbor at 10 A.M. for a cruise, far from the suspicious eyes of Noriega's officer corps, which North believed to be infiltrated by Cuban agents.

That morning, Noriega had phoned José Blandón to ask him to meet him at Pier 17 for a meeting with "a U.S. delegate" to talk about Central America. Oliver North brought an attractive woman with him and a similarly attractive interpreter.

As the yacht cruised slowly toward the Bridge of the Americas, North and Noriega discussed Central America for one and a half hours. Blandón and North drank Cokes, and Noriega sipped oriental tea. He never drank alcohol when discussing sensitive subjects in unfamiliar territory.

The meeting began with North's expounding upon the Sandinista threat to democracy, an odd problem to be explaining to Panama's dictator. North wanted to bolster the Southern Front. He said that he had more than 2,000 new Contra soldiers ready to take arms, but they needed training. He lacked the leaders who could train and then command them. He wanted the Panamanians to take on a relatively small job: to train a small cadre of Nicaraguans—perhaps 200—as commanders of small units and communications units. They in turn would train and lead these 2,000 men for an invasion of Nicaragua from the Southern Front. To stop this incursion, North hoped the Nicaraguans would cross into defenseless Costa Rica. That would provoke international outrage and increase sympathy for the Contras, said North.

North needed the Panamanians for three reasons. The Nicaraguans in Honduras were from a different geographical area and class than the troops on the Southern Front, and they "were mixing like oil and water." The CIA's Cuban trainers also clashed with the Contras. North thought he could overcome some of these problems with Panamanians. What went unspoken was that training couldn't take place on an American base in

Panama. Noriega knew that the U.S. Congress had banned American military involvement.

Noriega thought North's confidence in the Nicaraguan resistance fighters in Costa Rica was foolhardy, but he feared that saying so would damage his relationship with the CIA, so he brought Blandón along as the front man to express his own reservations.

"From a military point of view, your plan makes sense," Blandón told North, who immediately disliked this short, arrogant Panamanian. "The problem is that you don't have the Contras to carry it out. I don't know where your two thousand men are. The Southern Front doesn't exist." Blandón said Edén Pastora was the only commander with perhaps a few hundred followers, but the CIA had turned against him.

"We know the Southern Front well," Blandón said. "This is a zone where the Contras are more interested in making business and sleeping with prostitutes than fighting. We call them café guerrillas. They fight for two hours at the border and return to Costa Rica to enjoy themselves."

North defended the Contras' abilities on the Southern Front. He said he had heard a far rosier analysis from Contra leaders Francisco Locayo and from Edgar Chamorro, a former Jesuit priest and intellectual who had been assigned to the Contra directorate by the CIA. Blandón argued that those weren't credible reports. He told North that American intelligence in the region had been abysmal for years because it had relied on such people.

Noriega interrupted. "We have reservations about your plan, Colonel," Noriega said. "But we are going to help the Contras. We'll do that for you. We are friends. We are in the same boat. If something bad happens to you, it happens to us." Noriega said that they could use training facilities at the Pana Jungula school in Bocas del Toro and the José Domingo Espinar school in Colón. The Bocas del Toro school provided special jungle training, while the Colón facility focused on training unit commanders.

North then asked Noriega if his president, Nicholás Ardito Barletta, would receive the five leaders of the Contras. They had a document they wanted to present him. North was trying to rally more regional diplomatic support for the Contras. Two weeks later, in July 1985, Barletta did receive them, and thereafter the Contras' leaders held a press conference in Panama City.

Limited training of would-be Contra officers, according to Blandón, began late that month on the island of Bocas del Toro. The officers in charge of the Colón training were to be Lieutenant Colonel Elias Castillo and Lieutenant Colonel Ojone. Training in Colón began somewhat later.

The deeper Noriega's domestic troubles grew, the more dramatic were his offers to help the Contras. After the killing of Spadafora and the ouster of Barletta, he contacted Roberto Cordovez in late September to urgently arrange a second meeting with North.

Noriega's economy was in trouble. International financial organizations were balking at helping him. His ousted president had been the World Bank's vice president. U.S. and international economic authorities were giving him the cold shoulder. This time it was Noriega who was seeking help, not North.

When Noriega wanted to keep meetings secret, he held them on his own turf at "El Ocho," his windowless, cement command building at Fort Amador, and he wore his uniform. In October 1985, Noriega received North in "El Ocho," dressed in full military regalia, with one of his captains serving as translator.

North was in a hurry. He was making an unscheduled stop at Noriega's request and had to fly on to Washington immediately. Noriega started the meeting by claiming that he had started some training. "We have made progress in our work," he said. "The reason I've called you is we need your support now. We have some problems with the economy. We need your help." Noriega wanted Uncle Sam's payoff.

At Noriega's instruction, Blandón outlined what Panama was seeking from the World Bank and the International Monetary Fund. Until it could get IMF blessing, he said, its private bankers wouldn't extend new loans or reschedule old ones. Noriega requested North's help in gaining American support for this package of financial assistance. North, the primary speaker on the yacht in June, now was primarily listening.

Noriega offered North more help for the Contras in return. He proposed to prepare a Panamanian unit to be put inside Nicaragua to carry out certain sabotage missions. The members would appear to be Contras, but they would have the benefit of Panamanian intelligence and would be far better trained. He also mentioned that the Panamanians were acceding to the U.S. request to allow a political propaganda office to open on its territory. The office opened a month later, in November 1985.

Blandón was convinced that it was this meeting with North, and Noriega's new promises to help the Contras, that made possible a new package of loans from international financial institutions and private banks in March of the following year. North, whose role in gaining the financing had been tangential, never dissuaded Noriega from his belief that helping the Contras could have such direct financial rewards.

In retrospect, Leahy nevertheless believes Noriega always got more out of the U.S. than the Contras got from Noriega. "Noriega played intelligence agencies and the U.S. government like a violin," says Leahy now. "It gave him a lot of protection to help out in a way no one else could. But they were also hearing what they wanted to hear. That's part of the reason the Contra war was such a fiasco. You didn't have to give them much to make them happy."

Yet intelligence agencies so well fed by Noriega were deaf to the growing thunder of information that Noriega was increasingly involved with Colombian drug bosses and had extensive business connections with the Cubans that allowed them to beat America's trade embargo at great profit to Noriega and his cronies.

"For short-term gains, people were willing to put up with him," says Leahy. "That allowed him to get stronger and stronger. I don't think we created him as much as we fed him, nurtured him, and let him grow up to be big and strong."

At about the same time, the State Department's new assistant secretary for Latin American affairs, Elliott Abrams, began to believe that Noriega's help for the Contras was overestimated and his general harm to democracy and human rights was underestimated. Abrams had come out of State's human rights office, and despite conservative credentials he would be the first to take on the Pentagon and CIA's unwavering protection of Noriega. Abrams wasn't yet ready to mount an all-out offensive on Noriega, after the Barletta ouster, but he argued at several interagency meetings that backing the Contras could only be one part of an overall strategy of promoting democracy in the region. He wanted to put more pressure on Panama to democratize, but without endangering the good relationship that existed. More cynical voices, such as that of Pentagon official Nestor Sanchez, argued that Panamanians themselves weren't pressing for democracy, and that Abrams hence would be like a Don Quixote chasing windmills until Noriega's people themselves showed they were ready to fight. And anyway, he would argue, Panama would be worse off when Noriega left. His number two, Roberto Díaz Herrera, was a communist, and without Noriega, Panama would shift even further left.

Nevertheless, the administration agreed to sanction the first tough message to Noriega to democratize. It was the first in a long string of botched and halfhearted messages to Panama's dictator, the intention of which was to promote democracy but whose outcome was just the opposite. The first spear-carrier was William Casey. The State Department figured Casey was a man Noriega would be sure to respect. What Abrams didn't realize then was that Casey didn't want to carry his diplomatic weapon.

Casey brought the General to the CIA headquarters in Langley, Virginia, on November 1, 1985, less than two months after he had ousted Barletta. Noriega was prepared for the worst.

A secret assessment of Noriega's criminal activities was wired to Langley on that same day from the Southern Command—ostensibly to be given to Casey before his meeting. It provided clear evidence that the U.S. knew about Noriega's drug trafficking activities, but wanted to deal with them quietly. This was more than two years before he would be indicted in Florida.

The memo's seventh point read: "Although relatively effective, the leadership of the FDP [Panamanian Defense Forces] disregards human rights, is often arbitrary and high-handed, and is involved in illegal activities (e.g., drugs). The U.S. Government is aware of this situation and in one form or another attempts to change the behavior and attitude of the Panamanian military."

But the CIA director never intended to deliver the tough message. Instead, Casey had a friendly chat with Noriega. He didn't mention drug trafficking or democracy. One Panamanian official said they discussed the Contras and North's October meeting with Noriega, at which he had offered more help. It was a cordial session.

Casey then turned Noriega over to subordinates, who made him feel at home. The subordinates took Noriega to an expensive lunch at a Virginia countryside inn. Assuming their boss had dressed down the dictator, they were particularly cordial, hoping to heal any wounds inflicted on their longtime "asset." Noriega returned to Panama bragging about how the CIA had flown him all the way to Washington to wine and dine him.

Casey prepared a memorandum about the meeting on November 20, almost three weeks later and only after prodding by the State Department, which had heard from Panamanians that Noriega had received far too warm a CIA welcome.

"It was a CYA [cover your ass] memo," said Francis J. McNeil, who at the time was the deputy assistant secretary of state for intelligence and research. "He scolded Noriega only for letting the Cubans use Panama to evade the trade embargo, but he never mentioned narcotics, nor, if I recall correctly, democracy." Mr. Casey's memo noted that Noriega had been nervous when he arrived but he departed reassured, said McNeil.

The memo said that Casey had complained that Panamanian firms were being used by the Cubans to circumvent the trade and economic embargo of Cuba. Casey said he hadn't raised the concerns about narcotics or democratization because he was sure that Noriega was well aware of the American position. Such issues were a matter for the State Department and the ambassador in Panama. "The memo made clear that Casey let Noriega off the hook regarding drugs," McNeil would say later. "Noriega knew if he kept us happy regarding Nicaragua, he could do what he pleased."

National Security Adviser John Poindexter flew to the region in Decem-

ber to promote the Contras. His stop in Panama was also aimed at correct-
ing the misperceptions of the November meetings. It was Poindexter who
delivered the "talkers" that had been intended for Casey. The two men met
at Howard Air Force Base in the distinguished visitors lounge, along with
Abrams and Ambassador Briggs. Noriega came alone. "He didn't want his
other guys to hear him called on the carpet," said Abrams.

But again there were mixed messages. At the same time Poindexter was
seeing Noriega, National Security Council staff member Constantine
Menges was delivering a message to Noriega's American consultants, Joel
McCleary of Sawyer-Miller Group and Bill Hecht and Craig Hellsing of
Hecht and Associates. It was far tougher and more threatening than what
Noriega heard in Panama City.

Menges had been Casey's national intelligence officer for Latin America
before joining the National Security Council in 1983. He had become too
much of a lightning rod at the CIA. In his early forties, Menges was a
scholarly and supremely confident Hudson Institute conservative, whom
Casey considered even more to the right than himself. Menges saw the
forced resignation of Barletta in September 1985 as the beginning of a
reversal of democratic progress in the region—the first Latin American
military coup of the Reagan years. He was frustrated that national security
advisers Robert MacFarlane and John Poindexter, who took over in December 1985, weren't paying enough attention.

"I had warned that a Noriega-led military regime in Panama would
make it more vulnerable to destablization and ultimate takeover by radical
pro-Cuban/Soviet elements," he said. "I tried unsuccessfully for months
to get this issue before President Reagan." Menges did convince Reagan's
anti-drug chief, Carlton Turner, to investigate.

However, McCleary says that Menges made clear to the visiting consultants that the president had decided Noriega had to go. Menges said
officers involved in the Spadafora killing would be shipped out of the
country. He threatened military force if Noriega didn't clean up and democratize the country, McCleary said. It seemed to McCleary that they were
being told exactly what Poindexter would be saying to Noriega in Panama,
and that worried him.

Menges denied this version of events, and he considered the meeting
with the consultants, in retrospect, to have been a great misunderstanding.
He insisted that he wasn't even told by Poindexter about his mission to
Panama. Menges had been removed as the NSC's Latin American chief the
previous July, and he had been cut out of the loop and placed in a vague
job devoted to promoting democracy globally. Yet at the time, McCleary
was certain that Menges knew of the Poindexter meeting.

As for the military threat, well, Menges can only think that he said that military intervention might someday be necessary if the Panamanian situation wasn't addressed.

The confusion was increased by the fact that the consultants, at first, thought Menges was delivering a message from the president. They insisted Menges said as much. But Menges said he couldn't speak for the president on Panama because he couldn't even get a meeting with him to discuss the issue. "There was an unwillingness to deal with anything that wasn't a visible crisis," he said later.

In the hallway after the Menges meeting, Joel McCleary wanted clarification. He would have to report afterward to Major Daniel Delgado, Noriega's ally, who was visiting Washington. "If you want me to communicate a message to my client, Mr. Menges, then I must understand it clearly. I'm going to communicate this message, but speaking as an American, this is very dangerous stuff."

I don't know what kind of American you are, Menges replied, with apparent disdain for this man who was selling his services to Noriega.

Indeed, McCleary was an unusual kind of American. He was a North Carolina pol with a Harvard education and a taste for good wines, dark pin-striped suits, and political intrigue. His abiding belief in Buddhism was just part of a collection of esoteric interests, ranging from computer software to oriental philosophy. McCleary was the man you wanted beside you at a dinner party and on your side in a political street-fight.

A gregarious Irish-American with ruddy cheeks and curly hair, McCleary had a penchant for finding action. He rose from campaigner for the Youth for Muskie in North Carolina at age twenty-four to being the youngest Democratic party national treasurer at age twenty-eight, where he discovered that politics is really about money. As a protégé of Hamilton Jordan, he was made deputy assistant for political affairs to Jimmy Carter. McCleary first found his way to Panama in 1983, when Jordan's friend Gabriel Lewis sought help in running the ruling party's presidential campaign.

Jordan thought McCleary would be perfect. Two years earlier, McCleary had started work as an international consultant at D. H. Sawyer Associates, later to be the Sawyer-Miller Group, and he had a taste for political conspiracies. "Joel is the gringo who knows how to get things done," Jordan said. "He sees things in terms of plots and intrigue, and that's not a bad way to operate in Panama."

McCleary abandoned Barletta in early 1985, frustrated that Barletta wouldn't listen to advice and convinced that he would be ousted. He told

Vice President Delvalle when he left, "Call me when you become president. It's only a matter of time. Nicky's going to fall." So following the scandal surrounding Hugo Spadafora's beheading and the ouster of Barletta, Delvalle called McCleary back to Panama.

McCleary insisted two years later, when he had turned his skills to an effort to unseat Noriega, that he had believed Noriega was innocent of the Spadafora killing. A prominent Senate staffer, who briefed McCleary on the affair, said the culprit was more likely to be a right-wing Cuban with close ties to the CIA, whom he named. In fact, McCleary was so determined to help Noriega's new president, Eric Arturo Delvalle, who participated in the plot against Barletta, that he hired on President Reagan's former campaign manager and friend, Stuart Spencer.

McCleary later would blame himself for having fallen into the Panama trap. "Panama is a brothel for intelligence agencies, arms merchants, drug dealers, and soldiers of fortune," said McCleary. "Miami wasn't Casablanca. Panama was Casablanca. I got sucked into it and I loved it. Panama is the heart of darkness for me. I lost my political virginity in Panama."

When McCleary walked into Delgado's room after the Menges meeting, he prepared Noriega's military aide for the worst. "I've got to tell you an Alice in Wonderland story," said McCleary.

Delgado phoned Noriega immediately to relay the unbelievable message and get his orders. He feared armed conflict was near.

"I've just been given the same message you got [from Poindexter], and I am very concerned," Delgado told Noriega.

The truth was that Poindexter's message was relatively tough, but not threatening. The soft-spoken, pipe-smoking national security adviser told Noriega that Panama was running against the tide in Latin America through its increases of human rights abuses and the growing role of the military. He said drugs were an increasing problem in Panama, and that the military was involved, but he didn't blame Noriega directly for narcotics trafficking, said Elliott Abrams, who attended the meeting with U.S. Ambassador to Panama Everett Ellis Briggs and Southern Command chief John Galvin.

Noriega replied calmly. You are victims of disinformation from the Panamanian elite who are trying to regain power, he said. They are telling you bad things about the PDF because they want to go back to the good old days, before the revolution in 1968, when they were running Panama. The meeting was primarily Poindexter reading his points in a very unthreatening manner, and Noriega politely and articulately rebutting. It didn't seem all that bad to the General.

Hecht called McCleary a little later, after visiting with Casey and Nestor

Sanchez. Hecht said that Casey advised them to ignore Menges, who was now always out of the loop.

McCleary was shocked, however, at how close one official, exaggerating a presidential message, had come to triggering a foreign policy crisis. Maybe that is what Menges had wanted, he thought: a military confrontation that would have stopped the transfer of the Panama Canal to the Panamanians.

When Marcos was ousted in the Philippines on February 25, 1986, McCleary knew his Panamanian client Noriega had some troubles ahead. He thought the Elliott Abramses of the world now had the emotional boost they needed. Seeing Marcos on his way out and the general U.S. pressure on dictators, ten days earlier McCleary had written a seventy-five-page document, in neat computer graphics, offering Noriega a battle plan of how to make his regime work, how to strengthen civilian rule, and where his enemies were in Washington.

Noriega, feeling he had the Reagan administration on his side, was unhappy with some of McCleary's advice, even though it appears relatively soft in retrospect.

"The Barletta resignation and Spadafora murder sparked a disproportionately strong reaction from the U.S.," the report said. "These events energized negative historic and ideological feelings which had lain dormant during the first years of the Reagan administration."

The paper also let Noriega know who were his U.S. enemies—Elliott Abrams and departing Ambassador Briggs—and who were his friends: "[Pentagon official] Nestor Sanchez is an ally. Casey is a quieter but real friend. . . . Defense and CIA have clout in Washington, but they are not as strong as Panama believes."

But McCleary rebuked Noriega's regime: "The government stumbles from crisis to crisis because it has no agenda. . . . The government appears stalled and defensive."

And he even chided Noriega: "[Noriega's] intelligence background gives him a persona and working style not particularly suited for popular politics. His instinct is to be quiet, not to explain actions and motivations. . . . Noriega comes across badly in both domestic and international media because he has not been properly presented. . . . The press builds a dark, almost oriental, image of him which will undermine him if not changed."

It warned Noriega of dangers ahead from the U.S., though it softened the critique by agreeing that some of them were unfair: "The anti-Panama sentiment has, until recently, come from the far-right ideologues. That is now changing and creating real problems. . . . [Liberals] use the models of 'Marcos's Philippines' and 'Somoza's Nicaragua' to describe 'Noriega's Panama.' To today's liberal ideologues, all people in uniforms are fascists and corrupt. They are sadly blind to the differences between Pinochet and Noriega. . . . It is a new, strange, and dangerous alliance: the far right and left. This alliance against the current government must be taken seriously. . . . The facts, well explained, will bring the liberals back home."

The report then tried to soften the blow to the thin-skinned General: "Noriega is aware of his image problems, works to solve them, and, given time, will solve them, but at this moment his image is not one of a caring, sympathetic leader."

The written advice was bad enough, but then McCleary scolded Noriega in person a little later, just after Ferdinand Marcos's February 25 ouster and the removal of Haiti's despotic ruler Jean-Claude Duvalier two weeks earlier. It wasn't a good time for dictators, and McCleary advised Noriega to burn files in his office that might be embarrassing. "Get rid of the documents you don't want," he said.

But Noriega laughed him off. "We don't have your security problems," he said.

McCleary looked him in the eyes. "That's what Marcos thought."

Noriega hated being compared to Marcos, and his chief of staff said what the General was thinking. "How dare you lecture the General like a schoolchild?" said Colonel Marco Justine.

Noriega thought he had the CIA and Oliver North on his side, and he had consultants cozy with the Reagan administration, Frank Gomez and Richard Miller. McCleary's was a voice he didn't want to hear, so he quit listening. And Stuart Spencer found Noriega wouldn't even see him on his visits to Panama.

Noriega didn't change his nondemocratic ways in the weeks that followed, yet the Reagan administration, obsessed with Nicaragua, put the problem on the shelf. When the U.S. shift against Noriega began, in the spring and summer of 1986, it was because of former National Security Council staffer Norman Bailey, *New York Times* investigative reporter Seymour Hersh, and, most importantly, Republican Senator Jesse Helms of North Carolina. Thereafter, Massachusetts Senator John Kerry, a liberal Democrat, pursued Noriega in his narcotics subcommittee and gave anti-Noriega forces the bipartisan punch they had long lacked.

Helms had long sought an opportunity to vindicate his long-standing belief that Panamanian leaders were simply too corrupt to be entrusted with America's canal. At Canal Treaty hearings in 1978, he'd argued that the evidence was sufficient of Torrijos's and Noriega's involvement in drug trafficking, illegal trade with the Cubans, and other nefarious activities.

His warnings had been dismissed then as the exaggerations of a reactionary right-winger, but new evidence was mounting that could vindicate him. Even so, Democratic colleagues still feared that the conservative senator from North Carolina cared more about regaining the Panama Canal than promoting democracy.

Helms's interest in Panama was revived when Hugo Spadafora's brother, a thoughtful lawyer named Winston, visited him at his Capitol Hill office. The conservative maverick lit up one of his Lucky Strikes as Winston Spadafora recounted the grisly details of his brother's beheading and the evidence that led to Noriega's doorstep. Then Winston showed Helms the photographs from the Costa Rican autopsy. He described the six hours of torture, the fact that Hugo had been decapitated while alive, and that leg muscles had been professionally severed to facilitate homosexual rape.

"I don't think I've ever seen Helms so moved," said Deborah De Moss, his Latin American specialist who had arranged the meeting. "He looked at the photographs a long time, and then he put them down and shook his head. That's when he decided to do something."

Winston Spadafora had been frustrated that no other senator or government official would meet him in November 1985. Most hadn't ever heard of his brother. Two months after Hugo was killed and President Barletta was ousted, Washington just wasn't interested in Panama. Senator Helms emerged as his only ally.

"Nobody listened to me before about Panama," Helms told De Moss. "I've talked about this problem for years, and now we're seeing it."

During the Senate Foreign Relations Committee markup of the foreign aid bill, Helms proposed an amendment to impose economic sanctions on Panama. He cleverly used the same language Democrats had used not long before to withhold certain aid from El Salvador until the killers of three Catholic nuns had been brought to justice. He argued the Spadafora killing was at least as heinous and that Panama was far less democratic.

Connecticut Democrat Christopher Dodd, the committee's leading Latin American expert, jumped to his feet and accused Helms of using the Spadafora killing to revive the Panama Canal Treaties debate. "You want to take back the Canal," said Dodd.

The Helms amendment gained only one other vote in committee. Helms tried to pass the amendment again on the floor and only two other members voted with him.

But Helms wouldn't give up. He scheduled hearings on Panama the following spring as chairman of the Western Hemisphere Subcommittee of the Senate Foreign Relations Committee. The Democrats on the committee boycotted most of the sessions, rallying around Senator Dodd. Assistant Secretary of State Elliott Abrams unsuccessfully lobbied against Helms's plans to hold the hearings. So did the Pentagon's Nestor Sanchez, who told Helms staffers that Noriega had been helpful to the Reagan administration. None in the administration wanted to let Helms loose on Noriega.

Dodd's staffers even successfully blocked Spadafora's sister, Laura, from testifying on the infrequently used grounds that foreigners weren't allowed as witnesses. So Helms introduced Laura, who was sitting in the audience. Then he asked the American aunt of a prominent Panamanian opposition leader to read her moving testimony. The moment was all the more dramatic; listeners watched Laura's face wince as she heard the emotional message read aloud.

One of Helms's witnesses, former National Security Council staff member Norman Bailey, did more than any of the others to shift the debate on Panama, with his testimony on March 10, 1986. Bailey revealed for senators the details of Barletta's ouster for the first time. He said it was "triply" dangerous. First, it could begin the reversal of the recent process of democratization in Latin America. Second, Noriega had used the excuse that Barletta was wrestling with the country's economic and financial crisis improperly—a handy excuse to justify a coup that could be used by Latin American militaries more generally. Finally, he said, Noriega was widely suspected of drug dealings and the murder of Spadafora.

Bailey detailed Panamanian government corruption and said that drug trafficking was a problem "endemic in the PDF." Said Bailey, "The ingredients are there for Panama to become the first country to institutionalize the drug traffic and laundering of narco-dollars under the auspices of a government run by the PDF."

Senator John Kerry of Massachusetts, breaking ranks with other Democrats, chose to sit through a couple of Helms's hearings. After hearing convincing testimony, he turned to his aide Richard McCall. "You know, Helms may be onto something here," he said. "A lot of what Jesse is saying makes sense." Kerry was breaking ranks with other Democrats and beginning a bipartisan consensus against Noriega. Two years later, his narcotics subcommittee would be the focus of the Senate's war on the General.

The *New York Times* accelerated the political landslide. On June 12, 1986, investigative reporter Seymour Hersh delivered the most important blow of the early fight against Noriega. Hersh, as a free-lancer, had shifted the debate on Vietnam and won the Pulitzer Prize for his reporting on the

My Lai massacre. His article on the *New York Times* front page had similarly explosive impact in Panama, reporting more convincingly than ever before on Noriega's manifold criminal activities. Hersh and his editors timed the article for maximum impact—to be printed while General Noriega was in Washington, where he was presenting a Panamanian medal to the American head of the Interamerican Defense Board, Lieutenant General Robert L. Schweitzer.

Noriega first heard the charges when he turned on ABC's *Good Morning America* in his hotel room. A fellow officer said Noriega threw his breakfast on the floor in anger, and shouted at an aide that he had been set up by "elements" of the American government. He immediately flew home, canceling a series of other meetings, and rallied his government around him. He smelled a conspiracy, and he forced his president, Eric Arturo Delvalle, to issue a late-night statement expressing his full support.

At a cocktail party the day after the article appeared, Delvalle, the man who two years later would turn on Noriega on the basis of charges by Hersh and others, said, "I personally think that they, the *New York Times,* have lied. . . . We have the proof, here, and in due time it will be made public."

Under the headline "Panama Strongman Said to Trade in Drugs, Arms, and Illicit Money," Hersh drew upon a wide range of sources to make the toughest charges yet against the CIA's long-time ally. They included illicit money laundering, drug trafficking activities, providing guerrilla groups with arms, and acting as a secret investor in Panamanian export companies that sold restricted American technology to Cuba and East European countries. He also revealed that Noriega had transferred highly sensitive National Security Agency espionage materials to Cuba. Many of the charges weren't new, and many of them had appeared in a series of articles a year earlier written by journalist Knut Royce, then of Hearst Newspapers. But the high profile of a front-page *New York Times* article shook Panama and the U.S. Congress, and it hit a nerve with Noriega.

Yet even that article wasn't enough to shift the Reagan administration into open opposition to Noriega. The White House was still fighting the Sandinistas, and it didn't want a second front against Noriega.

Humiliated and in a rage, Noriega ordered his subordinates to strike at the administration's heart by seizing a shipment of arms passing through the Canal that his government-controlled press said had been bought by the Saudis and were en route to the Contras. The weapons were actually en route to Peruvian military rebels—a boatload, on a vessel called the "Pia Vesta," that the Peruvian government wanted to stop, according to Panamanian intelligence sources. Noriega's seizure of the *Pia Vesta,* two days after the Hersh story, was engineered to send the Americans a stark message: Noriega had the power to cause the Americans problems if they didn't come to his defense. North's response, though, was characteristically cavalier about Panamanian democracy. He asked Noriega if he could buy the weapons for his Contras. "I understood at the time that Lieutenant Colonel North approached Noriega to get him to spring the cargo for use by the Contras and that wiser heads at the CIA blocked the idea," said McNeil later.

Hersh's article prompted Noriega to offer the *Times* a rare interview, published on June 18, in which he criticized the paper for not naming his accusers. He charged the reporter was a tool of his political opponents and of those who opposed the Panama Canal Treaties. "It's a fight for political power," he said. After all, he added, "Manuel Antonio Noriega isn't the issue. Noriega is just a man in time and space."

To Casey's chagrin, however, Noriega had become the issue. The Hersh article was shifting the Panama policy further out of the hands of the pro-Contra warriors. The administration agreed that Noriega was corrupt, but a policy review nevertheless decided that the problem could wait, and even Noriega's future enemy, Assistant Secretary of State Elliott Abrams, went along. Nestor Sanchez of the Pentagon argued that Panamanians weren't going to the streets against Noriega: this wasn't the Philippines. "A decision was made to put Noriega on the shelf until Nicaragua was settled," said McNeil. "Clearly the obsession with Nicaragua overwhelmed our national interest."

However, the politics were shifting. Helms, who once couldn't find a friend regarding Panama, now lined up a number of cosponsors for another try at legislation against Noriega. It would trigger a personal war with Casey that the CIA chief couldn't win.

Helms used the unorthodox means of amending the Intelligence Appropriations Bill on the Senate floor. Changes in the bill are usually scribbled in behind the closed doors of the Senate Select Committee on Intelligence. The bill itself is usually passed by the Senate without debate. However, on September 24, 1986, during deliberations of the bill, Helms—not a member of the Intelligence Committee—introduced Amendment 2897, asking the director of central intelligence to provide a report "not later than March 1, 1987, whether and to what extent the Defense Forces of the Government of Panama have violated the human rights of the Panamanian people, are involved in international drug trafficking, arms trafficking, or money laundering, or were involved in the death of Hugo Spadafora."

Casey phoned Helms to stop the amendment, arguing that more vital foreign policy considerations were at stake. He said the action would destroy a useful relationship with Noriega. He said Helms's action was humiliating to him and demeaning to the CIA.

In his Carolinian drawl, Helms said he "only wanted a little report." He was surprised how strident Casey was—much more so than he had ever been in pushing the Senator or his colleagues for Contra support.

When Helms resisted, Casey turned angry. I'd rather not have an intelligence bill than have that amendment, he said.

"You might as well pull down the intelligence bill then," said Helms. "I have no intention of removing my amendment."

Casey hung up on Helms. When the CIA director later protested that he had done no such thing, Helms merely responded, "All I know is that the phone went dead, and I was still jabberin'."

Helms was finally a winner. The anti-drug Democrats joined him, as did almost all of the Republicans. On September 24, his amendment passed 53–46. Two Democrats—Senator Kerry of Massachusetts and Edward Zorinsky of Nebraska—signed on as cosponsors with an even dozen Republicans.

Senator Kerry's Foreign Relations Subcommittee on Terrorism, Narcotics, and International Communications would also begin shifting its work from the politically perilous and uncertain pursuit of a Contra drug connection to the richer vein of Noriega's links to the drug world. Kerry, a decorated Vietnam veteran who later campaigned against the war, was a liberal senator who made an unlikely ally for Helms, who Kerry suspected had a hidden agenda of scuttling the Panama Canal Treaties. But he joined forces with Helms anyway, because of the larger benefit of exposing Noriega for what he was. After Kerry broke the ice, other Democrats quickly followed. "I thought we should act right away, rather than let the problem linger until the point of a transition of the Canal administrator to Panamanian hands in 1990," said Kerry later. While Helms was out to make the Canal an issue again, Kerry schemed to preempt a painful revival of an issue that had cost many Democratic supporters of the treaties their seats in the 1970s.

The report that was issued several months later, on the day of the deadline, was innocuous and unsatisfying. But as Casey had feared, the political importance was far greater than that of a "little report." From that point forward, the administration would be playing catch up. The Senate had started the war on Panama's dictator, and Noriega knew it.

Noriega's role with the Contras intervened again. Even as the Senate was debating its bill, Noriega was in London, where North was anxiously drumming up support for his failing war. It was then that Noriega proposed to North that he would assist in assassinating members of the Sandinista directorate, to help clean up his image.

However, this time Noriega had gone too far. North passed the request to Poindexter and to Abrams, who gave it to Secretary of State George Shultz. Poindexter said assassination wasn't something the Americans could countenance. Shultz told Abrams that Noriega could help the Contras if he wanted, but cleaning up his image was his own business.

Noriega made an unscheduled stop in Washington on his way back from Europe, to complain about Helms's legislation. His intelligence counterparts explained to him that Helms was a crazy right-winger, certainly not representative of the administration or the Senate. They tried to reassure Noriega that their own ties with him would be preserved.

Noriega mapped out a characteristic strategy: he would plant press articles and make statements attacking Helms's credibility, and he would threaten and—in a thinly veiled way—blackmail the administration to halt this turn of events against him by revealing enough misinformation about the secret Contra war to show his Reagan administration friends how much harm he could do them. Noriega was sending a message to the CIA: he would reveal their most secret operation if they didn't back him and stop Helms.

On September 26, Panamanian National Assembly members allied with Noriega told Panamanian journalists that Americans were training Contras on their soil, at Fort Sherman on the Atlantic Coast. On October 2, Foreign Minister Jorge Abadía said the government would launch an investigation into these charges, since training Nicaraguan insurgents on Panamanian territory would violate the Canal Treaties.

On September 27, the Panamanian government protested the "unacceptable meddling" in their affairs in a diplomatic note to the U.S. ambassador to the United Nations, Vernon Walters.

Yet Noriega, eager to preserve his close relations with the U.S. at a time of domestic trouble, carried a conciliatory message back to Panama, even while he used subordinates to attack Washington.

"While in the United States, I met with the top-level officials who make the decisions," said Noriega on Panamanian television on October 2. "They have stated their support of Panama because they are aware of our constant efforts for an overall democratization. I could perceive that Jesse Helms is a missile without a range adjustment, and he is a madman who is causing many problems for President Reagan's government. I quote these expressions, which were underscored by those top-level [American] officials."

For the next month, Panama's newspapers were full of attacks on Helms. Politicians burned him in effigy across from the U.S. Embassy, while Noriega continued to try to please the CIA and the Pentagon with his cooperation.

"We feel that the security and defense groups are acting cautiously and wisely," Noriega said in the same television interview. He then explained that the Senate action was the result of Panamanian lobbyists working against him. He put the blame on them, these Panamanians "ready to sell their country," and on the "gullible senators" who listened to them.

He still counted the CIA and Pentagon as his friends, and he expected that they would defend him. What Noriega and his friends in the United States hadn't realized yet was that an irreversible process had begun. The Iran-Contra scandal, which would erupt in December, two months later, would remove the last barrier to taking on Noriega. Oliver North would be forced to resign; William Casey would die in May 1987; and Noriega's other friends would retreat and stop fighting on his behalf.

A conservative senator, a former NSC staff member, and an investigative journalist had begun a process that was drawing the Reagan administration into a fight it never wanted.

CHAPTER
TWELVE

THE FIFTH
HORSEMAN

The theologist Saint John wrote, on the island of Patmos, the testimony of Christ and the word of God. And in the apocalypse, the gallop of the four symbolic horses is described as the catastrophes and sufferings of man. . . .

As hunger, the plague, war and death are the first four horsemen, drugs could well be the fifth horseman of the apocalypse foretold by the prophet.

—LIEUTENANT COLONEL NORIEGA, 1973, AT THE INTERNATIONAL CONFERENCE ON NARCOTIC DRUGS, VIENNA

Pablo Escobar Gaviria was enraged that General Noriega was dodging his phone calls. The portly Colombian drug boss, known as "El Padrino," had become one of the world's richest men through an entrepreneurial cunning and a brutal enforcement of discipline.

Escobar had begun his career modestly as a small-time thief of headstones from graveyards in Medellín, Colombia. He shaved off the names and resold the blank slabs at cut-rate prices. By the mid-1980s, however, his cocaine production network prompted *Fortune* magazine to list him as one of the world's ten richest men. His Medellín cartel had become a drug force that few dared double-cross.

Nevertheless, Noriega had ordered his men to raid Escobar's new cocaine-processing facility in the Darién jungle, which violated a multimillion-dollar agreement Noriega had reached with Escobar just a few months earlier. Furthermore, Noriega had disappeared on a trip to Israel, and now he wasn't taking Escobar's phone calls.

Enraged, Escobar lifted a Chinese vase, a gift from Noriega, and hurled it through the picture window of the comfortable home that Noriega was leasing him. He had been losing his patience with Panama's dictator anyway. He complained to friends about the princely sums he had paid for the quarters at Fort Amador, which had once housed American officers. He had also begun to suspect that the bodyguards Noriega had given him were really spies, and that his movements were being reported to the CIA or, worse yet, to the Drug Enforcement Administration.

Escobar was believed to have ordered the murders of many men. The list began with his first arresting officer and—most Colombians thought— included the killing on April 30, 1984, of Colombia's justice minister, Rodrigo Lara Bonilla. The national outrage after Lara Bonilla's killing had forced him in early May to seek refuge in Panama, where General Noriega had rolled out the red carpet for him and other cartel members. Noriega knew a business opportunity when he saw it.

"They were upset," said Floyd Carlton Caceres, Noriega's partner in drugs, who would later be convicted in Miami. Several cartel members had been staying at Carlton's beach house at the time of the raid. "They had not been expecting the raid. They had helicopters as well as many of their assets seized . . . and they were ready to go to the end to get Noriega to answer for this."

Major Luis del Cid, who handled Noriega's relations with the cartel, was nervous. The General had left him alone to calm Escobar's rage. Del Cid, a handsome, and street-smart officer, was still little more than a glorified bagman for Noriega, and was ill-equipped to deal with this crisis. (Four years later he would be the only PDF member to be indicted with Noriega by the Miami grand jury.) Del Cid couldn't reach Noriega either. Noriega often left town when he felt a crisis coming, as though in a tropical evacuation before a hurricane. That forced others to clean up his messes, which they did faithfully to protect and promote their own careers. Noriega had often lectured del Cid that most storms pass for those patient enough to wait them out.

Del Cid was convinced, however, that this problem required his boss's urgent attention. What he didn't know was that Noriega really had had little choice about the matter.

On May 21, 1984, Panamanian air force helicopters had swooped down on an estimated $1 billion worth of new prefabricated buildings, generators, and labs in the thick of the El Sapo mountain range in Darién jungle, less than fifty miles from the Colombian border. They'd arrested and then imprisoned twenty-one cartel workers and confiscated plant and laboratory equipment, a French helicopter, and two twin-engine planes. Luis Quiel, Noriega's liaison with the DEA, had supervised the Darién raid with his honored guest, the U.S. Drug Enforcement Administration's chief for Panama, James Bramble. Noriega was making Darién his gift to the Americans.

The U.S. had discovered the Darién facility through blind luck. Some local Indians had started complaining about new intruders with lots of equipment, and their concerns had reached Panamanian justice officials, who had alerted the American embassy. Despite mounting evidence that Noriega was involved in drug trafficking, the Reagan administration had continued to protect him, partly because he was more cooperative than any leader in the region with American drug enforcement efforts.

Noriega was engaged in an increasingly perilous balancing act between the growing needs of the cartel in Panama and increased requests for cooperation from the Drug Enforcement Administration. He also needed Washington more than before. His political opposition was up in arms about his stealing of the May 1984 elections, and he needed to keep Washington on his side. He couldn't ignore Washington's complaints about Darién.

The raid was a headache, but it was one of the costs of staying in the drug business at all. Noriega hoped the cartel wouldn't take it too hard: he had fingered only one production facility, which hadn't even started operating yet, while leaving another facility intact and fully operative. He had also ignored DEA requests that he hold off on the raid for at least another month, so that the facility could have been completed and have begun production. The cartel's loss could have been far dearer. The problem was that he never told his Medellín partners that he would double-cross them to please the U.S.

Several months earlier, cartel intermediaries had negotiated the Darién project with Colonel Julian Borbua Melo, Noriega's right-hand man who for years had been his chief deputy at G-2. Melo was the filter for Noriega, who never dealt directly with drug lords. They had paid Melo $4 to $5 million to facilitate the building, the delivery of materials by Noriega's and their own pilots, and the protection of the Darién facility. The location was perfect, just fifty miles from the Colombian border, and its thick overgrowth prevented either satellites or planes from detecting it. Escobar had originally complained that the price was unfairly high, but it was cheap if it meant he was buying Panama's dictator.

The negotiations had also come at a difficult time for Escobar. The cartel's golden years in Colombia had been shattered when an electronically bugged shipment of ether—a radio device had been hidden in a false-bottomed drum—had led Colombian police to the biggest cocaine-processing facilities in the world. The raid had begun on March 10, 1984, in an isolated area of central Colombia known as Tranquilandia—"Quiet Village." The total take had been 13.8 tons of cocaine with a street value of $1.2 billion.

The cartel responded on April 30, killing Justice Minister Lara Bonilla. It was the first killing ever of a Colombian cabinet minister, and President Belisario Betancur struck back. Under a May 1 state of siege, drug defendants were tried in military courts without recourse to bail or parole after conviction. Police arrested drug world patriarch Fabio Ochoa Restreop, and Betancur signed the extradition order for drug boss Carlos Lehder Rivas, who would thereafter be tried and convicted in Tampa. The government invaded Pablo Escobar's apartment; seized his planes, cars, and trucks; and eventually took over his zoo and its starving animals, reopening it as a tourist attraction. On the morning of the Lara Bonilla murder, Escobar had escaped to Panama.

Escobar, the Ochoas, and other cartel leaders were on the run for the first time ever, and it was Noriega who threw out the welcome mat. The entrepreneurial dictator recognized the ultimate business opportunity. Billions in riches were moving his way. One of the most powerful forces in the world needed him.

The cartel moved 120 people to Panama: accountants, bodyguards, lawyers, and families. Noriega provided them housing, advice, and even Panamanian passports. When Jorge Ochoa was arrested the following year in Spain, he and his family were traveling with Panamanian diplomatic passports. The cartel bosses who most needed security and secrecy rented former U.S. officers' homes at Fort Amador, which had reverted to Noriega under terms of the Panama Canal Treaties. Others stayed in plush suites atop the Caesar Park Marriott Hotel.

Noriega was helpful at first, providing bodyguards and advice. On May 6, he even arranged a meeting between cartel leaders and Alfonso López Michelsen, a former Colombian president who was in the country to observe Panamanian elections. The drug bosses wanted to make a deal under which they could come home.

By the time of a second meeting, however—in Panama on May 26, with Colombian Attorney General Carlos Jimenez Gomez—Escobar and Ochoa were more desperate. They had just experienced the Darién raid a few days earlier, which had taught them the perils of depending on Noriega. They proposed to dismantle their drug operations and repatriate as much as $5 billion for a pardon, and handed the attorney general a six-page letter that said they would develop crop substitution projects to replace coca and marijuana. They also promised to assist anti-drug campaigns and to fund addict rehabilitation. Yet Escobar and Ochoa heard nothing from Colombia, while around them their world turned darker. About that time U.S. Customs in Miami seized 1.2 metric tons of cocaine in freezers aboard a cargo jet belonging to INAIR, a Panamanian charter company linked to Ochoa. A week later Panamanian police would confiscate 6,159 drums of ether in the Colón Free Trade Zone.

Escobar's worst fears about Noriega seemed to be coming true; and he told del Cid he wanted an "immediate business meeting" with Noriega.

Del Cid dialed Noriega's bedroom number, which was relayed automatically to wherever in the world the General happened to be—this time Israel. The Israeli army was giving Noriega a decoration, apparently for his help in providing end-user certificates for arms Israel was sending to Iran to help keep its war with Iraq alive. Noriega had brought friends and family along for the ceremony, which had been arranged by Michael Harari, the former Mossad agent who had organized the General's security and had long provided him political advice.

Noriega couldn't be reached, so del Cid talked to Colonel Julian Borbua Melo, the negotiator of the Darién deal, who was traveling with Noriega. They talked carefully even over scrambled lines, particularly since the Panamanian equipment had been bought from Israel. It was a dangerous situation, said del Cid. "El Padrino" wanted talks right away.

Noriega's first response was to work out a cover story. It said Melo had conspired on his own with the Medellín cartel to build Darién. The story had it that a friendly European intelligence agency had uncovered an assassination plot against Noriega that Melo had hatched with the Colombian drug bosses. The errant colonel was promptly shipped home early from Israel for "investigations."

Not surprisingly, Melo didn't much like the plan, but he had no choice. His whole career was tied to Noriega.

Melo's life had been saved by Noriega after he had been on the wrong side of an abortive 1969 coup against Omar Torrijos. The dictator, a forgiving man, had shipped him off to internal exile in Chitré province, but Melo had allegedly angered local businessmen by extorting protection money from them; and in 1976 Torrijos sent him to Colombia. Noriega had seen promise in this amoral officer, and put him on the G-2 payroll, giving him $450 a month above his somewhat smaller PDF salary. Melo's primary assignment was to monitor the growth of the drug business, which Noriega believed had the potential to become a new power factor in the region. Melo had studied at the Santander Police Academy in Colombia, the country's most influential breeding ground for enforcement officials, and he looked up fellow classmates, many of whom had ties to new drug businesses.

In 1979, Noriega rewarded Melo by promoting him to the sensitive position of his deputy G-2 chief. When Noriega took over as commander of the defense forces in August 1983, he made Melo his right-hand man, executive secretary to the Comandante.

So when the story of Melo and the cartel appeared, his friends knew he was taking the fall for Noriega. But the story would buy Noriega some time. Now he had to make peace with the traffickers.

How did Noriega become involved with the drug lords in the first place? Like most stories of Noriega's corruption, it is an intriguing tale of an opportunistic intelligence chief spotting an irresistible chance to increase his power and profits. Drugs didn't corrupt Noriega; rather, corruption led Noriega to the drug dealers. Again, the United States for years ignored intelligence on Noriega's links to the drug world; and agencies that had information, such as the CIA, didn't always share it with others. Noriega seemed to be encouraged by Washington's cavalier attitude toward his misadventures.

Noriega's ties to the Medellín cartel were a direct outgrowth of his increasing importance in trafficking arms to guerrillas in the late 1970s.

In 1976–77, some Colombian businessmen began transforming the embryonic cocaine trade from a relatively small business carried out by criminals to a major industry organized by self-styled civic leaders and entrepreneurs. In a Colombian prison in 1974, Carlos Lehder had outlined it all between games of Monopoly and tokes of marijuana with a young American hippie named Stephen Yakovac, whom he was recruiting to this new business.

Lehder had been locked up for smuggling Chevrolets into Colombia, a small-time infraction that fell short of his grand dreams. He told Yakovac that he would form "a conglomerate of small-time cocaine producers," who would pool their merchandise into a huge shipment, so as to help meet the costs for the more sophisticated equipment that they all needed in order to get drugs safely to their U.S. buyers through Coast Guard patrols using radar.

"He wanted to pull Colombia up by its bootstraps," Yakovac would testify years later. "He wanted to oust the imperialist Yankees and build a kingdom based on cocaine in Colombia." Lehder respected and idolized Adolf Hitler. "And he likened himself to Hitler in that he was a small man and could take over the world," said Yakovac. Lehder recruited Yakovac, and others in prison, to his new enterprise.

In the mid-1970s, Noriega watched the developments in Colombia from afar, with fascination. As drug traffickers grew richer and bolder, Noriega's interest also grew. He monitored their Panamanian bank accounts through G-2 agents placed in banks, and he started files on these Colombians, betting they would become a new, powerful elite. He also pressed his military attaché in Colombia, Julian Borbua Melo, for more intelligence. Noriega shared some of the reports with Torrijos, but he kept most of them for himself. Noriega's intelligence allowed him to see something in the mid-1970s that Torrijos didn't: drugs would shape Latin America's economic and political future.

The first hint the U.S. had that Noriega was dealing with Colombian drug interests came in 1977. DEA agent Tom Zepeda, on temporary duty assignment in Medellín, was surprised to see Noriega and Torrijos arrive in a Panamanian government plane at the Medellín airport in 1977. They were picked up on the landing strip by a Mercedes without license plates— the usual modus operandi for drug dealers. A reliable informant had reported several other Noriega trips to the region over a six-month period, sometimes with Torrijos and sometimes without him. Noriega was sticking his toe into the water, but he wasn't yet ready to jump in.

In fact, a U.S. intelligence officer said Noriega provided Washington some of its best reports on the early days of the new drug cartels and their development in Colombia. It was good cover for Noriega, providing him with a ready excuse if the U.S. uncovered any more of his secret meetings with the *narcotraficantes.*

At the same time, as a liaison officer with Washington's Drug Enforcement Administration, Noriega could obtain sensitive intelligence reports on the drug trade.

Noriega moved from the fringes to the focus of the drug world on a mission that originally had nothing to do with drugs. He was acting as the middleman, appointed by Torrijos, in an effort to help solve a Colombian political dispute.

In early 1980, former Colombian president Alfonso López Michelsen decided he wanted the presidency again and he wanted the backing—or at least the neutrality—of the M-19, an emerging force of leftist guerrillas headed by Fidel Castro. López Michelsen summoned his friend Omar Torrijos to a secret meeting in Bogotá, with José Blandón, Major Felipe Camargo, and then–Colombian defense minister, General Luis Carlos Camacho Leyva.

He asked Torrijos whether he would arrange negotiations in Panama with Jaime Bateman, the head of the M-19 guerrilla group. Bateman was a combination of Zorro and Ché Guevara, and his M-19 was a relatively popular force. Its members at that time were largely middle-class children with social-democratic instincts; many were medical students. They fought against government corruption and growing links between the army, politicians, and drug interests.

But the M-19 was evolving into a more radical force. In 1980, its guerrillas held hostage a group of ambassadors, including Washington's Diego C. Asencio, in the embassy of the Dominican Republic in Bogotá.

Soft-spoken and scholarly, Michelsen told Torrijos that he wanted the M-19 guerrilla group to transform itself into a political party that would renounce violence and back his candidacy. Michelsen told Torrijos that he would satisfy the M-19's goals of rooting out corruption in government and drug trafficking after his election. Torrijos liked the idea. He wanted more peaceful revolutions like his own in Panama. And he owed Michelsen a favor. As Colombia's president, Michelsen had been a key ally in pushing through his Panama Canal Treaties in Washington.

Torrijos asked Noriega to arrange the meeting with the M-19. Noriega invited Bateman through intelligence contacts in Spain, Mexico, and Cuba; and in September 1980, the dashing Colombian arrived in Panama via Cuba with his latest girlfriend and with an entourage of twenty-one. Noriega made the introductions on the first day of their meeting, and then provided whatever was needed: communications facilities, typists, lawyers. The M-19 agreed to form a political party to back Michelsen.

The political alliance was soon undermined, however. After the Panama talks, Noriega and Major Luis del Cid traveled back to Cuba with Bateman to brief Castro on the agreement; but Castro didn't like the pact and urged the M-19 to continue its armed revolution. That was fine with Bateman; and Noriega, sensing an opportunity, agreed to provide a conduit for weapons and infiltration of guerrillas into Colombia.

The Colombians first got wind of Noriega's help for M-19 guerrillas in March 1981, when two simultaneous rebel assaults in two rural areas were beaten back by the army. Several of the captured fighters said they had been trained for three months in Havana and then infiltrated into Colombia through Panama. The March attacks, in which 150 insurgents were killed or captured, shocked Colombians. Despite some thirty years of some sort of guerrilla activity, until that time Colombian governments had never considered insurgent activity a threat to existing political systems.

Then in November 1981, the freighter *Karina* and its East European crew and captain sailed into the Panama Canal from the Atlantic. Instead of passing quietly through the channel, however, it anchored at the Vacamonte fishing port—long controlled by Cuba—to take on some revolutionary cargo: a captain from Panama's G-2, some M-19 guerrillas, and tons of weapons.

The mission had been organized by a Colombian named Jaime Guillot-Lara. U.S. intelligence would later discover that Guillot-Lara received $700,000 from Cuba to buy the arms and transfer funds to guerrillas through an employee of a Panamanian bank.

The *Karina* passed safely through the Canal and transferred the weapons to another, less conspicuous, Colombian ship that planned to offload some 100 tons of weapons on Colombia's northern coast. The aim was to move the M-19 into the El Cacatan region, where the guerrillas hoped to establish a stronghold from which they could expand their power. But the Colombian navy intercepted the ship and sank it and the Panamanian captain was captured. Before dying during interrogation, he made the Colombians certain that Noriega's fingerprints were all over the shipment.

Torrijos was embarrassed. He had nothing against arming guerrillas, but he felt Noriega was taking too much private initiative. Torrijos feared that Noriega had arranged the shipment with Cuban intelligence, and he was also angry that the bungled operation had set back the M-19 and had undermined Michelsen's agreement. Michelsen would later lose the 1982 elections to Belisario Betancur Cuartas, the Conservative party candidate and no friend of Torrijos. Torrijos sent Noriega to Colombia to apologize personally to the government, and had Blandón and Panama's ambassador to Cuba, Marcel Salamin, deliver an angry message to Castro. It was the first open strain between the two leaders. "Torrijos believes in revolution through concessions," Castro sneered. "I believe in armed revolution."

Despite this M-19 muck-up, Noriega was becoming a bigger player every day, with closer links both to the Cubans and to their favorite revolutionaries. However, those ties put him in the middle of the war between the M-19 and the drug bosses.

The M-19 had become demoralized by its failed invasion, and it had lost whatever public favor it had enjoyed. It badly needed money and publicity to revive its waning power and credibility, and so it launched an offensive of high-visibility kidnappings and attacks.

On November 12, 1981, it did the unthinkable. Guerrillas kidnapped Marta Nieves Ochoa, the youngest sister of drug boss Jorge Ochoa, from the campus of the University of Antioquia. They demanded $15 million for her release. The kidnapping came as a second shock, after the M-19's attempted kidnap a few days earlier of drug boss Carlos Lehder, who survived a shot in the back during a dramatic escape. The Ochoas declared war on the M-19, and took the first steps toward creating the Medellín cartel.

Family patriarch Fabio Ochoa summoned more than 200 of the country's top drug traffickers for a secret session. Fabio's son, Jorge, a corpulent man nicknamed "El Gordo" for his girth, ran the meeting. The result was the founding of a new organization called Muerte a Secuestradores—"Death to the Kidnappers." The organization issued a statement: "The basic objective will be the public and immediate execution of all those involved in kidnappings beginning from the date of this communiqué." It said the guilty would be "hung from trees in public parks or shot and marked with the sign of our group—MAS." From that point, the cocaine traffickers started behaving less like competitive adventurers and more like Mafia-type businessmen facing a direct threat to their industry. Each contributed $30,000 and ten men for a new vigilante force.

Although the M-19 held on to the Ochoa girl, the vigilantes' success was immediate. They killed or turned in more than one hundred guerrillas and their supporters in six weeks. Police counted thirty murders in Medellín in the first two weeks of 1982 alone. The new cartel's thugs murdered, among others, three union bosses close to the M-19, and two men in prison involved in M-19 kidnappings.

The M-19 wanted peace. Through Fidel Castro, it asked Noriega to help arrange a deal.

Noriega contacted cartel representatives through Cuba's former ambassador to Colombia, Fernando Ravelo Renedo, who had been ousted from Bogotá three months earlier for assisting guerrillas. The Ochoas flew to Panama to negotiate with the M-19. Noriega provided three beachside houses not far from Panama City. One was for the Ochoa party and one for Bateman and the M-19, and the house between was used for negotiations. On February 17, 1982, Marta Nieves Ochoa was released unharmed.

The Ochoas paid more than $1 million in ransom, far less than the $15 million the M-19 had sought. The portly Ochoa family patriarch appeared at horse shows later that year on a pony called *Rescate,* or "Ransom." Del Cid joked to one fellow officer that it was bought with the money Noriega had saved the Ochoas. But Noriega, whom the cartel viewed as a valuable new contact, was paid a generous sum for facilitating the meeting. This was a contact the cartel wanted to keep. He had been efficient and discreet, and was trusted by both sides.

By mid-1982, the cartel and the M-19 had made peace. They had reached an agreement of nonaggression and mutual cooperation that had begun in the beach houses of Panama. Very soon, cartel planes loaded with drugs were being allowed to stop in Cuba en route to the U.S.

Significantly, Noriega had advanced his new and prosperous alliance. He had helped save Jorge Ochoa's sister and had helped end the cartel's war with the M-19. Now the Medellín cartel could emerge as the cocaine industry's guiding force and one of the world's most profitable conglomerates. Noriega wasn't a major player in the drug business, but he was an important friend.

Torrijos's death in July 1981 removed the last constraints on Noriega's ambitions. A power struggle was still under way within the Panamanian National Guard about who would be Comandante, but Noriega now had a virtually free reign over intelligence operations that no other officer knew about.

Several months after Marta Nieves was freed, Noriega sealed his first known deal with the Medellín cartel.

Cartel bosses did their homework on Noriega. They discovered that one way to arrange business with him was through pilots whom he trusted and with whom he owned front companies. The pilots had plenty of experience on perilous missions. They had helped him transport weapons, first to the Sandinistas in Nicaragua in the late 1970s and later to the El Salvadoran guerrillas.

The pilots were Floyd Carlton Caceres, César Rodriguez Contreras, and Enrique Pretelt, all friends of Noriega's since he had been a junior officer in Chiriquí province.

Carlton was serious and reserved, a man who squirreled away wealth without flaunting it. Rodriguez was all flash, a playboy who ran the city's hottest disco and an international call-girl service and who seemed always in search of a new thrill. Yet the two were inseparable friends. Pretelt was the businessman, whom Noriega had brought with him to Panama City in 1970 and helped set up with a high-class jewelry shop and other ventures.

Everyone in Panama knew the three as Noriega's pilots. They flew missions for their adventurous boss ranging from parachuting outings (he loved to jump) to high-altitude sex with partners of both sexes.

In June 1982, a Colombian visited Carlton in his office at Paitilla airport, a small landing strip in Panama City. The Colombian, Francisco Chavez, chartered planes from Carlton to fly to Medellín. He suggested that Carlton should meet some "very powerful individuals" in Colombia who wanted him to ferry money from the U.S. to Panama. "They had seen we enjoyed a certain type of immunity," Carlton said.

When he arrived in Colombia, Carlton was royally received by cartel bosses Pablo Escobar and his cousin Gustavo Gaviria. They told him they wanted to transship drugs through Panama en route from Colombia to the United States. Carlton protested. He thought they had wanted to transport cash. Without mentioning a name, Carlton said he'd have to consult higher-ups before accepting. Go ahead, said Escobar, ask Noriega.

Escobar knew he needed Noriega's cooperation. The Panamanian colonel's link to the DEA was causing problems. One of the cartel's ships carrying 800 kilos of cocaine had been seized outside the Colón Free Zone, and Escobar had been forced to pay Noriega about $1 million to free the vessel and its crew. Escobar didn't get back any of the cocaine. He wanted a more lasting arrangement with Noriega, and he was betting on Carlton as the connection.

Carlton briefed Noriega upon his return from Colombia. Noriega was angry. Why did Carlton go without Noriega's approval? The subject was dropped, and Carlton was relieved. But two or three weeks later, Noriega asked Carlton to a party at his beach house at La Playita, or "Little Beach." It was Noriega's most secure house, used for sensitive meetings.

Noriega wrapped his arm around Carlton's shoulder, and he laughed a little too loud, treating him in a more friendly manner than usual. He asked Carlton what had become of the Colombian deal. "So I explained to him the little that I had learned of the business and that I wasn't going to do anything, and he knew very well that we didn't do anything without first getting his approval," said Carlton.

Noriega instructed him to find out more. He said he didn't want Carlton to mention his name. "Be careful," Noriega said, "and don't forget: I don't know anything." He told Carlton never to use planes with Panamanian markings on his trips to Colombia. They had a few more drinks and talked about women.

Carlton returned to Medellín. Escobar told Carlton that the person who approved the deal—no one said the name Noriega—would receive $20,000 or $30,000 per flight. Carlton would earn $400 for each kilo delivered. Carlton and the cartel also agreed on the use of several small landing fields near Panama City, all of which were owned or run by members of the defense forces and clear of casually passing traffic.

Noriega laughed derisively when Carlton returned and told him of the deal. He chided Carlton for taking so little for himself. If the cartel thought Noriega was begging, they were wrong, he said. Noriega wouldn't take less than $100,000 for the first trip, and he wanted it in advance. Carlton flew to Medellín and told Escobar that he had spoken to "a person" and that the person wouldn't give his approval for less than one hundred grand.

Escobar "scratched his head, and he said, 'Oh, Noriega, Noriega,' so I asked him what Noriega had to do with it. And he said, 'Oh, Floyd, Floyd.' " Escobar said the price was acceptable, and he introduced Carlton to the pilot who would train him. It was late in the summer of 1982, and Noriega had reached his first known agreement with the Medellín cartel. Torrijos had only been dead one year, and Noriega wouldn't be Comandante until the following year. He would use the tens of thousands of dollars he would earn in the coming months to grease his way to the top, enriching a spoils system that had already gained him the allegiance of key officers and civilian allies.

Noriega received $100,000 for the first flight, $150,000 for the second, and $200,000 for the third. Carlton stayed with $400 per kilo.

The General was fastidious about the business details. At one point, he exploded when he discovered that the cartel had tried to add a planeload of drugs for transshipment through Panama that wasn't part of their agreement. He demanded full payment, and he got it. "Noriega told me about this and he was very displeased," said Carlton. " . . . According to him, these people thought that Panama was a group of Indians—that they could come and do whatever they wanted."

Noriega threw Escobar's men in jail and released them only when the cartel paid a considerable fee in amends. "Those persons were captured, and they were very much struck and beat around by the G-2 and mistreated," said Carlton.

Once when Noriega raised the price, Pablo Escobar said he wanted to hand him the money personally. Noriega "asked me whether they were crazy," said Carlton. "He didn't want to know or hear anything." Noriega angrily cut off flights for a while, and the relationship cooled some, until the cartel needed Noriega again.

However, Carlton knew Noriega also had other drug contacts, and that he earned money from other connections. His flights were just a small slice of the pie. "Nothing goes on in Panama and nothing happens in Panama that this gentleman doesn't know about," he said of Noriega.

Consequently, when news of his raid on a Medellín cartel laboratory in Darién province hit the press, most of the Panamanian public was certain that Noriega must have known about its construction. They were baffled at why he then would have shut it down. What they didn't know was the dispute had given rise to a dangerous feud between Noriega and the Medellín cartel or that Escobar, frustrated at his inability to reach the General, in a fit of temper, threatened Noriega's assassination. Word of the plotting reached Noriega through the French intelligence contacts of his Israeli friend, Michael Harari.

Yet Noriega's cover story blaming Julian Melo did little to reverse the Panamanian public's impression that Noriega was involved in this drug deal. Melo's closeness to Noriega was well known, and for the first time anti-military political forces could point to evidence that a senior PDF officer was linked to drug dealing. It recharged an opposition that was already steaming about fraudulent elections.

Noriega had moved to Paris from Israel to watch events from a safe distance. He phoned his keen political analyst José Blandón to take a reading. Blandón was a master at devising strategies and dissecting problems. CIA files painted him as a communist with troublesome political ambitions, but Noriega viewed him as a nonpareil back-room schemer. In his compartmentalized style of running Panama, however, Noriega had cut Blandón out of his drug dealings, although Blandón was intimately aware of his links with leftist guerrilla groups and Castro. Now Noriega asked Blandón to fly to "The Island," the code word for Cuba.

Blandón was as confused as other Panamanians by the Melo story. He turned for counsel to César Rodriguez, the dashing pilot and long-time friend of Noriega's whose flashy life-style of long-legged women and never-ending nights was financed by narcotics trafficking.

Rodriguez told Blandón that Melo was only the fall guy for Noriega—what other choice did Melo have? Noriega is big in this drug business, he said. We are all into it.

Then Rodriguez grew worried. Noriega would spread the blame further to keep himself clean, the pilot said. To save his own skin, Noriega would let his friends hang. Blandón could tell Rodriguez was thinking only about new dangers to himself. His too lavish life-style was making him an embarrassment to a dictator who would now try to distance himself from his most sordid partners.

On June 23, less than a month after the Darién raid, Blandón flew to Cuba with Felipe Camargo.

Blandón, who had often visited Castro before, usually brought gifts for the Cuban leader. Castro especially liked the latest electronic gadgetry, ranging from Israeli listening devices to a Japanese recorder that could simultaneously dub five cassettes. His other favorites were the latest videotapes of spy movies or the latest episodes of *Miami Vice*. But this time Blandón came empty-handed. This trip was all business.

Blandón and Camargo walked into Castro's spacious but spartan third-floor office at the Palace of the Revolution, a sprawling structure with a broad front staircase built by Batista for the Cuban supreme court. It stood at the center of a closely guarded government complex, from which Castro monitored his country. He often showed off his computer room, down the hall from his office, where his IBMs spewed out all manner of detail from the number of troops in Angola to the amount of hard currency taken in by a particular restaurant on a given evening. Castro's exuberant bear hugs made Blandón and Camargo feel shorter and meek in the Cuban leader's imposing shadow.

Joining them was Manuel Piñeiro Losada, his red beard by now grown white. The former head of the country's political secret police, he had become the powerful chief of the Central Committee's Department of the Americas, which meant he was the chief coordinator for all Cuban covert operations in the Hemisphere, including Nicaragua, Panama, Colombia, and the United States. He was Castro's constant comrade, and one of the few men with open access to his office.

The four sat at a conference table intended for twenty, at the end of Castro's office. Castro, sitting at the table's head, spoke first, opening with some small talk about Jesse Jackson, who had just begun a visit to the region in Panama that day and would fly to Havana three days later. Castro liked Jackson, and he was going to release some political prisoners to help him with his campaign for the Democratic presidential nomination. Castro said it was a shame that Jackson was black. If he were white, he could be elected president and advance Cuban interests in Washington. Blandón disagreed with this favorable assessment. He told Castro that Jackson was vain and superficial. "Jackson was more interested in his ego, his beautiful boots, and television coverage than substantive conversation," Blandón said.

As usual at their meetings, Castro wanted Blandón's detailed analysis of the defense forces' situation. "For the first time a top-ranking officer of the defense forces is involved in public in drugs," Blandón said. "This puts the defense forces back at the forefront of public controversy after an election that has left the country divided almost in half . . ." Castro cut Blandón off. He spoke quickly, as if the words were too dirty to dwell upon.

"The information that we have is—and I'm telling you this like family; this is very sensitive—is that Noriega decided to allow the cartel to build this Darién plant in Panama in 1983. They paid $5 million for the right. And you understand that the Medellín cartel is made of businessmen. They don't want problems." Castro said Melo had worked together with Escobar, who oversaw the operation. Melo was handed $5 million, from which $3 million went to Noriega, $1 million to himself, and $1 million to Panamanians involved.

Castro said "the Colombians" were enraged by the Darién raid. "And that's a dangerous situation—for Panama and for everybody." Castro didn't need to add for Blandón that Noriega also protected Cuba's myriad interests in Panama.

"The cartel could transform Panama into a battle zone if Noriega causes it problems," he said. "It would be between the defense forces and the cartel."

Blandón was surprised to hear Castro talk so knowledgeably about the cartel. He'd long suspected Noriega was in deep with drug interests, but he had long admired Castro, even when they differed ideologically, as the leader of "the most important historical movement in Latin America." Blandón had discounted reports of Cuba's ties to drugs as CIA propaganda.

Blandón was frightened, but kept his usual exterior of studied boredom and arrogance. "This is my first knowledge of Noriega's drug involvement," Blandón lied, and then followed with the truth: "I haven't received any instruction from Noriega about how to handle this."

Castro said the Colombians were most anxious that the imprisoned cartel members be freed. The last thing they wanted were more witnesses against them in U.S. courts. He said one of those who had been arrested was particularly important to the cartel. He didn't mention the name or say why, and Blandón didn't ask. Castro said the cartel also wanted back the money, the two planes, and the helicopter, and it wanted immediate negotiations over new ground rules.

Blandón cautiously asked Castro how he knew what the cartel wanted. Castro didn't answer, but kept talking. "There's someone in Havana that Noriega wants you to meet. You could arrange things with him. I'm just trying to prepare you."

Castro said that Fernando Ravelo Renedo—Cuba's former ambassador to Colombia, who'd been indicted and tried in absentia by a U.S. federal court on drug charges a year earlier—would brief Blandón on Colombia, the cartel, and its relations with Panama, before his meeting. "It's very important for you not to do anything wrong," said Castro. "You are working in a minefield. I don't want you to make a misstep and explode a bomb." It was clear to Blandón that this meeting would take place only if Blandón did what Castro wanted, and it was also clear that Noriega had turned the problem over to Fidel for resolution. He wondered to what extent both Noriega and Castro were involved together in the drug business. Why else would Noriega have called Castro for help first? Blandón, a man who prided himself on his inside knowledge, worried that he was in over his head.

Blandón asked for a short recess to talk things over with Camargo. They retreated to the far end of the long room, near Castro's desk. Camargo whispered that he didn't know anything about these Noriega drug connections. Blandón protested that he also knew very little. Noriega so compartmentalized his businesses that only he knew everything he was into. But now, said Camargo, we are part of it, whether we like it or not. He worried that Noriega didn't understand the gravity of what he had done.

When they returned to the table, Blandón said he'd face the problem the way Castro wanted. However, he also wanted to find a way to get Panama out of its problems with Medellín more generally. Blandón asked whether it would be possible for Noriega to resign from the drug world.

Castro said nothing. Piñeiro laughed wickedly at the naive question. He had never liked nor trusted the arrogant Blandón. He ran his finger across his throat and grimaced in mock pain. "These people can—*Crrrrr, Crrrrr*—they can kill you. And they can kill Noriega."

Early the next morning, Ravelo briefed Blandón for his negotiations with the cartel's representative. The briefing became an ideological debate. Piñeiro argued that drugs were a U.S. problem and their sale hastened America's downfall and raised money to advance "the revolution." Piñeiro's anti-Americanism had been born while he had studied at Columbia University in the early 1950s, where his radicalization was hastened by his loss to a rich South American in elections for leadership of a student association. His first wife was American. Piñeiro said that he didn't like drugs, but the money was valuable to "progressive forces" in Colombia, whose ends were noble. If you use the wrong means to achieve the right goal, that is not wrong, Piñeiro argued.

But the Cubans cautioned Blandón against talking politics with the Colombian. You have to understand this is not a political problem for them, Ravelo said. You aren't talking with Fidel or with Omar Torrijos. You are discussing matters with a businessman. This has to be a very short meeting.

Blandón repeated that he would say everything Castro had suggested. Ravelo hugged him. Piñeiro shook his hand.

At 2 P.M. on June 24, Blandón was driven to the Colombian intermediary's bungalow, one of a row of comfortable homes that once belonged to rich Cubans, behind the Palace of Non-Alignment in central Havana. The Colombian wanted to meet with only one Panamanian. Camargo went target shooting with a Cuban officer—a favorite pastime.

The Colombian stopped Blandón before they could exchange names. Names wouldn't be needed. I represent the Escobar interests, he said. He sat erectly, in a sharply tailored, dark European suit, which seemed out of place in the Caribbean. We are concerned about the situation in Panama, he said. We don't want to have trouble. We understand that we are dealing with serious people. All that we want is an explanation and a solution, because in our organization these disturbances aren't needed. You work for the military. You understand. You need discipline and can't allow disobedience. I don't have to explain that. So I'm here to listen to you. I'm willing to cooperate."

Blandón said he represented Noriega. Blandón apologized for what happened, and said Panama didn't want problems either. "We will formalize our proposals to your people as soon as Noriega arrives," he said, "But I'm authorized to tell you that we are going to return the money, the prisoners, the planes, and the helicopter. And Noriega will appoint someone to talk about the new rules."

The Colombian readily accepted the arrangements. They chitchatted for a few awkward minutes. The Colombian suggested, without meaning it, that the two might sit over dinner and discuss the two countries' relations. "But it's not necessary," he said. "Only if you have time." The two never met again. Their twenty-minute meeting had solved the immediate crisis.

Castro was pleased when he visited Blandón later that evening. Castro wanted to be sure everything was ready for the General's arrival the next day. He had an abundance of fruits and cheeses spread out for his guests on the living room table. He lectured Blandón in detail about how he had imported techniques and technicians from Europe to produce the finest-quality cheeses—"just like Switzerland."

Castro was clearly relieved the Darién raid crisis seemed to be over.

Noriega, not yet briefed on Blandón's handiwork, arrived in Havana from New York at about noon on June 25. A Panamanian government plane, a ninety-five-seat Electra, had been flown to La Guardia airport in New York to meet him. As usual, Noriega had flown to New York on a British Airways Concorde from Europe and had stayed in his usual suite atop New York's Helmsley Palace Hotel on Madison Avenue. BCCI bankers provided the usual limousines with Spanish-speaking drivers. Noriega invited his traveling guests to fly with him on this detour home through Cuba, hoping to avoid any alarm that might be transmitted to Panama because of his suddenly changed plans. They had flown with him to Israel, France, and London. But the added Cuba leg surprised his guests, who were already concerned by Melo's disappearance, the drug controversy at home, and Noriega's unusual nervousness; yet they all consented to join him on this impromptu adventure. They were adaptable parasites.

Noriega's wife Felicidad boarded with her usual shopping companion, Dayra Carrizo. Her husband, Celso, who was National Assembly president and Noriega's financial adviser, was also along. Noriega also brought Enrique Pretelt, a man widely rumored at the time to be his homosexual boyfriend as well as his business partner. Pretelt, the owner of a high-priced jewelry store, wore gold chains around his pale neck and wrists. He was the only traveler in a suit—a French-tailored one—and he was the most nervous. Colonel Alberto Purcell, who commanded Panama's air force, and Colonel Elias Castillo, in charge of his ground forces, were also along. By traveling with the men who controlled troops, Noriega avoided coup threats.

When Noriega arrived at the protocol house, he was more nervous than

Blandón had ever seen him. Nothing bothered Noriega more than being out of control of a situation. He threw back seven or eight frozen daiquiris, prepared by the house staff with sweet and potent Cuban rum. Felicidad was worried. "Stop drinking," she said. "Fidel is coming." But Noriega ordered another.

Blandón took Noriega aside and briefed him on the agreement. He told the General he had also asked Castro and Piñeiro what would happen if Noriega retired from the drug business. Piñeiro had laughed that Noriega would be killed.

"Is that true?" Blandón asked Noriega.

Noriega chose not to answer.

Did you ask the Colombian the same question? he said. He was relieved that Blandón hadn't done so. Always the intelligence agent, Noriega was as concerned with who knew about Blandón's talks as he was about their substance. Noriega was particularly troubled that Blandón didn't have the Colombian's name.

Castro picked up Noriega at 6 P.M. The large, confident Cuban always seemed to dwarf the small, introverted Panamanian. Castro's body language left no doubt who was superior. Blandón and Camargo were ordered to stay home in case their counsel was needed. Noriega's entourage that evening went to the Tropicana show, one of the last garish holdovers of Cuba's casino days.

Noriega was groggy and tipsy when he returned, after midnight, to the protocol house where they were staying. Castro was still fresh and exuberant. "The deal will be as we discussed," Castro told Camargo and Blandón as they saw him to the door.

Blandón and Camargo were alone with Noriega. As so often after he blundered, Noriega was the repentant schoolchild. He was very rarely the stubborn dictator who refused to concede fault. Look, José, he said, we made a mistake. We aren't going to do it again.

He never said whether the mistake was dealing with the cartel, being caught by the Americans, or double-crossing the Colombians.

But before Noriega could return home, he had one more crisis—with his wife. His mistress Vicky Amado, who was slowly replacing Felicidad in Noriega's life, had phoned the protocol house while he was out with Castro. During his travels, she kept him briefed on high-society gossip. The Cuban staff had left a note pinned to Noriega's door: call Señora Vicky. The drunk General never saw it. His sober wife did.

"Don't you respect me?" she shouted the following morning in front of several of Noriega's guests. She waved the note like a scarlet letter. "How did she have your number? What was she calling about?"

Noriega quietly calmed her, while his guests feigned indifference. Blandón smiled to himself, realizing that Noriega feared nothing, not even the Medellín cartel, as much as his wife's rage.

And for good reason. Over the years, Felicidad had become plumper and meaner, and legendary not only for her extravagant shopping trips to Europe and her lording it over diplomats' wives, but for her violent actions toward Tony's mistresses. She'd dug her fingernails into the face of one, an attractive, Canal Zone native named Carol who was married to a well-known Panamanian painter. Felicidad had scratched her face so deeply that Noriega had sent Carol for plastic surgery, at government cost, to his Swiss doctor. There have even been rumors floating around Panama, which have never been substantiated, that Felicidad pushed one of Noriega's mistresses out a window to her death. The woman's death had been ruled a suicide, but Felicidad was said to have been the last to see her alone.

Felicidad saw her Sieiro family was losing ground to the Amados, who were emerging as the new imperial clan. Without family of his own, Noriega had instead adopted the families of others. He had made Felicidad rich, but he had also made two of her brothers officers and he gave a third, Ramón, a political party Noriega had stolen from a rival. But the Amados were on the rise. Vicky's stepfather David Amado had been suspected of being involved in a Social Security scandal in the early 1980s, where millions of dollars had disappeared (although no charges were ever brought against him), and her mother Norma was head of Ersa, which published government newspapers. Even Vicky's younger sister was influential, running the politically powerful National Mortgage Bank at only age twenty-nine. However, Noriega's family problems were merely one of the many distractions for a military ruler who was getting caught up in the tangled webs of his own long years of manipulating so many others.

For many Panamanians, the Darién raid's aftermath was proof positive of Noriega's drug complicity. Panamanian authorities released the prisoners and returned the equipment and the money. Since the facility hadn't been operational, no real crime had been committed other than the entering of Panama without proper documentation.

At Washington's behest, PDF officials razed the warehouse in the Colón Free Zone that had held the ether, but the ether itself—enough to produce 100 tons of cocaine—disappeared. Noriega claimed it had been poured into the sea, but another PDF officer said it was returned to cartel bosses.

Noriega's friend, American marijuana dealer Steven Michael Kalish, helped to arrange the release of the Colombians, the recovery of the bribe money, and the mediation of new rules with the cartel that would prevent future misunderstandings and would establish percentages to be paid for laundering $50 to $100 million per month. Kalish, who would be arrested two months later, told investigators that the cartel had rewarded him with an Aero Commander 1000, valued at $1 million, as well as the helicopter from Darién and a "substantial amount of cash."

Colonel Melo was never tried or even dishonorably discharged. He quietly retired with a military pension and he soon thereafter was running a lucrative Panama City loan brokerage.

The cartel, however, never trusted Noriega completely again after the Darién raid. Like the U.S., the bosses had learned that Noriega was for rent, not for sale. For Noriega, his close call provided a different lesson: to protect his own interests he would forever be obligated to his drug trafficking friends.

The only way Noriega could maintain those ties with drug interests, however, was by continuing to convince American authorities that he was in their camp. It was a tricky game, but American agents in Panama were particularly easy to con, and staying on their good side made him all the more valuable to the Medellín cartel, as the only man within their circle with the latest intelligence from the DEA and the CIA. One drug lawyer in Panama called Noriega the cartel's "early warning system."

DEA agents, the CIA, and military intelligence in Panama didn't know the cartel bosses had moved to Panama in May 1984, or if they did, it wasn't reported to Washington.

The U.S. learned that the cartel bosses were in Panama only from Barry Seal, a legendary DEA informant. Seal was assassinated after providing U.S. courts with the most valuable testimony it had ever had on Colombian drug dealing. In three trials, his testimony brought seventeen convictions. Seal linked the Sandinistas to the cartel. His testimony led to the first indictment of a foreign head of government, the prime minister of the Turks and Caicos Islands, Norman Saunders. He directed the DEA record number of cocaine seizures in Las Vegas. But even after Seal had reported to the DEA on the cartel's Panama contacts, agents refused to be convinced.

In fact, with each major drug bust that Noriega assisted, and with each fugitive he helped to extradite, Noriega grew in the DEA's esteem, at the same time that he was expanding business with the cartel. It was a remarkable balancing act that can only be explained one way: Noriega was using the DEA as his own private enforcer.

After U.S. newspaper articles first focused on Noriega's drug ties in 1985 and 1986, and before Washington formally recognized his role, President

Eric Arturo Delvalle issued a 300-page collection of documents that defended his General. Entitled, "Panama: Sixteen Years of Struggle against Drug Traffic," it reads like an exchange of love letters between the DEA and Noriega. DEA officials call the letters "Attaboys"—pats on the back for foreign friends.

In a letter dated March 16, 1984, DEA administrator Francis Mullen's praise is fawning. The letter was written several months after Noriega had agreed to allow cocaine processing in Darién, and a little more than a month before the Medellín bosses and their families moved to Panama.

The note begins by mentioning the DEA's man in Panama. "Country attaché (James) Bramble has advised me of no small number of instances in which you have lent your personal support. It is very meaningful to us," the letter read. It got better. "Thank you very much for the autographed photograph. I have had it framed and it is proudly displayed in my office."

The regard didn't end there. After the cartel moved to Panama and then left, after the Spadafora murder, and even after prosecutors in Miami had begun the process of indicting Noriega, DEA administrator John C. Lawn continued to write friendly notes. One letter, dated May 8, 1986, followed up a private meeting between Lawn and Noriega in Buenos Aires at an international drug eradication conference. "Esteemed General," it said, "I would like to take this opportunity to reiterate my profound appreciation for the vigorous policy against drug trafficking that you have adopted and which [has] resulted in the numerous expulsions of accused drug traffickers, large confiscations of cocaine and chemical substances in Panama, and the eradication of marijuana plantations within the Panamanian territory. . . .

"While our respective governments generally maintain different standpoints on the matter of investigating the finances related to drugs, I am confident that a continued study of the subject will help us find the procedures that will be beneficial for all governments."

As late as July 1986, even as Senator Jesse Helms was pushing through an amendment requiring the CIA to investigate Noriega's drug ties, the DEA's country attaché was praising Noriega for help in shutting down the Roberto Suarez drug organization in Bolivia, another competitor of the Medellín cartel. The letter cited Noriega's involvement in the undercover strategy, although it also noted that Noriega's office retained a "small amount of the cocaine" for use in joint DEA/PDF "reverse undercover operations." No one knows what ever became of that cocaine.

"DEA considers this case to be one of the most successful cases done anywhere in the world in recent years and looks forward to continued cooperation with your office," the letter read.

On May 27, 1987, almost exactly a week before revelations by Noriega's chief of staff focused the world on the General's corruption, DEA administrator John C. Lawn was still issuing praise: "Drug traffickers around the world are now on notice that the proceeds and profits of their illegal ventures are not welcome in Panama."

The notes, however, were like heavy makeup that could only inadequately mask an increasingly ugly mien. Despite his best efforts at concealment, Noriega's true face began to show through.

The first setback was the Darién raid in May 1984, when PDF involvement in the drug world first came to public attention. Then two months later, U.S. drug agents arrested Steven Michael Kalish. Kalish had ample documentary evidence that Noriega had facilitated his money-laundering operations. His testimony three years later would be the core of one Noriega indictment in Tampa, Florida.

Noriega's friend and pilot César Rodriguez was the next to go. He was openly flaunting his riches, appearing in bars with briefcases full of $100 bills and throwing too many lavish parties at the exclusive club he opened with Noriega's backing atop the Bank of Boston building. Whenever anything was refused him in Panama, he quoted Noriega's name and barriers were withdrawn. Rodriguez was murdered in Medellín in March 1986 along with Rubén Paredes, the son of Noriega's predecessor as military chief.

After being refused protection by DEA agents in Panama in January 1986, Floyd Carlton was arrested in Costa Rica six months later in a sting operation arranged from the U.S. After his extradition four months later, his testimony would be key to the second indictment of Noriega. More than anyone else's, Carlton's testimony would make it impossible for the U.S. to ignore Noriega's drug ties any longer.

Noriega also hurt himself. His predilection for turning in to the DEA those he didn't want in Panama created at least one witness against him. Acting on a tip from Noriega, U.S. officials arrested money launderer Milan Rodriguez Ramón at a Fort Lauderdale, Florida, airport on May 4, 1983.

Rodriguez, an accountant seen with Noriega in Panama, would testify to giving Noriega a percentage of one to ten percent per transaction, amounting to a "ballpark figure" of fees between $320 and $350 million. He said Noriega gave him the use of Panamanian airports, the banking system, and security officers to facilitate the money laundering. However, Rodriguez, a Cuban-American in his early thirties, rubbed Noriega the wrong way. Noriega had recently hired the Pakistani-owned, Luxembourg-based Bank for Credit and Commerce International, or BCCI, as his private bankers for transactions ranging from the deposit of his CIA checks paid in by unsuspicious-sounding front companies, to transfers from Medellín drug lords. So Panamanian agents of Noriega turned in Rodriguez to the DEA.

"I'm paying him back now," Rodriguez told investigators. "If you wish to call that a personal vendetta, well then, that's fine."

Noriega's venture into the drug world made him and others in the Panamanian Defense Forces richer than they ever thought possible. But now Noriega had trapped himself. The same drugs that increased his power now threatened to dethrone him.

CHAPTER THIRTEEN

PLAYING THE U.S. CARD

A lie lasts twenty-four hours, not forever. Lincoln aptly said, "You can fool all of the people some of the time."
—NORIEGA ANSWERING CHARGES, MAY 1987

General Noriega had to stop the turn of events against him. It was late 1986, and his characteristic paranoia, a childhood scar, caused him to look constantly for enemies. By now, however, he had plenty of real ones, after having stolen an election, double-crossed the Medellín cartel, sanctioned the assassination of Hugo Spadafora, and ousted President Barletta.

What threatened him the most, though, was the continued threat of a coup within the PDF, whose control over Panama grew more lucrative and absolute evey year. Consequently, Noriega moved against his last rival for power, Colonel Roberto Díaz Herrera. Díaz Herrera, Noriega's chief of staff, shared Noriega's modest upbringing and grand ambitions. At five feet four, he was two inches shorter than Noriega, and both had been forced throughout their lives to outwit and out-macho physically larger opponents.

However, Díaz Herrera was more handsome, charismatic, and political than Noriega. He hobnobbed in Panamanian high society, and he picked mistresses from ballet troupes and acting companies. Díaz Herrera had the additional cachet of being Omar Torrijos's cousin, and he considered himself the natural inheritor of his mantle.

In 1981 Noriega had negotiated a deal with three other colonels under which Díaz Herrera would take military power on June 1, 1987. He needed to rid himself of this ambitious chief of staff before then, but Díaz Herrera had too many leftist friends in the ruling party and labor unions for the task to be simple. So Noriega devised a strategy to take the emotionally volatile Díaz Herrera and slowly drive him crazy. Noriega's U.S. intelligence allies, who considered Díaz Herrera too leftist for comfort, could only applaud this inventive approach.

He prohibited general staff officers from meeting with Díaz Herrera alone, and he cut Díaz Herrera off from any access to intelligence reports. He warned mistresses away from him, and gave him a desk job without important work. He forbade him to travel to provincial garrisons to curry support, and he discussed the most vital issues over lunches to which he hadn't invited Díaz Herrera. And when Díaz Herrera offered advice, he dismissed it as foolish.

One typical example of Noriega's approach came in September 1986. At a party for military attachés from foreign embassies in Panama, Noriega summoned Díaz Herrera to join a group of officers that he was regaling with stories. Noriega was drunk and aggressive, but his conversation was cold and calculating. He mentioned that he had just been discussing the recently ended visit of President Reagan's national security adviser, John Poindexter.

"Hey, Roberto, did I tell you that Poindexter asked me to retire you?" he said. The military attachés' ears perked up.

"Are they giving you that communism bullshit again?" said Díaz Herrera, trying to laugh off the uncomfortable situation. "Will they stop calling me a communist when I've acquired a billion dollars? I like beautiful women and five-star hotels. What more do they want?"

But Noriega had his teeth in. "I refused to do it," he said. "I didn't pay any attention, and I saved you. But do you know they have strong suspicions about you in the Spadafora case?" Díaz Herrera started shaking. Noriega was trying to destroy him with rumor and innuendo, his favorite weapons. The military attachés were hanging on every word, and the gossip would spread throughout Panama's diplomatic community the next day: the gringos thought Díaz Herrera had killed Spadafora.

The next morning, Díaz Herrera walked angrily into Noriega's private bedroom, behind his office at the Comandancia. "What was this shit you said about Spadafora last night in front of the attachés?" Díaz Herrera snarled. Sitting on his bed, drinking his morning cup of oriental tea, Noriega was upset at the intrusion. He was hung over, and his face was covered with a sickly green dermatological salve his Swiss skin doctor had given him.

Noriega exhaled a dismissive laugh. "What else do you have?" he said.

Díaz Herrera told Noriega that he didn't want to compete with him. He said he'd take an assignment abroad—that he would do anything to make peace. "Hatred is dividing us," he said. "I'm not deceiving you, and anyway I cannot do it because you have more spies than I have."

Noriega answered him with silence.

As Noriega's power grew, Díaz Herrera came to believe that General Noriega's strength came partly from Ivan Trilha, his Brazilian psychic and mentalist, and partly from Noriega's broad mixture of beliefs ranging from Buddhism to the Afro-Caribbean black magic beliefs subscribed to by many Panamanian officers. How else could such a small and insigificant man have come so far?

Consequently, in early October 1986 he went to Buenos Aires to find his own sorcerer. Friends put him in touch with an eighty-eight-year-old yogi named Indra Devi, whose powers convinced Díaz Herrera there was another way to take on Noriega—through Prana, the vital breath that sustains life and is issued as energy from pure substances such as fruit. She made him hold an apple in one outstretched, clenched fist and a cigarette in the other. The frail woman was unable to pull down the arm with the apple, but the fist with the cigarette fell easily. Díaz Herrera was converted.

Through this elderly yogi, Díaz Herrera met a California psychic who would become his constant companion and secret weapon against Noriega. She was Shama Calhoum, whose exotic, brown-skinned beauty in a white sari and white fingernails captivated the colonel. She and the old woman were both disciplines of Satya Sai Baba, who they said was a human reincarnation of God who lived in the Indian desert near Bangalore. A cobra had entered his crib as a child, but never hurt him. Ever since then, the boy had performed miracles: making instruments play by themselves and food appear from nothing.

Surely, thought Díaz Herrera, Noriega could do little to combat such power. Shama Calhoum read Díaz Herrera's future. She asked him to look at her third eye, located at the middle of her forehead, so she could read his aura. "Your mission in life is an historic one," she said. "Nothing can stop you from an inevitable battle. Don't expect to win right away, for you will be victorious in the end." The Californian, whom he affectionately called "La Gringa," didn't even know Noriega, but who else could she have meant?

"So I started a metaphysical war with Noriega with the assistance of my psychic from California," Díaz Herrera laughed later. He set up a Sai Baba temple in his home, complete with lighted candles; he meditated; and he read. Shama Calhoum also put Díaz Herrera in touch with a spiritualist masseuse from Miami and a Los Angeles nutritionist, whom the chief of staff flew to Panama at government expense.

Díaz Herrera hoped Noriega would see his enemy was now armed for spiritual warfare. By early 1987, Díaz Herrera all but forgot he was chief of staff. His passion was Sai Baba, whose color photograph—complete with crossed legs, long black hair, beads, and bare chest—he posted on his bedroom wall.

José de Jesús Martínez ("Chuchu"), who gained world fame for being the central figure in Graham Greene's book *Getting to Know the General,* thought Díaz Herrera wanted to believe so badly he overlooked Shama Calhoum's mistakes. On a long-distance call, Díaz Herrera asked the Californian to tell Chuchu what his ailments were. "You are having problems with your eyes."

"She's brilliant, isn't she?" asked Díaz Herrera. Chuchu, who had nothing wrong with his eyes, remained silent. He understood the attraction when Calhoum arrived in Panama for personal service.

"She was the most beautiful woman I have ever seen, with skin so soft that it should only have been touched by a blind man," Chuchu would say later.

Yet the crazier Díaz Herrera acted, the less Noriega worried about him. Noriega knew his plot was working when he heard that Chuchu, long a friend to Díaz Herrera, alleged that he had been chained like a dog in Díaz Herrera's basement and made to bark. Noriega's own psychic, Ivan Trilha, also told him that Díaz Herrera's astrological chart showed he was in trouble with his balance. Trilha showed Noriega on an astrological map that, as an Aquarius, he had a strong field of protection and mental clarity that Díaz Herrera lacked.

Some of Díaz Herrera's allies, fearing their friend's psychological decay, wanted to help. Martín Torrijos, the former dictator's son, and Dominican Republic politician Peña Gomez, a key player in the international socialist movement, tried to broker a deal with Noriega.

Peña Gomez told Noriega not to underestimate the problems Díaz Herrera could cause him, and in mid-May of 1987, Gomez actually drew up a solution negotiated with Noriega that would make Díaz Herrera ambassador to Japan and chief of the Yokohama and Kobe consulates—the most lucrative positions in the Panamanian foreign service. Díaz Herrera would keep his rank, which would increase his prestige in protocol-conscious Japan, but he would resign from the general staff and renounce all claims to Noriega's throne.

Initially, Noriega liked the idea, and he profusely hugged and thanked Gomez as he walked him to his car. Díaz Herrera accepted the agreement as well, although he worried that his inability to speak English would handicap him in the diplomatic world.

Peña delivered the final papers to Noriega on Friday, May 29, but by Monday, June 1, the General had changed his mind. He rejected the agreement, fearing the Tokyo job would give Díaz Herrera too much money and power, and retired Díaz Herrera the next day without offering him any substitute.

For the next three days, Díaz Herrera tried in vain to reach Noriega. On June 4, he finally scrawled Noriega a note in his childlike writing. Díaz Herrera wouldn't even write "General" on the letter, but instead addressed it to "Señor Manuel Antonio Noriega."

"You want to begin a total war with me, and I am trying to avoid it, for Lorena, Sandra, and Thais," the letter said, mentioning Noriega's daughters, who went to school with Díaz Herrera's own daughter. "But I am not afraid of you. If you don't talk to me, you are going to confront a total war on my behalf. Don't run away from me. Call me. I can't locate you."

Noriega, however, never dealt with his messiest problems directly. Colonel Marcos Justine, his new chief of staff, told Díaz Herrera to stay calm until they could find him an embassy in Europe and some "financial assistance." He spoke of a million dollars in a suitcase.

One senior officer, though, told Díaz Herrera that nothing good would come of his confrontation with Noriega. The friend had heard that the General was thinking of arresting Díaz Herrera and charging him with high treason, an executionable charge.

"Be patient, and everything will sort itself out," said Justine.

But Díaz Herrera feared for his life. He had to act.

"Stick it up your ass," he replied.

On Friday, June 5, 1987, Díaz Herrera began a desperate war against his oldest enemy through public revelations, some true and some false, about Noriega's crimes against the country. His words would set off a storm of public protests—the biggest demonstrations the country had ever seen—that would begin a political landslide against Noriega. Díaz Herrera's motivation to attack Noriega, however, wouldn't be anything as noble as democracy or justice, two concepts he'd vanquished as PDF chief of staff. His motives were survival and revenge. The irony was that it was a perceived enemy of the CIA, Díaz Herrera, whose charges would in the end prompt the agency to sever its contractual ties to Noriega.

In fact, Noriega's problems with Washington in the weeks that followed didn't come at the hands of longtime warriors for democracy. Rather, three of the men most instrumental in shifting policy in Washington in the second half of 1987 came from the military's inner circle. Díaz Herrera was the trigger, but the anti-Noriega strategy in Washington was developed by Ambassador Gabriel Lewis, the entrepreneur who had worked closely with Panama's military dictatorship for years; José Blandón, the military's political strategist; and Joel McCleary, the colorful North Carolinian consultant who had once been the Noriega regime's political adviser.

They were enemies Noriega never needed to make. Noriega turned these men against him through his most fatal flaws: greed and paranoia. He was jealous of the positions each had gained, and he wanted to block their continuing influence. He also feared, at first unjustly, that they were conspiring against him.

"This was a crisis of our own making," said McCleary months later. The General's opponents had seized a concept hard for congressmen to oppose—the removal of a drug-dealing dictator and the promotion of democracy—and along with the congressmen, U.S. policymakers were shifted into a confrontation they had long tried to avoid. The General's opponents also showed how easily resourceful individuals, seizing the right political issue at the correct moment, could shift debate in Washington and push an administration into a conflict for which it was ill-prepared. "This was a war of conspirators and Panama was the loser," said former President Nicholas Ardito Barletta.

In June 1987, this circle of regime collaborators first began more seriously to turn on Noriega when the hot-tempered Díaz Herrera, who had no troops to command, launched a media offensive.

First came confession. Díaz Herrera said he had bought his house, in the ritzy Altos del Golf neighborhood, with profits from his illegal sale of visas to Cubans. And yes, Díaz Herrera had carried out Noriega's orders to fix the 1984 elections. The final touches had been applied in his own home.

Then he turned to Noriega. He said the General was responsible for Spadafora's murder and for the plane crash that had taken Torrijos's life, in which the CIA was involved as well. He claimed that Southern Command chief Wallace Nutting had planned the Torrijos murder together with Noriega and Colonel Alberto Purcell, the head of the air force. Díaz Herrera also said that Noriega had stolen $12 million the Shah of Iran had given to Torrijos for giving him refuge.

Díaz Herrera threw out the charges so quickly that reporters couldn't keep up. The Godfather's second-in-command was ratting on the Mafia. "I attacked Noriega with information, disinformation, and misinformation," he said. "When you are being mugged by a gang of hoodlums in a dead-end street, you're not going to count how many punches you're landing or whether all of them are entirely fair."

Díaz Herrera's former enemies came to his house to pay their respects and try to rally opposition to Noriega. The first was Winston Spadafora, the brother of the beheaded Hugo.

In gossip-mad Panama, however, the initial crowds outside came less for a revolution than out of curiosity. Díaz Herrera lived among the country's wealthier class, and most of them had only a short walk or drive to find out what was happening. Díaz Herrera loved the attention, and he dubbed his home "the headquarters of dignity." He stood outside, handing out photocopied handbills with his latest charges against Noriega. Some were written as epistles, likening his war with Noriega to the story of Cain and Abel. Others were in verse. Others couldn't be understood at all.

The Panamanians that gathered, however, were surprised when a force most of them had never seen before arrived on the scene. They were riot troops who demonically called themselves "the Dobermans." They looked like characters off the cutting-room floor of a bad B-movie. A Doberman pincher's head was the insignia on their black trucks, and visored helmets gave them a Darth Vader look. They toted plastic shields, tear-gas bombs, shotguns, and rubber hoses.

When the Dobermans attacked the crowd outside Díaz Herrera's home, the surprised protesters dispersed, and then came back for more, so the Dobermans fired bird shot and tear gas. The people retreated again. They weren't accustomed to such open violence in placid Panama, where Noriega's dirty deeds had so long been hidden from public view. This was their political baptism. The Dobermans stumbled forward, some having trouble seeing through their fogged-up gas masks, the result of the midday heat and their own sweat. They were new at this, too.

Díaz Herrera's revelations also helped give birth to the Civic Crusade, the nonpartisan group that would lead protests against Noriega in the weeks that came. Chamber of Commerce president Aurelio Barria organized the first meeting, inspired by a trip earlier that year to the Philippines that had been arranged by the National Democratic Institute, the Democratic party's international arm.

When he'd returned in April, he'd begun organizing a vote-monitoring organization for the May 1989 elections. However, events forced him to move more quickly than he had planned. He brought together 200 professional, business, and civic organizations in a coalition that would bring more Panamanians to the street in protest than ever before.

The Civic Crusade grew out of a movement that had banded together to oppose the general decay of public morality under the Noriega rule. One of the original members of this movement, the president of the Rotary Club, had been found dead with *both* wrists cut to the bone. Somehow, police reports said, he had committed suicide in this fashion. At a press conference regarding the killing later, chief of investigations Nivaldo Madriñan was wearing the victim's distinctively designed ring. Madriñan would be formally charged with this murder after Noriega's ouster.

However, Díaz Herrera had given these businessmen new courage. Barria wanted to organize Manila-like street demonstrations that might force the dictator to resign or, as in the Philippines, prompt a coup that could speed his ouster. But Panama was no Philippines.

Indeed, the protests all seemed a little civilized to reporters accustomed to war zones and peoples' revolutions elsewhere. With the enthusiastic honking of horns and waving of white handkerchiefs, the Panamanian middle class was going after a drug-financed thug, but the demonstrations were usually at lunchtime or just before cocktail hour. People got out of their cars or came down from their offices to join what journalists came to call the "clock-watching revolution."

"Panama has the damnedest anti-government protestors," wrote *Rolling Stone* correspondent P. J. O'Rourke, who had the right forum and style to describe the bizarre scenes. "They're all dressed up in nice ties or linen dirndl skirts and driving around in BMWs and Jeep Wagoneers. . . . Opposition HQ is that infamous center of treachery and sedition worldwide, the Chamber of Commerce."

Yet, for the first time the world saw that Panamanians were fed up. Noriega sent out his Dobermans regularly to pelt the demonstrators with water cannon and American-made tear gas. Sold to the PDF to douse communists, the U.S.-supplied riot equipment was now fighting democracy. The canisters read: TRIPLE CHASER GRENADE/FEDERAL LABORATORIES/SALTSBURG, PENN.

Gabriel Lewis couldn't believe his luck. He had begun plotting against Noriega a few months earlier, but what he had lacked were street protests to convince his American friends that they couldn't continue to ignore Panama.

In late 1986, Lewis had launched a furtive war on Noriega, after the General had begun to take contracts and business opportunities away from him. Lewis had warned other businessmen that Noriega was out to destroy the traditional oligarchy and build a new business class that was beholden only to him.

Lewis was everything Noriega hated. He was bred by one of Panama's oldest oligarchic families, his great-grandfather had been part of the junta that ruled the country at independence, and streets were named after his grandfather, Samuel Lewis. Lewis had been born privileged, with all life's advantages. Light-complected and of noble Spanish descent, he considered Noriega a low-life whose rule of Panama was an international embarrassment.

Lewis was a bulldog in appearance and approach. His short legs supported a hefty body and a large, round head. He also latched on to ideas and projects with unyielding teeth. That stubbornness and a gracious charm made him so successful as Panama's ambassador to Washington during the Panama Canal Treaties negotiations that to this day Senator Edward Kennedy believes the Treaties might have failed without him.

Though he was born well-off, he had an entrepreneurial bent that made him even richer. He saw too many Panamanian bananas were being damaged when shipped on their stems to U.S. markets, so he converted his father's soap box factory and launched what he calls "the package revolution of bananas"—corrugated banana boxes. The first shipment sank in Balboa harbor, spreading a cardboard slick for miles around, but Lewis stuck with it, and the idea made him a multimillionaire, with banana box plants in Panama, Guatemala, Nicaragua, Costa Rica, Ecuador, and Surinam.

Noriega, jealous of Lewis's economic power and political muscle, began to cut him down to size. The General's first target was Contadora Island. Lewis loved the tropical island, where he'd entertained senators and millionaires, like a child he'd raised from birth. He'd bought it in the 1960s for $6,000 from Panama's equivalent of two old ladies from Pasadena. In time Lewis bought ten other nearby islands at similarly cut-rate prices.

Dictator Omar Torrijos had provided the soldiers and dynamite to blast away a huge boulder that stood in the way of a landing strip. Contadora began their famous friendship—the odd couple of the well-bred millionaire and the populist dictator. Torrijos dreamed of Contadora as a place "where French women would walk around without their tops," laughed Lewis years later.

But Lewis's project to develop the island's tourism, promoted by Torrijos, flopped. The government swallowed the debt and much of the property, and Lewis kept some land and two small islands, one for himself and one for his wife.

Noriega would have liked to sink Contadora, which he called "the oligarchy's luxury liner," but he settled for control of it. In 1984, Noriega named as his island manager Carlos Wittgreen, who had once been indicted in the U.S. on arms-smuggling charges and had grown rich helping the Cubans break the U.S. trade embargo. Noriega named drug trafficker César Rodriguez as manager of the island's airline. Island residents feared they were watching a Mafia takeover. Waiters in tuxedos served champagne on Rodriguez's opening-day celebration. A huge photograph of Noriega in white uniform and gold braid decorated the wall, and shocking-pink rugs lined the floors. Rodriguez, who would later be killed by drug world assassins in Colombia, would fly planeloads of models to Contadora Island for parties. He bought endless rounds of drinks for hangers-on at the hotel bar from a suitcase filled with $100 bills. For the first time, planes started landing on Contadora's airstrip in the middle of the night, refueling and sometimes off-loading large boxes, some filled with cash and others with drugs, and then flying on before dawn.

In 1986 Lewis tried to arrange the island's sale to Japanese businessman John Aoki. The plan was that Aoki would develop the island, but that Contadora residents could buy up to 20 percent of the shares of the newly-created company. Noriega undermined the sale, however, announcing that an Arab buyer had emerged who would pay more. When that deal collapsed, Noriega's people came back to Aoki themselves, but they cut out Lewis and other Contadora residents.

Noriega's move was part of a broader effort to separate Lewis from the Japanese, whom he considered Panama's new gold mine. At about the same time, he instructed his ambassador to Japan, Alberto Calvo, to tell Japanese businessmen to stop dealing with the traditional oligarchy. "Those names are dead," Noriega said one night. "Tell the Japanese I want them to deal with the new business class. People at this table." Sitting with him were business partners Carlos Duque, Carlos Wittgreen, Enrique Pretelt, and his mistress Vicky Amado.

With drink, Noriega grew angrier about his lack of control over Far East trade. At one point, he threw to the side a bowl of fish soup Vicky had put before him. She cowered in a corner. Then he ordered that an aide phone his ambassador in Taiwan so he could issue him instructions. When told it was 3 A.M. there, he burped, "So wake the son of a bitch." After the call was put through, Noriega said he didn't want to talk to the envoy anymore. The more his position was threatened, the more he wanted to humiliate any who thought they influenced him.

Noriega's second strike on Lewis came in early 1987. Lewis had bid for land on which he wanted to build an American military housing project, again with Aoki as one of his partners. Another partner was Roberto Eisenmann, the editor of the anti-Noriega paper *La Prensa*. The land would be a gold mine in the year 2000, when the housing could be sold on the open market. Noriega killed the project in March, before the bids could be opened.

Lewis sent his son Sammy to protest to President Delvalle, who was Sammy's father-in-law. Relations were already strained between Lewis and

Delvalle. The strains would worsen in the weeks to come, as Sammy divorced Delvalle's daughter while Lewis tried to bring down his government from Washington.

Only over Noriega's dead body would he allow these homes to be built by his enemies, said Delvalle.

Lewis sent back a message to Noriega through Delvalle. "This is the beginning of a fight. You are taking too much control of everything."

Lewis's original aim was to undermine Noriega through the May 1989 elections. He, like Barria, had flown to the Philippines for schooling on how to overthrow a dictator and he thereafter organized several meetings with leading opposition members, who had long criticized his complicity with the military. One American official joined them: John Maisto, the U.S. embassy's deputy chief of mission in Panama and a State Department veteran of the Philippine experience, who had been one of the first American officials to turn on Marcos. Maisto coached Lewis and others about why Filipino protests had worked, always stressing that nothing could be accomplished without a greater outpouring of public opposition to Noriega.

Lewis regarded his first big success as the lobbying of General Frederick F. Woerner, a soft-spoken, four-star general he'd known for years, who was about to take over the Southern Command in Panama. They had fished together often, and Woerner happily accepted Lewis's invitation to lunch at Maison Blanche, the expense-account watering hole for White House lobbyists. Lewis remembered Woerner, who fancied himself a soldier-diplomat, promising that he'd knock Noriega down to size. Woerner said later he'd never say such a thing, but he conceded Lewis had had "influence" on his June 5 change-of-command speech at Howard Air Force Base.

It was the first time the U.S. military had distanced itself from Noriega, and the message to Panamanian society was immediate: the gringos were no longer protecting Noriega.

Woerner carefully crafted the short speech, in both Spanish and English, to focus on "the proper role of the professional military in a democratic society." He disregarded protocol by not mentioning Noriega or complimenting him and after the speech, Noriega walked out in a huff without staying for the reception. One thousand prominent invitees spread the story around Panama the next day: the gringos were finally abandoning their pet, Noriega. Some, including Noriega, would see U.S. conspiracy in Colonel Díaz Herrera's revelations the next day. General Woerner, however, said Díaz Herrera's actions "were as much a surprise to me as I think they were to Díaz himself."

* * *

Lewis now had the street demonstrations he needed.

On Saturday, June 13, Lewis phoned U.S. senators and lobbyists from Panama to get the ball rolling against Noriega. The General, who was monitoring the calls, phoned Lewis and asked to discuss the crisis. Lewis consented, but warned Noriega he must be prepared to "make some personal sacrifices" to save Panama. He told Noriega to send someone senior enough to negotiate important matters.

Before the meeting, Lewis drove to Banco del Istmo to talk over the situation with his brother, Samuel, chairman of the bank, which was jointly owned by the Lewis family, the Delvalles, and other partners. Shortly after Lewis left the bank, three trucks full of Dobermans rolled up for an attack—just missing Lewis.

They broke through its one-story-high picture windows and tossed in a couple of tear-gas canisters to shake things up. They broke picture frames over antique prints of Panama Canal scenes, tellers' glass windows, and anything else that would shatter. The Dobermans focused immediate attention on the most attractive teller, Katya Poshol, who at twenty-nine was everything their class wanted to deflower: fair, shapely, elegantly dressed and coiffed. They beat her, and then threw her in the back of a paddy wagon with thirty Dobermans and a couple of other bank employes.

One Doberman forcibly held her on his lap while telling her that she'd be put in a cell with 200 criminals who hadn't had sex in months. Another covered his hands with blood oozing from his gashed leg, and then rubbed it on her breasts. Still another took her hand and put it over his crotch and laughed. The bank's manager of operations, who was in the paddy wagon as well, tried to stop them. They beat him back. "You are the bank manager and we are just the cops," sneered one, "but who is beating whom?"

The Dobermans stopped at a hospital to have their own wounds treated, and one of their number took pity on her. He released her. He wanted this pretty girl to like him. Katya Poshol needed a cast for her broken arm, but that was the least of her scars. A psychiatrist worked for months thereafter to heal her psychological bruises, and she still shakes whenever she sees a Doberman uniform.

It was a typical Noriega act, to weaken his negotiating partner before beginning talks. Lewis angrily phoned Noriega. "You want to have a dialogue, but then you break into my bank," said Lewis. "But I will put my feelings aside if you send people here to talk." Noriega's business partner, Carlos Duque, arrived twenty minutes later with a small delegation led by Colonel Alberto Purcell. Lewis sat with three opposition figures. Purcell reminded them of Idi Amin: fat, six feet tall, black, and wearing a camouflage-colored uniform and a .45-caliber pistol at his side. Lewis told Purcell that the only solution was Noriega's resignation. Idi Amin sneered. "There is nothing to discuss with you. Noriega is not negotiable," he said.

After the meeting, Noriega ordered an intelligence officer to phone Lewis. "You have become Enemy Number One of the defense forces," he said.

Lewis knew it was time to get out of the country. He had underestimated Noriega's strength, and officers were rallying around their General. But Noriega had also underestimated Lewis. The former ambassador worked the phone like a machine gun, firing off pleas for help to his powerful international friends.

One call was to Lewis's banker, Jackson T. Stephens, in Little Rock, Arkansas, who was desperate to get his friend and client to safety. Jack Stephens had accumulated one of the world's biggest fortunes at his investment banking firm of Stephens, Inc. by quietly disregarding Wall Street. He provided special services to customers, but seldom of the kind he gave Lewis that day. Stephens phoned his former classmate at the Naval Academy, chairman of the Joint Chiefs of Staff Admiral William Crowe. Stephens asked Crowe to help get Lewis out of the jam. Crowe phoned the Southern Command, and within minutes General Woerner sent over a black-paneled truck with some plainclothes bodyguards to protect Lewis and help him escape Panama.

They brought a secure mobile phone, over which Lewis worked out with Woerner the logistics of his escape. When two PDF helicopters hovered over Lewis's home, two of the American soldiers came out, so that Noriega would see what he was facing. And the Costa Rican ambassador held a huge national flag from his country, like a crucifix intended to ward off the vampires overhead. Lewis sped away in the ambassador's car to the city's Paitilla airport, where an American businessman had provided his plane to Lewis for his departure to Costa Rica. Seymour Millstein, another friend and the former head of United Brands, sent his Gulfstream II to Costa Rica to pick up Lewis and bring him to the United States.

Lewis had moved his war to Washington, with the help of a Pentagon military escort and American businessmen's private planes.

In Washington, Lewis hit the ground running. He called lobbyist and friend John "Riverboat" Campbell to put together a strategy to bring down Noriega. Campbell, a retired army colonel, was well connected from his years as the Pentagon's liaison to Congress, and he also knew the military after three tours of Vietnam and service as an instructor of psychological warfare at West Point. Lewis saw his character as a combination of John Wayne and Jimmy Stewart. "He was helping me like a brother," said Lewis.

The Reagan administration, however, wasn't yet ready for war on Noriega. National Security Adviser Frank Carlucci wouldn't even meet with Lewis. The meeting Lewis and opposition activist Roberto Eisenmann had with the NSC's Latin American specialist, José Sorzano, was disastrous.

Sorzano suggested that the opposition ought first to take on Noriega itself before involving Washington. "Why don't you solve your own problems first?" he said, reflecting the view of some others that Lewis was carrying out a personal vendetta.

Lewis blew up, saying that so long as Noriega was on the CIA payroll, Panamanians alone couldn't unseat him. "You are the source of his power," argued Lewis. "You have to cut yourselves off from Noriega."

Lewis and Campbell thereafter focused on the Senate. Lewis had long-standing ties to Democrats who backed the Panama Canal Treaties; most prominent among them was Edward Kennedy. He had also grown close to Senator Alfonse D'Amato through a business friend. D'Amato would rally the Republican right behind him and keep the issue alive. With Lewis's help, Kennedy aide Gregory Craig drew up a resolution that would begin the political landslide against Noriega.

Campbell lined up a series of conservative Republicans who had been Lewis's opponents on the Treaties, but whom he now needed as allies. Lewis would say later that Campbell had personally lined up at least forty votes.

Kennedy submitted the resolution, but he also found sponsors ranging from North Carolina's Jesse Helms and Senator D'Amato on the right to John Kerry of Massachusetts on the left. Kerry was quickly becoming the most active Democratic campaigner against Noriega, as his narcotics sub-committee continued to find more traces of Noriega's drug dealings.

The resolution noted that demonstrations had been set off by charges that the Panamanian Defense Forces and its commander were involved in the murder of Spadafora, the stealing of 1984 presidential elections, drug trafficking, and money laundering. It called for a "public accounting" of the allegations. It even asked the U.S. government to "direct the current commander of the Panama Defense Forces and any other implicated officials to relinquish their duties pending the outcome of the independent investigation."

Christopher Dodd, a Connecticut Democrat who was one of the Senate's leading experts on Latin America, thought Lewis and his allies on Capitol

Hill had gone too far, and that the resolution, by personalizing the problem as Noriega, overlooked deeper problems in Panama. He also believed that singling out Noriega restricted U.S. and Panamanian room for maneuver and negotiation with the General.

Dodd, a Spanish-speaking senator, knew Noriega better than anyone on the Hill. He had spent several long sessions with Noriega in the past, uncharacteristically sending away his aides during these meetings, and he flew to Panama now for some damage control, with a draft of the amendment in his hand. During a three-and-a-half-day stay, he talked with more than 150 people. Noriega liked and trusted this senator, who had taken the controversial position of defending him when other senators had wanted Panama decertified as being uncooperative in America's war on drugs in March 1987. That would have cut off some aid to the country. Dodd had succeeded in getting the Senate to table the amendment by a vote of 49–48. However, Dodd felt that Noriega had misunderstood what was a pragmatic position, aimed at preserving national interests, as political sympathy.

Noriega was oddly jovial when Dodd arrived at his headquarters with Washington's ambassador to Panama, Arthur H. Davis. The General complained that Americans misunderstood Panama because they spent too much time with the opposition. Dodd protested that his schedule was also packed with government meetings. "In fact, General," said Davis, "he's seen everyone here except Miss Panama."

Noriega snapped his fingers. Within a couple of minutes, a stunningly beautiful woman, the former Miss Panama, walked in. She worked in his office. "Talk about oneupsmanship," Ambassador Davis said later. They all laughed.

Dodd told Noriega the Senate resolution was a serious matter. He told Noriega he needed something to take back to Washington to turn the resolution around: this was a tactic that Congress had used with some success in moving Marcos toward reform and elections. Isn't there something you can give me? Dodd asked.

But Delvalle and Noriega weren't convinced the Senate would act. They underestimated the depth of emotion emerging against Noriega. They also miscalculated the lobbying power of Gabriel Lewis. Dodd told Noriega that turning Lewis against him had been a grave error. "He knows more senators than I do," he said, only half in jest.

When Dodd returned to Washington empty-handed, he nevertheless fought to erase Noriega's name from the resolution. "If we make the General the sole and absolute target of this resolution, we run the risk of denying those other elements, both civilian and military, in Panama the room to maneuver," he said. His staffers felt Lewis was using the Senate as his private battlefield.

But Lewis had lined up his ducks. "I think it is important that we not let General Noriega set the agenda for debate and discussion in terms of this particular resolution," Senator Kennedy countered, taking a swipe at Dodd. "Mr. President, I think that to leave General Noriega out would be like going to the North Pole and not talking about the ice and snow."

The resolution passed 75–13, with Dodd casting one of the baker's dozen votes against it.

Four days after the Senate resolution, Noriega struck back.

His puppet legislature rescinded his State of Emergency, aimed at stopping opposition demonstrations, in order to clear the way for anti-American protests.

When Ambassador Davis arrived at the embassy at 7:15 A.M. on June 30, riot policeman stood about four or five feet apart from each other around the entire embassy complex. All but a handful disappeared, however, when demonstrators arrived, along with a load of rocks that had been conveniently moved from a construction site at a nearby hospital.

At 10:45 A.M., a couple of dozen demonstrators began to stone the embassy and to destroy and overturn employees' cars. Policemen merely looked on. Davis fumed from his second-floor vantage point. He wanted to order the marines to fire.

Davis was an eccentric political ambassador, whose first try at diplomacy had come at age sixty-four after President Reagan's 1980 election. He was a self-made man, who'd made millions in Colorado supermarket developments and who'd gained his first ambassadorial posting in Paraguay, he imagined, through his friendship with Joe and Holly Coors of the conservative beer-making family. Yet his only Latin experience had been as an armed services weatherman in Chile after World War II. He certainly had never prepared for this.

The ambassador turned to John Maisto, his deputy chief of mission. "If those sons of bitches come onto the yard, I want the marines to kill those bastards," Davis said. At another point, he shouted at Maisto, "Give me the goddamned gun. I want to shoot these suckers."

Maisto calmly apprised the ambassador of the embassy's engagement rules. The marines couldn't fire until demonstrators had entered the building. Maisto's experience in the Philippines had prepared him for such violence.

"But, John, they are destroying public property," the ambassador protested.

"That's not enough, Mr. Ambassador," Maisto replied, repeating the rules.

Davis smiled. "John, I'm glad you're here." Davis conceded later that he would have ordered the marines to shoot if Maisto hadn't intervened.

The embassy's military attaché tried without luck to call someone at the PDF to call off the attack or protect the embassy. Davis called President Delvalle and Foreign Minister Jorge Abadía.

"Send the bill to the U.S. Senate," said Delvalle. "It is their resolution that caused all this."

Foreign Minister Jorge Abadía was more measured, offering to pay the bill once the problem was over.

"The bill is going to be higher than you think," Davis fumed. Without any instructions from the State Department, he suspended all economic and military assistance on behalf of the president. It was a highly unusual move for an ambassador: in fact, it hadn't ever been done before. Many thought it was illegal.

When Secretary of State Shultz called, however, Ambassador Davis was only encouraged. "Tell Delvalle this has happened in only one other place," Shultz said. "That was Iran. If that's the kind of relationship they want, that's the kind of relationship they'll get."

Davis demanded a meeting with Noriega the next day.

The General blamed the attack on a leftist faction of the ruling party. "They were very angry at the U.S. Senate resolution and the difficulty it was causing the country," he said.

By then Davis knew from his intelligence staff that the G-2 had organized the attack on Noriega's orders. "I had an embassy shattered, people under great strain, under attack, and you gave us no protection at all," he complained.

Noriega insisted the police hadn't been removed intentionally. "There was some trouble at the demonstration in the city and they had to leave," he said.

Davis saw he wasn't getting anywhere, so he tried another approach. He told Noriega his problems with the U.S. would end if he would seriously work toward democracy.

"We are working toward a firm democracy, a solid democracy that will last," said Noriega. "The Reagan administration and Elliott Abrams don't know what kind of democracy it will have to be. Only we do." Noriega told Davis that of the Latin American democracies that then existed, most of them would soon disappear. "They are weak democracies," he said. "They will be replaced by the military."

*　*　*

Unlike Iran's Ayatollah, Noriega had been on the CIA payroll when he ordered the attack on the American embassy. Senior officials, who had been discussing whether to cut off the CIA-Noriega relationship, now knew the payments had to end before they became an embarrassment through press leaks. However, the CIA didn't like the idea of ending a "liaison" relationship with an intelligence service that had provided valuable data on Nicaragua, Cuba, and other countries, as well as passports for undercover work.

The setting for the CIA's divorce proceedings was a "PRG" meeting—a Policy Review Group made up of sub-cabinet officials in the situation room in the White House basement. Deputy National Security Adviser Colin Powell sat under the presidential seal. He asked the CIA representative about Noriega's contractual relationship with the U.S.

The CIA representative said the General had been on the U.S. payroll for years. His G-2 was paid by two U.S. intelligence services, the DIA and CIA, to "defray the costs" of joint operations. The CIA man said the G-2 was an "inactive account," and that payments hadn't been made for about a year. He said Noriega wasn't paid personally anyway. But what he didn't say was that the money was put into a private account at the Bank for Credit and Commerce International, or BCCI, that only the General controlled. The CIA official didn't discuss Noriega's price, but others in the room knew it to be about $200,000 annually—equal to the president's salary.

It wasn't an unusual arrangement, the CIA's man said. The U.S. was paying military intelligence groups all over the world. Panama was one of the most valuable as a base for CIA and DIA regional operations, including an important electronic listening post.

The CIA official was then asked to outline the consequences of cutting ties. First, Noriega might disrupt use of military and intelligence facilities. Second, the U.S. would lose access to information Noriega had provided. Other military leaders with arrangements similar to that of Noriega might also now balk at helping the CIA.

"The CIA made an honest case," said one of the meeting's attendees. "You cannot have a relationship with people for many, many years and suddenly sever it without repercussions. The U.S. was like a spider in a web, and every little move in the net had repercussions."

Despite that, everyone at the meeting agreed that the relationship wasn't politically sustainable. Powell directed the CIA to cut Noriega off. No one protested. However, the CIA official warned them, "This is going to be a lot more difficult than is assumed in this room. Don't underestimate this guy. This man is a tough son of a bitch."

* * *

A few days later, Noriega displayed his personal rage in a crackdown that became known as "Black Friday," the single worst day of repression the country had known.

Noriega no longer felt constrained. The U.S. had cut him off, and the Civic Crusade was growing too bold. It had scheduled its planned July 10 demonstration one day ahead of the wedding of Noriega's daughter, and the General was convinced the timing was intentional.

Felicidad had orchestrated the grand event in the country's most elegant hotel, the Caesar Park Marriott. A chartered jet would bring the bridegroom and his family from Santo Domingo, where his father had been a general. Moët & Chandon had prepared the wedding invitations for 3,000 guests as a label on bottles of its best French champagne, delivered to the doors of the invitees with a Baccarat crystal champagne glass engraved with the couple's initials.

Now, however, the Marriott was filled with journalists covering the anti-Noriega rallies. It was no place or time for a wedding. Noriega moved his daughter's wedding forward to July 8; it was celebrated with only a couple of dozen guests at the Fort Amador chapel, where security was more certain. At a reception afterward, Noriega was morose and drunk when he complained to a friend that Díaz Herrera "and his Indian guru" had ruined his life. Just look at this wedding. Is this the sort of wedding the daughter of a Comandante should be having?

But that wasn't the only humiliation. At the same time, the opposition had taken to hanging pineapples from telephone poles, fruity effigies of "Pineapple Face" Noriega. When restaurant owner Sarah Simpson complained to her supplier a few days later that there were still no pineapples, despite the fact that all of them had been removed from Panamanian streets, he explained that Noriega's troops had bought out the whole market—thus disarming his opponents. Two days after the humiliation of his daughter's wedding, Noriega lashed out with all his anger.

What followed was the most drastic and longest-lasting suspension of constitutional guarantees in Panamanian history, including the closing of opposition press and radio. Over 1,500 protesters were arrested, dozens were tortured, and between 500 to 1,000 suffered bullet or bird-shot wounds.

Then on July 27, after six weeks of indecision, Noriega's Israeli-trained shock troops stormed into Díaz Herrera's mansion with hand grenades, tear-gas bombs, and Uzi submachine guns. Military helicopters hovered overhead. Díaz Herrera was on his bedroom floor with his wife,

Maigualida, under a half-smiling color photograph of Sai Baba, his Indian guru, in saffron robes. Noriega's Benedict Arnold was under arrest.

Fear spread through Panama like tropical heat. Noriega was back in control, and the war moved back to Washington.

Throughout the summer of 1987, Gabriel Lewis watched in frustration as Noriega regained confidence and Washington began to lose interest.

Lewis had never expected Noriega to survive so long, and now he feared his own exile could be permanent. He needed to revive pressure on the administration in Washington and on Noriega in Panama, so in September 1987 he called a man he would later refer to as his secret weapon: American political consultant Joel McCleary.

Lewis had watched McCleary help transform a colorless World Bank official, Nicholás Ardito Barletta, into a credible presidential candidate in 1984. Barletta had won by 1,713 votes, amid charges of fraud, but most Panamanians had considered it miraculous that he had come so close at all to legitimately beating Arnulfo Arias, a legendary Panamanian politician. Barletta charged that McCleary was more of a self-promoter than a genius, but Lewis was effusive in his praise.

"Joel's one of the greatest conspirators the world has never known," Lewis smiled. "He's out of a Le Carré novel. He plans all these things that belong in movies, and they turn out in real life."

McCleary and Noriega had fallen out in the summer of 1986, when the General had told a secret general staff meeting—McCleary says falsely—that the American consultant had begun conspiring to overthrow him. According to McCleary, Major Daniel Delgado said that Oliver North had planted the idea in the General's head, so as to get the former Carter aide out of Panama. North had feared word of his Contra dealings with Noriega might leak out and undermine the whole secret project. McCleary's friends in the Panamanian military advised McCleary to leave Panama. They said he was in danger.

So McCleary traveled about as far from Panama as humanly possible during 1986–87, to Dharmsala, India, a hill station on the way to Mount Everest. The Dalai Lama lived there, in exile from Tibet, and McCleary joined him, in exile from Noriega.

McCleary had converted to Buddhism after he graduated from Harvard College in 1971, but his short-lived fantasy of becoming a monk had disappeared during long chess matches on the New Jersey porch of Geshe Wangyal, the chief disciple of the Buddhist adviser to the last Russian czar. Wangyal had said that monks deluded themselves that they were doing good, but twentieth-century living demanded participation. He'd said that the Tibetans' problem was they weren't political enough—that's why they had lost the kingdom.

So McCleary had chosen politics on the advice of a Buddhist scholar. "On the way to Damascus, I got caught in a brothel," said McCleary.

However, McCleary's retreat from politics was still Buddhism. He flew to India to study Tibetan texts, a long-ignored passion, but within weeks he was helping the Dalai Lama plot his return to Tibet. McCleary even drew up a 170-page plan, which had three parts: how to save the intellectual tradition of Tibet; an overview of the Tibetan refugee community and its problems; and an action program that outlined how the Dalai Lama could bring the Tibet issue back to international attention. McCleary was conspiring for a new client.

However, in September 1987 Lewis wanted to bring McCleary back into Panamanian affairs, this time with a brief to destroy his former employer. McCleary had already returned from India, but Lewis had been reluctant to bring on a consultant who had been so close to men like José Blandón, who were still Noriega's allies. By autumn, however, Lewis had decided he could get rid of Noriega only with the military's help. McCleary had the contacts and knowledge he needed to pull it off. Again, Lewis's American banker, Jack Stephens, for whom McCleary had done work in the past, helped bring the two together and overcome any lingering distrust, during a meeting at the Westin Hotel in Washington.

McCleary said he would help, but first he gave Lewis a warning. "In my view, we could run up against the administration. There's a lot more involved here than you all realize. Noriega's worked for the CIA for years, and he's got friends all over."

Prodded by McCleary, Lewis called together a meeting of his inner core to revive the conspiracy against Noriega. On September 26, they all gathered at his home: former Carter White House aide Hamilton Jordan, former ambassador to Panama William Jorden, Washington lawyer and former Canal Treaties negotiator William Rogers, and Washington lobbyist and former army officer John Campbell. Lewis was pleased. His war cabinet was in action.

McCleary had convinced Lewis that the key to bringing down Noriega was forming an alliance with Blandón, whom Noriega had shipped off to New York as consul officer earlier that year, because of concerns among other officers about his loyalty.

Lewis had the muscle in Washington and Blandón had the know-how of Noriega's camp. Lewis was the lobbyist, and Blandón the computer-smart conspirator. But Lewis was a proud capitalist and socialite, and Blandón was a scheming leftist intellectual who hadn't yet decided to make the break with Noriega. They didn't much like or trust each other. Lewis said he'd meet Blandón only if McCleary would "attend every meeting I have with that bastard." Blandón had fewer misgivings. Without Lewis, the Americans wouldn't trust him.

The three men met at Lewis's Washington home on October 3. Blandón said that Noriega had just asked him to find a way out of his current political crisis with Washington in a way that would prevent future criminal indictments. Noriega's intelligence channels had reported that a Miami grand jury was making progress in putting together drug charges against him and that a Tampa grand jury was close behind.

Noriega told Blandón he wanted a plan that would allow him to leave politics, give him the right to stay in Panama and assure immunity from prosecution.

He would later give him specific written instructions: "I recommend that you be careful, cautious, conceptual in setting forth the issues," Noriega cabled to Blandón. Noriega told Blandón that all dealings with the plan "must be kept under your strict control, so that it does not appear as a formula of understanding on the part of the government." Noriega didn't want to give his political enemies the impression that Panama was like "the Japanese empire in World War II, signing its capitulation on the decks of the *Missouri.*"

Lewis arranged his first meeting with a senior administration official, Deputy Assistant Secretary of State William Walker. They met secretly at the United Nations mission in New York. Walker was impressed with Blandón's knowledge and his rich store of information on Noriega.

On October 26, at Sawyer-Miller's Fifth Avenue offices, Blandón, Lewis, and McCleary met again to draw up the outline of the "Blandón Plan." Blandón and Lewis threw out ideas, and McCleary put them down on large legal pads.

As usual, Lewis found his concentration in a glass of Diet Coke. The fluid was little more than a setting for ice cubes. Lewis focused on them entirely, picking each one out of a half-full glass, pinching it between his thick, round fingers, and then tossing it absentmindedly into his mouth. His teeth then ground the cubes into disintegrating bits. The conspirators littered the room with yellow legal pads.

They knew they were producing something historic. The two Panamanians then left McCleary at his Macintosh desk-top computer, where he spent the night hacking out what he thought was only a rough draft for his partners' perusal. Instead, it became a blueprint from which U.S. officials and Panamanian oppositionists labored for months.

Lewis was so excited by the draft that he ran over to the State Department to brief officials, without telling either McCleary or Blandón. Before

long, the "Blandón Plan" was circulating around Washington and becoming the basis for all future strategies for removing Noriega. McCleary was
angry that their team had lost control of the plan's circulation, and Blandón was doubly nervous. Before long, the worst happened: Noriega got a
leaked copy from an American friend with contacts at the Pentagon.

Two versions had been prepared, one for Noriega's consumption and the
other for those who wanted to undo him. Blandón's version for Noriega
was sugarcoated: "This plan is good because, first, it is a Panamanian
solution and it is our plan, not the opposition's. Second, you can buy time
and get [an agreement] from the opposition that you will leave in April
1988. And we can negotiate with the U.S. that there will be no indictments.
For you, it is the best, and we can transform this into the idea that you
are giving a gift to the Panamanian people."

The Blandón Plan called for the retirement of all general staff members
with twenty-five years' service, along with the "Gang of Six," Noriega's
closest cronies. The plan would have stripped the PDF of control over
immigration, customs, prisons, and civil and criminal investigation—generally castrating it of immense powers and profit-making capability. The
carrot for Noriega was that President Reagan would grant Noriega criminal immunity.

However, McCleary had made the administration's version a conspirator's recipe to unseat the General. Its primary points sent Noriega into a
fury when he saw them.

—Under the heading, "Selling the plan to Noriega," the plan said any
explanation to Noriega should be timed to coincide with a series of events
(strikes, protests) which would "remind him of his tentative hold on Panama. . . ."

—Before November 4, Pentagon official Nestor Sanchez must be recruited to carry the message. The logic was that only a good friend could
carry such a tough message. "Noriega trusts Nestor," the plan read. "He
will see him immediately."

—Within two days, the U.S. Southern Command leader Fred Woerner
should carry the same message to Noriega and three other senior officers.
"Important to give to all four, so Noriega has no freedom to freely interpret
message to others." The message would say there is no support in the CIA
or Pentagon for Noriega.

If Noriega was angry, however, other officers were even angrier. They
suspected that Noriega would get a rich exile, but that they would be left
behind to face jail or execution. With members from the "Gang of Six" in
the room, Noriega phoned Blandón, and screamed at him for pursuing an
unauthorized course with Washington.

"You can't talk to me like a sergeant," Blandón bristled, knowing

Noriega was speaking for the benefit of other officers in the room, in order to wash his hands of the plan to end their careers. To make his loyalty to fellow officers clearer, he even locked up one of Blandón's two sons, a teenager who already hated his father for his links to the military and Noriega. For some time Noriega wouldn't even take Blandón's calls. Two weeks after the arrest, Blandón finally flew to Panama and gained his son's release.

The Blandón Plan gasped its final breath when an old friend of Vice President Bush's came to town looking for business. In November, retired admiral Daniel Murphy called on Noriega, ostensibly to drum up clients for a new consulting business he wanted to start.

Noriega regarded the mission as a sign that the Reagan administration wasn't as determined to remove him from power as Blandón was saying. He also regarded Murphy as his back channel to Bush. Murphy had been Bush's deputy director at the CIA in 1976 and his chief of staff during President Reagan's first term. It was Murphy's third trip to Panama, and he had told friends during his frequent tennis outings that Noriega could become his newest client.

The trip's most bizarre twist, however, was that it was arranged and paid for by Tongsun Park, the South Korean lobbyist who had been indicted in 1977 in the Koreagate influence-peddling scandal. To give the trip a shadier aspect yet, the two flew to Panama using the borrowed private plane of an international arms dealer, Sarkis Soghenalian, who had often carried out missions in the Middle East for U.S. intelligence agencies. Soghenalian's passenger manifest for the November 7 mission included Murphy, Park, Park's girlfriend or secretary Miss Oh, and a mysterious G. Lebarge. Soghenalian pegged Lebarge as an intelligence agent, both because of his mannerisms and because of the fact that Park and Murphy delayed their departure by nearly two hours while they waited for him to arrive with documents.

Murphy had known Park socially for years, a man who had long been friendly with the Bush crowd and who entertained Washington's pretty and powerful at the exclusive Georgetown Club, which the South Korean had founded and where he still entertained. Murphy insisted later that he didn't even ask Park who was paying for the trips. "Tongsun Park is a respected international businessman who deals with some very fine people," Murphy explained. "When you analyze how he maneuvers around the world, he seems to be generally accepted everywhere but in the U.S."

Park had been trying to expand his business contacts in Panama, and the South Korean's delivery of Murphy would prove his usefulness to Noriega. The South Korean and Noriega were already friends, having hit it off so well they were frequently spotted together betting at cockfights.

The South Korean, with Murphy in tow, proudly told Soghenalian that they were carrying a message to Noriega from the vice president. Park liked telling this plugged-in arms dealer about his adventures. The more important Park appeared, the more likely Soghenalian would be to bestow favors. Murphy stood quietly to Park's side, not contradicting the story until he later had to explain himself before Senator Kerry's narcotics subcommittee.

When Park and Murphy appeared without prior notice—not unusual in Soghenalian's clandestine business—he lamented that he had only his personal Boeing 707. He wouldn't charge them for the crew or flying time, but they'd have to retank, and the plane burned $2,600 worth of fuel per flight hour. Park said that would be fine. Noriega would be all the more impressed with such a large plane. In the end, Noriega refueled the aircraft gratis anyway.

The arms dealer would lose money in the venture, but two important people would owe him favors. ". . . It goes that way, that one hand washes the other and they both wash the face," Soghenalian would say later.

For a trip he portrayed as a private mission, Murphy was unusually well briefed before departure. He spoke to senior officials at the State Department, the Pentagon, the CIA, and the NSC and to Bush's national security adviser Donald Gregg.

Murphy, senior Panamanian officials said, gave Noriega a surprisingly positive assessment of his outlook. He mentioned a series of reforms Noriega should undertake, but he didn't insist that Noriega needed to resign. He mentioned a date for possible retirement, but it was months later than the Blandón Plan's April 1988 target. Murphy told Noriega not to worry about Abrams, who didn't carry that much weight in Washington, the Panamanian government officials said.

Those who met Murphy in Panama were surprised and angered at the relatively soft line he was taking vis-à-vis Noriega. At one party, former Panamanian foreign minister Fernando Eleta was aghast at Murphy's "naive and unprobing" view of Noriega. He left the party early, in disgust. "The man was over his head," said Eleta.

Murphy backed off his Panama mediation only after Lewis leaked the details to Washington newsmen in early 1988. However, in mid-1988 Murphy attended a party that Tongsun Park was throwing at the Georgetown Club for the visiting Panamanian ambassador to Japan, Alberto Calvo. He raised a toast to Panama, apologizing for all the harm that misguided U.S. policies had caused the country. Murphy's words were dutifully reported back to Noriega.

The Murphy meeting gave Noriega confidence he could weather the storm with Washington. He felt festive as he flew to the annual conference of Latin American military chiefs at Mar del Plata, Argentina, in late November. To tweak the U.S. just before he left, he had granted the Soviet airline Aeroflot landing rights for the first time and he had given Muammar el-Qaddafi the green light to open a Libyan People's Bureau.

He phoned Blandón from Argentina. To hell with Elliott Abrams, he said. He said that Murphy was on his side, and that the retired admiral had assured him that Abrams and Ambassador Davis weren't important. Murphy said, according to Noriega, that he had enough contacts to get Ambassador Davis fired. Murphy and Park had offered him a deal under which the Japanese would help Panama economically. The strategy was for Prime Minister Takeshita, who was a friend of Tongsun Park, to convince President Reagan to ease the pressure on Noriega and he would make democratic reforms. Murphy denied Noriega's claims. Whether they were true or not, General Noriega was using their meeting to his advantage.

As usual, Noriega arrived late at the conference, with a delegation far larger than rules allowed. The General ignored all protocol, and put his entourage into a five-star hotel. They began drinking and whoring upon arrival. Other Latin officers saw Noriega as a misfit in their European-influenced ranks. He reveled all night and then slept through most of the substantial discussions.

Noriega was turning Mar del Plata into a publicity stage. At noon one day, other generals were surprised to find Noriega outside his hotel in a French-designer jogging suit, Lecoq Sportif, in baby blue. A camera crew was in tow. But Noriega didn't join fellow generals jogging on the beach. Instead, he ran in place in front of his hotel for no more than three minutes while cameras rolled. Then he returned to his suite for an afternoon nap.

State Department officials say Woerner had been instructed to carry a tough message to Noriega in Argentina, but that he cabled back that the atmosphere wasn't right for such a talk. Woerner argued that he wasn't ever given orders to dress down Noriega, and so he didn't. He never thought it a good idea to carry the poison personally, anyway. Whether Noriega were forced out or not, his relationship with the Panamanian military was better protected by staying in the shadows. "I could best serve by being separated from the message," he said.

Lewis lobbied hard for an official mission to Panama that would undo the comedy of mixed signals that had encouraged Noriega to fight on. Someone finally had to tell the General he was finished.

Then the administration had to argue about who should be the spear-carrier. A State Department official wasn't convincing enough; the Pentagon didn't want to send a man in uniform, and the Iran-Contra aftertaste prompted the CIA and NSC to decline any involvement. One official suggested Vernon Walters, who had known of Noriega for years as the CIA's deputy director and had been familiar with the original intelligence relationship with Noriega's G-2. He declined the honor, saying he didn't want to be Noriega's "undertaker."

The opposition wanted to send Nestor Sanchez, the former CIA official who knew Noriega better than anyone, but the State Department didn't trust him and Sanchez didn't want the job.

The administration chose Richard Armitage, the Pentagon's assistant secretary for international security affairs. Every agency had a veto, and only Armitage survived the blackball. He was macho enough, a Vietnam veteran and a weight lifter, but so much time had been spent on choosing the man that no one could agree on a very tough message. And Armitage didn't speak Spanish. So, through an interpreter, he delivered a toothless message that Noriega could and did see as a bluff.

Noriega opened the late morning meeting by pouring Armitage and himself a drink of Old Parr scotch. Davis declined a tumbler. Armitage committed the tactical error of saying he didn't know much about Panama. Noriega lectured him ad nauseam, recalling his past relationship with the U.S. He talked of the U.S. officers who had trained and befriended him. He spoke of how he and General John Galvin, the former Southern Command chief, had organized more and bigger joint maneuvers than ever before. "Torrijos tried to keep the two militaries apart, but I have brought them closer together," he said. Now, after all this work, the U.S. was turning against Noriega, he said, referring to himself in the third person.

"We don't want a confrontation with you," said Armitage. "We want to solve this problem, and we want you to be part of the solution." He then outlined a plan under which Noriega would retire and democracy would be promoted, but the message was far softer than the General had expected. And there was no ultimatum.

Noriega had stage-managed the result in advance anyway. After three hours of largely unstructured, casual chitchat, they said good-bye. Noriega gave Armitage some Cuban cigars with his name on them to give to his "friend Nestor" (Sanchez).

The General then appeared before his officers in the courtyard of his headquarters complex, holding the bottle of Old Parr like a trophy. He declared the Pentagon to be on his side in a battle against Elliott Abrams and the State Department. Surely, the officers thought, the Americans wouldn't down a bottle of scotch with a dictator they wanted to depose.

Noriega laughed that Armitage had only come to warn him against Blandón.

It was a warning Noriega ought to have heeded. Instead, the falsely confident Noriega fired Blandón as his New York consul at the end of the year. He then ordered Blandón to return to Panama, where he could monitor him more closely.

Blandón refused, and he told two emissaries sent by Noriega to Miami on New Year's Day that he would be forced to testify against Noriega now that his diplomatic immunity was gone. He sent the message that Noriega should either announce retirement plans or face Blandón's testimony against him.

Noriega didn't believe Blandón would dare act against him, but to be safe, he ordered one of Blandón's best friends to lure the would-be rebel back to Panama. "José, don't make a terrible mistake," said Didio Sosa, who had worked with Blandón in supporting leftist groups throughout the region. "It's not too late to mend fences." Sosa, whose voice was tense, knew he was summoning Blandón to either prison or death. Sosa said he wanted to meet Blandón in a neutral place, Costa Rica. "No obligations," he said.

Blandón lied that he could come. That would buy him just enough time to testify and get under witness protection. He would then testify the following week before a Senate subcommittee on narcotics.

Lewis's weapon against Noriega was the Senate, and now Blandón's would be the judicial system. And both found ready allies in senators and U.S. attorneys who had much to gain politically in taking on Noriega.

The next voice Blandón heard from Panama was that of his retarded twenty-year-old son. He was weeping uncontrollably.

It was less than a week after Noriega's once-loyal adviser had testified before a Miami grand jury against Panama's dictator. Blandón had expected some trouble, but he thought the handicapped boy was beyond harm at his farmhouse near the Atlantic port of Colón.

The modest home had been customized for the boy, whose birth defects had left him prone to frequent seizures. The edges of tables and shelves were rounded or padded, and the walls hadn't any electrical sockets. Blandón's son lived quietly and spent his days feeding and playing with the farm animals, each of which he had given a name. But the boy's voice had a desperation Blandón hadn't ever heard before.

A dozen soldiers had invaded the farm, slaughtered his pet calf, and carried off his other pets—a horse, a cow, and a goat. They then began to burn down the house with all his special furniture. The soldiers only stopped in fear once the boy went into seizures.

"Help me, Daddy," he sobbed. "Please help me."

Blandón, the cold conspirator, cried.

* * *

The attack on the farm was born more of frustration than strength. General Noriega's worst nightmare had now come true. For years he had been putting crooks on planes to Miami to face prosecution. Now he was the fugitive from U.S. law. And it had all begun two years earlier, undramatically, when a resourceful anti-drug agent had gone under cover in Miami.

CHAPTER
FOURTEEN

FOREIGN POLICY BY INDICTMENT

*A Latin American poet once said, "Good belongs to all,"
and there is nothing more universal than the threat of
drugs and the necessity to combat and destroy this men-
ace.*

—NORIEGA, SUMMER 1984

Danny Martelli confidently steered his mauve Jaguar—a shiny, new twelve-cylinder SJX with all the trimmings—to the back door of the Cessna dealership. He checked his gold Rolex watch and saw that he was just late enough to appear cool. A gold bracelet dripped from his wrist, and a gold chain dangled from his neck. Martelli's black beard was neatly trimmed and his garb was chic Banana Republic. It was enough to suggest wealth but not to arouse undue attention. It was January 1985, but the summery Miami sun was beating down. He looked through his Porsche Carrera sunglasses to see that the hangers-on of the drug world, all dressed more or less as he was, were registering the arrival of his unfamiliar face.

Alfredo Caballero, the owner of DIASCA, Inc., sold used and new Cessna airplanes and parts. He also ran one of Miami's most successful front operations for a burgeoning drug business. Caballero took Martelli into his office, and they spoke over the noise of planes taking off from Miami International Airport's noisy southern runway. Caballero wanted to make sure this Italian-American was what he claimed to be: a man who could launder drug money risk-free. Martelli's price was fair enough: three percent for wire transfers and five percent for cashiers' checks. He also refused sums of less than $100,000. That showed seriousness. And when two Cubans appeared unexpectedly with money for the first deal, Martelli exploded, just as he should have. "Hey, look, pal, I don't like to be surprised," he complained. "I don't like seeing faces I don't expect." Caballero calmed the money launderer, and they sealed their first deal: the laundering of $250,000.

On his way out, the elated Martelli automatically began flirting with the Nicaraguan-born secretary, Patty. She seemed interested, and he smiled to himself. It was the final act of a perfect day's performance.

Martelli—a.k.a. Daniel E. Moritz, undercover agent for the Drug Enforcement Administration—had worked his way inside a drug operation that would lead U.S. prosecutors to an indictment of General Manuel Antonio Noriega three years later. Although Moritz didn't know it then, he would be the key player in an investigation that would alter American foreign policy toward an ally who had been on American intelligence payrolls for two decades. "Moritz started it all," said then–assistant U.S. attorney Richard Gregorie. "He's about the best I've ever seen."

In early 1985, Moritz was taking it one step at a time. He knew his ultimate targets were Noriega and cartel boss Pablo Escobar Gaviria, but he could only get to them through Floyd Carlton Caceres, whose organization in the U.S. worked out of Caballero's office. An informant, Edgar Espinosa, had tipped Moritz off to the Noriega connection. Espinosa wanted some money and a U.S. visa, and Moritz had promised both if Espinosa could get him inside the business.

As one of the most convincing actors in the DEA, Moritz made drug dealing look easy. Over the next year he would be the middleman in twelve money-laundering deals, amounting to $3.8 million. He'd buy and sell several aircraft for the Carlton organization and he'd even set up a used-car company as a front for couriers driving cocaine to Florida from Texas. Moritz had so won his partners' trust that when they decided to retire, fearing a federal crackdown, they wanted to turn the business over to him. One of the dopers was even arrested carrying tens of thousands of dollars in a $200 leather briefcase Moritz had given him. Moritz had had the doper's initials engraved on the outside.

Moritz knew an undercover cop's major mistake is overanxiousness. When he met his target, Floyd Carlton, in March 1985, he nonchalantly offered his services for his usual price. Take it or leave it. Noriega's pilot looked Moritz over suspiciously. He wanted to know what banks he used and how he insulated his clients. "That's not your affair," said Moritz. "If you had that information, you'd have no reason to come to me. I don't ask you how you do your business." Carlton liked Moritz immediately.

Danger wasn't new to Moritz: friends thought it was *his* drug. He had been a Special Forces Green Beret in South and Central America in the early 1970s, so he'd learned some Spanish before joining the DEA in 1981. He'd also seen some action in the Middle East, "but nothing that's on the record." He was a veteran of commando training in Turkey, underwater demolition in Greece, mountain ski warfare instruction in Spain, and jungle survival school in Panama. He liked challenges, and few beat going after Noriega.

Moritz's investigation of Carlton hit serious snags in mid-1985, however, when Carlton vanished unexpectedly. Drug bosses falsely accused him of running off with an $18 million shipment of cocaine, after the plane's pilot and Carlton's close friend, Teofilo Watson, disappeared in Costa Rica, having landed on a field used for shipments of arms to the Contras. They backhoed a field of his Panamanian ranch to search for the drugs, and a hood kidnapped and tortured his cousin—clubbing him with rifle stocks and prodding him with electric wires—to get Carlton's whereabouts. "I gave him a few little jolts just to relax him," said the torturer, later, when he was questioned by prosecutors.

Carlton was safely hidden in Panama, however, protected by General Noriega himself. So Moritz decided to close in on the rest of the group. He had heard that a big shipment was coming in a twin-engined Cessna 441 with the tail number N703US, so he put into the intelligence computers to be on the lookout for it. On September 22, 1985, he got word from Customs that the plane was in Brownsville, Texas, and preparing to fly to Florida. An airport security guard bought by the traffickers opened up the landing field after midnight so that the pilot, Tony Azpruia, could take off. Moritz asked Customs planes and helicopters to follow, and a cross-country chase began that had Azpruia hopscotching from Texas to Florida until, out of gas, he landed his plane with more than 500 kilos of cocaine on an unfinished stretch of I-75.

Azpruia escaped into a swamp, submerging himself for five hours while breathing through reeds. Metro-Dade dive teams, DEA agents, and assorted other law enforcement officers gave up the chase after a couple of hours, dissuaded by alligators and water moccasins. Azpruia called his Miami contact, who was a Moritz contact, for safekeeping. Moritz logged his every move. He wasn't ready to bring Azpruia in yet, but he now had a cocaine shipment and a trail of enough other evidence to charge Carlton, Caballero, Azpruia, and others in sealed indictments.

Moritz came out from undercover long enough to visit assistant U.S. attorney Richard Gregorie. "I can give you General Noriega," he said flatly. Gregorie was always skeptical of agents who talked big, but Moritz's story was too good to disbelieve.

"There's my next target," smiled Gregorie, whose beard and balding head gave him an oddly monkish appearance. "Let's get to work."

As a prosecutor, Gregorie had always looked for ways to work up the line—to get from the dealers, the pilots, and the middlemen to the source of trouble. He pursued Noriega with prosecutorial zeal. He had first heard about Noriega and his ties to the drug world from super-informant Barry Seal, who had had several business meetings with Medellín cartel members in Panama in 1984.

Gregorie knew from watching Panama that the cartel operated there with impunity. From May 1984, however, Gregorie had been frustrated in any attempts to link it to Noriega. He had wearied of cutting off branches but never getting to the roots of the drug trade.

His most troubling struggle had been pursuing drug boss Jorge Ochoa, and finding that U.S. officials either didn't want to help or refused assistance outright. He told friends that he felt "a lot like the soldiers in Vietnam must have felt. We aren't being allowed to win this war. The higher I go, the more reluctance there is. The closer to the target, the less we want to hit it."

That only made him want Noriega's head all the more.

Gregorie and Moritz agreed they had to bring in Carlton, wherever he was, and Gregorie assembled a grand jury to indict Carlton's allies on the strength of Moritz's undercover work. They returned sealed indictments on all the major players.

In January 1986, Moritz's business partners thought it was time for them to retire. The September bust had frightened them, and they had been so impressed with their friend Danny Martelli that they invited him to take over the business. He consented to do at a festive celebration of their retirement at the Coral Gables home of drug trafficker Cecilio Saenz-Barria, with whom Moritz had grown increasingly friendly. Over lobster and champagne, they told Martelli that the last shipment was coming in the next week. After he laundered their profits, the business was his.

On January 23, 1986, the plane full of cocaine was seized near the border in Mexico before it could leave for Texas, and a sweep of arrests brought in Carlton's allies. As each was brought to DEA headquarters and saw the familiar face of Moritz greet them, they knew they were in deep. Moritz flew to Texas three days later to identify Cecilio Saenz-Barria. Saenz-Barria smiled when his friend walked into the Houston courtroom, believing Moritz was there to bail him out. But when the judge referred to Moritz as the "DEA agent from Miami," Saenz-Barria's face turned ashen. "He put his head in his hands," said Moritz.

Moritz's knowledge frightened them enough to agree to cooperate in bringing in Carlton. But the end game was still Noriega—something neither these convicts nor Washington yet knew.

Having heard rumors that an indictment was being prepared against him, Floyd Carlton came out of hiding briefly in early January. He feared for his life, and he was looking for protection. His friend General Noriega wouldn't see him, apparently figuring that what he didn't touch couldn't make him dirty. When Carlton told Noriega through a mediator that he might have problems, Noriega only sent back the message that Carlton should keep his mouth shut, no matter what happened.

So Carlton looked elsewhere for help. Through friends, he organized a clandestine meeting with the DEA's local station chief, Tom Telles, and two other agents at the Holiday Inn on Panama's exclusive Paitilla Point. They chatted while driving in the DEA agent's car.

Telles asked what he wanted to talk about.

"Have you not heard my name?" Carlton asked.

The agents conceded that they had.

Carlton complained that Telles had ignored several of his requests for a meeting through middlemen. "You have always told them you have nothing to talk to me about. And the fact is that I believe that I can go before the American judicial system and speak of a lot of things that are happening in this country, and I can even prove them." He offered documents and cassette recordings that would prove Noriega's complicity in the drug war.

One of the agents asked what he could prove.

"Money laundering, drugs, weapons, corruption, assassinations," he said. But when he mentioned General Noriega's name, Carlton saw they were upset. Then he grew nervous himself, fearing that Noriega was too close to this group of Americans. The agents contacted Carlton only once more, and when he returned their calls he was unable to get through.

"They did not try to contact me again, and the only thing I had asked for was protection for myself and my family," he said. "And at that time I didn't have any problems with the American judicial system."

At least none that Carlton knew of. In fact, Telles was already working secretly with Moritz to put together indictments against Carlton's friends, yet he couldn't inform Carlton—who was the next target.

Shortly after Carlton's rejection by DEA agents in Panama City, he got word of the January 23 arrests of his friends and learned that his name was atop the indictment against them. Then in March his friend and fellow trafficker, César Rodriguez, was assassinated in Medellín. He was certain Noriega had set up the killing. Rodriguez and Noriega had run afoul of each other. Rodriguez had been openly flaunting his riches, running a club atop the Bank of Boston building where members paid an annual fee of $1,000 a head. Noriega had inspired the idea, but now he wanted to divorce himself from it and Rodriguez. He even told Rodriguez to sell his home, which was beside Noriega's in the elite Altos del Golf section of Panama City. Noriega, belatedly, was trying to repair his image.

Rodriguez, having been sent the message by Nivaldo Madriñan, Noriega's chief investigator had recorded a conversation with the General in which Rodriguez had said to Noriega "Don't send me that little fag. I've got the balls to meet you face to face, so don't send me messages like a kid."

Said Carlton: "The only person that would scream and say vulgar things to Noriega was César."

Rodriguez had known too much about Noriega. Carlton had even sat in on a meeting where Rodriguez had discussed with Paraguayans the possibility of assassinating Somoza for $5 million, apparently to be paid for by Noriega. Another group had done the killing in the end, but those were the types of matters Rodriguez had known about Noriega.

He'd kept tapes of their conversations, imagining that he might need protection someday. Both Carlton and Rodriguez had known that Noriega was impetuous, and now he wanted to forget them. "Since he went up to being a general, little by little he tried to free himself of certain friends."

Carlton began to fear for his own life. "All of us were a danger to General Noriega," he said. "He was trying to clean up his image and we—those of us who at some point had done something illegal for him—were a danger for him."

While DEA agents in Panama were putting Carlton off, DEA agents in Miami were closing in. After two uncomfortable weeks in prison, Alfredo Caballero had decided to cooperate with Moritz, the man who had put him behind bars. In June 1986, Caballero called his friend Carlton and promised him valuable information on the investigations into his drug trafficking, and asked him to meet him in San José, Costa Rica, at the exclusive Cariari Hotel.

Caballero called room service to order a mixed drink for himself and beers for Carlton and three friends, but the call was switched automatically to a nearby room, where Moritz, three DEA agents posted in San José, and Costa Rican agents waited. Moritz, uncomfortable in a waiter's outfit, nervously took the tray of drinks to the door, careful not to spill them. But when one of Carlton's friends opened it, Costa Rican agents stormed past and arrested Carlton, and Moritz dumped the tray and came face-to-face with his erstwhile business partner.

Even at this late point, the State Department knew nothing about a case that would end up permanently altering its policy toward Noriega and his

Panama. Gregorie's boss, U.S. Attorney Leon Kellner, didn't tell State
about the Noriega link even after he was seeking Carlton's extradition from
Costa Rica. "All they had to know was that this guy was a defendant, and
so that's what we told them," Kellner said. "I've always been concerned
about State's commitment to the drug fight. I never told them at the time
that this was about Noriega, and I don't think anyone else did."

Noriega later would brand his drug indictment political, but from the
beginning, prosecutors regarded administration officials as their enemies.
They moved quietly so as not to alert officials who might try to undermine
their work.

Carlton still needed to be extradited, however, and U.S. agents had
picked up intelligence that Noriega wanted to break Carlton out of jail.
They grew more worried when a prison informant told authorities that
Carlton had offered the prison warden a $1 million bribe. Carlton was
transferred to a higher security prison. They had no reason to be worried,
however. Noriega had distanced himself from Carlton. He calculated that
he was well enough insulated from prosecution and that involving himself
in the Carlton mess would only suggest complicity.

Carlton sent Noriega several letters requesting help, but the General sent
back messages through intermediaries that he would get Carlton out of the
United States through a prisoner exchange agreement. "By that date, he
was supposedly going to be president of Panama, and there wouldn't be
any problems," said Carlton.

It was a critical miscalculation on Noriega's part. More than six months
later, after mountains of paperwork and tens of phone calls, Moritz was
finally given the go-ahead to pick up Carlton in San José in January 1987.

It had been six long months since Moritz had helped arrest Carlton the
previous June at the Cariari Hotel. Gregorie had doubts that Carlton
would be willing to talk, but Moritz—partly to promote his own case—
continued to insist that he wouldn't have any choice once he was in U.S.
custody. As Carlton stepped out of the back door of the Costa Rican police
wagon, which looked more like a camouflage-colored Good Humor truck,
he exchanged a smile with Moritz. They were together again. "Well,
Danny, what happens next?" Carlton asked in Spanish.

As the DEA plane lifted off, a Cheyenne turboprop, Moritz read Carlton
his rights over the roar of the twin engines. Their faces were only two feet
apart in its small backseats, and Carlton looked into Moritz's eyes. "What
do you want," asked Carlton.

"*El General,*" said Moritz.

Carlton smiled. "We'll talk later."

First, Carlton wanted a cigarette. But Kenneth Kennedy, Moritz's superior, who had come along to pick up Carlton, was quitting, so he could only

offer him a Nicorette. Carlton tried one, then spit out the bitter gum in disgust.

So he pulled out a hand-held, computerized game called Donkey Kong. Kennedy joined him, but Carlton won every time, having had little else to occupy him during his months behind bars. Kennedy wanted to win this man's confidence, and if it took losing at Donkey Kong all the way to Miami, it was a small price to pay.

Gregorie and Moritz began debriefing their new witness almost immediately, in a large grand-jury room at the Miami courthouse. Neither of them was prepared for the rich bank of information they had captured. They feared this might be the only shot they got at Carlton, if he decided later not to testify or was somehow freed or killed by Noriega. So they pumped him all day for an entire week.

Regarding Noriega, he was an encyclopedia. Carlton had provided them details of how Noriega had orchestrated arms deliveries to the Sandinista guerrillas starting in 1977, and how Carlton had flown many of the supply missions through 1979. Carlton later flew at least seventeen missions for Noriega to supply El Salvadoran guerrillas. "We did nothing without his approval," Carlton said.

He said Noriega's salary was $2,200 to $2,500 a month, but that he supplemented that income from illegal earnings. He owned at least five homes, a couple of apartment buildings, two BMWs (both model 735), a collector's item Corvette valued at $50,000, a Grand Wagoneer station wagon, and a van supplied "with all the luxury items." He also owned several airplanes, apartments around the world, and many businesses, both legal and illegal.

Carlton spoke of how he helped introduce Noriega to the Medellín cartel, and he outlined Noriega's role in helping drug dealers launder money, transship drugs, and set up a cocaine-processing laboratory. Carlton provided dates, descriptions of meetings, and names of those who attended, and he delivered all the information in such a deadpan style—never exaggerating—that none of his interrogators ever doubted his credibility.

During breaks in his debriefing, Gregorie and Moritz would retreat to the hallway and shake their heads. They had captured a prosecutor's gold mine. "We'd look at each other and say, 'Holy shit'," said Moritz. "We knew what he was saying would forever change the relationship between the United States and Panama. This was going to be one of the best CIs [confidential informants] in history. He had a photographic memory, full of too much detail to be invention." Carlton also knew enough about Noriega's personal life to turn his listeners' stomachs.

Senate aides got a small taste of the sordid stories Carlton was privy to a few months later, when staffers from Senator Kerry's narcotics subcommittee pressed him to explain why he didn't like to spend time with Noriega. "Aside from the fact that he's a repulsive person," Carlton reluctantly answered, "you're near him and you feel death near you. That person inspires you with terror. César [Rodriguez] on one occasion told me.—I don't want to say it—that Noriega grabbed him, went for his penis, and then sucked it." The sexual attack came on a flight in Rodriguez's Piper Navajo turboprop, and Rodriguez returned to Carlton on the ground to tell him about it with a sickly pale face. Rodriguez hadn't dared stop Noriega, who was a man who got what he wanted.

After the translator recovered her composure, and asked the staffers if they wanted her to continue, Carlton went on. "He's a dangerous person because he reacts unexpectedly like that. Now you understand why I don't want to be near him."

Senator Helms's foreign policy aide, Deborah De Moss, smiled at the embarrassed Carlton. "We don't want to be near him either."

Up the road in Tampa, Florida, another U.S. attorney was putting together a separate case against General Noriega. Robert Merkle, nicknamed "Mad Dog" for his aggressive pursuit of drug dealers and political corruption, was already moving toward the first U.S. trial ever of a Medellín cartel kingpin, Carlos Lehder. He salivated at a chance to indict Panama's Noriega as well.

His narrower case focused on Noriega's role in facilitating the drug money laundering of a major U.S. marijuana dealer, Steven Michael Kalish. The Miami case was aimed at far broader racketeering charges, involving the Medellín cartel.

Kalish's claims were bountiful—and even better, many of them could be proven with documents. He had been arrested in Tampa in July, 1984, six months before Moritz started his undercover work. However, he only started testifying before a Noriega grand jury three years later, after reaching a sentence-reduction agreement with Merkle and after Miami prosecutors were already homing in on Panama's General.

Kalish had turned to Panama only after he had been overwhelmed by his profits in 1983 and was expecting $300 million more from new operations that were on line, including shipments of marijuana in an oceangoing tug and barge up the Mississippi.

The lead fumes from the millions in cash he hadn't yet laundered were already making his counters sick; they were mostly trusted friends from his high school days. Even counting machines couldn't handle the volume. Kalish finally gave up counting and sent the cash directly to banks in the Cayman Islands, where the banks weighed the money and then deposited the amount in dollars that the poundage suggested.

But his Cayman Islands banks couldn't handle the volume, either. One had recently balked at a $12 million load of $20 bills. Kalish already had rooms full of cash in Tampa, totaling $35 million at one time, and he wasn't about to risk putting the money in U.S. banks.

"I began to seek out banking havens in earnest," he said. "I was aware of changing relations between the United States and the Cayman Islands and feared a loss of bank secrecy. The Cayman banks were simply not capable of dealing with this volume of money."

Kalish arranged "a trial run" in Panama through two intermediaries. They instructed Kalish to fly to Panama with $2 million for deposit, to show his seriousness. On September 22, 1983, he had his first meeting in Panama with César Rodriguez, who was known to be Noriega's business partner. Rodriguez put him in touch with lawyers, bankers, and government officials, who offered a package of corporate, banking, and investment services together with armored car delivery from the airport of the cash to be laundered.

Kalish quickly learned of another advantage in working with Noriega. The G-2 passed information to Rodriguez, gained from U.S. intelligence contacts, that Kalish's Lear Jet was on the DEA's watch list. So Kalish had it sent back to the U.S.

For Kalish, Rodriguez was the sort of find drug dealers dream about, the high-rolling middleman who had direct contacts with a country's government. Rodriguez and Noriega owned several companies together, including the club in the penthouse of the Bank of Boston for their common friends. It cost $1,000 to become a member, and there were only 100 members. Noriega authorized the general manager of the bank to give Rodriguez a loan for the club, which he never paid back.

Rodriguez would regularly receive PDF checks of $20,000 or more, whose proceeds he would divide with Noriega. The money was often used to pay for transporting a large number of models for Noriega's private parties—beautiful white American girls—who would fly down for the weekend on chartered jets.

Kalish visited Noriega at his home the day after his arrival. Rodriguez instructed him to bring a gift for the General, "large enough to show how serious I was about doing business in Panama." Kalish brought $300,000 in a briefcase. Kalish told the General that he wanted to live and invest in Panama, and he made clear he was "intending to bring extremely large amounts of cash" to Panama. After a thirty-minute chat, Kalish left his briefcase and started to leave the room.

"You've forgotten your briefcase," Kalish recalled Noriega saying. Kalish told the General it was for him, and Noriega smiled.

Kalish was invited to a party at the Panama Canal Commission offices that same night. Noriega was friendly and told Kalish to continue dealing with Rodriguez and his partner, Enrique Pretelt. He said he would do whatever he could to help. And he thanked Kalish for the gift.

Kalish moved into a plush home just around the corner from Noriega. He paid $400,000 to buy 25 percent of Servicios Turisticos, a business that he established with Rodriguez, Pretelt, and Noriega. Half of the payment for his share went to Noriega. As a favor to the General, he arranged the purchase of an executive helicopter and a Boeing 727/100 plane. The PDF budget didn't have the funds for the helicopter, so Kalish bought it. The helicopter was worth $1,650,000, but the National Bank of Panama—on Noriega's instruction—issued Kalish a letter of credit for $1,995,000. The $350,000 surplus was paid in kickbacks, one-third of which went to Noriega. The PDF continued its $50,000 monthly payments to Kalish's account, which were automatically transferred to government escrow accounts, even after he was arrested in summer 1984.

Kalish also made a half-million-dollar payment for the Boeing 727/100, an aircraft which Noriega later agreed to use for money laundering. Noriega said that Kalish could fly planeloads of money from Washington, D.C., to Panama under diplomatic cover. Kalish also allowed Noriega to use his own Learjet on frequent flights to Washington, New York, and Las Vegas. Gifts were the way to a Latin American dictator's heart, and Kalish gave the General and his wife jewelry one Christmas that was valued at $25,000. At Noriega's birthday party in 1983, Kalish gave the General a rifle and two pistols, valued at more than $20,000.

But for Kalish, this was an acceptable cost for buying a country. At one point, he had three Panamanian passports, including a diplomatic passport that allowed him to travel unhindered through airports throughout the world. The fee for the diplomatic passport was $60,000—modest compared to the potential returns. His planes filled with money would land at Panama's main airport, but then they would taxi to a far corner that was controlled by the air force. An officer would supervise the unloading of money into armored cars that PDF escorts then would accompany to banks.

Noriega and Kalish grew close. On February 18, 1984, Noriega invited Kalish and his fiancée, Denise, for a weekend at his ranch in Chiriquí province. Noriega came with a mistress and a sergeant who would cook all their meals. He ordered a generous bouquet for the fiancée, with which he left a note: "Miss Denis: [sic] Welcome to Panama. Your friend, General Noriega." The note was found in Kalish's wallet when he was arrested.

Noriega's purpose for the weekend outing wasn't social, however; Noriega had recently agreed to a $1 million fee up front for facilitating the transshipment of marijuana. Kalish had already paid $250,000, but Noriega wanted additional assurances that Panama's role was insulated well enough so that the U.S. wouldn't discover it. He was starting to get nervous. He feared his role was becoming too apparent.

In dry, legal language, the Miami and Tampa grand jury investigations would produce "cases of first impression." This would be the first time that the ruler of a friendly sovereign country would be indicted by a U.S. federal court.

However, from the beginning the cases were more of political importance than a blow to the drug world. Noriega was indeed an important facilitator for drug dealers, but in truth he was never as big a fish as the publicity surrounding the indictments would suggest. He made life easier for drug traffickers in exchange for payment, but there's no sign he actively involved himself in the drug business. His role also had apparently grown smaller since 1985. "Noriega was never a major player in the drug war," conceded U.S. attorney Leon Kellner, who was Gregorie's boss in Miami. "He got paid like everyone else did."

Yet those officials who might have blocked the indictment on foreign policy grounds were powerless because of shifting priorities in Washington and the shadow of the Iran-Contra affair. Officials also knew that two ambitious U.S. attorneys and one assistant U.S. attorney would fight in the press whatever the officials did to block an indictment of General Noriega. Each of these prosecutors had pursued the investigation for his own private reasons, but now the attorneys had moved to the center of an escalating foreign policy crisis over Panama. They wouldn't give up their indictments without a fight that no U.S. official was willing to wage.

What Noriega never understood until it was too late was that he was up against the sort of enemies that Washington could stop only at great political cost: ambitious U.S. attorneys who would have leaked to the press any hint of political meddling in their judicial affairs. The chief prosecutors in Miami and in Tampa were both Republicans with political ambitions. Leon Kellner in Miami, who was Gregorie's boss, was looking to make a positive reputation for himself, ahead of 1988 elections, that would erase charges that he had dragged his heels in pursing cases that might have uncovered Oliver North's Iran-Contra scandal earlier. Robert Merkle in Tampa was already making a name by prosecuting Carlos Lehder, the biggest drugpin to yet face an American jury. With plans to run for the 1988 Republican Senate nomination in his district, a Noriega trial could only help. Both Kellner and Merkle had much to gain from the indictments in a prosecutorial world where U.S. attorneys are like princes independently ruling provinces, often in a manner most likely to gain them publicity and to grease their political careers.

For Leon Kellner, the Noriega case appeared to be the perfect way to repair what he considered his unfairly tarnished image.

Kellner had gotten off to a slow start in Miami as the Southern District's chief prosecutor. He had been an international bank lawyer on Wall Street, and nothing in his previous life had prepared him for Florida's underworld of drug dealers and international criminals.

He would never have abandoned the relatively safe and lucrative world of corporate law had not his Harvard classmate, Stanley Marcus, offered him a job after Marcus was named southern Florida's U.S. attorney. Kellner was a conservative Republican with political ambitions, and a stint in a U.S. attorney's office during the Reagan administration couldn't hurt. When Marcus was named a federal judge in 1985, Kellner took Marcus's job. That's when his troubles began.

After he brought the first indictment anywhere that named the Medellín cartel, the FBI tracked down Kellner and his new wife, while they were traveling, to issue them a warning: the cartel had targeted them for assassination. Kellner's wife Ellen phoned their house-sitter in Coral Gables and told her, "Take the dog, take my personal telephone book, remove all the family photos. Leave the house. And don't say anything to anybody." With all the evidence that could help an assassination team safely removed from their home, Kellner moved his family to Eglin Air Force Base.

The move to Eglin made sense to Kellner, but it infuriated his staff. Many had worked dangerous cases for years, and some had been Mafia prosecutors for over a decade. They figured everyone was exposed, and that Kellner was looking after only himself. Kellner's chief assistant, Richard Gregorie, warned him that he was spreading panic through the office.

Even after that, his wife couldn't sleep at night because of her fear, and they both suffered from the work load, mounting morale problems at the office, and new charges in Washington that Kellner had dragged his feet on an investigation that might have stopped the illegal arming of the Contras before it became a national scandal.

Kellner's problems grew when Massachusetts Senator John Kerry's subcommittee on narcotics started investigating allegations that he had blocked a young prosecutor's pursuit of Oliver North's secret Nicaraguan arms supply network during a trip to Costa Rica eight months before the Iran-Contra scandal became public. The prosecutor, Jeffrey Feldman, had raised alarm bells in Costa Rica when he had sought interviews with rancher John Hull, one of the key links in the arms network. The Costa

Rican station chief, Joe Fernandez, had asked for a meeting with Feldman to find out how much he knew, and in a panic Hull contacted North about the probe, who then informed National Security Adviser John Poindexter.

Feldman had written a memo to Kellner in August 1986. "We have sufficient evidence to begin a grand jury investigation . . . [which] would ultimately reveal criminal activities including gunrunning and Neutrality Act violations." Kellner had sent back the memo with a handwritten notation. "I concur that we have sufficient evidence to ask for a grand jury."

He later reversed himself, however, and ordered Feldman's memo rewritten so it said, "A grand jury at this point would represent a fishing expedition." Feldman quotes Kellner as telling him "politics are involved." But other prosecutors in the office, including Gregorie, agreed with Kellner's decision to delay the grand jury. What Feldman found especially suspicious, however, was that he was then sent off to Thailand for a deposition. "Most young prosecutors consider such trips a reward," countered Kellner.

The subcommittee's chief investigator, Jack Blum, also charged that Kellner had sidetracked an investigation of Southern Air Transport which might have led to North's illegal arms network far earlier. Indictments weren't finally handed down until 1988, after Kellner had announced his resignation. "Kellner saw his job in Miami as keeping the lid on," said Blum. "We were all over him. He had been part and parcel of covering up what the administration was up to in Latin America. Kellner felt the heat from us."

Charges against Kellner were never proven, but the allegations nevertheless tarnished his reputation and threatened his career. Kellner was damned if he would be slowed in his Noriega investigation. Justice Department officials knew Kellner would go ballistic before the entire press corps if they blocked his Noriega case. He told his chief assistant, Richard Gregorie, to go ahead full tilt.

Stopping Kellner in Miami would have been hard, but blocking Merkle in Tampa was impossible. Merkle was just the type of man to take perverse pleasure in his nickname "Mad Dog," given him for his rabid litigious style. "If he had evidence against God Himself, he'd take Him before a grand jury," said Blum.

Most Americans haven't any idea who the U.S. attorneys are for their districts, but middle Florida knew Merkle. The burly, forty-three-year-old former Notre Dame running back with a bulldog's mien and jawline put his head down and broke through lines of political opposition with a sense of abandon that prompted at least one local newspaper to impugn his sanity.

In five years Merkle more than doubled the number of criminal cases in his district. He raised his office's overall conviction rate 67 percent to more than 80 percent. He'd indicted two judges, six county commissioners, three prosecutors, one sheriff, four deputies, two federal agents, and dozens of lawyers, bankers, and businessmen.

Yet his almost evangelical fight against drugs, political corruption, child pornography, and abortion had won him powerful enemies and made him one of the most controversial U.S. attorneys in the country. By the time the Noriega case rolled around in 1987, Florida's Governor Bob Martinez had already tried to get him ousted. In one trial on political corruption, Merkle had converted Martinez from witness to defendant as charges had arisen that he had been taking bribes. Two-thirds of Florida's sheriffs had approved a resolution calling for his resignation and a veteran state prosecutor in Jacksonville had called him a "reincarnation of Joe McCarthy."

Merkle, however, survived this threatened political slaughter, neutralizing most of his opponents by trying the biggest drug kingpin ever to go before a U.S. court, Carlos Lehder.

"This is just not the time to be making political moves when as big a drug case as this is being handled by Bob Merkle," said Republican Congressman C. W. "Bill" Young. And Governor Martinez agreed to a truce until after the trial.

The Noriega grand jury would give Merkle a little more armor for his political breastplate, and would allow him to make what would turn out to be an unsuccessful run for the Republican Senate nomination. In 1988 his loss there against Representative Connie Mack was predictable; he'd alienated most of the Republican establishment.

Although Merkle's attack on the drug lords freed him from his domestic enemies, it gained him a slew of new, more dangerous adversaries. He took to driving rented cars, which he traded in every few days to evade potential assassinations, and he drove circuitous routes to work. Robert Merkle might be "mad," but he wasn't crazy.

Back in Miami, Kellner's chief assistant, Dick Gregorie, was the engine of the Noriega investigation. Kellner was a politically astute operator who had never known a criminal case before moving to Miami. Gregorie was the antithesis: an apolitical, streetwise veteran of nearly two decades of prosecuting drug traffickers. He had a strike-force mentality, and nothing was more important than the case. While many prosecutors considered themselves above the drug cops, Gregorie played third base on their softball team in Miami.

He viewed himself as the Man in the White Hat, taking on all the evils of Miami, the Casablanca of the 1980s. "Just as that North African city became the meeting place for refugees, spies and criminals during the Second World War," Gregorie wrote in Senate testimony. "Miami during the 1980s has become the central location for drug smugglers, money launderers, mercenaries, revolutionaries, and refugees from political and economic disaster in other parts of the world."

In October 1987, Gregorie knew it was time to let higher-ups know that the Noriega case was getting closer to indictment. Assistant Attorney General Stephen Trott saw a strong case in its early stages and was supportive. DEA administrator John Lawn, who saw elements that could embarrass the DEA and him personally, was less enthusiastic. The DEA never blocked the Miami investigation, but it also never seemed very excited about pursuing it.

Of course, it didn't help when the DEA transferred Moritz to the Midwest at just the time he was most needed to find the witnesses and set the traps that would bring in the corroboration for Carlton's testimony. The DEA claimed it was normal procedure—nothing against the Noriega case—but Gregorie bristled that the policy ought to be changed in a place like Miami, where familiarity breeds success. "They're moving all these people around the country for what purpose?" said Gregorie. "Certainly not to stop drug trafficking."

Gregorie found his DEA team lacked skills and experience for such a critical investigation. One of the new supervisors, Kenneth Kennedy, was extremely talented, but didn't know the area and couldn't speak Spanish. One of the agents had just been sent to Miami after sixteen years of working in airports. Another had been transferred to his first street work after doing documents and records. The best of the group was a Spanish-speaking agent who would help the Floyd Carlton debriefings, but he had endurance problems due to injuries when a bale of marijuana fell on him. "Here was a chance to get Noriega," said Gregorie, "and one kid has never seen a case in his life, a second was injured so badly he has a hard time working, I've just lost the lead agent on the case for three years to a transfer, and I've got an airport detail guy who was just sent from Chicago."

Gregorie also found that the FBI and CIA were little interested in a slew of other information his prosecution was coming up with, ranging from data on illegal technology transfers through Panama to Cuba to intelligence information on Noriega's arms dealings in the region. "Our government discouraged every other investigation that could have grown out of this," said Gregorie.

Gregorie also had difficulty getting cooperation from DEA agents in Panama in gathering evidence against Noriega, who was still helping them bring in drug busts. "We kept asking, and they kept coming back empty-handed," Gregorie said. "It was very dissatisfying to keep asking for this stuff and not to have all the power of the U.S. government to turn it up." One DEA supervisor said racial tensions grew between the non-Latin DEA agents in Miami who were pursuing the case and the Spanish-speaking agents in Panama.

One of the Panama agents, Alfredo Duncan, was so reluctant to cooperate with agents in Miami that he fired off cables to Washington that insisted his Miami colleagues were on the wrong track. His cables vouched for Noriega's assistance on a wide range of drug enforcement matters. Duncan considered the Noriega drug case to be a political matter. He said in one cable that the Miami proceedings could prompt Noriega to shut down the DEA office in Panama, which was one of the most productive in the region in terms of arrests and seizures. The truth was that Noriega had so manipulated the DEA in Panama that the agency did nothing he didn't know about through his liaison to them, Luis Quiel, whom they had wined and dined during the DEA-sponsored tour of the country organized by Noriega's pro-Contra lobbyist in Washington, former State Department official Frank Gomez.

At one point, Gregorie threatened to bring the DEA's agents in Panama before the grand jury, after one informant provided proof that they had tampered with a box of documents that the informant had given them to ship to Miami. The matter was serious enough for an internal DEA investigation, which found no wrongdoing. But the informant, who passed a lie detector test over the matter, said Noriega's bank records had been removed from the box, and the agents conceded that they had opened the box, although they were vague about what they were trying to find.

Despite all the problems, Gregorie appeared in October 1987 to have a case with lots of promise. Trott's only warning was that he needed more corroboration and, most of all, needed to find out what connection Noriega had to U.S. intelligence agencies and whether his work for the CIA could undermine the case.

Despite repeated efforts, the CIA didn't let Gregorie at its files until months thereafter, in May 1988, when the Miami grand jury had already indicted Noriega. Even then, Gregorie was disappointed. He had left a whole day free to sort through what he imagined might be two boxes full of documents. Instead, he received two thin file folders, whose "secret" documents included reproductions of *Washington Post* articles. Gregorie never stopped worrying that Noriega could end his entire prosecution in court by mounting a "Brady defense," now better known as the "Oliver North defense," which would require the government's prosecutors to turn over any material favorable to the defense—particularly information on drug traffickers that Noriega might have provided to CIA intelligence as part of his contractual intelligence relationship.

"The major weakness of the Noriega case is that he was an agent of the U.S. government for years," said Gregorie. "We have a myriad of intelligence agencies; some I've heard of and others I haven't. I have requested the right to see certain things. I can honestly tell you that I am convinced that we have not seen even a small percentage of what we should see."

Gregorie knew his grand jury case had gone over the top, however, when José Blandón and two other key witnesses appeared in late December and early January. They provided corroborating evidence for every key point in the indictment.

José Blandón's testimony, however, gave the investigation its first clearly political twist. Blandón's decision to testify was a carefully calculated political move, first to exert leverage on Noriega and then to protect himself from the General after he was fired from his New York consul's job. Kellner grew impatient, as on several occasions Blandón rescheduled his first appearance before the grand jury while maneuvering Noriega, the opposition, the Kerry committee in Washington, and their own grand jury.

Oddly enough, Gregorie had first heard of Blandón from a CBS Television *60 Minutes* producer. The producer had told Gregorie he would offer a disaffected Panamanian diplomat who could be a star witness in exchange for an interview with Floyd Carlton, the government's strongest witness. Gregorie liked the deal, and he provided Carlton. But Blandón was still playing games with Noriega. The producer couldn't deliver Blandón.

Joel McCleary had counseled Blandón against making any move until he hired a lawyer. Blandón wanted to know how to best use the grand jury process and the upcoming congressional committee sessions to best protect his future and promote Noriega's downfall. McCleary wanted the meeting in a place where assassination was unlikely.

The lawyer, a former Detroit strike-force attorney named Atlee Wompler, who had prosecuted Jimmy Hoffa, picked the second floor restaurant of the Miami department store Burdine's. Blandón had met earlier with Panamanian opposition leaders to announce he was joining their cause. Now over the cold plate special, talking amid the chatter of overweight shoppers seeking midweek sales, the criminal lawyer and the Latin conspirator laid the groundwork for Blandón's testimony. As far as Blandón was concerned, at that meeting he had crossed the point of no return.

Blandón felt alone and confused. Congress wanted the political dynamite of his testimony in public hearings; U.S. attorneys in Panama needed him to juice their grand jury case against Noriega; and Wompler wanted to make sure he was fully protected by federal marshals prior to making any move.

Wompler arranged a secret meeting with Blandón, DEA agents, and prosecutors Kellner and Gregorie in a small conference room at the Sofitel Hotel at the Miami airport. Blandón's tale so transfixed his listeners that the DEA agents dropped to the floor and drew their guns when a loud rap on the door disturbed their session. It was only a waiter delivering coffee.

The memo Gregorie drew up was for a RICO indictment that named the Panamanian Defense Forces as a criminal enterprise. The Noriega case was in the political realm now, though, and the State Department feared such a prosecution would dissuade fellow officers from turning on Noriega. So Justice officials rewrote the document. This RICO business isn't going to stick, Justice Department official Paul Coffee told Gregorie. Draft it another way. Gregorie wrote the indictment for fifteen individuals and Noriega as "an association in fact" with the Medellín cartel, and that seemed to do it.

In a hurry to beat Senate subcommittee hearings the next week, Kellner and Gregorie put the finishing touches on their indictment at Kellner's home on Super Bowl Sunday, January 31, 1988. Kellner had grown to hate Blum, and he didn't want to give him the satisfaction of hitting the news first with his Panama hearings. He also didn't want to be accused of having issued the indictment as part of a general political campaign against Noriega: he was going to get out first if he had to work around the clock.

The Washington Redskins beat the Denver Broncos 42–10; the attorneys found their own game far more stimulating. They chomped Domino's pizza and once had to clean some tomato sauce off a document that made America's war on Noriega irreversible. They began at 7 A.M., and by midnight Kellner and Gregorie inspected the final version of *United States of America* v. *Manuel Antonio Noriega* and fifteen others.

"At all times relevant to this Indictment, there existed an Enterprise . . . a group of individuals associated in fact which utilized the official positions of the defendant MANUEL ANTONIO NORIEGA in the Republic of Panama to facilitate the manufacture and transportation of large quantities of cocaine destined for the United States and to launder narcotics proceeds."

The indictment said drug traffickers purchased Noriega's use of his official position to "influence and assist and protect their narcotics and money laundering operations." It charged him with obtaining "substantial personal profit" to offer safe use of Panama for transshipment of cocaine and of ether and acetone, chemicals needed for drug production. It also said he allowed the building of cocaine laboratory facilities and then protected them, that he provided a safe haven for drug traffickers, and that he allowed them to deposit millions of dollars of narcotics proceeds in Panamanian banks.

"Manuel Antonio Noriega, directly and through intermediaries, negotiated with narcotics traffickers," it said. "Failure to make adequate payment to, or the failure to obtain the prior approval of, Manuel Antonio Noriega for narcotics operations resulted in the seizure of drugs or other retaliatory measures by Manuel Antonio Noriega." It then mentioned his negotiations with Castro in Cuba.

Not to be left out in Tampa, Merkle stepped up his indictment plans. Justice Department officials knew it would have made more sense to combine the cases, and thus make one, stronger indictment against Noriega. But U.S. attorneys Kellner and Merkle greedily demanded their own individual stages. The indictments, if approved by Washington, would be unsealed simultaneously so as not to bruise the prosecutors' egos.

The Miami grand jury would indict Noriega and fifteen others on twelve counts of participating in a criminal enterprise in violation of U.S. racketeering and drug laws. Kellner charged the General with accepting $4.5 million in payoffs for allowing Colombia's Medellín cartel to ship more than two tons of cocaine through Panama to the U.S. Noriega was also charged with allowing the cartel to set up a cocaine-processing plant in Panama and to move its headquarters there after the Colombian justice minister's penalty of 145 years in prison and $1.1 million in fines.

The Tampa grand jury's less ambitious indictment charged Noriega on three counts of allegedly assisting a U.S.–based marijuana smuggling operation in return for about $1 million in payments.

The documents looked good. Kellner and Gregorie were ready to fly to Washington, and they were prepared for a fight. They let some journalists know they were coming. If senior officials were going to knock down their work for political reasons, the media would know about it. "The journalists brought a certain amount of accountability," Gregorie smiled.

Senior officials, however, were surprisingly submissive. Only C. Nicholas Rostow, the president's legal adviser, was openly critical. At a White House staff meeting, he angrily asked Kellner, "Since when does some assistant U.S. attorney start making foreign policy?"

When Kellner relayed this conversation to Gregorie after the meeting, Gregorie steamed. "Did you ask him, 'Since when does U.S. foreign policy say a banana republic's dictator can help dope trafficking that's killing hundreds of thousands of American youth? Did you tell him I started making foreign policy when the foreign policy makers started breaking the law?" Kellner conceded that he hadn't put it quite that way. He liked Gregorie's fire, but he was glad he was handling the politics.

Kellner had scores of his own to settle. After all the talk that he had been manipulated by Washington regarding Contra-related prosecutions, he didn't want anyone saying he was bending to the Reagan administration on this one. He convinced Trott to let him brief officials at the February 2 Policy Review Group meeting, where sub-cabinet officials would debate his indictment. "If they are going to force me to kowtow, I want them to do it to me face-to-face," he said.

As important as the indictment issue had become, President Reagan wasn't ever informed about a decision that would push his administration into a foreign policy corner. Asked several months later about Reagan's role, White House spokesman Marlin Fitzwater said he wanted to keep out of the legal process.

"Certainly NSC officials and others were aware of the indictments coming down and the legal process that had been in the works for many months," said Fitzwater. But he added, "It did not go to the president."

In fact, the final decision was laid in cement at a sub-cabinet level meeting chaired by Deputy National Security Adviser John Negroponte. The former ambassador to Honduras called Kellner forward from the back of the room. "You sit at the table," he said impatiently. "You are the reason we are having this meeting."

Kellner briefed them generally about what the indictments would say and said that they would be handed down in two days—on February 4, 1988—and then unsealed at a noon press conference the day after. The Tampa indictment would be released at the same time. What Kellner didn't say was that the two ambitious U.S. attorneys had refused to combine their cases and the timing had been agreed upon to avoid rivalry. Kellner couldn't provide senior officials with copies of the thirty-page indictment nor could he read it, because of grand jury secrecy.

"Does anyone have a problem with what this man is going to do," asked Negroponte.

Kellner had looked forward to seeing government at work, and he had prepared himself to defend his action. "But no one even wanted to talk about it," he said, "In government, you learn that no one makes the hard call. We were allowed to go ahead, not because every official thought it was a good idea, but because those who didn't like it wouldn't dare argue against it. There were good arguments to be made against the indictment, but I didn't hear any of them."

After the meeting, officials complained to each other that the indictment was the height of foreign policy folly, and one guessed it would paint them and Noriega in a corner. The threat of an indictment has always been more useful than the fact, he said. But none dared speak out for the meeting's note-taker, fearing he would be quoted, either the next day in the newspaper or in a future congressional hearing, as having backed a drug-dealing dictator. In the atmosphere of Iran-Contra, silence was the best policy. Only technical questions were asked.

One official wanted to know if the indictment could be moved up by one day because of the danger of leaks. Kellner said that that wasn't possible, because twenty-four citizens on the grand jury needed to vote, and they all had to get off work to do so.

The State Department's representative, Deputy Secretary of State John Whitehead, asked if he could inform the U.S. ambassador in Panama, whose embassy might be the target of retribution. They agreed that the embassy could be put on alert.

However, Kellner said that President Delvalle couldn't be informed. State Department officials had wanted to tell him, hoping the news would finally prompt him to turn on Noriega. Delvalle's frequent promises of action, and then his cowardly backing down, had started to irritate some State Department officials.

Another official asked how U.S. diplomats and military officers should deal with Noriega when they talked to him. "Read him his Miranda rights," Kellner laughed. "Anything he says can be used against him."

No one even smiled.

The Reagan administration now had an indictment against Noriega. But it still lacked a policy to remove the General from power.

CHAPTER
FIFTEEN

THE WRONG HERO

*I am the frog and he is the scorpion. Maybe I should
swim underwater and let him drown.*

—PRESIDENT ERIC ARTURO DELVALLE

General Noriega's U.S. informant phoned Mario Rognoni from a down-town Washington phone booth at just after 10 A.M., February 25, 1988. Rognoni, the General's trusted friend and adviser, had given his secretary instructions to switch through all calls immediately from this American, who had used his contacts in the Reagan administration to keep the Noriega crowd informed of the myriad inconsistencies of U.S. policy. Rognoni could hear the sound of Washington's morning traffic in the background.

The voice said that President Eric Arturo Delvalle would try to fire Noriega that afternoon in a twenty-minute-long televised speech, which he had prerecorded a day earlier. The speech would be shown at 1 P.M. that day on Channel 5, the TV station that Delvalle owned.

Rognoni smiled at this valuable tip. Noriega had long expected a Delvalle defection, but knowing the means and timing was a tactical advantage. Noriega was always happy with good intelligence.

Rognoni made two calls. The first was to Noriega's office. The second was to a little-known shadow government that Noriega had established on the fifteenth floor of Panama City's Bank of Boston building, made up of some forty of his most trusted civilian allies. Noriega had formed the group in October 1987 after he had received word of Delvalle's secret meetings with U.S. officials on "medical" visits to Miami. Noriega's shadow president was his education minister, Manuel Solis Palma. Solis Palma had two advantages: he was a shrewd clandestine operator and he had no domestic political base with which to challenge Noriega. Rognoni had convinced

Noriega of the need for such a group, fearing the General was losing all civilian backing.

Rognoni was one of Panama's complex, half-American products. He was a round, jovial, slap-you-on-the-back figure who seemed more of a southern good ol' boy than a Latin dictator's flunky. His first wife had been American, and a photo of his blond son in an American football uniform decorated his inner office wall beside a Confederate flag. Rognoni had graduated from Georgia Tech, and he still wore its class ring.

In his conference room, one wall was covered by photographs of himself with Noriega, one hand inevitably holding a glass of scotch and the other arm around the General. The wall beside it was papered with General Douglas MacArthur's Credo and kitschy U.S. bumper stickers: "Is That Really Your Face, or Did Your Neck Throw Up," "Poverty Sucks," and, perhaps most fitting, "I Don't Lie, Cheat, or Steal Unnecessarily."

Upon hearing Rognoni's news, the provisional government split into two groups to put its contingency plan into action. Noriega's two fears were that civilians would take to the streets to support Delvalle and that Delvalle himself would seize the presidential palace, forcing him to storm it with troops. So one group, including Rognoni, rushed to occupy the palace. The other, headed by Solis Palma, drove to Noriega's headquarters to help him plot street control and to organize a legislature session that would appoint a new president.

Their victory that day, however, would be a far easier task than any of them had expected.

Delvalle's taped message wasn't played until 5 P.M., four hours later than the informant had expected. For a while, Noriega thought Delvalle had backed down. He'd come close to turning on Noriega several times in recent weeks, and each time had gotten cold feet. Noriega even started driving out of town late that afternoon, only to turn back when he was radioed that the tape had finally aired. Delvalle, looking stiff and anything but combative, had said that he had asked Noriega to step down voluntarily, and Noriega had refused. What he didn't say was that, through the papal nuncio, he had tried twice to meet with Noriega the previous week, but Noriega wouldn't even give his president an audience.

"There is no other alternative but the use of the powers that the constitution gives me, to separate General Noriega from his high command and to encharge the leadership of the institution to the current chief of staff, Colonel Marco Justine. . . . No one can be above the nation," he said. Delvalle then retreated to his home with his wife and family rather than fight it out at the Presidencia with an AK-47 in hand, in the spirit of Chile's slain Salvador Allende. The only vestige of the presidency that he carried was the sash, and U.S. embassy officials thereafter took to calling their reluctant hero "Have-Sash-Will-Travel."

Delvalle had expected Panamanians to take to the streets, as they had after Colonel Díaz Herrera's revelations, but the Civic Crusade, the heart of the popular opposition to Noriega, hated Delvalle so much that it wouldn't give him the satisfaction of an uprising. At the time, most people suspected his speech was another Noriega trick. His speech was stolid and stiff and shown only once: it was hardly the stuff of revolution. "We didn't look for him," said Aurelio Barria, a Chamber of Commerce leader and Civic Crusade chief. "He jumped onto our wagon, and he did it only because the Americans guaranteed him support."

For Barria, this was the man who had held a pro-Noriega rally the day after President Barletta had been ousted in September 1985. Delvalle had led his supporters in a march to the Comandancia to thank the General, who stood accused of having ordered the beheading of his most outspoken political opponent. "No puppet president has dragged himself any lower than that," said Barria.

And it was Delvalle who had as president given his blessing to the country's worst repression ever. He even congratulated Noriega after his brutal "Black Friday" crackdown on July 10, 1987. "Yes, I wrote a letter congratulating the armed forces for not killing anyone," Delvalle would say later. "That was quite an accomplishment. And why shouldn't Noriega repress the demonstrators? The Civic Crusade wanted law and order, but then they break the law against demonstrations."

He derided the Civic Crusade leaders, businessmen who were the heart of the street demonstrations against Noriega, as "cabezas calientes." He considered Noriega's opposition as a bunch of fainthearted "people in the street waving hankies and throwing over garbage cans. It wasn't serious and, if I had been Noriega, I wouldn't have gone either."

And when Barria was arrested, stripped, and humiliated while interrogated, Delvalle had told Ambassador Davis that Noriega should lock him up and throw away the keys. "It would have been great if Noriega had done so," Delvalle said later. "Davis sent Barria to the Philippines to fill his head full of a lot of baloney about democracy. Panama wasn't the Philippines." But perhaps even more irritating was that Delvalle, after a half year of Noriega's repression, decorated the General with "The Harpy Eagle," a new medal that Noriega invented himself. Delvalle argued that he traded the medal for Noriega's agreement to reopen the press, but while the press was quickly closed again, the medal remained long after in Noriega's trophy case.

Delvalle's desire for the presidency had been congenital. His father had created Panama's Republican party with the aim of becoming president—the first Jewish president outside of Israel. The father never succeeded, but his son inherited the ambition and the party, and in the process he'd sold some of his soul, first by conspiring in the ouster of a president and then by acting as accomplice in Noriega's repression.

Delvalle's own elite class had begun to disown him. During one lunch at the Union Club, the traditional watering hole for Panama's upper class, diners had hit their utensils against crystal glasses in protest until the ringing drove Delvalle to the microphone to explain himself. But the diners had shouted him down, and he'd left in disgrace. His wife, the daughter of one of Panama's most elite families, had wept and begged him to distance himself from Noriega. There was also another motivation: Noriega would remove Delvalle if he didn't act first. Delvalle's fears were clear in December, when he talked to Rognoni.

"You know the story of the frog and the scorpion?" he asked Rognoni. "The scorpion asked the frog to give him a ride to the other side of the river. The frog thought the scorpion, who couldn't swim, wouldn't dare sting his means of survival. The frog starts swimming, but in the middle of the stream, the scorpion stings the frog. Before he dies, he turns to the scorpion and says, 'Now we will both die. Why did you sting me?'

"'For the hell of it,' said the scorpion."

Delvalle frowned. "I am the frog and he is the scorpion. Maybe I should swim underwater and let him drown."

The month after his December conversation with Rognoni, the frog was still balking at going underwater. He flew to New York in January and met with Elliott Abrams and his deputy, William Walker. Delvalle complained about new Senate action that robbed Panama of its sugar quota, thus striking at the heart of Delvalle's private business. He knew his former friend Gabriel Lewis, whose son was divorcing Delvalle's daughter, had arranged for this attack. "You should instead open your resources to me and make me stronger," he said.

But Abrams and Walker wanted Delvalle to fire Noriega, something Delvalle considered a fool's mission. He knew he didn't have the power to make it work, and Gabriel Lewis was only out to rob Noriega of his puppet president. He felt that Noriega would sink of his own weight, that matters would gradually grow so bad that he would resign or be ousted by fellow officers.

But after the February 4 indictment, Delvalle was persuaded that he had to act. His family and friends from Panama's upper classes had become unbearable, with all their complaints about his continued protection of Noriega. He flew to Miami a week after the indictments, for clandestine meetings with Joel McCleary, who was the opposition's intermediary, and Elliott Abrams, at his dentist's home off Biscayne Boulevard. McCleary waited for three days in Miami for the dentist's furtive call. "The dentist was acting like he was in a Le Carré novel," laughed McCleary later. "But I knew we were in a Beckett play"—*Waiting for Delvalle.*

McCleary told Delvalle that he had two private jets, sent by Gabriel Lewis, waiting nearby to whisk him to Washington to make the announcement before the Organization of American States that he was firing Noriega. Lewis even arranged for Senator Kennedy to call while Delvalle was talking to McCleary, and Kennedy expressed his support for such a move. But Delvalle would have nothing to do with Lewis's choreography at that time. He was tired of the aggressive entrepreneur's efforts to push him around. "Gabriel likes to control everything," said Delvalle. "He is money-conscious twenty-four hours a day, and I think his whole conflict with Noriega was economic."

Abrams met with him afterward. Delvalle complained about the indictment. "You have left me with no way out," Delvalle said. "I can't stay with him, yet I don't have the power to remove him. Can you lift the indictments in exchange for his resignation?"

The word is quash, said Abrams, adding that the adverse publicity President Reagan would suffer prevented such a move.

"I'll have to fire him, and then I'll be fired," said Delvalle. "Democracy will suffer a big setback." But Lewis would finally have his way, and Delvalle would have to step down.

Yet Delvalle wanted to take one more shot at talking Noriega down from power. He invited the diminutive General to his porch atop the Moorish presidential palace, and they looked over the Pacific while Delvalle suggested Noriega step down and clear his name.

Then he would be playing into the U.S. hands, said Noriega. This is all about the Americans wanting to keep their military bases; it has nothing to do with me. Noriega was immovable, so Delvalle decided to act, knowing the only result could be his firing. He secretly taped his message to the nation at the papal nuncio's residence, having sneaked his presidential sash out of the presidential palace in a shoe box; then he escaped from his home through the back door to avoid the notice of his chauffeur. He wasn't about to take the risk of going on TV live. "Do you think I'm suicidal?" he asked later.

For Noriega, ousting Delvalle was easy. His biggest dilemma thereafter was whether to take over the presidency himself or name another puppet. He gathered his advisers in his private bedroom behind his main office at the headquarters, where he retreated in times of trouble. Rognoni argued that he should stop the charade and take over power himself.

But Noriega's deeply trusted Israeli adviser, Michael Harari, had consistently told him to remain behind the scenes, where he was safer and devoid of direct political responsibility. This was also the personal instinct of the shy and withdrawn leader. Noriega also told his advisers that he had promised Peruvian leader Alan Garcia and "American political leaders" that he would maintain constitutional rule.

Noriega opted to remain where he was most comfortable: backstage. He rounded up thirty-eight of the sixty-seven legislators in his puppet national assembly and at 2 A.M. on February 26 they unanimously approved a resolution dismissing Delvalle and his vice president, Roderick Esquivel, from office. The resolution said Delvalle's dismissal of Noriega "was carried out disregarding the legal procedure demanded by the Constitution and the Organic Law regulating the Defense Forces."

The cabinet then appointed Manuel Solis Palma as the "Minister in Charge of the Presidency" under Article 184 of the Constitution. The Constitution wouldn't allow the unelected education minister to inherit the simple title "president," and Noriega wanted everything to be constitutional. Solis Palma was sworn in at 2:30 A.M., during a fifteen-minute cabinet meeting. In his eagerness to be president, Delvalle had allowed Noriega to control most of his cabinet. Hence, twelve of the fourteen cabinet ministers approved his removal and Solis's appointment.

The Civic Crusade only reluctantly endorsed Delvalle ten days later, following a series of meetings at the papal nuncio's with U.S. embassy officials. The nuncio's diary reads: "For some of them, it was very hard, because they hated Delvalle as much as they hated Noriega. But the State Department guaranteed them there would be clean, decisive intervention and they would get rid of Noriega now. You could see all of them understood the importance of their decision. But you could see on their faces how painful it was for them to accept Delvalle. He had put them in jail and supported laws that repressed them, while he profited from ownership of companies gained while in the presidency."

The most tireless political warrior against military rule, Ricardo Arias Calderón, found Delvalle so reprehensible that he wouldn't even utter his name in public at first. Interviewer Ted Koppel, of ABC's *Nightline*, tried without luck to get Calderón to endorse the underground president. "As hard as I try, I can't get you to say that you're going to support Delvalle, so I must conclude that you don't support him," said Koppel.

President Reagan had fewer hesitations about endorsing Delvalle than Noriega's Panamanian opposition. Immediately following Delvalle's television announcement, White House spokesman Marlin Fitzwater expressed "unqualified" support for civilian rule. The backing grew more explicit each day. On February 26, a White House statement said: "We condemn all efforts to perpetuate military rule in Panama, including efforts to remove President Delvalle from office." Then on March 2, prompted by Delvalle's legal suit in U.S. courts to freeze Panamanian government funds, the State Department, for the first time since World War II, certified the legitimate government of a regime to be led by a president who was in hiding. When the dust finally settled, the U.S. found itself the only country in the world that still recognized Delvalle.

From February 1988 U.S. policy toward Panama would be ruled by two historically unusual moves: the unprecedented indictment of a previously friendly dictator and the continued official recognition of the president Noriega had ousted as constitutional leader.

As exceptional as both moves were, neither was debated much within the Reagan administration. Yet those two decisions soon transformed what had largely been a domestic Panamanian conflict into a U.S.–Noriega struggle. Not only was Washington now party to the Panamanian conflict, but a solution was far less likely to be reached without the U.S. government's participation.

The indictments prompted Noriega to refuse any compromise with his internal opposition that didn't include the U.S.'s lifting the legal charges against him. The certification of the Delvalle regime saddled policymakers with a tarnished hero, around whom they could not rally domestic Panamanian enthusiasm. The millionaire socialite didn't like living underground, and he did not have any experience fighting for a cause. U.S. intelligence agencies even took to bugging his home when they heard he was privately negotiating with Noriega representatives. During one session between Ambassador Davis and the papal nuncio, Monsignor José Sebastian Laboa, Delvalle's lack of courage was an item of gossip. The Vatican's representative offered Davis two marble eggs from a bowl in his entry hall. "Give these to Delvalle," he said, placing them playfully below his own waist. "He doesn't have any of his own."

The cost of this U.S. policy course, however, was that the critical interagency debates didn't begin in earnest until the time for decisive action had already come. The State Department and Pentagon launched a guerrilla warfare of press leaks and accusations, while President Reagan stood to the side and failed to intercede. For six weeks, from Delvalle's action on February 25 to President Reagan's imposition of limited economic sanctions on April 8, there was no coordinated and coherent U.S. government policy and no presidential direction. There was a goal—to get rid of Noriega—but there was never any agreed-upon set of policy instruments to accomplish it. The result was heavy rhetoric backed up by feeble means. That approach raised the ire of Latin America, but it didn't budge Noriega.

* * *

In fact, Noriega's greatest danger in early March didn't come from the Reagan administration. Instead, in a scheme cooked up by Gabriel Lewis and his friends, he was almost brought down by a series of suits filed by lawyers at the Washington law firm of Arnold & Porter. Ironically, these suits would make President Delvalle far more powerful in exile than he ever was while in power.

Joel McCleary knew a foreign policy vacuum when he saw it. On the weekend after Delvalle tried to fire Noriega, he saw the Reagan administration wasn't prepared to act. The opposition had to move, he thought, before the moment was lost. But how? It struck McCleary that if the Reagan administration continued to recognize Delvalle's regime as constitutional, perhaps Delvalle would also continue to control Panamanian government assets in the United States.

McCleary called Lewis. Whenever Lewis heard an idea that excited him, his response was the same. "Yeah, yeah, yeah," he would say, and then he would hang up, too excited to talk about the plan any further or even say good-bye. Less than twenty-four hours after McCleary's suggestion, Lewis assembled a core of allies at his home on Washington's exclusive Foxhall Crescent: McCleary, Blandón, former ambassador to Panama William Jorden, and the former U.S. military officer and lobbyist, John Campbell. The main character in the day's work, however, was Lewis's old friend William D. Rogers, the former assistant secretary of state for Inter-American affairs.

Delvalle's ambassador to Washington, Juan B. Sosa, wasn't at the initial meeting, although he and the opposition later endorsed the course Lewis had chosen. Lewis, moving into the political vacuum again, had taken over and decided that Delvalle and Sosa should hire Rogers to find a legal basis for freezing Panamanian government assets in the U.S., thereby squeezing General Noriega until either he quit or, more likely, his military allies ousted him in fear for their country's and military's well-being.

Rogers and his orthodox firm would become the spear-carrier for an extremely unorthodox legal fight. Housed in a modern building in downtown Washington, Arnold & Porter was replete with gray-flanneled Ivy League graduates. Rogers had represented clients ranging from Henry Kissinger to the government of Brazil, but the Panama case provided him the liberal lawyer's fantasy: the chance to try to bring down a tyrant and promote democracy in an American courtroom. "Noriega's the closest thing to the incarnation of evil in power of any leader in the twentieth century," Rogers said. "Thank God his grip is only on a small nation."

Rogers was enthusiastic enough to refer to his efforts as "revolution by litigation." In an interview at the time, he boasted, "As King Lear said,

I shall do the most wonderful things." Arnold & Porter would take over, not only as Delvalle's lawyers, but also as his foreign office, filing suits in U.S. courts and sending diplomatic messages around the world. "I am an instrument in their hands," he said.

Rogers's first step was to draft a declaration for President Delvalle that declared the Noriega regime to be illegitimate under the Panamanian constitution. The proclamation put all parties dealing with the Noriega regime on notice that their transactions would not be recognized by nor binding upon the Delvalle government. The proclamation was drafted February 29, and it was released to the press and printed as a full-page advertisement in *The Wall Street Journal* on March 1. By this time, Rogers was forming a Panama team at Arnold & Porter that would expand each day. Lawyers at the large firm were phoning the team captain, Kenneth I. Juster, asking if they could help. "Lawyers usually do not volunteer for more work, but many saw this was the most exciting case at the firm, and perhaps in the country," said Juster, who at age thirty-three was keeping tabs on a multifaceted approach that included gathering intelligence on Panamanian government assets, filing lawsuits against banks, seizing assets of the national airline (Air Panama), drafting diplomatic notes, and drawing up an economic assistance package that would be aimed at repairing the damage caused in part by the efforts to bring down Noriega. "We thought from the outset that the best chance for success would come in the first few weeks, so we sought to apply as much pressure as we could," said Juster.

The most critical job was to identify and gain control of Panamanian government assets in the United States. Anti-Noriega moles at the National Bank of Panama, as well as other opposition bankers, provided Delvalle's people with a list of U.S. banks where Panamanian accounts were known to be held. On behalf of Ambassador Sosa, the Rogers team faxed the chairmen of the board of four of these banks and twenty of the U.S. companies most involved in Panama to inform them that debts and taxes paid to the Noriega regime wouldn't satisfy obligations due the Republic of Panama.

The letters, however, would not be enough. A source in the U.S. government informed Rogers that the Republic National Bank of New York was transferring $10 million to Panama on the day the faxes were transmitted, and that it planned to wire another $10 million the day after. Twenty million dollars was a lot of money for a country of only two million people. The Arnold & Porter team thus realized that they would have to institute emergency litigation against the banks in order to stop the flow of funds to the Noriega regime. The team, therefore, labored throughout the night

to draft papers for a lawsuit to be filed the next day in New York, seeking
a temporary restraining order against Republic National. Judge Lloyd F.
MacMahon of the Southern District of New York promptly issued such
an order, stopping the transfer of the second $10 million.

Arnold & Porter needed to make the restraining order permanent. Banking lawyer Robert Mannion dug up the precedent that Rogers needed. The
Edge Act of 1941 had allowed the U.S. to recognize governments forced
into exile by Adolf Hitler, so that they could maintain gold and other assets
in Allied banks. The act had last been used in 1953 to settle a dispute
between Taiwan and mainland China over Wells Fargo Bank accounts:
Taiwan had won, as the State Department did not recognize the commu-
nist-ruled mainland. The law, however, had never before been used as
effectively to bring substantial economic pressure on a de facto government
as it now would be with Panama.

The Rogers team drafted a diplomatic note for the State Department
that said that Ambassador Sosa was the only person "with authority to
receive, control, or dispose of any property held in any Federal Reserve
Bank for an account of the Republic of Panama or any central bank
thereof." Acting Secretary of State John Whitehead (Shultz was traveling
in early March, and continued to be out of the country on other business
during much of the early weeks of the Panama crisis) provided the necessary certification, which gave notice "to any Federal Reserve Bank or to
any federally insured bank" that the United States accepted the authority
of Ambassador Sosa "with respect to such property." That certification
would prove to be more damaging to Noriega than any U.S. official sanction against him that would follow. It immediately cut Noriega's regime
off from $40 million in U.S. banks and also cut Panama off from using the
New York banks to perform essential clearing house functions for Panama's international transactions—a necessity, because the country's currency is the U.S. dollar. The certification also made it impossible for
Noriega's lawyers to appeal in court. Only lawyers representing the Delvalle government had legal standing to appear on behalf of the Republic
of Panama.

The court scenes themselves often resembled the old TV panel show *To
Tell the Truth*. A number of different lawyers would stand to say, one after
another, that they each represented the Republic of Panama. The judge
then had to decide who the imposters were. Arnold & Porter's lawyers
would object the moment one of Noriega's lawyers opened his mouth,
arguing that he had no legal standing as a representative of Panama's
government. "It's the first time I've seen lawyers make an objection before
the court when an opposing lawyer stood up to introduce himself," laughed

Melvin Garbow, an Arnold & Porter lawyer who helped gain control of Air Panama's operations in the United States for the Delvalle group.

In the Air Panama case, Garbow eventually found himself representing both the plaintiff (the Republic of Panama) and the defendant (Air Panama), once the judge ruled that Noriega's lawyers had no standing. That raised some novel issues. If the Republic of Panama was suing an entity of itself, how could it do so in an American court? "In twenty-six years of law practice, I've never seen anything like this," said Garbow. "There were no precedents to a lot of what was happening."

As the de facto foreign office of Delvalle's regime, Arnold & Porter often acted on tips from the U.S. government. Its fourth-floor conference room had been converted into a "war room," and Panamanian opposition fighters wandered in and out all day, comparing notes and plotting new strategies with the legal team.

A minor sideplot also developed between two firms as dissimilar as their clients. Arnold & Porter is Washington establishment. Noriega's banking interests were represented by, among others, the maverick New York firm of Rabinowitz, Boudin, Standard, Krinsky, & Lieberman. The firm first gained fame defending victims of the 1950s anti-Communist campaign of Senator Joseph McCarthy. It has since represented Alger Hiss, the Church of Scientology, Fidel Castro, Muammar Qaddafi, the Ayatollah Khomeini, and Amy Carter.

Rabinowitz, Boudin lawyers prepared arguments outside court that cited passages of the U.S. Foreign Policy Act and the Treaty of the Organization of American States to back up his case that the Reagan administration had acted unconstitutionally in recognizing Delvalle. They also were prepared to cite the restatement of the Foreign Relations Law of April 6, 1985, by the American Law Institute: "When a state recognizes or treats a rebellious regime as the legitimate government while the previously recognized government is still in control, that constitutes unlawful interference in the international affairs of the other state." He figured his legal basis was solid enough to take the case to the Supreme Court.

But one judge after another ruled that Rabinowitz, Boudin's lawyers couldn't be heard. At a star-studded March 7 hearing in New York, Judge Lloyd F. MacMahon was faced with three sets of lawyers. Arnold & Porter was defending what the State Department viewed as the Republic of Panama. Rabinowitz, Boudin appeared representing what it claimed was Panama, and subway gunman Bernhard Goetz's goateed defense lawyer, Barry Slotnick, made a surprise appearance on behalf of National Bank of Panama.

Anthony Baratta of Rabinowitz, Boudin was shut down when trying to argue that the U.S. recognition of Delvalle was illegal. "I cannot hear that," said the judge. "I am bound by the State Department here. . . . So you are just wasting your time and mine arguing it."

Baratta tried again. "Would Your Honor allow me respectfully—"

"No, I will not," the judge said. "I will not hear your application to intervene and that's all."

Baratta persisted, arguing, "The question is who is Panama and who legitimately—"

"I won't hear you any further. That issue, as I have told you, clearly is not before this court. You're through. Next?"

Barry Slotnick had another approach. Having spent the Chinese New Year with Noriega in 1988, he had been appointed to represent the bank only that morning. He apologized for not having had time to prepare legal documents, but he did give the judge a tear-jerking letter: "I have been informed that there are many households that are unable to purchase food, milk, and other necessities for their families and children." He tried to argue that some of the funds that had been frozen belonged to private depositors. "As Your Honor knows from my letter, there are people in Panama who do not have the money to feed their children," he said.

An exasperated Judge MacMahon finally extended his restraining order by ten days and asked all interveners to give him briefs within three days. Slotnick objected, "Your Honor, we ask most respectfully that all briefs be submitted by tomorrow morning, due to the devastation that is occurring. . . ."

"No, that is not much help to the court," said the judge. "I have had enough off the cuff. Three days. Three days."

With State Department certification in place, the Rogers team moved to amend the complaint against Republic National to include three other New York banks. As a direct result, Panama's banks were closed on March 3, 1988. "We have brought the Panama banking system to its knees," said Rogers.

Additional lawsuits were also successful against another bank in Boston and four in Miami. By the second week of March, the Delvalle government had successfully obtained temporary restraining orders against nine U.S. banks and one airline.

Policy makers stood by with admiration and encouragement as this group of Washington lawyers took the lead against Noriega. "Ambassador Sosa and his lawyers could be stopped definitively only if the United States chose publicly to recognize Noriega," said Arnold & Porter's Juster.

Ironically, however, Delvalle's successful lawsuits may have taken some of the pressure off Reagan and thus delayed decisive and effective U.S.

action. It was only on March 11, nearly three weeks after Delvalle's ouster, that President Reagan took the first, limited measures to complement Arnold & Porter's actions. Reagan said the United States would put into escrow monthly payments due Noriega from the Panama Canal Commission, amounting to some $80 million a year. Reagan also suspended trade preferences available to Panama that, over the course of the year, would affect $96 million in exports from the country. More significant U.S. sanctions, however, that might have hit Noriega when he was weakest, wouldn't come for another month.

Federal courts had put Noriega on the ropes, but the Reagan administration failed to deliver the knockout blow. While Panamanians joined general strikes, U.S. officials were involved in a seemingly endless series of interagency disputes. Juster was disappointed to see the effect of the firm's handiwork dissipated, leaving Panama's economy wilting and Noriega still in place. "Different groups in the Reagan administration bickered openly and vociferously about what to do, thus playing out in public what should have been debated in private," Juster said later. "This distracted from the effort to push Noriega from power and, instead, only emboldened him."

To answer Arnold & Porter, Noriega's regime was organizing an all-out counteroffensive to get money to Panama. The drama was an international one.

For its part, Noriega's family was firing off a series of letters to protect its own accounts and assets, which amounted to at least $300 million worldwide, and to move them to safer locations. The family shifted much of its money into accounts in foreign banks listed only under the National Bank of Panama, which was slowly becoming Noriega's personal institution.

However, more important to Noriega's survival, he ordered his subordinates to come up with money quickly so that he could pay public employees; and he shipped emissaries overseas to find emergency loans.

On March 3, 1988, Panamanian banks had closed to avoid panic withdrawals. Noriega's desperation for cash had become so clear that several American banks, fearing that he would raid their vaults, organized a secret meeting with American military officers at a baseball field at Fort Clayton. They wanted help to get the money out of their coffers and safely to the United States. As a result, on the following Saturday a garbage truck pulled up behind each of their banks, and large garbage bags filled with $20, $50, and $100 bills were tossed in the trucks by workers who hadn't any idea what was inside. The bags then were spirited to an American military base, where they were flown on Air Force cargo planes to the United States. One banker says some $100 million was sent out in the shipment.

Even as money was going out, however, Noriega was finding clever ways to bring some in. On March 13, he held a strategy session in his overly air-conditioned office with shivering international financial advisers: Ambassador to Japan Alberto Calvo, Ambassador to London Guillermo Vega, merchant marine boss Hugo Torrijos, Ambassador to Paris Gaspar Wittgreen (his wife's first cousin and the brother of Carlos Wittgreen, Noriega's partner in arms dealings and Cuban embargo-breaking), and a half-dozen others, including his finance minister. They had all become millionaires through their alliance with Noriega; and they all had keen financial minds that would turn to finding funds for Noriega's regime.

They planned how to tap the sources of income that the U.S. couldn't touch: horse racing, the lottery, unpaid taxes, and fees from the Colón Free Trade Zone. Each reported how much was in the pipeline, and then suggested ways of raising money quickly. One sure source of income was licensing and the associated fees for Panamanian-flagged merchant vessels. Noriega turned to Calvo, who had converted the Japanese embassy into a multimillion-dollar business in less than ten years. How could he get the incoming payments—and prepayments from cooperative Japanese friends—to Panama quickly?

Calvo explained that normal banking channels had been closed off by the Americans. That was a problem because all dollar transfers to Panama had to be sent through U.S. commercial banks as clearing houses, because of Panama's lack of a central bank of its own.

But Noriega wasn't interested in discussion of details. He trusted this team's vested interests to motivate them. He just wanted to see results. "You are the experts," he said. "You take care of this."

Albert Calvo, a short, meaty, and disheveled lawyer, put his brilliant mind to work. Calvo was a master conspirator, an international-class bridge player who had dueled Larry Tisch in New York, Omar Sharif in southern France, and Deng Xiaoping in Beijing. He used his valuable connections as a board member of the World Bridge Association to gain entree to powerful political circles as Noriega's ambassador to Tokyo.

Calvo came up with some money for Noriega in Japan, but then he needed to get it out of that country, so he contacted two friends in Tokyo's diplomatic community: the Soviet and Cuban ambassadors. He wanted to ship hundreds of thousands of American dollars from Tokyo to Panama via Havana. They both replied that their countries wouldn't inspect Panamanian diplomatic bags. They would be even less likely to do so in an operation whose ultimate aim was to undermine U.S. policy. The money was carried by a courier on Aeroflot to Moscow and then through Havana to Panama. Some months later, President Solis Palma would decorate Calvo for his counter–economic warfare.

A senior Panamanian official confirmed that at least $2 million—and probably much more—traveled through this channel in March and April. It was a significant sum for such a small country. In May, Calvo created a less cumbersome channel. Money from Panamanian consulates all over the world was sent primarily through National Bank of Paris accounts to Hong Kong. Ambassador to Paris Gaspar Wittgreen helped make arrangements. These consulates earned hefty fees, not only from shipping but also from selling passports, end-user certificates for sensitive materials, and other clandestine services. When money landed in Hong Kong, the Banco Nacional de Paris issued it in cash. A Hong Kong courier service, accustomed to such secret dealings, then carried it to Panama on KLM Airlines, in simple cardboard boxes. KLM is the only European airline that flies directly to Panama without an intermediate stop in the U.S.: this reduced the risk of seizure.

By hook or by crook, the money came—but it came too late. The general strikes were called, the general unease grew, and soon Noriega found himself faced with his first full-fledged coup attempt.

CHAPTER
SIXTEEN

THE KEYSTONE
COUP

There are no unsolvable problems, only incapable people.

—GENERAL NORIEGA, MARCH 1987

General Manuel Antonio Noriega needed to calm his cabinet ministers and political allies and reassure them that he was in control. It was March 15, 1988, and on that morning he had missed payment of public employees' salaries for the first time. Noriega and his staff were exploring ways to find the funds and stifle unrest. A general strike was to begin the next morning.

Noriega picked Major Fernando Quezada, one of his brightest and most articulate officers, to brief the cabinet about the dangers ahead. Quezada, who had recently returned from a year of study in Washington at the Inter-American Defense College, drew an alarming picture. He was running an operations center that was monitoring public unrest and the American military threat, and both were escalating dangerously. He described in detail every new piece of military equipment brought in by the Americans. He spoke of five new helicopters with firepower sufficient to blow up all of Panama City. He outlined U.S. plans to build refugee camps that would house 100,000 people and could be assembled in two hours. The arriving troops were potent and highly mobile. He said the Panamanian air force and army "could do nothing" if the U.S. decided to attack. "Nothing," he repeated, his eyes searching throughout the room to measure the response. Noriega's general staff were all there, and no one disagreed.

The presentation was so alarmist that many of those attending guessed that Noriega wanted to exaggerate the threat. Noriega's motive was clear:

273

the greater the perceived danger, the more license he could take in repression and in the demands he would make of his government officers. Quezada, however, was playing a different game. He was setting the table for his coup against Noriega the next morning. He wanted cabinet members and other officers to see that Noriega had brought the country to such danger that his removal was the only alternative.

At the same time, Joel McCleary and Costa Rican politician Enrique Carreras were nervously waiting in their hotel rooms in Panama City for a secret rendezvous with a Panamanian officer. Noriega had sent a message to Gabriel Lewis that he wanted to negotiate, but Lewis had sent McCleary as his cannon fodder instead.

Ever since McCleary's arrival the night before, however, it had been clear something was afoot. An old friend, who had heard through the G-2 that McCleary was in Panama, visited him in the predawn hours. He put a sizable finger to his lips to ensure that McCleary remain silent. He knew the American consultant's room at the Caesar Park Marriott was wired for sound. They walked down the hall to the elevators. "I have a message from a friend," the man said. "Get the fuck out of here before tomorrow. You are in big danger. Stuff is going to happen."

"Stuff?" McCleary felt elated. He instantly knew his friend was talking about a coup. Now he had to decide what to do. Would he stay for his scheduled meeting the next day with Noriega? Or should he get out on the first morning plane? With the arrogance that infects political consultants, he wanted to remain to give the rebels post-coup advice. They were potential clients.

By that evening, while Noriega was meeting with his cabinet, McCleary and Carreras stood in the saw grass at the end of a landing strip at Paitilla airport. McCleary was in a blue suit with broad pinstripes, more befitting Washington than the tropics. Carreras was all in white. They left their taxi waiting and stood alone in the open, worried that they were easy targets for sharpshooters and wondering if they could trust each other.

A major they both knew arrived with an armed bodyguard. "The General can't meet with you now," he said. "He wants to, but he can't." They exchanged some small talk in this odd setting. The major complained about Noriega's legal fees in the U.S. "He's pissed off because he thinks they are charging him too much," the officer said. "They're leeches."

"Noriega was always cheap," McCleary said. They all laughed in agreement.

McCleary then delivered the message he'd been assigned to carry. Would Noriega be interested in negotiating with members of the U.S. State

Department? He mentioned State Department officials William Walker and Michael Kozak. Noriega's lawyers were already making the same offer in Washington.

"Noriega will deal with people in the U.S. government," the major said. "But not right now."

McCleary had carried out his task. Now he wanted out. If the coup failed, he was certain that Noriega would lock him up as a co-conspirator. The two mediators caught the last plane to San José.

Noriega ended the marathon cabinet meeting at 1 A.M., but his actions thereafter suggested that he knew about the plot. In fact, assigning Quezada to brief the cabinet—rather than doing so himself—was to be his last attempt to expose the ambitious Quezada and frighten him from his treason. Noriega lied to Quezada that he'd be sleeping at his bedroom in the well-guarded Comandancia that night, and that they should meet there at 8 A.M. for a strategy session with the general staff about how to deal with the day's general strike. Noriega and Quezada then put their opposing plans into action.

Noriega stayed at a PDF guards' quarters across from the presidential palace until after 3 A.M., but he moved his cars from the area so that the coup plotters would think he had left. He drank a few Old Parr whiskeys with the night watch, and he acted so nonchalantly that no one would guess he was counterplotting. He even sent his personal driver back to the Comandancia, so that the men Quezada had posted there would think he had returned.

Noriega needs little sleep. Throughout his crisis, he would rest for an odd hour or two when and where possible, and he'd often change the places where he slept. His backup driver thus didn't think it unusual for the General to stay out until 4 A.M. or to change his destination at the last moment from the Comandancia to his more secure office at Fort Amador.

At 5 A.M., Guillermo "Willy" Cochez, a Christian Democratic politician received a phone call from a friend who had acted as his middleman for secret meetings with PDF officers. "My friend of the restaurant wants to talk to you," he said in a code they both understood.

The politician raced to his car, and he drove to the home of a restaurant owner, who then gave him details of a meeting he would have just a few minutes later at the Bridge of the Americas. When the politician arrived, Major Quezada was jogging nonchalantly across the span that binds North and South America. He liked running there at that time in the morning, where he could look down 200 yards to the water below, and gaze out at the Pacific to his left and the Panama Canal to his right. On this morning, it was also important that he could see for miles in each direction, to spot any suspicious cars. Traffic was light when the politician stopped and Quezada jumped in, certain that no one had paid much attention. He spoke as they drove.

"We are beginning a coup at 7:15 A.M., and we need your help," he said. Quezada wanted to ensure that the opposition would voice its support for the coup makers, and they in turn would support democratic elections. He also wanted the Civic Crusade to send demonstrators to the streets after the coup was announced, to help prevent Noriega's troops from coming to rescue him. Quezada's only request was that Delvalle not be included in the transitional government. "We are against Delvalle and his people," said Quezada. "They are crooks."

Quezada said the rebels were getting rid of Noriega because he was destroying the institution and the country. When Cochez asked if the Americans were helping, Quezada said he had contacted General Woerner, the chief of the Southern Command, to ask for weapons and other assistance. "I'm not sure we'll get those weapons or anything else," Quezada said in a disappointed tone. The Americans had been, for him, surprisingly uncooperative.

The politician knew all the officers who had been involved in the coup. Ironically, Noriega had created this Frankenstein monster that was trying to destroy him. Many had been associated with his G-2, which had become a political school for officers. They watched over and mixed with student leaders, political officers, and business groups.

Torrijos had kept his officers at arm's length from the political opposition, but Noriega hadn't liked it that military officers were considered second-rank citizens, and he'd wanted to politicize them and offer them more power. In his attempt to control society, he had assigned his smartest officers to interact with National Assembly members, to push through bills he wanted and to attend diplomatic parties, where they were assigned to pick up the latest rumors and gossip. The problem was that, through their contacts, Quezada and others began to learn that the men of the opposition weren't the dangerous ogres or enemies that PDF propaganda painted.

Major Aristides Valdonedo, another key member of the rebellion, had made the PDF's first contacts to the Christian Democrats, the only opposition party that had a sound structure and conducted political operations between electoral periods. Major Moisés del Rio, another of the rebels, had been head of the ministry of natural resources. Others, and some whose involvement Noriega hasn't yet discovered even now, had similar backgrounds.

The rebels had other elements in common. Several, including Quezada and Valdonedo, had recently completed military courses in the U.S., and they feared Noriega's slide to the left. Most were near or already past twenty-five years of service, at which point Noriega could retire them. All the officers involved had been passed over for promotions. Most also had better upbringings than many in the pro-Noriega crowd. A handful of the majors had attended the La Salle Catholic School instead of the more populist Instituto Nacional.

They were Noriega's smartest and most capable officers, and it was their General's decision to put them among Panamanian politicians that had made them the freethinking rebels they had become.

The only officer who didn't fit this mold was Colonel Leonidas Macias, the head of Panama's police. The coup makers needed Macias, whose reputation was that of a brutal oaf, because none of them controlled troops. He had the police who would control the roads and shut off Noriega's headquarters complex. Macias's men were also responsible for monitoring Noriega's movements that night for the coup makers. Macias falsely reported that Noriega had fallen into their trap by choosing to sleep at the Comandancia.

The coup plotting had only started a couple of weeks earlier. Some like-minded majors knew the risk of proceeding quickly with a half-hatched plan, but they wanted to seize the opportunity of the March 16 general strike, an opportunity that might not come again. Roads would be blocked; protesters who hadn't been paid would clog the streets; public sentiment was behind them. The port authority and railway unions would paralyze transportation, and the electrical union was planning to cut off power to the city. The U.S. was augmenting its troops, and many Panamanian officers feared an invasion that would destroy their institution and their careers. More practically, these majors feared higher-ranking officers might preempt their action with a coup of their own.

Noriega's growing links to Cuba concerned many of the officers, who tended to be anti-communist. Major Augusto Villalaz, an air force pilot, had flown three shipments of arms from Cuba to Panama in the first half of March. Each trip had brought sixteen tons more of weaponry to Panama—his Boeing 727 cargo plane's maximum load. The plane carried AK-47s, RPG-7s, ammunition for mortars, and other munitions. Villalaz dropped each of the shipments at a different location, where they would be stored away for armed conflict with the Americans or internal enemies. Noriega was preparing to fight to the end with the help of the Cubans, Villalaz thought. Villalaz joined the coup plotters, and his intelligence on the Cuban weapons deliveries fueled their sense of urgency.

The coup planning was a nervous affair. Most believed Noriega's ears were everywhere. At general meetings, he would often announce a small piece of information—sometimes as innocuous as congratulations on an officer's newborn or questions about a sick relative—confirming that he either had informants or was bugging phones. Officers couldn't trust each other or talk freely.

Villalaz remembered an evening in November 1987, when Noriega called his accompanying officers to a typical all-nighter in his hotel room in Taiwan, where he was receiving a medal (the "Propitious Tripod Award"). Noriega would chastise any officers who drank too slowly or refused refills. "A good officer has to be able to drink," he would chortle. But his own scotch would be a lighter hue of brown, refilled only by his personal aides and not by fellow officers. He would say little, merely asking occasional questions and flushing out discontent, while he stuck his finger in his glass and methodically stirred the ice cubes. Before each such session, officers reached a private pact to kick each other if they started talking too much. Villalaz, because of his close contacts to former General Paredes, was particularly suspect.

Villalaz eagerly joined the conspirators. His job as the number two man in the air force was to keep planes and helicopters grounded during the coup. His contact in the coup was the middleman for much of the planning, Major Fundora. Fundora was second in command of the PDF treasury, so it wasn't unusual that a large number of majors should be visiting or calling him to get money for the troops' food, boots, or any other extraordinary costs.

After each flight to Cuba, Villalaz would report to Fundora on how many arms he had brought and where they had been delivered. Fundora's brother-in-law had been born in Cuba, so Villalaz would phone to say he had a present from his uncle. If the shipment was 16 tons, or 32,000 pounds, he would say the package weighed 32 pounds. The last shipment came on the day before the coup attempt.

Fundora phoned Villalaz through his beeper that night, waking him from a sound sleep. "The party will be held tomorrow," he said. "I hope you can make it."

Villalaz's first concern came at 5 A.M. when 200 of Noriega's most loyal troops, a company from the Battalion 2000, arrived at his airfield for parachute training. Villalaz panicked. They could undermine the whole operation. He quickly woke up two pilots to get those paratroopers to their jumping area earlier than they had expected. The first near-crisis had been avoided, but the coup makers' woes had only started.

At 6 A.M., Colonel Macias easily took the headquarters' armory.

Noriega's loyalists would now be without weapons. Having accomplished his first task without much trouble, Macias used the armory phone to complete step two. He called radio stations to announce the coup and to appeal for supporters to take the streets. But while he was dialing, Lieutenant Colonel Euclides Corro, who was in charge of the armory, walked out and locked Macias in. It was just 6:30 A.M., and the coup's senior officer was out of commission.

The coup makers arrested Captain Jesús George Balma and put him in the strategy room while they started discussing their next steps. Balma overheard the details, and he easily walked out of the building, called a cab, and drove off to alert Noriega at Fort Amador. At the time, however, the coup makers worried little about his escape. They thought Noriega was still sleeping in the adjoining building, in the bedroom behind his office.

Major Jaime Benitez had been assigned the critical job of arresting Captain Moisés Giroldi, the most loyal and dangerous of Noriega's allies, who controlled the 200 men who protected the headquarters. Benitez put an AK-47 to Giroldi's head as he slept, and told him to make his troops surrender. Giroldi said his troops would obey him only if he faced them. But as soon as Giroldi reached the courtyard, he screamed to his men that they should grab Benitez. Fifty men were soon pointing guns at him. Giroldi grabbed a 7-millimeter machine gun, mounted in the courtyard to protect Noriega's headquarters, and he fired in the air to wake everyone. These were the only shots of the coup. The incident would later be reported by the press as gunshots and a firefight, but nothing of the sort ever occurred.

The coup makers never got far enough along to discover their biggest error: Noriega's bed was undisturbed and their target was absent.

By 9 A.M., the coup was over and Noriega returned from El Ocho. He emerged confidently from his windowless bunker and drove the few miles to his headquarters, past the grave and bust of Omar Torrijos, and then past the Fort Amador golf course where American officers seemed to have pushed back the jungle with an army of lawn mowers. Some officers were teeing up for the first morning rounds, oblivious to who was driving by them or what had happened. Noriega's blue Mercedes, followed by a tail vehicle with his bodyguards, drove past mango trees and royal palms, and the YMCA in the former Panama Canal Zone, and then entered what U.S. officers called "Indian territory"—Panama City's slums. The last two blocks of the five-minute ride took him past the dilapidated French canal-worker housing, where the wood is decaying and the rusty, corrugated steel roofs leave huge gaps over their destitute tenants. Noriega drove by the sentries guarding the Comandancia only after the danger was over. When it was clear all was secure, he came out on a balcony of the whitewashed Comandancia to show he was in charge. Reporters, who had been tipped off of a possible coup in the early-morning hours, waited below. Wearing civilian clothes and looking relaxed, Noriega appeared with several members of his general staff.

The shots? "They were kisses," he answered to a reporter's shouted question. Noriega laughed.

The failed coup showed cracks in the PDF, but it also helped him. It uncovered the General's opponents; and it gave him an excuse to dismiss officers of uncertain loyalty and promote those he trusted.

"That failed coup gave him new oxygen," Paredes would say later. "At the time of his greatest weakness, this was a godsend. The civilian government, which was growing cautious of him, was demoralized and rallied back around him. The undecided officers closed ranks behind him." Both dictators Ferdinand Marcos and "Baby Doc" Duvalier had fallen after army coups had altered the balance against them. Noriega had conquered this initial threat.

Noriega seized the moment to create a new leadership council, based more on personal loyalty to him than on rank. Noriega had always been wary of giving too many senior officers too much power. The PDF had only one general, five full colonels, twelve lieutenant colonels and fifty-five majors at the time of the coup. Yet financial rewards and power always came to officers closest to him. Noriega paid less attention to rank than perhaps any other Latin officer.

The March 16 coup allowed him to institutionalize this informal arrangement under a new council called the Strategic Military Council, or CEM. Although Noriega's general staff wasn't disbanded, its responsibilities were now limited to strategic military affairs, which had never been very important to the PDF. The CEM became Noriega's de facto parliament. At its inception, it was made up of one colonel, three lieutenant colonels, ten majors, and six captains. The group would meet at least once a week formally and more often informally.

From that point forward, it would scrutinize speeches planned by Noriega, critique them, and then return them to the General. It would invite experts to lecture on topics ranging from Panama's printing its own currency (an idea abandoned on economic grounds) to how hard to attack Bush during the U.S. election campaign (it opted to hold its punches). It would often call in union leaders to defuse strikes by catching unrest early.

Noriega imprisoned more than a dozen officers for twenty-year sentences, and thereafter tortured the officers and lodged them in underground cells without lights or toilets to dissuade other would-be rebels. He made sure news of their mistreatment was broadly circulated.

Paredes doubted that the military would be able to repeat this act very soon. "When a woman is pregnant," said the former commander, "you have to wait nine months before she is ready to be pregnant again. The coup was a premature birth, or an abortion if you want to be more honest. It will take a longer time to get pregnant again because the woman is wary."

With his own military back under control, Noriega searched furiously for international help. One of Washington's greatest errors in 1988 was underestimating the strength of Noriega's friends and their willingness to continue doing business with him. Noriega's international allies were a diverse lot, unified only in their distrust of—or opposition to—American policies, and their opportunistic hope for economic gain. They included the Japanese, Taiwanese, French, Israelis, Cubans, Nicaraguans, and Colombian drug dealers. All had profited from their relationship with Noriega; some owed him debts; and others were looking for favors.

The French had given Noriega their Medal of Honor for clandestine assistance; the Taiwanese honored him with the Propitious Tripod Award; and the Israelis decorated him as well. The Cubans, Nicaraguans, and Libyans, all longstanding enemies of the U.S., actually had him on their intelligence payrolls before Noriega's crisis, and, unlike the U.S., they never took him off.

In its efforts to isolate Noriega, Washington had pushed him more closely toward its traditional enemies. Now, Noriega reached out to these groups to support his claims that he was fighting American imperialism and to send a message to Washington that its confrontation with him could be politically costly.

Noriega's first financial help in the worst weeks of winter 1988, came from the Libyans. Moammar Qaddafi provided Noriega a $20 million emergency loan with a one-year grace period before repayment. U.S. intelligence types worried that the Libyan money would also free Qaddafi to make greater use of Panamanian banks and territory to support terrorist operations.

The State Department's annual survey for 1987, published in August 1988, had already called Panama a banking and transit site for many terrorist and insurgent groups, facilitated by the Cuban and Nicaraguan embassies and the Libyan People's Bureau. Noriega had always been careful not to condone this activity, since much of the Jewish business community in Panama supported him; and until the U.S. turned against Noriega, the activities had been carefully circumscribed. Now, however, although still cautious, Noriega began expanding opportunities for the Libyans and their friends.

In mid-October 1988, American CIA operatives delivered a startling report. It said that the Hawari/Special Operations Group, an intelligence branch of the PLO's relatively moderate al-Fatah faction, was planning terrorist operations against U.S. interests around Panama. The group was run by a former bodyguard of Yasir Arafat named Abdallah Abd al-Hamid Labib.

The report read: "Three Lebanese Palestinians, traveling on genuine, true-name passports, have departed Lebanon for Panama where they intend to mount terrorist operations against U.S. registered ships in the Canal Zone. Following this, they plan to travel to the U.S. A second team of three Palestinian operatives departed Beirut for Panama in early September. While in Panama, the six operatives also will attempt to infiltrate other operatives into the U.S. by stowing them away on ships headed for U.S. ports."

A Defense Intelligence Agency memo two days later questioned the credibility of the CIA report, claiming that neither Arafat nor Noriega would support such strikes on U.S. shipping. The two agencies agreed, however, that Qaddafi viewed Noriega as a valuable ally.

"The strategic interests of Libya are currently well served by maintaining its presence and contacts in Panama," said the report. "Tripoli uses Panama to facilitate financial transactions, intelligence collection, and the movement of trainees from radical groups in Latin America to and from Libya. A terrorist attack would represent a dramatic reversal of relations between Tripoli and Panamanian leader Noriega."

The attack never came off, but the Libyans and the Hawari group continued to use Panama as a staging area, and U.S. intelligence agents feared that if Washington escalated its fight against Noriega, these terrorist assets might be deployed against U.S. targets. These groups owed Noriega a debt. In fact, it seemed to American intelligence agents in Panama that dark characters of every ilk were indebted to Panama's dictator. In a dirty war, they reported to Washington, Noriega would have the upper hand.

Noriega and Castro also moved quietly to strengthen already close ties, although it was in both sides' interests to play down the connection. The Pentagon played along with this effort to keep their tightening links secret. Pentagon spokesmen religiously reported that they had been unable to confirm numerous reports that more Cuban advisers and arms were reaching Panama. They also failed to reveal information that proved beyond any reasonable doubt that Cuban troops, in live-ammunition war games, were infiltrating an American tank farm at night to spook American troops and increase their feeling of vulnerability.

Yet what the Pentagon was denying in public, it was confirming to senators in intelligence sessions. "I have no doubt the Cubans were involved," says Senator Alfonse D'Amato, a New York Republican who had taken on the Panama issue as a favorite issue. "I think the information was repressed simply because it would have heightened the tension and brought [the Panama crisis] to greater public visibility. People would want some action if they knew that the Cubans were attempting to infiltrate our bases. . . . But the Joint Chiefs absolutely want to keep the situation status quo."

For Castro, Panama had become perhaps his most important economic outlet to the world, providing him a means to market his own products through the Colón Free Trade Zone—products often sent to American buyers with labels from other Latin American countries. Panama had also provided Fidel Castro the easiest means to buy American spare parts and high technology that were banned by the United States trade embargo of Cuba.

With Noriega's crisis, however, he expanded these long-standing business and economic links into a closer political and military relationship. Initially, the Cubans sent thirty-nine advisers to help Noriega on issues ranging from propaganda and psychological warfare to the technical operation of a government and the possibility of his printing his own money. Panama's continued use of the American dollar as its only paper currency had helped the banking sector's success, but it had made Noriega vulnerable to American economic pressure.

The first dramatic signal of increased Cuban activity came on April 14, 1988, when the Cubans helped Noriega provide their answer to the Americans' "Total Warrior" exercises, which had been designed to increase the psychological pressure on Noriega. A little-known Department of Defense intelligence group, the Anti-Terrorist Alert Center (ATAC) reported:

At approximately 0120 hours on April 13, U.S. Marines at Arraijan fuel farm, near Howard AFB, were attacked by 50–70 unidentified individuals wearing black camouflage uniforms and using small arms and mortars. Fighting continued for approximately 2½ hours. No *U.S.* casualties were reported.

An American intelligence agent said the uniforms, tactics, and arms that were used hadn't ever before been seen among Panamanian soldiers. A "Panama code word briefing" for U.S. senators and cleared staff was more explicit. One source with access to U.S. military intelligence reports provided the following account:

> The first April attack started from the estate which abuts the Arraijan tank farm owned by a leftist member of the Panamanian Congress [National Assembly member Rigoberto Paredes]. It was primarily Cuban commandos, Cuban Spetznaz special forces. The operation was staged out of the estate and the Cubans retreated back through the estate. Three of the Cubans were wounded in the attack. They were taken to a PDF military hospital and registered under [false names]. One died, and after some hospital workers became suspicious, the other two were transferred to a Cuban ship transiting the canal.
>
> The [U.S.] Marines at the tank farm were ordered by the commanding Army general not to go out and collect the bodies of the others killed during the attack. They waited for nine hours before going out, and there were only blood trails left to be found.

A report prepared in Key West, Florida, by the intelligence arm of the U.S. forces in the Caribbean, drew an ominous picture under the heading, "Cubans in Panama." It said:

> Cuba has strong economic and political reasons to get directly involved in Panama and to ensure that events turn out favorably for Noriega. Politically, Castro views Noriega as an ally in Cuba's struggle against the United States. While Noriega is extremely disreputable and the type of corrupt leader Castro used to condemn, Castro can ill afford another setback in Latin America. The America Department [of Cuban Intelligence] is probably orchestrating the Cuban support of Noriega through many avenues. Humint [human intelligence] reporting indicates that there are Cuban political and Military Advisors to Noriega and Cuban soldiers in Panama as well. The number of personnel at the Cuban Embassy has been increasing slowly. . . .
>
> Two First Rate Cuban media personnel have arrived in Panama to advise the government-controlled news media in their specialty, news manipulation. There have been several reports alleging that Cubans are conducting guerrilla warfare training for Panamanian soldiers.
>
> All of these trends indicate that Cuba has a vested interest to ensure that the government of Panama stays friendly with Cuba. What is striking is the quality of the people Cuba is sending into Panama. Cuba is following much the same pattern it has historically used when executing covert operations in Angola, Ethiopia, and Nicaragua. While it is unlikely that Cuba will commit a large number of troops to Panama, Cuba has apparently committed itself to providing as much expertise as possible to shore up the Noriega regime.

The intelligence report made clear the importance of this closer relationship: "If Noriega is able to stay in power, Cuba's help will not be forgotten."

Perhaps most alarming to American policymakers, however, was the quiet ability shown by the Japanese and Taiwanese—countries flooded with cash seeking a home—to keep an American enemy afloat simply by refusing to join U.S. sanctions.

Under pressure from Secretary of State George Shultz, Japan had stopped providing officially guaranteed credits for large new investments; yet it sent signals to Noriega that it wasn't abandoning him. In the spring of 1988 it contributed $50,000 to the Panamanian Red Cross for food to "help feed the hungry" after American sanctions started taking their toll. At about the same time, the Japanese sent another $100,000 in hurricane relief. The U.S. embassy protested both times. The propaganda was as valuable as the money to General Noriega, who could show fellow officers and Panamanian businessmen that Japan was on his side.

Foreign ministry officials continually told their Panamanian counterparts that they considered Washington's war on Noriega another example of whimsical U.S. policy that they had to humor to some extent, so as not to cause further strains with their major trading partner. Japan's ambassador to the U.S., Nobua Matsunaga, used his weight initially to overrule the foreign ministry's desire to disregard efforts to unseat Noriega, but as it became clear that Washington wouldn't unseat the General, the Japanese grew less circumspect about their dealings with him.

The Japanese firm Pioneer moved its regional headquarters to Panama, at a time when U.S. law wouldn't even allow American companies to pay taxes to Noriega's regime, and other Japanese companies maintained or expanded ties. All that held Japan back was business sense: Panama had become a financial risk. Yet strategically, Panama remained the financial and transactional base from which Tokyo wanted to promote relations throughout the region. Its companies had invested many millions of dollars in the country's Colón Free Trade Zone.

In addition, many Japanese businessmen had grown obsessed with the idea of building a sea-level waterway through Panama, which would cut Japanese transportation costs and make goods even more competitive. Furthermore, the bulk of the construction contracts would likely go to Japanese companies. If a new waterway wasn't possible, they wanted at least to manage the Canal for the Panamanians when it reverted to them at the turn of the century.

Throughout all that, characteristically, Noriega had his own back channel to the Japanese. It had been established during the 1970s, and grew out of Noriega's odd fascination with oriental philosophies and fringe sects. Noriega's judo teacher in the early 1970s, a Chinese-Panamanian named Chuh Yih, had taught the young intelligence chief Buddhism. He introduced Noriega to a highly disciplined, quasi-fascist lay sect known as Soka Gakkai—the "Value Creation Society."

A disciplined, orderly, and private group, Soka Gakkai was established in 1930 "to save the unhappy in the entire world and achieve peace" through the propagation of the teachings of the fierce Japanese monk Nichiren, who died in the thirteenth century. In 1963, *Look* magazine called the sect "an alarming new religion that wants to conquer the world." It said the sect had strong overtones of the Hitler Youth and of Nazism in its organization and tactics. In 1964, *Time* magazine said, "The movement mixes the evangelism of the Moral Rearmament with the get-out-the-votes discipline of the Communist party and lots of show biz." Recently, Soka Gakkai has been made all the stronger through the rise of its Clean Government party, or Komeito, now the third-largest political party in Japan.

From the mid-1970s, Noriega often visited the sect's Taiseki Temple at the foot of Mount Fuji, where white-shirted believers with white armbands and sneakers worshiped. As Noriega's powers increased, he grew closer to the sect's leader, Daisaku Ikeda, and a life-sized statue of Noriega was erected in a garden at one temple in Japan in honor of his generous contributions. Noriega chanted the prayer there time and again in Panamanian-accented Japanese: *Namu myoho renge kyo* ("adoration to the scripture of the lotus of the true law"). The prayer is hypnotic, and those who repeat it often enough are assured by Soka Gakkai that they "can obtain vitality and wisdom as well as good fortune in leading a happy life."

Noriega hosted Ikeda on several visits to Panama, and treated him like a visiting head of state, despite the fact that he was merely a sect leader. The men were drawn to each other—both of them had great intellectual pretensions but only modest education. Like Noriega, Ikeda had risen from the ranks of the country's disaffected. Noriega's friends say that Ikeda provided him several million dollars' worth of assistance during the worst part of his crisis in 1987 and 1988. Soka Gakkai spokesmen deny Ikeda helped Noriega. They say he never officially converted, though he visited the temple. Whether official or not, Noriega considered himself a member of the sect. Better yet, Ikeda boosted Noriega's ego by calling him "Shogun." Japan was a place where Noriega never had to apologize for human rights violations or repressing democracy.

* * *

In his darkest days, Noriega also tapped old friendships elsewhere in the far east. One of the Panamanian General's oldest friends, Taiwanese Admiral Sung Ch'ang-chih, took over as Taiwan's ambassador to Panama in 1986. Admiral Sung had been one of Noriega's trainers at special courses for officers in Taiwan, though Noriega told friends that they had first met at a training course in the United States. For years, Noriega had provided the Taiwanese with Panamanian passports for intelligence-gathering missions in the People's Republic of China. Panama also remained as one of the few countries in the world that recognized only Taiwan and not the PRC. As a port open to Taiwan, the Colón Free Trade Zone was becoming one of the major transit points for Taiwanese goods, including an expanding weapons manufacturing industry that was seeking South American and Central American clients.

Taiwan became critically important to Noriega and others in Central America who had been cut off from American weapons shipments because Taiwanese military equipment was copied from U.S. originals; and Taiwan was eagerly seeking new markets for air defense missiles that Noriega and others couldn't find elsewhere. Admiral Sung, the former defense minister, eagerly promoted this business, and in March 1987 was instrumental in his government's decision to award Noriega its "Propitious Tripod" decoration, largely for his contributions to this effort.

Nevertheless, U.S. pressure on Taiwan to stand back caused a dispute to erupt between Taiwanese ministers over whether to expand economic relations with the Panamanians. Those favoring Noriega won out, partly because they didn't expect retribution from Washington.

A classified State Department cable from Taipei, sent to various intelligence agencies, confirmed that economics minister Chen Li-an, a frequent visitor to Noriega, carried the day, extolling the virtues of Taiwan-Panamanian relations. He overruled the head of the council for planning and economic development, Frederick Chien, who argued that such a course endangered U.S.–Taiwanese relations. In fact, the U.S. never took strong action against Taiwan, even when its loans—sometimes made through third countries to conceal them from the Americans—and the expansion of its export processing zone, helped undermine American sanctions.

Taiwan's quiet help for Panama culminated in May 1989 with a government announcement that Taiwan had offered Panama access to a whopping $1 billion fund for a series of projects, beginning with a $300 million export processing center at Coco Solo on the Atlantic coast. That followed an agreement for $40 million in loans the previous year, according to Rognoni.

"The Taiwanese were the ringleaders of those helping us," said Mario Rognoni. "The others followed." Indeed, some of America's best friends were acting like worst enemies in Panama, but Washington was doing nothing to combat their actions.

As Noriega's commerce minister, Mario Rognoni had been responsible for finding much of this international help. Even he, however, concedes that none of it would have made any difference if the U.S. had been determined to finish off Panama's dictator. "We were really a lot more worried during this time than we ever needed to be," he said months later. "The U.S. was never very determined or consistent in its war against us."

Which didn't mean, of course, that in its own bumbling fashion, the U.S. wouldn't try again. . . .

CHAPTER
SEVENTEEN

U.S. POLICY
FOLLIES

*You rope them into the idea of the invincible gringos
getting rid of Noriega, and then they find out it's not to
be like that.*

—ELLIOTT ABRAMS, 1989

William Walker's life as a deputy assistant secretary at the State Department didn't have much cloak-and-dagger to it. Most of his wars were bureaucratic, and survival meant lasting through the drudgery of meetings and memos that are the stuff of diplomacy.

So for him, this mission to Israel in late March 1988, was extraordinary. Michael Kozak's first talks to negotiate Noriega from power had failed on March 19; and now, just a few days later, Elliott Abrams and his allies wanted to escalate the pressure, perhaps even risking military involvement. The State Department was engaging in covert action, secret at first even from the CIA. Walker's job was to spirit Panama's Ambassador to Israel, Colonel Eduardo Herrera Hassan, to Washington for secret meetings to plot the military overthrow of Noriega. Colonel Herrera Hassan would then slip back into Israel and resume his ambassadorial duties until the plan was ready to be set into motion.

Walker's mission was made more perilous because one of Noriega's closest allies, former Mossad agent Michael Harari, was Panama's honorary consul in Jerusalem. In July 1985, when political events began to turn on Noriega, the General shipped Herrera Hassan to Tel Aviv as ambassador expressly to get him under Harari's wing. "I was the ambassador, but

Harari was in charge," said Colonel Herrera Hassan later. "I played stupid."

But all the time, Herrera Hassan was hoping he'd get a chance to exact his revenge on Noriega. He had been Torrijos's chief of security, and he was convinced that Noriega had planned the airplane crash that killed the dictator. He had long wanted revenge, and now the U.S. was offering him the opportunity. "He was honest and straightforward," said one U.S. intelligence agent. "We had the feeling he could inspire opposition in the defense forces, that he could serve to attract and prosyletize the military."

U.S. Ambassador to Israel Thomas Pickering had made the initial overture on March 20 at the instruction of Secretary Shultz. Pickering had grown friendly with Herrera Hassan through diplomatic parties and a natural chemistry. Pickering knew about Eduardo Herrera Hassan's tense relationship with the former Mossad agent, but he had counseled the Panamanian to remain patient. U.S. intelligence officials also knew that the Mossad was secretly training Herrera Hassan, realizing that it might need a friend close to the military should Noriega be ousted.

Listen, Eduardo, said Pickering, would you be willing to receive a visitor from the State Department?

Colonel Herrera Hassan sensed immediately the reason for the question, although Pickering wouldn't provide any further details. "Why not?" he said. "We—the State Department and I—are not enemies."

Herrera Hassan had never been an officer with political motivations; all he cared about was getting back at Noriega and reviving his stunted military career. Herrera called a CIA agent in Israel, however, to make sure the operation was genuine. He found it unusual that his contacts for a covert mission had been an ambassador. Yet the Americans must be serious, he thought. Why else would a superpower go to the trouble of recruiting him and then secretly escorting him back to Washington? The CIA man in Israel, who knew nothing about the plan, was suspicious. When queried by the CIA in Washington, Abrams confirmed the plan. He didn't tell the CIA that he had kept it secret to ensure that Harari didn't discover his handiwork from his friends in American intelligence who might owe him favors.

Three days after Pickering's initial contact, Walker was sitting with Herrera Hassan at his comfortable home in the beachside community of Herzliya, near Tel Aviv. His mission was to get Herrera Hassan to fly to the U.S. while only providing him the bare minimum of explanation why. "Many people want you to help us," said Walker. "We have a problem with Noriega, and we want to fly you to the United States to see what can be done." Even Walker didn't know the final details of what might be done.

But in Washington, the Abrams plan had already taken shape: Herrera Hassan and Delvalle would set themselves up as alternative military and political leadership in an area that is jointly administered under provisions of the Panama Canal Treaties. U.S. soldiers, as allowed by the Treaties, would ring the area on the pretext of protecting American civilians living there. Delvalle would then call for the backing of National Assembly members, many of whom would be lured over to the opposition by their longtime friend, José Blandón. Herrera Hassan would call for military defections. And all the time, the Civic Crusade would be demonstrating in the tens of thousands outside the National Assembly building, which was very near where these alternative leaders would set up shop, to show Panama was behind Delvalle's government and Herrera Hassan's military. The target date for the plan was April 3, Easter Sunday, when Noriega's military forces would be less ready to strike and the opposition could more easily call its workers, teachers, businessmen, and lawyers to the streets.

The plan had plenty of flaws. Delvalle was discredited with most Panamanians; Herrera Hassan had been away from Panama long enough to have lost intimate contacts with fellow officers; and José Blandón's hold on the ruling party was doubtful. On the other hand, opposition strategists thought failure could serve them as well. They would establish an exile government within Panama under U.S. protection. Washington would be dragged even further into their fight. And a foolish Noriega might undertake some action to provoke military action against him.

"I know it sounds farfetched," conceded Gabriel Lewis afterward, "but we had to try something, and this made as much sense as any other plan. It might have worked."

Even without knowing the details of this imperfect scheme, Herrera Hassan was reluctant. "I have to speak to my wife and family," he said. Colonel Herrera Hassan had spent twenty-three years in the Panamanian military and was just two years from retirement. However, if the U.S. was serious, Herrera Hassan wouldn't be able to resist the risk. He wasn't a diplomat made for the Tel Aviv cocktail circuit, but a forty-five-year-old officer, a paratrooper with commando training eager for this ultimate battle against his nemesis.

After talking to his wife and his seventeen-year-old son, he opted to sign on. He told his household staff that he was going to the beach resort of Eilat for the Passover holiday week, but instead Walker and Herrera Hassan flew on a TWA plane to Paris and then on to Washington. They sat across the aisle from each other in business class, not paying any attention to one another, and Herrera Hassan flew under the false name of Emilio Hassan. Herrera Hassan's heart raced as the TWA flight lifted off from Charles de

Gaulle airport, secure only in the fact that he was doing the right thing with the right adversary.

What Herrera Hassan didn't know was that he was just another piece in an interagency battle that the State Department was losing. By the time Herrera Hassan landed in Washington, and was whisked through customs by Walker, the Pentagon had successfully killed Abrams's plan, after a brutal interagency fight. The State Department was furiously working up other schemes, but no one needed the Panamanian anymore. No one had even booked him a hotel room.

Herrera Hassan, who had set off thinking he was to be the instrument of a coordinated U.S. policy, became another victim of America's bungled policy toward Panama. The Pentagon railed that the State Department had unfairly used Herrera Hassan as its pawn. Abrams argued that he couldn't believe that the administration would now turn back, once President Reagan had so clearly committed American prestige to removing Noriega. Since Herrera Hassan's hosts didn't have a hotel room for him, Gabriel Lewis checked him into the Key Bridge Marriott in Rosslyn, Virginia, listed as John Campbell, Lewis's lobbyist friend who would guarantee payment.

"We screwed up," said one senior State Department official, who was responsible for such intelligence missions. "It was badly managed. We didn't do well by him. We acted precipitously, partly out of frustration that nothing was happening."

Without a plot to participate in, Herrera Hassan was instead ushered around Washington by State Department officials who were trying to sell their candidate for leader of the Panamanian military against Noriega. After a week of meetings without any apparent purpose, Herrera Hassan turned to his escort, Colonel Gerry Clark, and said, "Listen, I'm going back. If Noriega finds out I have been here, he will have my head. If you have something, call me."

Herrera Hassan was angry inside, knowing he never would have made this risky trip if he had known agencies in Washington hadn't agreed on a course of action. On April 2, he flew back, and two weeks later, Noriega fired him. Herrera Hassan has told friends that he suspects that Pentagon officials, perhaps including Nestor Sanchez, passed word to the General of his mission.

Yet Abrams puts responsibility for Herrera Hassan's forsaking at the Joint Chiefs of Staff's doorstep. "His abandonment was simply the fallout from a larger problem," said Abrams. "Our policy was fraying. It was our state of political confusion that endangered his future. All the agencies had signed on to a policy of removing Noriega, but then they adopted approaches that went against it—that willy-nilly let us get into that mess and then stopped us from winning. We made a mistake, Walker and I, in bringing Herrera in. It had literally not occurred to us at that late date that the policy would be turned off.

"It's one of the things I feel worst about," said Abrams. "You rope them into the idea of the invincible Yankees getting rid of Noriega, and then they find out it's not to be like that. Herrera was abandoned and left out to dry."

The Herrera Hassan fiasco marked the climax of the six weeks of U.S. foreign policy follies that followed Noriega's indictment and Delvalle's ouster. Those events began a bureaucratic war between a pacifist Pentagon and a militarist State Department that for several weeks neutralized Washington in its war with Noriega. In fact, Noriega's most dangerous opponents in early 1988 weren't American officials but rather the two U.S. attorneys in Florida who indicted him and the private lawyers of Arnold & Porter who froze his U.S. assets on behalf of Delvalle. By spring 1988, American foreign policy makers all agreed Noriega had to go, but they couldn't determine how to arrange it. Individual ambitions and bureaucratic rivalries overshadowed national security interests, and America's allies, as usual, were the victims. President Reagan failed to intervene until Noriega's weakest moment had passed.

Other agencies took a back seat. The new CIA director, William Webster, who had been confirmed in May 1987 after William Casey's death, directed his people to play a primarily analytical and advisory role. Chastened as a result of Oliver North's schemes, the NSC acted as a broker that avoided any role even vaguely operational.

The State-Pentagon conflict was made more bitter by the central characters involved: Abrams and the chairman of the Joint Chiefs of Staff, Admiral William Crowe. Despite having a rank far more junior than that of Crowe, Abrams carried the ball on Panama policy, both because of his own forceful nature and because of Secretary Shultz's relative lack of interest in Central American affairs.

The State Department policy, articulated by Abrams, argued that Noriega must be removed at all costs as a matter of international prestige. But Pentagon officials considered the crisis one of Washington's own making; they never considered the Noriega threat to be worth the risks involved in bringing him down. Noriega, as distasteful as he was, wasn't endangering American lives, U.S. property, or regional security interests. Moreover, the post-Vietnam Pentagon knew the costs of inaction were far less than those of action, and officers didn't want to be drawn into a battle by politicians who might not be willing to carry through.

Abrams was assistant secretary of state for Inter-American affairs at the time, and he wielded his intellect like a rapier. During the worst part of the Panama crisis, Shultz had to appeal to the president to get some senior White House officials to stop giving briefings aimed at destroying Abrams. After the meeting, Shultz turned to Abrams with a quizzical look. "Is there any cabinet member this week who doesn't want me to fire you?" he asked. One State Department official argues that the major subplot of the policy fight over ousting Noriega in Panama was a bureaucratic fight waged by other American officials to remove Abrams from the State Department, which had started much earlier.

From the beginning of the June 1987 demonstrations against Noriega, José Sorzano viewed Abrams as the "engine" behind the anti-Noriega policy at State. "Elliott was a fighting cock," said Sorzano, biting the air so his point wouldn't be missed. "He's always on the attack. I never heard anything come out of Shultz on Panama that I hadn't heard Elliott say more articulately and brilliantly."

Since early in 1986, Noriega also had known Abrams was his most determined opponent. Curiously enough, it was his consultant Joel McCleary who'd first tipped him off to the Abrams danger, in a seventy-five-page February 1986 briefing paper he had written for Panama's government. "Policy toward Panama is strongly shaped by Abrams," he wrote, "who is a favorite of Secretary Shultz and who has unusual strength with the U.S. media. Abrams is obsessed with Nicaragua. He sees all Central America in terms of that single issue. . . . Abrams has also been strongly influenced by his experience as assistant secretary for human rights. He knows the human rights community and is sensitive to those issues, especially in cases in which left or left-of-center governments are seemingly in violation. . . . He, more than any other individual in the U.S. government, has a world view that will make it impossible to ever have an understanding and sympathetic view of the Republic of Panama."

Admiral Crowe, then a sixty-three-year-old navy man with four hard-earned stars, considered Abrams a dangerous man pursuing a perilous policy. He told friends that Abrams represented the Reagan administration's most frightening problem: ideologues out of control. Crowe would in any case have devoted great energy to opposing military involvement in Panama. Abrams's high profile, however, made Crowe hate the policy all the more. He couldn't understand why a relatively balanced man like George Shultz had given Abrams so much power.

Crowe's demeanor was the antithesis of Abrams's. He concealed his keen intellect behind a rumpled professorial facade. The tougher the scrape, the more he exaggerated his Oklahoma drawl to disarm opponents with a brilliant, aw-shucks point. He won over enemies by making jokes on himself, commenting once on his own lack of military bearing by comparing his looks to those of "an unmade bed."

Crowe had also handpicked an astute vice admiral to lead his blocking at lower bureaucratic levels. His personal representative at sub-cabinet meetings was Vice Admiral Jonathan Howe, a man who was humorless, brilliant, calculating, and arrogant. He was the perfect foil to Abrams. He knew the State Department bureaucracy, having directed its Political-Military Bureau. He had his Ph.D. from the Fletcher School of Diplomacy at Tufts University and had been the military assistant to Vice President Nelson Rockefeller in the Ford administration.

Howe and Crowe also had the built-in advantage of all military men: presidents usually don't know enough about their work to second-guess their analysis. When the chairman of the JCS argues that the risks are too great for an operation, it is a brave president who dares question him.

Abrams was outgunned from the beginning, and he knew his effort to remove Noriega depended on political turns in Panama and the U.S. that could shift the balance in his favor. For Abrams, the February indictments and Delvalle's ouster were two tactical victories that he hoped would turn the tide in his favor in the bureaucratic war. He thought it would now be impossible for Pentagon opponents to impede an oust-Noriega policy. But Abrams had overestimated his ability to logroll the Pentagon.

With the Iran-Contra scandal having destroyed his hopes of Nicaraguan success, Abrams had shifted his passions to Panama. His critics charged that going after Noriega was also a good way to win back favor on Capitol Hill, where congressional committees had banned him from testifying after he had lied to them on Iran-Contra. Abrams argued, however, that fighting Noriega was another side of the same coin: the need to reverse anti-democratic forces in Latin America. He didn't understand why the U.S. had put up with Noriega's double-agent work for the Cubans. He was also convinced Noriega was backing leftist guerrillas in the region and promising far more in help to the Contras than he ever delivered.

Abrams's strongest argument at interagency meetings in February and March was the most obvious one: President Reagan had said Noriega must go, and hence the administration must come up with a policy to bring that about. Yet while Reagan's initial rhetoric was clear and strong, the limited sanctions he enacted on March 11 were far milder than Abrams had hoped, doing far less damage than Arnold & Porter's lawsuits. Only the rhetoric was tough for the speak-loudly-but-carry-a-small-stick president. "Until such a time as democratic government is restored in Panama, the United

States cannot proceed on a 'business-as-usual' basis," said Reagan. "Today, therefore, I have taken a number of steps against the illegitimate Noriega regime. . . ." He withdrew trade preferences for Panama under two government-approved programs, and he impounded $80 million paid each year to Noriega's regime for use of the Panama Canal.

At a press conference after Reagan's statement, Secretary Shultz drew reporters' attention to the president's use of the word "illegitimate" to describe Noriega's regime. "That's a very strong word," he said. "What we think should happen is that he should leave Panama, and we want to see a return to civilian democratic rule." Later at the press conference, he repeated the central refrain: "We are anxious to see General Noriega get out of there."

Abrams, however, was unable to capitalize on these strong statements, partly because their chief proponent, Shultz, was rarely in Washington to help him. Shultz's absence in those pivotal six weeks of 1988 left Abrams to do much of the battle against Crowe on his own. In the wake of the Iran-Contra scandal, Shultz had been spending most of his time on the road and was expending his efforts on the Soviet Union and, to a lesser degree, the Middle East. He left Panama largely to Abrams, giving him rare power for an assistant secretary of state. During that period, at National Security Planning Group meetings, the cabinet-level forum at which the most important policy directions are set, the State Department chair revolved between Deputy Secretary of State John Whitehead, Undersecretary of State Michael Armacost, State Department counsellor Max Kampelman and, once, even Abrams himself—something virtually unheard of. The State Department lacked a consistent and strident voice to back up Abrams.

Crowe had him outgunned from the beginning. He virulently opposed using his troops to help oust Noriega; and he was almost as adamant in opposing Abrams's plan that the opposition use his bases as a setting for covert actions against Noriega or as the home of a government-in-exile.

His arguments were simple enough for President Reagan's satisfaction: any such action would endanger U.S. base rights in countries all over the world. His second argument cut right to Reagan's heart: 50,000 Americans lived in Panama, including 10,000 troops, and Noriega would threaten them or even take hostages if the U.S. gave him no alternative. His third argument—this seemed more of an afterthought, to his State Department critics—was that other Latin American officers would revolt against Washington if American force were used to remove a fellow military leader.

"We have military bases not just in Panama, but in Portugal, Spain,

Turkey, and Greece," Crowe argued at one critical March meeting. "In all of those places there are sensitive political issues. How do you expect those governments would react to the specter of the U.S. using its bases to overthrow a country's leadership?" Secretary of Defense Frank Carlucci and his aides would generally back the JCS arguments, but it was Crowe and Vice Admiral Jonathan Howe who carried the ball against Abrams and the State Department.

At one NSPG meeting, Crowe argued to the president that Noriega's opposition, made up primarily of well-off Panamanians, didn't see much point in dying to remove Noriega and neither should the U.S. "Why should good ol' boys from Peoria, Illinois, go down and die for people in Panama driving in Mercedeses?" he said. "It just doesn't make sense."

Crowe knew Reagan's language. And the president, born just 120 miles southwest of Peoria in Tampico, Illinois, was obviously moved.

Abrams was also up against the CIA, although this opposition was indirect. Judge Webster didn't take sides in the policy discussions, but his lack of interest in the Panama issue and the characteristic caution of the post-Casey CIA worked against Abrams.

The CIA played Panama relatively straight. The Iran-Contra scandal's emergence in December 1986 and William Casey's death on May 7, 1987, both acted to return the agency to a more limited and less political role. However, the agency's new caution and its legalistic approach to any requests State had for covert action resulted in implementation of plans that was so slow that the CIA, de facto, became an impediment to State.

William Webster also cared little—and knew less—about Panama. His performance at interagency meetings revealed that he didn't know his brief. His role was usually restricted to reading reports that aides had prepared and then listening to others.

At the first National Security Planning Group meeting shortly after Delvalle went underground, Webster read a report on Manuel Solis Palma. He said Solis, Noriega's puppet president, was a good man who was considered pro-American and pro-Western. "He's somebody we can work with," he said.

The State Department's Max Kampelman couldn't believe his ears. "What are you talking about?" said Kampelman. "Panama doesn't have a new president." Kampelman reminded Webster that the U.S. recognized only Delvalle as president.

The CIA's lack of intelligence on the Panamanian military also impeded action. Up until the March coup against Noriega, it was reporting new fissures in the Panamanian Defense Forces. When asked to draw up a list of officers who might foment a coup against Noriega, the CIA was at a loss. Over the years Noriega had slowly reduced U.S. infiltration of his officers corps, partly through agreement with the CIA, and he kept tight control on any officers who had private contacts with U.S. intelligence agents. The CIA knew little more than what Noriega fed its agents.

The same was true of other agencies. U.S. intelligence capabilities in Panama were divided into four parts: the Southern Command's J-2, the Defense Intelligence Agency's 470th Military Intelligence Brigade, the station chief at the U.S. embassy, and the Drug Enforcement Agency. When the State Department suggested a policy aimed at fomenting a military coup against Noriega, the other three agencies were just as incapable as the CIA of identifying potential allies in the Panamanian military.

One senior intelligence officer in Panama said the problem was "humint," or human intelligence. They still had plenty of wiretap information and other intercepts. But military intelligence operatives on the ground were largely Puerto Rican, and the Panamanians didn't like them or respect them. "It's like using a New York black to infiltrate the southern whites," said the intelligence source. "A liaison relationship with a foreign intelligence service is only as good as your deepest penetration of that service. And we just didn't have Noriega's G-2 penetrated at all by the mid-1980s. He shut us out, and we went along with it."

What defense intelligence services did know a lot about was Noriega. They had boxes full of information on him. CIA warned that Noriega wouldn't roll over easily, and that, based on his psychological profile, he would fight even harder when cornered. The CIA's analysis generally backed up JCS arguments. "This wasn't a question of intelligence failure," said John Negroponte, who was then deputy national security adviser, "It was a question of not listening to the intelligence."

The best example of CIA bureaucracy's undermining the opposition was the State Department's efforts in March to get a radio transmitter for President Delvalle, so he could communicate directly with Panamanians.

At an NSPG meeting, the president approved the idea. He then instructed the CIA to provide the opposition such a radio and train Panamanians to use it. But the CIA responded that providing the radio wasn't in the scope of its mandate for Panama as outlined by presidential policy. It would need a presidential finding redefining objectives in Panama, in order to provide such equipment. The State Department wrote the finding, a process that took another three days—a critical amount of time, at the height of Noriega's worst troubles.

However, the office of the legal counsel of the president said that providing the transmitter would be illegal. In 1987, Congress had banned all assistance to Panama's government. Although that was done before Delvalle became Washington's chosen president, the legal ban still applied to him, since he was the officially sanctioned Panamanian leader.

The NSC found a way around the problem. It could skirt the restrictions on national security grounds under the Foreign Assistance Act. It need only consult with Congress. But with whom? The NSC wanted to contact the chairmen of the foreign assistance committees of the Senate and the House. "Over our dead body," said one CIA official. "This is a covert matter. You can deal only with the appropriate intelligence committees."

After some debate, the national security adviser invited the various chairmen of the foreign assistance committees and intelligence committees to the Old Executive Office Building for tea. The chairmen said they first wanted to know what sort of radio it would be. The CIA said it couldn't tell them. After some haggling, the CIA man gave a general description. The CIA didn't deliver the transmitter until a month and a half later—after Noriega's greatest problems were over and long after the time when it would have been most useful to Delvalle.

"This was all over a radio transmitter you and I could have bought at Radio Shack," said an NSC official at the time.

Yet throughout this period, it was the Abrams-Crowe standoff that held center stage. Abrams never concealed his disdain for Crowe's conservatism, interpreting this as the ill-guided, post-Vietnam military caution. Crowe would argue to friends that like many of Washington's young conservatives, Abrams hadn't fought in Vietnam and hence didn't understand military risk. Abrams had had an educational deferment at Harvard.

Abrams would later blame the JCS point-blank for policy failure in Panama—not because of any subterranean plot, but rather because of lack of will. "The problem was a failure of nerve of the JCS, not protection of Noriega. The PDF is a corrupt police force; it's not an army," he would say later. "JCS wanted to know how we could defend bases from the PDF. Give me a break. The PDF is like a Mississippi police force in the 1960s. It's vicious, corrupt, and incompetent. It is a group that never carried out a military operation."

Crowe didn't like Abrams telling him how his troops should be used or assessing the danger from Panamanian troops, who had been trained and equipped at a cost of millions of dollars to the U.S. taxpayer. He told one friend that Abrams was an "arrogant young man, still wet behind the ears" whom Shultz had given power that "exceeded his capability."

Abrams's Harvard law degree also didn't impress him. Crowe had a master's in education from Stanford and a Ph.D. in politics from Princeton. And he didn't need lessons from Abrams on solving disputes. Abrams had failed with the Contras. And Crowe, as commander in chief of NATO forces in southern Europe, had helped strengthen the alliance's southern flank by mediating conflicts between Greece and Turkey. Just that year, he had been the key figure behind U.S. policy of keeping the Persian Gulf open, partly by putting the American flag on Kuwaiti tankers.

Another quirk of history had given Crowe a much stronger voice at NSPG meetings than the JCS chairmen before him. A landmark Pentagon reorganization bill in 1986 had increased the chairman's role and independence. Before the bill, the chairman could only express the collective views of the Joint Chiefs, thus diminishing his individual power. Effective October 1, 1986, the chairman became the principal military adviser to the president, the secretary of defense, and the National Security Council. He was now authorized to express his own opinions and to unilaterally solve conflicts among the chiefs of each of the services. Crowe had become the most powerful peacetime military officer in American history.

Crowe was also strengthened in his feud with Abrams by a persuasive ally and source of information in Panama. His information came in clear, well-argued form from the seasoned officer-diplomat who ran the Southern Command, General Frederick Woerner. Woerner had a host of intelligence officers and analysts serving under him.

Woerner, a fluent speaker of Spanish who had a Bolivian wife, had a degree in Latin American history from the University of Arizona and had long taught future officers Latin American policy courses at the Army War College. He was an articulate soldier-diplomat who spoke extemporaneously with confidence.

Abrams's link to Panama was Ambassador Davis, a septuagenarian Reagan political appointee whom other embassy officers shielded from the press for fear that he would embarrass himself and the State Department. And he lacked the secret power of many political ambassadors: access to the president. He rarely even spoke to Shultz and had few other high-level allies in Washington, while Woerner could speak to Crowe whenever the situation called for it.

Davis was a political ambassador whose first try at diplomacy came in Paraguay after President Reagan's 1980 election. He came to Panama in 1986, shortly after his wife had died in a plane crash, and Panama's crisis cut his time of mourning short, thrusting him onto an unforgiving stage. The embassy's press section went to lengths to keep their ambassador out of the public limelight because of his inarticulate, shoot-from-the-lip approach to sensitive diplomatic matters. They were even more upset that he couldn't control his daughter, and new first lady, Susan, who had become one of the opposition's most boisterous backers: she'd go to the front lawn of the embassy residence to bang pots and pans, and embassy personnel complained that she often released classified information to reporters in an effort to promote the anti-Noriega cause.

Woerner looked down on Ambassador Davis, and struggled hard to hide his impatience at their weekly Friday meetings. Davis, a man moved by individual cases of repression and human misery, viewed his task as getting rid of Noriega. Woerner was concerned about how the crisis was hampering his broader responsibilities for defense in the whole region, and he thought getting rid of Noriega wouldn't necessarily bring Panama democracy. He thought the crisis had been overpersonalized.

Between Crowe and Woerner, the JCS took on every Abrams proposal with detailed descriptions of costs, risks, and obstacles. When State called for a crash evacuation to get all military dependents moved to base to clear the decks for action, Vice Admiral Howe presented astronomical estimates of the moving costs and the difficulty in scheduling van lines. He said the cost could be as high as $100 million, including overtime for movers, payments for prematurely ended leases, and costs of damaged goods from the quick moves. And anyway, he said, the van lines are so booked up that the whole move would take seven months.

Michael Armacost, the undersecretary of state for political affairs, lost his patience with one of Vice Admiral Howe's mobilization estimates. "This is not serious," said the usually soft-spoken Armacost. He charged that the JCS was saying Washington couldn't approach step 1 until it had step 100 solved. Armacost suspected the Pentagon was engaging in "Aw, shit!" politics.

"That's when you tell the president a reason why he can't do something that is so overwhelming that he says, 'Aw, shit,' " explained a State Department official.

The JCS study helped shoot down the idea.

The Pentagon had good reason to balk at attacking Noriega, who had served its interests for years. Noriega had looked the other way at American uses of the bases that were far broader than the only purpose allowed under the treaties, which was defense of the Canal. America's major listening post in the region was in Panama, and the U.S. regional defense—including CIA secret operations, anti-terrorist activity, and even support for the Contra war—were waged from Panama.

And Noriega was sending clear messages that this could end if the U.S. pushed him. A secret Defense Intelligence Agency report to Admiral

Crowe worried that Noriega was challenging the "Total Warrior" military maneuvers scheduled from March 12 to April 12. Noriega had said that under the treaty Puerto Rico and the Florida National Guard wouldn't be allowed to participate, because their involvement "is not related to defense of the Canal." Noriega also told U.S. officers that U.S. military convoys would be restricted to between midnight and 6 A.M. "to prevent angry Panamanians from attacking them."

The message was clear: you turn against Noriega only at your own risk. DIA faithfully relayed this message to Crowe and others in the memo: ". . . Attempts to place legal restrictions on US Southcom operations do not seriously jeopardize the safety of U.S. personnel. Nonetheless, they serve as a reminder of the PDF's potential for escalating the crisis, which General Noriega has characterized as a U.S. attack on Panamanian sovereignty. For the near term, tension will continue to mount, and no resolution is in sight."

Some intelligence reports were outright alarmist. One report from the 470th Military Intelligence Brigade, which is known to pass on information planted by Noriega, said that a leftist political front and union were planning to foment a confrontation between U.S. troops and workers. It said that the union would use military personnel to fire upon American troops, "hoping that return U.S. fire will kill several innocent demonstrators. This will provide Panama with martyrs and will hopefully unite the Panamanian people against the U.S."

The net result of these personal and bureaucratic differences was inaction. The U.S. didn't respond when Noriega declared a "state of emergency" March 18, following the failed coup against him, which suspended constitutional rights. Opposition leaders responded with an indefinite general strike beginning March 21. It paralyzed an economy that had already been hit by the closing of the banks March 3. Yet while Panamanians were rallying, the White House again faltered.

It was then, on March 29, 1988, that the climax came to the State-Pentagon dispute. While Walker was bringing Colonel Eduardo Herrera Hassan from Israel to lead an exiled military against Noriega, a climactic National Security Planning Group meeting was occurring in the White House situation room. Abrams had built up tension at the time of the meeting, saying he expected Noriega would be out "in a matter of days."

Marlin Fitzwater, responding to the beatings of American citizens in Panama, said Washington patience "was not unlimited." Panamanian Ambassador to the U.S. Juan Sosa called for a commando raid to take Noriega out of his country. But the crisis atmosphere would turn out to be nothing more than the usual Washington storm before a calm of inaction.

Reagan listened silently as Shultz went over the details of the plan that he had worked out with Abrams and the Panamanian opposition. Crowe and Defense Secretary Carlucci held forth on the dangers of retribution from Noriega against the 50,000 Americans in Panama. Crowe spoke of a hostage-taking plan Noriega had developed (nothing frightens a president more than hostages), and he outlined the number of troops that it would take to protect Americans against the Panamanian threat. They included commandos, perhaps a carrier task force, and amphibious assault teams, Carlucci and Crowe said. They would need "at least two brigades" of additional U.S. troops to guard bases, American residents, and the Canal, augmenting the 10,000 troops already in Panama by adding 6,000 more.

Shultz's face reddened with anger a little more with each escalating estimate of the troops required. He said that he was a marine himself, and he knew it didn't take all that much force to get rid of one small dictator. "It just isn't that way," he said. Shultz said all that was needed was one well-trained, well-prepared commando group to grab Noriega and bring him to justice in the United States. Officials at the meeting can't remember whether he used the word "kidnap," but that was the message.

Abrams's complex plan to set up an exile military and political leadership in jointly administered Panamanian territory was being ruled out because of its logistical impossibility. Instead, Shultz was now pushing for a "snatch" operation. Delvalle would waive normal extradition procedures, giving Washington the legal basis it needed.

Reagan hence tasked his administration to draw up plans aimed at such a snatch operation. The Pentagon opposed this as well, on the grounds that Noriega and his people would take retribution on American civilians. Yet in the next days, Special Forces planners and intelligence agents would participate in drawing up several scenarios. One was patterned on the successful U.S. kidnapping of Honduran drug kingpin Juan Ramón Matta Ballesteros, which would not occur until April 1988 but was already being planned at that time. A CIA source said the proposed scenario would differ from the Matta Ballesteros plan, in which Honduran officials would assist, in that this operation would be carried out in the Dominican Republic. Noriega's daughter was married to the son of a powerful Dominican general, and Noriega felt safe on that Caribbean island. A Special Forces paramilitary officer involved in the planning called the "DR Plan" nothing less than a "snatch operation."

Another idea was an *Achille Lauro* plan, which would call for American aircraft from Panamanian bases to force Noriega's plane down on extraditable territory, just as U.S. navy jets had forced down a Palestinian hijacker in Sicily. After Noriega's arrest, he would be shipped off to Miami for a "public arrival in handcuffs," a State Department official said.

In all, five options grew out of the May 29 meeting, intelligence sources said, but in the end, none of them would be acted upon. At a meeting two days later, the president decided not to pursue any of the more dramatic actions. Instead, he was slowly moving toward imposing economic sanctions—which had become the chosen method of showing American impotence. In addition the Pentagon announced it would send 1,300 more troops the week after Easter, including 500 military police and a large number of patrol dogs with their trainers. "This is not meant to be a message to General Noriega," said Southern Command spokesman Ronald Sconyers.

The message was clear: America wasn't ready to come after him yet.

Furthermore, the Pentagon began leaking to reporters in order to ensure that such plans, which senior Pentagon officials termed as "harebrained," didn't come up again. Abrams, a master at using the press to promote policies, accurately charged that Crowe and Howe were fighting him with his own weapon of press disclosures, by having lower-ranking officials tell reporters about Abrams's "reckless" approach to Panama.

"All the leaks have come in articles in the *New York Times* and the *Washington Post* written by their defense correspondents, who often quoted unnamed uniformed military," Abrams said. Some of the most detailed and troubling stories to the State Department were written by the *Washington Post*'s Pentagon correspondent George Wilson, long a favorite reporter of the uniformed military.

Shultz, who had withdrawn again from the bureaucratic battles he'd grown to hate—this time to Rome for an Easter celebration en route to the Middle East—was nevertheless forced to answer leaks about his "snatch" proposals. "We debate various options," he said. "I never comment on speculative newspaper articles . . . on particularly harebrained-type proposals."

Nevertheless, the opposition's belief in late March that the U.S. was on the verge of dramatic action against Noriega caused some tragic comedy in Panama City. At the center of it was Ambassador Davis, who fed Panamanian expectations.

In an effort to keep restless anti-Noriega campaigners mollified, the U.S. often exaggerated to the opposition its readiness for tough—even military—action to unseat Noriega. "We continued to reassure the opposition that we were doing something, if only to keep their morale up," said one National Security Council staff member at the time. "Some people were telling them a little more than what was true. They believed we were on the threshold of a major decision."

And the gossipy Panamanians spread the word around, so that by the week before Easter, many expected U.S. forces to descend on Noriega at any moment.

Delvalle was a key target of these reassurances. An internal State Department memo, marked "eyes only" for Secretary Shultz, carried the flash line: "Delvalle Depressed and Desperate." Ambassador Davis was passing on a letter which Delvalle had sent to his own wife, requesting her to share it with Davis. He said in the letter that he needed more U.S. pressure on Noriega. He said the U.S. needed to act by Easter Sunday, April 3, to "avoid an anti-America backlash."

"He writes he has 'paid his dues' so if the U.S. does not 'work out' its 'plan' he will consider seeking asylum in the U.S. and not play the 'role of a stupid jerk'," said Davis's memo.

On March 25, the papal nuncio first became convinced of plans for strong action during a dinner with opposition activist Roberto Eisenmann in Miami. Gabriel Lewis phoned excitedly from Washington to say Herrera Hassan now had all the backing of the State Department to prepare for the invasion of Panama.

According to his diary, the papal nuncio, José Sebastián Laboa, indicated that he became sure of the plans after conversations with Ambassador Davis upon his return from Miami. According to the diary, Ambassador Davis told the nuncio that the U.S. was going to kidnap Noriega just after midnight on Easter Sunday.

The nuncio came home at noon after his Easter mass. Nothing had happened. Davis seemed apologetic that afternoon, the diary reads. The plan to kidnap Noriega from his beachside home at Rio Ható had fallen through. Noriega wasn't there. The Americans couldn't find him. The nuncio laughed. "If you had asked me, I could have told you where he was."

You could have? asked Davis.

"He was with his mistress," the nuncio proudly announced.

He had seen the general visiting his mistress, Vicky Amado, at the plush condominium of her mother, Norma Amado. She lived in a building near the nuncio's residence. He had seen the General's car and his bodyguard outside.

The diary said that Davis then told the nuncio "the action" would take place the following day. There was no doubt about Reagan's decision to go on with this, he said. The problem was that the General was always changing his whereabouts.

The nuncio later discovered that no such plan was ever that close to being executed. He wondered why Ambassador Davis was that explicit about something that wasn't in the works. Davis denies he ever said any of the things that are logged for posterity in the nuncio's diary.

"We never talked about snatching or military invasion," said Davis. "This office has never heard a word from Washington about a snatch. I told him that Easter week would be a busy week. That's all I told him. If he thought there was a kidnapping planned, it never came from us."

Davis said that the U.S. was waiting until more happened on the streets. The strike was being billed as the final push to get Noriega out. "The U.S. was waiting to see that happen," he said, "but that never happened. That never materialized."

In the end, President Reagan opted for caution. On the Friday following Easter, after Noriega's worst troubles had subsided, Reagan took the only step that neither State nor Defense would block: economic sanctions. President Reagan declared a national emergency under the authority of the International Emergency Economic Powers Act (IEEPA) and issued an executive order prohibiting certain transactions with Panama.

The measures blocked all assets of the government of Panama in the United States, except transactions authorized by Ambassador Sosa and President Delvalle. It prohibited payments by individuals and organizations in the U.S. to the Noriega regime, and it banned payments by U.S. people and organizations in Panama, including U.S. branches and subsidiaries.

Its impact was limited, however, because of the timing. It came six weeks after Noriega had ousted Delvalle, four weeks after Delvalle's lawsuits had been filed, three weeks after the failed coup, and more than one week after the twenty-day general strike had collapsed.

The moves made permanent what lawyers spending hundreds of hours and being paid hundreds of thousands of dollars had achieved at Arnold & Porter a little over a month earlier. "The irony is that, because of its belated timing, the executive order had much less impact on the situation in Panama than the Delvalle lawsuits," said Arnold & Porter lawyer Kenneth Juster. By the first week of April, Noriega had overcome a coup attempt, crushed a general strike, and found enough dollars to keep his economy afloat.

Nobody much liked the measures or thought they'd work.

Secretary of State Shultz didn't like sanctions generally. He said they were difficult to enforce and rarely achieved their ends. James Baker, the secretary of the treasury, liked the idea even less. "You are using an atomic bomb to kill a fly," said one Treasury official at an April meeting. "These are sanctions we use in general warfare. They shouldn't be used in a limited offensive."

Not even the Pentagon enthusiastically endorsed sanctions.

"But there was tremendous pressure by Congress to do something, and sanctions were all we could do," said Abrams.

The National Security Council's José Sorzano wasn't surprised with the sanctions' outcome, although this was the natural decision to come out of the impasse in the White House situation room. "It's the one decision that no one sitting around the table in the room has to pay for," he said. "Economic sanctions have become a weapon of choice because no one in the decision-making group is directly affected. The Pentagon doesn't need to risk its soldiers or use its facilities. The State Department can say it is taking action, and the White House can say to a domestic audience that it is tough with a drug dealer. It's people outside the room—Panamanians, American businessmen, and bankers—who get hurt. Economic sanctions are generally the result of not knowing what else to do or not being able to do something else. It isn't an effective way to bring down governments. Fidel Castro has been strangled for thirty years, and where has that got us?"

Panama's opposition liked sanctions even less. Roberto Brenes, a stockbroker and the owner of a financial newspaper that had been closed by Noriega, said they would damage the private sector, which was the heart of Noriega's opposition. He warned State Department officials that the Noriega clique's well-being didn't depend on the local economy. "When you earn your cash from money laundering, drug trafficking, and arms dealing for the Iran-Iraq war, you aren't as vulnerable personally to sanctions. The money he hands out to his soldiers doesn't depend much on economic activity."

The Civic Crusade in the end backed the sanctions, after being assured they were merely another rung in an escalating ladder of measures against Noriega. "It's only as such that they would make sense," said Brenes.

The worst possible result is what followed. Panama was hit with sanctions, but the expected panoply of other measures never followed. The U.S. had given Noriega an excuse to put the country on a war economy and to paint himself as a modern-day Simón Bolívar fighting for Latin American causes against gringo imperialists, but it hadn't hit his own pocketbook or that of his closest allies.

And the U.S. bureaucracy would now be tied up for months by the mess the president's decision had created and all the requests for exceptions. What happened to refineries on the U.S. Gulf Coast if the U.S. pipeline company didn't pay its taxes to the Panamanian government? That was exempted. What if the U.S. embassy didn't pay its electricity bill and Noriega turned out the lights? That bill must be paid. "There was one special pleading after another," says Sorzano. "A bureaucracy that should have been finishing Noriega was instead putting out sanctions fires all over the place, and in the process reducing the impact of the squeeze on Noriega."

That shifted some control of Panama policy from the State Department to the Treasury. The Treasury Department's Office of Foreign Assets Control, or OFAC, got off to a slow start. It took almost two months for it to promulgate regulations that would implement the executive order. U.S. companies complained that they lacked regulatory guidance, and the sanctions drifted.

OFAC's first move, in fact, was to announce a series of exemptions on April 30. They included allowing companies to make payments to Panama for travel-related services, postal fees, and such items as utility bills (to keep embassy lights on). The amount of money in the exemptions was small, but the announcement created the impression in Panama that the U.S. was easing its pressure on Noriega under pressure from U.S. companies.

The administration was skeptical about its own sanctions from the beginning, and they always seemed more a domestic political palliative than an element of a serious policy. White House Chief of Staff Howard Baker pooh-poohed them even as President Reagan was announcing his executive order.

The actions "undoubtedly hurt the people of Panama more than they hurt him [Noriega]," former Senator Baker said. "General Noriega, no doubt, has money squirreled away, who knows where, and I doubt very much that we have done much to interrupt his life-style or diminish his assets."

It seemed the Reagan administration was conceding defeat at the same time that it was declaring war. Because the U.S. government couldn't force Noriega out, it decided it would try to negotiate him down from power.

CHAPTER
EIGHTEEN

THE MISSED
OPPORTUNITY

As long as those indictments are around, you'll have to come after me. And you'll find some guy like me to come get me.

— GENERAL NORIEGA, MAY 1988

President Reagan impatiently interrupted his national security adviser, Colin Powell, as Powell recited U.S. policy options on Panama. It was 7 P.M. on Sunday, May 22, 1988, and the president wanted to dispose of his Noriega problem quickly so he could concentrate on the coming week's Moscow summit, the crowning event of his presidency.

"I know what my options are," he told Powell and other cabinet-level officials who had gathered in the living room of the White House's private quarters. "I wanted you all to go home and think about them yourselves so you would understand why I've reached the decision I have reached. I don't think many of you are going to like it," the president said, with an accusatory sideward glance toward his vice president, George Bush.

Tension charged the room, because of an unusual disagreement between Reagan and Bush over one of the administration's most delicate policy issues. Two days earlier, George Bush had come out publicly against the president's plans to trade two Florida drug indictments against Noriega for the Panamanian strongman's resignation. It seemed a good bargain to Reagan—some legal charges that could never be enforced in exchange for the departure of a disagreeable dictator—but the vice president's aides had decided it would be political suicide for Bush's presidential chances to go soft on a "drug dictator." As a result, for the first time in eight years, Bush had come out publicly against his president.

Bush was particularly worried over a deal under which the U.S. had encouraged a Colombian bank, flush with drug dollars, to deposit some $20 million in the National Bank of Panama as part of the lure for Noriega's departure. It looked suspiciously like bribing Noriega. So over lunch on Friday, Bush had asked Reagan to bring home his negotiator, the State Department's Michael Kozak, from Panama, where he had just settled the last details of an agreement. Now, just two days later, Bush and his allies wanted to stop Kozak from going back.

It was a summery May evening as the cabinet members and their staffs arrived in the living room of the President's private quarters, whose large French doors opened onto the Rose Garden. Reagan sat comfortably in an antique armchair in front of the large, unlit fireplace in the oval, pastel-blue room. George Bush fidgeted at the president's left, knowing the president was displeased by the inconvenience he had caused. Beside him was Kozak, who as the primary briefer had been put near the president, because of Reagan's hearing difficulties. Chief of Staff Howard Baker, Treasury Secretary James Baker, Deputy Chief of Staff Kenneth Duberstein, and Defense Secretary Frank Carlucci were also arrayed to the left on chairs and sofas. George Shultz, Reagan's only friend in the cabinet on this issue, sat as a lonely defender beside the president on the right, next to CIA director William Webster, Attorney General Ed Meese III, and NSC adviser Powell. The State Department's Elliott Abrams and Powell's deputy, John Negroponte, took notes at the back of the room.

The president had reviewed his alternatives since his stormy session with the same group twenty-four hours earlier. Led by Treasury Secretary James Baker, acting as George Bush's campaign director–elect, the members of the group had rattled off the myriad political difficulties that lifting the indictments would cause Reagan with Congress and the American people in an election year. The unspoken message had been clear: the Bush-for-President campaign was moving in on President Reagan's foreign policies.

That Sunday, however, Reagan stood his ground. He said he was ready to take the political heat. He said that once the American people heard his logic, they would change their minds. He wasn't letting off a drug dealer; he was getting rid of a dictator. Reagan had always been convinced of his powers of persuasion. He said that he believed in Jeffersonian democratic principles—that leaders can take controversial decisions if they are explained properly to the citizenry. "Maybe I'm a little naive," he said, "but that's what I've always thought."

Elliott Abrams, a neoconservative admirer of the president, was surprised by the president's eloquence and emotion, and he thought it was a shame that the president's biographer, Edmund Morris, wasn't there to record it. "I've just never seen him so deeply engaged in a foreign policy argument," Abrams said. "You've heard all the stories about Reagan's general passivity, his lack of grasp of the facts, but if you had come down from Mars and seen Ronald Reagan that day, you would assume all those arguments were made by morons."

In past sessions on Panama, Reagan had been passive, sometimes almost uninterested. His inaction had allowed a State Department–Pentagon feud to paralyze policy toward Panama for weeks. Panama had caught his attention only when it threatened to be the center of a domestic political crisis. And the prospect of the Moscow trip seemed to have taken years off him and sharpened his mind, so that a solution to the Panama problem—the faster and simpler the better—seemed clear.

The president carried the conversation. "Well, the way I see it we have three basic options," he said. "One, we can hold on to these precious pieces of paper, these indictments, which are worthless as long as Noriega's in Panama, because under the extradition treaty you can't extradite a Panamanian from Panama anyway. It's prohibited under their constitution and their law. Much less can you expect to do it when the head of the police force is the man you're trying to extradite. Who's going to arrest him? So that option involves me hanging on to these precious pieces of paper and leaving in place a man you tell me is a murderer and a drug dealer—so that he can keep on murdering and drug-dealing.

"The second option is that we can make an arrangement where we give up those pieces of paper and get him out of there so he can't continue in his business, then we've accomplished something at the expense of giving up those pieces of paper.

"And the third is that I can start counting up the bodies [by ordering a military strike on Noriega].

"So those are the three options. And it's obvious to me which one is the right one, if it can be done. And that's why I've made my decision. I know a lot of you don't agree with that. But I have come to that conclusion."

Mike Kozak was elated. His task for the previous two months had been to negotiate Noriega out of power, but he had felt like a hunter without a gun. He hadn't any convincing answer to Noriega's unspoken question: "So what if I don't go?" No less an official than the White House spokesman had trumpeted that America's military wouldn't attack him. The military wouldn't even allow its bases to be used by the opposition to mount covert actions against Noriega. All Kozak had to lure Noriega from power were the indictments. Now he had final clearance to give these up in return for Noriega's departure.

Yet officials in Washington continued to mistrust the cagey dictator's intentions. When they asked Kozak if Noriega was sincere, Kozak avoided a direct response. He only knew that Noriega had pursued the negotiations despite press leaks that had brought heavy pressures from his allies, and despite his anger over Washington's frequently changing negotiating positions, which shifted with the political winds. Americans all knew Noriega was the bad guy, but U.S. negotiators realized they had been the less consistent party in talks. Noriega, who had shipped many criminals off to American justice, had grown obsessed with the danger of arrest and trial in America. He wanted to rid himself of the dreaded indictments. And in May 1988, domestic pressures on him were great and American sanctions had taken a heavy toll. Noriega had even told his mistress Vicky Amado to prepare for a move to Paris, where he owned several luxury apartments, and Noriega had shown the conspiratorial and playful papal nuncio in Panama, Monsignor José Sebastián Laboa, portions of a resignation speech he was writing. Noriega's family and friends had convinced him that he was finished for now and that he should retreat, perhaps to return later, once civilians proved incapable of ruling Panama. His closest friends and the American negotiating team of Kozak and army Colonel Gerald Clark were convinced that he, for the first and the last time, was ready to resign.

With apparent success only a few commas away, however, Kozak had gotten the call to leave Panama, without giving Noriega any explanation, and to come home to brief cabinet members and their staffs. Kozak could feel the political space closing around him. The domestic politics of hanging tough on drugs in a campaign year was overwhelming the foreign policy logic of settling the Noriega problem peacefully.

The details of Kozak's painstakingly negotiated pact with Noriega were that President Reagan would trigger the agreement by suspending economic sanctions against Panama, and within one hour Noriega would make a speech in which he would call for enactment of a law establishing five years as the maximum term for Panamanian Defense Forces (PDF) commanders. It would be retroactive; and Noriega would resign no later than August 12, 1988, the fifth anniversary of his rule. Civil liberties would be restored, amnesty would be granted to political prisoners and exiles, and Noriega would leave the country at least through the May 7, 1989, elections. He would have the freedom to portray this temporary exile as a long vacation, however, and he could return for Christmas, just to show he wasn't being bullied by the gringos.

Panama's political parties would negotiate a national reconciliation government to prepare for new elections and begin economic recovery. The opposition's leverage would come from continued U.S. recognition and its hold on tens of millions of Panamanian government funds in escrow accounts. The Kozak settlement didn't determine who would take over the military, but it was assumed in talks that Noriega would be followed by the PDF chief of staff, Colonel Marco Justine.

But the whole deal rested on Reagan's lifting of the indictments, the details of which Justice Department officials had hammered out the previous week with Noriega's American lawyers. Political pressure was building against the plan, after leaks to the press the previous week, and almost all of Reagan's assembled advisers lobbied against the deal on political, legal, and moral grounds.

"It's the sentiment of the law enforcement community that making such a deal with an indicted drug dealer is like dealing with terrorists," said Attorney General Ed Meese, careful not to make this a personal disagreement with Reagan but rather the view of his troops in the field. Reagan had loyally defended his besieged attorney general during a Justice Department influence-peddling scandal, and Ed Meese didn't want to appear ungrateful. "The law enforcement community believes that this will demoralize those on the front lines fighting against drugs if it is allowed to go forward." He said U.S. attorneys in Miami were already raising hell with the press over reports the indictment would be dropped.

Treasury Secretary James Baker was most outspoken against the president's decision, arguing that it was political suicide in an election year. "The Democrats will eat us up on this," he said. Baker's well-earned nickname was "Mr. Cautious," and he considered dealing with Noriega this close to November far too great a risk.

George Bush backed him up, trying to reach President Reagan's emotions by recalling a visit he had made that week to a Los Angeles drug rehabilitation center. "I could never tell those kids that I'm letting off a drug-dealing dictator," he said. Late the previous week, Bush had decided with his advisers that he'd use the Noriega negotiations to satisfy two campaign needs: to overcome charges that he was merely Reagan's lackey and to head off potentially poisonous but unproven charges that he was protecting Noriega because of dark secrets they shared from his time as CIA director in 1976, and again regarding the Contras in the 1980s. Bumper stickers were already rolling off his opponents' presses: "Bush-Noriega '88—You Know They Can Work Together."

A few days earlier, Bush's national security adviser Donald Gregg had warned him that Panama could be a millstone around his neck. Gregg's deputy, Sam Watson, had been even more strident. "We have really got to pull the plug on this one," he said. "George Bush is going to be trapped by Panama." Watson had been Bush's man monitoring the Panama Working Group meetings: his assignment was to alert the campaign whenever anything was afoot that could hurt Bush. Now he was sounding the alarm.

Chief of Staff Howard Baker warned the president that Congress almost unanimously opposed lifting the indictments. Kansas Senator Robert Dole, Bush's chief opponent in Republican primaries, had pushed through a non-binding amendment to the 1989 Defense Authorization Bill on May 17 that read: "No negotiations should be conducted, nor arrangements made by the United States Government, with Noriega, which would involve the dropping of the drug-related indictments against him."

Dole had sensed his opponent's vulnerability. "The evidence appears to be overwhelming: Noriega deals drugs, protects drug traffickers, launders drug money," he had said. "Pick your title, Noriega fits them all: drug kingpin, drug overlord, drug godfather." Dole said Noriega should go, but he argued that the U.S. ought not "send him off with a legal. golden parachute." The amendment had passed 86–10.

Kenneth Duberstein, Reagan's deputy chief of staff, tried to convince the president that he would so anger Congress with his decision to drop the indictments that, in retaliation, senators would vote down his historic short-range arms agreement with the Soviets, the foreign policy centerpiece of his administration. Everyone groaned, knowing that Duberstein had overstepped in his eagerness to join the pro-Bush majority.

Yet President Reagan held the line, with only George Shultz and his two aides to back him up. ("I hope I didn't go too far," Shultz would tell his aides later, "but I couldn't leave the president out there all alone.") Shultz's team seemed out of place, and not only because of their minority backing of the president. Abrams, who had been gardening, wore a soiled T-shirt, jeans, and sneakers. Kozak wasn't much better, in slacks and an open-necked Latin American guayabera. The State Department operations center officer had told them Shultz wanted them urgently, but he had failed to say that it was for a meeting with President Reagan. So they'd arrived at Shultz's home in their Sunday worst, and Shultz joked to Reagan that they might just be the worst-dressed government officials ever to brief the president.

Kozak was all the more embarrassed by his martial haircut, which he'd arranged at a U.S. base in Panama before his return. The military barber had mistaken Kozak for an officer, and his co-negotiator Colonel Clark had caught the error too late. "Well, I kind of like the haircut," said Reagan. "I think he's the only decent-looking one in the room."

* * *

When Reagan's opponents couldn't budge him on the indictments, they attacked on another front. They argued that a portion of the agreement that would bring $20 to $25 million dollars in new deposits from Banco Cafetero, Colombia's coffee growers' bank, to the National Bank of Panama was nothing short of bribing a dictator with drug money, and that General Noriega could easily just pocket the cash and run.

The monetary portion of the Noriega resignation pact, which had at first gained little notice, had become its most troublesome and controversial aspect. At first Noriega had demanded that the U.S. turn over all of some $70 million frozen in escrow accounts at the Federal Reserve because of U.S. economic sanctions. Kozak had explained that wasn't possible. So Panamanian negotiators had asked the U.S. to use its influence with Japan and Taiwan, who Noriega said would give him money if only the U.S. would make clear it hadn't any objections. Shultz had passed the word that the U.S. would consider such deposits to be "fully compatible with the proposed solution to Panama's crisis," but the Taiwanese and the Japanese had wanted more: a U.S. government guarantee on their deposits, which Shultz couldn't give.

The Panamanians had then suggested Banco Cafetero as an alternative source of capital. Shultz had phoned Colombian Foreign Minister Julio Londonio to make clear he hadn't any objections to the bank's depositing money in the Noriega-controlled state bank. At the time of Reagan's Sunday meeting, Noriega's intermediary to Washington, Guillermo St. Malo, was in Bogotá to work out the final arrangements. Shultz knew the political dangers of such an arrangement, but his aquiescence was just another sign of the State Department's desperation to settle the Noriega problem.

Shultz had also checked out the bank. He'd made his "no obstacles" call to Bogotá only after CIA stations and U.S. embassy officers in Panama and Colombia had said they hadn't any adverse information on the state-run Banco Cafetero. But at the Sunday meeting, the CIA director reversed himself. Webster's people now alleged the bank was indeed engaged in significant drug money laundering. The Bush crowd was horrified. They could see the morning papers' headlines: "Reagan Administration Bribes Noriega with Colombian Drug Money."

President Reagan, however, still wanted to go ahead. He joked lamely that every bank in Miami was probably laundering drug dollars, whether they were aware of it or not. He didn't see this as a major impediment. Shultz, however, was troubled. He complained that if Webster had given him this information earlier, he never would have approved this facet of the deal in the first place. Shultz withdrew his instructions to the Colombians that evening, thus undermining the cash transfer.

With that out of the way, Reagan turned to Kozak. He wanted the whole deal sealed before he left for Moscow on Wednesday, so at 9:30 Sunday night, he asked, "Can you wrap this thing up by then?"

Kozak frowned. That gave him only two days. "Realistically, Mr. President, no."

Kozak said that from the beginning Noriega had said he would need four or five days after an agreement to sell it to his military and other supporters. Kozak also said the reversal of the Banco Cafetero agreement would cause some last-minute problems in negotiations. Washington was essentially reneging on two portions of his agreement with Noriega that both sides considered final. "We've got some loose ends, because of things that have come up here, that we need to clarify or refine. And it's going to take me a couple of days to do that." He apologized that he needed about a week, and that he knew that would put the president in the middle of the summit.

Reagan sympathized. "But why don't you go back and give it a shot and see if it can't be done before then," he said. Reagan wanted to be on hand in Washington to defend this controversial move. "It's clear to me no one else will do it for me," glancing again at Bush and others in the room, many of whom were already angling for jobs in the Bush campaign or a future administration.

Kozak made his way to the nearest phone and called Colonel Gerry Clark, his co-negotiator. Clark was about Kozak's height at five-nine, but he was more handsome and stocky. He was a likable military officer and veteran of covert operations who a little over a month earlier had orchestrated the dramatic arrest and extradition of drug kingpin Juan Matta Ballesteros from Honduras. Clark was picked for Kozak's mission to Panama by default: the Pentagon and General Frederick Woerner of the Southern Command didn't want to join the negotiations, but Clark could join Kozak's team since he had been detailed to the State Department months earlier.

And Clark was a valuable addition, a man who spoke fluent Spanish and knew the region. Yet Clark, who had already seen the politicians pull the rug out from under his effort to help the Contras, had one request of Kozak. "Just promise me that we won't do to the Panamanian people what we've done to the Nicaraguans," he said, a sadness overcoming him.

Kozak said he couldn't promise that politics wouldn't prompt the U.S. to abandon the Panamanians, but that he would do his best to prevent it. "Okay, I guess that's the best you can do."

Little did Clark know that American domestic politics would again undermine him just when he was convinced that Noriega's departure was within reach.

Kozak's negotiating history with Noriega had begun two months before his fateful weekend meeting in Washington. On March 19, three days after an abortive coup attempt against the General, Kozak had traveled to Panama with Deputy Assistant Secretary of State William Walker and a contract psychiatrist for the State Department's crisis management team, Steve Pieczenik, who was there to read Noriega's mood and dream up psychological operations against him.

At the last minute, Kozak and Walker had been told Noriega would see them only if his U.S. lawyers were present, so the government plane had stopped in Miami to pick them up. They were an unusual couple: Neil Sonnet, a respectable-looking former U.S. attorney in a European-tailored suit, and Ray Takiff, whom Walker pegged as a stereotypical Miami lawyer. A gold chain dripped from Takiff's neck, and his shirt opened to a hairy chest. "And he sweated a lot," said Walker.

Their first session was in the kitchen of a G-2 safe house along a Panama Canal causeway. It looked innocently suburban, but Noriega's officers used it for their most sensitive interrogations and most secret sexual liaisons. The U.S. officials hardly recognized Noriega. He seemed frail, reticent, and shy. He was swimming in a guayabera that seemed a couple of sizes too big, and his handshake was limp. He was visibly down, waiting to hear a message that he feared. Contrary to Latin etiquette, he didn't offer his guests coffee or any food—not even in the kitchen. For hours, they sat by the sink and refrigerator without a drink of water.

Yet Kozak was pleased to see that his negotiating partner was Rómulo Escobar Bethancourt, with whom he had hammered out the gritty details of the Panama Canal Treaties more than a decade earlier. Despite their contradictory political beliefs and backgrounds, the two had grown close and believed that their mutual trust had helped overcome minor problems in the Treaties that could have grown into national disputes.

Escobar, then sixty-one years old, had been the rector of the University of Panama. He was a brilliant intellectual, a former member of the Communist party and a close friend of Fidel Castro. His life had been devoted to finding a way to get U.S. troops out of Panama and the country's oligarchy out of power. Torrijos had cleverly chosen him as treaty negotiator as protection from leftist political attacks.

Kozak hadn't been long out of the University of California at Berkeley law school when, at the age of twenty-eight, he'd met Escobar. Kozak had an energy and optimism that was odd in the State Department. He maintained a sense of humor about Washington bureaucracy, a world that engulfed him and often frustrated him. He had quietly impressed his superiors with his legal mind and attention to detail. And when negotiations went badly, he cheerfully retreated to his Virginia garage, where, an amateur auto mechanic, he loved to tinker.

"You are too young to be a lackey of the fascists," Escobar had told Kozak upon meeting him.

"And you are too old to be a snotty-nosed college radical," Kozak retorted. "We can either do business together or continue calling each other names."

They'd both laughed, and a friendship had been born.

To Noriega, who was then Panama's intelligence chief, Kozak seemed to be the CIA man on the U.S. delegation. Noriega's misleading tip-off was when Kozak, an amateur radio operator, jimmy-rigged a communications outpost during negotiations. So Noriega set out to know Kozak better. Noriega's brother Luis Carlos, then a foreign ministry official, had invited Kozak to meet with Noriega privately, and Noriega had watched Kozak closely ever after, looking for a chance to snare him in a honey trap. On a flight back to Washington, an attractive woman had moved over to take the seat next to Kozak. They had been over Cuba, and she'd pointed out installations they were overflying and seductively proposed to share more information. Kozak hadn't taken her up on the offer.

On that day in March, Noriega had thanked Kozak as an "old friend of Panama" for coming to seek a solution, but Kozak's message to the General was an unwelcome one. He'd opened the kitchen table talks with a forty-five-minute description of the deteriorating Panamanian situation and the U.S. offer: asylum for Noriega in Spain and a promise of non-extradition from that country. President Reagan wasn't willing to drop the indictments, Kozak said.

He knew immediately, however, that Noriega wouldn't negotiate unless the indictments were on the table. Escobar launched an ideological harangue about U.S. efforts to regain the Panama Canal and to rebuild its old alliance with the oligarchy. In the give-and-take, Noriega sought more ironclad assurances of non-extradition. "I am an intelligence man," he said, "and I know that your CIA has prepared kidnap plans in the past and that you have prepared them again now for me. Your government has no scruples. We know what your Oliver North has done."

After a noontime break, Noriega returned more confident and alert. The U.S. negotiators thought he might have taken some drugs, or at least a little coffee, to boost his spirits after the morning session. His own friends say he was merely encouraged that the U.S. message wasn't more threatening. He took the offensive, denouncing the indictments and U.S. imperialism. His departure wasn't on the agenda, Noriega said. A few minutes later, the previously animated Noriega almost fell asleep during Kozak's counterargument. His eyes slowly closed as he leaned forward on his crossed arms, and Walker thought he looked very much like the frog figures that he collected, called *sapos,* a word meaning toads that was also the slang for "informant." The General would slowly open and shut his reptilian eyes, always seeming as though he was watching for a passing insect to lash with his sandpapery tongue.

Noriega was clearly playing games with his U.S. counterparts. Having just defeated a military coup against himself, he wasn't yet ready to talk. He was confident the Americans wouldn't take military action to force him out. "I never want to talk to that bastard again," Kozak had told Walker when they left Panama.

Nevertheless, Kozak had returned in mid-April. By then, American sanctions and Panamanian street protests had made Noriega readier to deal; and the U.S., unable to force Noriega out, now had a better offer to make. This time, Kozak also insisted on an agenda in advance in order to avoid the March failure. For the first time, it included the issue of Noriega's departure, phrased by the Panamanian side as "Noriega's Relief and When He Will Take Over."

The talks this time took place in Noriega's plush offices at "El Ocho"—Building 8—at Fort Amador, a windowless cement facility that had been used by U.S. military intelligence before it reverted to Panama under the Canal treaties. Noriega used it as his bunker, and he retreated there behind a wall of security for his most sensitive discussions.

Noriega was troubled. "It's getting so I wake up in the morning and I think I am just going to go into the office and tell Justine, 'Marco, this whole pile of shit is your pile of shit. I'm walking away, *tranquilo.*' But no, my people say that would be irresponsible and destabilize the country, and of course they are right. But that is how I feel."

For two days, Kozak hammered away on the issue of Noriega's departure. But the Panamanians wouldn't discuss it. "If we can't reach an understanding on that issue, then there is no point in discussing anything else," Kozak said.

Noriega, almost choking on his own words, finally said he would be prepared to resign on August 12 if the U.S. suspended sanctions and dropped the indictments. The General grimaced and left the room. His friends say it was the most difficult sentence he had ever uttered. However conditional, it was a surrender to the Americans.

Kozak turned to the two Panamanians left in the room, Escobar and co-negotiator Marco Justine, the Panamanian Defense Forces' financier and hence Noriega's bagman. He said the timing was too far off. He said the lifting of sanctions was doable, but dropping the indictments was impossible.

When they next met, Kozak offered Noriega a chance to defend himself against the drug charges without facing imprisonment, if only he would step down from power. "You keep telling me you have all the evidence to prove your innocence," Kozak said. "Maybe we can make a non-extradition pledge while an independent counsel looks into the charges. We will pick someone you consider to be an objective and impartial American lawyer. It will still be our pick, but we wouldn't pick someone who was committed against you. If he recommended that the charges be dropped, you would have your wish. If he recommended otherwise, you'd still be able to take asylum somewhere else."

Noriega's eyes glazed over. "If the day comes for me to step down and those indictments are still in place, I'm not stepping down," he said flatly. "No deal. *No deal. No deal!*"

"Why?" Kozak asked.

"Because I know what indictments mean in your country. I've spent the better part of my career rolling up men you've indicted. If I step down, you'll lose your political motivation to come after me, but you won't lose your legal motivation. And about independent counsels and non-extradition promises and all of this—that's not how it works. You can't extradite a Panamanian from Panama, but I do it for you all the time. You just grab a guy and put him on a plane to Miami. That's how it works.

"As long as those indictments are around, you'll have to come after me. And you'll find some guy like me to come get me. So I'm not going to do it. *No deal.*"

Kozak protested that indictments were holy things in the U.S., and dropping them was politically impossible.

"I hear you," said Noriega. "But will you please carry my message to your president? You should be the star pitcher on the team. You tell them this is the best deal they'll get."

"I'll carry the message," said Kozak. "That's my job. But you had better make it goddamned attractive if you want me to carry a message like that."

Kozak said Noriega should, for instance, give the specific date of his resignation and say when he would leave the country.

"Panamanians aren't very good at long-range planning," Noriega said.

"I think you are in a position where you should start making an effort at it," said Kozak.

In the end, Noriega said he would step down on August 12, the fifth anniversary of his rule; but he balked at saying when he would leave the country. The problem was partially one of saving face: Noriega didn't want to be seen as being forced into exile by the U.S.

Kozak tried to convince Noriega that he needed to leave the country for the good of his own ruling party. Kozak agreed with Noriega that his ruling party might win a fair election, but Kozak contended that the opposition would consider it stolen if Noriega were still in the country. "For better or worse, you've convinced people you are Superman—that you manipulate everything that goes on in this country," said Kozak. "If you lived a hundred and eighty years and worked twenty-four hours a day, you couldn't have done all the things you are accused of doing."

Kozak likened Noriega's situation to that of President Nixon during Watergate. Like Americans then, Panamanians were blaming all their country's problems on Noriega. "Nixon had enough sense to get out of Washington and politics and lie low for a couple of years," said Kozak. "People began to realize all the problems in the country weren't his fault, and they talked about all the good things he had done. Now he has some real respect."

Kozak said his teenage son was even wearing a T-shirt that was promoting Nixon as a presidential candidate. "It reads: 'Nixon in '88: He's tan, rested, and ready,'" laughed Kozak.

Noriega smiled at this story, and his negotiator Escobar seized upon it. "Yes, General, you can leave and let the civilians take over the government and ruin everything. By 1995, people in the country will look back on your leadership fondly. You'll be a natural as a presidential candidate." And then Noriega would satisfy his real dream. He would lead Panama in the year 2000, when the gringos would have to give him the Panama Canal under provisions of the 1977 Treaties. It was a prize that would put his name in history books along with those of military leaders like Simón Bolívar and San Martín, he told Escobar.

Kozak had returned to Washington in early May with Noriega's first concrete offer yet to step down. Noriega had said he would need a month after his August 12 resignation to put his personal affairs in order, and then he would travel outside Panama until after the May elections, except for a visit home for Christmas. Secretary Shultz authorized Kozak to work on a plan that would include the lifting of the indictments, without Reagan's yet giving his formal approval of the policy.

During the talks that followed, Noriega was often more the charming host than the hostile dictator. He threatened and wooed adversaries with equal pleasure. Noriega arrived one morning at talks with little meringues and cashews that he claimed to have roasted himself over an open fire. He spoke of their health benefits—no preservatives or other additives "like one finds too often in America." On another occasion, when the U.S. staff pleaded hunger, he sent his staff to pick up empanadas. He was disappointed, however, to find they had come from the American-run YMCA. "You see the mentality in this country," he laughed. "All I can offer you is gringo empanadas."

Noriega saw his predicament clearly throughout negotiations. "I can either remain in uniform and in power," he told Kozak, "with all the risks and pressure that now exist. Or there is the certainty of going to jail in Miami." He was also swayed by two other sources. One senior Panamanian official said Noriega had been told by Medellín cartel emissaries that he couldn't step down unless indictments were dropped, because they feared his potential testimony against them. They knew Noriega's protection before a U.S. court would be to tell all that he knew about the drug lords. Meanwhile, the Cubans and Nicaraguans were telling him that if he hung on, Latin American history might remember him as the man who stood down the Yanquis.

Without a military threat, Kozak also had little leverage on Noriega. At one point, Kozak received a call from his boss, State Department Assistant Secretary Elliott Abrams, saying that Noriega had to agree to the deal right away. It was one of many ultimatums Kozak carried from Washington, most of which turned out to be bluffs. Noriega had ceased believing them.

"He's got to agree right now or else," said Abrams.

"Or else what?" countered Kozak sarcastically. "Should we torture him by insisting he sit through our interagency meetings?"

"You've been sitting with him too long," answered Abrams. "You've become sadistic."

Yet on May 11, Noriega approved a provisional plan that traded his power for the indictments. Noriega's negotiating team had been surprised how many concessions the Reagan administration was willing to give in its hurry to solve the problem. Inability to remove Noriega had become a major embarrassment. President Reagan approved the plan two days later, and lawyers for both sides went to work on hammering out the final arrangements on May 15.

Both sides were sworn to secrecy, of course, but the news leaked in Washington on May 14, and an uproar quickly erupted. Hurriedly, Noriega asked for an emergency meeting with Kozak, without lawyers present. The dictator of Panama was sneaking around so his American lawyers wouldn't chide him for meeting alone with Kozak. He shed his uniform for this private session, and he looked forlorn in his beige double-knit pants and yellow shoes.

"Jesus, Mike, you are killing me with your leaks," he said. "I'm going to be tarred and feathered." He said that secretaries were running up and down the halls crying and that junior officers were accusing him of abandoning them to save his own skin. "The press is outside," he said, "and I'm a prisoner in my own building."

Kozak saw Noriega's assessment was true. Noriega asked Kozak to help him by making a press statement that talks had broken down. Kozak said the State Department couldn't lie, but that he'd ask Washington to issue a statement saying that no agreement had been reached. That was technically true, since Kozak and Noriega hadn't yet shaken hands on the package that was almost totally negotiated. Noriega, unconstrained by the truth, put out a lie that the whole deal had collapsed.

But the leaks began to shrink the "political space" for an agreement. Forewarned, the U.S. attorneys in Florida who had brought the indictments launched a campaign against Kozak's deal, and senators who had long pressed the administration to force Noriega out were now just as enthusiastically against the use of the indictments as a tool to achieve that end.

"What you have here is an administration that has set its hair on fire and is trying to put it out with a hammer," said Senator D'Amato of New York, the most outspoken anti-Noriega campaigner on Capitol Hill, who preferred military force to judicial surrender.

United States attorneys were livid that White House Chief of Staff Howard Baker was referring to the Kozak negotiations as the perfect plea bargain, something only they were supposed to do.

"If the indictment produced his leaving Panama and paving the way for democratic government in that troubled country," Baker said, "that would be the most fruitful and productive plea bargaining I've ever seen in a long, long time, if ever."

The Justice Department countered by arguing that it was proper to trade indictments for assistance in law enforcement, but not to achieve foreign policy goals. Yet two Justice Department lawyers quietly beavered away at drawing up the final agreement with Noriega in a rundown suite at the Continental Hotel in Panama City, chosen to keep them a safe distance from reporters.

On Friday, May 20, Kozak received a call from Washington over his scrambler radio, through which he had been relaying news of new negotiation progress. The radio allowed Kozak to avoid Noriega's advanced interception devices by means of tactical satellites that beamed signals into a small, compact dish, small enough to be checked as baggage. The U.S. team in Panama had concealed the radio dish behind a bush at their hideaway inside Albrook Air Force Base, a safe distance from journalists and Noriega's prying G-2 men.

Charlie Hill, Shultz's executive secretary, was on the line. He had been one of the few cool heads in the past weeks, translating for Kozak the often contradictory messages and shifting positions.

As Shultz grew more nervous about the political costs of the negotiations, hence wanting closer control, he relied more on Hill as his liaison to Kozak. Shultz was caught between his loyalty to President Reagan, who wanted to negotiate Noriega out, and an abiding loyalty to the Republican party, whose chief strategists thought the Kozak negotiations could harm their 1988 chances. Tall, thin, and taciturn, Hill had the even manner and experience that Shultz trusted. He had been Ellsworth Bunker's special assistant in Saigon during the most critical weeks of the Vietnam war, and thereafter Kissinger drafted him as his speech writer.

"I have a very odd instruction for you," Hill said. "Don't question it; just do it. The president wants you to come back and explain this all to him. And you're not to tell Noriega that you're breaking off the negotiations; you're not to tell them that you're going to be back, either. You're just to say that you have to leave and go consult with the president."

The fateful weekend meetings in Reagan's private living room, that followed that phone call would make Kozak's job in Panama both easier and harder. He could now assure Noriega that the president would drop the indictments in exchange for his resignation and temporary departure from Panama. But time was short.

Based on the president's guidance, he told Escobar that a deal needed to be concluded before Wednesday "if possible" and that the political space for such an arrangement was closing swiftly. The president was having a hard time defending the agreement politically, Kozak said.

"Is that an ultimatum?" Escobar asked.

"No," said Kozak, knowing that whenever threats were not backed with a specific commitment to action, Noriega's reaction was to dismiss his partner's seriousness entirely. Escobar and Justine, nevertheless, worked throughout the night Monday and all day Tuesday to finalize the agreement.

Noriega, however, was relieved not to be under the pressure of an ultimatum. He spent Monday evening with the papal nuncio, who would hold the agreed-upon documents. He asked the Vatican's representative to show him the safe where the papers would be stored. An aide to the nuncio wondered if Noriega needed to know their location in order to pilfer them. Noriega told the nuncio not to lose track of the documents, but that he wouldn't sign anything until he was totally satisfied. "Reagan has told me that there is no hurry to sign the documents and that the signing can take place after the Moscow summit," he said. He was pleased with the agreement's two main points: the dropping of the indictments and the right to return to Panama, occasionally at first and permanently later.

The Panamanian negotiators didn't tell Noriega about the U.S. rejection of the Colombian money deal, not wanting him to know anything was amiss. Even his negotiators wanted to avoid giving the General any excuse to back off an agreement they thought was in their country's best interest. Kozak, however, began to think that even entering into talks about the money had been a mistake. An aspect he had considered relatively minor was now the biggest obstacle. State Department officials were surprised their superiors hadn't killed such an explosive idea before it got so far.

The whole history of Noriega's demand for money had been an unhappy one. It had begun when, early in May, Colonel Justine had said that Noriega wanted Panama's government revenues, held in escrow accounts in the United States because of American sanctions, to be released on the day that the General announced his resignation. He argued that if civil liberties were restored and people could not cash their checks, civil unrest could disrupt Panama. Kozak said President Eric Arturo Delvalle, who was in hiding after Noriega had ousted him, controlled those funds as the only Panamanian leader that Washington recognized. Delvalle wasn't likely to release the funds until Noriega had left the country and an acceptable transition regime was established. "I can't give you that money," said Kozak.

Justine offered an alternative. He said Japan and Taiwan were ready to deposit funds in that amount if Uncle Sam gave the green light. Undersecretary of State Michael Armacost called in the Japanese Ambassador to Washington, Nobua Matsunaga, to tell him the U.S. wouldn't object to such deposits in the context of a settlement that involved the suspension of U.S. sanctions, and the same message was carried to Taiwan.

Noriega enjoyed the rich irony of this cash chase. He joked to one of his ambassadors that he had "Abrams out trying to find me money, just like he did for the Contras." Noriega knew that Abrams, his biggest enemy in the administration, had solicited $10 million from the Sultan of Brunei in August 1986. "Maybe Abrams can raise some money in Brunei for us," Noriega chortled. He also knew the cash infusion would be good propaganda: the U.S. paying for the damage it had done Panama's economy.

After efforts were already well under way to convert the Japanese and Taiwanese, Shultz also began to fear that Noriega was toying with the U.S.

and might pocket the funds himself. Over Shultz's signature, State cabled Deputy Secretary John Whitehead in Paris to call him off plans to raise the issue with Japanese officials he would be meeting there. "Mike Kozak remains in Panama waiting for Noriega's decision," he said. "It is possible the whole thing will fall through. Please note that despite the approach to the Japanese and others to deposit money in Panamanian institutions, the Secretary has decided that this is not the way to go, and has killed the idea. You should therefore not mention the idea when you meet with Japanese Vice Minister Murata. Apparently the concern is that such funds would do more to line pockets than help liquidity, and other options are being studied."

The other option was Banco Cafetero. The bank's chief in Panama was the head of the country's bankers' association and a close friend of Guillermo St. Malo de Arias, the scion's son who had facilitated the talks. The bank director said a letter from the State Department to his board in Bogotá could clear the way for a sizable deposit in the National Bank of Panama. Shultz's letter was received; and St. Malo was ready to collect the money when Shultz, at the last moment, backed out of that deal as well.

In the end, St. Malo and the other negotiators finessed the problem with some quick Monday and Tuesday footwork. Commerce Minister Mario Rognoni gathered information on how much money in taxes U.S. companies had been withholding from Noriega's government and which therefore would be made available to Panama's government once sanctions were suspended. Ambassador Arthur Davis called the chairmen of the largest of these companies and ascertained that they would pay these taxes to Panama's regime as soon as the political disputes were solved, in order to maintain good relations with the government. With this, the language of the agreement concerning deposits was deleted; the U.S. promise to suspend sanctions would be the best Panama could do to deal with its liquidity problem.

Late Tuesday afternoon, State Department Under Secretary Michael Armacost changed U.S. instructions to Kozak again. What had originally been a strong hope that Kozak could finish by Wednesday was now an ultimatum. This wasn't Reagan changing his mind, but rather it was senior officials reinterpreting what Reagan had said to Kozak on Sunday. The political space had closed. When Kozak told Noriega's negotiators he would have to sign Tuesday night, they balked. "But you assured us this was not an ultimatum," Escobar said.

Kozak was relieved when at 8 P.M. Tuesday, Billy St. Malo announced that they had a deal. Noriega had even phoned the nuncio that evening to say that he had written his speech to be delivered the next morning and that he wanted the nuncio's assistant to be ready to accept the documents. He visited his mistress Vicky Amado and her mother Norma Amado, who had become an important adviser to him, and he told them to pack their bags for Paris. Vicky called a friend to gossip about it.

Shortly thereafter, Kozak got the fateful call from Washington that turned U.S. demands into an ultimatum. Charlie Hill, ever methodical and calm, told Kozak that Shultz would stay Wednesday morning until the deal could be concluded. "It's got to be done now or you are instructed to pull everything off the table and get out of there," Hill said. Kozak wasn't surprised by the ultimatum, but he advised against Shultz's waiting. He knew Noriega's reputation for delays, and he didn't think it was a good idea for Shultz to sit and wait impatiently. But Shultz wanted personally to defend the controversial decision to trade away the indictments and not leave the job to Armacost, who thereby might have been hurt politically in his hopes to land a big job in a Bush administration.

Kozak kept news of the ultimatum from Noriega's people that night. He felt he had an agreement anyway, and he knew any new strong-arming could only undermine the fragile accord.

But Noriega didn't like making decisions, and he often delayed them. This was the biggest decision of his life, and his instinct to procrastinate was proportional. He tried to buy time by telling his negotiators that he feared the documents had been doctored while Kozak was in Washington. Hence, Noriega's lawyers were flown in from Miami in the middle of the night to compare the documents, but were so bleary-eyed that they made little progress. Kozak proposed a work-saving method: they should hold the originals and their own copies up to the light to see if all the letters matched. They did, and this crisis was solved. But Noriega had disappeared.

When Kozak and Colonel Clark came to Escobar's office at 7 A.M., they still hadn't heard from the General and, worse, they saw a disturbing headline on the morning government newspaper: "CEM [Strategic Military Council] Issues Declaration Demanding Their Commander Not Leave Under U.S. Pressure."

At just after 9 A.M., Escobar answered the phone. "The General wants to see you," said Rómulo. "But he's not ready yet." It was clear from Rómulo's face that matters were going wrong. Noriega didn't receive Kozak and Clark until 11 A.M. Reagan was already en route to Moscow; and Shultz, who had delayed his departure, was angrily and impatiently waiting for word from Panama. Reagan's comments on departure only confused the negotiations with Noriega more, making the dictator believe the ultimatum was only another trick. While Kozak was saying Noriega had to agree "now or never," Reagan shouted to reporters yelling at his helicopter, "It's not the timing of the agreement that's the problem; it's the quality." Kozak watched the report in horror on *Good Morning America,* beamed over the Southern Command Forces Network.

The conflicting instructions to Kozak over the past week, shifting after every major interagency meeting, had brought Noriega to doubt American ultimatums. The negotiating team had grown frustrated, tossed like a small boat on an angry political sea. The Reagan statement made Noriega all the more suspicious. Just an hour before his talks with the U.S. were to be broken off entirely, he still didn't believe he was facing his final chance.

Noriega chose a dramatic stage for the final meeting. He greeted Kozak and Clark at former dictator Omar Torrijos's home on Calle Cincuenta, which had become a museum, and he invited them into Torrijos's bedroom. The legendary Panamanian dictator's bathrobe still rested on the bed, his slippers still lay flat on the floor, and his uniforms still hung in the closet. Nothing had changed from the day he had died in a mysterious plane crash on July 31, 1981. Kozak had known Torrijos personally, and he found the setting weird if not haunted. He and Clark sat opposite Noriega on facing couches near the foot of the bed.

"I was ready to do this," frowned Noriega. "I had prepared myself and my family psychologically for this. I told you, though, from the beginning that I was going to need some days to prepare my people. And you haven't given me that time. And you can't say we haven't tried. Rómulo did a good job with the popular sector leaders [unions and other leftist organizations]. Some don't like it, but they'll live with it. I've talked with the general staff. They don't like it either. But they'll acquiesce. But I'm having real problems with the junior officers. They're reacting emotionally, not logically. They're immature. They don't have good political sense."

Kozak interrupted. "Under instructions, General, we don't have any more time. My instructions are that we either do this thing now or I am instructed to pull everything off the table and to leave." Noriega protested that he hadn't thought he was facing an ultimatum. He felt the rug was being pulled out from under him and their agreement, and his American negotiating partners feared he was right. They'd never be able to say this to the American public, but Noriega had been jerked around and misled.

"I understand you," said Kozak. "But these are my orders. Either you sign, or everything's off." Many officials in Washington thought Noriega was just stringing them along, but if he was, Clark thought he had carried the bluff a long way.

Noriega complained to Kozak that it was Washington's leaks that turned his junior officers against the plan before he even had a chance to brief them. "I wanted to wait and brief the officers only after we'd gotten a deal. What they're reacting to is your leaks, not my presentation. . . . Based on your propaganda, they think this is a deal where I'm giving up the command and the security of the country and the defense forces to save my own skin."

Kozak tried one more time to convince Noriega to act. He didn't know whether the General was telling the truth—whether it was the junior officers who were stopping him or himself—but he didn't think Noriega yet realized that this was his last chance.

Kozak said the leaks weren't done to hurt Noriega. "They present exactly the same problem for us," he said. Kozak said the president was being accused of being too willing to give up the indictments, but that he'll go out to "defend this agreement like crazy." He suggested Noriega do the same. "The president is quite confident that once the American people understand what this agreement is all about, they will support it. He's willing to take that risk, and I think that would be good advice for you, too."

"Yes, that is generally good advice, but I have a problem that your president doesn't," Noriega frowned. "I don't think your military is going to engage in a coup. These officers are saying, if we go ahead with this deal, they will no longer feel bound by the rules of military discipline."

About that time, Colonel Marco Justine walked in. He was agitated. "I had to get out of there," he said of a meeting with junior officers. "I realized they thought I was promoting this agreement so I could get you out and take over your command myself," he told the General. Justine's entrance was either elaborate staging or the convincing final proof for the Americans.

At one point, Clark jumped in. "Look, General, Mike is under instructions that it's now or never. So he can't even ask you hypothetical questions. But on a personal basis, I want to ask you a hypothetical question. If we could give you more time, how much would you need?" Noriega was vague. A few days, he said.

Kozak cut the conversation off after two and a half hours. "Look, the secretary of state is waiting: the president has already left the country. The secretary is going to leave. I need to tell him it's over."

Noriega and Justine shook the hands of Kozak and Clark. Nobody was happy.

Kozak stopped at Escobar's office to pick up his car and to phone Washington. Under Secretary Michael Armacost and Abrams got on the line. Shultz was in the press room waiting to make his announcement. Was it thumbs up or down? Shultz was impatient and angry, fed up with what he viewed as Noriega's machinations.

"It's over," Kozak said.

"What do you mean?" Armacost asked. "Is it successful or not?"

"No. Over. Negative," Kozak replied.

Just then, Noriega phoned on another line while Kozak was talking. It had finally hit the dictator that time had run out. Maybe the Americans really meant this, the last of many ultimatums.

"Tell Mike I wasn't as precise as I should have been in answering your question," he told Clark. "To be precise, I will make the agreement with you today. We'll sign the papers; we'll deposit them with the nuncio."

Clark whispered the new offer to Kozak. It seemed Noriega had realized that this was indeed his last chance. Kozak's voice couldn't conceal his excitement.

"Same deal?" Kozak asked Noriega through Clark, while keeping Armacost and Abrams on the other line.

"Yes, same deal," replied Noriega to Clark.

Noriega said they would need to add one more provision. The speeches would be carried out the day the president returned from Moscow. Reagan would come back in ten days. "I don't need that much time," Noriega said. "I can do it in a few days. But I understand from your side that it's important for your president to be there to defend this. So let's do the deal now, we'll deposit it, we'll just keep quiet about it. Then on the day the president gets back from Moscow, I'll make my speech. And I'm ready to sign that agreement and deposit it today."

Kozak spoke to Armacost again. "He's offering to sign today, but execute in two weeks."

But the matter had grown too politically hot to handle, Reagan wanted to concentrate on success in Moscow, and few in Washington trusted Noriega's sincerity. No one realized this would likely be Washington's last chance to remove Noriega peacefully.

"Get out of there," Armacost told Kozak.

Kozak heard the click and put down the receiver. Clark passed the rejection to Noriega and apologized. Another click.

What they didn't know was that the rejection had come without Shultz's consulting with Ronald Reagan, who was on his way to Helsinki, his way station before the Moscow summit.

Kozak and Clark, thinking the U.S. may have missed a key opportunity, walked out of Escobar's office and climbed into their broken-down Subaru, a rental car without diplomatic plates that they had used in Panama City to remain incognito. As they steered toward their secret home at Albrook Air Force Base, Clark drove quickly, complaining that the Subaru's "wimp horn" wasn't loud enough for Latin traffic.

"We were that close," said Clark, holding two fingers less than an inch apart. "Would we have been better off just to ignore our instructions and have signed the thing and given Noriega the time he wanted?"

Kozak laughed, and recalled for Clark a historical precedent for just such insubordination. In 1848 an American minister to Mexico had ignored presidential instructions not to sign the Treaty of Guadalupe Hidalgo, which had ended the Mexican-American War. When he came home with the signed treaty, the president had backed it and the senate had ratified it.

Kozak and Clark were tempted, but they opted to play by the rules. Clark figured they'd be back in two weeks anyway to pick up the pieces. "Don't bet on it," said Kozak.

CHAPTER
NINETEEN

BUSH'S TAR BABY

Noriega was one of those issues that fell under the category of the less you had to say about it, the better.
—CRAIG FULLER, VICE PRESIDENT BUSH'S
FORMER CHIEF OF STAFF, 1989

Six months before the end of President Reagan's term, in June 1988, the drive to get Vice President Bush elected shaped any decision regarding Panama. The only way to get Noriega out was through negotiations or military force; yet the Bush campaign opposed both solutions.

Negotiating with Noriega again would raise charges that Washington was offering concessions to a drug dealer, and military action risked failure or the possibility of so aggravating Noriega that he revealed intelligence he was supposedly holding on Bush. Whether true or false, a Noriega offensive against the vice president could tie the campaign in knots of rebuttal and explanation.

And all George Bush's top campaign strategists remembered what had happened to Jimmy Carter when his hostage-rescue attempt had blown up in the Iranian desert in 1980. The world had grown accustomed to adjusting its political clock around the overriding priorities of American presidential politics, and Panama's crisis would have to wait.

In this new atmosphere, the Reagan administration answered a number of new overtures from Noriega with one simple message: provide us a detailed list of the conditions you would accept regarding your resignation, and we will look at them and decide if talks are warranted. Noriega never sent the document. In the late summer and fall, with Secretary Shultz helping to get the ball rolling both times, Spanish and Uruguayan officials tried to engage Noriega in discussions aimed at his resignation, but on both occasions Noriega cut them off. Noriega wanted to talk directly to the Americans, but the gringos weren't talking.

For the Bush campaign, Noriega was a tar baby. Any way you touched him, you got stuck. To the vice president's campaign strategists, there were three potential land mines that could explode underneath their presidential hopes. The first was the Iran-Contra scandal. The second was long-standing but never publicized rumors of an extramarital affair. The third was Noriega.

"Noriega was one of those things that fell into the category of the less you had to say about it, the better," Craig Fuller, Bush's chief of staff at the time, would say later. "There was almost nothing you could say that could help. If you suggested that you should find another way to get rid of him, that conjured up in people's minds American troops and Panama, and that scared them more than Noriega. There wasn't a proposal you could come up with in the political environment that was going to be popular. Hence, we were just as happy that it not be discussed.

"We felt at all times that George Bush was vulnerable on the issue, in the sense that we thought the other side would raise it," Fuller added. "It's not that George Bush had done anything wrong; it's just that he had to deal with the issue. Dealing with narcotics traffickers became a stock phrase that was thrown at us."

The Bush campaign's message to put Noriega on the back burner reached all quarters of the administration.

Embassy officials in Panama, including Ambassador Arthur H. Davis and Deputy Chief of Mission John Maisto, were told to tone down their activities and statements so as not to aggravate Noriega.

At a meeting in the White House in late summer, National Security Adviser Colin Powell listened impatiently as Southern Command chief General Frederick F. Woerner discussed the region in a manner Powell considered typically tedious. After Woerner finished listing alternatives for action, Powell paused before telling his military chief for Latin America that Panama was to be put on the back burner until after the election. Woerner's aides say the message was repeated by telephone by Admiral Crowe, the chairman of the Joint Chiefs of Staff, and by Defense Secretary Frank Carlucci. "No one ever put it on paper," said one Southern Command officer. "But General Woerner had no doubt of his instructions."

Woerner, in turn, told aides that the Bush fix was in: no action was to be taken by his 12,000 troops to foment a conflict with Noriega. And when Noriega threw sand in military faces, and harassed the Americans, he instructed troops to turn the other cheek, thus diminishing troop morale and encouraging Noriega to tweak the Americans even more.

The Panamanians detained troops illegally, beat some soldiers, stopped the delivery of mail, and on at least one occasion seized military equipment arriving in the country. Once they even stole Ambassador Davis's diplomatic mailbag as he was driving through town. It wasn't ever returned. In a single nine-month period in 1988, Southcom registered more than 1,000 separate incidents of harassment, but the U.S. did nothing.

The go-slow message also reached members of the anti-Noriega opposition. In August, the Defense Intelligence Agency's officer for Latin America, Colonel James V. Coniglio, told opposition operatives that they "should expect nothing, nothing from the military forces of the U.S. And the U.S. will not use military force itself."

The Bush campaign staff got unexpected assistance from Panama's ambassador to Washington, Juan Sosa, whose best friends in Washington were leading Republicans. As a member of the small Republican party in Panama, ties to the George Bush crowd were his insurance against an uncertain future, and he instructed his embassy staff to do everything possible to keep Panama out of the headlines. Even President Delvalle, for whom Sosa technically worked, would privately criticize his ambassador's overenthusiasm for helping the Bush campaign. And Sosa, as if hoping to confirm these connections, had leading Republicans as his first clients when he shut down the embassy and opened his own consulting business a year later.

But in the service of Bush, Sosa stood by silently as federal authorities relocated José Blandón, who was talking openly about the alleged ties between Bush's national security adviser Donald Gregg and Noriega's adviser Michael Harari. That put Blandón out of the press corps' reach.

And again, Colonel Eduardo Herrera Hassan, who had been plotting with the Israelis and Venezuelans to overthrow Noriega, suffered. Sosa, who paid Herrera Hassan's bills, instructed Herrera Hassan to take a vacation from the overthrow business until the election was over. "While Bush was campaigning, I was taking my children to see Mickey Mouse in Orlando and watching soap operas," Herrera Hassan laughed. "I was very worried all these months—about what would happen next on the soap opera."

When Herrera Hassan continued plotting anyway, he was visited by one of his CIA minders. They told him to stop planning anything even vaguely resembling the assassination of Noriega or the FBI would put him behind bars. Eduardo, be careful, the CIA man said. These senators are very worried about you.

Herrera Hassan was slowly growing convinced that Noriega did have Bush by the balls, just as he had said, and that was preventing the administration from going after him in a way that might backfire and hence prompt him to reveal what he knew. "I know Noriega well," Herrera Hassan said.

"When Noriega says he has something on someone, he has it. I don't know how big it is, but Noriega has a file on everyone."

Panama's underground president, Eric Arturo Delvalle, later would blame the Bush campaign for setting back Noriega's opposition. "The Bush campaign took the steam out of the whole thing," he said. "It's a real problem: this country was constantly talking about election and reelection."

The Bush campaign's handling of the Noriega issue is a case study in how presidential politics takes precedence over virtually all other issues in Washington. This is the story of how the Bush campaign handled the Noriega issue—first working to undermine negotiations that came closest to a peaceful resolution of the crisis, then moving to avoid military confrontation with Noriega that might go awry, and thereafter working to keep the issue out of the headlines until Bush could be elected. All along, national security interests came a distant second to domestic presidential prerogatives.

Kansas Senator Robert Dole, Bush's Republican challenger for the presidential nomination, immediately seized the issue in late February, when he demanded the vice president reveal whether Noriega had been in the CIA payroll when Bush had headed the intelligence operations in 1976. "Part of what I don't do," replied Bush, "is go out and discuss [such matters] when I take an oath of office at CIA to protect sources and methods of intelligence."

Then at a House subcommittee hearing, former National Security Council staff member Norman Bailey indirectly questioned Bush's claim that he hadn't known about Noriega's drug involvement years earlier. "The only possible reason or excuse for being ignorant of [Noriega's ties to drugs] would be because the person involved did not want to know or find out, or willfully ignored the overwhelming evidence," Bailey said.

Bailey added that wire intercepts and other intelligence in 1983 and 1985 had resulted in references to meetings between Noriega and drug traffickers in a daily summary of top secret U.S. intelligence known as the NID, or National Intelligence Daily. "Available to me as an officer of the NSC, and available to any authorized official of the U.S. government, is a plethora of human intelligence, electronic intercepts, and satellite and overflight photography that, taken together, constitute not just a smoking gun, but rather a twenty-one-cannon salute," Bailey said. "Clear and incontrovertible evidence was, at best, ignored and, at worst, hidden and denied by many different agencies and departments."

The political heat on Bush continued to build.

By April, Democratic candidate Michael Dukakis—the most likely challenger to Bush—had seized on the Noriega issue. "How about telling us who in this administration was dealing with Noriega," he asked at a Democratic debate. "Who was paying Noriega? Who was ignoring the fact that we knew he was dealing in drugs and making millions and we're still doing business with him?"

Bush's supporters were caught in a maze of contradictions. Initially they said that the vice president had never met with Noriega, and then, after a photograph appeared showing Bush and Noriega together, were forced to concede at least two meetings—one in 1976 and another in 1983.

They claimed that Bush hadn't known anything about Noriega's drug ties until the time of the indictment, but then a memo emerged that suggested that in December 1985 Bush had discussed those ties in a meeting with America's then-ambassador to Panama, Everett Ellis Briggs. Bush aides had Briggs tell the press that he hadn't talked about drugs then, to which Bush readily agreed; but Donald Gregg, Bush's foreign policy adviser, contradicted his boss. In a sworn deposition to answer a Christic Institute lawsuit, Gregg testified that Bush and Briggs had discussed drugs, but only in a general way.

"I think we came away from the meeting with Ambassador Briggs with the sense that Noriega was a growing problem politically, militarily, and possibly in the drug area," he said.

Bush aides felt compelled to reinterpret the vice president's confusing and contradictory statements on Noriega and drugs, but their statements often fed uncertainties. "I don't think the vice president is trying to suggest that he didn't know Panama had a narcotics problem and that Noriega, as a key player in Panama, might have some involvement," said Fuller at the time. "What he's really saying is that *certain* knowledge didn't come until after the indictment of Noriega."

It was in this atmosphere that Bush decided to collide with the president over Panama. With each news leak about the Kozak negotiations, Bush had come under increasing pressure from his campaign handlers, Lee Atwater and Robert Teeter, to come out openly against the president on the Noriega issue. Although Bush had won the Republican primaries soundly, opinion surveys showed that the public perceived him as Reagan's patsy—a man without his own views or policies—and May opinion surveys showed that Dukakis had surpassed Bush as Americans' president of choice by as much as 10 percentage points. The polls cited drugs as Americans' primary worry.

Atwater and Teeter saw the Noriega negotiations as an opportunity to address two of the vice president's greatest vulnerabilities. First, Bush could distinguish himself from Reagan—without cost to Republican causes—and second, in doing so he could defuse the whole issue of his supposed intelligence links to Noriega.

On May 13, a day after the press leaks about an initial agreement with Noriega, Bush phoned Fuller with his concerns about the course of the Kozak negotiations. From a barn at a campaign stop in Escondido, California, Fuller phoned the White House to relay the vice president's misgivings.

The Bush team feared that Kozak, with Shultz's authorization, was exceeding his original negotiating instructions by promising to allow Noriega to remain in Panama once he resigned from power. This raised the vice president's greatest fear: that the U.S. would give up the indictments and not remove Noriega from power. Pressures from the Bush camp and other sources had already sent often-changing instructions to Kozak, but now the vice president's men began to believe the negotiations should be cut off altogether. "If that's where negotiations are headed, the vice president thinks they should be stopped," said Fuller.

Yet Teeter and Atwater wanted more. They pressed Bush to go public against Reagan. He's got to say something publicly, Teeter told Fuller. And he's got to do it soon.

Publicly defying the president wasn't Bush's style, however. Every time Fuller raised the issue with Bush, the vice president said he didn't want to undermine President Reagan's efforts to remove Noriega from power.

A rash of newspaper stories on the negotiations made Bush's continued silence increasingly costly. Reporters were questioning him and his staff on Noriega at every turn. On the morning of May 18, Fuller unhappily reviewed the text the vice president would deliver on drugs that night before the Los Angeles Police Academy. It didn't include any reference to Noriega.

"This whole Noriega story had really reached a crescendo," Fuller remembered months later. "And here was a whole speech on drugs that didn't even mention Noriega. I told the vice president, 'You can't give the speech and not make reference to this issue, in my view.' "

Bush reluctantly wrote in cautious language that said he wouldn't "bargain with drug dealers, either on U.S. or foreign soil." Even as Bush read the language to Fuller over the hotel telephone, however, the vice president was reluctant to commit himself to delivering it that evening.

Don't tell anybody I'm thinking of putting this in, said Bush, because I may change my mind.

According to Fuller, what finally convinced Bush to keep the new language in his speech was a visit later that morning to a Los Angeles crack house with the tough-minded Los Angeles Police Chief Daryl Gates. Gates proselytized Bush in the backseat of their limousine as they struggled through Los Angeles traffic. The vice president was sickened by the destitution of the crack house. The Noriega language would stay in.

A few hours before the evening speech, Fuller passed the word to the White House that the vice president was "moving out" on the Noriega issue in opposition to President Reagan. "The vice president isn't going to object to people's indicating that he feels differently about this Noriega business," Fuller told National Security Adviser Colin Powell, Chief of Staff Howard Baker, and Baker's deputy Kenneth Duberstein.

It was a dramatic moment. For the first time in eight years, Bush clearly and publicly differed with his boss. But the vice president hadn't bothered to tell Reagan personally. The president was disturbed; and he publicly suggested the vice president didn't understand all the details of the talks. He understood Bush's political need to show himself as independent, but the president was upset that Bush had staked out a position that undermined his policy course at such a sensitive moment.

Bush still hadn't decided if he wanted to try to stop the negotiations in Panama, however—a step his aides urged him to take, particularly since the parties seemed near agreement. It wasn't until the day after his Los Angeles speech that Bush's confrontational stance was fixed. U.S. Attorney Leon Kellner, the politically ambitious prosecutor who had indicted Noriega in Miami, had grown so desperate to preserve his indictment that he had called a major Bush fund-raiser in Florida named Alex Courtelis, and asked Courtelis to arrange a meeting with the vice president. Bush's handlers jumped at the opportunity.

That morning, Kellner played surprisingly tough with the vice president. He told Bush that President Reagan's plans to drop drug indictments against General Manuel Antonio Noriega, in exchange for the dictator's resignation, would be political suicide for Bush's presidential campaign.

"Do you want it straight?" he asked.

Bush nodded.

"The voters would think you were a crook—that you had been blackmailed by Noriega," he said. "I don't believe that. If I did, I wouldn't be here. But that's the way the Democrats will use it."

Bush fumed. "That's a crock of shit," he said. "That's just a lie." Kellner was shocked at Bush's strong language, which sounded unnatural coming from the vice president's Brahmin mouth.

Bush conceded to Kellner that he had only recently begun focusing on

Panama. What Bush didn't say was that he thought that indicting a foreign ally had been a stupid idea from the beginning. The foreign policy consequences hadn't been thought through.

Yet Bush explained to Kellner that President Reagan believed the indictments were a small price to pay for gaining Noriega's departure from power. Bush hadn't made up his own mind yet, he told Kellner, but he thought the president's arguments held merit. Perhaps it made sense to drop the indictments in the country's broader national security interests.

Kellner was strident in defending his indictments, however. He told Bush that using the threat of indictments as a negotiating tool would have been fine before they were unsealed, but now the indictments were Holy Grail. The Reagan administration was "politicizing" American law.

The Kellner-Bush meeting itself, of course, couldn't have been more political. Kellner was looking to repair his image and build a political career. Bush was looking to protect his campaign and make voters believe he was his own man. Foreign policy was an afterthought.

By the time Kellner walked out of Bush's office, he believed he had the vice president on his side, and indeed, Bush immediately began to push to end the negotiations altogether. He wanted Reagan to bring back Kozak from Panama. His eager accomplice was James Baker, the treasury secretary who would soon be his campaign manager.

After his meeting with Kellner, Bush informed President Reagan over lunch that he had to take him on over "this Noriega thing." Reagan appealed to Bush to change his mind, but former Reagan aides say the master politician understood the politics of Bush's move. That afternoon Bush met with his image maker, Roger Ailes, to see how he could get the most mileage out of it.

Fuller, Bush's chief of staff, issued a statement confirming news reports that "the vice president favors ending the negotiations and bringing the envoy back to Washington." If Bush's influence ended talks in Panama, that would suit the campaign fine, he thought. If talks continued, Bush at least had washed his hands of the negotiations politically.

On May 20, Bush's misgivings and the growing political heat in Congress prompted the White House to call Kozak back from Panama for weekend consultations. Although the president sent Kozak back the following Monday to conclude a deal with Noriega, the pressure of the Bush campaign had taken hold. By the following Wednesday, the political space that allowed the negotiations had closed so rapidly that Noriega was given an unexpected twenty-four-hour ultimatum either to sign a deal right away or to have all offers swept from the table. Noriega balked, and those opposed to President Reagan's negotiating course took their chance to shut down the talks before they could do the vice president any more political harm.

The campaign's decision was clear: it was politically riskier to Bush to get rid of Noriega by trading the indictments than it was to keep the indictments and Noriega. "That's clearly what the campaign was saying," agreed Fuller later. "And George Bush, who always understood the details [of the negotiations], was most concerned about a situation in which we would give up the indictments and not get rid of Noriega."

Despite all the odds going against it, the State Department did try to put together one last shot at dealing with Noriega before the November elections, this time through the military action of exiled Panamanian officers and some rebels within Panama that were led by Eduardo Herrera Hassan. However, campaign fever also overcame this scheme: members of the Senate Select Committee on Intelligence felt the plan was so ill-considered that they had no alternative but to reject it. Some even suspected they were being set up by the White House and the Bush campaign to block action against Noriega, thus absorbing some of the blame for the failed policy that was harming Bush's campaign.

The fifteen members of the committee muttered angrily among themselves as they walked by the armed guard and through the vaulted, microwave-proof steel door into their austere chambers—Room 219 of the Senate's Hart Office Building. While Noriega consolidated his position in Panama, they braced for bureaucratic warfare.

It was July 26, 1988, just six weeks after the breakdown of the Kozak negotiations and a little more than three months before the elections. The last thing committee members wanted to see cross their tables at this point in an election year was the president's newest "finding," requiring the CIA and others to prepare a blueprint for covert action against Noriega. It would include psychological operations, propaganda, and—most controversially—support for a coup against Noriega led by exiled Panamanian Colonel Eduardo Herrera Hassan, who had been so unceremoniously abandoned when the Pentagon had shut off any military option three months earlier.

A "finding" is a presidential directive that calls for covert action to achieve a specific foreign policy goal. In this case, however, some Intelligence Committee members considered the proposed action poorly planned, and others said the hidden goal—the assassination of Noriega—was illegal.

The senators impatiently prepared to attack the three witnesses sent by the Reagan administration to brief them: State Department Undersecretary for Political Affairs Michael Armacost, CIA official Dick Stolz, and the Pentagon's Assistant Secretary for International Security Affairs Richard Armitage. The senators sat in their shallow armchairs, arranged around a horseshoe-shaped table. The three administration officials sat at the table's opening, like gladiators unhappily waiting for the crowd's thumbs down.

They were a veteran group of clandestine campaigners. Armacost, the senior of them, sat at the center and presented the administration's case in his methodical monotone. This soft-spoken but tough-minded former ambassador to the Philippines knew what it took to remove a dictator. Dick Stolz, who ran the CIA's covert operations directorate, had been brought out of retirement by the new CIA director, William Webster. Secret missions of all sorts were his specialty, although his expertise was in Eastern Europe. Armitage was also a veteran of clandestine operations, and his role in the Iran-Contra affair had raised some eyebrows; the weightlifting Naval Academy graduate ran the Pentagon's military covert operations branch.

Expertise there was aplenty, yet these three men's chances of success were so bleak that Armacost suggested to Secretary of State Shultz that he should not stake his prestige on a favorable outcome. A secret memo sent to Shultz before the session read in part: "The initial reactions we have gotten back from the [CIA] consultations with the intelligence committees suggest that we face an uphill battle on this one. . . . There is some feeling over in the White House that our chances of securing congressional support for this—and their support is required, since monies must be reprogrammed—would be enhanced if you and Bill Webster handled the testimony. . . . But I would urge you not to take this one on. . . . Rich, Dick, and I are ready to give it our best shot."

Their best shot fell far short. Without Shultz or Webster to defend such a controversial plan, it was a dead letter.

Democratic Senator Bill Bradley of New Jersey and Republican Senator William Cohen of Maine led the bipartisan charge against the finding, but their arguments were buttressed by the outspoken opposition of more than half of the committee members in the room.

What assurances could the briefers give that Noriega wouldn't be killed during the kidnap attempt? Bradley asked. What assurances were there that Americans in Panama wouldn't be taken hostage? What would the Panamanians do if Noriega pulled a gun on them when they tried to arrest him? Wouldn't the covert action be as likely to bring about the assassination of Noriega as his arrest?

Indeed, the coup's would-be leader, Colonel Herrera Hassan, told CIA officials quite honestly that he would be just as happy to take Noriega dead as alive. As Torrijos's former security chief, he was certain Noriega had plotted the plane crash that had taken his idol's life, and he was bent on revenge. He had already started plotting with one foreign country, and some members of Israeli intelligence were helping as well. "There was no assassination plot," Herrera said months later. "What we wanted to do was enter Panama with a force and stage a coup. We would have seized him, arrested him, maybe burned him. We didn't know what would happen."

That wasn't good enough for the Intelligence Committee. Bradley and Cohen both knew that some covert actions risked loss of life, and that was permissible when the circumstances demanded, but Executive Order 12333 banned U.S. involvement, either direct or indirect, in assassination, and this finding clearly violated that order.

In addition, Cohen had often thought that the intelligence community sent its most troublesome matters to the committee just before recess, hoping that vacation-bound senators would sign off without much scrutiny. This was one of his pet peeves, and he considered the Panama finding the worst example of this bad practice. The finding had been ready on July 15; yet it hadn't been brought to the Senate until more than ten days later. Cohen suggested that this had been deliberate, so that the senators would not have adequate time to hash out a perhaps more acceptable alternative with the administration and the Intelligence Committee.

This mistrust was fed by several circumstances, including the fact that the administration sought a "reprogramming" of funds, instead of simply taking the money out of the CIA's contingency account, which is normally used for urgent actions. Reprogramming requires approval of several committees, most important among them being the intelligence committees. And it takes more time.

For his part, Armitage denied charges of a setup. He, Stolz, and Armitage protested that the administration was briefing the committee so close to its recess only because the plan for covert action had been put together in just the six weeks since the Kozak negotiations had broken down— pretty fast work by Washington standards.

He acted baffled at the senators' consternation. The beauty of the plan, he thought, was that it would be orchestrated and executed by Panamanians with only some equipment, training, and logistical help offered by the Americans. They wouldn't even use U.S. bases to launch their activities, thus avoiding the Pentagon's sensitivities that such action could harm its base rights elsewhere in the world.

The administration officials denied that murdering Noriega was the aim—but they also couldn't guarantee the senators that deaths wouldn't occur. The officials wanted to avoid another controversy such as the one that had followed the mining of Nicaraguan harbors in 1985. Some CIA officials felt that the Intelligence Committee had been properly notified of that clandestine scheme, but senators insisted that the only hint had been a single sentence buried in a long opening statement by William Casey. This time the administration wanted to be explicit, but their honesty only increased the senators' suspicions.

Armacost, Stolz, and Armitage ended the surprisingly short session disappointed but not surprised at how easily the Intelligence Committee members had dismissed the president's finding. "There wasn't any serious consideration or debate," said one official involved in preparing the briefers. "The senators just threw it out. Sure, we gave them every possible worry we had. We had to say there was a chance of violence and, if there was violence, someone could get hurt. They wanted to be tough with Panama, but they wanted to solve the problem without pain or risk."

Within two hours, a senior administration official had leaked news of the Intelligence Committee session to journalists, hoping by his timing to have Congress blamed for its characteristic talkativeness on sensitive matters. The stories that appeared in the next day's editions of the *Washington Post* and the *Los Angeles Times* included reports that President Reagan had called Panamanian President Eric Arturo Delvalle on July 15 to inform him about the new covert action. The only problem was that an account of the Delvalle conversation, and several other facts in the articles, had never been given to the senators during their briefing.

"It was not even subtly done," said Senator Boren of Oklahoma. "It was so heavy-handed, the items leaked so obviously came from the administration." Even the Republican Senator Alfonse M. D'Amato of New York said at the time that the details of the finding had obviously been leaked by White House officials in an effort to "minimize the political damage" to Vice President George Bush.

Noriega, however, who didn't really understand American domestic politics, still believed that former CIA director George Bush was his best chance at improving his standing in Washington, and he went to extraordinary lengths to create a back channel to the vice president. Reagan was too ideological, and Michael Dukakis and the Democrats were too naive. Bush was more his style—the pragmatic former intelligence chief.

Noriega assigned several Panamanian officials to work on this link. Among them was Alberto Calvo, Noriega's ambassador to Tokyo, whose disheveled hair and protruding stomach masked a brilliance and charisma that had made him an effective operator in the Orient. Calvo's ingeniously chosen target was George Bush's businessman brother, Prescott Bush, who walked into Calvo's lair looking for Japanese business connections.

Calvo's introduction to Prescott Bush came through Robert Trent Jones, Jr., a golf-course architect and political player in the Far East who had done much to help Cory Aquino find friends in the United States. Jones was a longtime friend of the Bush family, and when Prescott came hunting for business, he introduced him to Calvo. The Panamanian, one of the wealthiest and most senior diplomats in Japan, had a rich store of connections.

And Calvo knew an opportunity when he saw it. To open doors to the Japanese business world for Prescott Bush was to curry favor with the brother of the man who might be the next president. Among others, Calvo, according to Trent Jones, was the one who introduced Prescott Bush to John Aoki, Noriega's favorite Japanese businessman. Aoki, who spoke Spanish well and was married to a Brazilian, took some of the projects Panama couldn't sell elsewhere, such as the tourist development of Contadora Island. In return for handling some of Noriega's less attractive projects, he gained rich construction deals such as a hydroelectric dam, projects in the Colón Free Trade Zone, and he hoped to share in any new Panama Canal project. Aoki had told Calvo that he didn't much respect Prescott Bush, but he wanted entree to his brother. Trent Jones said that it didn't take long for Calvo's matchmaking to produce results. On May 12, 1988, Prescott Bush and Aoki signed an agreement with a government-run Chinese construction company to build an $18 million golf course and resort in Shanghai. Trent Jones Jr. would be the designer.

Now that Calvo had done Prescott Bush a favor, he wanted a favor in return. He wanted a conduit to George Bush. When first asked about his ties to Calvo, Prescott Bush's secretary denied he even knew about Calvo. Thereafter, Prescott Bush said he knew Calvo but he hadn't introduced him to Aoki (Trent Jones insisted that it was Calvo who made the introduction). Finally, the Bush brother even conceded they had talked Panama politics. Calvo "was interested in my getting the vice president interested in Panama to bring about a certain situation," Prescott Bush said. "But I don't get involved in those things." Calvo told friends the contact failed because Prescott Bush wasn't shrewd or influential enough. Noriega's aides did say they gained one important message from President Bush: that the American military didn't plan to intervene in Panama. But Noriega could read that in newspapers. Whatever resulted from the Calvo-Bush link made less difference to Noriega than the fact of the connection. It delighted Noriega's perversely conspiratorial mind that one of his most important allies helped make the connections for a deal for the vice president's brother.

The Panamanian dance with Prescott Bush—and earlier with the vice president's former chief of staff, Daniel Murphy—showed the lengths to which Noriega would go to find a conduit to the vice president. It also demonstrated how imaginative Noriega could be in finding conduits. None of it worked, however: George Bush kept his distance.

Having circumvented Noriega's back-channel efforts, and gotten out in front of the drug-dictator issue, Bush should have been feeling pretty good about the whole Panama situation as his election drive came to a close—at least one would have thought so. In September 1988, however, the Bush Panama watch started becoming apprehensive again. They feared that the campaign might be charged with holding back administration efforts to unseat Noriega—a true and potentially damaging charge—but, even more, feared that administration inaction would prompt President Eric Arturo Delvalle to resign. Delvalle, the well-bred millionaire who loved the social life, was growing tired of the underground. The threat of resignation was the only leverage he had, and he used it frequently; yet such a move as his retirement so close to election could undermine the campaign's efforts to keep Panama out of the headlines.

Throughout the 1988 campaign, Bush strategists had monitored Panama policy closely to make sure nothing occurred that could hurt them. The point man was Colonel Samuel J. Watson III, who attended most interagency sessions on the vice president's behalf. "If you see anything happening, we want to know about it right away," Craig Fuller told Watson. Watson's new importance was so openly acknowledged that, before one session, officials jokingly bent to kiss his ring.

The secret minutes from one of the weekly working group meetings on Panama, held at the State Department in mid-September, provide insight into how the campaign shaped almost every decision in the matter. "Again the notion was raised of deferring decisions until after the election," the minutes said. "Sam Watson of the vice president's office sought to make clear that there is no desire to avoid putting pressure on Noriega prior to the election. Quite to the contrary, the kind of pressure they want to avoid is stories about bickering between the U.S. agencies. They do not mind in the least stories manifesting greater pressure on Noriega."

The meeting reviewed a decision made by the Southern Command, the U.S. embassy, and the local CIA station chief that military television, which reaches most Panamanians, be used as a means of presenting accurate news on Panama. "Too bad we didn't have support six months ago," the State Department report said. "We will follow up with [the Pentagon] and try to structure a useful program."

But like many meetings at that time, worries revolved around Delvalle. He was the administration's Achilles heel—a vain man who had always played all sides of the political spectrum before deciding what served his interests best. Washington's own wiretaps of Delvalle's phone conversations indicated that he might start trying to play the Noriega card again and that he was giving up on Washington. Officials talked about him like a wayward child who had to be brought back into line.

The Pentagon's Robert Pastorino suggested at the meeting that the working group come up with a contingency plan for the very real possibility of Delvalle's resignation. "We also recognize the problem of staffing such a contingency plan for fear of creating a self-fulfilling prophecy," the memo recounting the meeting said.

The officials at the meeting outlined a two-pronged strategy to deal with Delvalle. First, it would fly him to Washington and treat him presidentially, thus massaging his ego. Second, it would explore means of damage control in case he abandoned ship anyway.

Many of the U.S. officials had lost any respect they had once had for Delvalle. He had made several trips to the U.S. on American military aircraft during the crisis, but he often seemed more interested in horse-buying and horse-racing than overthrowing Noriega. Stories to that effect had appeared in the Panamanian press, making light of the underground president and his U.S.-sponsored outings. Only the United States continued to recognize him as the rightful leader of Panama.

"Delvalle is scheduled to come to the U.S. October 7 to receive our promised intelligence briefing," the memo from the working group meeting said. "DoD [the Department of Defense] asked whether he will be counseled against foolish activities such as buying racehorses. I answered yes, he had learned his lesson." The Pentagon argued that the visit should be delayed until after the election, the memo said. Why take a chance when the Bush campaign was going so well? But others at the meeting successfully argued against any postponement. Their argument: Why risk Delvalle's resignation?

Yet the Americans wanted to keep Delvalle on a short rein. They wanted to ensure that Noriega's former puppet president now responded to their string-pulling. "The visit will presumably proceed on schedule," the memo said. "The CIA rep said that several European journalists have expressed interest in interviewing Delvalle. I agreed this was a good idea, provided Delvalle was willing to do it and we carefully coached him beforehand."

For Delvalle and the Panamanian opposition, the U.S. post-election period was the greatest disappointment of all. Senior officials had promised Delvalle that if he remained patient, the Reagan administration would use the transition period either to negotiate or to leverage Noriega out, but Delvalle soon discovered the promises had been designed primarily to keep him quiet.

Nothing would happen while Reagan remained in office. The U.S. president didn't want to risk any operation that might result in his leaving office on a sour note. In addition, some of his advisers were resentful that Bush and James Baker, the new secretary of state, had undermined the president when he appeared to be within days of gaining Noriega's removal.

The reasoning was: Why help Bush after he's hurt us? "They didn't let us get rid of the turd," said one Reagan administration official at the time, "so let's hand it over to them, warm and steamy. We might have acted differently if we had seen Bush as being on our side on this issue."

Secretary of State George Shultz pressed for action, and sought cabinet-level meetings on the matter, but National Security Adviser Colin Powell wouldn't even schedule a session with the president over Noriega.

Delvalle felt humiliated and depressed in late November. Pentagon official Robert Pastorino and Michael Kozak flew to Miami to try to cheer up him. "Let's put the cards on the table," said Delvalle. "You aren't going to do anything between now and the inauguration."

Kozak frowned. "You are probably right about that."

So Delvalle decided to shake matters up with a little private negotiating. He wrote a letter to Noriega, requesting talks, but first called the papal nuncio, who was visiting the pope in Rome to ask for advice on the wording of the letter.

"What are you trying to tell Noriega?" the nuncio asked.

"I want to touch his heart," replied Delvalle.

The nuncio held back a wicked chuckle. With the military, he suggested, Delvalle must touch some other organ.

However, the nuncio took the letter upon his return to Panama, and he passed it on to Noriega. Noriega sent a letter back to the nuncio, not even addressing it to Delvalle. He named two mediators, including the father of his mistress, David Amado.

The nuncio could see the talks wouldn't be serious. "I don't want to take part in a farce," he told Noriega. "Not with you and not with Delvalle."

Delvalle backed down once he realized Noriega's intention was to humiliate him. Noriega told the nuncio that he had no respect for a man whose place in history was as a puppet, first to him and then to the Americans. "Delvalle is no one," he said.

Nevertheless, Washington was worried about Delvalle. What would the United States do with all the money in escrow accounts, held by Delvalle's government in exile, if Delvalle himself resigned? The result could be a financial windfall for Noriega that would make ousting him all the more difficult. One intelligence report filed from Panama, dated early December, read:

> Noriega has dispatched two envoys to Miami to negotiate with President Delvalle, who had let it be known he was going to the U.S. for a medical checkup. According to sensitive special intelligence, Noriega told the envoys to adhere to his plan at all times and press Delvalle for concessions.
>
> Comment: Noriega probably sees Delvalle as the weakest link in U.S. Panama policy and will try to persuade him to give up his claim to the presidency, thereby unfreezing Panamanian assets in the U.S. Delvalle's apparent agreement to a secret meeting with the envoys raises questions about his determination to continue resisting Noriega.

To massage Delvalle's ego and prevent his feared defection, the White House finally consented to schedule a meeting between Delvalle and President Reagan on December 22. Delvalle wanted American action, but what he got was a photo opportunity.

"We admire your courage and what you are doing for democracy in Panama," said President Reagan. He said that he and the Bush administration would continue to support Delvalle's efforts. "It is unacceptable that Panama is in the hands of a dictator. What can we do to end this situation?"

Delvalle, taken aback by the tardiness and naiveté of the question, said Noriega would only be removed by force or through negotiations. He suggested reopening the negotiations through a third country, preferably through President Julio Maria Sanguinetti of Uruguay or, as an alternative, Spanish President Felipe Gonzalez.

When president-elect Bush asked him about Noriega's hold on the military, Delvalle replied sadly, "There are no cracks." Delvalle also warned that the opposition, by joining the May elections, was essentially recognizing Noriega's regime. "Noriega will not have an election only to lose it," said Delvalle. Delvalle knew. He had been elected vice president in a fraudulent election in 1984.

Bush used the meeting politically to counteract reports that he had unknown ties to Noriega that the dictator could use against him. The General would remain persona non grata under the Bush administration, the president-elect promised.

"During the campaign, there were rumors, no doubt spread by him, that he has my goods from the time I was director of the CIA," said Bush. "Well, nothing was forthcoming because he has no goods on me."

Delvalle asked that Bush's remarks be made public. National Security

Adviser Colin Powell remarked that other rumors should be cleared up in the press as well; any suggestions that people close to the vice president were talking to Noriega's envoys ought to be denied point-blank. "There are no negotiations nor are we thinking of negotiations," said Powell.

However, the superficial nature of the meeting convinced Delvalle that Panama was a secondary issue for incoming and outgoing administrations, a topic that would be attended to only when it couldn't be ignored.

Delvalle's aide, José B. Cardenas, ended the meeting in the superficial spirit in which it had been held. "Mr. President, it is important that this problem be solved now," he said. "I went to the University of Notre Dame and I remember the movie about Knute Rockne. So let's win one for the Gipper."

The meeting ended with some nervous laughter. The Gipper saw his guests out of the room, stage right. The drama returned to Panama, where Noriega prepared to steal an election.

CHAPTER TWENTY

PSYCHOLOGICAL WARFARE

The masses have a great weakness: their scarce or nonexistent ability to think. . . . They have abdicated this power to the elites. . . . We can make them think as we want and move in the direction we like.

—LIEUTENANT COLONEL NORIEGA, IN HIS BOOK
PSYCHOLOGICAL OPERATIONS, 1975

President Manuel Solis Palma walked nervously across the spacious living room of Panama's presidential palace. He threw open the two large glass doors that opened onto the second-floor stone balcony, and surveyed the disturbing scene below.

The panorama below the whitewashed, Moorish-style palace was usually placid: waves gently lapping against mossy restraining walls, small fishing boats trailing nets, and lovers strolling along the pier. Below him on May 10, 1989, however, were three armored personnel carriers emptying out armed soldiers with guns locked and loaded. Some set up machine-gun positions, and others looked through binoculars for unseen enemies. Solis Palma's lunch guests slowly followed their worried president onto the balcony. They included senior officials and a couple of Panamanian ambassadors home on leave. They and Solis Palma feared a coup d'état had begun. They didn't know who had launched it—only that they were likely to be some of its intended victims.

Solis Palma had reason to feel guilty. Two days earlier Noriega's candidates had fared miserably in presidential elections, and he had begun to plot quietly against the General. Solis Palma was one of the old foxes of Panamanian politics. He'd spent the early 1970s in exile after opposing military rule; but time had tempered his combativeness, and opportunism and economic misery had prompted him to accept Noriega's offer to supplant ousted President Eric Arturo Delvalle in February 1988. Solis Palma's lifetime dream had been to become president, and reaching a Faustian compromise with Noriega had been an acceptable cost. However, after the landslide vote against Noriega's candidates, by a margin of more than two to one, Solis Palma and his friends figured the General's luck had finally run out.

General Noriega was weaker and more isolated than ever before. Election rules had allowed him to send soldiers to vote several times at different polling places, but ballot counts showed that even they had turned on the Comandante. In desperation, Noriega had ordered his troops to storm ballot-counting places after dark, firing their guns in the air and pilfering tally sheets. Women had fled so quickly that the floors of polling places were littered with high heels. Yet more than two days after the election, the Electoral Tribunal still hadn't dared declare a result, and puppet President Solis Palma hadn't heard a word from his vanished puppeteer. Over lunch, Solis Palma had been exploring alternatives with his closest allies that would leave him and the ruling party in power. Almost all of the ideas required Noriega's resignation.

Solis Palma's guilty conscience made him fear the worst, so he sighed in relief when the soldiers pointed the machine guns away from the palace and didn't climb the stairs after him. These troops had come to protect him. But from what? And why hadn't Noriega told his president he was sending troops? Now Solis Palma was angry. His headquarters had been surrounded, and—as was usual—Noriega's president hadn't the slightest idea what was going on.

Noriega wasn't down and out, as Solis Palma and his friends thought. He had merely made a tactical retreat after a disastrous battle. Now he was determined to come back and win the war. The troops were at the palace because opposition candidates were making their way in that direction in a car caravan. Noriega was at war, and his president's sensitivities were the least of his troubles.

Solis Palma's lunch guests, talkative and conspiratorial before their interlude on the balcony, returned to their dessert uncertain and silent. They were paralyzed by concern that the General knew they had been engaged in high treason. They feared Noriega's eyes and ears were everywhere. Certainly his hand seemed to be.

"... *Sun Tzu (in his book "The Art of War," 500 B.C.), in that distant epoch, mentioned that true war is waged in the minds of man, and that if man succeed in gaining such a mind, man has won the war. So for him, the best war does*

not require violence. For example, if one succeeds in terrifying a certain coun-
try, victory can be had without yielding men, money, or arms, thus reaching
the objective without resorting to violence. " —Noriega

The General was hidden away with two or three of his key advisers and officers. From his bunker at Fort Amador, he was toiling to undo his most serious mistake yet: letting elections proceed and then bungling the fraud. Advisers, unwilling to tell Noriega how unpopular he was, instead said the election was winnable or at least pilferable. Noriega had convinced himself that the Americans had exaggerated opposition to his rule. Noriega wouldn't allow pollsters to include his name on any survey, however, so the government's preelection estimates only partially predicted the extent of the public mood against him.

Noriega had made several critical miscalculations during the run-up to the May 7 elections, a democratic inconvenience the Panamanians had agreed to as part of the bargain to gain control of the Panama Canal. Put most simply, he had miscalculated his own ability to manipulate voting rolls and buy votes in the face of national opposition to his rule.

In the interest of maintaining absolute control, his ticket had included his business partner Carlos Duque as president, his brother-in-law Ramón Sieiro as vice president, and, as his second vice president, Aquilino Boyd, the man who had given him his start by recommending him for a spot at the Peruvian Military Academy. These three men's closeness to Noriega drove home the fact that the vote was a plebiscite on his rule.

Two days before the election, at a meeting of his top advisers, one Noriega adviser, Rodrigo Espino, recommended that Noriega cancel the vote. He presented a disastrous poll by the University of Panama that predicted the extent of sentiment against him. However, National Assembly candidates argued against such a move, having been promised seats as payoffs for loyalty and for services such as breaking strikes.

The military officers preparing the fraud also assured Noriega that they had cheated enough to bring a victory.

"We have only three days until the election," said Noriega. But that was all he said. The chronically indecisive dictator never decided whether the vote should go ahead or be canceled—so it went forward.

And anyway, his allies had put hundreds of known opposition voters' names on registration lists far from their homes; he had changed rules so that military men could vote at any polling station (and they voted early and often); and he created enough parties to give him an edge at tabulation time. By law, the parties each had a vote to settle disputes, and Noriega had an 8–3 edge. He had also dealt American efforts to help the opposition a severe blow by spreading the news that the Americans had funneled $10 million to his opponents, and by arresting the American coordinator of an altogether ineffective clandestine radio operation a month before elections.

Despite all that, Noriega's vote-watchers, led by Major Daniel Delgado, began to panic when the first returns showed a more than 2–1 landslide against their candidates. After the polls closed at 6 P.M., Noriega plotted an uncharacteristically heavy-handed assault on counting stations. Bands of armed men, many in civilian clothes, raided schoolhouses, gymnasiums, and boxing rings to confiscate the tabulation sheets. At a boxing ring in the Atlantic port city of Colón, where Roberto Duran had begun his career, they fired their guns into the air and frightened off the local men and women quietly counting. All that was left behind were new tabulation sheets, with unrecognizable signatures. The military stole most of the ballots, but the opposition ran off with plenty.

The opposition's representatives in Washington were oblivious to the tragedy taking place, however, and their actions showed why they had been so ham-handed in forcing Noriega from office. President Delvalle, Ambassador Sosa, and their cronies and families partied in the conference room of the embassy. They had already run up bills of several thousand dollars during the weekend at Washington's elite Jockey Club. Now, many of them laughed about the previous night's episode of *Miami Vice,* in which the FBI and CIA had tried to save a tropical dictator with whom the vice president was deeply involved. Drunk and oddly jubilant, they opened up bottles of Dom Perignon, paid for out of an escrow account filled with Panamanian state funds. The blasts of the corks flying coincided oddly with the paramilitary troops shooting up vote-counting places in Panama.

Even the opposition's ineptness, however, couldn't hide Noriega's blunder. One of the first of the international observers to cry foul was former President Jimmy Carter, a national hero in Panama for his signing of the Canal Treaties.

Noriega figured Carter wouldn't condemn the vote, for fear of fueling new opposition to the implementation of his treaties in Washington. Carter had met with Noriega for more than an hour on the day before elections, and he was shocked that Noriega didn't even entertain the prospect of defeat. When Carter tried again to reach Noriega after the balloting ended, hoping to mediate some sort of a solution, the General wouldn't even take his calls. Carter had even convinced the Roman Catholic Church to delay the release of its own private count to allow a mediated solution.

Carter saw ballots that were fraudulent and heard tales of the violence. He wanted to speak out, but Noriega's people locked him out of the Atlapa Convention Center. That only made him angrier. So the former president walked across the street to attack Noriega at a relocated press conference in the lobby of the Marriott Hotel, where journalists circulated in the lobby. Carter confirmed the Catholic Church's private vote count that said the opposition had won by a 3–1 margin, and reported that Noriega's "military dictatorship" was replacing original tally sheets with false ones and "taking the elections by fraud."

Back at Fort Amador, the pockmarks that scarred Noriega's face had deepened, the only sign to the outsider that he was feeling stress. Noriega's ruling party colleagues were demoralized and fighting with each other, each trying to escape blame for the election disaster. Noriega's brother-in-law and his vice presidential candidate, Ramón Sieiro, blamed the ruling party, and the ruling party leader, Carlos Duque, blamed Sieiro. Even officers were uncertain, muttering to each other that this time *El Viejo*— the old man—wouldn't survive.

But Noriega was at his best when he was down. He seemed attracted to crisis like a moth to a flame. He had lived most of his life as an underdog, and he had seemed uncomfortable on those rare occasions when he was unthreatened, sinking into bouts of depression and drunkenness.

After forty-eight hours out of view of even some of his closest advisers, Noriega reemerged in characteristic fashion. On the morning of Solis Palma's lunch, he phoned three or four officers to relay birthday greetings and, at least in one case, congratulations on a newborn. His secretary, Marcella Tason, invited Noriega's close friends to a weekend party at his beach house. Those two moves sent a message of quiet confidence to his more doubtful supporters. Within hours, Panama's rumor mill, affectionately known as "Lip Radio," would spread the word throughout the country that Noriega was back. Rumors that Noriega was through disappeared overnight, and possible rebels came back into line.

> *"The duty of all members of the National Guard is to inform the directorate level immediately of any dangerous rumor and explain in detail what was heard. . . . The National Guard must systematically orient people against these rumors that tend to create dangerous activity and divisions among our population. You have to hold your guard against this enemy* [of rumor]." —Noriega

Later that same morning, Noriega met with his most important allies— his Strategic Military Council, known by the Spanish acronym CEM—to discuss the options. He knew that rallying the military behind him was the first priority, so he told fellow officers that the civilians had failed in their election. The military would have to intercede and restore order to the country. For them, it was an attractive message. Most had never liked the idea of elections in the first place. Noriega, the master manipulator, was back at work.

Noriega didn't participate in their debate, but merely listened. He wanted to measure his subordinates' loyalty. Major Daniel Delgado thought the General should use whatever force necessary to enforce the election victory of his candidates. Delgado, an officer charged with ensuring election victory, considered the success of the government candidates a personal test. A representative of a group of younger officers, Captain Joseph Balma, had a more ingenious and conspiratorial alternative. He said Noriega should allow the opposition's presidential candidate, Guillermo Endara, to be named president, arguing that this would prompt Washington to lift the sanctions and thus break Panama's international isolation. Balma argued that once the sanctions were lifted, Noriega could find a pretext to block Endara's succession.

However, Noriega wanted an option that restored his power to manipulate matters from backstage. An option to annul the election appealed to him most; yet, as usual at critical moments, he was wracked by indecision. He ended the meeting and put off any verdict. He told one aide that he had until September 1 to make a final decision, when Solis Palma's term ended.

But events forced his hand.

Against all his expectations, the usually cowardly opposition candidates were showing uncharacteristic physical courage. Standing in the flatbed of a red Toyota pickup, the three opposition candidates were leading a caravan throughout the city. G-2 agents stationed along the Avenida Central radioed that the candidates were headed toward sacred Noriega territory— the poor barrios of the city's Chorrillos sector. Panama's poor cheered the candidates as they snaked their way toward the neighborhoods near Noriega's headquarters and the presidential palace.

General Noriega had never seen such courage among his opposition, and he had to stop it. He feared they would seize his presidential palace. It was time to remind the opposition who was in charge. His civilian opponents had usually been timid, but they smelled the General's blood. Like Solis Palma, they sensed that Noriega was on the ropes, and that a couple of bold actions might deliver the final blows that could bring him down.

The American embassy, which had closely followed and privately advised opposition candidates, was monitoring every move. To a certain extent, U.S. officials had prompted the caravan. Diplomats made clear to the candidates that the Bush administration would have trouble backing them more strongly if the candidates couldn't rally Panamanians behind them. The candidates protested that the Roman Catholic Church's private vote count showed they had won with some 70 percent of the vote—wasn't that enough? But what the State Department needed was a Philippines-like people-power demonstration. The candidates, however, didn't want to risk Panamanians' lives, and frankly didn't think thousands would come into the streets to march on their behalf. So they set out in a car caravan with a relatively small number of followers.

Washington had much invested in the opposition's election victory. In one of his first covert-action programs, Bush had authorized a $10 million operation designed to force Noriega from office, a largely unsuccessful effort that relied on sporadic clandestine radio broadcasts and campaign funds funneled through third countries. The U.S. organizer of the broadcasts had been captured, however, and a news leak about the covert program resulted in Noriega's getting more mileage from attacking American intervention than the opposition got from the money.

The embassy kept in constant contact with the candidates' caravan as it traveled through the city. Billy Quijano, an opposition activist with close ties to the Americans, spoke through a secure cellular phone to political officer Michael Polt. The officer riddled the Panamanian with questions about the caravan's location, the number of cars, and the strength of PDF resistance.

"People are on the streets cheering us," he said in English. "Some are coming to balconies. The caravan is of some fifty vehicles, perhaps a few more or less. There are very few military. Just some on the sides of the streets. And some of those wave to us."

The embassy official asked a question.

"No," answered Quijano. "No problems yet. Wait a minute. They are stopping us. We are at Santa Ana Square. We are getting out. The candidates are getting down from their truck. We are being stopped by troops."

The candidates clambered down to confront the officer in charge of some two dozen troops who were blocking their path to Santa Ana Square. The symbolism was rich. Panama's first president had been inaugurated there, and much of the country's history had occurred within a stone's throw of Santa Ana cathedral. The poor residents of the area were shouting taunts at the soldiers and encouraging the candidates to hold their ground.

Presidential candidate Guillermo Endara's ample stomach rested against the shield of one of a dozen riot policemen. He was a kindly lawyer who had fought military rule for more than two decades, but never from such close quarters. His taller, lanky vice presidential candidate, Ricardo Arias Calderón, began negotiating with the officer. With a philosophy degree from France's Sorbonne and a lifetime of studying language and ideas, he measured each word carefully and enunciated his requests carefully. It was an oddly humorous scene: "Laurel and Hardy meet the Panamanian Military."

Beside Endara and Arias Calderón was Billy Ford, the third man on the opposition ticket but by far the most popular among Panama's people. He was the feistiest and most charismatic of the candidates, a playboy entrepreneur who was complimented by questions about his amorous reputation. "Well, I don't like little boys," he would say, referring to the rumored predilections of Panama's dictator. Ford's nickname was "Pica Gallo"— the fighting cock.

"We only want a peaceful manifestation," said Arias Calderón to the lieutenant, whose orders were obviously coming from a senior officer. "Can we have permission to turn around in the square and turn back?" Calderón laughed to himself about the symbolism of the standoff: the opposition's unarmed willingness to talk versus the military's weapons and inflexibility.

For about an hour, the candidates stood at the center of the road leading into the square and riot police stood nervously across from them, flinching at the taunts from the crowd. Calderón continued to request an intermediary with whom they would negotiate the peaceful end to their march. But as the candidates patiently waited, Noriega was preparing to spring a carefully orchestrated trap. He opted to send his opposition a violent message they wouldn't forget. He ordered his "Dignity Battalion" into action. The Dignity Battalions, known more descriptively as "the Digbats," were an irregular paramilitary group that had been created in 1988.

"Strategy is carried out deceptively by combining wit and skill against an enemy and thereby winning more easily when the combat turns to a direct clash of the battling masses. The surprise factor can be executed militarily in concert with psychological operations, which together diminish the fighting power of the enemy." —Noriega

The Digbats had been trained for weeks for just such an event by Panamanian officers who had been separated from their PDF duties for this special assignment. Noriega's new Cuban advisers, who had started arriving in February 1988, had trained the officers. The model was the Cuban national revolutionary militias, which had been copied in Nicaragua as Turbas Divinas.

Noriega lacked Cuba's and Nicaragua's ideologically fervent cadres, so he'd filled Digbat ranks with a motley collection of psychopaths, criminals, and unemployed toughs from the barrios. Their ranks also included soldiers from Noriega's Special Forces, who could use the appearance of violent chaos to carry out specific missions. The Digbats arrived on the scene like violence-bent thugs in a bad B-movie. Some carried two-by-fours pierced with rusty nails, and rubber hoses bent from misuse. Other wielded steel reinforcing rods, which they beat against their palms menacingly as they awaited the order to attack. They wore purple-and-blue polyester T-shirts, still creased from their boxes. White letters were stenciled on the shirts: BATALLÓN DIGNIDAD. The shirts, which hadn't been seen before, were a pragmatic necessity, allowing soldiers to differentiate the Digbats from their Panamanian targets in the melee that followed. Their ranks were sprinkled with women—a clear effort to show that these pro-Noriega "volunteers" represented society—but the women would hit the ground when the fighting began.

The Digbats trainers had prepared them to attack Americans, and their angry voices screamed, "*Yanquí,* no, *Yanquí,* no." But the only enemies before them were the small collection of mostly Panamanian businessmen who surrounded the candidates. Some began to slip away down side streets as the confrontation neared.

A middle-aged man in the midst of the Digbats, not wearing their identifying T-shirt, almost imperceptibly lowered his hand. That was the signal. Noriega's thugs charged through the riot police line toward the shocked candidates. It was the sort of attack Panama's elite business class hadn't ever seen before and never expected. And the attack would come near Noriega's childhood home at the mouth of the mean-streets alley of "Sal Si Puedes"—"Get out if you can." They failed to heed the advice.

> "*Surprise is a way of attaining superiority. . . . When surprise is greatest, confusion and the decay of the enemy's spirit are the natural consequences, and the maximum result is that the enemy offers practically no resistance.*"
> —Noriega

When the swarm of Digbats attacked, Endara bent over to reach for his glasses, which had been knocked to the ground. The kindly lawyer, who had quietly opposed military rule for more than two decades, could see only a violent blur around him. One of the Digbats crushed the glasses before he could reach them. When he tried to stand again, the same thug hit him over the head with a steel pipe. Endara, a rotund 240 pounds, looked like the class nerd being beaten by the schoolyard bully. Endara's bodyguard amazingly lifted the hefty presidential candidate over the prone bodies of the fearful and injured to escape down a side street.

The scholarly Arias Calderón was toppled by the crush of bodies before he could be hit. He remembers now fearing that he might "suffocate for Panama" before being spirited away by his bodyguards into a nearby shop. He was later smuggled out of the area on the backseat floor of a taxi.

But Noriega feared Billy Ford most, and Ford got the worst of it. Among the three, he was the most dangerous to Noriega—the only one among them who had the charisma and force to motivate Panamanians of all social classes. Besides, Noriega's resentment of Ford predated the election. When Noriega was fourteen, he had been a frequent houseguest of Demetrio Porras, the country's Socialist party leader. Porras had considered Noriega a boy of potential, yet Porras's three daughters had been much more taken with the young, dashing, well-off Billy Ford than the homely and poor Noriega.

Before the 1984 elections, Noriega had met Ford for the first time in years and said he wanted to discuss Panama's future with him. Ford, who had been exiled by Noriega's G-2 in the mid-1970s, said he would talk only on one condition: that the spirit of Norita—Porras's most beautiful daughter, who had died in an automobile crash—would be their silent witness. Ford's was a psychological ploy to protect against the General's usual duplicity. Noriega sneered that no witness was needed, and the two men never spoke again.

When the uniformed military let Noriega's paramilitary through their lines, Billy Ford jumped into the rear seat of his car. One bodyguard, Alexis Guerra, sat with his back to the window, facing Ford. Just a few weeks earlier, he had been guarding American embassy official Terence Kneebone, the head of the United States Information Service in Panama. The company that employed Guerra provided all the bodyguards for embassy officials in Panama. At Ford's request, however, Kneebone had released Guerra to protect Billy Ford. Ford wanted someone he could trust.

Wild shots rang out, windows were shattered, and voices screamed.

"*Viejo* [old man], I am shot," Alexis gurgled to Billy Ford.

Ford protested. "Alexis, hold it, hold it, you are not shot."

Alexis gave him a fixed look. "I am dying," he said. Alexis threw up blood on Ford's white shirt and the seat.

When Ford saw his other bodyguard was shot, too, he climbed into the front seat and out the driver's side. One of the Digbats hit him with a clenched fist, throwing him back against the seat. Ford bounced back, like a punching bag, and he was swinging. Another punch sent him back against the seat. Shaken, bloody, and disoriented—half of his white shirt saturated in his bodyguard's blood—Ford stumbled along the sidewalk past a video shop and its posters advertising Sean Connery's thriller, *The Presidio*. As he was pushed forward by a uniformed soldier, apparently trying to lead him to safety, yet another attacker took a swipe at him with a pipe. An angry, bloodied Ford, with his arms outspread, tried to avoid the swinging pipe. He threw yet another punch at the phantom attacker through the haze of his blood-covered eyes. Ironically, it was a military officer who finally rescued Ford, pushing him in the back of a paddy wagon which would take him to jail, where, during a post-midnight session before a groggy but obedient judge, he would be booked for disturbing public order.

U.S. Ambassador to Panama Arthur H. Davis later said that the attack on Ford had been an assassination attempt gone wrong. That was good anti-Noriega propaganda, but U.S. intelligence officials said the Digbats killed the man they had targeted. They wanted Alexis Guerra's head, to send a message to all Panamanians who chose to defend the Americans and, according to their indoctrination, their oligarchic allies. U.S. intelligence officials said the assassin put the gun against Guerra's back and then pulled the trigger. "This was a grudge killing," an intelligence source said. "The man who shot Alexis knew exactly what he was doing. Ford went free because he was intended to go free."

"The German poet Schiller said that war is glorious because it is the impulse of human destiny. In any war, regardless of the winner, the defeated are always the Philistines, the 'bourgeois,' the men in whose hands social life freezes and hardens. They find that their birthrights or that which strengthens their lifelong privileges—ideas, institutions, values, customs—must have an immutable permanence. These are the restraining elements of the historical process. However, all wars produce a revolution for both the triumphant and the defeated." —Noriega

Noriega's attack on the candidates was a master stroke in a psychological war to regain control of Panama. It was a calculated risk that paid Noriega immediate dividends. Noriega, a man who understands the power of television perhaps better than any dictator before him, had given his senior officers directing the operation instructions to allow television cameramen to continue rolling, and to give still photographers room to record all the violence. "Didn't you ever wonder why journalists were allowed to continue to work there, and why all their film was allowed to be shipped out of Panama without a problem?" his spokesman Mario Rognoni would ask later. "It wasn't an accident."

Noriega reckoned he had more to win than lose through the publicity of his ruthlessness. The bloody photographs of Billy Ford, reprinted in magazines around the world, became the symbol of Noriega's repressive Panama. In another country, the action might have brought the disgusted masses onto the streets to rebel against Noriega, but in Panama, where the opposition is largely made up of well-off Panamanians who would rather make a buck than a revolution, Noriega had delivered an efficient and economic blow. What appeared to be a dictator out of control to the world was really a dictator carefully measuring every blow.

By attacking the most courageous of his Panamanian opponents so brutally, he had frightened tens of thousands into submission. He had struck the head of the opposition, and the whole body shuddered. Opposition legislative candidates disappeared into hiding; government officials who had considered resigning were now cowed into continued submission; and Washington wasn't ready to risk military action to unseat him.

"It is not without reason that Hollywood and Broadway are the greatest causes of the 'Americanization' of modern customs. . . . Don't we know that it has almost become a vice of modern man that he can not live without his cinema and TV set? . . . There is not even the smallest doubt that by using this power we can impose our ideas and influence on the masses." —Noriega

Noriega couldn't delay a decision on the elections any longer. He couldn't allow Endara to take office, but he also couldn't impose his own candidates on a country that had so totally rejected them. In his own curious mind, he was left no choice but to annul the elections. It would buy him time and remove the opposition's rallying point: a stolen election.

The annulment would also defuse some of the international outrage that he expected to follow the attack on the candidates. "You run out of time when you see violence at that level," his spokesman Mario Rognoni would say later. "He was already moving toward annulling the elections, but that event was an accelerator."

Noriega had craftily combined the shock of physical attack with the confusion of the annulment to paralyze his enemies and buy himself time.

"Using a stratagem, one tries with crafty skill to deceive and conquer the enemy, thus avoiding direct physical combat between the battling masses. Militarily, the so-called 'surprise' factor can only complement psychological operations, since both seek to diminish the enemy's combat power."
—Noriega

Again, Noriega's enemies had underestimated their resourceful opponent, who by mid-1989 had mastered the art of survival. His country was sinking, his circle of supporters was shrinking, and his international opposition was growing. It seemed obvious to all that somehow, some way, Noriega had to go. But the General hung on, sometimes seeming to endure by the strength of his wits alone. At other times, he patiently waited for his enemies to tire or lose interest.

Noriega's intimate knowledge of the United States, his rich sources of illicit income, his manifold international ties from two decades in intelligence, and his own quiet patience in the face of adversity allowed him to become the Bush administration's first and most enduring foreign policy problem. Outmanned and outgunned, he deployed his secret weapon of psychological warfare.

With the Americans unwilling to use their military might against Noriega, this became the most important field of battle; and Noriega's psychological-warfare arsenal was far richer than theirs. Noriega was so obsessed with the importance of the ancient art of psychological warfare that in 1971 he had created a special department within Panama's G-2 Military Intelligence body devoted only to this science. In 1975, he had written the book on psychological warfare that is quoted in italics throughout this chapter: *Psychological Operations.*

Like his speeches, it rambles and name-drops, citing in a positive light the likes of Genghis Khan, Hitler, and Lenin, whom he cites as experts who used psychological operations to rule nations and conquer enemies. But by 1988, Noriega considered himself one of the world's leading authorities on this ancient art. American officials came to agree. Even if in the end he should falter and be deposed, Noriega was humiliating the United States as no dictator had before him, turning up his pockmarked nose at all manner of threat and pressure.

In his psychological war, he was also acquiring new weapons. By manipulating tax laws, he was able to shut down the last relatively balanced television station, Channel 4, which was owned by former foreign minister Fernando Eleta. He said Eleta owed back taxes far in excess of what he would be able to pay. Without resorting to the heavy-handed act of seizing the station, he had taken control of it.

Hoping to counter Noriega, the Bush administration undertook some "psy-ops" of its own. In answer to Noriega's attack on the candidates, Bush dispatched 1,882 army and marine reinforcements to Panama to augment some 10,000 that were already there. Since he had already decided not to risk American lives to unseat Noriega, his move was primarily aimed at defusing domestic criticism of his inaction and increasing the psychological pressure on Noriega.

It was President Bush's first major decision to use military force, yet it looked like nothing more than old-fashioned gunboat diplomacy. Army riflemen, marine assault troops, armored vehicles, and navy warships were all heading to Panama as a result of the White House's decision to beef up its presence. The ostensible reason for all this force was to protect the more than 40,000 Americans living in Panama. Ironically, however, Bush's action did more to help Noriega than hurt him—a critical misstep in a psychological confrontation.

Less than two days after the Digbats had attacked opposition candidates, the televised images of a badly beaten Billy Ford, his shirt saturated with his slain bodyguard's blood, had been replaced by the eager, camouflage-painted faces of American soldiers. The global story switched from Noriega's repression to America's gunboat diplomacy. And the Panamanian opposition, already cowed by the attack on the candidates, was content to wait for the American cavalry to save them.

Far more serious than the troop reinforcements were Bush's new instructions to the Southern Command, which seemed engineered to clear the decks for action and trigger an armed conflict with Noriega.

General Frederick Woerner, following orders from his superiors, had for many months instructed his officers to avoid confrontations with Noriega. When his troops had been harassed, he hadn't responded. When his treaty rights had been violated, he'd filed unanswered protests. Southcom soldiers started calling Woerner the "Wimpcom" commander, and they joked among themselves that their commanding officer's slogan was "Kiss Ass and Take Names Later." Woerner explained he only was following orders.

Now, however, Bush planned to get rid of Woerner and revise Southcom's orders. Woerner had angered Bush in March when he had given a speech suggesting that a policy vacuum in Washington made it impossible to formulate policy toward Panama—a true but unauthorized statement. From a trip to the Far East, Bush rifled off an angry telegram to the chairman of the Joint Chiefs of Staff, William J. Crowe, Jr., reprimanding the disloyal general. Woerner then sealed his own demise when he boarded a plane full of senators and congressmen who had come to observe the Panamanian elections, and lectured them on the dangers that they faced in Panama. Since they didn't have proper papers, he said, they were likely to be arrested. When Woerner told them that "diplomatic" means would have to be used to gain their release, the senators interpreted this as a warning that he would do nothing to help them.

When Woerner was relieved of his command, Noriega seized the moment to float rumors in the Panamanian press. One newspaper said Woerner had been removed for dealing in drugs; and another article said the Bush administration had removed Woerner as part of an agreement with Noriega. Noriega had long sought Woerner's replacement. Some of the value that might have been gained by Woerner's removal from Panama was defused by a clever campaign of disinformation.

"The rumor is like a tactical weapon, helping to 'Divide and Rule.' The bigger the lie, the more it is believed. That was part of Hitler's strategy of terror.

*The Nazis infected their country with defeatist rumors to create confusion and
a sense of demoralization; so that they could then carry out their smashing
victories. This way they created optimism and hope in their policies, however
blind and irrational they actually were."*   —Noriega

The tougher Bush policy began with the order that Southcom should
withdraw its 2,160 service members and their dependents who lived off-
base to military installations by July. These troops and dependents had
been de facto hostages; Noriega even had plans known to Southcom to
kidnap some of them should U.S. pressure on him increase. For months,
the military had balked at State Department requests to reduce this vulnerability, arguing that the costs and inconvenience were prohibitive.

The move theoretically cleared the decks for military action against
Noriega, so in mid-July the Southern Command started a series of military
exercises over a six-week period that were clearly engineered to remind
Noriega of his vulnerability. Operations were staged along the fifty-one-
mile Canal, and a causeway was stormed at a jointly used U.S.-Panama
base near the Pacific Coast (and beside Noriega's bunker). Troops even
mounted a helicopter-borne assault to show that they could protect or
evacuate Americans at the U.S. embassy complex in downtown Panama
City. The operations had several purposes. The maneuvers worked out
bugs that might cause problems if an operation were carried out against
Noriega, and they demonstrated to Noriega's fellow officers how vulnerable he was. Some hoped they might provoke the General into action
American troops would be forced to answer.

But Noriega even played the American maneuvers masterfully. He
backed off his long weeks of tweaking the American military, realizing that
the army was now willing to be provoked. "He was clever enough not to
be taunted by us into throwing the first punch," said one senior administration official months later. "It might all be over now if he'd taken our bait."

Instead of giving the Americans the excuse some officials wanted,
Noriega appeared on Panamanian television carrying mangoes to offer to
American soldiers at a guard station. "Do you dare eat this Panamanian
fruit, given in the spirit of peace?" he asked.

Noriega even turned the American maneuvers against Washington's
effort to find a "Latin solution" to the Noriega problem. In an effort to
internationalize pressure on Noriega, Bush had turned negotiations with
the dictator and his opposition over to the Organization of American
States. However, when delegates from the OAS came to Panama, Noriega
on at least three occasions organized meetings with them at a location that
he knew in advance would be shut off by the exercises. On one occasion,

the delegates arrived at his offices at Fort Amador just as American helicopters were bearing down and armored personnel carriers rumbled by.
Lack of coordination between the embassy and the Southern Command
had failed to alert Washington of this public relations danger.

Other times, Noriega would cancel a meeting with the OAS, apologizing
that it would need to be rescheduled because of American interference in
Panama's internal affairs—longhand for "maneuvers." When the General
finally did meet the OAS delegates, he preempted their efforts to bring
about his resignation by showing them video tapes of the exercises. It was
something none of them could publicly condone, no matter how much they
hated Noriega: the American heavy hand in action.

Washington, hamstrung by congressional restrictions and American
law, had more difficulty than Noriega with psychological warfare, which
at its best included the planting of lies and misinformation and the use of
government machinery to relay false messages. The CIA also lacked independent "assets" within the PDF that could be manipulated against
Noriega. America's efforts to convince PDF officers that Noriega was their
biggest threat were thus often ham-handed. They had to resort to the less
subtle means of a presidential news conference.

After the attack on the presidential candidates, Bush called reporters to
his compartment on Air Force One, on his way to a commencement
address at Mississippi State University, to call for Panamanian military
rebellion. "They ought to do everything they can to get Noriega out of
there," he said. "He's one man, and they have a well-trained force."

Noriega's psychological warfare was more intricate and subtle.
Noriega's message to his troops was that the U.S. and its Panamanian allies
were out to destroy the military, and only Noriega's continued rule could
ensure their protection. Noriega also spread tales of the brutal beating and
torture of officers who had betrayed him. Before the May 1989 elections,
he had sent the dozen or so officers who had participated in the March 1988
failed coup against him to provincial garrisons, so soldiers around the
country could see their desperate and emaciated state. He'd paraded them
in the garrison courtyards, wrapped in nothing but American flags, and
PDF officers had then taunted and beaten them. And it was clear to
Noriega's many allies that another Panamanian leader might make them
pay for their long years of corruption.

"Among the oldest examples [of psychological warfare] *we can mention is
Phillip of Macedonia and his son Alexander the Great, well known by all.
. . . Under the advice of his father, Alexander perfected a method of psychologi-
cal torture that was the hidden cause of many of his unexpected victories. It*

has a great resemblance to psychological operations of today used by certain modern totalitarian systems." —Noriega

With each week that Noriega remained in power, his psychological warfare grew more convincing and the American effort became less so. Troops had heard many American threats, yet Noriega remained in power, and a certain mystique came to surround him among his own troops. In the world of Caribbean superstition and Noriega's own carefully cultivated world of oriental mysticism, his troops grew to believe Noriega was invincible. This only increased their fear of him. Why stand up to a man whom even the Americans couldn't remove?

"In terms of psychological warfare, we have been outgunned and outmanned," said Lieutenant Commander Stephen Bloch, a naval intelligence officer at the U.S. Southern Command. Bloch noted that while Noriega had an entire division of his G-2 dedicated to psychological warfare, the Southern Command had assigned only two officers to the job.

Bloch had found many of his plans to take on Noriega psychologically were blocked in Washington, where the idea of psychological warfare was still an uncomfortable one. For instance, after the March 1988 coup, General Frederick Woerner had proposed to Washington that Southcom launch a psy-ops campaign against Noriega, but the idea had been rejected, as had a proposal by Woerner to withdraw all dependents from Panama City—a ploy designed to pressure Noriega by showing that the U.S. was clearing the decks for action. Washington turned down some of the plans, and simply didn't act on others. Senior officials hadn't wanted to disrupt ongoing negotiations with Noriega regarding his resignation.

Southcom had also found itself paralyzed when it needed to respond to Noriega's psy-ops measures. Traffic violations that resulted in $25 fines for Panamanians were bringing $250 fines for American soldiers. One soldier was stopped by PDF officers, and his American girlfriend was raped. Noriega's troops stopped American school buses full of children at gunpoint, because of licensing irregularities that had come about as a result of sanctions preventing Americans from paying taxes to Noriega's regime. Most gruesome, Noriega's regime had dropped a headless torso on the front driveway of a Panamanian lawyer, Marcus Ostrander, who had been pressing the Noriega regime hard on treaty-violation charges. The neatly wrapped body was only a few feet from the dark head. The message wasn't subtle, but it was effective.

In every case, the U.S. either didn't respond at all or responded slowly and ineffectively. "Because we wouldn't stand up, we were losing ground," said Bloch. "Noriega was nibbling away at our treaty rights."

"The inefficiency of American psychological operations has been demonstrated. Their radio broadcasts incited towns under Soviet domination to rebellion. When that rebellion occurred in Hungary and Czechoslovakia, the North Americans abandoned them. The same thing occurred with the Bay of Pigs invasion and on the 31st of March, 1975 in South Vietnam. Now nobody trusts the North Americans for similar operations." —Noriega

Noriega's confidence grew, while the morale of soldiers sank. Even after the May 1989 elections, the U.S. again found itself without alternatives, once the exercises failed to spook Noriega. But the exercises had to be abandoned because they had begun to be counterproductive: Noriega had seen the threat wasn't real and other Latin American countries were condemning the U.S. military pressure.

The Americans appeared to be muscle-bound giants trying to swat the troublesome gnat Noriega, yet every time one of the giants took a swipe, he seemed to hurt himself more than the General. Noriega responded quickly to every opportunity, while Southern leaders, fearful of a misstep, sent every decision to Washington; and responses were tardy when they came at all.

Despite the American missteps and Noriega's psychological warfare prowess, however, the General's troubles continued to worsen. Economic problems mounted, and the morale of Noriega's military continued to decline. The Bush administration, failing to cow Noriega militarily, decided to tighten its sanctions to isolate his closest supporters and allies. In early September, the U.S. Treasury listed the names of all the members of the Strategic Military Command and many other officials, all of whom were to be included in sanctions that had thus far only been aimed at the Noriega regime.

The aim was the same as the military exercises: to encourage fellow officers to rise up against Noriega and either kill him or remove him in a coup. U.S. intelligence agencies weren't sure how or when this strategy would work, but they had no other strategy: their own intelligence contacts were so poor and their knowledge of the PDF so limited that they could only hope that their show of military power, the increased international criticism of Noriega, and the new sanctions would convince officers that Noriega was more of a cost than a benefit.

But when American measures and Panamanian distress reached a critical mass in October, resulting in another coup attempt, Washington found itself too cumbersome, ill-prepared, and ham-handed to take advantage of a situation it had done so much to create.

"Von Clausewitz, in his classic work 'About War,' says, 'The less powerful the forces, the easier craftiness and wit will serve them. . . . The decidedly weak and small, who can't be saved by prudence, wile, and trickery present themselves as a last resort.' "   —Noriega

CHAPTER
TWENTY-ONE

UNFINISHED
BUSINESS

I blame the North Americans for my husband's death.
They only had to show off their power and equipment,
and his coup would have worked.

—ADELA BONILLA DE GIROLDI,
DECEMBER 1989

General Manuel Antonio Noriega had invited about a hundred of his closest friends to the christening of his new granddaughter. It was Sunday, October 1, 1989. The setting was San Jorge church, a tastelessly modern though mercifully small chapel that he had built inside the secure walls of his headquarters complex two years earlier. It was his answer to a Roman Catholic hierarchy that had begun to turn against him, and had been built without the Vatican's permission.

At just before 8 A.M., the first light broke through the blue stained glass onto the jewels that adorned the necks and wrists of the wives of Panamanian millionaires and politicians whose fates were so tied to Noriega that he could summon them to any event. Their husbands buzzed around the exultant and already drunk grandfather-General like flies circling the source of their survival.

Major Moisés Giroldi Vega, in charge of security for the event, mumbled his disgust to a fellow officer as he watched no less than five priests conduct the much-too-elaborate christening ceremony. Noriega, not able to co-opt the Catholic Church as a whole, had bought off enough priests to show that at least a percentage of God's servants were on his side. Everyone in Panama seemed to have a price. Giroldi also believed rumors that Noriega

369

had blackmailed Panama's archbishop, Monsignor Gregorio Marcus McGrath, whom Noriega had protected after he had run down and killed a man while driving home drunk from an outlying village a few years earlier.

But there really wasn't much Catholic about the ceremony. It seemed more to Giroldi like the celebration of a monarch who had collected this large swarm of parasites to worship himself. The child was adorned in a lace and satin christening gown that stretched several times further than its own length. Noriega was acting more like a king than a general looking after the welfare of his soldiers and people.

This self-styled king walked up to Giroldi at the rear of the chapel and barked some orders in a voice calculated to be overheard by others at the ceremony. "If you see any American helicopters come near, shoot them down," he said, his eyes appearing to Giroldi to be dilated and crazed. In the past, Giroldi's security officers always had been told to avoid confrontation with the gringos. Seeing Giroldi's look of disbelief, Noriega barked the order again. Then he laughed, intoxicated by his own power and, perhaps, his trademark Old Parr whiskey.

Major Giroldi laughed with the others when Noriega ordered his sentries to fire on American choppers, but inside he shuddered. He began to think that Noriega, who seemed constantly to be drunk or on mood-stabilizing injections, applied by his omnipresent doctor, was so crazed with his own power that he would order his troops to fire on Panamanians and—far more perilous—Americans. Giroldi would later tell CIA agents that it was at Noriega's christening party that he passed the point of turning back in a coup plot that he had been piecing together for several months.

Noriega had kept close watch on his officer corps, like a parent who has ample grounds to suspect delinquency among his children. Israeli intelligence, through Mike Harari, had tipped him off to the danger of an American-backed coup three weeks earlier.

However, even the master spy Noriega hadn't thought to suspect the soft-spoken Giroldi, who, in March 1988, had been the hero in blocking another coup attempt against Noriega. For that, he had been rapidly promoted from captain to major. He was a handsome officer, in a swarthy, chiseled way, trained at a military academy in Nicaragua during the anti-communist heyday of dictator Anastasio Somoza. At age thirty-eight, he'd never shown any signs of disloyalty to Noriega. Noriega had been the witness and sponsor at his wedding at the same San Jorge church just a year earlier, when Giroldi—at the request of Noriega—had joined other officers who were having their own marriages resealed in Catholic ceremo-

nies conducted by Noriega's puppet priests. But most of all, Giroldi owed
Noriega for protecting him after a serious dispute with the General's
brother-in-law, Major Manuel Sieiro, over which of them would run a
defense forces training academy. Instead of firing him, Noriega had promoted Giroldi to be chief of his headquarters security. Giroldi was one of
a half-dozen men Noriega allowed near him with a submachine gun.

Giroldi, a quiet man in whom fellow officers liked to confide, won allies
to his plot over a number of weeks. One was Captain Jesús George Balma,
the chief of special forces, who provided much of the brains behind the
venture. He was an ambitious and articulate leftist officer who had angered
the Americans with his arrogance while serving on a joint military committee that dealt with Panama Canal affairs. Giroldi's key ally in the scheme,
however, was Major Federico Olechea, a friend of Giroldi's who ruled the
most potent pro-Noriega force: the Battalion 2000. Giroldi needed Olechea's support or, at least, his neutrality if the coup were to succeed. He
thought he had it, and this, as much as anything else, prompted him to act.
Olechea even planned to dispatch many of his troops far from the scene
of the coup in San José, three hours from Panama City, where they
couldn't be summoned to save Noriega.

The remaining dangers to his coup could be handled only if the Americans were willing to block key roads and prevent helicopters and planes
from leaving vital airfields. The threats included the Israeli-trained Special
Forces, known as the UESAT, and the 5th Rifle Company at Fort Amador, led by one of Noriega's most loyal men. More troublesome yet was
the Cuban-trained 7th Rifle Company based near RíoHató, better known
in Panama as the Machos del Monte—"Macho Men of the Mountains."
No group was more loyal to Noriega or less influenced by his opposition.

The American help would be a simple affair: Giroldi would only be
asking the gringos to repeat their frequent, cage-rattling military exercises.
And Giroldi expected help: a not-so-quiet U.S. covert program had aimed
at encouraging a coup, and public statements suggesting U.S. support for
Panamanian coup-makers convinced Giroldi that Washington would be on
his side.

It was a critical miscalculation that would begin a course of joint action
with the Americans that would end in disaster after a series of misunderstood messages, communications botch-ups, intelligence failures, presidential indecision, and then a post-coup cover-up, during which the Bush
administration at first tried to deny any involvement at all and thereafter
attempted to discredit a man who was trying to achieve one of the Bush
administration's toughest foreign policy goals—ousting Noriega.

The U.S.–Giroldi drama began when the rebel major turned to his attractive wife to make his first furtive contacts to the gringos.

Adela Bonilla de Giroldi wasn't the usual Latin military wife. Shrewd and intelligent, she masked her inner toughness with an outer femininity. She worked as operations manager at the National Bank of Panama, where she served as a de facto intelligence agent for her husband. He would send soldiers in plainclothes out on the streets to take the pulse of Panama City by listening to gossip and recording their gripes. His wife would then act as a sounding board against whom he could compare what he learned in the headquarters with what she was hearing at the bank. Together, they saw how much Panamanians hated Noriega, and how much they were coming to resent any officer in uniform.

However, for a long time Major Giroldi kept secret from his wife his plans for a coup against Noriega. In fact, his secret meetings gave rise to concerns of a far different sort. Señora Giroldi had caught her husband in an affair the previous March, and she suspected his frequent absences and lame excuses suggested that he had resumed it.

She had married her husband at age sixteen, and she knew his moods better than her own. He had turned tense and distant. Adela Giroldi would push her husband to talk about any problems, but he answered with silence. That could only mean another woman. He was supposed to be looking around the country to buy a farm for their family, so she could start her own agricultural business. But when Major Giroldi said he was farm-shopping, he would return smelling of smoke and without anything to report about farms. In fact, talk of buying a farm had become Giroldi's code word to summon fellow plotters to secret meetings. Adela de Giroldi, however, became convinced the other woman was back, and she began a fight to hang on to her husband.

She insisted on driving her apparently errant husband to work, picking him up, delivering his lunches, and making weekend plans—all to prevent contact with the other woman. Finally, Major Giroldi was compelled to explain that he wasn't two-timing, he was coup-plotting. Adela was relieved and frightened, particularly when her husband asked her to make the first contacts with the Americans.

Adela had what her husband lacked: links to the U.S. Southern Command. The Giroldi home was in Diablo Heights, just a short walk from Albrook Air Force Base; and one of Adela's best friends worked as a secretary for a military intelligence officer. In fact, American intelligence-gathering in Panama had so declined, because of restrictions on contacts with the Panamanian military, that the best reports were the gossip of such women. "We were reduced to conducting intelligence gathering operations through our women," complained one intelligence officer at the time. "Some of them were spying for Noriega, too, but that's Panama." The intelligence officer said that eleven such women were removed from their jobs in 1988 because of evidence that they were working for Noriega.

But Señora Giroldi's friend was firmly on the American side. For weeks, she had been urging Adela to turn her husband against Noriega, so she would be receptive to helping her now. Señora Giroldi first approached the woman in early September, when she suggested that her husband and a group of other Panamanian officers wanted to talk to "a decision maker" in the Southern Command.

The meeting was set for the following weekend in mid-September, between two CIA agents and two or three Panamanian officers. According to U.S. officials, however, Major Giroldi apparently got cold feet. The meeting never came off. The contacts continued between the two women, but the Americans didn't aggressively follow up. They suspected a Noriega ploy to draw them out. Adela de Giroldi also assumed her husband's adventurism was over.

That was until Friday, September 29, when Adela de Giroldi was waiting impatiently in her bedroom, dressed to attend an accordion concert at the Atlapa Convention Center. Her husband came home too late for her to catch the beginning of the concert, and she exploded as he walked in the door. She still suspected he was keeping a mistress. Major Giroldi went to the refrigerator, grabbed a cold can of beer, and used it as a cold pack on his neck and face as he told his wife that he and other officers, meeting at a veterans' club at Corundu, had laid out the final plans for their coup. Noriega was sending out orders to shoot civilians the next time they protested. "There is going to come a day when we have to shoot the people," he said. "We must stop this."

The Giroldis went to the concert late, not wanting to alarm any friends by their absence. Adela wanted to dance, but her husband refused. So she turned to talk to another man. Tense and angry, Major Giroldi accused his wife of flirting, and he stormed out of the convention center. It was a believable act in passionate Panama, and it gave him more time to meet rebels and refine his plan.

Major Giroldi returned home after midnight. He was restless in bed, and Adela tried to reassure him. She asked whether Noriega would be killed. Would Giroldi himself be in danger? "There's not going to be one dead person," Major Giroldi reassured his wife. He said that if Noriega wouldn't quietly resign, he'd give him to the gringos for trial. "Everything is under control. I just need one thing. I need your contact to the Americans."

They made love more passionately than they had for months. Giroldi's only mistress now, thought Señora Giroldi, was danger.

At midday on Saturday, Adela de Giroldi drove to the fashionable La Boca district, under the Bridge of the Americas, where her friend lived. Adela used this friend, an American who worked with U.S. military intelligence, to take readings of the gringos. If she ever moved from Panama, Adela would get her family out as well. Adela was the one to watch now, however. For the first time ever, she told her friend that she thought Noriega had to go. She wanted to see the American's reaction, but she didn't yet make her husband's request for a contact.

It wasn't until after the Sunday christening that Major Giroldi's plans were made definite. He returned home at just after 11 A.M., and immediately left again to meet with other rebels to lay the final groundwork. He seemed excited and optimistic when he returned at 5 P.M., the danger acting as adrenaline. He gave his wife detailed instructions about what to request from the Americans, and she drove to her friend's home, but her gray Mitsubishi van wasn't in the driveway. Nervously, she waited for more than an hour before her friend returned home; and it took another hour before she could arrange the meeting that Major Giroldi wanted. The secretary couldn't reach her own boss, who was out of town, so she reached her father, who knew the secretary of General Maxwell Thurman, who had just taken over leadership of the Southern Command on the previous night.

Thurman sent over a colonel to screen Adela de Giroldi. After he was satisfied the woman was worth the CIA's interest, he left to arrange a meeting with intelligence agents. He phoned back to the house less than a half hour later. "The beans are cooking just fine," he said in an impromptu code. "They will be delivered shortly, and you should trust the cooks."

At shortly after 7 P.M., Adela de Giroldi smiled as two very American-looking CIA agents (although they didn't introduce themselves as such) walked into her friend's home. The secretary lived with another woman, and the home was filled with feminine pastels and pinks; ornate mirrors decorated the walls. The two CIA agents seemed oddly out of place. They were a Mutt-and-Jeff–looking duo. One was extraordinarily tall, with a large build, dark hair, and a thick mustache. He spoke Spanish fluently, with a Mexican accent. The other was blonder and slighter. He didn't speak at all, but merely listened. For the first time, the plot against Noriega seemed real to Señora Giroldi.

"My husband wants you to fly over three airports after the coup begins—Chiriquí, Paitilla, and Tocumen," she said. "And he wants you to close all the access roads to the headquarters." The two men scribbled notes.

And who's your husband? the larger man asked.

"Major Giroldi," she said.

The CIA man misspelled the name on his notepad.

Where does he work? asked the CIA agent, a man relatively new to his post.

Adela de Giroldi was surprised these men didn't know more about her husband. She would have been more disappointed if she had known that their job was to know just such intelligence. But she nevertheless patiently answered their elementary questions. She also relayed her husband's request for a private meeting with a "decision maker" to confirm what he needed. She looked at the Americans' eyes, however, and she feared they weren't taking her seriously.

Several weeks after her husband's coup attempt, sitting in urban squalor at a characterless apartment complex in Miami, she was surprised to hear that her account of conversations with CIA officials had contradicted the Bush administration's story. Since she herself was unfamiliar with the Bush version of events, and relatively unsophisticated, there seems little reason to doubt that Mrs. Giroldi was telling the truth and that American officials revised for public consumption their account of what Giroldi requested of them so as to conceal just how deeply they had failed him.

Most contradictory to the Bush administration version is Mrs. Giroldi's claim that she requested the U.S. to block *todos los vías*—"all of the roads—" over which rescue troops could reach Noriega: a phrase she says she repeated several times to the CIA men. The U.S. claim was that Giroldi asked for only two roads to be blocked. The point is critical because the troops that would rescue Noriega arrived on a third road, which the Americans left free. "Why would my husband only have wanted one or two roads blocked while his enemies came in on others?" she asked with some incredulity.

Señora Giroldi also says that she asked for U.S. air cover at the three airfields most crucial to the coup, but instead the U.S. kept its planes grounded. Her statement flies in the face of the U.S. claim that no request for air cover was made. This point too is critical, since the crack jungle troops that rescued Noriega arrived by air at Tocumen airport while American officers watched their arrival, first on their radar screens and then through binoculars.

But Señora Giroldi does concede a major oversight on her husband's part. Thinking he could talk Noriega down from power, he didn't make any specific plans that evening for the Americans to take custody of the

General. However, in an interview with the *Miami Herald* later, she contradicted the U.S. version that Giroldi insisted he wouldn't give up Noriega under any conditions. "My husband said they had to either turn Noriega over to the Americans or kill him," she said. "He said he didn't want to kill him, because that wasn't his nature."

After relaying her husband's requests to the CIA men during an hourlong meeting, Mrs. Giroldi said her husband wanted to meet with a "decision maker": he wanted to eyeball the man who was going to insure his coup's success. The CIA officials also wanted to check out Giroldi, so they sent her to get him, and suggested that General Maxwell Thurman would be there when they returned.

She phoned from a booth on her way back to her husband's headquarters. "Your sandwiches are ready," she said in a prearranged code. "Just like you wanted them."

"So why don't you bring them over," Giroldi said in as casual a manner as possible.

A few minutes later, Adela picked up her husband at his office, where he was dressed down for Sunday—white shorts, tennis shoes, and a T-shirt. After a casual chat in his office, they drove to the parking lot of a bank not far from their home. They switched cars there, and drove to the secretary's home. When Major Giroldi arrived, however, General Thurman still wasn't there. Adela Giroldi doesn't think the CIA men had even moved.

The CIA men said they wanted to take a drive with Major Giroldi. He refused, not entirely trusting them. The intelligence officers didn't want to stay indoors, not trusting Giroldi. But Giroldi wouldn't even get in their car. So they compromised by sitting in the secretary's gray Mitsubishi, in the driveway, as they talked. Their meeting lasted only fifteen minutes; it was kept brief by a rebel major who deeply feared discovery.

Knowing his wife had provided most of the details of his requests, Major Giroldi made it clear he wanted U.S. help to be as limited and unapparent as possible. "I want a Panamanian revolution," he said. American actions over the past two years had so soured military officers toward the U.S. that the rebels stood a better chance of winning allies to their side by maintaining the coup's home-grown nature. When the CIA agents asked whether the coup was contingent upon their assistance, he said it wasn't. He would try to remove Noriega from power whether or not the gringos helped. But without the gringos, his chances of success were far less.

A senior U.S. military official said the CIA men had come to their meetings with the Giroldis without any clear instructions except for two: they were to listen—and not to provide advice or promises—and they were to avoid

American involvement in any coup attempt that could end in Noriega's death.

Despite long months of encouraging the PDF to organize a coup against Noriega, these CIA men had no clear instructions to help the coup makers.

In fact, the Reagan administration had agreed to Senate Intelligence Committee restrictions on mounting a coup against Noriega that were so strict that Bush may technically have had to inform Panama's dictator ahead of time if he knew an operation was being planned that might result in Noriega's death, as any coup was likely to do.

"The net effect was that U.S. officials were nervous about even sitting in the same room with Panamanians who were talking among themselves about coup plans, fearful that they were violating laws," said one administration official. "Our hands were tied, and in the post–Iran-Contra atmosphere nobody wanted to misstep."

When the CIA agents, now ever cautious, spotted flaws in Giroldi's plan, they bit their lips. This wasn't William Casey's CIA, where agents looked for chances for covert action. This was Judge William Webster's CIA, where everything was by the book.

"Their standing instructions were that if anyone plotting a coup comes to talk to you, you listen," said one intelligence official. "You don't make suggestions or offer help. You don't even ask leading questions. We weren't being asked for our opinion and we didn't provide it."

Under those instructions, however, the CIA agents made clear that they couldn't assist a plan that included Noriega's death. American officials worried later that this warning played a role in Giroldi's decision not to kill Noriega—making him fear that if Noriega were killed U.S. support would then be withdrawn. "How else could a Panamanian who doesn't understand all this congressional mumbo jumbo have interpreted our warnings during a half-hour meeting?" said one intelligence official.

More critically, the CIA men didn't offer a secure means of radio or phone communication to the coup plotters: again, legislation wouldn't allow it. They left Giroldi with a phone number or two, and asked him to dial in case of emergency. The numbers were almost impossible to reach from Panama City, even at the best of times. However, Giroldi didn't seem concerned about this lack of contact. U.S. officials asked whether Giroldi could give them a number at which they could reach him. He declined, wanting to maintain the integrity of his coup.

In reporting this contact to Washington and General Thurman, the agents had a problem. They knew little about Giroldi, not even the spelling of his name. Lacking hard intelligence, the CIA men relied on their instincts.

They were convinced they weren't being set up, because of Giroldi's fear when meeting with them. He shook, and his eyes darted nervously around the house, which had the feel of American suburbia: a video machine, some cheap art, department store furniture, and a rack full of paperbacks. He didn't like being there. During their meeting with him, the CIA men wrote words in their notebook such as "scared" and "nervous" to describe the rebel major as he outlined his plans. If Giroldi was a plant, he was a damn good actor, they thought. They also trusted Giroldi, because of his insistence that U.S. participation remain limited and start only after the coup had begun. His request that Southern Command take his family on base on the morning of the coup gave them added reassurance.

On Monday, October 2, at just after 2:30 A.M. Washington time, Thurman relayed Giroldi's plans and requests to the chairman of the Joint Chiefs of Staff, Lieutenant General Colin Powell. Thurman hadn't expected such a challenge so soon in his tenure, and neither had Powell. It was Thurman's second day on the job and Powell's first. Powell woke Defense Secretary Richard Cheney with the news, and at 3 A.M. called Bush's national security adviser, Brent Scowcroft.

Before daybreak Monday, Thurman and the chief of the Southern Command's army contingent, Brigadier General Marc Cisneros, had positioned tractors and graders by the side of the road that crosses the Bridge of the Americas and by the gate of Fort Amador. By 6 A.M., U.S. marines, who had been sent to Panama in May from Camp Lejeune, were poised near the Arraijan tank farm, where they would stop the Machos del Monte from rescuing Noriega by blocking the road to the Bridge of the Americas and Panama City. And by 8 A.M., twelve transport helicopters of the 5th Battalion, 87th Infantry Company, had set down on the Fort Amador golf course to face off against the 5th Rifle Company on planned "maneuvers." (One golfer, with two holes to play, threatened to take a club to one of the soldiers.)

By 9:40 A.M., their planned training had ended, but the coup still hadn't begun, so the troops were ordered to remain on scene in full battle gear throughout the day, in the Panamanian sun. Some officers worried the U.S. was showing its hand.

"We were in a forward-leaning position," said one officer responsible for logistics.

President Bush readjusted that forward lean a few notches backward when he was briefed Monday morning.

President Bush first heard of the coup plans during his 8 A.M. morning briefing. More detailed outlines were drawn for him during a conference call a half-hour later with Baker, Cheney, and Scowcroft, who felt the situation was serious enough to call for a larger meeting in the Oval Office at 9 A.M. Joining the original group were Vice President Dan Quayle, Powell, Bush's chief of staff John Sununu, two senior State Department officials, and three generals. CIA Director William Webster was out of town, so Scowcroft's deputy Robert Gates—a former CIA boss—acted as the de facto representative of CIA interests.

None of the cabinet officers was able to tell Bush much about the coup makers. The president was frustrated by the lack of intelligence, but he nevertheless gave his blessing to Giroldi's request for limited assistance. "We should do the things that they asked for," said Bush. His logic was that it would be easier for civilians to promote democracy with any military leader other than Noriega, since none other could wield his dictatorial power. And anyway, said Bush, "We are being asked to do something we do routinely anyway."

Yet Bush and his aides entered enough notes of caution about risking American lives to let Powell and his generals follow their post-Vietnam instincts—to avoid direct military confrontation at all costs.

Defense Secretary Richard Cheney fed this caution by questioning Giroldi's bona fides. "The individual who was allegedly plotting the coup was the only source of information we had and he was a noted confidant and crony of Noriega's," Cheney would say later.

Secretary of State James Baker worried about legal entanglements with Congress over assassination prohibitions. "Get the lawyers," said Baker, upon being told of the coup.

The meeting never discussed in much detail the alternatives for American response. Only fifteen minutes into the discussion, an aide walked in with a note that said the coup had been postponed. The note didn't say until when. The meeting was adjourned. Why take up any more of the president's busy schedule over a no-go coup? "It was very apparent nothing was going to happen when they said it was going to happen," said an official who was at the meeting. Some doubted whether the coup would come off at all. "The inclination was to think it was just another of the periodic coup reports we were getting."

Very little had been decided during that short meeting. Senior officials didn't discuss in any detail how far American military involvement should go—the key question that would face them a day later. "You can't make that kind of decision unless you know the specific circumstances," Cheney said later in his own defense. "You didn't know how many people he had with him. You didn't know whether he would be able to get hold of Noriega. You didn't know whether you would find yourself in the middle of a Panamanian civil war. There were just too many uncertainties."

Yet when the coup began twenty-four hours later, the lack of detailed preparation Monday would handicap Bush's ability to respond quickly. Operatives in Panama waited in vain for more precise contingency instructions. "We should have gone into more details then," said one of the briefers. "That really hurt us later."

In Panama later that same Monday, General Thurman was getting cold feet. Fresh to his command, he began to suspect that General Noriega was plotting to humiliate him—and the United States. When the coup didn't happen Monday morning, Thurman grew more nervous. "Noriega's setting a trap for me," he said to one officer. "They're trying to suck me in. He wants to embarrass me." Thurman noted that Noriega's newest puppet president, Francisco Rodriguez, was in New York at the United Nations. He theorized that Noriega had planned the sting operation while the United Nations General Assembly was in session, so the whole world could watch.

"He thought it was all about him, and he failed to realize this was about Panama," one of his senior officers later complained. "People were risking their lives and he was fearing his own personal embarrassment. What an enormous ego that takes! And his staff was feeding that machine."

Thurman, at age fifty-eight, delayed his planned retirement to take over command from General Frederick Woerner. Thurman was a soldier-warrior who would ask few questions and follow Washington's orders. The joke went that he had remained single his entire life because he was married to the army, and that he only took time off to attend church on Sunday. In Panama, Thurman was living up to his reputation. He regarded his newest assignment as war duty, and he put his 12,000-odd troops—many of whom had never left their offices—on battle footing. His first act after taking command on Sunday was to require all soldiers and officers to wear camouflage-colored battle dress uniforms, or BDUs. One naval intelligence officer complained that he had to spend the morning the coup was scheduled to occur trying to find a uniform his size. Thurman's second act was to remove the vending machines from the area outside "The Tunnel," the long corridor dug into the side of Quarry Heights hill, where officers collected and processed intelligence. The area around the machines provided a place for officers to smoke and relax during breaks, but Thurman saw a security threat in a place where officers chatted too casually.

In addition, Thurman's new staff, which lacked Latin American specialists, arrogantly disregarded the counsel of Woerner's old hands in the Southern Command until, in the midst of the coup attempt, Thurman urgently needed some expert advice. The lack of experience around Thurman was immediately clear. Turning to his senior advisers in the secure intelligence briefing area, he asked the senior Latin American expert to identify himself. General Michael Schneider, the chief of the Southern Command's J-2 intelligence arm, spoke up. General Schneider, alas, had been in Panama only two months. His officers worried about backing a man who had never been an intelligence "asset" for Washington—an informer. They knew little about him. When the U.S. had been more in the coup business in Latin America, the leader of the ouster effort was usually a man known to the Americans and often was already on their payrolls. This coup didn't fit the mold.

Giroldi fed their doubts by not carrying off the coup on his earliest target date. Giroldi feared both that Noriega had found him out and that the U.S. would not support him. He also didn't know where Noriega was at the time the coup was to have started.

Thurman remained in the tunnel from dawn to midnight, waiting for information and action. His doubts were relayed to Washington, where they were amplified as they ran through the bureaucracy. Thurman fed the characteristic caution of Washington, where the political risks of action are always greater than they are for inaction.

By late Monday, Washington began to worry about being associated with rebels who hadn't committed themselves to democracy. Bush sent a message to Mrs. Giroldi through the Southern Command that Washington would like a declaration of democratic principles and an effort to get international support in the coup makers' first statement after seizing power. It sure would be good if they would say they were in favor of new elections monitored by the Organization of American States.

Giroldi considered that message and other news on Monday night to be Washington's nod that the Southern Command would help. He had been told not to expect any clearer message. The Southern Command, as required by the Panama Canal Treaties, notified the Panamanian Defense Forces at 6 P.M. that it planned to engage in exercises of mechanized forces at Fort Amador and Howard Air Force Base the following morning. To Noriega, it was just another of the frequent American maneuvers that were designed to rattle him. To Giroldi, however, it was the go-ahead. The Americans would be blocking roads en route to the headquarters. "By our actions, we signaled them that we weren't averse to their going ahead," said one White House official later.

In bed that night, Adela de Giroldi turned to her husband, who seemed more relaxed than he had been for weeks. He was relieved the time for action had come. "If you do this, you will have to kill Noriega," Adela said to her husband.

Giroldi reassured his wife that with the Americans carrying out their part of the bargain that wouldn't be necessary. "Noriega will understand he needs to leave," said Major Giroldi. "There is no need to kill him."

What Giroldi didn't know was that his American allies had become much more reluctant warriors since his meeting with the CIA agents on Sunday night.

On Tuesday morning, General Manuel Antonio Noriega drove into the headquarters complex at 7:40 A.M., an hour earlier than Giroldi had expected him. His dark-blue, armor-plated Mercedes-Benz drove ahead of a similar car carrying his bodyguards. Because he was an hour early for the 9 A.M. General Staff meeting, the captain who was assigned to arrest him in the parking lot hesitated. When one of Noriega's two bodyguards heard the clicking of the captain's gun, the bodyguard wheeled around and drew his pistol.

"Just a security exercise," the cowed captain said.

But Noriega knew there was trouble. He walked to his office, back to back with a bodyguard who kept his pistol trained on the captain. Major Giroldi was waiting inside. Surprised that Noriega hadn't been arrested, Giroldi at first stuttered that Noriega was being deposed "for the good of the country." He spoke of people going hungry, and the country needing relief. He said he was pursuing an institutional solution under which everyone with twenty-five years' service, including Noriega, was being retired.

"You're crazy," Noriega responded, and ordered his bodyguards to fire their guns out of the windows to sound an alarm. They were the first shots of a five-hour drama. But when his loyalists fired, Giroldi's carefully positioned troops from the 4th "Urraca" Company, the Dobermans (the country's riot police), and the cavalry all answered, on cue, with a hail of gunfire.

"That's when Noriega knew he was in more trouble than he thought," his friend and spokesman Mario Rognoni would say later. "He was just shooting warning shots. He never expected his shots to be returned in such force. Giroldi had planned the first part of the coup perfectly."

Watching from a hilltop of Quarry Heights only 600 yards away, American officers saw the Dobermans in their black berets and the Urraca Company in its green berets take control of the headquarters building by building. The routine was simple. They would shoot out the windows of an office, and then demand its occupants give up. A number of men would then stream into the courtyard with their arms folded on their heads. "No one seemed particularly concerned," said one of the Americans watching. "It worked smoothly."

Before Giroldi seized Noriega, the General was able to place two phone calls to civilian allies. The intercepted calls were the first sign American intelligence had that the General was inside. Noriega pleaded with the civilians to phone the Battalion 2000 and the 5th and 7th rifle companies for help. "Noriega phoned civilians because he didn't know whom to trust in the army," said Rognoni.

Olechea had sent the bulk of his troops on maneuvers in Darién province, and he had promised Giroldi neutrality—but if Giroldi failed, Olechea was a dead man. He hedged his bets. He prepared his remaining troops and their heavy equipment to roll into Panama City with the Machos del Monte. Mrs. Giroldi believes now that Olechea's strategy was to put himself in a position either to be the force that saved Noriega or to seize power himself from Giroldi by storming the headquarters after Noriega either was killed or was taken by the Americans. And if the Americans blocked the road, he would stop and wait to see who won the fight at the headquarters. Olechea, one of Noriega's cleverest and least principled officers, had all fronts covered.

At 9:15 A.M. in Washington, Deputy National Security Adviser Robert Gates got reports from the White House situation room of gunfire around Noriega's headquarters. Until that point, Gates and other senior officials hadn't taken the Giroldi coup seriously.

George Bush was told of the coup on the fly at about 9:30 A.M. National Security Adviser Brent Scowcroft and a handful of other officials trailed behind him from his Oval Office through the West Wing of the White House and onto the South Lawn, where he was to greet arriving Mexican President Carlos Salinas de Gortari.

There is shooting in the Comandancia, Scowcroft told the president. The coup is going down. Thurman's troops are already blocking the roads.

There wasn't much time to give Bush any more news, let alone discuss options. And he didn't ask for a fuller report at that time. "Yes, good," said Bush almost dismissively.

"It was a walking briefing," said one of the officials. "There wasn't much depth to it."

No one suggested Bush cut short or reschedule any meetings with the Mexican leader, who ironically had been one of the Latin leaders who most strongly opposed American policy toward Panama. At a critical point in the coup, Bush engaged in twenty minutes of pomp and circumstance on the White House South Lawn, while operatives in Panama impatiently waited for guidance.

Defense Secretary Richard Cheney wasn't even in Washington. Colin Powell reached Cheney with word of the coup while he was sitting beside Soviet Defense Minister Dimitri Yazov in a bus touring the Gettysburg battleground. Although he had been told Monday afternoon that the coup would begin Tuesday morning, Cheney opted not to reschedule his super-power tour guiding.

General Thurman would later brief congressmen in secret sessions that the key problem during the coup was the lack of any contingency plan. If he had had clearer instructions, he wouldn't have needed Bush or Cheney. But he hadn't any idea how he should react to events on the ground, and all his superiors seemed to be tied up fulfilling the demands of their appointment calendars.

In crisis centers at the State Department, the Pentagon, and the CIA, second-tier officials toiled in isolation from the White House. Their reports often contradicted each other, but Bush saw few of them during the day anyway, because of poor communication between the White House and its agencies and the absence of a CIA official at decision-making sessions.

Led by Deputy Assistant Secretary of State Michael Kozak, the State Department task force furiously collected what information was available from Panama City, and passed it on to Secretary of State James Baker at the White House. Kozak kept a line open to U.S. chargé d'affaires in Panama John Maisto. Maisto did the same with General Thurman.

One of the task force's first discussions was what to do if the coup makers offered to give them Noriega. Maisto and Thurman decided that the president had three alternatives: (1) They could take delivery of Noriega. "Giroldi would wrap him up nicely and then put him in a truck to be driven to the Southern Command," said one official. (2) The U.S. could send its own troops in to pick him up, either with helicopters or by convoy. (3) They could take Noriega by force. Maisto and Thurman communicated those options to Washington for President Bush's consideration.

Initially, U.S. participation in the coup came off like clockwork. U.S. forces at Fort Amador neutralized General Noriega's 5th rifle company and the Israeli-trained UESAT special forces. These units didn't even try to break out to rescue Noriega. "We provided them an excuse not to join a fight they didn't want to participate in," said one U.S. officer. And American marines blocked the land approach of the Machos del Monte. The first hint that American planning was flawed occurred when Major Giroldi's wife, his three children, and his invalid father—under an arrangement made Sunday night with CIA officials—showed up at the gate of Fort Clayton seeking refuge. The escort that was to have been waiting for them wasn't there. Initially, guards attempted to turn them away, since they hadn't been informed of the arrangements, and Mrs. Giroldi feared the worst: the abandonment of her husband and the coup. The escort arrived, but her fears would return after only a short while.

Communications would be even worse in the old section of Panama City, where General Noriega maintained his military headquarters complex, a series of boxlike, three-story, whitewashed buildings that stretched for more than a city block. Without any preestablished means to communicate with the rebels, U.S. officers furiously tried to phone the Comandancia to find out what was happening. Some military officers' outgoing calls were interrupted by their own switchboard operators, who chastised the officials for using lines they had been ordered to keep free.

But at 9:30 A.M., Panama time, Major Giroldi still thought he could pull off the coup without much more American assistance, particularly if American forces were blocking roads and keeping Panamanian aircraft grounded, as he hoped. His forces had secured the headquarters building, were holding Noriega, and had fanned out into the poor neighborhood surrounding the complex to head off what they considered their only threat: the infiltration of special forces loyal to Noriega.

Giroldi tried to talk Noriega down from power. "Giroldi explained to Noriega that he respected him a great deal, and out of honor to the PDF, he had to say that the public was hungry, that people didn't have jobs, and that we were heading toward total ruin," as recalled later by Captain Javier Licona, a rebel officer who commanded Panama's cavalry, when he arrived in exile in the United States. Giroldi even told Noriega that he could name three officials to lead the PDF. But Noriega, who had come to believe that his only safety was in uniform, refused. "You've got to kill me first," he said. "If you are so macho, kill me." But that is exactly what Giroldi didn't want to do to the godfather of his son and the best man at his wedding.

At 11 A.M. Giroldi went on Panamanian radio to announce the coup in an attempt to attract American support and that of troops loyal to Noriega. But he made two critical mistakes. First, he didn't say what had happened to Noriega—sending a message to loyalists that their General still hadn't surrendered power—and, second, by saying that Noriega's puppet president would remain in power, he failed to bring opposition activists onto the streets. His only nod to democracy was that OAS-supervised elections could take place, and that officers with twenty-five years' service—like Noriega—would be retired.

Licona was growing impatient with the Giroldi-Noriega talks. "The General entered into a discussion with the major [Giroldi] in order to stall him and buy time for his loyal troops, who were loyal only out of fear," said Captain Licona. Licona, losing patience, entered the discussion, saying the General had to step down because the people were destitute and the soldiers were against him.

"You can't speak for the fifteen thousand men of the PDF," Noriega said.

Licona said troop morale was so low that he often told soldiers lies about the future to maintain peace. But Licona didn't want to debate. He told Giroldi, his superior, to give Noriega five minutes to decide to resign or be taken to Fort Clayton. Licona left the office to arrange for a truck to transfer Noriega.

Licona started loading the several colonels allied with Noriega onto the truck. Giroldi came out of the headquarters angry. He said that he didn't think the roads had been safely closed by the U.S. He already had reports that loyalist troops were en route to save Noriega. He doubted whether he had the men both to transfer Noriega to the Americans and to continue holding the headquarters. Giroldi ordered Licona to bring the officers down from his truck.

Major Giroldi didn't know that he was missing his last chance to send Noriega to the Americans, something that his wife insists had been a fail-safe part of his plan all along.

At about 10:30 A.M., John Maisto and General Thurman were "getting geared up" to put some A-37 reconnaissance planes in the air, one senior official said, to prevent a rescue effort of Noriega. Southern Command had been watching for air activity, and it had reported no signs of trouble. Yet the U.S. officials were too late. By the time they thought to block air traffic, the most serious threat to Giroldi was on its way.

Giroldi had counted on a show of U.S. power to dissuade troops from rescuing Noriega. He properly gauged that most officers wouldn't come to the General's assistance unless they saw Giroldi's coup was failing and they feared Noriega's retribution. However, after sitting on the fence in the first few hours of the coup, and seeing that U.S. support was partial and halting, some troops began to throw their lot with Noriega; and some of Giroldi's men outside the headquarters began to defect.

"The decisive factor at 10 to 11 A.M. on the day of the coup was U.S. inaction," said one Southern Command officer, who waited in vain for instructions from Washington to block roads or head off air traffic.

Senator Sam Nunn, the chairman of the Armed Services Committee, had no doubt where to place the blame after being briefed by administration officials on this period of time. "I do not believe people on the ground had clear policy guidance from Washington," Nunn said. "We had a public policy for encouraging a coup, but no real plans for our people on the ground on how to proceed if it occurred. . . . We did not have coordination of intelligence activities on the ground or back here in Washington."

On the ground, it was clear the coup was turning against Giroldi. Radar screens at the U.S. installation on Taboga Island spotted what appeared to be a civilian 727 take off from the Panamanian base at Río Ható. The American radar watchers at Taboga Island are a strict bunch, tasked with guarding the Panama Canal from their small tropical station floating in Panama Bay. No Panamanian pilot dares pass without identifying himself, but this flight remained unidentified, and senior military officers said their men at Taboga didn't send out an alert as the suspicious plane flew near the U.S. Howard Air Force Base and then landed at the military portion of Tocumen airport at Panama City.

Southern Command officers didn't worry at first as they watched the white plane with red trim. It didn't appear to be a military aircraft. But through their high-powered lenses, they saw the plane disgorge tens of heavily armed troops in black T-shirts: the Machos del Monte.

Commanded by Captain "Cholo" Gonzalez, these troops were the meanest and most loyal under Noriega's command. They were trained by Cuban commandos, and video clips of their initiation had horrified the upper crust of Panamanian society and even fellow soldiers: black-bearded commandos in shorts and black T-shirts poured buckets of blood over their heads while grunting fiercely and indecipherably.

Giroldi's plan foresaw two means to stop the Machos. U.S. troops had blocked their road across the Bridge of the Americas and, he assumed, A-37s would be circling over Tocumen and Paitilla airports to stop them from flying in. And if that didn't work, his men in the apartments would gun them down as they neared the Comandancia. Without heavy artillery support, they could never reach him, and the only group that could provide that support was the Battalion 2000, whose commander had promised neutrality.

The Machos drove to the nearby Battalion 2000 base. Captain Gonzalez's arrival convinced Major Olechea he had to offer whatever troops he hadn't sent on maneuver, to join the rescue attempt. The military spotters watched as Giroldi's doom roared down roads General Thurman opted not to block. Washington wasn't leaning forward on this one, and he wasn't about to risk American lives without his superiors' blessing.

At about noon, Maisto's voice grew frantic as he looked out of his embassy window, which usually had a placid view of the Pacific over Balboa Avenue. "Holy shit," he told a senior official over an open line to Washington. Tens of tanks and personnel carriers of the Battalion 2000 were roaring by, he said, and held the phone out so the Washington official could hear.

"Are they coming to rescue Noriega?" the official asked.

"I have a bad feeling they are on the wrong side," said Maisto. The chargé d'affaires, whose last posting had him supporting a much neater and more promising revolution in the Philippines only two years earlier, reported that the Battalion 2000 was right behind the Machos del Monte.

"Is there anything we can do to restore the balance?" asked Washington. Maisto passed the phone to Jerry Dunbar, the embassy's military attaché.

Dunbar said the two forces were forming a pincer. The Battalion 2000 had gone up the Avenue of the Poets, and the Machos del Monte were positioned on what had once been Fourth of July Avenue, renamed by the Panamanians "Avenue of the Martyrs" for the deaths of students rioting against the U.S. in 1964. Dunbar said the only hope would be to deploy troops at the edge of American-controlled territory at Fort Amador, to intimidate the Panamanians. The troops could come within a football field's distance of the Machos del Monte.

Giroldi was in trouble and Uncle Sam wasn't much help. The Americans were reacting too slowly. The gringos were doing the bare minimum—and that wasn't enough. He was losing control of the area around the headquarters, and many of his troops outside the Comandancia were defecting to Noriega's side.

Yet he still held the headquarters itself and, more importantly, he had Noriega. If Giroldi had killed Noriega then, the coup would have been over and loyalist forces might never have stormed his headquarters. But he still thought he could strike a deal.

As a prisoner, Noriega now had become a bargaining chip. Major Giroldi, still sensitive to the anti–U.S. feelings of the military, had instructed his emissaries to ask that the U.S. take Noriega but promise not to send him to the U.S. to be tried. By giving assurances that the U.S. wouldn't extradite Noriega, perhaps the outflanked rebels could convert some Noriega loyalists to their side. Giroldi requested two cease-fires from Noriega, and allowed him to talk to officers outside over the radio, so that he could continue his negotiations.

"I have the General, and he may get hurt," Giroldi pleaded to the loyalist troops that surrounded his headquarters. His only way out was with Noriega.

Giroldi tried often to call the numbers he had been given by the CIA officials, but he couldn't get through. The Americans had failed him in blocking the roads and airports, and he wanted to find out why. The Americans' failure in satisfying those smaller requests now meant he might need the gringos to take Noriega off his hands. American officials said they also tried without luck to phone in to Giroldi, but the truth is that several of their calls did reach the rebels.

One call whose occurrence the Pentagon maintained as secret was from the Southern Command's deputy chief of intelligence, Colonel William McDonough, to his counterpart in the G-2, Nicasio Lorenzo Drake, who would later pay with his life for the call, which had been recorded on Noriega's monitoring equipment. McDonough won't say what they discussed. American officials insist he merely wanted an update on the coup, but rebel officers said Drake passed on a request that the Americans take Noriega off Giroldi's hands. Panamanian government officials, who claim to have heard the tape, confirm this. Two other U.S. sources close to the Southern Command told William Branigin of the *Washington Post* that, in addition, the rebels twice phoned Brigadier General Marc Cisneros's office to reiterate the custody request.

Frustrated at the apparent failure of the Americans to block all roads and stop air traffic, and at the communications difficulties, Giroldi sent Licona and four others to Fort Clayton to find out from Brigadier General Cisneros where the gringos' assistance was. Licona was happy to leave, fearing Giroldi's coup was failing. Giroldi's message was that he needed the Americans to deliver on their Sunday promises. To Licona, Cisneros seemed oddly aloof and ignorant of what was transpiring or what had been promised. Cisneros made a phone call, and he talked for twenty minutes while Giroldi was under fire.

"It bothered me when he said he had to consult the blueprint of Giroldi's plans," said Licona, who thought Cisneros should have known the situation better by then. Licona complained that Cisneros was concerned that world opinion might chastise the United States for intervening and that blocking more roads might inconvenience Panamanians.

Licona couldn't understand this. The situation was "very special," he pleaded, and there would be "no problems" with Panamanian citizens.

The request for a non-extradition promise was passed on to Washington, a senior U.S. official said. "We didn't have any contingency plan to deal with this," said the official. Apparently, neither did officials in Washington. "It was being worked, and there was a delay," said a military officer in Panama. "There was no outright rejection, but no quick response."

State Department official Michael Kozak, whose attempt to negotiate Noriega from power in May 1988 had been derailed, got word from Panama that he now had a chance to take custody of the dictator. Chargé d'Affaires John Maisto phoned from the U.S. embassy with the most important news of the day: the rebels wanted the Americans to take Noriega off their hands. Maisto was passing the message on from Brigadier General William Hertzog, the deputy chief of intelligence for the army in Panama, who was sitting in on the meeting with Licona.

Kozak relayed the request to Secretary of State James Baker at the

White House. Only after the coup was over would Kozak and Maisto be told that Hertzog had given them an inaccurate report because he misunderstood what was said at the meeting. Hertzog told Maisto he had walked out prematurely, before the message was clear. Yet Hertzog never phoned Maisto back to reverse the message once it did become clear. To add to the confusion, Pentagon officials would later say that Hertzog was merely phoning to relay to Maisto what alternatives were available to the U.S.— absent any request from the rebels.

As so often in government, the difficulty of agreeing to the right cover story suggests that someone was trying to hide the truth. Put simply, says one U.S. intelligence source, the rebels wanted U.S. help in getting Noriega out, and Washington didn't want to provide it. "The last thing the Bush administration wants is Noriega on trial in Miami subpoenaing intelligence documents, revealing CIA secrets, and perhaps even beating the drug charges against him," he said. "No one would be too eager to take custody of Noriega, no matter what they say publicly. Bringing Noriega to justice is exactly what they *don't* want to do."

Later, the Bush White House would insist that the president had gotten the right message from Southern Command all along—that the rebels didn't want to turn over Noriega—although the White House would also send out a different version of the misunderstanding, saying that a cable had falsely reported the rebels "want" (the U.S. to take custody) instead of "won't" (allow the U.S. to take custody).

In any event, in Washington, Bush finally sat down to discuss more effective ways to help the rebels at about the time Giroldi was losing all hope, and operatives on the ground had given up on hearing any instructions from their superiors. Officials' meetings with the Mexican president and Soviet defense minister, and a haphazard effort to make sense out of intelligence from the crisis control centers at the Pentagon, the State Department, and the Central Intelligence Agency only delayed and complicated the decision making.

Bush called one meeting for about 11:30 A.M. in Washington. Loyalist troops were already well on their way to rescuing the General, but officials still hadn't sent any guidance for action to their troops in Panama. Cheney had returned from his field trip to Gettysburg, but officials still weren't even sure where Noriega was. Intelligence was contradictory, and no one available at the meeting could determine whose data was most reliable. The CIA still wasn't participating.

"Why do we have an intelligence agency if they're not going to be in the situation room at the time decisions are being made?" bristled Senator David Boren, the Oklahoma Democrat and Intelligence Committee chairman, after the coup had failed.

Bush's first full-fledged meeting on the coup didn't occur until about 1:30 P.M., after Licona had reached Fort Clayton. Defensive officials later would term this their third meeting of the day on Panama, but senior officials have said it was the only substantive session. Cheney dropped Yazov in the outer office of the White House before he briefed Bush and his top advisers on the Licona meeting in Panama. By this time, the officials felt confident Noriega was being held at the headquarters by the rebels. This time, Cheney brought a large map, on which he would review options.

Bush ruled that Washington should take Noriega "if he was delivered F.O.B." by the rebels, said one official. Bush also said the U.S. could go pick up Noriega if they could find a workable way to pull it off. Thurman hadn't called in the Delta Force from Fort Bragg, so any blitzlike operation would be difficult. And Bush ruled out taking Noriega if the rebels weren't offering him.

The president had made his most important decision of the day after it no longer made any difference.

Cheney got back into his car, with Yazov, to drive to the Pentagon. By the time he'd made the ten-minute drive, Noriega had regained power. Seldom had a Soviet defense minister been so close to American crisis management, and Moscow's fears of the Washington threat could only have receded even further.

Backed by the Battalion 2000's armor, the crack jungle troops began to storm the headquarters at just before 1 P.M. Panama time. Major Olechea, still trying to play both sides, told Captain Gonzalez of the Machos that he didn't want to go in for fear of killing Noriega. Gonzalez announced that the Machos were going forward anyway.

Giroldi's troops, outnumbered and surrounded, surrendered without a real fight. To make the combat seem a little more ferocious, Battalion 2000 lobbed one mortar into a warehouse, and a black plume of smoke filled the air. Gonzalez also ordered his men to fire their guns at the blue sky above, just to add to the atmosphere. Noriega's spokesman Mario Rognoni and a military officer who was at the scene described Noriega's actions:

Noriega looked out the window of Giroldi's office, where he was being held, to see the Machos del Monte taking the courtyard. When he saw their black T-shirts and beards, he knew he had won. After five hours of Giroldi's detention, he had almost miraculously emerged a victor—if Giroldi didn't shoot him.

The recharged Noriega walked across the office toward Giroldi, who stood four feet from the wall with his machine gun pointed at Noriega. You know something, Giroldi, you will never be a general, said Noriega. The troops want someone with balls. But you don't have balls. Not even to shoot me.

Giroldi backed up slowly.

Look, Giroldi, you are sweating, said Noriega. You are afraid. People sweat when they are afraid. You've lost the headquarters now. All you control is the second floor.

At that point, a Noriega loyalist walked into the room, Major Rufito Cedeño. A nervous corporal standing next to Giroldi ordered the major to hit the floor, which he dutifully did. Giroldi barked the same order at Noriega. But Noriega laughed, gambling his life that Giroldi wouldn't kill him.

You are giving me orders? he chortled malignantly. I am the General. *I* give the orders. All you control is the second floor of this building.

Noriega walked toward Giroldi. He told him to lay down his machine gun. He had been misled, said Noriega, suggesting that he would show mercy to Giroldi and his men. Giroldi couldn't pull the trigger. He set his gun on a desk. Noriega had regained control of Panama. "My husband may have had a moment of weakness," Mrs. Giroldi would say later of his failure to kill Noriega.

Noriega took a pistol from one of his security guards. He walked up to two rebel officers. I'm tired of these bastards, he said, with Giroldi watching helplessly. Then he shot one officer in the left temple, killing him on the spot. Blood splattered on the wall. As Giroldi cried openly, Noriega shouted at him, "Kill yourself, kill yourself, or I'll kill you."

But Giroldi didn't kill himself, and Noriega didn't pull the trigger. A crueler fate awaited the coup's leader.

U.S. officers watched helplessly from the hill overhead as they saw Noriega walk into the courtyard unarmed, as Giroldi's troops surrendered to him.

They talked about how easy it would have been to preserve Giroldi's victory. One mentioned that only two or three armored vehicles would have been needed to block the only three roads the Battalion 2000 would have taken. Only a few A-37s circling would have stopped the Machos del Monte. Any sign of U.S. intercession would have frightened off most of the Noriega loyalists. Why hadn't Washington given them the orders to act?

"The rebels did their share, but the Americans didn't do theirs," said Noriega's friend, Mario Rognoni. "The Americans wanted a white-glove coup, American-style. The U.S. behaved like a lady in a whorehouse."

Noriega shipped Giroldi off to Battalion 2000 headquarters, according to U.S. military intelligence, where Major Olechea, the man who had abandoned Giroldi at the most critical moment, oversaw his torture and interrogation. The demonic Noriega was punishing and testing the untrustworthy Olechea.

Noriega was there as well to listen in. "Giroldi was the goose who laid the golden egg. He knew who had participated in the coup, what the U.S. had done, and who had promised to remain neutral."

If Noriega's bullet killed Giroldi, it was merely one of several. To dissuade other would-be traitors, Noriega invited a handful of officers—including the fence-sitting Olechea—to participate in gunning Giroldi down. His body was buried with several gunshot wounds, a cracked skull, and broken legs and ribs. Noriega wanted to send a signal to whoever might turn their guns against him in the future that this General wouldn't show mercy.

No matter who pulled the trigger, Adela Bonilla de Giroldi hasn't any doubt the gringos were the villains. "I blame the North Americans for my husband's death," she said later in Miami, looking worn in her Super Bowl XXIII T-shirt, while tending to three children with chicken pox. "They only had to show off their power and equipment and his coup would have worked. There would not have been a confrontation. No Panamanians are so stupid as to confront the North Americans."

The aftermath of the coup demonstrated why it had been so difficult for the United States to unseat Noriega despite more than two years of sanctions and threats.

While Washington concentrated on bickering and agreeing on its own version of events, Noriega brutally repaired his position. The coup was a political problem in Washington, but it was a matter of life and death for Noriega. Nothing could have made that clearer than when Bush's chief of staff, John Sununu, gave Noriega 8–5 odds against survival at a time when Noriega was torturing and executing opponents.

The Bush administration's war to protect its political self began with a flurry of false administration statements that claimed that the administration hadn't been involved at all in the coup. Even when reporters persistently questioned this version of events, State Department spokesman Richard Boucher stood his ground: "I think if we come out here and in good faith tell you that the U.S. government is not involved in these events in Panama, we're not trying to shade the truth and mislead people with statements like these."

White House spokesman Marlin Fitzwater dutifully reported that the Bush administration had never been directly informed of a coup plot. "If we were," he said, "the president doesn't know about it, the secretary of state doesn't know about it, and the secretary of defense doesn't know about it." He added later, "We never did have direct discussions with the leader of the insurgency at any point."

Once U.S. involvement was revealed, the Bush strategy shifted from cover-up to damage control. Senior officials tried to destroy the credibility of the coup makers to convince Americans that they hadn't deserved support. And for those who wouldn't swallow that, administration officials blamed the Senate Select Committee on Intelligence for preventing it from supporting any coup that might end in a leader's death.

Finally, a frustrated President Bush sent out the edict that his top advisers should stop all internal administration criticism over his handling of the coup. Deputy Assistant Secretary of State Michael Kozak phoned the embassy in Panama with the orders, and other officials did the same, until the carping all but dried up. The Defense Investigative Service began an investigation of reporters who were leaked details of American involvement in the coup.

However, the political sideshows continued to sap energy that Bush could have been using on Noriega. Perhaps the most intriguing—and most important—was the feud between two usually soft-spoken Washington warriors. Senate Intelligence Committee chairman David Boren, a Rhodes Scholar and astute political operator, criticized the administration for walking loudly and carrying a small stick. National Security Adviser Brent Scowcroft, a veteran Washington official who'd served in the same job for President Ford, responded by accusing the Congress of withholding the president's stick.

"Here you have brave people in Panama . . . trying to rid themselves of a drug dealer and thug who's taken over the country," said Boren. He argued it was "wrong" for the U.S., with all its belief in democracy, to stand by only two miles away "and do nothing."

Countered Scowcroft, "The Congress, by its actions and demeanor, certainly leaned us against the kinds of things they're now saying we should have done."

They never came out and said that their argument was about the interpretation of an executive order banning U.S. participation, direct or indirect, in political assassinations. However, President Bush, fearing chinks in his political armor, read a letter from the Intelligence Committee to President Reagan dated the previous October that implied the U.S. not only couldn't participate in a coup against Noriega but would have to inform him if it had knowledge that a coup was being hatched that could result in his death. Boren privately fumed that Bush might be violating the law by releasing such intelligence information.

Despite Bush's protestations that he would respond exactly the same way again in terms of using force, the Panama fiasco prompted a rash of rethinking and reorganizing. American officials worked furiously behind the scenes to draw up what didn't exist before the coup: contingency plans.

In addition, the White House and the Intelligence Committee began working on more liberal rules that would allow the president more leeway to back the next coup in Panama. One official likened the process, after Noriega had so totally purged his defense forces, to shutting the barn door after the cows were all gone.

Yet within a month after the coup, the administration was trying to corral the escaped cows with vigor. The Bush administration dispatched the highest-ranking entourage it had sent to date to the House and Senate intelligence committees to launch a new covert attempt to oust Noriega. President Bush had authorized the CIA, in what is known as a presidential "finding," to spend $3 million initially to recruit Panamanian officers and other dissidents to mount a coup against Noriega. It was the clearest confession of failure the Bush administration could have made.

The authorization also reflected a new interpretation of a thirteen-year-old executive order banning U.S. involvement in assassination of foreign leaders. For the first time, the prohibition did not prevent U.S. intelligence agencies from involvement in a plot that might indirectly lead to the killing of foreign political figures.

The senior member of the administration's briefing team was CIA Director William Webster, but Deputy Secretary of State Lawrence S. Eagleburger was its most articulate and forceful spokesman, because of Webster's reluctance to discuss any policy issues. They were accompanied by the Pentagon's Undersecretary for Policy Paul Wolfowitz, and Assistant Secretary of State for Inter-American Affairs Bernie Aronson. Three weeks after the coup failed, the administration was turning its big guns on Noriega.

Eagleburger, a twenty-five-year veteran of the State Department and of senior political positions in three Republican administrations, drew the outlines of the toughest policy yet toward Noriega, between feverish puffs on an endless chain of low-tar Vantage cigarettes. Eagleburger was a man known for his ready wit, likable demeanor, brilliant analytical skills, and self-destructive health habits.

When one congressman asked him whether Washington could compromise with Noriega, allowing him to seek exile in Spain or quiet retirement in Panama, Eagleburger's face reddened in anger. "There will be no compromise," he said. "He's going no place, unless it's to the United States."

Indeed, although Noriega won big in October, his victory was a hollow one. His circle of supporters grew even smaller, and he was forced to arrest or execute many of his best officers. That left many other soldiers and families with reason enough to go after Noriega. Ultimately, the Americans could afford far more mistakes. One mistake could cost Noriega his life.

Noriega had often said that only weak dictators use wholesale brutality. By his own measure, Noriega was in trouble.

Leaping more often into rages, sinking into bouts of drunkenness and mistrust, Noriega ordered the execution of at least seventy Panamanian troops in the days following the coup, and he arrested 600 others.

He fired more than a third of the government workers, many of whom had broken into celebration when Major Giroldi announced over the radio that he had seized power. That helped him cut a public payroll he could no longer meet and also sent a message throughout society that opposition to Noriega carried a heavy price.

Noriega also knew that his enemies had learned a key lesson: the General would leave office only on a slab. It had become clear that Noriega didn't want the graceful exit from power that Giroldi had offered him.

He continued to change the place he slept every night, sometimes several times nightly. His meals were most often prepared by the only women he trusted entirely, his full-time mistress, Vicky Amado, and her mother, Norma.

Noriega had found little joy in victory. He had grown rich beyond his wildest hopes, but he couldn't savor the luxury. American extradition papers waited in U.S. embassies around the world, so he couldn't travel, and at home, he feared even to fly between towns.

General Noriega had always been unlike other dictators: less brutal, more savvy, and preferring to remain in the background while pulling civilian politicians' strings. He was too complex to be easily understood. However, Giroldi's failed coup had finally transformed Noriega into a dictator whose means of holding power were simple and brutal. He murdered enemies, seized total power, and ruled by brutal caprice.

Noriega expressed his new and brutally simple policy in a speech two days after the coup: "Clubbings for the undecided, bullets for the enemies, and money to friends."

With every month, the Noriega story gained more the feel of Shakespearean tragedy than political science. The tragic General increasingly behaved like a man imprisoned by a strange fate. If he relinquished power, he feared his enemies would kill him; yet if he held on to it, he suspected that sooner or later some usurper would pull the trigger. He had become trapped in a world he had created himself, one of criminals, torturers, corrupt politicians, and opportunistic sycophants. They realized their own salvation required the General to stay in power.

Like Shakespeare's hunchbacked Richard III, Noriega had overcome his defects of birth to rise to power through misdeeds and an amoral passion for power. As did Richard III, he had "set the murderous Machiavel to school" and added "colors to the chameleon."

However, as with all virtuosos in evil, his power can only be temporary. His psychic, Ivan Trilha, was shipped abroad in mid-1989 when he told the General that he saw dark, threatening clouds over his future—the first time he had offered a pessimistic assessment of the General's outlook.

And like the tragic Richard III, Noriega was caught on a battlefield without escape, without a horse to carry him into war or to a safe retreat.

As Richard III said shortly before he was slain by Richmond:

> *Go Gentlemen, every man unto his charge.*
> *Let not our babbling dreams affright our souls;*
> *Conscience is but a word that cowards use,*
> *Devised at first to keep the strong in awe:*
> *Our strong arms be our conscience, swords our law!*
> *March on, join bravely, let us to it pell-mell,*
> *If not to heaven, then hand in hand to hell.*

CHAPTER
TWENTY-TWO

NORIEGA AND
THE NUNCIO

Life goes on. . . . We are just molecules.
—GENERAL NORIEGA, DECEMBER 27, 1989

It was December 24, 1989, although it didn't seem much like Christmas Eve to the American troops that had invaded just four days earlier. The weather was humid and tropical. The 25,000 American troops on the ground in Panama were sweating buckets. The real combat had lasted less than a day. Now, with their camouflage-painted faces and Kevlar helmets trailing shreds of camouflage cloth, they'd become the largest, best-armed, and most unusual posse in history, all hunting down one wanted man: General Noriega.

At the Vatican's embassy, known better as "the Nunciatura," three nuns and their helpers were preparing a holiday dinner for two dozen uninvited guests—mostly Noriega's officers and cronies who had taken refuge after the fighting began. The visitors' cots were lined up across one end of the downstairs dining hall; the long table had been pushed to the other end of the room. They were a rogues' gallery of asylum-seekers: a military chaplain who had sold his Catholic soul to the General; a corrupt banker with his two children and nanny; an immigration minister whose offices housed a cocaine lab; a half dozen officers suspected, among other things, of murder and torture; and four Basques from the ETA terrorist group whom Noriega had granted asylum. Almost as an afterthought, a Cuban worker straggled in, having shelled out $3,500 for a work permit, only to have the Americans oust the corrupt officials he had bribed.

Monsignor José Sebastián Laboa, the Vatican's ambassador to Panama, joked to friends that he was beginning to regret his return to Panama. He felt more like a hotelier, or perhaps a warden, than a nuncio. He had been vacationing in San Sebastián, a Spanish port city in his Basque homeland, when the morning news had brought word that the gringos had invaded. One American official had told the nuncio to delay his holiday because "something will happen." But he had heard U.S. saber-rattling too often before. When Panamanian rebels and the U.S. had blown the opportunity of the Giroldi coup three months earlier, the nuncio had grown convinced of two things: the Panamanians would never oust Noriega on their own and Bush wouldn't risk American lives unless Noriega directly threatened the lives of American citizens. So, after a short delay, he went on his vacation.

What the nuncio had not counted on was that Noriega's rhetoric would so quickly escalate that he would declare himself "maximum leader" and Panama as being in a state of war with the United States. The direct result had been a tense atmosphere in which Panamanian troops had shot one U.S. marine, beaten a navy lieutenant, and threatened the lieutenant's wife with sexual abuse. The unpreparedness of U.S. troops at the time of the Giroldi coup made the Bush administration determined not to balk, or to fail, when these provocations came.

The nuncio, who had been a key political figure in Panama ever since he had arrived seven years earlier, called his superiors and got clearance to return to Panama. He flew from Madrid to Miami on Spanish Iberia Air Lines. The problem was that from Miami only the U.S. air force could get him to Panama City. The nuncio, never much a friend of American foreign policy, swallowed his pride. He called Civic Crusade leader Aurelio Barria in Miami, who arranged through the State Department to get the nuncio a seat on a C-141 flying from Homestead Air Force Base the next night—the second night after the invasion. The nuncio frowned when an officer put a bulletproof vest over his cassock and quietly said a prayer. And when he arrived at 4 A.M., he withheld his anger when his baggage came up lost—including a fifteenth-century crucifix he carried everywhere. He arrived at the Nunciatura at dawn on December 22, 1989, two days before Noriega's desperate flight would bring the nuncio to the center of world attention.

When General Noriega walked through the two large, carved wooden doors of the papal residence at just after 2 P.M. on Christmas Eve, his cronies and other officers came to attention. The nuncio was surprised at the respect they still showed Noriega, although he was exhausted and defeated and hardly dictatorial in his Bermuda shorts and a tattered gray V-neck T-shirt. Many of them believed a special, supernatural power had allowed Noriega to survive so long. Noriega sat silently in the reception hall, under a painting of Pope John Paul II, and he drank a bottle of beer—then was ushered upstairs to the spartan room where he would spend his last eleven days in Panama.

A single crucifix hung on one wall, and a small desk rested against another. Noriega's only diversion would be a color television with cable channels but a badly blurred picture. There was sublime irony in the choice of rooms. Guillermo Endara, who had just been installed as president, had slept there less then two months earlier, during Noriega's rampage following the failed Giroldi coup. And the Church official Noriega disliked most, Panama's Archbishop Marcus McGrath, had slept there just the night before, taking shelter from the remaining members of Noriega's paramilitary. The nuncio mentioned this to his new houseguest.

"My God," Noriega exclaimed incredulously, "I'm going to sleep in McGrath's bed."

The General could at least take some comfort in the presence of his bodyguard, Captain Eliecer Gaytan, one of the few underlings who remained loyal to Noriega. Most of Noriega's allies were sycophants who had abandoned him in the first hours of the U.S. invasion, but Gaytan had profited little financially from his links to Noriega. Gaytan was motivated by devotion to his General. That loyalty without price was what had prompted the distrustful General to choose him to run his personal security and special forces.

Thirty minutes after Noriega arrived, another close ally followed in more dramatic fashion. Colonel Nivaldo Madriñan, the chief of the secret police, leaped over the back wall just a few hundred yards ahead of pursuing troops. His reputation for cruelty far exceeded that of Noriega. "Save me, save me, please let me in!" he shouted, shaking with fear.

One of the nuncio's friends, a Panamanian businessman named César Tribaldos, flung the door open. "Come in, you son of a whore," sneered Tribaldos. Tribaldos hurried upstairs to tell the nuncio of the latest uninvited check-in.

"Oh, dear lord, what am I going to do with all these people?" the nuncio groaned, shaking his head in despair. Noriega, Gaytan, and Madriñan—three men bound together by history—would be the key actors in the drama that unfolded at the Nunciatura in the coming days.

A little more than an hour after Noriega arrived, the nuncio phoned his friend Major General Marc Cisneros, the Mexican-American head of the Southern Command's army forces. The two had grown close over the previous three years, occasionally meeting for lunch and trading stories. The nuncio liked this Texas-born general who understood Latin cultures better than his counterparts. Cisneros wanted Noriega to surrender to the

U.S. immediately, but Noriega told the nuncio he had to rest before he could decide anything. "Just let me sleep for a while," Noriega pleaded softly and politely, hardly the blustering dictator.

News of Noriega's surrender at the Vatican residence was broadcast soon thereafter over Panamanian radio and television. Neighbors in high-rises overlooking the red-roofed Nunciatura, along with Panamanians all over the city, took to their balconies to bang pots and pans in joy, and the tinny cacophony could be heard clearly by the nuncio's guests. But Noriega heard nothing. He was sound asleep, and would be for more than twelve hours.

Laboa, one of the world's more Machiavellian monsignors, immediately began plotting. He thought about the problems Noriega would cause for each of the parties involved. For the Holy See, Noriega was an unwanted visitor who couldn't be thrown out, due to a nearly two-thousand-year history of providing asylum. This history was vitally important to John Paul II, a Polish pope whose views of the Church as a place of refuge from communist oppressors were deeply ingrained in his East European mind. Noriega certainly couldn't be turned over against his will to what a Vatican spokesman had publicly referred to as "an occupying power."

For Panama's new government, Noriega was a man who couldn't be allowed to take asylum in a foreign country, for fear that he'd still be able to cause problems for a new and fragile government. But he also couldn't be tried in Panama; it was doubtful the country had a jail that could hold him.

For the U.S. president George Bush, Noriega was the brass ring of a costly invasion. Because Noriega hadn't died in the fighting, bringing him to trial to Miami was a political necessity.

And the nuncio had his own problems. He had taken Noriega without consulting the Vatican; he argued to his superiors that he simply hadn't had time, having been given only ten minutes to decide by General Noriega. Now he had to get the pope out of the mess without creating any new precedents regarding asylum. The nuncio needed a solution that was both Christian and timely. "I had a hot potato on my hands," said the nuncio, "and the danger was that I could be juggling him for a long time."

Yet he saw only one solution. He had to create the right atmosphere in his embassy for some *mano a mano* talks with Noriega, and then he had to convince the General to turn himself in voluntarily to the Americans. That would be tricky, because Noriega had come in to the Nunciatura thinking he might gain asylum in a third country, as had so many others who had passed through during his rule.

"From the first moment, the key dangers were evident," the nuncio would say later. "Noriega couldn't be allowed to think about political asylum [in a third country]. Panama wouldn't let him go, nor would the United States. And I couldn't bring myself to hand him over—not to the U.S. and even less to the Panamanians."

Laboa was a hyperactive, gregarious archbishop who had been at the center of Vatican intrigues for years. After moving to Panama in 1983, several months before Noriega came to power, he had quickly established himself as the best-informed envoy in town. Everyone talked to the nuncio. A small group of diplomats collected every morning for breakfast at his table to exchange information. They took to calling themselves *le levée,* "the getting up," after the regular breakfast meeting of Louis XIV's advisers.

And the nuncio knew Noriega. He was one of the few men in the world whom the General trusted. The nuncio had been at the middle of some of the most sensitive negotiations aimed at Noriega's resignation. When Noriega had nearly stepped down in May 1988, it was the nuncio to whom he had shown portions of his resignation speech for approval. The nuncio had become a sort of Dutch uncle to Noriega—a man who spoke plainly to him, rebuking him when he erred but always leaving his door open. "The nuncio sometimes says things we don't like to hear, but he is always moved by a higher motive," Noriega would often tell officers who warned him against the man.

Those who knew the nuncio's history with Noriega couldn't believe the U.S. had unintentionally left the Vatican embassy unguarded. The fact that the nuncio had flown to Panama in a U.S. military plane only increased suspicion. And the nuncio said that he had mentioned to several American officials the possibility that Noriega would come to him in such a crisis. But senior U.S. officials and the nuncio insisted afterward that leaving Noriega this option was simply an oversight. The military had come to believe its own propaganda that only Cuba, Nicaragua, and Libya would provide Noriega shelter. And officers wanted to use their troops only at a limited number of fixed locations, thus leaving most soldiers free to go after Noriega's stubborn paramilitary.

Now, however, the nuncio was crucial to the Bush administration's thinking. The ultimate triumph of the largest American military action since Vietnam rested on his shoulders.

When the nuncio's talks with American authorities began on Christmas Day, he already knew what approach he wanted to take. He met with General Cisneros and the State Department's David Sciacatano across the street from his residence in the spartan principal's office of the St. Augustine School. The nuncio had thought about the concept of "asylum," and he'd decided that its broad definition would allow Noriega to be turned over to the American justice system. To him as a religious man, asylum meant saving someone's life and ensuring the person's human rights were protected. He saw only one way out. "My plan was to convince Noriega that the best way out was to give himself up, not to the U.S. or a military power, but to the legal system of the United States, which is fair and would respect his human rights," said the nuncio. "This plan would satisfy everyone's needs and wouldn't hurt anyone."

To implement this plan, the nuncio's first request was for American and Panamanian help to rid his embassy of its asylum-seekers, particularly of Gaytan and Madriñan. The two officers wanted asylum in Peru or Spain, and the nuncio wanted a response to their requests as soon as possible.

"I'm convinced that if the atmosphere in my embassy is the way I want it," said the nuncio, "I can probably convince Noriega to give himself up." But the nuncio needed time, the confidence and help of the U.S. and Panamanian governments—and the forbearance of his own pope—and he needed Gaytan and Madriñan out.

But no response would come from the U.S. representatives for more than a week.

The problem was in converting U.S. generals to this subtle strategy. The idea of their war being brought to a close through the conniving of a Spanish Basque nuncio was, well, heresy. And the generals resisted the embrace of a plan over which they had no control and which had no timetable. The nuncio would be the only one talking to all parties in the negotiations: the Vatican, the Bush administration, the new Panamanian government, and Noriega. U.S. officials never talked to Noriega directly; the Vatican wouldn't negotiate directly with Panamanian or American authorities. And Noriega wasn't talking to anyone but the nuncio.

The nuncio's plan brought a direct clash between a Mediterranean monsignor and the American military mind. General Maxwell R. Thurman was the most skeptical about the nuncio's sincerity, but he wasn't alone. Both he and General Carl Stiner, the operational master who oversaw the invasion, were unwilling to accept the nuncio's promises at face value. Intelligence files revealed some shady history from his days in the Vatican, Thurman told other U.S. officials. He was particularly chagrined by the nuncio's close links to Basque terrorists, four of whom were taking asylum in his embassy. Under an agreement with Spanish leader Felipe González, Noriega had granted asylum to these Basques when they had laid down their guns. The nuncio was the Spanish government's liaison. His relationship was so warm with these accused terrorists that visitors to the Nunciatura saw them setting the dinner table, hanging draperies, and otherwise helping out around the house.

When challenged in the past about his hospitality to such nefarious characters, the nuncio had quoted a story about a transformed thief from the Book of Luke in the New Testament. Christ, too, had been harshly criticized by his followers when he had visited the home of Zacchaeus, a thieving tax collector. But Zacchaeus had repaid Jesus's act by giving half his goods to the poor and repaying what he had stolen fourfold.

That wasn't good enough for Thurman, an unreconstructed pre–Vatican II Catholic whose brother was a "good" priest, not like the loose Latin clerics with political ambitions and loose morals. Thurman fumed when, on December 26, he saw Lieutenant Colonel Valarde leave his asylum at the Nunciatura and immediately ask the whereabouts of a woman U.S. officers believed to be his mistress. Valarde, a Catholic priest and Noriega's military chaplain, had been given his stripes and a healthy salary when he had sold out to the General.

"Laboa has been fishing in murky waters for fifteen years," Thurman argued to other U.S. officials at one meeting. "He had his own agenda at the Vatican, and he's had his own agenda in Panama." Thurman didn't trust Laboa to deliver on his promises. Neither did General Stiner nor John Bushnell, the acting head of the U.S. embassy, who had arrived in Panama only two months earlier. In fact, Bushnell had suggested another solution. He thought the U.S. should recruit Gaytan to carry his own General bodily out of the Nunciatura. Senior officials said a generous payment would have been required.

Only Cisneros believed in the nuncio. He understood from the beginning what Monsignor Laboa was trying to do, and he tried to find ways to assist him and explain him to Thurman. Yet Cisneros, a fluent Spanish speaker, had long been the object of suspicion by some of his superiors for being too close to the natives, and his backing for the nuncio only raised more eyebrows. The nuncio regarded him as his undeclared ally in a struggle with the military's inflexibility. They were up against an inbred American predilection to take big decisions to the top when the lower ranks don't give the desired result.

"Let's just kick this up to the pope and he'll make the decision," Thurman asserted. "The Vatican is where the action is."

At Thurman's urging, Secretary of State James Baker fired off cables to the Vatican asking for Noriega, an indicted criminal, to be turned over to American hands. Three cables came back from Rome, but they only acknowledged receipt of the U.S. messages, a polite cold shoulder in the diplomatic world. Unwilling to be dragged into a mess that might set some unwanted precedents, the Vatican wasn't responding. By Vatican design, the nuncio was on his own.

The nuncio shrugged when told of a threat of American attack on his residence, a danger he never believed existed. "If you invade us you will solve the problem for me," the nuncio said to General Cisneros. "But you will be left with a stain that will never go away. But if I hand him over, I would stain the Holy See. I prefer you bear the stain."

Laboa was playing clever poker, and President Bush would strengthen his hand. It just wasn't good politics to take on the Church at Christmas. "I don't want a war with the Vatican over this," Bush told a senior State Department official. The president was willing to be patient. Congress and the American people were busy with their holiday vacations.

What frustrated U.S. officials most was that the nuncio couldn't provide them any timetable for his strategy. Time and again the State Department would ask how long it would take to get Noriega out if they found a way to rid the nuncio of the two Panamanian officers, Gaytan and Madriñan.

In the first few days of Noriega's stay, the nuncio would only say the time wasn't ripe. For his plan, the nuncio believed, timing and atmosphere were everything. If he asked Noriega to decide too early, the General would say no and the consequence could be a perhaps irretrievable setback to his plan.

Moreover, in the first few days, Noriega was too shaken by his rapidly altered fortunes to plan ahead. "It all happened so quickly for him," said a deacon who works with the nuncio, Hermann López Arias. "He just couldn't absorb it. At first, Noriega expected he would gain asylum in a third country—like others who had taken refuge at the embassy."

But it was soon apparent he was a different sort of guest. On the evening of December 26, Noriega cowered under his blanket as American psychological operations hit a fever pitch. Blackhawk helicopters, sweeping in from the Bay of Panama, flew low enough to shake the windows of the Nunciatura, and troops set alight a field next to the residence, just outside Noriega's window, to create a new landing pad. The blaze turned Noriega's opaque windows a fiery red. "Are you listening?" Noriega shouted to two young Panamanian lawyers who had come to help the nuncio with his overcapacity crowd. "The gringos will climb over the wall. They're burning up the lot next door. Please go and check."

The helicopters continued to circle, like vultures. And an armored personnel carrier, its engines gunned, pulled up to the back gate repeatedly, with its headlights ablaze, braking and nudging the gate in threatening fashion. The next day Noriega complained about unheard intrusions: men with binoculars watched Noriega's window from the apartment building carport just outside it, and men with supersensitive microphones picked up his every whisper. Yet he seemed curiously untroubled by the loudest disturbance, which came from troops outside, blasting in rock music. The day's broadcast opened with a loud "Good Morning, Panama," after the Robin Williams Vietnam film. And the songs were chosen appropriately: "I Fought the Law (and the Law Won)" was a frequent repeat. Mock newscasts, played at high decibels, reported Panamanians breaking into the Vatican residence and taking Noriega apart limb by limb.

The nuncio was certain the music and news programs were intended to unsettle Noriega, despite American assurances that the broadcasts merely prevented eavesdropping. But all it seemed to do was disturb the nuncio. "I'm up all night, but Noriega is sleeping like a baby," he complained to a U.S. embassy official. The nuncio said it was the only time he was angry about U.S. actions during Noriega's stay.

What the nuncio wanted to do was carry out his low-decibel psychological warfare in peace. He wanted to bring Noriega slowly to the conclusion that a courtroom in Miami was his best, and only, alternative. Some of the measures were crude: despite the hot, tropical climate, Noriega's air conditioning was cut off. The nuncio's aides also removed the phone from Noriega's room and watched closely to prevent him from using the nuncio's phone or telefax down the hall. They kept him dry; the nuns emptied all the liquor from the cabinet. The Uzi machine gun that Noriega had carried into the papal mission was securely locked in the safe. And the General was left without his closetful of French-made uniforms. For Noriega, a man who had thrived in the underworld of corruption, prostitution, and intelligence-gathering, the Nunciatura must have seemed a lot like Dante's Hell.

Nevertheless, the General tried to take it philosophically.

One of the young Panamanian lawyers walked into General Noriega's room on December 27, three days after he had arrived and at a time when the fallen dictator still wasn't mixing with the nuncio's other guests. On television, the General was watching the blurred images of children ice-skating at Rockefeller Center. "Have your days been long?" the lawyer asked.

Noriega nodded to the television, and he pointed to an open Bible and a book by the daughter of the late Chilean president, Salvador Allende, who had fallen more dramatically in 1973 when he had reportedly killed himself as troops rocketed and closed in on his presidential palace.

"Well, I've learned nothing is so important in life that you can't do without it," said Noriega, a man who by then had lost everything. "Life goes on. . . . We are just molecules." The lawyer, Enrique Jelenzsky, soon stopped fearing Noriega. He only pitied him.

Some psy-ops were engagingly clever, often applied by the nuncio's visiting friends. A West German diplomat, Klaus Meixner, visited almost every day with food cooked by the nuncio's favorite chef: Meixner's Spanish wife. Upon leaving one evening, he made a remark outside Noriega's door that was intended for overhearing. "Good night," said Meixner, "and tell Noriega that if he likes life, he'll surrender to the Americans. History never lets cruel dictators survive. Just look at Anastasio Somoza," he said, referring to the Nicaraguan leader who, after being overthrown, had been blown up by a bazooka as he drove his luxury car in Paraguay.

The nuncio's pressures carried more subtlety and humor. "Do you want nuns washing your underwear for the rest of your life?" he asked the fallen dictator.

The nuncio slowly started pushing Noriega to make a decision, arguing that the Americans would treat him better if he didn't make them wait too long. "You may get a comfortable prison—a Colorado castle with all the amenities," he told Noriega, "but if you wait too long, you will be sitting in Alcatraz," the famously tough former federal prison.

The nuncio then faced another danger to his plan, this time from the Vatican. A Vatican spokesman suggested that the Holy See could never turn Noriega over to Washington. "An occupying power cannot interfere with the work of a diplomatic mission or demand that a person who is seeking asylum there be handed over to it," papal spokesman Joaquin Navarro said.

The Vatican seemed to be tailoring its response to third-world outrage over American intervention, instead of to Panamanian realities. In his effort to turn off this approach, the nuncio found two ready allies: the Panamanian bishops' conference and newly installed President Guillermo Endara.

In a statement, the Panamanian bishops' conference suggested that Noriega was a criminal who had to be brought to justice. The document persuaded the Vatican to treat Noriega as a common criminal, without any intrinsic right to be in the embassy, rather than as a political prisoner. What the Vatican probably didn't know, however, was that the nuncio had written the letter himself to fit neatly into his plan. But the Vatican preferred to have Noriega turned over to the Panamanians, if to anyone.

That's where Endara's letter came in. Its aim was to win the Vatican to the idea of Noriega being tried in the United States, where he would be more secure than in Panama. He argued that Noriega's continued stay in the Nunciatura raised the prospect of terrorism launched by followers who thought his continued survival was born of some "black magic." In the letter, he said Noriega had been "justly accused of homicide and narco-trafficking." He called upon the pope to end the sanctuary provided Noriega, after which the United States could arrest him. "In our judgment, this solution would save innocent Panamanian lives," he said. The Vatican was hence put on notice that the new Panamanian government didn't want to handle the merchandise. The letter was sent through the nuncio's fax machine, and it was leaked to the press, just in case the Vatican wasn't paying attention.

"We don't have a functioning judicial system," Endara had told the nuncio. "If we put him in jail, he'll either bribe or kill the guards." Another possibility, he said, was that Panamanians might lynch him—not the way he wanted to begin a government based on human rights.

The U.S. military made the Vatican's previous position all the more uncomfortable by releasing the sordid details of what it had uncovered at Noriega's homes and offices: collections of pornography, a "witches' house" full of voodoo objects, fifty kilograms of white powder (which was announced as cocaine, but, embarrassingly, was tamale flour), and a drug laboratory at the immigration ministry.

With the other parties under some control, and Noriega less on edge, the nuncio stepped up his subtle pressures. He knew he was up against the man who had written the psychological warfare manual for the Panamanian military. Yet he wasn't daunted. "I considered myself much more of a psychologist than him, and I had much more experience at it," he smiled later. In the past, the nuncio had managed to convince Noriega to allow his fiercest opponents to seek refuge at the Nunciatura and from there gain easy passage out of Panama.

The nuncio was surprised by the American obsession with the possibility that Noriega might take him hostage, something he thought his relationship with Noriega precluded. Thurman believed Noriega must have had a hidden reason for coming to the Nunciatura, and he could only assume taking hostages was a prime possibility. "They feared Panama would become an Iran or Vietnam," the nuncio said.

Nevertheless the nuncio used the Americans' fear to advance his own plan. At American request the nuncio signed a release that would allow U.S. troops to storm his residence if Noriega or his men should take him hostage. American officials, with the nuncio's blessing, released news of the agreement, and the reports were broadcast on Panamanian television, which Noriega was watching in his room. He trooped out the door immediately and asked the nuncio if the reports were true.

The nuncio shrugged. "I have done this, but I can assure you that I never believed you would come to this point," said Monsignor Laboa. "It is as if someone asked me whether they could put out a fire, if someone should start a fire. I don't expect the fire, but our safety is of the most importance. . . . I am ready to give my life for Jesus Christ, but I am not willing to die for a political cause."

The nuncio never lost his sense of humor or his pragmatism. At one point, two State Department officials walked to the gate and suggested that, considering the threat of hostage taking, he at least get the three nuns out of the building. "I'm sure I should do it," he said, then reconsidered. "But if I let them go, who will do the cooking and laundry?"

The nuncio's bigger concern was that Noriega would commit suicide, another potential stain on the Vatican and himself. He had heard that Noriega had threatened suicide the night before he had come to the Nunciatura, but he nevertheless considered this outcome only a faint possibility. "Noriega was more cunning than that," he said later. In fact, preserving his own life was Noriega's obsession in the days following his capture. The nuncio restricted Noriega from roaming around most of the mission, but Noriega limited his own movements even further. He avoided windows and even the shaded palm court out of fear that snipers would gun him down.

As Noriega grew more comfortable at the Nunciatura, he began to move around. Ever a Christian, the nuncio provided a sumptuous New Year's Eve meal with special Panamanian trimmings. West German diplomat Klaus Meixner delivered a turkey through U.S. military lines in the early afternoon, cooked by his wife.

A crowd outside, demonstrating against Noriega's continued asylum, offered to replace the bird with one of the vultures that were symbolically circling overhead. When Meixner came inside, Colonel Madriñan asked what was for dinner. "For the good visitors, I have turkey," Meixner said, "and for the bad visitors, the people outside are chasing down some vultures." Noriega and his two officers didn't laugh.

New Year's Eve dinner was the first time since Noriega's arrival, a week earlier, that he joined the others at the table. They all ate from the same carcass—the good visitors and the bad visitors. Noriega recalled a conversation with the nuncio, during which he had asked whether he believed Panamanian reports that in a painting, the image of the Messiah was perspiring. "Why not," the nuncio had answered. "Everyone sweats in

Panama." They laughed. The nuncio saw Noriega's resistance was fading. Now would be the time to start convincing him to leave.

By New Year's Day, though, the Bush administration still hadn't answered the original requests of Gaytan and Madriñan to obtain asylum. Without that the nuncio couldn't get them or Noriega to focus on the next move. The problem in Washington was partly mistrust of the nuncio and partly bureaucracy. Cisneros' requests, relayed by voice, were slowed by being passed through a couple of layers in Panama and then a couple in Washington. On December 31, State Department official Michael Kozak finally entered the fray to help break the apparent impasse, once again embroiling himself in an effort to get Noriega out of Panama.

When Kozak arrived, General Thurman still wanted the State Department to press the Vatican. But Kozak quickly discovered the Vatican route was futile. "It's clear nothing is going to happen in Rome," State Department Undersecretary Robert Kimmit, who was working the problem in Washington, told his men in Panama. "The way we understand it, the action is on the ground."

Kozak knew the U.S. answer was no to asylum. The committee approach had merely failed to deliver the response. The nuncio was growing frustrated and demanding a response. Now the trick was getting Washington to say no as quickly as possible, so that the negotiators could move on to other things. Kozak and Cisneros drafted a proposed one-page response rejecting the asylum requests, and they sent it to Washington for approval. They also prepared a response to Noriega's concerns about facing the death penalty and/or a "loan back" to Panama for a trial there.

It took another thirty-six hours for Washington to respond. On January 1, the Americans called for a meeting with the nuncio, as usual in the principal's office. The nuncio embraced Kozak. "I told Noriega you were here," the nuncio said to Kozak, who had talked to Noriega for hours in previous negotiations that would have yielded a far happier conclusion. "He remembers you sympathetically and with big confidence," the nuncio told Kozak.

Kozak laughed. "I keep getting embraced by skunks."

Kozak tried to show good faith to the nuncio by revealing details of covert activities that Noriega had run against the Church under the code name "Operation Judas." Anti-Noriega priests were being portrayed as homosexuals, Kozak said, quoting documents American troops had found after the invasion. But the nuncio, it turned out, knew even more than Kozak. He named the officers in charge of the operation, and he said the former chief of intelligence had told him all.

The Americans then passed word to the nuncio that asylum for Gaytan and Madriñan had been refused. They'd have to go through American processing at Fort Clayton, just like all other prisoners of war. Regarding Noriega, the U.S. wanted him in the hands of U.S. forces, to be brought to a fair and safe trial. The document noted that none of the charges against Noriega warranted the death penalty. Others in Washington had resisted that language, but Cisneros and Kozak argued successfully that it was merely a statement of fact. The statement also helped the nuncio with the Vatican, which feared turning the General over, only to have him executed later. The Americans couldn't satisfy Noriega's request for assurances that he not be given over to the Panamanians, whom he apparently feared more than the gringos.

"As a practical matter, Noriega can avoid being sent back to Panama only by pleading guilty and asking for the maximum sentence," Kozak told the nuncio. He said the U.S. then wouldn't be able to loan back Noriega for trial. "The only guarantee we can give him is the U.S. justice system itself," said Kozak. For some reason, the nuncio liked that line, and he rehearsed it a couple of times.

Late on New Year's Day, the nuncio, still seeking room to maneuver, proposed to clear his embassy by "loaning" all his asylum-seekers except Noriega to other embassies. The U.S. negotiators said no. It was too complicated. So he proposed instead that the Panamanian government award diplomatic immunity to a second location for the Vatican—not an unusual request, since most ambassadors have both an embassy and a residence that is protected. The nuncio proposed that a wing of the St. Augustine School be used to house Noriega's henchmen while he kept Noriega isolated at the Nunciatura. The Americans considered this a far better idea.

But by the morning of January 2, the nuncio didn't want to move anyone. An anti-Noriega demonstration scheduled for the following day had raised such fears in Gaytan and Madriñan that they were both counseling Noriega to turn himself in to save his own life. They worried that Panamanians would come in after Noriega or, worse yet, the Americans would use the entry of Panamanians as a pretext to come in themselves. Noriega had been watching reports on television about the ouster and murder of Romanian leader Nicolai Ceaucescu, and that only made him more nervous.

"Gaytan is being very helpful," the nuncio said. "I want him to stay. I think I can settle this thing in two days."

Thurman and Stiner were still skeptical. They doubted Noriega could be talked into American captivity. The only alternative was storming the Nunciatura. Thurman's men were practicing just such a mission in the field outside Panama City, using smoke bombs as a fog to conceal their entry. But the fact was that such an attack was improbable, and when a Vatican emissary arrived to boost Monsignor Laboa's confidence and individual authority, Thurman grew more convinced that he had to rely on the nuncio.

Kozak gave the nuncio a message to carry to the General. "Last year, Noriega and I worked very hard together," Kozak said. "But Noriega lost a very good alternative for him and everyone else because he dithered. Now the General is down to his last alternative, and if he delays, he's going to lose that and he's going to lose a whole lot more."

The nuncio was chastened. He said that he would declare to Noriega the next morning that he "would have to leave within four hours" or unspecific American actions might follow. Kozak said it would be better if the nuncio could pass the message that night. The nuncio, an endlessly talkative man, was silent. Thinking better of it, he never issued any ultimatum, but instead continued to play his more subtle psychological game.

On the evening of January 2, the nuncio had the first of his two longest meetings with Noriega and his two officers in the front reception hall of the embassy. A portrait of the pope hung overhead. Nearby was Archbishop Laboa's coat of arms, whose inscription he had often pointed out to Noriega: *Solvitur in Excelsis*—everything is solved from above.

The nuncio doubted any danger to Noriega from the Panamanian demonstration due the next day. But the nuncio deliberately didn't dissuade the three Panamanian officers from their fears that the gringos would let through a bloodthirsty crowd.

"I had to point out to him all the dangers present in any other solution," said the nuncio. "I told him he would be able to remain here; I would never kick him out." The nuncio added pointedly, however, that he could provide no security. How long would U.S. forces remain around the embassy and not let a mob come in and lynch him? A situation might arise where the U.S. soldiers would have no control, or the U.S. might provoke an incident, the nuncio suggested.

"I'm sure U.S. soldiers will never open fire on Panamanians if the masses get in," the nuncio told Noriega. (In fact, he had been told as much by military officers just a few hours earlier.) "And then you would face the fate of Mussolini," the nuncio said, referring to the Italian leader whose people had shot him and hung him from a lamppost after his World War II defeat. "That would be a very undignified end for you."

Colonel Nivaldo Madriñan agreed that Noriega should leave. Gaytan, a man Noriega trusted and respected perhaps more than any other, told the General to save his own life by giving up. Miami, Gaytan said, was the only way.

That evening Noriega told the nuncio he was prepared to leave. Noriega's fear was so great after disclosing the decision that he asked his loyal bodyguard to sleep on the hallway floor outside his door. By that point Gaytan didn't know what to fear more: Noriega's suicide or American troops and Panamanians outside.

The nuncio didn't sleep well that night. He knew his next day's task was to prevent Noriega from changing his mind. To isolate Noriega from any influences that might dissuade him, he or a member of his staff talked to the General nonstop throughout the day. "They talked to him in his room, in the hallway, in the kitchen, everywhere he went," said César Tribaldos, a close friend of the nuncio, who spent some of the day at his mission. "Noriega is a man who changes moods like others do undershirts." And in Panama, that's at least twice a day.

At 10 A.M. on January 3, President Endara pulled aside Kozak at a meeting at the presidential palace. "An emissary from the nuncio just visited me," Endara said. "He talked to Noriega last night and he agreed to leave tonight or tomorrow morning. He wants me to shut down this demonstration." Endara was skeptical Noriega would carry through. But the new Panamanian president was also worried about the demonstration. American intelligence had picked up reports that members of Noriega's paramilitary would infiltrate the crowd to plant a bomb or open fire on American troops around the Nunciatura to provoke a bloodbath.

Kozak said the U.S. embassy was trying to have the organizers at least break up the protest by nightfall, to prevent the risk of sniper fire by Noriega loyalists.

At about noon the nuncio urgently sent for Kozak. While he sat in the room, the nuncio watched another priest call a Civic Crusade leader, begging him to postpone the demonstration. "Ask him to put it off for just forty-eight hours," the nuncio implored. "You tell them that if Noriega doesn't go through with this deal, I'm going to have the American troops come in." The nuncio didn't mean it, but he was growing desperate to head off anything that might undermine Noriega's decision to leave.

Noriega might have feared the crowds. But the nuncio worried that a too modest protest—always possible among the civilized Panamanians—might stir Noriega's legendary stubbornness and prompt him to dig in his heels. He also feared that Noriega might decide that walking out in the face of protests was an unacceptable humiliation.

In the early afternoon Noriega outlined some further conditions for surrender that were carried to the Americans by Father Joseph Spiteri, the nuncio's executive secretary. Some had been inspired by Gaytan, who wanted to preserve his General's dignity even upon surrender.

—Noriega wanted to wear his uniform. "He can come out dressed however he wants," said Cisneros.

—He wanted to call his family. Cisneros said it was the nuncio's phone, so he could decide.

—The General didn't want press coverage, and he wanted to come out at night to ensure that the cameras poised overhead, on the balconies of the Holiday Inn, wouldn't record his surrender. "We have no interest in coverage either," said Cisneros. "We aren't inviting the press to the cere- mony." But U.S. officials did want Noriega to move up his departure from 9:30 or 10:00 P.M. to just after nightfall.

—Noriega wanted a general officer to be present, at least giving the pretense of military surrender by a defeated commander. Cisneros didn't formally agree, but he assured the nuncio that the generals would be there.

When the the Panamanian demonstration began, with chants of *"jus- ticia"* and "no mercy," it was far smaller and gentler than expected. The nastiest display was the carrying of skewered pineapples, a reference to the pockmarked dictator's nickname, *La Piña*. The nuncio took undeserved credit for having reduced the size and quelling the heat of the protests. Noriega hardly noticed the protests, though, engaged as he was in constant meetings with the nuncio and his staff. His decision to surrender stayed firm.

From 2 P.M. to 5 P.M. the nuncio met nonstop with Noriega in the upstairs library, interrupted only by occasional phone calls. Monsignor Laboa was seeing to it that his influence prevailed. "Up to the last minute in the meetings with his people and me, there was no ultimatum," said the nuncio. "My last words were, 'You have to decide, I will never tell you to leave. But if you want what I think is wise advice, you will make your decision as soon as possible.'" Noriega, as usual, listened silently.

After their meeting Noriega called his wife at the Cuban residence, where she had taken refuge. He wrote letters to his family. He wrote the pope, to whom he declared his innocence and then praised the nuncio for treating him justly.

When it was clear Noriega was leaving, one of the lawyers who had been helping the nuncio asked the General if he would mind posing for a photograph. "Would it be dangerous for you if we take a picture?" asked the lawyer, Enrique Jelenzsky.

"Not at all," Noriega replied. "Just let me put on a clean shirt." He returned shortly thereafter and posed with them, and then with Madriñan, and afterward with one or two others. He was patient and serene.

At about 6 P.M. on January 3, the nuncio held mass in the Vatican residence's small chapel. Noriega attended, for only the second time since he had come to the Nunciatura. In an effort to assuage Noriega's sense of being deserted, the nuncio talked about loyalties. About how friends sometimes disappoint us. Noriega had talked to one of the nuncio's friends about abandonment. He had lost his erstwhile American sponsors, his own officers, and then his many friends who had so richly profited from their relationship with him. "Our only assurance and loyalty," the nuncio said, "is that God will never abandon us."

After mass, Noriega prepared carefully for his surrender. He climbed the stairs calmly, and put on his neatly pressed uniform, which had been delivered him that day from the apartment of his mistress Vicky Amado. Four stars were stitched on each of its shoulder boards, and his name rested over his heart. Simply NORIEGA. The time passed slowly. The nuncio still feared Noriega might change his mind.

As Noriega prepared to leave the Nunciatura, Monsignor Laboa asked for one last search of his room. Under the bed he found an AK-47 and plenty of ammunition, apparently left behind by one of the officers who had left the refuge earlier. Laboa was horrified. Noriega could have taken hostages at any time, it seemed—or he could have killed himself. Yet he had taken neither course. He had simply seen no point in either route, but he had kept those options open to himself until the very end. Laboa felt tricked by the General.

At about 8 P.M., Father Joseph walked across the street and told the huddled Americans that Noriega would come out at 8:30 P.M. They had already landed a helicopter on a small baseball field just behind the school. No helicopter had landed in that small area since Noriega had taken refuge at the Nunciatura, eleven long days earlier. Journalists watching from balconies overlooking the Nunciatura in the Holiday Inn spread the word.

The helicopters' blades whirred in anticipation, and soon Panama City was buzzing with rumors that Noriega would soon surrender. Kozak and General Thurman sat on a bench in the courtyard in back of the St. Augustine School, waiting for word that Noriega had left his safe refuge. New instructions for dealing with him had arrived from Washington, but American officials had chosen to ignore them. None of the U.S. officials there was going to blow this chance.

Television cameramen moved to their balconies, adjusting their night lenses and squinting to see anyone, anything, through the dark. Editors called nervously. First-edition deadlines were passing, and everyone seemed to sense that the end was near. Then, some dark images could be seen moving into the night.

General Manuel Antonio Noriega, age fifty-five, walked into the dark courtyard at 8:44 P.M., wearing his uniform and carrying a Bible. He stumbled twice on the unfamiliar terrain outside the Vatican residence as two priests and the papal nuncio trailed a few paces behind. Monsignor Laboa and Father Joseph had promised Noriega they would walk with him to the helicopter. The third priest, the most outspoken cleric against Noriega, bade farewell at the gate. "I will pray for you every day," said Father Javier Villanueva.

"Gracias," General Noriega mumbled, his head hanging and his eyes glazed. The intelligence officer who once noticed everything now looked only at the ground in front of his next step.

He walked through the huge, black iron gates. He took one, perhaps two steps in freedom. Then members of the Delta Force trained their guns on him. One or two others frisked him for weapons. He was clean. Thurman and Cisneros stood nearby. But despite the trappings of military surrender, Noriega would be treated as a captured criminal. A soldier pulled behind Noriega and pushed the General gently on his way toward the waiting chopper. The priests walked just behind Noriega. The General, his head hanging forlornly, walked forward slowly on heavy legs.

Michael Kozak had expected to feel elation, but instead he felt an odd sadness. He'd never seen anyone look so utterly defeated in his entire life. He told a friend that it was like watching the neighbor's vicious dog, a hound you had wanted to shoot for years, get run over by a truck. "It's lying on the street with its back broken, and it's whimpering and crying," Kozak said. "You can't help but feel sorry for him."

The General and his captors walked around to the back of the school. They stopped before two short flights of cement stairs leading to the baseball field and the chopper. "Has there been a positive ID?" shouted a member of the Delta Force, which would transport Noriega to Howard Air Force Base, where he would be stripped, checked by doctors, handcuffed, and taken to Miami. Someone had to finger formally the most famous man in Panama, who at one time had eluded trackers by using a double.

Thurman told Kozak, who knew him best, to perform the task.

So when Noriega turned on the landing to descend the last set of stairs, Kozak hung back, above him, so he could see the General's face clearly. "Yeah, that's him," said Kozak, turning to Thurman. "They don't make too many who look like that."

Drug enforcement agents pulled Noriega's trembling hands behind his back. They slapped on wire handcuffs. Noriega, looking desperate and humiliated, turned to Father Joseph for explanation. "It's for your safety," Father Joseph shouted over the helicopter's roar. The agents hauled Noriega into the chopper.

Almost immediately, it pulled away. The wind swept the nuncio's white skullcap off his head. It flew off across the baseball field like a wild Frisbee, and a couple of soldiers scurried after it.

EPILOGUE

OUR OWN
WORST ENEMY

Noriega's downfall was also America's tragedy.

Never mind the old-fashioned Yankee euphoria conjured up by the vision of a manacled, fallen dictator, brought to justice on a U.S. Air Force C-130. And pay no attention to the U.S. officials engaging in self-congratulation, satisfied that American force was again righting wrongs and furthering democracy.

It was all a misplaced celebration of American might.

The use of massive military force in December 1989 that brought Noriega's rule to an end was the final proof of the failure of American foreign policy in Panama. After more than two years of trying to negotiate or coerce Noriega from power, the invasion was the last resort and the final surrender to a no-win policy that had envisioned success at far less cost and trouble. Even more, it was an indictment of the United States' thirty-year affair with General Noriega, a relationship that had begun with his furtive recruitment into espionage as a young military cadet and ended with Noriega as Federal Prisoner 41586.

U.S. political pressure, intelligently applied and mixed with appropriate incentives, might have avoided military action and eased Noriega from power earlier and far more quietly. Such an approach would have left Panamanians with more of the responsibility for reforming and rebuilding their economy and political system. Now the U.S., as the invading force, bears the responsibility of an invader—to rebuild what it has torn asunder. The price has been high: twenty-five American lives, perhaps a thousand Panamanian fatalities, and $1.5 billion in damages.

For more than two years, the U.S. followed an inconsistent course of halfhearted economic sanctions and unfulfilled threats that helped destroy one of the region's healthiest economies but left Noriega in place. And Washington's focus on domestic politics in the presidential campaign year of 1988 prevented the consistent, patient policy that might have been successful in negotiating Noriega from power.

Washington's bungled affair with Noriega might be the best case study yet to illustrate the cost to America of abandoning its democratic principles in implementing short-term foreign-policy goals. General Noriega isn't the only villain in this episode; it is also Washington's inconsistent and often unconsidered approach to international affairs, an unfortunate by-product of American democracy. America, not Noriega, is its own worst enemy.

The Noriega story is also a tale of good and evil. The United States helped create the evil, then made it worse by ignoring its existence until it had become a festering sore that couldn't be ignored any longer or healed with anything short of catastrophic surgery.

There isn't an administration in the last twenty years that can't share the blame. The Nixon administration had intelligence that Noriega was involved in drugs. The Ford administration, with George Bush as its director of Central Intelligence in 1976, discovered that Noriega was buying the services of its intelligence agents. The Carter administration caught him illegally shipping arms to Nicaraguan resistance forces in the late 1970s, on behalf of Panamanian leader Omar Torrijos. And when Noriega came to power in 1983, the Reagan administration was already paying him some $185,000 to $200,000 annually—equal to the annual salary of the American president—despite evidence that he was involved in drug trafficking, that he had stolen elections, sanctioned the beheading of a political opponent, and corrupted an entire military and political structure.

Yet Washington shrugged off the many favors Noriega had done once it decided to oust him. Now America was the force for good pitched against Noriega's evil. But, as the philosopher Blaise Pascal said, "Evil is flexible and has intricate forms." The corollary is that good was a muscle-bound giant, reluctant to throw its weight around and hopelessly awkward at matching Noriega's artistry in covert action and psychological warfare. When the U.S. finally did decide to act, it was with massive force that seemed excessive in stamping out this relatively minor threat to national security.

With the triumph of the moment in Noriega's downfall, it was easy to forget the closeness of the past relationship. Noriega was able to manipulate his U.S. sponsors and friends for nearly three decades because he knew what he wanted and he understood Washington well enough to get it. America failed because it never knew what it wanted from its relationship with Noriega and it never understood the dangers he represented until it was too late.

Noriega wanted power. He cleverly used the United States to help get it, through America's early sponsorship and development of his career, and ultimately through America's protection. He gained prestige and knowledge that helped him outflank opponents to rise to power. And once he had power, they helped him hold on to it. When he faced a backlash after stolen elections, or when a coup was being plotted against him, the U.S. not only held its punches but even occasionally provided intelligence that helped Noriega fend off foes.

What Noriega recognized was that American foreign policy most often is a complex result of individuals' ambitions and competing bureaucratic agendas. So Noriega fed American agencies and their representatives. He gave intelligence and a listening post to the CIA; he afforded the Pentagon surprisingly free use of bases; he turned narco-traffickers (often his own competition) over to the Drug Enforcement Administration, and he shipped off criminals to the FBI, despite the lack of any extradition treaty. In short, he consistently served America's narrowest interests, all the time satisfying his own agenda, which included facilitating money laundering, the sale of intelligence and high technology to the Cubans, and the transfer of arms to guerrilla movements throughout the region.

The United States was Noriega's earliest sponsor, promoter, and adviser until it became his final enemy. But Washington engineered the divorce as poorly as it had conducted the marriage. Instead of destroying the Frankenstein monster that it had helped to create, its halfway policies extended Noriega's political life by giving him a cause, an excuse for brutal repression, while never posing a significant enough threat to provoke U.S. action. America acted with the reluctance of a partner contemplating the cutting off of a little bit of itself.

The mishandling of the Noriega affair is also a broader indictment of the way the United States transacts its international business. Put most simply, American foreign policy isn't made, it just happens. Goals are seldom matched by the means to achieve them, and rhetoric is often unaccompanied by action. The best of intentions often produce the worst of consequences.

American foreign policy isn't the well-considered result of some deliberate process that can be explained on a chalkboard. It is messier and more cynical than that. Look first to the vaguer incentives of domestic politics, bureaucratic agendas, and the ambitions of individual officials. Then factor in the universal desire of officials in Washington to avoid the sorts of political risks that could shape history but might also ruin careers.

Domestic politics is America's strongest force. Yet such concerns command too short an attention span to inspire the difficult and comprehensive measures required against modern-day evils such as disagreeable dictators, drug dealers, and terrorists. Noriega's sins were quickly eclipsed by the television storm of a presidential election, riots in Beijing, and a San Francisco earthquake. He ceased to be a problem to the U.S. until the media discovered him again or until he became a campaign issue. Yet for Panama, he remained as an untreated, malignant tumor.

Washington's policies are shaped by a constantly shifting set of motivations, priorities, and forces that tend to confuse (and sometimes abandon) allies. That makes it difficult to promote, or even to define, national interests. The approach to Noriega over the years has shifted with the political whims of the moment. Promoting democracy, however, hasn't ever been the driving force of U.S. policy toward Panama.

President Theodore Roosevelt's decisive gunship intervention in 1903 to enforce Panamanian independence from Colombia was motivated by the desire to build a canal. During World War II, the U.S. backed the ouster of the country's most popular president ever, Arnulfo Arias, largely because he wouldn't allow his country and its merchant fleet to become adjuncts to the American war effort. Fighting communists and Castro thereafter prompted the United States to promote the development of a Panamanian military that grew far beyond the size needed to defend the country. After that military took power in 1968, the effort to conclude a new Panama Canal Treaty prompted officials to overlook increasing evidence of the military's corruption and Noriega's own nefarious activities. And the Reagan administration's obsession with Nicaragua and the Contras again resulted in support for Noriega at a time when his misadventures had reached historic proportions.

No, desire for democracy didn't turn the Reagan administration against Noriega. Drugs did. In "just say no" America, Noriega's two indictments on drug charges in February 1988 transformed him from a disagreeable dictator to a domestic political problem. In one judicial stroke, carried out in Florida, apparently without foreign-policy considerations, Noriega became untouchable. He had become a political symbol, a stereotype easy to hate and impossible to accommodate: a drug-dealing dictator. The Panamanian opposition even invented a new term to describe his rule: "Narco-militarism."

The papal nuncio, Monsignor José Sebastián Laboa, has good reason to be convinced that certain U.S. institutions would have happily continued the relationship with Noriega, had not the indictments and senate hearings brought the problem to the attention of the American public.

"The American people weren't ever to blame," said the nuncio. "When the people got to know who Noriega was, they not only rejected him but also insisted there be no relations or deals with him. The problem is that your institutions aren't as moral and ethical as your people. Had not this reached the American public, this situation would have gone on."

Perhaps the heart of the problem, once the U.S. turned on Noriega, was that American officials underestimated the General, a more complex and resourceful figure than his stereotype suggested. He was more of a master puppeteer than a military dictator. He was an intelligence agent at heart, who preferred spying on enemies to running a nation. He preferred pulling strings from backstage, and he relied upon psychological warfare far more readily than direct confrontation. He said in his high school yearbook that he wanted to become a psychiatrist and president; he became both.

Not understanding his hidden strengths, the Reagan administration thought this diminutive general would be just another easy notch on its anti-dictator handgun. The administration was intoxicated with its 1986 success in unseating Philippine dictator Ferdinand Marcos and Haiti's Jean-Claude "Baby Doc" Duvalier. Even Chile's Augusto Pinochet had been forced into a referendum that would put his rule on the line.

Surely, this five-foot-six-inch, uncharismatic, homely figure in Panama couldn't stand up to American pressure. Yet Noriega was a new breed of despot: a combination of ghetto street-fighter, Oriental mystic, intelligence agent, and Mafia godfather. And he had a host of opportunistic friends who—in a bid to profit—would extend his rule. The Israelis provided him intelligence and security advice. The Taiwanese and Japanese looked for business opportunities. The Cubans provided propaganda advice and special-forces training.

Even at the very end American military officers miscalculated the General. Some feared he'd go to the jungle to lead a guerrilla war; but Noriega was no Che Guevara. And when Noriega took refuge in the papal residence, the collective wisdom of American generals was that he would take hostages; but the General also wasn't the Ayatollah Khomeini. And others believed he would kill himself; but Noriega was no Adolf Hitler either.

General Noriega just never quite seemed to fit the American stereotype of a dictator. Noriega the survivor was the cunning manipulator, not the idealist or ideologue. He surrendered quietly, despite the fact that he had an AK-47 with plenty of ammunition hidden under his mattress at the Nunciatura to take his life—or the lives of others—at any time. Noriega, silently relying on his own cunning, realized that both courses were equally suicidal.

So he chose the best of the remaining alternatives. He left the war ground and his homeland to carry his combat with the United States to the courtrooms of Miami. The ultimate survivor was very far down, but he was not yet out.

Even in defeat and disgrace, General Noriega plotted another battle.

NOTES

FOREWORD: BLOOD UNDER THE PILLOW

I will only tell you honestly Noriega's interview with the Madrid newspaper *ABC*'s supplement, *Blanco y Negro,* May 26, 1989, pp. 24–29.

I found Ivan Trilha The bulk of the foreword comes from the author's two lengthy interviews with Ivan Trilha in November 1988 at his "clinic." Author also interviewed other Trilha patients and several of Noriega's friends regarding Trilha's influence on Noriega.

The lawyer told of one client The lawyer's allegations, made in November 1988, were confirmed with a senior Panamanian government official, who said that Madriñan came to work closely with drug interests and that he was at the forefront of efforts to crack down on any dealers or money launderers who hadn't reached some business agreement with the Panamanian Defense Forces.

But by Panamanian standards The body was dumped on the driveway of Marcus Ostrander, a Panamanian-American lawyer. The details came from author's interview with military intelligence source, March 1989.

Everyone was sleeping Author's interview with Joel McCleary, February 1988. Also see Frederick Kempe, "Panama Plotter: American Buddhist Aids Noriega's Foes," *Wall Street Journal,* April 8, 1988, p. 1.

CHAPTER ONE   LAST RESORT

Yet an unfamiliar tension Author's interview with military intelligence source and also official cables recounting the incident, January 1990.

Captain Haddad's foot Author's interview with military intelligence official, cited above, and interview with Haddad with Southern Command Television reporter, December 1989.

As the car raced William Branigin, "Marines' Wrong Turn Set Stage for Invasion," *Washington Post,* January 4, 1990.

They kicked me The quotes come from the lieutenant's videotaped interview with Southern Command Network, December 1990. His face was blurred electronically due to his sensitive position in Southern Command. Also see above, William Branigan, "Marines' Wrong Turn Set Stage for Invasion" and Walter Pincus, "Pair of Incidents Pushed Bush Toward Invasion," *Washington Post,* December 24, 1989.

On Sunday morning George J. Church, "Showing Muscle," *Time,* January 1, 1990, p. 20.

Business as usual George J. Church, *Time,* cited above.

Enough is enough Jack Nelson, "Enough is Enough, President Declared," *Los Angeles Times,* December 21, 1989.

Three military alternatives Bernard E. Trainor, "Gaps in Vital Intelligence Hampered U.S. Troops," *New York Times,* December 21, 1989.

Bush quizzed Powell David Hoffman and Bob Woodward, "President Launched Invasion With Little View to Aftermath," *Washington Post,* December 24, 1989.

In the end Thomas M. DeFrank and Ann McDaniel, "Bush: The Secret Presidency," *Newsweek,* January 1, 1990, pps. 26–27.

At 2 P.M. Tuesday Michael Gordon, "U.S. Drafted Invasion Plan Weeks Ago," December 24, 1989.

Further advance warning The reconstruction of the Noriega chase comes from author's interviews with two intelligence officials and one senior military officer, January 1990. Sources also provided access to sanitized versions of intelligence documents recounting Noriega's final hours.

A team from the crack Frederick Kempe, "Give Noriega This: He Adds New Twist to the Word 'Wily,' " *Wall Street Journal,* December 22, 1989.

At 7 P.M. Monday evening Author's interview with Rubin and two other members of his platoon, January 1990.

The attack on the Comandancia Molly Moore and George C. Wilson, "Bush's Maximum-Force Invasion Still Entails Risks," *Washington Post,* December 21, 1990.

Del Cid, a handsome Frederick Kempe, "How a Noriega Man Decided It Was Time to Cut His Losses," *Wall Street Journal,* December 27, 1989. The quotes and information regarding Luis del Cid's actions come from this *WSJ* article and lengthy interviews with del Cid and Gaytan carried out for the article.

An informant had come Author's interview with Axson, January 1990.

Axson doubted Author's interview with Axson. Also see Frederick Kempe and José de Córdoba, "Dictator's Dodge: Legalities Are Murky, But Panama Cheers Noriega's Downfall."

Noriega phoned The account of the phone call to Laboa and the events that followed comes from interviews with two close friends of the nuncio, Father Joseph Spitera and Monsignor José Sebastián Laboa, January 1990.

CHAPTER TWO   BUSH'S RECURRING NIGHTMARE

President Gerald Ford The Senate confirmed Bush's nomination to succeed William E. Colby on January 27 by a 63–27 vote. Bush was serving as U.S. ambassador to Beijing when Ford nominated him in November, 1975.

Idaho Senator Frank Church Walter Pincus, "Bush Nomination Cleared by Panel," *Washington Post,* December 19, 1975, p. A-1.

Lew Allen, Jr., then the head Stephen Engelberg with Jeff Gerth, "Bush and Noriega: Their 20-Year Relationship," *New York Times,* September 27, 1988.

Noriega must have appeared Author's interview with Stansfield Turner, January 1989. Also an Associated Press story reprinted in *Newsday,* "Turner: Bush Kept Close to Noriega," October 3, 1988, p. 4.

Even back in 1976 Torrijos's response to pressure and the Escobar quote come from William J. Jorden, *Panama Odyssey,* University of Texas Press, Austin, 1984, pp. 336–339. Noriega's role comes from interviews with Jorden and former U.S. intelligence source, June and July 1989.

Noriega's G-2 planted Jorden, *Panama Odyssey.*

A few days after Author's interview with William J. Jorden, June 1989.

The two met Account of the Bush-Noriega lunch comes from author's interviews with Aquilino Boyd, Nicholás Gonzalez Revilla, and a former U.S. intelligence official.

The last problem Author's interview with Aquilino Boyd, cited above; and William Branigin, "Pro-Noriega Candidate Details Amity with Bush," *Washington Post,* April 4, 1989.

Well oiled by his trademark Author's interviews autumn 1988, with two foreign officials who attended the celebration.

Interviewer David Frost "David Frost Talks with President and Mrs. Bush," Public Broadcasting Service, September 5, 1989: broadcast transcript from David Paradine Television.

CHAPTER THREE   THE ABANDONED CHILD

Felicidad Sieiro de Noriega wept The story of the near divorce of Noriega comes from author's interviews with lawyers involved, including Rodrigo Miranda Morales, February 1989, and from still existing divorce papers that were never filed. The story of their marital spat has been confirmed by two other family friends.

Noriega's scheme hit a glitch Author's interviews with two eyewitnesses, February, 1989.

Noriega came by all these traits Gathering the details of Noriega's early life presented one of the more difficult reporting projects for this book, involving interviews with family members and former childhood friends who primarily spoke anonymously because of fears of retribution from General Noriega, who endeavored to keep information about his early life secret. Those willing to speak on the record are quoted. This account includes many new details that haven't before been made public.

When Tony Noriega was born The stories of what happened to his mother after then differ. Details on Noriega's childhood life and the location of his early home come from two unnamed sources and from Hector Manfredo, a local doctor and former grade-school friend who played with Noriega at his home.

He was the only Instituto Nacional yearbook, 1952, author's translation.

The Bullet with a Soul Copy provided by a former teacher of Noriega's; author's translation.

Although Noriega's paper A former instructor provided access to the paper, dated November 8, 1951. Although the paper is unsigned—the cover sheet was missing—the handwriting matches that of other samples of Noriega's writing of that period. The quote from Machiavelli isn't a direct translation from the Spanish of Noriega's text, but rather the same excerpt from the English version of *The Prince* published by Viking-Penguin Books, Classic Edition, New York, 1981.

CHAPTER FOUR   A SPY IS BORN

He had an elegant Author's interview with Darién Ayala, March 1989.

During the summer Information comes from a Defense Intelligence Agency report which is coded with the letters IIR, or Intelligence Information Report. It was dated 1960 and still rests in Noriega's top-secret biographical files at the Central Intelligence Agency.

That summer, Noriega and two friends Much of the information on Noriega's years in Peru comes from author's interviews in 1988 and 1989 with Colonel Roberto Díaz Herrera, Francisco Rodriguez, Darién Ayala, and two sources who have asked to remain unnamed. One excellent novel gives a flavor of life at a Peruvian military academy: Mario Vargas Llosa's *The Time of the Hero,* Farrar, Straus & Giroux, New York, 1988.

What preceded this historic Author's interviews with two employes of Santo Tomás Hospital and with Pedro Brín Martínez, 1989.

Noriega turned Author's interviews with two Noriega family members, February 1989.

Then one day Author's interview with Boris Martínez, November 1988.

CHAPTER FIVE   THE NOT-SO-LOYAL SERVANT

The best preparation Manuel Antonio Noriega, *The Philosophy of the Talent to Be in Command,* Editorial Acuario, Panama City, undated.

Noriega was silent Details of Noriega's action on the day of the coup come from author's 1988 and 1989 interviews with three former Panamanian officials who had been involved in Torrijos's regime and then agreed to join the coup makers' government. They either personally heard the phone calls, or were told later by Noriega about his actions. Also author's interview with close friend of Luis Carlos Noriega, 1988 and 1989, provided confirmation of Luis Carlos's role.

Legend has it Author's interview with Mario Rognoni, Noriega's spokesman and friend, November 1988.

However, Noriega's new career Author's interview with former U.S. military intelligence agent, May 1989, and with Boris Martínez in Miami, January 1989.

In his position Interview with Boris Martínez, January 1989, cited above.

Now that Noriega Author's copy of Noriega curriculum vitae.

Major Boris Martínez Author's interview with Martínez January 1989, cited above.

Plotting against Arias began immediately An account of the coup appears in William J. Jorden's *Panama Odyssey,* University of Texas Press, Austin, 1984, pp. 128–140.

That same week Account of misleading intelligence being planted comes from author's interviews with Torrijos's closest friend, Rory Gonzalez, 1988 and 1989.

The 1968 coup Author's interview with two lawyers in David, Chiriquí province.

On February 24, 1969 Interview with Boris Martínez, January 1989, cited above.

Now, less than ten months Regarding American involvement in the coup, again officials who cooperated with the coup makers provided information about local cooperation by intelligence agents, but no proof could be found of higher-level involvement within the Nixon administration. A good account of the coup appears in William J. Jorden's *Panama Odyssey.*

In Panama City, coup leader Amado Sanjur The complaints of the coup makers are recounted in William J. Jorden's *Panama Odyssey,* p. 144.

The coup makers gave Author's interviews with four former Panamanian officials, including Fernando Manfredo and Nicholás Ardito Barletta, 1988 and 1989.

In Mexico City, Torrijos Author's interviews with Fernando Eleta, Rubén Darío Paredes, and Demetrio "Jimmy" Lakas, November 1988 and February 1989.

In Chiriquí province, Noriega Author's interviews with Lakas, cited above, and with Aristedes Abadía, November 1988.

Noriega participated Author's interviews with Rory Gonzalez, 1988 and 1989, cited above, and with a former U.S. intelligence agent, March 1989.

CHAPTER SIX THE NORIEGA UNDERWORLD

Well, do I look Sally Quinn, "The Name That Strikes Instant Terror," *Washington Post,* March 8, 1978.

Suddenly, banks were Author's interviews with Jack Blum, January 1989.

The head of air traffic Author's interview with former BNDD agent, March 1989, and with former Panamanian official, February 1989.

In May 1971, the White House Former Senate staffer for intelligence matters provided author copy of the memo.

In January 1972, Ingersoll The five alternatives were listed in an article by Jonathan Marshall, "The White House Death Squad," *Inquiry,* March 5, 1979, pp. 15–21. The author gained access to a copy of the five-page report, and interviewed a congressional investigator who has studied it.

Also see reports on Noriega assassination plan by Knut Royce, "Panama role in arms-drugs trade starts with corruption," Hearst News Service, appearing in the (Baltimore) *News American,* June 10, 1985, and other Hearst newspapers.

Linking the official to a fictitious Most of the information on the DEA in the early 1970s, the Noriega assassination plot, and Ingersoll's subsequent meetings with Omar Torrijos comes from portions of a secret document known as "the DeFeo report." It was named for its author, Michael DeFeo, a DEA investigator. The report carried the following label: "Pursuant to Attorney General's Order No. 600-75, Assigning Employes to Investigate Allegations of Fraud, Irregularity, and Misconduct in the Drug Enforcement Administration." It is still classified secret and is available only to those with special clearance.

All the transcripts, cassette tapes, and steno tapes of testimony taken by the DeFeo team, as well as all files reviewed by them, were turned over to then Assistant Attorney General Richard L. Thornburgh on September 10, 1975. Since then, they have remained secret except for leaks of small portions.

The mood was tense Ingersoll first complained to Torrijos. Ingersoll's conversation with Torrijos, except where otherwise noted in the next, comes from secret documents of the still classified DeFeo report cited above.

Ingersoll then raised Ingersoll quote from Elaine Shannon, *Desperados,* Viking Penguin, 1988, pp. 164–165.

Plots against Torrijos This account was pieced together from interviews with former intelligence agents; documents from the DeFeo report; Jack Anderson and Les Whitten, "Rumors of an Anti-Torrijos Plot, *Washington Post,* December 16, 1977, p. C-19; and Jonathan Marshall article in *Inquiry* March 5, 1979, cited above.

In June 1973, *Newsweek* reported that White House counsel John Dean was going to tell the Senate Watergate committee that low-level White

House aides had hatched a scheme to kill Noriega. Dean never made the statement, because all he had was hearsay evidence.

To deal with Panama Articles by Jack Anderson and Les Whitten and by Jonathan Marshall, cited above.

In February 1977, when asked Hunt had denied to Senate Watergate investigators any knowledge of a Torrijos death plot, but he made this statement after emerging from prison, in an interview with John Willis and Janet Langhart, co-hosts of the *Good Day* show on Boston's WCVB Channel 5. Also reported in article by Jack Anderson and Les Whitten cited above.

Noriega quietly placed Author's interview with two former Panamanian ambassadors and a former senior Panamanian official, 1989. Noriega's enrolling in Israeli courses is documented in a short chronology of foreign instruction that he listed at the end of a book issued to defend his role in stopping drug trafficking, called *16 Years in Struggle Against Drug Traffic,* 1986, author's copy. Further information on the Israeli connection from interviews with a former intelligence agent who served in Panama.

Noriega's fondest, and most Sally Quinn, *Washington Post,* March 8, 1978, cited above.

One such instance A fuller description of the U.N. meeting in Panama City appears in William J. Jorden's *Panama Odyssey,* pp. 184–197. The account of Noriega's role comes from author's interview with a senior Panamanian official, May, 1989.

As Scali was about to leave William J. Jorden, *Panama Odyssey,* pp. 190–196.

A little later, in mid-August 1974 Author's interview with Nicholas Gonzalez Revilla, February, 1989. Another good account of the opening of relations with Cuba is in William J. Jorden, *Panama Odyssey,* pp. 256–60.

In the first ten Steven Ropp, *Panamanian Politics, From Guarded Nation to National Guard,* Praeger Publishers, 1982.

CHAPTER SEVEN   THE CARTER COVER-UP

Noriega knows where we are Torrijos to his former Justice Minister, Juan Materno Vasquez, 1975. From interview with Materno Vasquez, December 1988.

From his first day on the job Author's interview with Stansfield Turner, December 1988.

The subcommittee issued subpoenas John M. Goshko, "Spy Tale Proving Troublesome for Panama Pact Advocates," *Washington Post,* October 1, 1977; and John H. Averill, "Eight Subpoenaed in Panama Bugging," *Los Angeles Times* article appearing in *Washington Post,* September 27, 1977, p. A-1.

But the inquiry fizzled John H. Averill, *Los Angeles Times* article appearing in *Washington Post,* October 6, 1977, p. A-27.

The Senate Intelligence Committee Author's interview with Ambler Moss, February 1989.

But the fight wasn't over *Congressional Record,* February 21, 1988.

In May, 1979, Jerome Sanford Author's interview with Sanford, in October 1989. Former *Wall Street Journal* reporter Clifford Krauss also made available a transcript from his own interview with Sanford earlier in 1989.

Washington wasn't as eager The warning to Noriega comes from interviews with a former military intelligence officer in June 1989, and a former State Department official in October 1989.

Before prosecutors could Author's interview with Sanford in October 1989, cited above.

Congressional hearings Hearings before the House Merchant Marine and Fisheries Subcommittee on the Panama Canal, June 6 and 7 and July 10, 1979, serial no. 96-22, U.S. Government Printing Office, 1980.

Agents planned to set up Jim McGee and Bob Woodward, "Noriega Arms Indictment Stalled in '80," *Washington Post,* March 20, 1988.

After prodding from Sanford The letter's existence was first revealed in the article by Jim McGee and Bob Woodward, cited above. A photograph of the letter appeared beside the article. The author thereafter was also given a copy of the letter.

After Sanford left his post Author's interview with Wes Currier, November 1989.

Carl Perrian, then a staff member Author's interview with Perrian, November, 1989.

In addition, the administration Mary Russell, "Panama Accused of Running Guns to the Rebels," *Washington Post,* June 7, 1979. As quoted in this article Atwood says there was "no evidence" that the Panamanian government was involved in gun smuggling.

Having saved Noriega The account of Noriega's role in protecting, monitoring, and trying to sell property to the Shah comes from author's interviews with Robert Armao, November 1988; Ambler Moss, February, 1989; and José de Jesús Martínez, March and April 1989.

Torrijos wanted to make A brilliant account of the Shah's final days is by William Shawcross, *The Shah's Last Ride: The Fate of an Ally,* Simon and Schuster, 1988. The Shah's account can be found in Mohammad Reza Pahlavi, *Answer to History,* Stein and Day Publishers, New York, 1980.

The Shah complained Mohammad Reza Pahlavi, *Answer to History,* cited above.

Noriega also did some pimping Noriega gave author Shawcross a different version. In an interview, he told Shawcross he had booked a suite in the Panama Hotel. He said he had arranged for a woman from a good family, not a Canadian tourist, to entertain the Shah.

But Paredes soon reported Author's interviews with Paredes, March and April 1989.

Noriega's knowledge Anecdote from author's interview with Enrique Carreras, long-time aide to Figueres, February 1989.

The pilots, Floyd Carlton Floyd Carlton testimony, taken in deposition before staff members of the Senate Foreign Relations Subcommittee on Terrorism, Narcotics, and International Communications, December 4, 1987. Declassified August 1989.

Also see Stephen Engelberg, "Salvador Rebel Arms: Noriega Link?" *New York Times,* December 18, 1987.

CHAPTER EIGHT   THE ARROGANCE OF POWER

Power in Panama Author's interview with General Paredes, March, 1989.

On the morning Account of Flores's ouster from author's interviews with Díaz Herrera, March 1989, and Paredes, March 1989.

The next step Author's interview with Royo family member and a former government aide, April 1989.

Noriega's pincer attack Interview with Díaz Herrera, March, 1989, cited above; and with de la Espriella aide, June 1989.

Noriega thereafter Larry Rohter, "Noriega Ordered Colombia Slaying," *New York Times,* February 5, 1988.

At first, Harari's David B. Tinnin, with Dag Christensen, *The Hit Team,* published by Dell Publishing, 1976, and reprinted by arrangement by Little, Brown and Co. "Mike" throughout the book is Michael Harari.

But Harari had grown David Gardner, "The Legendary Figure Haunting Shadows Behind Noriega," *Miami Herald,* May 5, 1988, p. 3.

Harari's official business Juan O. Tamayo, "Noriega Supported by Ex-spy," *Miami Herald,* January 19, 1988.

Pastora believed the July 31 Shirley Christian, *Nicaragua: Revolution in the Family,* Vintage Books, New York, 1986, pp. 311–13. Christian's book provides the best detail on Panama's ties to and cooperation with the Sandinistas.

Barletta wanted the job Author's interviews with Barletta, 1988 and 1989.

However, Noriega sanctioned Stephen Kinzer, "Panama's Long Count Stirs Up Some Old Political Tensions," *New York Times,* May 13, 1984, sec. IV. p. 5.

Author's interviews with Noriega's chief of staff Roberto Díaz Herrera in February 1989 revealed previously unknown details of how the election was stolen.

CHAPTER NINE   THE SPADAFORA KILLING

Major Córdoba: We have The exchange was part of a longer conversation between Córdoba, the chief of the Chiriquí garrison, who is alleged to have supervised the murder of Spadafora, and Noriega, who is thought to have ordered the killing. It was recorded by National Security Agency equipment on Panama's Galeta Island. The text convinced American intelligence that Noriega ordered and approved of the Spadafora killing.

Spadafora was a dashing Hugo Spadafora, *Thoughts and Experiences of a Physician/Guerrilla Fighter.*

A large-scale guerrilla war was fought against the Portuguese, starting in 1963. Spadafora fought with the guerrillas, led by Amílcar Cabral and directed by him until he was assassinated in 1973.

Spadafora and Noriega The story of the first Spadafora-Noriega meeting comes from author's interview February 1989 with Hugo Spadafora's younger brother, Winston, a lawyer who has led the campaign to bring Noriega to justice for Hugo's murder.

What made him most Author's interview with Carmelo Spadafora, February 1989.

Noriega tried to weaken Interview with Carmelo Spadafora February 1989, cited above.

On September 13, 1985 Author's interview with Joshua D'Baron, July 1989.

The restaurant's owner The account of Spadafora's last day comes from author's interviews with witnesses along his route; from the interview with Carmelo Spadafora; from depositions from witnesses; and from an interview with lawyer Rodrigo Miranda Morales, who was gathering data to file a writ of habeas corpus. Also, an excellent article on Spadafora's last day is Guillermo Sánchez Borbón's "Hugo Spadafora's Last Day," *Harper's Magazine,* June 1987.

Miranda viewed Spadafora This human rights violation incident and others that followed were compiled in an undated report given to American human-rights groups by Miranda and other local human-rights campaigners after the Spadafora killing. Author's copy.

In August 1985 "F-8 Terrorists Linked to Murder," Panama City Radio ACAN, September 17, 1985.

The pain wasn't over "Hugo Spadafora's Father Blames Noriega for Death," *La Prensa,* Panama City, September 17, 1985; and "Spadafora's Father Gives Ultimatium to Government," *Deutsche Presse Agentur,* Hamburg, September 19, 1985.

CHAPTER TEN   THE BARLETTA OUSTER

Listen to me Author's interviews with Nicholás Ardito Barletta and Roberto Díaz Herrera, 1988 and 1989.

Colonel Marco Justine Author's interviews with a senior Panamanian military officer and government official, 1989. These two men provided much of the information regarding Noriega's response to the Spadafora situation.

For Panamanians, Barletta Articles on Barletta's early problems as Panama's president include Roger Fontaine, "Pro–U.S. Panamanian Leader's Mandate Questioned," *Washington Times,* August 14, 1985, James Nelson Goodsell, "Panamanian civilians worry that generals are about to take power," *Christian Science Monitor,* March 21, 1985, p. 13.

Barletta frowned Regarding the F-8, a State Department report titled "Country Reports on Human Rights Practices for 1985," U.S. Government Printing Office, February 1986, p. 641, said, "Both Spadafora and Mauro Zuñiga, an opposition leader, kidnapped the previous month by unknown assailants, had the inscription F-8 on their backs. This link raises the possibility that there is some sort of death squad that may be operating in Panama. Some speculate that F-8 is a successor of the infamous Seventh Force, a progovernment squad that was active during the 1984 elections."

Noriega arrived in New York Author's interview with José Blandón, March 1989, and with former U.S. intelligence official, April 1989, to confirm Clarridge visit with Noriega.

I didn't kill him Noriega repeated the same excuse to various friends thereafter, including a U.S. intelligence official, according to interview with former Defense Intelligence Agency official. Bank documents from BCCI confirm Noriega's presence at the Helmsley Palace in New York on the days Blandón recalled, and another source close to Camargo confirmed the nature of Blandón's discussion with Noriega.

En route to Panama "Tom Castillo" was the cover name for Joe Fernandez, who couldn't be reached for comment. Fernandez was fired after a long investigation of his role in the Iran-Contra affair. In June 1988, he was the first CIA station chief ever indicted for exceeding his formal instructions, on charges of conspiracy to defraud the United States.

Noriega's office was The account of Barletta's meeting at Noriega's headquarters comes from author's lengthy interviews with both Colonel Díaz Herrera, who is now in exile in Venezuela, in February 1989, and with Nicholás Ardito Barletta, in both 1988 and 1989. Their separate accounts were similar in almost all respects, despite their mutual animosity.

Noriega came in at 7 P.M. Interviews with Barletta, cited above, and with Nestor Sanchez, April 1989.

To avoid any misunderstanding Reporting at the time on the Barletta ouster by Edward Cody: "New President Inaugurated in Panama," *Washington Post,* September 29, 1985.

CHAPTER ELEVEN   NORIEGA AND THE CONTRAS

Relations between Panama The quote comes from an interview with Noriega on Panama City's Televisora Nacional in Spanish on October 2, 1986, translated by Foreign Broadcast Information Service. Noriega was responding to Senator Helms's amendment to the intelligence appropriations bill that required an investigation into the defense forces' links to drugs, the Cubans, and the Spadafora murder.

On the sunbaked morning Description of the explosion from author's interview with a diplomat in Managua at the time; from Associated Press reports from Managua, and from "Uncle Sam's British Mercenary," *World in Action,* July 25, 1988, P568/845 Grenada TV, Ltd., Manchester, England.

By helping the March The Noriega role in providing technicians and his intelligence network in Managua for the top-secret mission was pieced together from interviews with intelligence sources; from documents released for Oliver North's criminal trial, including a forty-two-page stipulation, made public, of documents used in North's defense; and from North's testimony before the Iran-Contra committee.

Even while at Control Risks "Britain's Colonel North," *London Daily News,* July 14, 1987, p. 3. The British government conceded that it had hired bodyguards for diplomats from KMS, Ltd., but won't comment on whether KMS has provided paramilitary services.

In December 1984, North One of the best investigative reports on Walker, although it doesn't probe the Noriega connection, was "Uncle Sam's British Mercenary," on *World in Action,* Grenada TV Ltd., cited above.

A narrowly circulated *United States of America* v. *Oliver L. North,* United States District Court for the District of Columbia, Criminal no. 88-0080-02-GAG. pp. 38–39.

Noriega had become In IBC's Justice Department filing of September 30, 1986, Gomez writes that "IBC will not be conducting political activities" on behalf of Impulso Turistico. Yet Gomez's activities had little to do with tourism and everything to do with helping Noriega's regime. In author's interviews with José Blandón, Noriega's former aide, both in 1988 and 1989, Blandón said Noriega would use North through the Gomez-Cordovez conduit whenever he needed to send a message to North.

The services also included were assisting Noriega's chief drug enforcement official, inspector Luis Quiel, on a trip to the U.S. and the monitoring of the news media and translation of newspaper articles and documents regarding the Panama Canal and regarding "drugs and the Defense Forces."

Documents from the Justice Department show that Gomez and his partner, Richard Miller, were paid $35,000 a month plus expenses from September 1, 1986, through December 31, 1986, for their work on behalf of Impulso Turistico y Financiero. After IBC folded, Gomez picked up the contract for his own company, based in Bethesda, Maryland—which he at first called Gomez International, Inc.—for $21,000 a month plus expenses. His first billings began in May 1987. He changed the name of his firm to Public Affairs Resources, Inc., in September, 1987. But Gomez's work, done indirectly for Noriega, continued even after U.S. sanctions were imposed on

Panama after a government-sponsored gang attacked the American embassy.

In the later filing at Justice, Gomez conceded that he was involved in political activities, namely the "fostering of accurate public and official perceptions of realities in Panama." He only severed his long service to Noriega, which began with the blessing of Oliver North, after Panama's dictator was indicted by two grand juries in Florida in February 1988.

Congressional committees never found a direct connection between IBC's Panama work and its North connection, but a senior Panamanian official and José Blandón, Noriega's former aide, said that Noriega would use the Cordovez-Gomez conduit whenever he needed to reach Oliver North. Gomez wouldn't comment.

It was a time Background on the Israeli-Panama connection is given by Robert Parry, with Rod Nordland, in "Guns for Drugs?" *Newsweek,* May 23, 1988, pp. 22–23.

The Reagan administration's BCCI documents made available to author. The name of the company used to transfer the funds, which is still being used in CIA operations, is unnamed, by agreement with the source.

Casey had appointed Author's interview with former CIA official, August 1989. On Clarridge relationship to Casey, see also Bob Woodward, *Veil: The Secret Wars of the CIA 1981–87,* Simon and Schuster, 1987.

Noriega's importance A good account of the mining of the harbors and the political fallout appears in *Landslide,* by Jane Mayer and Doyle McManus, Houghton Mifflin, 1988.

William Casey and Oliver North The Iran-Contra committee dated the birth of Lake Resources as October 1985. Information gathered for this book, including access to checks written on the Lake Resources account, indicate that it was actually created more than a year earlier.

A senator's mission Bob Woodward, *Veil,* cited above, pp. 231–33. Author's interviews with Leahy and another source regarding the trip have provided details not included in Woodward's book.

Clarridge told Leahy The quote at the end of the paragraph and other information from the Leahy mission can be found in reports of the Senate Select Committee on Intelligence, January 1, 1983, to December 31, 1983, report 98-665, October 10, 1984, U.S. Government Printing Office.

As the Congressional Memo from documents released for the North trial. A U.S. intelligence expert, intimately familiar with Panama's role with the Contras, provided the country name that had been blacked out.

Casey's desire for Noriega's help Excerpts from Casey's appointment calendar released for the North trial.

The North trial stipulation Excerpt from *United States of America* v. *Oliver L. North,* cited above, paragraph 46, p. 17. The information comes from an analysis of Contra support that Casey asked to be prepared for Oliver North to assess recent performance and the near-term prospects for the Nicaraguan Resistance. Vice President Bush and National Security Adviser Robert McFarlane also received copies of this analysis.

After the Boland The Castillero connection, through his law firm Quijano Associates, was cited in a deposition for the Iran-Contra committee in Congress. It is unclear whether Noriega suggested Castillero to North.

In mid-January, 1985 North stipulation, cited above.

North and Noriega The account of the meeting comes from the author's interview with Blandón, cited above, and from his notes of the meeting. The timing and the fact of the meeting's occurrence was confirmed with officials at Balboa Harbor Port Authority.

But the CIA director Testimony of Francis J. McNeil, Senate Foreign Relations Subcommittee on Terrorism, Narcotics, and International Communications, April 4–7, 1988, Senate Hearing 100-773, part three, p. 41.

I had warned Constantine Menges, *Inside the National Security Council,* Simon and Schuster, 1988, p. 276.

In December, however Details of Menges meeting from interview with McCleary, January 1989, and with Daniel Delgado, March, 1989.

Jordan thought McCleary Author's interview with Hamilton Jordan, February 1988; for profile of McCleary and his role in Panama, Frederick Kempe, *Wall Street Journal,* "Panama Plotter: American Buddhist Aids Noriega's Foes," April 8, 1988, p. 1

When Marcos was ousted Joel McCleary, "Panama: Strategic Recommendations," Prepared by Sawyer-Miller Group for the Panamanian government, February 15, 1986. Author's copy.

Senator John Kerry For profile, see David Shribman, "The Right Sees Sen. Kerry as a Leftist Demon," *Wall Street Journal,* March 27, 1987.

The New York Times accelerated Seymour Hersh, "Panama Strongman Said to Trade in Drugs, Arms, and Illicit Money," *New York Times,* June 12, 1986, p. 1.

At a cocktail party Reuters article appearing in the *New York Times* under the headline "Panamanian Says Charges Are Aimed at Nation," June 14, 1986, p. A-3.

Yet even that Author's interview with Francis McNeil, January, 1989, and McNeil's testimony before the Senate Foreign Relations Subcommittee on Terrorism, Narcotics, and International Communication, cited above.

Senator Kerry's Foreign Author's interview with Senator Kerry, September 1989.

However, this time Author's interview with Elliott Abrams, April 1989.

On September 26, Panamanian See "Legislator Claims 'Contras' Training Locally," Madrid news service *EFE* in Spanish, 1454 GMT, September 26, 1986. Also see "PRD President on Proposed CIA Drug Inquiry," Panama City Domestic Service, 1815 GMT, September 25, 1986 (translated in *Foreign Broadcast Information Service* (*FBIS*), VI, September 26, 1986). Also see Defense Forces Communiqué on U.S. Resolution in *FBIS,* VI, September 30, 1986. Also see "Striking Legislator Threatens to Expose CIA," Panama City radio ACAN, 2235 GMT, September 29, 1986, translated in *FBIS,* VI, October 1, 1986.

On September 27 "Government Note to U.S. Condemns Investigations," Hamburg, *Deutsche Presse Agentur,* in Spanish, 2349 GMT, September 27, 1986, translated in *FBIS,* VI, September 29, 1986.

CHAPTER TWELVE   THE FIFTH HORSEMAN

For a more detailed account of the history of the Medellín cartel, several books are worthwhile reading: *Kings of Cocaine,* by Guy Gugliotta and Jeff Leen, Simon and Schuster, 1989; *Los Jinetes de la Cocaina,* by Fabio Castillo, Editorial Documentos Periodisticos, Bogotá, 1987; *Desperados,* by Elaine Shannon, Viking Books, 1988; *The Cocaine Wars,* by Paul Eddy with Hugo Sabogal, Sara Walden, W. W. Norton, New York, 1988.

Pablo Escobar was enraged The account of Escobar's feud with Noriega comes primarily from a senior PDF officer who knew Escobar's people well. Portions of the account were confirmed by José Blandón, such as the location of Escobar's housing. Another PDF officer confirmed Escobar's angry phone calls to del Cid and confirmed the replacement of the glass for the Fort Amador window. Portions were also confirmed in Floyd Carlton's depositions for a Miami grand jury in 1986 and his testimony to Senate investigators in February 1989.

They were upset Carlton's testimony before the Subcommittee on Terrorism, Narcotics, and International Communications of the Committee on Foreign Relations, Senate Hearings 100-773, part 2, February 8–11, 1988.

On May 21, 1984 *Critica,* Panamanian government newspaper, May 22, 1984, pp. 16–17.

The U.S. had discovered Floyd Carlton testimony, Senate Hearing 100-773, part 2, February 8–11, 1988 (cited above).

The raid was a headache Miami prosecutors have confirmed the existence of a second lab, with two witnesses who have testified to the Miami grand jury against Noriega.

Several months earlier In Carlton testimony before the Senate drug subcommittee, he claims the agreement cost $4 million. Author's interviews with José Blandón and his Senate testimony put the price at $5 million, an amount he first heard while in Cuba while negotiating a solution to the cartel-Noriega problem with Castro.

The negotiations For details of the Tranquilandia raid see Gugliotta and Leen, *Kings of Cocaine,* cited above.

By the time of Details of the second meeting are from Mario Arango Jaramillo and Jorge Child Velez, *Los Condenados de la Coca.* Editorial J. M. Arango, Medellín, 1985, p. 99, reprints Cartel's famous letter to Betancur in 1984 saying its members controlled "70 to 80 percent of all the cocaine produced in Colombia." Later, in July, President Betancur would dismiss any suggestion of a deal with the cartel, after news leaks turned the secret Panama meeting into an embarrassment.

Escobar's worst fears Author's interviews with a Panamanian lawyer who works with drug interests, and a PDF major, 1988.

In 1976–77, some *Kings of Cocaine,* cited above. Yakovac's account from court testimony *U.S.* v. *Lehder,* December 9–10, 1987.

The first hint Zepeda's April 6, 1988, deposition to the Subcommittee on Terrorism, Narcotics and International Communications, Senate Hearing 100-773, July 11, 12, 14, 1988, part 4, U.S. Government Printing Office, 1989.

In early 1980 Author's interview with José Blandón, June 1989, and with a senior Panamanian official, May 1989.

The Colombians first Account of rebel assaults, Warren Hoge, *New York Times,* August 13, 1981, p. A-3.

Then in November 1981 Knut Royce, Hearst Newspapers Service, June 10, 1985. Appeared, among others, in the *San Antonio Light.* Court records in Miami for *U.S.* v. *Jaime Guillot Lara.*

Torrijos was embarrassed Interviews with Blandón and a senior Panamanian official in May and June 1989, cited above.

Family patriarch Fabio The book *Kings of Cocaine* cites the organizer of the secret session as Jorge Ochoa. A former lawyer for cartel interests, in a June 1988 interview, insisted it was Fabio Ochoa, Jorge's father. Other details of the cartel's organizational period come from *Los Jinetes de la Cocaina,* by Fabio Castillo, cited above, pp. 111–14.

The Ochoas paid See the book *Kings of Cocaine,* cited above. Details of how the meeting was organized come also from author's interviews May and June 1989 with Blandón and a U.S. intelligence official. Details of monetary and other elements of the solution are from 1989 interviews with two Panamanian officials, one of whom has looked after relations with Colombia and the other of whom has close ties to the M-19.

By mid-1982, the cartel Author's interview with senior Colombian official, and with Blandón, 1988. In April 1984, the Colombian Defense Ministry was quoted by the Associated Press as saying guerrillas and drug dealers worked together with the Cubans in a drugs-for-guns deal that threatened Colombian democracy.

In June 1982 Carlton testimony to Senate subcommittee, February 1988, cited above.

Noriega wrapped his arm From Carlton testimony at closed hearing with

Foreign Relations Committee staffers, December 1987. Declassified August 1988.

Once when Noriega Carlton's testimony at closed Senate staffers' hearing, cited above.

On June 23, less than The account of the Cuba trip and Castro meetings comes from Blandón's memory, Blandón's notes, and a tape recording that Blandón prepared for a briefing that he was giving to the Miami grand jury. Castro's quotes couldn't be confirmed with Cuban sources. However, a Panamanian government source close to the military, and particularly to Major Camargo, confirmed the authenticity of the briefing tape made for Noriega and the general details of Blandón's mission to Cuba. The information's reliability was convincing enough for U.S. prosecutors in Miami, who confirmed many portions of Blandón's story, to include the Castro meeting in their February 4, 1988, indictment against Noriega. Blandón also made photographs taken at the meeting available to prosecutors.

Joining them was Manuel Piñeiro Losada A description of Piñeiro and more biographical information about him are given in Tad Szulc's book, *Fidel: A Critical Portrait,* William Morrow, New York, 1986.

Castro said that Fernando In *U.S.* v. *Jaime Guillot-Lara.,* cited above, four high-ranking Cuban officials, including Ravelo Renado, were indicted and convicted in absentia. Guillot-Lara is in hiding in Cuba.

The Colombian stopped Blandón identified the Colombian's face on a rap sheet put before him by prosecutors in Miami.

Noriega, not yet briefed To avoid raising CIA alarm, Noriega's flight logs showed his plane was going to the Bahamas. Flight logs were investigated by Miami prosecutors to confirm the dates and other elements of Blandón's story. Although the plane had intended to land in the Bahamas, airport authorities there don't have any record of its ever arriving.

And for good reason For vivid insight into Noriega's domestic difficulties, see T. D. Allman, "Unnecessary Evil," *Vanity Fair,* June 1988.

For many Panamanians Steven Michael Kalish testimony, Permanent Subcommittee on Investigations of the Committee on Governmental Affairs, Senate Hearing 100-654, p. 24. Kalish produced documents to support these claims, for the Tampa grand jury that indicted Noriega on February 4, 1988.

Noriega also hurt John Lawn, in an interview on CBS TV's *Face the Nation,* February 28, 1988, said, ". . . our attention was focused on Mr. Rodriguez, because the general, General Noriega, told us that he was concerned that this man may be a drug trafficker."

I'm paying him back Milian Rodriguez testimony, Foreign Relations Subcommittee on Terrorism, Narcotics, and International Communications, Senate Hearing 100-773, part 2, February 1988, pp. 219–67.

CHAPTER THIRTEEN   PLAYING THE U.S. CARD

In 1981, Noriega had negotiated Author's week-long interviews with Roberto Díaz Herrera, March 1989. Also, author's copy of the undated agreement between the colonels, entitled "Secreto Plan Torrijos, Cronogeama-Compromiso Historico de la Guardia Nacional."

Surely, thought Díaz Herrera Author's 1989 interviews with Díaz Herrera, cited above. Also see excellent article on the mystical war between Díaz Herrera and Noriega by Andres Oppenheimer, "Odd Man Out," *Miami Herald* Sunday magazine *Tropic,* August 13, 1989.

José de Jesús Martínez Author's interview with José de Jesús Martínez, July 1988.

When the Dobermans Guillermo Sánchez Borbón, "Panama Fallen Among Thieves," *Harper's Magazine,* December 1987, pp. 57–67.

Díaz Herrera's revelations Author's interviews with Aurelio Barria, 1988 and 1989.

Panama has the P. J. O'Rourke, *Holidays in Hell,* Atlantic Monthly Press, 1988, pp. 58–68.

Noriega, jealous of Lewis's Detail of Noriega's feud with Lewis over Contadora comes from interviews with a lawyer involved in the Aoki arrangements with Noriega, and with Lewis himself, his son Eduardo Lewis, and lawyer Jaime Arias, all in 1989.

Noriega's move Author's interviews with two Panamanians who were at Noriega's home when he issued his orders regarding the Japanese, March and April 1989.

Noriega's second strike Author's interview with Lewis, his son Eduardo, and a lawyer involved in arranging the deal, all in early 1989.

They broke through Author's interview with Katya Poshol, December 1988, and with Fernando Lewis, one of the bank's managers and Gabriel Lewis's son, December 1988.

Kennedy submitted the resolution 100th Congress, 1st Session, senate resolution 239. Excerpts from debate in *Congressional Record,* June 26, 1987.

The resolution noted Debate is in *Congressional Record,* June 26, 1987, pp. S8833–S8849. The text of the resolution is on pp. S8848–S8849.

Christopher Dodd Interviews with Senate staffers who accompanied Dodd on a trip to Panama, 1988 and 1989. Author's interview with Senator Dodd, July 1989, and with Ambassador Arthur Davis, February, 1989.

Dodd, a Spanish-speaking Dodd's statements of opposition to decertification are in *Congressional Record,* April 7, 1987, pp. S4661–S4667.

The ambassador turned to Author's interviews with Maisto and Davis, February 1989.

Unlike Iran's Ayatollah Author's interview November 1988 with two former

U.S. officials who attended the meeting at which Noriega's CIA funds were cut off.

Noriega no longer Guillermo Sánchez Borbón, "Panama Fallen among Thieves," cited above.

McCleary and Noriega Author's interviews with McCleary, Lewis, and Delgado, 1988 and 1989.

He would later give him Author's copy of Noriega cable to Blandón September 9, 1987.

The Blandón plan called "Thoughts on a Panamanian Political Solution," October 27, 1987, author's copy. A copy of the plan also appears in the report of Senator Kerry's Senate Foreign Relations Subcommittee on Terrorism, Narcotics, and International Communications, February 8, 1988, p. 276.

The trip's most bizarre twist Frederick Kempe, "Tongsun Park Finds an Embattled Client: Panama's Noriega," *Wall Street Journal,* January 29, 1988, p. 1. Also Sarkis Soghenalian testimony, Subcommittee on Terrorism, Narcotics and International Communications of the Senate Foreign Relations Committee, Senate Hearing 100-773, part 4, July 11, 12, 14, 1988, pp. 270–83, U.S. Government Printing Office, Washington, D.C., 1989. A copy of the passenger manifest is in the addendum to the hearing report.

Murphy had known Park In an interview, Murphy said he hadn't known Park until shortly before his trips to Panama. However, friends of his and Park's say their friendship dated back to Murphy's time at the Pentagon under Melvin Laird in the early 1970s. The quote from Murphy regarding Park appeared in Frederick Kempe, "Tongsun Park Finds an Embattled Client," cited above.

The South Korean, with Murphy Soghenalian's testimony and Murphy's testimony to the Senate Foreign Relations Subcommittee on Terrorism, Narcotics, and International Communications, Senate Hearing 100-773, part 4, July 11, 12, 14, 1988, U.S. Government Printing Office, 1989.

Murphy only backed off Author's interviews with two attendees at the Georgetown Club, March 1989.

As usual, Noriega arrived late Author's interview with General Frederick Woerner, July 12, 1989.

Noriega opened the late Author's interview with Davis February 1989; and in early 1989 with José Sorzano, former NSC official, and a senior Panamanian government official, with access to notes from the meeting.

Noriega didn't believe Account of Noriega's attitude is from Panamanian military officer and senior Panamanian government official, both in December 1988.

Blandón, the cold conspirator Author's interviews with Blandón and Lewis, October 1988. Lewis was in the room at the time of Blandón's phone call to his retarded son.

CHAPTER FOURTEEN   FOREIGN POLICY BY
INDICTMENT

A Latin American poet once said Quote comes from speech Noriega gave to 47th General Assembly of the International Criminal Police—INTER-POL—meeting in Panama City, at which Noriega suggested Panama as the site for an international drug-fighting center.

Danny Martelli confidently The details of the undercover operation explained at the beginning of this chapter come primarily from author's interviews with Daniel E. Moritz, Drug Enforcement Administration agent, July and August 1989, and interviews with former U.S. assistant attorney Richard Gregorie, February 1989 and July 1989. Other details come from Moritz deposition "in the matter of the extradition of Floyd Carlton Caceres," Dade County, Florida, Case No. 86-70-Cr.-Aronovitz, U.S. District Court, Southern District of Florida. Also from the February 4, 1988, Miami indict-ment itself, *United States of America* v. *Floyd Carlton Caceres and others,* U.S. District Court, Southern District of Florida, No. 86-70-Cr.-Aronovitz, August 27, 1986.

Moritz's investigation Author's interview with Moritz and Carlton testimony to Senate Subcommittee, cited above. Contra link comes from later Costa Rican court cases, in which the keepers of the airfield were indicted on drug trafficking charges in 1989.

Having heard rumors Author's interview with DEA agents who debriefed Carlton, and Carlton's testimony to Senate Subcommittee on Terrorism, Narcotics, and International Communications of the Committee on Foreign Relations, Senate Hearing 100-773, part two, February 8, 9, 10, 11, 1988, pp. 184–219, U.S. Government Printing Office.

He'd kept tapes Carlton's testimony in a deposition before staff investigators of the Senate Foreign Relations Subcommittee on Terrorism, Narcotics and International Communications, December 4, 1988, declassified August 1988.

Even at this late point Author's interview with Kellner April 1989.

Senate aides Carlton's testimony to Senate staffers on December 4, 1988, cited above.

Kalish's claims Steven Michael Kalish testimony, Permanent Subcommittee on Investigations of the Senate Committee on Governmental Affairs, Senate Hearing 100-654, January 28, 1988.

For Kalish, Rodriguez For information about Rodriguez, the best public source is Floyd Carlton's testimony to the Subcommittee on Terrorism, Narcotics, and International Communications of the Senate Foreign Rela-tions Committee, Senate Hearing 100-773, part 2, February 8–10, 1988.

Kalish visited Noriega Kalish testimony, cited above. Kalish's close relation-ship to Noriega was confirmed during author's interviews with Panamanian officials in 1988 and 1989. The grand jury also was able to corroborate much of Kalish's testimony from a rich store of documents he brought with him. Dates he provided of financial transactions were later corroborated from ledgers he kept that were recovered from Panama.

Noriega and Kalish The note to "Denis" was accepted as evidence, and it was reproduced with the transcript of Kalish's testimony before the Senate Foreign Relations subcommittee, cited above.

Kellner had gotten Kellner's profile is from author's interviews with Kellner July 1989; interviews with assistant U.S. attorneys in Kellner's office; and an article by Myra MacPherson in the *Washington Post,* May 20, 1988.

Most Americans haven't Profile of Merkle by Michael Allen, "Zealous Prosecutor: Robert Merkle Courts Trouble but Holds on to U.S. Attorney Post," *Wall Street Journal,* May 26, 1987. Also see Morley Safer, "Mad Dog Merkle," CBS News *60 Minutes,* January 10, 1988, transcripts vol. XX, no. 17.

Merkle, however, survived For account of Merkle's role in bringing in Lehder, see Michael Satchell, "A Narco-Traficante's Worst Nightmare," *U.S. News & World Report,* January 11, 1988, p. 30.

He viewed himself Gregorie testimony, Subcommittee on Terrorism, Narcotics, and International Communications of the Senate Committee on Foreign Relations, Senate Hearing 100-773, part 4, 1988, U.S. Government Printing Office. Also author's interviews with Gregorie.

Wompler arranged Author's interview with Atlee Wompler, March 1989. Story confirmed in interviews with Blandón, Gregorie, and Kellner.

At all times relevant *United States of America* v. *Manuel Antonio Noriega, et al.,* U.S. District Court, Southern District of Florida, February 4, 1988.

CHAPTER FIFTEEN   THE WRONG HERO

I am the frog Delvalle conversation with Mario Rognoni, December 1988.

General Noriega's U.S. informant Author's interviews with Rognoni, 1988 and 1989. Noriega on several occasions surprised his own aides and U.S. officials with his ability to garner information from inside the Reagan administration. State Department officials and Panamanian opposition members often complained about leaks, which they thought originated in the Pentagon, but no investigation was ever carried out nor was it convincingly proved that Pentagon officials were responsible. The more likely source of the leaks were consultants for Noriega who had friends that were well placed within the administration.

There is no other alternative Associated Press and Reuters wire reports, February 25, 1988.

But after the February 4 Author's interview with McCleary, January 1988. Account of the meeting also appeared in Frederick Kempe, "Panama Plotter: American Buddhist Aids Noriega's Foes," *Wall Street Journal,* April 8, 1988.

For Noriega, ousting Delvalle Details of the meeting from author's interview with Mario Rognoni, and with a senior Panamanian official, December 1988.

Noriega opted to remain Legislative Assembly, Republic of Panama, Resolution N.1, February 26, 1988, author's copy.

The cabinet then appointed Article 184 of the Political Constitution, in its third paragraph, says that if, for any reason, the vice presidents can't replace a president, the cabinet by majority must then choose one of its members to do so. That minister, however, can't become president, but only "Minister in Charge of the Presidency of the Republic."

The Civic Crusade Author gained access to portions of the nuncio's diary while in Panama in March 1989.

The most tireless ABC's *Nightline* with Ted Koppel, March 3, 1988, show no. 1769.

Rogers and his orthodox Frederick Kempe, "Noriega and His Foes Are Slugging It Out in U.S. Courtrooms," *Wall Street Journal,* May 24, 1988, p. 1.

Rogers was enthusiastic Unpublished portions of author's interview with Rogers for *The Wall Street Journal,* March 5, 1988.

Rogers's first step The best account and analysis of the impact of the legal actions is an unpublished paper written by Kenneth I. Juster of Arnold & Porter, entitled "U.S. Policy Toward Panama: The Premature Demise of Economic Sanctions." Author's copy.

The Rogers team The certification was in accordance with Section 25 (b) of the Federal Reserve Act, as amended, 12 U.S.C. s632.

The court scenes Frederick Kempe, *Wall Street Journal,* May 24, 1988, cited above.

The U.S. embassy Details of Bladex account and efforts with Brazil and Uruguay come from confidential memos and cables on the attempted transactions, provided to the author.

But one judge after another From a transcript of the March 7 hearing provided by Arnold & Porter.

On March 3, Panamanian Interviews with two American bankers involved in the clandestine cash evacuation, April and May 1989.

Even as money was Author's interview May 1989 with two senior Panamanian government officials who attended these meetings.

Alberto Calvo, a short Author's interview May 1989 with two senior Panamanian government officials familiar with the details of Calvo's operation.

CHAPTER SIXTEEN   THE KEYSTONE COUP

There are no unsolvable problems Noriega at the cabinet meeting on the eve of the failed March 16 coup attempt.

Noriega picked Major Account of the cabinet meeting from author's interviews with Mario Rognoni and two other Panamanian government officials, and a military officer who attended the session.

At the same time Unpublished portions of author's interviews with McCleary and Carreras, January 1988, for *The Wall Street Journal.*

At 5 A.M. Author's interview with Christian Democratic politician, November 1989, and with a senior military officer who was involved in the coup, March 1989.

The coup plotting The reconstruction of the coup that follows comes from various sources and numerous interviews with families of the coup makers, officers who participated and weren't jailed, and government officials. Most asked that their names not be cited. However, helpful information was provided in interviews with Noriega's aide Mario Rognoni and Major Daniel Delgado and by Major Augusto Villalaz (one of the coup makers who escaped to the United States thereafter) and another Panamanian officer involved in the coup.

Noriega's growing links Author's interviews with Villalaz, May 1988. Also see James Dorsey, "Cuban Arms Being Flown into Panama, and Hidden," *Washington Times,* June 10, 1988; and James Dorsey, "Cuba Helps Noriega Plant Seeds of War," *Washington Times.* March 21, 1988.

The shots? James Dorsey, "Noriega Crushes Revolt," *Washington Times,* March 17, 1988. He finished the quote by calling the shots "kisses for reporters."

The suspect party Author's interview with a senior U.S. diplomat in Panama in December 1988; with Gabriel Lewis in November 1988; and with an American military intelligence source in October 1989.

That failed coup Author's interview with General Paredes, February 1989.

The March 16 coup Author's December 1988 interview with Major Delgado provided details on the workings of the CEM.

Noriega's first financial Author's interviews 1988 with two senior Panamanian officials involved in the negotiations with the Libyans and with a U.S. official who monitored the deal. Author also had access to State Department and Pentagon cables regarding the Libyan arrangement.

In mid-October 1988 Author had access to this memo and other cables and memos quoted in this chapter, information from which hasn't previously appeared in print. Authenticity of the memos was confirmed with another senior U.S. official.

Yet what the Pentagon Author's interview with D'Amato, September 1989. D'Amato's allegations have also been confirmed by a Senate staff member with access to intelligence cables regarding the Cuban involvement in Panama.

Foreign Ministry officials Author's interview with three Japanese officials involved in trade and political relations with Panama, May and June 1989.

A disciplined, orderly Jerrold Schecter, *The New Face of Buddha,* John Weatherhill, Inc., Tokyo, 1967.

In his darkest Author's interview with senior Panamanian official, May 1989, and with U.S. intelligence source, February 1989.

Taiwan's quiet help Unclassified State Department cable, May 1, 1989, translating "Taiwan Technical Mission Offers $1 Billion Loan," *La Republica* (Panama City), May 1, 1989.

CHAPTER SEVENTEEN   U.S. POLICY FOLLIES

You rope them Author's interview with Elliott Abrams, March 1989.

William Walker's life Account of the Walker mission to Israel comes from interviews with Eduardo Herrera Hassan December 1989 and with two senior U.S. officials; also with Elliott Abrams and Gabriel Lewis, in 1988 and 1989. Also see Stephen Engelberg, "Panamanian's Tale: '87 [*sic*] Plan for a Coup," *New York Times,* October 29, 1989, section I, part I, p. 18.

But in Washington For an excellent account of Abrams's plan and the military options that grew out of it, see William Scott Malone, "The Panama Debacle—Uncle Sam Wimps Out," *Washington Post* (Outlook), April 23, 1989, p. C-1.

Yet Abrams puts Author's interview with Abrams, February 1989.

Since early in 1986 Excerpt comes from Joel McCleary, *Panama: Strategic Recommendations,* prepared by Sawyer-Miller, February 15, 1986, author's copy. The impact of this document on Noriega's thinking was confirmed in author's interview with PDF major, March 1989.

Admiral Crowe, then Author's interviews with senior Pentagon officials, National Security Council officials, and an aide to Admiral Crowe, 1988 and 1989.

With the Iran-Contra For an account of Abrams's relations with Congress, see *Landslide: The Unmaking of the President,* by Jane Mayer and Doyle McManus, Houghton Mifflin Co., 1988, pp. 366–67.

Abrams's strongest argument President's statement of March 11, 1988, in *Department of State Bulletin on the Western Hemisphere,* May 1988, p. 71, U.S. Government Printing Office.

At a press conference *Department of State Bulletin* cited above, pp. 71–72.

The best example The account of the radio fiasco comes from author's interviews with U.S. intelligence source, March 1989; with a senior State Department official January, 1989; and with José Sorzano, December 1988.

The message was clear Author gained access to the memo. It was one of many cables sent by uniformed military sources in Panama that were orchestrated to alarm the White House about the dangers of a confrontational course regarding Panama.

It was then, on March 29 Author's interviews in December 1988 and February 1989 with two State Department officials and one NSC official involved in the meeting.

Marlin Fitzwater Bill McAllister, "U.S. Patience 'Not Unlimited,' " *Washington Post,* March 30, 1988.

Reagan hence tasked William Scott Malone, *Washington Post* (Outlook), March 30, 1988, cited above.

Furthermore, the Pentagon See George C. Wilson, "U.S. considered Military Plan to Aid Delvalle," *Washington Post,* April 3, 1988. Wilson, one of the better-sourced Pentagon correspondents, was a frequent purveyor of the Pentagon's anti-Abrams leaks.

Shultz, who had George C. Wilson, *Washington Post,* April 3, 1988, cited above.

On March 25, the papal Author gained access to the papal nuncio's diary.

In the end Executive Order 12635, Prohibiting Certain Transactions with Respect to Panama, April 8, 1988, *Presidential Papers of the Administration of Ronald Reagan, 1988,* week ending Friday, April 15, 1988, pp. 441–42.

OFAC's first move U.S. Treasury Department news release, April 30, 1988.

The actions "undoubtedly Ellen Hume with Frederick Kempe, "U.S. Panama Sanctions Are Less Harsh Than Some Sought, But Still Pose Risks," *Wall Street Journal,* April 11, 1988.

CHAPTER EIGHTEEN   THE MISSED OPPORTUNITY

In chapter eighteen almost all of the information comes from more than twenty-five interviews with key participants in the talks, both Americans and Panamanians, and from their notes. Because Noriega was still in power at the time the chapter was completed, the sources, with rare exceptions, asked to remain anonymous.

Statements in quotation marks are either from the speaker's best recollection or from the memory of two sources present at the meeting. Some quotes are also taken from notes kept of the meeting or the negotiations.

As long as those indictments Noriega to Michael Kozak in late April 1988, during negotiations regarding his resignation.

President Reagan impatiently Account of Sunday and Saturday session with Reagan from author's interviews with four participants in the meeting. Reagan's and other quotes are from the best memories of the participants and, in some cases, from notes taken during the meetings or memos written about the meetings afterward.

Tension charged the room David Hoffman and Judith Havemann, "Bush Presses to Cut Off Talks with Noriega," *Washington Post,* May 20, 1988, p. 1.

Bush was particularly worried The details of the Colombian bank arrangements come from aides to Bush, senior U.S. officials, and a senior Panamanian official, who were involved in the negotiations.

Elliott Abrams, a neoconservative Author's interview with Elliott Abrams, June 1989.

The details of Kozak's The details of the plan come from author's interviews with Panamanian and U.S. negotiators and from a federal transcript service text of a background briefing by a senior State Department official on May 25, 1988. The official was Under Secretary for Political Affairs Michael Armacost.

Bush's national security adviser Author's interviews with Craig Fuller, Bush's chief of staff, July 1989, and Samuel J. Watson III, his deputy national security adviser, September 1989.

Chief of Staff Howard Baker Dole's amendment is cited in *Congressional Record,* May 16, 1988, vol. 134, no. 68, p. 5950. The debate appears in *Congressional Record,* May 16 and May 17, 1988, vol. 134, no. 69.

What you have here Joe Pichirallo, "Offer to Drop Noriega Case Decried," *Washington Post,* May 13, 1988.

United States attorneys were livid The Baker quote was from an interview with CBS News, May 12, 1988.

CHAPTER NINETEEN   BUSH'S TAR BABY

Noriega was one Author's interview with Craig Fuller, August 1989.

At a meeting in the White House Author's interviews with two officials who attended the meeting, August 1989.

The go-slow message Author's interview with U.S. intelligence source, December 1988, and with Panamanian opposition member involved in covert activities, July 1989.

Kansas Senator Robert Dole Jim McGee and David Hoffman, "Rivals Hint Bush Understates Knowledge of Noriega Ties," *Washington Post,* May 5, 1988.

Then at a House subcommittee hearing Dr. Norman A. Bailey testimony, hearing before the House Select Committee on Narcotics Abuse and Control, March 29, 1988, SCNAC-100-2-3, pp. 5–18. U.S. Government Printing Office.

I think we came away Joe Pichirallo, "Gregg Says Envoy Told Bush Noriega Was a Problem," *Washington Post,* May 21, 1988.

Bush aides felt compelled Joe Pichirallo, "Bush Broadens Noriega Explanation," *Washington Post,* May 10, 1988.

It was a dramatic moment Reagan's response to Bush's opposition comes from author's 1989 interviews with two NSC officials of the 1988 period.

That morning, Kellner Account of Bush's meeting with Kellner comes from author's interview with Kellner, March 1989.

Fuller, Bush's chief Steven V. Roberts, "Deal for Noriega to Leave Panama Reported Gaining," *New York Times,* May 21, 1988, p. 1.

On May 20, Bush's misgivings David Hoffman and Judith Havemann, "Bush Presses to Cut Off Talks With Noriega," *Washington Post,* May 20, 1988, p. 1.

The fifteen members Account of the SSCI meeting on July 26 comes from interviews with Senate staffers, intelligence sources, and State Department officials, 1989. Newspaper reports on the session that provided the first detail of the meeting include Stephen Engelberg, "U.S. Officials Say Senators Balked at Noriega Ouster," *New York Times,* April 24, 1989; William Scott Malone, "The Panama Debacle: Uncle Sam Wimps Out," *Washington Post* (Outlook), April 23, 1989; Carla Anne Robbins, "Taking Aim at Noriega," *U.S. News & World Report,* May 1, 1989.

Expertise there was aplenty The memorandum was made available by an administration official. Its contents and the thinking behind it were analyzed by two senior administration officials in author's interviews, July and August 1989.

Indeed, the coup's would-be leader Stephen Engelberg, "Panamanian's Tale: '87 Plan for a Coup," *New York Times,* October 29, 1989, p. 18. (The headline and article erroneously speak of an '87 plan for a coup. The plan was in 1988.)

That wasn't good enough Laws and Related Laws and Executive Orders of Interest to the National Intelligence Community (as Amended Through March 1987). Published in March 1987 by the Government Printing Office for the House Select Committee on Intelligence. Executive Order 12333 of the United States Intelligence Activities, December 4, 1981, 46 F.R. 59941, p. 421.

"2.11. Prohibition on assassination. No person employed by or acting on behalf of the United States Government shall engage in, or conspire to engage in, assassination.

"2.12. Indirect participation. No agency of the Intelligence Community shall participate in or request any person to undertake activities forbidden by this Order."

The committee's suspicion Details about the attached CIA assessment come from Stephen Engelberg, "White House, Noriega and Battle in Congress," *New York Times,* October 23, 1989, p. A-10.

Within two hours Lou Cannon and Joe Pichirallo, "Covert Action on Noriega Is Cleared," *Washington Post,* July 27, 1988; and James Gerstenzang, "Reagan Reportedly Authorizes New Action: Covert U.S. Anti-Noriega Plan

Told," *Los Angeles Times,* July 27, 1988. Author's own reporting confirmed the leak came from a senior administration official.

It was not even subtly For stories on the Senators' outrage about the leaks, see Sara Fritz and Doyle McManus, "Senators Angered by Leak of Anti-Noriega plan," *Los Angeles Times,* July 28, 1988 p. 12; Stephen Engelberg, "CIA Said to Plan Series of Steps to Put New Pressure on Noriega," *New York Times,* July 28, 1988, p. 12; Helen Dewar, "Senators Accuse Administration of Setup on Panama Leak," *Washington Post,* July 29, 1988.

Calvo's overture Account of the Calvo-Bush connection comes from interviews with two Panamanian officials and one Japanese businessman, May and April 1989.

It was late in 1987 Details of the golf course deal appeared May 17, 1988, in "First Chinese–United States–Japan joint venture to build golf course and resort facility in Shanghai," a press release issued by Business Wire.

The secret minutes Author gained access to a reporting memo to Secretary of State George Shultz, who was traveling. Two officials at the meeting expanded on its details in interviews, February 1989.

What are you trying From the nuncio's diary, to which the author gained access.

To massage Delvalle's ego The report on the White House meeting comes from author's copy of a transcript of the session that Delvalle's associates made.

CHAPTER TWENTY PSYCHOLOGICAL WARFARE

The masses have a great weakness The quotes at the opening of chapter twenty and set off in italics throughout its text come from Manuel Antonio Noriega's eighty-page book entitled *Psychological Operations.* It was written in 1975, when Noriega was in charge of the country's military intelligence, or G-2, and presented to the National Guard's chief of staff, Florencio Flores. It followed psychological operations training Noriega had in the United States, Israel, and, according to one senior National Guard officer of that time, Cuba.

President Manuel Solis Palma The report on Solis Palma's actions and his quiet plotting against Noriega comes from author's interviews with two eyewitnesses at the presidential palace, May 1989.

Noriega had made several For an excellent report on the elections and their aftermath, see article, by Joseph Galloway with Carla Anne Robbins in Panama and Kenneth T. Walsh, Stephen J. Hedges, and Andy Plattner in Washington, *U.S. News and World Report,* May 22, 1989. Also see "A Test of Wills," by Larry Martz with Charles Lane in Panama City, and John Barry, Thomas M. DeFrank, and Douglas Waller in Washington, *Newsweek,* May 22, 1989, p. 34.

Two days before Account of preelection meeting of Noriega's advisers is from author's interviews with two Panamanian government officials, May 1989.

The opposition's representatives Author's interviews April 1989 with two employees of the Panamanian embassy at the time of the election.

Carter saw ballots "Lead-Pipe Politics," by William Doerner, reported by Ricardo Chavira, Michael Duffy, and John Moody, *Time Magazine,* May 22, 1989, p. 42.

Later that same morning Account of CEM meeting comes from author's interviews May 1989 with Panamanian government official and military officer who attended.

The embassy kept in The author, chasing the caravan, was pulled into Kihano's car by two opposition activists. He overheard the conversation, and he interviewed the embassy official about it later that week.

For about an hour Author was on hand at the time of the attack on the candidates, and this account is his own. The first details appeared in Frederick Kempe, "Noriega's Dignity Battalion Attacks Opposition Candidates in Panama City," *Wall Street Journal,* May 11, 1989. Account also comes from author's interviews with Endara, Ford, and Calderón, May 1989.

When the uniformed Author's interview with Ford, May 1989, cited above.

Again, Noriega's enemies Regarding Noriega's art of survival, see Frederick Kempe, "A Master of Survival: Noriega Is Riding High as Panamanians Vote," *Wall Street Journal,* May 5, 1989, p. 1.

It was President Bush's George C. Wilson, "Bush Turns to Gunboat Diplomacy in Move to Protect U.S. Lives," *Washington Post,* May 12, 1989.

After the attack David Hoffman, "Bush Seeks Overthrow of Noriega; Panama's Military, Citizens Urged to Do Everything They Can." *Washington Post,* May 13, 1989.

CHAPTER TWENTY-ONE   UNFINISHED BUSINESS

General Manuel Antonio Noriega had invited Frederick Kempe, "Panama Tragedy: How the Inexperience of American Officials Helped Doom Coup," *Wall Street Journal,* October 6, 1989, p. 1. This piece was the earliest story to reveal the role of Mrs. Giroldi and the full extent of American involvement in the coup.

At just before 8 A.M. Account of the christening comes from author's five-hour interview with Adela Bonilla de Giroldi, December 6, 1989. Some details also came from author's interview with senior Panamanian official, October 1989.

This self-styled Giroldi's recollection of Noriega's words came in conversation with CIA officials later, recounted by a senior U.S. official in October 1989.

Noriega had kept close watch Smu'al Rosenblum, "Israelis Warn Noriega of a Coup Financed by the U.S.," in the Israeli newspaper *Hadashot,* October 5, 1989, p. 1. The Defense Ministry formally denied the information, provided to the reporter by an Israeli air force officer.

However, for a long time Personal details from the pre-coup weekend come from author's interview with Adela de Giroldi December 6, 1989, cited above.

But Señora Giroldi's friend Author's October 1989 interview with U.S. intelligence source provided detail of the first Giroldi contact. Confirmed by a second intelligence source. Mrs. Giroldi denies this early link.

Major Giroldi returned Andres Oppenheimer, "Coup Leader Planned to Give Noriega to U.S., Widow Says," *Miami Herald,* October 12, 1989, p. 1. Also author's interview, November 1989.

At midday on Saturday Author's interview with Mrs. Giroldi November 1989, and notes from six hours of discussions between Mrs. Giroldi and Deborah De Moss, Senate Foreign Relations Committee staff member.

But Señora Giroldi does concede Andres Oppenheimer, *Miami Herald,* October 12, 1989, cited above. U.S. officials deny that Mrs. Giroldi or her husband ever requested that the U.S. take custody.

Defense Secretary Richard Cheney David Hoffman and Ann Devroy, "Opposition Leader Detained; Noriega Threatens Crackdown," *Washington Post,* October 6, 1980, p. A-33.

Secretary of State James Baker David Hoffman, "Bush Used Characteristic Caution in Panama Crisis," *Washington Post,* October 15, 1989, p. 1.

The meeting never discussed A senior White House official's background briefing with Gerald Seib of *The Wall Street Journal,* October 12, 1989. Also author's interviews with senior administration officials, October 1989.

In addition, Thurman's The account of the tunnel session comes from Frederick Kempe, *Wall Street Journal,* October 6, 1989, cited above; and James Dorsey, "Confusion at Top Levels Foiled Decision-making," *Washington Times,* October 6, 1989, p. 1.

On Tuesday morning The reconstruction of events at the Comandancia comes from more than ten interviews with Panamanian government officials, a Panamanian military source, Mario Rognoni, U.S. intelligence officials, and U.S. diplomats with access to intelligence information. All interviews were conducted in October 1989.

At 9:15 A.M. in Washington Author's interviews with a senior official October 23, 1989; and Seib background briefing, October 12, 1989, cited above.

No one suggested Bush cut short David Hoffman, *Washington Post,* October 15, 1989, p. 1, cited above.

Initially, U.S. participation Frederick Kempe, *Wall Street Journal,* October 6, 1989, cited above.

Giroldi tried to talk From a nine-page report on the coup prepared by Captain Javier Licona for Colonel Eduardo Herrera Hassan, a Panamanian officer in exile. Other quotes from Licona also come from this report, unless otherwise noted. Author's copy.

One call whose occurrence Author's interview with Mario Rognoni and one senior Panamanian government official, October 1989. The Branigin information comes from Bob Woodward and Joe Pichirallo, "U.S. Move On Noriega Was Option," *Washington Post,* October 8, 1989, p. A-37.

Why do we have an intelligence agency Ellen Warren and Bill Arthur, *Miami Herald,* October 7, 1989, p. A-26.

The president had made Andrew Rosenthal and others, "Panama Crisis: Disarray Hindered White House," *New York Times,* October 8, 1989, p. 1.

Noriega took a pistol William Branigin, "Rebel Ignored Plea to Delay Coup," *Washington Post,* October 14, 1989, p. A-14. The information came from U.S. military intelligence reports.

Noriega shipped Giroldi off Author's interview with American military intelligence agents, October and November 1989.

The Bush administration's war State Department press briefing by Richard Boucher, October 3, 1988, as reported by the United States Information Service.

White House spokesman C. S. Manegold, with Charles Lane in Panama and others, "Amateur Hour," *Newsweek,* October 16, 1989, pp. 26–31.

Finally, a frustrated President Bush Ann Devroy, "Bush to Aides: Stop Second-Guessing," *Washington Post,* October 11, 1989.

Here you have brave people Ann Devroy, "U.S. Keeps Troops on Sidelines," *Washington Post,* October 4, 1989, p. 1.

Yet within a month Robin Wright, "U.S. in New Bid to Oust Noriega," *Los Angeles Times,* November 16, 1989, p. 1. The story wasn't the outcome of a deliberate leak, according to its writer; but rather, it grew out of a far broader interview with this intelligence source.

CHAPTER TWENTY-TWO   NORIEGA AND THE NUNCIO

Life goes on Noriega made the comment to a Panamanian lawyer who had come to the Nunciatura to help the papal nuncio. Enrique Jelenzsky and Rolando Domingo (as told to **David L. Marcus**), "Inside the Embassy with Noriega," *Dallas Morning News* (from Universal Press Syndicate), January 1, 1990, p. 1.

At the Vatican's embassy Unless otherwise noted, the account of Noriega's final days at the Nunciatura comes from various interviews with several sources who spent a great deal of time inside during Noriega's stay. The interviews included five hours with Monsignor Laboa, interviews with Father Joseph Spiteri, West German diplomat Klaus Meixner, with businessman César Tribaldos, with deacon Hermann López Arias, with two senior State Department officials and a military officer involved in the talks. These interviews were also instrumental in producing two stories written by the author that provided information for this chapter: Frederick Kempe, "So Noriega Is Ours; Give Some Credit to the Papal Nuncio," *Wall Street*

Journal, January 4, 1990, p. 1, and also "Noriega Walked Quietly into the Night," *Wall Street Journal,* January 5, 1990, p. a-4.

The nuncio, who had been Details of the nuncio's flight arrangements from interview with Aurelio Barria, a leader of the Civic Crusade who made the arrangements for Monsignor Laboa with the State Department.

I'm convinced Frederick Kempe, "So Noriega Is Ours," cited above.

When challenged See Luke 19:2–10. Originally reported in Kempe, "So Noriega Is Ours."

But it was soon Enrique Jelenzsky and Rolando Domingo, cited above.

Well, I've learned By Jelenzsky and Domingo.

The nuncio's pressures Kempe, "So Noriega Is Ours," cited above.

The nuncio then faced Jennifer Parmell, "Nuncio Urging Noriega to Leave, Vatican Says," *Washington Post,* December 30, 1989, p. a-11.

That's where Endara's Dana Priest, "Panama Asks Vatican to End Noriega's Sanctuary," *Washington Post,* December 28, 1989.

General Manuel Antonio Noriega . . . walked Kempe, "Noriega Walked Quietly into the Night," cited above.

INDEX

Abadía, Aristides, 69, 72
Abadía, Jorge, 150, 151, 181, 223
Abrams, Elliott, 33, 152–54, 169, 171, 173,
   174, 177, 179, 181, 223, 232, 233,
   310–11, 314, 322, 325
   anti-Noriega strategy, 289–97, 299–301,
   303, 304, 329–30
   Crowe's standoff with, 293–97, 299–301
   Delvalle and, 261, 262
   Herrera Hassan fiasco and, 289–93
Abrantes, José, 108–9, 122
Achille Lauro plan, 303–4
Adair, Charles, 63
Aguilar, Adolfo, 64
Ailes, Roger, 339
Air Force, U.S., 16, 270
Air Panama, 268
Alexander, Clifford I., 92
Alexander the Great, 365–66
Allen, James, 91
Allen, Lew, Jr., 28
Allen, Orlando, 13
Allende, Salvador, 406
Alvarado, Juan Velasco, 51
Alvarez, José Antonio, 97
Amado, David, 202, 347
Amado, Norma, 16, 161, 202, 305, 327, 396
Amado, Vicky, 16, 22–23, 161, 201, 216,
   327, 396, 415
Amaya, Edwin Eredia, 139
Amendment 2897, 179–80
American Law Institute, 268
Angueira, Efrain, 58, 63, 67, 71
Anti-Terrorist Alert Center (ATAC), 283
Aoki, John, 216, 344
Araúz, Maj. Alejandro, 55–56, 66–68
Arias, Arnulfo, 48–49, 57, 83, 226, 421
   coups against, 45, 49, 62–64
Arias, Jorge Abadía, 68–70
Arias, Robert (Tito), 81
Arias Calderón, Jaime, 111
Arias Calderón, Ricardo, 263, 356–58

Armacost, Michael, 296, 301, 325, 326,
   329–30, 340–43
Armao, Robert, 102–8
Armitage, Richard, 233, 341–43
Arms shipments (or smuggling), 95–101,
   109–110, 243, 277, 278, 419, 420
   Noriega's seizure of, 178–79
   to Contras, 161–62
Armudas, Rolando Armuelles, 128
Arnold & Porter, 265–70, 293, 295, 306
Arnulfistas, 57, 59, 62
Aronson, Bernie, 395
Arosemena, Diogenes, 134
Arosemena, Emilia, 68
Arosemena, Ramón (Tinto), 16
Arrco, Luis B. de, 139
Artime, Manuel, 80
Asencio, Diego C., 190
Assassinations (assassination plots), 5, 118
   against Kellner family, 248
   against Rodriguez, 118, 131, 240–41
   against Sandinistas, 160, 180–81
   against Somoza, 105
   against Torrijos, 78, 80
   against Noriega, 78, 80, 187, 195
Asylum, concept of, 401–4
Atlantic-Pacific Convention Center (Atlapa),
   32–33
Atlapa Convention Center, 353, 373
Atwater, Lee, 336–37
Axson, Lt. Col. Harry B., 21–23
Ayala, Darién, 47, 52–53, 82
Azpruia, Tony, 238

Bailey, Norman, 175, 177, 335
Baker, Howard, 87, 308, 310, 314, 323, 338
Baker, James, 11, 306–7, 310, 313, 339, 347,
   378, 379, 384, 389–90, 404
Ballestros, Juan Matta, 316
Balma, Capt. Jesús George, 371
Balma, Capt. Joseph, 355
Banana workers' unions, 60–61

457

Banco Cafetero, 315–16, 326
Banco del Istmo, 218
Bank for Credit and Commerce
    International, 147, 206, 224
Bank of Boston, 241, 245, 258
Banks, Panamanian, 4, 74, 270, 271, 302
Baratta, Anthony, 268–69
Barletta, Mrs., 155
Barletta, Nicholás Ardito, 67, 87, 111–12,
    123, 143–45, 212, 226
  Contras and, 167
  ouster of, 149–56, 168, 169, 171–74,
    177
Barria, Aurelio, 213–14, 217, 260, 399
Bateman, Jaime, 190, 192
Batista, Fulgencio, 51
Battalion 2000, 278, 371, 383, 387–88, 391,
    392
Bayh, Birch, 93–94
Bay of Pigs invasion, 80
Beatings, 10, 218, 365. See also Torture
  of Ford, 5
  of prostitutes, 47–48, 56–57
Bell, Griffin, 92
Benitez, Maj. Jaime, 279
Ben Or, Passat, 120
Betancur, Belisário, 186
Billings (woman), 59
Bisexuality, 83. See also Homosexuality
"black" communications, 58–59
Black Friday (1987), 225–26, 260
Blandón, José, 110–11, 114, 128, 147–49,
    162, 166, 189, 191, 334
  anti-Noriega strategy, 212, 227–30, 232,
    233–34
  arrest of son, 230
  Contras and, 163–64, 167, 168
  in Cuba, 196–201
  economic issues and, 168
  firing of, 234
  Noriega's attack on farm, 234–35
  testimony, 253–54
Blandón Plan, 228–30
Bloch, Lt. Comm. Stephen, 366, 367
Blum, Jack, 74, 249
Bocas del Toro, Panama, 57, 59
Boland, Edward P., 163
Boland amendment, 163, 165
Bombings, 59, 139–40
  in Panama Canal Zone, 29–32, 90
Bonilla, Rodrigo Lara, 184, 186
Bonilla de Giroldi, Adela, 369, 372–76, 381,
    383–86, 392, 393
Boren, David, 343, 390, 394
Borge, Tomás, 121–22
Boyd, Aquilino, 30–32, 50, 352
Bradley, Bill, 341, 342

Brady defense (Oliver North defense),
    252–53
Bramble, James, 185, 204
Branigin, William, 389
Brenes, Roberto, 307
Briggs, Everett Ellis, 156, 171, 173, 174, 336
Brín Martinez, Pedro, 40, 45, 46
Brunei, Sultan of, 325
Brustmayer, Ilor Rodriguez, 91
Brzezinski, Zbigniew, 93
Buddhism, 226–27
"Bullet with a Soul, The" (Noriega), 44
Bunker, Ellsworth, 86
Bureau of Narcotics and Dangerous Drugs
    (BNDD), 75–78
Bush, George (Bush administration), 8,
    10–13, 25–26, 91, 162, 230, 332–40,
    343–45, 347–49, 355–56, 362–65,
    378–80, 383, 390–91, 394–95, 399,
    401, 405. See also Invasion of
    Panama (1989)
  award offered by, 17, 21–22
  as CIA director, 11, 27–32, 419
  election of 1988, 32–33, 313–14, 332–40
  Giroldi coup and, 371–96, 399
  medallion given to, 32
  Noriega problem and, 27–34
  Noriega's 1976 meeting with, 30–32
  psychological warfare of, 362–66
  Reagan's disagreements with, 309–10,
    336–40
  as vice president, 32, 33, 165
Bush, Prescott, 344–45
Bushnell, John, 404
Business(es), 17
  destruction of, 139–40

Caballero, Alfredo, 236, 241
Cabral, Amilcar, 128
Caceres, Floyd Carlton, 110, 184, 193–95,
    237–44, 251
  extradition of, 242
  Moritz's investigation of, 237–42
Calhoum, Shama, 209–10
Cali, Colombia, 3–4
Calvo, Alberto, 216, 231, 271–72, 343–44
Camargo, Maj. Felipe, 128, 147–48, 189,
    196, 198, 199, 201
Campbell, John ("Riverboat"), 219–20, 227,
    265, 292
Canton Song (operation), 28–30
Cardenas, José B., 349
Carlton, Floyd, 205, 253
Carlucci, Frank, 220, 297, 303, 310, 333
Carreras, Enrique, 113, 118, 274
Carrizo, Celso, 200
Carrizo, Dayra, 200

Carter, Jimmy (Carter administration), 6, 12,
29, 30, 79, 90–112, 172, 332, 353–54,
419
Noriega as thriving during, 90–91
Panama Canal Treaties and, 91–94, 97, 98
Shah of Iran and, 102
Casey, William, 146, 148, 162–65, 169–71,
173–74, 179, 343, 377
CYA (cover your ass) memo of, 170
death of, 182, 293, 297
Helms and, 179–80
Noriega's meetings with, 156, 162, 169–70
Castillero, Juan Bautista, 165
Castillo, Col. Elías, 53
Contras and, 167
Castillo, Capt. Ivan, 18, 21
Castillo, Tomás. See Fernandez, Joe
Castro, Fidel, 6, 28, 51, 75, 80, 121, 255,
282–84, 307. See also Cuba
drug trafficking and, 196–201
Figueres visit to, 109
M-19 and, 189–92
Nicaragua and, 108
Noriega and, 109
Sandinistas and, 97
Torrijos and, 86, 87, 93, 112
Cayman Islands, 244–45
Caza y Pesca, 96–97
Ceaucescu, Nicolai, 411
Cedeño, Maj. Rufito, 13, 392
Celidor, 120
CEM (Strategic Military Council), 33, 280,
327, 354–55
Central Intelligence Agency (CIA), 6, 7, 50,
55, 71, 87, 96, 101, 112, 119, 132,
145–48, 162–65, 178–82, 282, 297–99,
318, 342–43, 365, 384, 390, 395, 420.
See also Casey, William
Bush as director of, 11, 27–32, 419
Contras armed by, 129
Cuba and, 51
Díaz Herrera and, 211
Giroldi and, 370, 374–79, 388
intelligence failings of, 297–98
Miami drug trafficking investigation and,
251–53
Nicaraguan harbors mined by, 163
Noriega on payroll of, 26, 28, 51–52, 61,
83, 119, 162, 220, 224
Noriega ties severed by, 90, 211, 224
Torrijos and, 57
Chamber of Commerce, Panamanian, 213,
214
Chamorro, Edgar, 167
Ch'ang-chih, Sung, 287
Chavez, Francisco, 193
Cheney, Richard, 10, 378, 379, 383–84, 391

Chiari, Adolfo, 45
Chicas Boutique, 140
Chien, Frederick, 287
China, 82, 267, 287
Chiriquí province, 18–20, 55–70, 102–3, 140,
147
Chishan, Teresita, 143
Chorrillos Military Academy, 47–48, 50–54
Christian Democrats, 276
Christopher, Warren, 97
Church, Frank, 27–28
Cisneros, Maj. Gen. Marc, 19–20, 24, 389,
400–5, 410, 411, 414, 416
Civic Crusade, 213–14, 225, 260, 263, 307,
413
Civiletti, Benjamin H., 92
Clark, Col. Gerald, 292, 312, 314, 316–17,
327–31
Clarridge, Duane R. (Dewey), 145, 162–
64
Cocaine, 183–87, 203–4, 238, 239, 254–55.
See also Drug trafficking
Cochez, Guillermo (Willy), 275–76
Coffee, Paul, 254
Cohen, William, 341, 342
Cold War, 51
Colombia, 96, 421. See also Medellín cartel
M-19 and, 189–93
Colón, Panama, 56, 127, 167
Colón Free Trade Zone, 74–75, 187, 194,
202, 271, 283, 285, 287, 344
Columbus, Christopher, 37
Comandancia, 15, 275, 277, 280, 383, 385,
388
"Combo, the," 62–64
Communism, 60, 67
Torrijos and, 76–77
U.S. fear of, 6, 51, 208, 421
Congress, U.S., 12, 76, 253, 299, 310, 314.
See also House of Representatives,
U.S.; Senate, U.S.
Boland amendment, 163, 165
Contra funding banned by, 161, 163, 165,
167
Coniglio, Col. James V., 334
Constant, Thomas M., 92
Constitution, Panamanian, 263
Contadora Island, 111, 215–16, 344
Shah of Iran on, 102–7
Contras, Nicaraguan, 122, 156, 421. See also
Iran-Contra scandal
CIA arming of, 129
Noriega and, 157–82
Panamanian unit as, 168
Reagan administration and, 6
training of, 166–67, 181
U.S. funding of, 146, 163, 165

Contreras, César Rodriguez, 110, 193, 196, 205
Contreras, Col. Armando, 114–16
Control Risks, 159
Coors, Holly, 222
Coors, Joe, 222
Córdoba, Domitillo, 148
Córdoba, Maj. Luis, 138, 139, 141, 148
Cordovez, Roberto, 161, 166, 168
Corozo, Panama, 136–37
Correa, Mayín, 82
Corro, Lt. Col. Euclides, 279
Corruption, 94, 128, 130, 188
    Torrijos and, 73–75, 88, 113
Costa Rica, 57, 96, 131, 133, 165, 167, 219, 238, 241–42
Courtelis, Alex, 338
Craig, Gregory, 220
Crédit Suisse, 163
Crowe, Adm. William J., 219, 227, 293–97, 299–304, 333, 363
Cuartas, Belisario Betancur, 191
Cuba, 13, 16, 51, 75, 76, 170, 196–202, 402, 422. See also Castro, Fidel
    Contras and, 166
    drug trafficking and, 196–201
    intelligence service of, 108–9, 191
    Noriega and, 108–9, 119, 178, 200–2, 255, 277, 281–85
    Panama's relations with, 86–87
    Sandinistas and, 108
    U.S. relations with, 80
Currier, Wes, 100
Customs, U.S., 83, 94, 99, 187, 238

Dalai Lama, 226, 227
D'Amato, Alfonse M., 220, 283, 323, 343
Darién plant
    construction of, 185, 197
    raid on, 183–88, 195–200, 202–3
David City, 18, 103
Davis, Arthur H., 221–23, 232, 260, 264, 300–1, 304–6, 326, 333, 334, 360
Davis, Susan, 301
D'Baron, Joshua, 131–33
DeBakey, Michael, 107
Defense Authorization Bill, 314
Defense Department, U.S., 7, 95–96, 119, 132, 169, 181–82, 232, 264, 283, 292, 301–4, 306–7, 342, 345, 346, 384, 388–89, 420
    State Department conflict with, 293–95, 311
Defense Intelligence Agency (DIA), 28, 95–96, 101, 282, 298, 301–2
Defense Investigative Service, 394
DeFeo, Michael, 77

DeFeo Report, 77–78
del Cid, Maj. Luis, 18–20, 105, 184, 187, 190
DeLeuze, Gabriele, 146–47
Delgado, Maj. Daniel, 172, 226, 353, 355
del Rio, Maj. Moisés, 276
Delta Force, 13–14
Delvalle, Eric Arturo, 140, 144, 149–51, 153, 173, 178, 204, 223, 257, 258–66, 293, 303, 305, 306, 325, 334, 335, 345–49, 351, 353
    Lewis and, 216–17
    Noriega attempt to fire, 258–62
    ousting of, 262–64
    radio transmitter for, 298–99
    U.S. recognition of, 263–64, 268–69
Delvalle, Mrs., 261, 305
Democracy, Panamanian, 6, 7, 87, 89, 111, 179, 223
    Abrams's views on, 169
    in Panama, 114, 116, 156
Democratic party, U.S., 163, 176, 177, 180, 313, 343
Democratic Revolutionary Party (PRD), 153
De Moss, Deborah, 176, 244
Denise (Kalish's fiancée), 246
De Puy, Edgar A., 139
Devi, Indra, 209
DIASCA, Inc., 236
Díaz Herrera, Col. Roberto, 53, 105, 111, 114–15, 117, 118, 122, 145–56, 169, 225
    arrest of, 225
    Barletta and, 145
    confession of, 212, 217
    coup attempt by, 146–50
    election of 1984 and, 123–25
    Japan job considered for, 210–11
    as leftist, 208
    Noriega compared to, 207
    Noriega's rivalry with, 146–47, 207–14
    spiritualism and, 209–10
Díaz Herrera, Maigualida, 226
Dignity Battalions, 5, 15, 17, 357–59, 363
Dobermans, 213–14, 218, 381
Dodd, Christopher, 176–77, 220–22
Dole, Robert, 314, 335
Dolmy Business, Inc., 163
Dowd, Maureen, 12
Dreams, Noriega's, 141–42
Drug enforcement, 75–81
    in Nixon administration, 76–78
    Noriega and, 4, 5, 94, 183–84, 203–6, 420
Drug Enforcement Administration, U.S., 7, 20, 75–80, 83, 122, 132, 237–45, 298, 420
    Miami investigation and, 251–52
    Noriega and, 185, 189, 194, 203–6

undercover investigations by,
237–44
Drug trafficking, 3–4, 75–81, 92–93
del Cid and, 18, 20
Him Gonzalez and, 75–76
Noriega and, 94, 128–30, 170, 175–80,
183–206, 220, 237–57
Spadafora's accusations about, 128–30
Drummond, William, 30, 31
Duberstein, Kenneth, 310, 314, 338
Dukakis, Michael, 33, 336, 343
Dunbar, Jerry, 388
Duncan, Alfredo, 252
Duque, Carlos, 33, 42, 129, 216, 218, 352,
354
Duran, Roberto, 353
Durkin, William, 77, 78
Duvalier, Jean-Claude (Baby Doc), 175, 280,
422

Eagleburger, Lawrence S., 395
Eastland, James, 92
Echeverría, Juan José (Johnny), 128
Economic sanctions, 306–8, 419
Economy, Panamanian, 65, 419
Barletta and, 145, 149
problems of, 168
Edge Act (1941), 267
Ehrlichman, John, 78
82nd Airborne, 14, 19, 20, 22
Eisenhower, Dwight D., 51
Eisenmann, Roberto, 216, 220, 305
Elections, Panamanian
candidates attacked in, 357–61, 363
1952, 45
1964, 58, 59
1968, 62
1984, 122–25, 139, 165, 185, 212, 220
1989, 213, 350–63
Elections, U.S.
1972, 80
1976, 27–28, 30
1988, 32–33, 313–14, 332–40
Electoral Tribunal, 82
Eleta, Fernando, 68, 231, 362
El Ocho (Noriega's offices), 168, 319
El Salvador, 148–49, 176
Emerson, Ralph Waldo, 43
Endara, Guillermo, 355–58, 361, 400, 407–8,
413
Energy Resources International, 163
Escobar Bethancourt, Rómulo, 29, 41, 71,
87, 154, 155, 199, 317–21, 324,
327–28
Escuela República de Méjico, 39
Eskenazi, Jack, 100
Espino, Rodrigo, 352

Espinosa, Edgar, 237
Espinoza, Rodolfo Miguel, 128, 129
Espriella, Ricardo de la, 116, 117, 122, 162
Esquivel, Roderick, 150, 263
Evil eye, 17

FARC guerrillas, 96
FDN. See Contras
Federal Aviation Authority, 76
Federal Bureau of Investigation (FBI), 83,
99, 248, 251, 420
Federal Reserve, 315
F-8 (secret society), 140, 145
Feldman, Jeffrey, 248–49
Fernandez, Joe (alias Tomás Castillo), 148,
162, 249
Fierro, José, 145, 150
5th Rifle Company, 371, 378, 384
Figueres, José "Pepe," 109
First Company of Engineers, 64
1st Special Operations Wing, 15
Fitzwater, Marlin, 10, 256, 263, 302, 393
Flores, Col. Florencio, 114, 115
"Flying Whorehouse," 103
Foley, Thomas, 160
Ford, Billy (Pica Gallo), 5, 357–60, 363
Ford, Gerald (Ford administration), 6,
27–30, 419
Fort Bragg, 58
4th "Urraca" Company, 381
470th Military Intelligence Brigade, 28, 57,
58, 63, 298, 302
France, 281
Franco, Luis Nentzen, 66
Frost, David, 33
Fuller, Craig, 332, 333, 337–38, 340, 345
Fundora, Maj., 278

G-2 (Panamanian intelligence service),
31–32, 57, 70–72, 75, 77, 110, 195,
223, 245, 274, 276, 298, 362, 366
growth of, 81–82
gunrunning and, 96–97
Medellín cartel and, 189
Melo and, 187–88
Noriega named head of, 70
Shah protected by, 104–6
Spadafora's criticism of, 129
Turner's severing of relations with, 90,
91
U.S. funding of, 26, 29, 82, 224
Gallegos, Father Hector, 81
Galvin, Gen. John, 150, 173, 233
Gang of Six, 229
Garbow, Melvin, 268
Garcia, Alan, 263
Garcia, Carlos, 147

Garcia, Col. Rodrigo, 71
Gates, Daryl, 338
Gates, Robert, 379, 383
Gaviria, Gustavo, 193–94
Gaviria, Pablo Escobar (El Padrino), 183–87,
    193–95
Gaytan, Capt. Eliezer, 19, 400, 403, 410,
    411, 413, 414
Gaytan, Maj. Ivan, 18–19
Gaytan, Moisés, 19
Giroldi Vega, Maj. Moisés, 8, 279, 369–93,
    396
    murder of, 392–93
    Noriega's talk with, 385–86
    U.S. help expected by, 371, 381–82
Gomez, Carlos Jimenez, 186
Gomez, Francis G., 161
Gomez, Frank, 166, 175, 252
Gómez, Lucho, 16
Gomez, Peña, 210–11
Gonzalez, Capt. Cholo, 387, 391
Gonzalez, Diomedes, 139
Gonzalez, Felipe, 108, 348, 403
Gonzalez, Francisco Eliecer (Bruce Lee),
    135, 136, 138
Gonzalez, Israel, 13
Gonzalez, Ivan Garcia (El Guapo), 133–35
Gonzalez, Natividad, 139
Gonzalez, Rafael Richard, 77
Gonzalez, Rory, 111
Gonzalez López, Guillermo, 79
Gonzalez Revilla, Nicholás, 30, 71, 85, 86
Good Morning America, 178
Gorgas Army Hospital, 9
Gorman, Gen. Paul, 165
Gray, Red (Gallo Chiricano), 69
gray communications, 58
Greene, Graham, 210
Gregg, Donald, 163, 231, 313, 334
Gregorie, Richard, 237–39, 242, 243, 248–56
Grenada, U.S. invasion of, 12
Grove, Brendon, 98
Guatemala, 96, 132
Guerra, Alexis, 359, 360
Guerrilla warfare (guerrillas), 126
    gunrunning and, 95–98, 109–10
    M-19 and, 189–93
    in Nicaragua, 95–98. *See also* Contras
    Noriega's combatting of, 64–65
    U.S. invasion and Noriega's rejection of,
    17–19
Guillot-Lara, Jaime, 191
Gunrunning. *See* Arms shipments

Haddad, Capt. Richard, 9
Hakim, Albert, 163
Harari, Celi, 120

Harari, Dor, 120
Harari, Michael, 161, 163–64, 187, 195, 263,
    289–90, 334, 370
Hawari/Special Operations Group, 282
Hecht, Bill, 171, 173–74
Hellsing, Craig, 171
Helms, Jesse, 175–77, 179–81, 204, 220
Helmsley, Leona, 147
Heroin trade, 76–77
Herrera Hassan, Col. Eduardo, 289–93, 302,
    305, 334–35, 340–42
Hersh, Seymour, 175, 177–79
Hertzog, Brig. Gen. William, 389–90
H-Hour, 12–14
Hill, Charlie, 324, 327
Him Gonzalez, Joaquín (Chino), 75–76, 80
Hitler, Adolf, 188–89, 267
Hoffa, Jimmy, 253
Homosexuality, 40, 83, 127, 146, 200, 244,
    410
Homosexual rape, 134–37
Hong Kong, 82, 272
House of Representatives, U.S., 299, 335
    Intelligence Committee of, 160
    Merchant Marine and Fisheries
        Subcommittee on the Panama Canal
        of, 97–98
Howe, Vice Adm. Jonathan, 295, 297, 301,
    304
Human rights abuses, 134–41, 169, 170, 173,
    225–26
Hunt, E. Howard, 80–81

Ibarra, Juan B., 64
"If I Call Myself Your Friend" (del Cid), 20
IFMA Management Company, 162
Ikeda, Daisaku, 286
Illueca, Jorge, 41
Impulso Turistico y Financiero, 161
INAIR, 187
Ingersoll, John, 77–80
Inouye, Daniel K., 92
Instituto Nacional, 39–46, 50
INTERCOMSA (International
    Communications Satellite), 68
International Business Communications
    (IBC), 161
International Emergency Economic Powers
    Act (IEEPA), 306
International Monetary Fund (IMF), 144,
    149, 153, 168
Interpol, 78
Invasion of Panama by the United States,
    9–26, 277, 398–418
    casualties in, 11, 12, 25, 418
    costs of, 25–26
    headquarters attacked in, 14–15

Noriega's advance knowledge of, 12–14
Noriega's flight and, 13–14, 16–18, 20–25
Noriega's plans and, 17–18
Paz killing and, 9–11
plans for, 11–12
property damage and, 17, 25
oversights and, 17
success of, 25
telephone warfare and, 19–20
Iran, 223
Empress of, 106, 107
Shah of, 95, 98, 101–8, 120, 212
U.S. hostages in, 102, 106, 332
Iran-Contra scandal, 160, 162, 182, 232–33, 247, 248, 249, 257, 295–97, 333
Israel, 58, 82, 119–20, 129, 281, 422
CIA and, 162
Contras and, 161–65
Noriega in, 187

Jackson, Jesse, 197
Jahanbini, Col. Kiumars, 103, 105, 107
Japan, 210–11, 216, 281, 285–86, 315, 325–26, 422
Jelenzsky, Enrique, 407, 414
John Paul II, Pope, 401
Joint Chiefs of Staff (JCS), 283, 292–97, 299–301
Jones, Robert Trent, Jr., 344
Jordan, Hamilton, 102–3, 120, 172, 227
Jorden, William J., 30, 86, 227
J-2, 298, 381
Juliao, Abdiel, 129, 131
Juster, Kenneth I., 266, 270, 306
Justice Department, U.S., 77, 100, 249, 255, 313, 323
Justine, Col. Marco, 143, 144, 150, 151, 175, 211, 259, 313, 319, 320, 324–25, 329

Kalish, Steven Michael, 202–3, 25, 244–47
Kampelman, Max, 296, 297
Karina, 190–91
Kelley, Clarence M., 92
Kellner, Ellen, 248
Kellner, Leon, 242, 247–49, 254–57, 338–39
Kennedy, Edward, 215, 220, 222, 262
Kennedy, John F., 3, 51, 71
Kennedy, Kenneth, 242–43, 251
Kerry, John, 74, 175, 177, 180, 220, 244, 248
Khomeini, Ayatollah, 101, 102
Kidnapping, 159, 191–93
Kimbler, Donald, 100
Kimmit, Robert, 410
Kissinger, Henry, 30, 31, 86, 324
KLM Airlines, 272
KMS, Ltd (Keeny-Meeny Services), 159–6
Koppel, Ted, 263

Kozak, Michael, 20, 29, 275, 289, 336, 337, 339, 340, 342, 347, 384, 389–90, 394, 410–13, 416
anti-Noriega strategy, 310–31
Krupnick, Jorge, 16–18, 22
Krupnick, Mrs. Jorge, 22–23

Labib, Abdallah Abd al-Hamid, 282
Laboa, Msgr. José Sebastián, 23–25, 312, 324–325, 347, 398–99, 401–16, 421–22
Delvalle and, 263, 264
diary of, 305–6
Labor unions, 60–61, 67, 208
Lackland Air Force Base, 102
Lakas, Demetrio Basilio (Jimmy), 32, 63, 81, 86
Lake Resources, 163
Land reform, 65
"Law 20," 120
Lawn, John C., 204, 205, 251
LD (line of demarcation), 15
Lewis, Gabriel, 86, 93, 103, 107, 111, 150, 172, 274, 305
anti-Noriega strategy, 212, 214–22, 226–28, 234, 261, 262, 265, 292
Delvalle and, 261, 262
emigration of, 219
family background of, 214–15
Noriega's strikes against, 215–17
Leahy, Patrick, 164, 168–69
Lebarge, G., 230
Lehder, Carlos, 244, 247, 250
Lehman, John, 159
Lewis, Sammy (nephew), 216–17
Lewis, Samuel (uncle), 218
Leyva, Gen. Luis Carlos Camacho, 189
Li-an, Chen, 287
Libya, 281–82, 402
Licona, Javier, 385–86, 389, 391
Liddy, G. Gordon, 80
Linowitz, Sol, 93
Lip Radio, 354
Locaya, Francisco, 167
London Daily News, 160
Londonio, Julio, 315
López, Edgardo, 96–97
López Arias, Hermann, 405
Losada, Manuel Piñeiro (Barba Roja), 108–9, 121, 197, 199, 201
Loyalty Day, 8–9, 70

McAuliffe, Lt. Gen. Dennis P., 98, 101
McCall, Richard, 177
McCarthy, Joseph, 268
McCleary, Joel, 7, 171–75, 253, 294
anti-Noriega strategy, 212, 226–28, 262, 265

background of, 172
Delvalle and, 262, 265
in Noriega negotiations, 274–75
Noriega battle plan written by, 174–75
McDonough, Col. William, 389
McFarlane, Robert, 164–65, 171
McGrath, Archbishop Gregorio Marcus, 370, 400
McNeil, Francis J., 170, 179
Machiavelli, Niccolò, 45–46
Machos del Monte, 8–10, 371, 378, 383, 387–88, 391, 392
Macias, Col. Leonidas, 277–79
Mack, Connie, 250
MacMahon, Lloyd F., 267–69
Madriñan, Col. Nivaldo, 4, 136, 148, 214, 241, 400, 403, 409–11, 413, 415
Mafia, 75, 93
Maisto, John, 217, 222–23, 333, 384, 386, 389–90
Managua, 1985 attack in, 157–58, 160
Manfredo, Fernando, 67, 123
Manfredo, Hector, 39, 41, 42, 44, 45
Mannion, Robert, 267
Marcos, Ferdinand, 174, 175, 217, 221, 280, 422
Marcus, Stanley, 248
Marijuana, 244, 247, 255
Marines, U.S., 9, 222–23
Martelli, Danny. See Moritz, Daniel E.
Martinez, Bob, 250
Martínez, Boris, 42–43, 50, 56–57, 62–66, 68
Martínez, José de Jesús (Chuchu), 75, 101, 210
Martinz, Louis, 83–84
Massages, 3
Materno Vasquez, Juan, 88
Matsunaga, Nobua, 285
Matta, Juan Ramón, 303
Matta Ballesteros plan, 303
Maylin, César Rodriquez, 42
Medellín cartel, 3–4, 119, 183–89, 192–203, 239, 243, 254, 255, 322
creation of, 192–93
M-19 and, 192–93
Noriega's first agreement with, 193–95
Meese, Ed, 310, 313
Meir, Golda, 119
Meixner, Klaus, 407, 409
Mejía, Bertilo, 139
Melo, Col. Julian Borbua, 129, 185, 187–89, 195–96, 203
Menges, Constantine, 171–72, 174
Merkle, Robert (Mad Dog), 244, 247, 249–50, 255
Mexico, 87
Michelson, Alfonso López, 186, 189–91

Militarism, cult of, 52
Military intelligence, U.S., 47–48, 57–59, 63
Military Police, 17
Military Zone Five, 18
Miller, Richard, 175
Millstein, Seymour, 219
Miranda Morales, Rodrigo, 35–36, 64, 134, 135, 137–39
Miskito Indians, 131
Miss Panama affair, 146–47
M-19 guerrillas, 189–93
Moisés Clinical Laboratory, 139–40
Money laundering, 4, 162, 220, 236–37, 239, 246, 254, 315
Monroe, Marilyn, 83
Moreau, Vice Adm. Arthur, 165
Moreno (Noriega's mother), 38–39
Moreno Guillén, Armando, 78
Morgan, Juan David, 63
Moritz, Daniel E. (Danny Martelli), 236–44, 251
Morris, Edmund, 311
Morse, Mark, 106
Moss, Ambler, 83, 88, 92, 98, 103, 105–6, 120–21
Mossad, 119–20
Muerte a Secuestradores ("Death to the Kidnappers") (MAS), 192
Mullen, Francis, 204
Murata, Vice Minister, 326
Murgas, Rolando, 124
Murphy, Daniel, 230–32, 345
Murphy, John, 101

National Assembly, Panamanian, 41, 54, 181, 276, 352
National Bank of Canada, 246, 266, 268, 270, 310, 315, 326, 372
National Congress of Students, 41, 43
National Democratic Institute, 213
National Guard, Panamanian, 45, 53, 111
Arias and, 62–63, 123
"the Combo" in, 62–64
expansion of power of, 88
Flores and, 114
Noriega's control of, 118–20
Noriega in, 36, 55–70, 116
Noriega's promotions in, 64, 68
Spadafora's views on, 129, 130
transformation of, 56
National Intelligence Daily (NID), 335
National Mortgage Bank, 202
National Security Agency, 28, 90, 178
National Security Council (NSC), 157, 233, 256, 293, 299
National Security Planning Group (NSPG), 296–98, 300, 302–4

Navarro, Joaquin, 407
Negroponte, John, 122, 256, 298, 310
New York Times, 177–79, 304
Nicaragua, 121, 357, 402, 419, 421. *See also* Contras; Sandinistas
  CIA mining of ports, 163
  gunrunning to, 95–98
  Paredes mission to, 108
  Torrijos death and, 112, 121
Nixon, Richard M. (Nixon administration), 66, 67, 71, 76, 91, 321, 419
  drug enforcement and, 75–81
  Panama Canal Treaties and, 76, 79
Noriega, Felicidad Sieiro de (wife), 17, 35–37, 59–60, 161, 200–2, 225
Noriega, Gen. Manuel Antonio, 14. *See also specific topics*
  ambitions, 42, 48, 55, 70, 193
  appearance, 6, 40, 42, 43, 47, 84, 102, 146, 207, 317, 354
  arrest (1960), 47
  asylum sought by, 23–25
  awards of, 260, 278, 281, 287
  Catholicism, 24
  coup attempts against, 8, 11, 34, 173, 272–81, 298, 302, 340–43, 367–96
  cruelty, 48, 64, 128
  double-dealing, 119, 122, 158, 295
  drinking, 59–60, 141, 166, 208, 216, 275, 278, 354, 370
  drug enforcement and, 4, 5, 94, 183–84, 203–6, 420
  drug trafficking and, 5, 170, 175–80, 183–206, 185, 206
  education, 39–46
  facial treatments, 143
  family background, 6, 31, 36–40
  father figures, 44, 52, 55, 122
  files kept by, 57, 61–62, 72
  flight, 13–14, 16–18, 20–25
  Florida drug indictments, 30, 33, 94, 184, 247–57, 261, 309, 313, 318, 320, 322, 323, 421
  as Frankenstein, 5–6
  growth of power, 81–83, 88, 109
  gunrunning, 95–101, 109–110
  headaches, 2, 6
  high school yearbook, 35, 42
  homosexuality, 83, 127, 200, 244
  humiliation of, 225
  image problem, 84, 85, 126
  infidelities, 22, 35–37. *See also* Amado, Vicky
  as informant, 48, 51
  introversion, 113, 146
  manipulativeness, 37, 63, 419–20

  marriage. *See* Noriega, Felicidad Sieiro de (wife)
  as maximum leader, 8, 54
  military education, 47–48, 50–54
  monetary counteroffensive, 270–72
  nightmares, 141–42
  paranoia, 17, 207, 212
  patience, 37, 116
  poetry, 43–44
  as police transit chief, 35–36, 57–58
  political career, 41–43
  as rapist, 47–48, 56–57, 64
  as "rent-a-colonel," 158
  resentment of, 38, 49–50, 130
  as Richard III, 6, 396–97
  ruling style, 5, 73, 258–59, 262–63
  Santeria and, 4–5, 24
  spiritualism and, 1–3
  in succession struggles, 114–18
  U.S. training, 6, 18, 26, 31, 58, 82, 87–88
  as Wizard of Oz, 6
Noriega, Julio (half-brother), 38, 40, 49, 50
Noriega, Lorena (daughter), 211
Noriega, Luis Carlos (half-brother), 46, 49, 83–84, 318
  at Chorrillos Military Academy, 50
  in coup attempts, 66–68, 70
  death, 41, 122
  homosexuality, 40, 83, 146
  U.S. intelligence and, 48, 51
Noriega, Ricaurte Tomás (father), 38, 40
Noriega, Rubén (half-brother), 38, 40, 49, 50
Noriega, Sandra (daughter), 17, 37, 211
Noriega, Thais (daughter), 211
Noriega, Tomás (half-brother), 38, 40–41, 49, 50
North, Oliver, 175, 226, 318
  Contras and, 146, 156–61, 165–68
  Iran-Contra scandal and, 165, 182, 247–49
  Noriega's meetings with, 166–68
  resignation, 182
  Walker and, 159–60
Nunciatura (Vatican embassy), 398–416
Nunn, Sam, 386
Nutting, Wallace, 212

Ochoa, Jorge, 186–87, 191, 192, 239
Ochoa, Marta Nieves, 191–93
Oh, Miss, 230
Ojone, Lt., 167
Olechea, Maj. Federico, 371, 383, 391–93
"Oliver North defense" ("Brady defense"), 252–53
Operation Judas, 410
Operation Just Cause, 12
Organization of American States (OAS), 86–87, 268, 364–65, 381

O'Rourke, P. J., 214
ORPA guerrillas, 96
Ostrander, Marcus, 366

Palestine Liberation Organization (PLO),
    282
Panama. *See also specific topics*
  capital flight from, 4
  democracy, 6, 7, 87, 89, 111, 114, 116,
    156, 169, 179, 223
  failure of U.S. policy, 418–23
  independence, 30
  Murphy's trip to, 230–32
  protests, 213–14, 222–25, 356, 413–14
  "state of war" with, 8
  Switzerland of Latin America, 74–75
  U.S. economic sanctions, 306–8
  U.S. invasion. *See* Invasion of Panama by
    the United States
  U.S. restraining order on assets, 266–67,
    269–70
Panama, University of, 41–42, 352
Panama Canal, 11, 28, 43, 74–75
  Kissinger-Tack Principles and, 86
  "Law 20" and, 120
  sabotage plan for, 87–88
  World War II base agreement and, 41
Panama Canal Commission, 270
Panama Canal Treaties, 6, 9, 73, 91, 108,
    321, 381, 421
  Lewis and, 215, 220
  of 1903, 71
  Senate and, 175–76, 180
  Senate investigations and, 91–94
  signing of, 91, 102, 111
  talks on, 29, 30, 76, 77, 79, 81, 85–90
  Torrijos and, 2
  violations of, 5
Panama Canal Zone, 63, 76, 79
  bombings in, 29–32, 90
Panama Civil Aviation Authority, 76
Panamanian Defense Forces (PDF), 15, 119,
    123, 141, 149, 155, 156, 162, 173,
    184, 202, 219, 227, 220, 245, 246,
    275, 278, 298, 299, 302, 312, 365,
    367, 377, 381, 385–86
  Blandón Plan and, 229
  coup attempted by, 276–80
  Spadafora detained by, 134–38
  U.S. government ban on, 160
"Panama: Sixteen Years of Struggle Against
    Drug Traffic" (DEA-Noriega letters),
    204
Paredes, Rigoberto, 153, 284
Paredes, Gen. Rubén Darío, 108, 111,
    113–19, 130, 205, 278, 281
Park, Tongsun, 230–32

Pascal, Blaise, 419
Pastor, Robert, 98
Pastora Gómez, Edén (Commander Zero),
    112, 121–22, 127, 131, 132, 167
Pastorino, Robert, 346, 347
Paz, First Lt. Robert, 9–11
PDF. *See* Panamanian Defense Forces
Peace Corps, 76
Pedreschi, Carlos Bolívar, 42
Pérez, Carlos Andrés, 97, 121
Periñan, Balbina, 16
Perrian, Carl, 100–1
Peru, 87
Philip of Macedonia, 365
Philippines, 214–15, 217, 221, 222
"Philosophy of the Talent to Be in
    Command" (Noriega), 55
Pia Vesta, 178–79
Pickering, Thomas, 290
Pieczenik, Steve, 317
Pineapple effigies, 225
Pinilla, José María, 67
Pinochet, Augusto, 422
Poetry, 20, 43–44
Poindexter, Vice Adm. John, 160, 161,
    170–71, 173, 181, 208, 249
Policy Review Group (PRG), 224
Polt, Michael, 356
Porras, Demetrio, 44, 359
Poshol, Katya, 218
Powell, Lt. Gen. Colin, 10–12, 224, 309,
    310, 333, 338, 347, 349, 378, 379,
    383
PRD (Democratic Revolutionary Party),
    153
Prensa, La, 129, 130, 135–38, 216
Pretelt, Enrique, 111, 193, 200, 216, 246
Prince, The (Machiavelli), 45–46
Project Democracy, 161, 163, 165
Property, destruction or damage, 17, 25,
    139–40, 222–23
Prostitutes, 47–48, 56–57, 84, 103–4
Protests, 356, 413–14
  anti-American, 222–24
Psychics, 1–3, 209
Psychological warfare, 31, 58, 65, 81, 85–86,
    350–68, 408, 422
  election of 1989 and, 350–63
Puerto Armuelles, Panama, 57
Purcell, Col. Alberto, 200, 212, 218–19

Qaddafi, Moammar, 232, 281, 282
Quayle, Dan, 4, 5, 379
Quezada, Maj. Fernando, 273–77
Quiel, Luis, 185
Quijano, Billy, 365
Quinn, Sally, 84–85

Rabin, Yitzhak, 119
Rabinowitz, Boudin, Standard, Krinsky, &
    Lieberman, 268–69
Radio Continente, 128–30
Radio La Republica, 130
Ramón, Milan Rodriguez, 205–6
Rangers, 14
Rape, 366
  homosexual, 134–38
  of prostitutes, 47–48, 56–57
  as torture, 59
Reagan, Ronald (Reagan administration),
    25–26, 28, 33, 119, 156, 159, 229,
    232, 256, 262, 263, 264, 293, 295–96,
    303, 305–16, 322, 324, 326, 327–28,
    330, 348
  Bush's disagreements with, 309–10, 336–40
  Contras and, 6
  economic sanctions announced by, 306–8
  Noriega and, 157–82, 185, 220, 223,
    256–57, 258–70, 289–332, 346–47,
    419, 421, 422
Remón, Col., 45, 49
Renedo, Fernando Ravelo, 192–203, 198,
    199
Republican party, U.S., 27–28, 163, 247
Republic National Bank of New York,
    266–67, 269
Restreop, Fabio Ochoa, 186, 192
RICO, 254
RíoHató Air Base, 16
Rivas, Carlos Lehder, 186, 188–89, 191
Rodriguez, César, 118, 131, 215–16
  assassination of, 240–41
  Kalish and, 245–46
  Noriega's sexual attack on, 244
Rodriguez, Felix, 132
Rodriguez, Francisco, 53–54, 380
Rodriguez, Yolanda Pulice de, 124
Rogers, William D., 227, 265–67
Rognoni, Mario, 258–59, 261, 262, 287–88,
    326, 360, 361, 382, 391, 392
Roman Catholic Church, 353–56
Roman Catholicism, 369–71
Romero, Carlos Humberto, 98
Roosevelt, Theodore, 30, 421
Rostow, C. Nicholas, 255
Royce, Knut, 178
Royo, Aristides, 71, 106, 115–16
Rubin, Lt. Doug, 14–15

Saenz-Barria, Cecilio, 239
Sai Baba, Satya, 209–10, 226
St. Malo de Arias, Guillermo, 315, 326–27
Salamin, Marcel, 191
Salinas de Gortari, Carlos, 383
Sal Si Puedes, 38, 358

Samudio, David, 62
Sanchez, Luisa (Noriega's adoptive mother),
    2, 6, 39
Sanchez, Nestor, 145, 154, 162, 169, 173–74,
    177, 179, 229, 233, 292
Sánchez-Borbón, Guillermo, 135, 137
Sandinistas, 91, 95–98, 105, 108, 119
  arms suppliers to, 243
  assassination plans and, 180–81
  Medellín cartel and, 203
  Miskito Indians vs., 131
  Noriega's support for, 120–22
  Victoriano Lorenzo Brigade and, 127–28
Sanford, Jerome, 95, 99–101
Sanguinetti, Julio Maria, 348
Sanjur, Amado, 66–68
San Martín, José de, 53
Santeria, 4–5, 24, 131–33
Santo Tomás Hospital, 48–50
Sardinia, Walter, 64
Saunders, Norman, 203
Sayre, Robert, 76
Scali, John, 85–86
Schneider, Gen. Michael, 381
Schweitzer, Lt. Gen. Robert L., 178
Sciacatano, David, 402–3
Sconyers, Ronald, 304
Scowcroft, Brent, 10, 12, 85, 394
Scowcroft, Brig. Gen. Marc, 378
Seal, Barry, 203, 239
Second Infantry Company, 64
Secord, Richard V., 163
Senate, U.S., 77, 88, 175–82, 299
  Carlton testimony, 243–44
  Foreign Relations Committee, 176, 177
  Hersh revelations and, 177–79
  Intelligence Committee of, 77, 92–94, 164,
    179, 340, 342, 343, 377, 394, 395
  Lewis's lobbying, 220–22, 234
  Panama Canal Treaties and, 91–94,
    175–76, 180
  "public accounting" resolution of, 220–23
  Terrorism, Narcotics, and International
    Communications Subcommittee, 180
7th Rifle Company, 371
Sexual abuse, 10. See also Rape
Sexual torture, 59, 60
Shawcross, William, 104, 106
Shultz, George, 123, 125, 156, 181, 223, 267,
    285, 290, 293, 294, 296, 300, 303–6,
    304, 310, 314–16, 321, 323, 325–27,
    332, 337, 341, 347
Sieiro, Maj. Manuel, 371
Sieiro, Ramón, 37, 202, 352, 354
Sieiro family, 36, 202
Silvera, Ramiro, 6, 68
Singapore, 82

Singing Sergeants affair, 28, 91–92
Slotnick, Barry, 268–69
Smith, Phillip, 77, 78
Socialist party, Panamanian, 44, 45
Softball, 75–76
Soka Gakkai (Value Creation Society), 286
Solis Palma, Manuel, 258–59, 263, 297,
    350–51, 355
Somoza, Anastasio, 77, 95, 97, 105, 118,
    127, 241, 407, 409
Sonnet, Niel, 317
Soraya (Shah's former wife), 83
Sorzano, José, 220, 294, 307, 308
Sosa, Didio, 234
Sosa, Juan B., 265–67, 269, 302, 306, 334,
    353
Sossa, Sarita, 23
Southern Air Transport, 249
Southern Command, U.S., 9, 66, 98, 170,
    217, 219, 227, 276, 298, 333–34, 345,
    363–66, 366, 372–73, 378, 380–81,
    384, 386–87, 390
Soviet Union, 13, 232
Spadafora, Aris, 127, 131, 133
Spadafora, Carmelo, Jr., 130, 133–37, 140,
    141
Spadafora, Carmelo, Sr., 133–34, 140
Spadafora, Hugo, 121, 126–42, 128
  murder of, 5, 132–50, 152, 168, 173, 174,
    176, 208, 212, 220
  Noriega compared with, 126
  Noriega's first meeting with, 126–27
  Noriega's rivalry with, 5, 126–30
Spadafora, Laura, 177
Spadafora, Winston, 141, 176, 213
Special Forces, U.S., 14, 21, 303
Special Investigative Unit, 80
Spencer, Stuart, 173, 175
Spiritualism, 1–3, 209–10
Spiteri, Father Joseph, 24–25, 414
Spying, 28–32, 47–48, 50–52. *See also*
    Central Intelligence Agency (CIA);
    Panama, intelligence service of
State Department, U.S., 76, 79, 93, 95–96,
    100–1, 125, 154, 158, 169–71, 223,
    232–33, 241–42, 254, 257, 263, 264,
    267–69, 274–75, 306–7, 314, 326,
    340–42, 345, 356, 364, 384, 399, 405,
    410
  Defense Department conflict with, 293–95,
    311
  Herrera Hassan fiasco and, 289–93
  Munitions Control Office of, 97
Stealth F-117 fighters, 16
Stephens, Inc., 219, 227
Stephens, Jackson T., 219, 227
Stiner, Gen. Carl, 403, 411–12

Stokes, Louis, 160
Stolz, Dick, 340–43
Strategic Military Command, 367
Strategic Military Council (CEM), 33, 280,
    327, 354–55
Strikes, 302
Suarez, Roberto, 204
Sumner, Lt. Gen. Gordon, 97–98
Sununu, John, 379, 393
"Supplemental Assistance to Nicaragua
    Program" (CIA memo), 164–65
Supreme Court, U.S., 268

Tack, Juan Antonio, 77, 86
Taiwan, 58, 216, 267, 281, 287–88, 315, 325,
    422
Takeshita, Prime Minister, 232
Takiff, Ray, 317
Tason, Marcella, 21, 354
Tason, Ulysses, 21
Teeter, Robert, 336–37
Telephone warfare, 19–20
Television, 362, 364
Telles, Tom, 240
Thatcher, Margaret, 165
Thoughts and Experience of a Medical
    Guerrilla (Spadafora), 126, 131
Thurman, Gen. Maxwell R. (Mad Max), 11,
    374, 377, 380–81, 384, 386, 403–4,
    408, 410–12, 416
Tighe, Lt. Gen. Eugene, Jr., 92, 95
Torres Arias, Leonides, 122
Torrijos, Hugo, 271
Torrijos, Martín, 121, 128, 210
Torrijos, Moisés, 61–62, 76, 78–79, 94
Torrijos, Omar, 2, 6, 28, 29, 32, 55–59,
    61–99, 104, 112, 207, 419
  anti-Americanism of, 71
  Armao and, 103–4
  coup against Arias, 62–64
  coup attempts against, 55–56, 66–70, 187
  death, 111–14, 112–14, 121, 128, 130, 193,
    212
  Harari and, 119–20
  "the lazy dictator," 83
  leftist, 66, 76–77, 82, 86, 98
  Lewis and, 215
  Martínez ouster and, 65–66, 68
  M-19 and, 189–91
  Noriega compared to, 73, 81, 120–21,
    276
  Noriega's first meeting with, 56
  Noriega mistrusted by, 109–11
  Noriega's relationship with, 2, 6, 46, 98,
    104, 109–12
  Panama Canal Treaties and, 2, 79, 81,
    85–89, 91, 102, 108

Panama Canal Zone and, 29–31
personality, 65, 73
return, 69–70
Shah and, 101–2, 105, 106, 120
Spadafora and, 127–28
succession struggles after death, 114–18
U.S. legitimization, 88–89
U.S. wiretaps, 91
Torrijos, Raquel, 57, 71, 112, 119
Torrijosism, 70
Torture, 126, 140, 238, 280–81
sexual, 59, 60
of Spadafora, 134–38, 176
"Total Warrior" military maneuvers, 302
Tranquilandia (Quiet Village), 186
Treasury Department, U.S., 308, 367
Tribaldos, César, 400, 413
Trilha, Ivan, 1–4, 209, 210, 397
Trott, Stephen, 251, 252
Turner, Carleton, 171
Turner, Stansfield, 29, 90, 92, 162

Udall Research Company, 165
UESAT (anti-terrorism forces), 115, 371, 384
United Fruit Co., 57
United Nations Security Council, 85–86
United States. *See also specific presidents and other topics*
anti-communism, 66, 75–77, 91
failure of Panama policy, 418–23
Noriega as creation, 5–7
Noriega resignation plan, 312–13, 315–31
Panamanian demonstrations against, 222–23
Torrijos legitimized by, 88–89
United States of America v. *Manuel Antonio Noriega,* 254–55

Valarde, Lt. Col., 404
Valdonedo, Maj. Aristides, 276, 277
Vallarino, Gen. Bolívar, 57, 62, 63
Vance, Cyrus, 97
Vatican, 401, 404–5, 407–8
embassy (Nunciatura), 23–25, 398–416

Vega, Guillermo, 271
Victoriano Lorenzo Brigade, 127–28
Villalaz, Maj. Augusto, 277–78
Villanueva, Father Javier, 24–25, 416
Voice of America, 88
Voodoo, 141

Walker, David, 158–61
Walker, William, 228, 261, 275, 289–93, 302, 317, 319
Wall Street Journal, 266
Walters, Vernon, 181, 233
Wangyal, Geshe, 226–27
Washington Post, 84–85, 304
Watergate scandal, 80
Watson, Col. Samuel J., 313–14, 345
Watson, Teofilo, 238
Webster, William, 293, 297, 310, 315, 341, 377, 379, 395
Wells Fargo Bank, 267
Whitehead, John, 257, 267, 296, 326
White House Special Projects Fund, 80
Wilson, George, 304
Wilson, Jerry, 153
Witchcraft, 59, 131–32
Wittenberg, Manfred Hoffman, 148–49
Wittgreen, Carlos, 95–97, 99, 215, 216, 271
Wittgreen, Gaspar, 271, 272
Woerner, Gen. Frederick, 11, 85, 300, 316, 333, 363, 366, 380
Lewis and, 217, 219, 229, 232, 276
Wolfowitz, Paul, 395
Wompler, Atlee, 253–54
World Bank, 149, 153, 168
World War II, 41, 421

Yakovac, Stephen, 188–89
Yazov, Dimitri, 383, 391
Yih, Chuh, 286
Young, Brig. Gen. Robert S., 92
Young, C. W. (Bill), 250

Zepeda, Tom, 189
Zorinsky, Edward, 180
Zuñiga, Mauro, 140, 145